D0793769

PRESIDENTIALISM IN COMMONWEALTH AFRICA

PRESIDENTIALISM

IN

COMMONWEALTH

AFRICA

BY

B. O. NWABUEZE

C. HURST & COMPANY, LONDON
in association with NWAMIFE PUBLISHERS, ENUGU

First published in the United Kingdom by
C. Hurst & Co. (Publishers) Ltd., London

in association with Nwamife Publishers Ltd.,
10 Ibiam Street, Uwani, P.O. Box 430, Enugu, Nigeria

© 1974 by B. O. Nwabueze

ISBN 0-903983-16-8

PRINTED IN GREAT BRITAIN BY OFFSET LITHOGRAPHY BY
BILLING AND SONS LTD., GUILDFORD AND LONDON

PREFACE

The tendency of a lawyer writing on government is to approach it from the standpoint of rules of law. His training and orientation incline him to view government in terms of its formal framework as embodied in the constitution and other laws, almost disdaining its practice as the concern of political scientists. To the political scientist, preoccupied as he is, on his side, with the practice of government, this is a sin, and one that makes much legal writing on government unappealing, if not unedifying. Not that the lawyer's approach is altogether indefensible. And, paradoxically, the best defence has come from a political scientist. When Professor Ridley of the Department of Political Science at the University of Manchester spoke about the importance of a constitution at his inaugural in 1966, he meant to admonish his fellow political scientists for their undue preoccupation with the practice of government to the neglect of its rules, but he was, perhaps without knowing it, also defending the constitutional lawyer's position.

In line with Professor Ridley's advocacy of the importance of a constitution, this book attempts a thorough analysis of the formal structure of presidential rule in Commonwealth Africa: the nature of the state organisation whether unitary or federal, and the relation of the centre to the local units in both their modern and traditional forms; the internal structure of the executive — the presidency, the cabinet, ministries, departments, armed forces, etc. — and its relation to the legislature and to the individual. The picture that emerges is of a highly centralised governmental structure — 'democratic centralism', as some of the government leaders rather euphemistically describe it. Every kind of separation or division in governmental authority is rejected. Starting with the abolition — for good reason — of the separation of the Head of State from the Head of Government and the diffusion of executive power among cabinet members, the whole apparatus of power is concentrated in the executive. The legislature is subordinated to the executive; bicameralism where it existed before is replaced by unicameralism, and federalism or regionalism by unitarism. The judiciary is subordinated to the executive as regards appointment, and sometimes even as regards dismissal too. All this is but a foundation for the emergence of that political monolith, the one-party state, which itself finally consummates the personalisation of rule, that is, the centralisation, within the single party, of all power in the hands of the leader.

In many cases the constitution still guarantees individual rights, but two countries in Commonwealth Africa, Tanzania and Malawi, have since followed the example of Ghana (1960–9) in rejecting a constitutional guarantee. The whole concept of 'checks and balances' is largely abandoned. Thus, for example, in many of the countries, the President has replaced the independent public service commissions, set up at independence, as the authority for the appointment, removal and disciplinary control of public servants, and his authority is not limited, as in the United States, by the necessity to obtain the approval of the legislature. This centralising feature of presidential rule in Commonwealth Africa – centralism in the organisation of state power, and in the organisation of politics, centralism in the administration of government, and the subordination of the legislature – is thus a central thrust of the discussion in this book. The primacy of the presidential executive and its overweening power also manifests itself in its fearsomely vast security powers and in its arrogation of the constituent power of the state, that ultimate mark of the sovereignty of the nation.

While recognising its importance, the study of the constitution, it may be admitted, can be a dreary exercise. Rules are lifeless and cold, and it is perhaps understandable that the political scientist should prefer the excitement of action and its stimulating dynamics. Yet, studied comparatively, rules are not altogether without fascination. All the Commonwealth African constitutions have been drafted with the same drafting technique, often in identical language, adopted from the original draftsmen of the early independence constitutions. But the variations in phraseology and definition, even of the same institutions or procedures, the different approaches to the relation between governmental structures and agencies, and the diversity of local qualifications on the rights of the individual, are mentally engaging and stimulating, the more so when we begin to probe their underlying motivations and explanations. Indeed the Commonwealth African presidential constitutions discussed in this book perhaps exhibit more diversity than uniformity, more localism than conformity to a common Commonwealth pattern – a fact that challenges the comparative student whose task is thereby made more daunting by the sheer complexity of the material. Yet the task is infinitely rewarding, for this diversity and localism throw a flood of light on the significance and implications of expressions that might otherwise be taken for granted. The simple lesson is that comparative study of constitutions deserves more attention than it has so far received.

However, rules are not to be regarded as a self-sufficient subject of study. Insofar as he tends to glorify rules to the utter neglect of practice, insofar as he fails to set the rules in the context of the real world of politics and the politician and the forces that condition them, the constitutional lawyer cannot hope to compel the attention and the respect of those outside his profession. For rules may be poles apart from the reality of the power they confer. For a rounded picture of any institutions, in particular governmental ones, the distortions and perversions of practice, and the underlying political and social forces motivating them, are as vital as the rules. The reality and vitality of the powers of the presidency in Africa, for example, cannot be perceived solely by reference to the provisions of the constitution creating and defining them. Equally important are the informal determinants of power, such as, for instance, the relative impotence of extra-constitutional sanctions against the abuse of power in Africa, the African's traditional attitude towards power and his conception of authority, the colonial experience, and the mystique and charisma which the nationalist struggle has bestowed upon the leader, the circumstances of under-development and the newness of the state, the heterogeneity of its society and the tensions of modernisation, and the personality of the individual Presidents. These factors are also discussed in the book, but of course in the context of the law of the constitution, since the play of social and political forces cannot completely nullify or supersede the law.

The need to blend rules with practice has thus determined the approach adopted in this book. It is two-dimensional, combining the analysis of rules with an inquiry into practice and the political and social forces that condition it. This has made necessary a heavy reliance on primary sources, reports of parliamentary debates, government white papers, reports of commissions of enquiry, etc.

The book also focuses on the relative suitability of presidentialism in bringing development to the new nations in Commonwealth Africa. The paramount need of an African country is for development. It wants to develop its economy, to modernise and integrate its society, to secure and promote stability in the community. Economic development and modernisation loom large in discussions about development, but they are not enough, or even capable of achievement, without national integration and social stability, which together provide the foundation for economic and social development. Progress can only be achieved within an ordered society, and order in turn presupposes unity among the people. These considerations run right through the book. But, whatever its advantages for this purpose, the establishment of a presidential constitution does not end the need for further constitu-tional development. Politics in the developing countries have tended increasingly to be preoccupied with how to win and retain power, overriding the need for a due sense of balance and restraint. Along with economic development, national integration and stability, there is a need for ideology, for principles of government; in short for constitutionalism. Government must aim not only at providing the individual with the basic needs for a decent existence — food and clothing, water, shelter and light, education and medical services. It must also afford him the opportunity to develop his personality — his initiative and creativity, his power of thought and expression. The need for constitutional development in the emergent states is thus a quest for constitutionalism, a quest for appropriate restraints upon the powers of government in the interests of the protection of individual liberty. The book makes suggestions to this end.

I have three apologies to make, all of which relate to certain omissions in the book. The chapter on the relation of judicial to legislative and executive power has had to be withdrawn for reasons partly of space but mainly in order to avoid duplication of material which is more suitably designed for another volume, *Judicialism: The Role of the Judiciary in Government*. This work is to be the third and final volume in a series of which this book is the second, and *Constitutionalism in The Emergent States* was the first. Secondly, Sierra Leone's Republican Constitution of 1971 has been omitted from the discussion in this book. Efforts to secure a copy of it have proved unavailing, and it was only in July 1973, after the typescript had been delivered to the publishers, that while in Europe on a conference, I chanced upon a Sierra Leonean carrying a copy with him, which he was willing to lend me, but only for a night as we were due to part the following day. Although I made copious notes from it, the material came too late for inclusion in this volume. Thirdly, it has not proved possible to incorporate all the changes in Zambia's one-party state-constitution which came into force in August 1973, and on the drafting committee of which I had the privilege to serve.

Now to the customary acknowledgments. My thanks go first to the University of Zambia which provided a grant that made it possible for me to visit Kenya, Tanzania and Uganda in connection with my research on the book. I also wish to thank my colleagues in the University of Zambia: Professor J. T. Craig and Dr E. Jones for reading all but one of the chapters, Professor R. B. Seidman and Mr S. V. Mubako for reading chapters 1–4. Their comments, especially those of Jimmy Craig, were extremely useful to me. As with *Constitutionalism*, Mr Christopher Hurst of C. Hurst & Co., Publishers, London, has been forthcoming with encouragement and insightful advice and comments.

Lusaka   BEN O. NWABUEZE
September 1973

CONTENTS

CHAPTER I

THE NATURE OF EXECUTIVE POWER

The executive in a presidential system of government – its powers, functions and its relations with the other organs of government and with the individual – is the main focus of this book. The reference to the executive and other governmental organs at once implies some notion of structure in the organisation of government. It implies that government is not the function of just one undifferentiated, monolithic organisation, but rather that its various functions may be separated and assigned to different organs. It has been customary to conceive of the functions of government in terms of legislation, execution and adjudication. This has provided the pattern for the needful separation. And from this too has emerged the tripartite structure – legislature, executive and judiciary. The functions involved in legislation and adjudication are easily delineable. The one is concerned with the making of laws and the other with its interpretation and adjudication. With the function of execution, however, such precise delineation is difficult. Executive power is indeed a term of uncertain meaning. Perhaps no other term in the science of government is so much taken for granted and yet so difficult of precise delineation. Does executive power embrace all functions that are neither legislative nor judicial? More important, can executive power be exercised independently of a law – a provision of the constitution or statute or other law? Three views are held upon this question.

1. *The Residual Power Theory*

The widest view of executive power is that it embraces every power which by its nature is neither legislative nor judicial. Professor Alan Gledhill has put the point quite simply, almost as if the matter admitted of no controversy. 'Executive power', he writes, 'is what remains of the functions of government after the legislative and judicial powers have been taken away. It is not limited to execution of the laws and, provided it is not forbidden by law, action by government need not wait upon legislation expressly empowering government to do it. The formulation of policy and the preliminary steps necessary to implement it by legislation come within the executive power.'[1]

The characteristic point in this view of executive power is that it is not limited even by the inherent implication of the word 'execute'. The *Concise Oxford Dictionary* defines 'execute' as to 'carry (plan, command, law, judicial sentence, will) into effect'. This, like every other definition of the word, suggests physical action of some sort, and would therefore exclude any function that does not involve such action, such as thought. It would be an abuse of language to say that thinking is execution or that a person is executing anything when he is thinking out a plan. Thought is of course a vital element in a process that may eventually produce a definite plan or policy which is to be executed. The thinking out of a plan or policy partakes of the same nature as the deciding of cases by the courts. The adjudication function cannot be said to involve execution. That arises when the court has given a decision and the decision is being carried into effect. The same is true of the function of administering a law. Much of it is quasi-judicial or quasi-legislative, involving merely the taking of decisions which operate to determine individual cases or to lay down general regulations.

The residual power theory has merit nevertheless in that, by classifying the thinking out of policy and the administering of laws as executive, it conforms to the general practice of modern government. For these are today among the most vital functions of executive government. One cannot imagine an executive that is excluded altogether from the thinking out of policy and its formulation. The executive has the primary responsibility for government, and policy is squarely implicated in governing. So also the filling in of the details of complex, modern legislation and the determination of a variety of issues arising in its administration can only be undertaken by the executive. Neither the legislature nor the judiciary is really well suited for the task, because of their procedure and the limited time and personnel available to them.

However, the fact that, for reasons of convenience, governmental efficiency and the logic of the executive's responsibility to govern, it has become customary for the executive to assume these functions should not brand them with the character of executive power. While generally recognised practice has brought them under the umbrella of the executive, by nature they are still not executive; they fall therefore outside the ordinary meaning of executive power. A distinction is to be made between functions which are executive by their nature. and those that do not partake of that nature but are merely treated as such by modern governmental practice. The latter is not part of the *executive power* strictly so-called. This distinction appears to have the support of the United States Supreme Court.[2] The Constitution of the United States, like almost every other written constitution, vests executive power in the head of state (i.e. the President). It also vests legislative power in the legislature (i.e. Congress). The vesting of executive power in the President operates unquestionably as a limitation on Congress' legislative power, precluding it from using the power to divest the President of any function that properly forms part of the executive power.[3] The competence of Congress to confer on persons other than the President functions arising under a law that it enacts would depend therefore on whether such functions are executive in nature. The question arose in *Humphrey* v. *United States*.[4] The Federal Trade Commission Act, 1914, created a commission charged with responsibility for the prevention of unfair methods of competition in commerce. The commission is empowered to prefer and try charges of unfair competition, to issue a 'cease and desist' order against any person, partnership or corporation found guilty after due hearing of using unfair method of competition. If the order is disobeyed, the Commission may apply to the appropriate circuit court of appeals for its enforcement, subject to the right of the person against whom the order is made to apply to the circuit court of appeals for a review of the order. The commission also has wide powers of investigation in respect of certain matters; when it investigates any matter it must report to Congress with recommendations. Its members are appointed for a fixed term of years by the President by and with the advice and consent of the Senate, and may be removed by him for inefficiency, neglect of duty or malfeasance in office. Humphrey, a member of the commission, was removed by the President before the expiration of his normal term, not for any of the causes specified in the Act, but because he and the President entertained divergent views with respect to matters of policy. Humphrey then sued for arrears of salary for wrongful dismissal. For the President it was argued that the provision of the Act prescribing the grounds upon which a member of the commission may be removed was unconstitutional as being an interference with the President's executive power.

In its opinion on the case, the Supreme Court defined the status of the commission to be that of an agency, created by statute to carry out the policy, not of individual Presidents but of the law; accordingly it is to be independent of executive authority and direction, whether it be that of the President or any regular executive department. Its functions, the court held, are purely administrative, and do not involve the exercise of 'executive power'. 'In administering the provisions of the statute in respect of 'unfair methods of competition' – that is to say filling in and administering the details embodied by the general standard – the commission acts in part quasi-legislatively and in part quasi-judicially.... To the extent that it exercises any executive function – as distinguished from executive power in the constitutional sense — it does so in the discharge and effectuation of its quasi-legislative powers.'[5] Since they are not comprehended in the President's executive power, therefore, the functions of the commission and the tenure of its members are unquestionably within the power of Congress to prescribe. 'The authority of Congress,' the Supreme Court declared, 'in creating quasi-legislative or quasi-judicial agencies, to require them to act in discharge of their duties independently of executive control, cannot well be doubted; and that authority includes, as an appropriate incident, power to fix the period during which they shall continue, and to forbid their removal except for cause in the meantime.'[6] The court explained its earlier decision in *Myers* v. *United States*[7] as being confined to 'purely executive officers' such as postmasters, i.e. officers whose functions form part of the executive power vested by the Constitution in the President.

The objection to the residual power theory is its assertion that the executive has an inherent authority, independently of an enabling law, to 'execute' any action necessary for the government of the nation, so long as this is not positively prohibited to it by law. There is at this point an overlap with another theory, the inherent power theory.

2. *The Inherent Power Theory*

According to this theory, executive power confers an inherent authority to exercise any function which is *inherently* executive in nature. It presupposes, therefore, that the function in fact partakes of the nature of execution. This would exclude functions that are not inherently of that nature, such as policy and administration of law. In this respect it differs from the residual power theory but it shares with the latter the assertion that, within its proper field, the executive has an inherent authority to act without prior authority conferred in every case by a specific legislation or other law. Perhaps the most eloquent statement of the theory is that by President Theodore Roosevelt:

> The most important factor in getting the right spirit of my Administration, next to the insistence upon courage, honesty, and a genuine democracy of desire to serve the plain people, was my insistence upon the theory that the executive power was limited only by specific restrictions and prohibitions appearing in the Constitution or imposed by the Congress under its constitutional powers. My view was that every executive officer, and above all every executive officer in high position, was a steward of the people, and not to content himself with the negative merit of keeping his talents undamaged in a napkin. I declined to adopt the view that what was imperatively necessary for the Nation could not be done by the President unless he could find some specific authorisation to do it. My belief was that it was not only his right but his duty to do

anything that the needs of the Nation demanded unless such action was forbidden by the Constitution or by the laws. Under this interpretation of executive power I did and caused to be done many things not previously done by the President and the heads of the Departments. I did not usurp power, but I did greatly broaden the use of executive power. In other words, I acted for the public welfare, I acted for the common well-being of all our people, whenever and in whatever manner was necessary, unless prevented by direct constitutional or legislative prohibition.[8]

This proposition is both startling and dangerous, for it means that the executive can interfere with private rights without legal authorisation so long as what it does is not prohibited by law. This is quite contrary to the Anglo-Saxon conception of governmental powers. The executive, Lord Atkin has said, 'can only act in pursuance of the powers given to him by law. In accordance with British jurisprudence no member of the executive can interfere with the liberty or property of a British subject except on the condition that he can support the legality of his action before a court of justice'.[9] Lord Bryce expresses exactly the same point when, in his epochal book, *The American Commonwealth*, he writes: 'The doctrine that all executive power is strictly limited by the law ... is indeed a cornerstone of English liberty.'[10] It should be even more a cornerstone of American liberty. For the idea of an inherent executive power sounds somewhat contradictory in a written constitution, a contradiction which many Americans have been at pains to point out. Thus, in 1789 in the very first Congress under the Constitution, Congressman Stone, in a debate touching upon this question, said:

If gentlemen will tell us that powers, impliedly executive, belong to the President, they ought to go further with the idea, and give us a correct idea of executive power, as applicable to their rule. In an absolute monarchy there never has been any doubt with respect to implication; the monarch can do what he pleases. In a limited monarchy, the prince has powers incident to kingly prerogative. How far will a federal executive, limited by a Constitution, extend in implications of this kind? Does it go so far as absolute monarchy? Or is it confined to restrained monarchy?[11]

In another debate upon the same question in 1835, Senator Clay exclaimed in alarm: 'Inherent power! Whence is it derived? The Constitution created the office of President, and made it just what it is. It had no power prior to its existence. It can have none but those which are conferred upon it by the instrument which created it, or laws passed in pursuance of that instrument. Do gentlemen mean by inherent power, such power as is exercised by the monarchs or chief magistrates of other countries?'[12] It is difficult to equate the position of a head of government created by a written constitution with that of a hereditary monarch, whose office and powers have their origin in unwritten custom. To argue therefore, as the advocates of the inherent power theory do, that the vesting of executive power in the President 'confers upon him all that power which, in any age of the world and under any form of government, has been vested in the chief executive functionary, whether King or Czar, emperor or dictator'[13] is a startling and untenable proposition. For it would mean implying into a written constitution all the prerogatives, originating in immemorial custom, which appertain to and adorn the kingly office. In this connection we may note an interesting provision which appears in most of the presidential constitutions of Commonwealth Africa, to the effect that 'where under any existing law, constitutional custom or convention any prerogatives or privileges are vested in Her Majesty in respect of Malawi or in the Governor-General on behalf of Her Majesty, they shall with effect from the appointed day vest in the President and, subject to the Constitution or any other law, the President shall have power to do all things necessary for the exercise thereof'.[14] Does this import into Malawi all the prerogatives of the British Crown? That would seem certainly to follow from the rather wide sweep of the provision. Commenting on a similar provision in respect of Uganda under its 1962 Constitution (as amended in 1963), Morris and Read have said that 'such questions as whether the President of Uganda can create peers, confer honours and decorations under the prerogative, create corporations by "Presidential" (rather than Royal) Charter, claim treasure trove, grant franchises or the right to print the Bible, demand personal service in time of formidable insurrection or exercise the right of angary ... depend upon whether the Queen or the Governor-General enjoyed such powers in respect of Uganda before October 9, 1963, and whether, and if so how far any such powers had been restricted by the Constitution'.[15] 'These questions', they add, 'raise a number of imponderable problems'. Typical of Nyerere's unpretentious nature, the provisions in Tanzania, unique in all the Commonwealth African presidential regimes, vest the Queen's prerogative or privileges, not in the President, but in the Republic, which also stands for the Queen (or the Crown) in all references to her in any existing law, though the President is given power to do all things necessary for the exercise of such prerogatives.[16] This is the right equation, for, given the conception of monarchy as a personification of the state, it is the Republic itself, rather than the President, that corresponds to the monarch.

Among the classical writers upon government, the great authority of John Locke, who unquestionably was one of the dominant influences upon the framers of the American Constitution, is sometimes cited in support of the inherent power theory. It may be useful therefore to examine somewhat closely what Locke wrote upon this point. This is what he said:

> Where the legislative and executive powers are in distinct hands, as they are in all moderated monarchies and well-framed governments, there the good of the society requires that several things should be left to the direction of him that has the executive power. For the legislators not being able to foresee and provide by laws for all that may be useful to the community, the executor of the laws having the power in his hands, has by the common law of Nature a right to make use of it for the good of the society, in many cases where the municipal law has given no direction, till the legislature can conveniently be assembled to provide for it; nay, many things there are which the law can by no means provide for, and those must necessarily be left to the discretion of him that has the executive power in his hands, to be ordered by him as the public good and advantage shall require; nay, it is fit that the laws themselves should in some cases give way to the executive power, or rather to this fundamental law of nature and government — viz., that as much as may be all the members of the society are to be preserved.[17]

This passage is far from precise. It is possible to interpret it as meaning that the executive can do whatever the 'public good and advantage' require; nonetheless the kernel of Locke's thesis seems to lie in what he calls the fundamental law of Nature, namely the necessity to preserve society against any situation threatening its safety or peace. The power is a temporary one to be exercised during an exceptional situation until the legislature can conveniently be assembled to provide for it. Thus the basis of the power which Locke claims for the executive is simply necessity, which is a well-recognised doctrine of law, providing justification for action otherwise unlawful. Its rationale is that in an emergency imperilling public order or public security, the safety of the people is the supreme law — *salus populi est suprema lex*. By this supreme law of necessity, the organs of the state are entitled, in the face of such an emergency, to take all appropriate actions, even in deviation from the express provisions of the constitution, in order to safeguard law and order and preserve the state and society. The doctrine does not operate from outside the law, but is implied in it as an integral part thereof. It is 'implicit in the constitution of every civilised community'.[18] This is so because 'no constitution can anticipate all the different forms of phenomena which may beset a nation'.[19] Thus the doctrine has been held to be incorporated into the written constitutions of Pakistan, Cyprus, Nigeria, Rhodesia, Italy, Greece and the United States of America; and that, as so incorporated, it operates to qualify, though not to abolish, the concept of the inviolability of the constitution's supremacy and consequently of the limitations which the constitution imposes upon governmental power. The sort of situation which gives rise to a necessity justifying otherwise unlawful action as well as the type of act which can be done in pursuance of it may vary from country to country,[20] but the doctrine has been held not to be confined to the executive; it also applies to enable a limited legislature to exceed the limits of its power.[21] Clearly therefore necessity does not support any claim of a general inherent executive power, and if that is all Locke meant to say, his authority does not avail the inherent power theory.

By attributing to the executive power to do anything that is not prohibited by law, the inherent power theory equates the executive to a natural person. This is clearly untenable. The government (i.e. the executive) is an artificial legal person, and like all artificial legal entities, whether a registered company or a statutory corporation, its power is limited by the doctrine of *ultra vires* to what it is authorised by law to do; a natural person, on the other hand, is not subject to the limitation of the doctrine. Thus, whereas the only relevant question with which an individual intending to undertake a business need concern himself is whether the particular business is prohibited by law or requires a licence from the state, an artificial legal person, including the government or any ministry or department thereof, has in addition to ask whether it has power conferred by law or, in the case of a registered company, by its constitution, to do the thing in question. The matter may be better perceived if it is remembered that government is a collective term for the ministries or departments of which it is composed, and that powers are seldom conferred on it as such. Considered from the standpoint of its individual constituent units, it seems indisputable that the ministry of communications, for example, cannot lawfully run a nursery school any more than the ministry of education can operate postal and telegraph services.

No doubt vast extensions to the powers of the executive would result from the doctrine of implied powers. The doctrine is a rule of construction according to which every grant of power is construed as including by implication all such powers as are reasonably incidental thereto and not expressly excluded.[22] Thus, when a government department or ministry is constituted and assigned definite functions and responsibilities by law, there would accrue to it power to do such things as are incidental to those functions, such as power to acquire office accommodation, office equipment, to employ staff and to do all other things necessary for the execution of its functions. The incidental powers of all the government departments add up to a total nearly as comprehensive as the powers of an individual. From this it is easy to move to a notion of an inherent power, for the comprehensiveness of the totality of the incidental powers of all the government departments makes the executive appear different from other artificial legal persons, approximating it very closely to a natural person. The affinity is made all the more close in Commonwealth Africa by the fact that ministries or departments are seldom established by an act of the legislature as in the United States and Britain but by executive instrument. The constitutions of the Commonwealth African presidential regimes empower the president to establish offices of minister,[23] and to constitute and abolish offices in the public service.[24] This power only enables the president to structure the administrative machinery of the government, but certainly not to confer substantive powers upon the structures or offices so created. This latter can only be done by act of the legislature. It is from specific enactments of the legislature that the ministers and public officers derive their substantive powers as distinct from routine administrative functions.

The advocates of the inherent power theory might well argue further that the executive's responsibility for government should include as a necessary incident power to do anything necessary to that end. The doctrine of implied power cannot be predicated upon the executive's general responsibility to govern. That would be carrying the idea of incidental power beyond its proper scope, thereby obliterating the basic difference between it and the notion of an inherent power. For inherent power is conceived by reference to the totality of the executive's powers of government, whereas an implied power is judged by reference to its being necessary for the accomplishment of a particular grant of a main power. The nature of incidental powers is well illustrated by the Privy Council decision in *Balewa* v. *Doherty*,[25] a case arising under the federal Constitution of Nigeria, 1960. The federal scheme of the constitution limited the power of the federal parliament to certain enumerated matters listed in a schedule to the constitution. These did not include the creation of offences, this being a matter reserved to the regional legislatures. However, as incidental to the matters in the legislative lists parliament was empowered to create offences, but only as an incident of its main power. The question was whether, before it enacted a legislation on any of the matters in the lists, say, banks or banking or railway or trunk roads, which were among matters so listed, the federal parliament could create offences relating to them. To this question the Privy Council returned an emphatic negative:

> One cannot talk sensibly of an offence being incidental or supplementary to banks or banking, or to railways (Item 37) or to trunk roads (Item 39). But if there has been legislation about trunk roads, one can ask oneself whether the creation of the particular offence can properly be called an incidental or supplementary part of that legislation. . . . There must be actual legislation in being . . . ,

only then can the connection between the two matters be examined to see whether it is sufficiently close. It can ... readily be appreciated that a statute authorising the Prime Minister to create any offence in relation to any subject on the legislative lists would be too wide; it would enable him to remodel the criminal law.[26]

3. *Executive Power as Power to Execute the Laws: The Specific Grant Theory*

The third view of executive power is that it is simply power to execute the laws, to carry into effect the provisions of the law, either by enforcement against persons contravening them or by doing work or taking some other action required thereunder. Accordingly executive power presupposes some law which is to be executed. There must be in existence a law in execution of which the action of the executive is done. The government can no more incorporate a parastatal organisation to operate industrial and commercial undertakings without the authority of an enabling law than it can abolish private contracts without legal authority. It can no more operate postal services without the backing of the law than it can expropriate a citizen of his land without a similar authority.

But the laws which the executive is to execute are not confined to laws enacted by the legislature, although unquestionably they form the preponderant proportion. There is also the law of the constitution as well as the law of nations. This has always been conceded. Thus in all the Commonwealth federal constitutions the executive authority is defined to extend to the execution and maintenance of the constitution. So also in the leading case of *In re Neagle*, it was admitted by both the minority and majority of the United States Supreme Court that 'the laws he [the President] is to see executed are manifestly those contained in the constitution, and those enacted by Congress'.[27]

From the power to execute the law of nations flows the conduct of relations with other nations which comprises as one of its important aspects the making of treaties and of diplomatic negotiations. The constitution itself may of course restrict the power of the executive to conduct foreign relations. The U.S. Constitution, for example, makes formal treaty-making the joint responsibility of the President and the Senate; the President, the Constitution declares, shall have power, by and with the advice and consent of the Senate, to make treaties, provided two-thirds of the Senate present concur.

The execution of the law of the constitution is apt to give, and has in fact given, rise to much dispute regarding the nature and extent of acts that may be done in pursuance of it. This is because of the uncertainty as to what provisions of the constitution amount for this purpose to a 'law' capable of being executed. A constitution, for example, creates legislative, executive and judicial powers, and vests them in specific organs. Are the relevant provisions by which it does this 'law', a contravention of which calls for some executive action on the part of the government? Suppose a person by a murderous attack tries to interfere with a judge or a member of the legislature in the exercise of his duty under the constitution, cannot the President, even without specific legal authorisation, take whatever action he deems appropriate to protect the judge or legislator? If there is in the constitution an express provision to that effect, then that will clearly be a law, which the President can execute by, for example, detailing a constable or some other law-enforcement officer to guard the judge or legislator wherever he may go. But does not such a provision arise in the constitution by necessary implication?

This was in effect the issue in the Neagle case just referred to. A justice of the U.S. Supreme Court, while on circuit in California, was threatened with assault and murder by a person against whom he had given judgment. To protect him against the threatened attack, a marshal of the United States was, on the instruction of the U.S. Attorney-General, assigned to act as bodyguard to the Justice. While the Justice was at a railway station in the course of travelling from one circuit court to another, he was attacked by the author of the threats, whereupon the marshal shot and killed the attacker. The question before the Supreme Court was whether the Attorney-General, on behalf of the President, had power to assign a marshal to act as bodyguard to a justice of the Supreme Court travelling on circuit, so as to constitute the killing of the attacker an act done in pursuance of a law of the U.S., which would entitle the marshal to be released on a writ of *habeas corpus* from the custody of the authorities of the State of California. There was no statute or any specific provision of the Constitution enabling the President to protect judges, but it was argued that the action was justified by his power to execute the Constitution, because the assignment of the marshal was made in discharge of an obligation fairly and properly inferable from that instrument, namely the preservation of the Constitution against a person seeking to interfere with the discharge of his duty by a member of one of its agencies.

The argument was accepted by the majority of the court which held that the power to execute the laws extended to all the rights, duties and obligations growing out of the Constitution and to all the protection implied by the nature of the government under the Constitution. And the protection of the judges was essential to the existence of the government, since it would be a great reproach to the system of government of the United States if there was to be found within the domain of its powers no means of protecting the judges in the conscientious and faithful discharge of their duties from the malice and hatred of those upon whom their judgments might operate unfavourably.

A minority of two, while admitting that the President's executive power extended to the execution of the law of the Constitution, held that the Constitution established no law specifically requiring the protection of judges in their official capacity against murderous attacks. On the contrary, the Constitution vests in Congress the power 'to make all laws which shall be necessary and proper for carrying into execution [its own powers] and all other powers vested by this Constitution in the government of the United States, or in any department or officer thereof'.[28] Accordingly, in the absence of any enactment by Congress providing for protection as being necessary and proper for carrying the judicial power into execution, the President could not assign a marshal to act as a bodyguard to a judge and to follow him in his journey while in circuit. 'The protection needed and to be given must proceed, not from the President, but primarily from Congress',[29] and 'the right claimed must be traced to legislation of Congress, else it cannot exist'.[30]

At least two comments may be made on the decision of the majority in this case. First, the proposition that the power to execute the laws extended to all the rights, duties and obligations growing out of the Constitution and to all the protection implied by the nature of the government under the Constitution comes dangerously near to the inherent power theory. Secondly, it may be questioned whether the special protection of a judge is essential to the existence of the government. No doubt, if a situation arises imperilling the existence of the government or of society, as where a group of persons unlawfully establish powers of government over some part of the country or attempt by force of arms to prevent one or more of the established organs from exercising their functions under the Constitution, the executive will be entitled to take such action as may be necessary to deal with the situation and save the government or society from ruination. This is the law of necessity, of which we have already spoken. But the situation necessitating the invocation of the power must be a grave one; it must be a situation of present and imminent danger to the existence, peace or well-being of the state or society. It seems clear that the protection of the judge in the *Neagle case* cannot be rested upon the law of necessity. In the absence of necessity the proposition seems incontestable that the power to take action in execution of the Constitution must arise either from specific provisions of the Constitution or from express statutory enactment.

The Attorney-General had argued that the U.S. Constitution contained such specific provision in the oath which it requires the

President to take 'to preserve, protect and defend the Constitution'.[31]
It may be remarked here that the Constitutions of many Commonwealth African countries also prescribe a similar oath for the President.
Now, while an oath attaches criminal sanction in the event of its
violation, the question is whether it also operates as a grant of power.
Neither the majority nor the minority in the *Neagle case* dealt with this
question directly. Edward S. Corwin has, however, pointed to 'the
obvious difficulty in claiming for the President powers that the
Constitution otherwise withholds from him, simply on the score of his
obligation to protect and preserve it',[32] and he concludes both on
logical interpretation and upon available historical evidence that the
oath is not an independent source of power.

The other question that has arisen on the effect of the oath is
whether the obligation which it imposes upon the President to preserve
and protect the Constitution is a legally enforceable one. The
President's oath may be compared with the Queen's coronation oath by
which she swore 'to conform to the people of England the laws and
customs granted to them by the ancient kings of England', and to 'hold
and keep the righteous customs' of the realm and to 'defend and
strengthen the same'. Edward Corwin has again expressed the view that
the 'purpose, definitely, was to put the King's conscience in bonds to
the law'.[33] In other words, the normal consequences of a violation of
an oath do not apply in the case of the Queen or President. This
interpretation is supported by a decision of the Ghana Supreme Court
in 1961 in *Re Akoto*[34] which, likening the declaration of fundamental principles, which the President of Ghana was required to make
on assumption of office, to the Queen's coronation oath, held that
'neither the oath nor the declaration can be said to have a statutory
effect'.[35]

A further question that arises upon this view of executive power is
whether the authority to execute a law must be specifically granted by
the law in question or whether the authority flows from the general
executive power clause. If the legislature enacts a law without expressly
empowering the president to execute it, can he nevertheless exercise the
power by virtue of the vesting of executive power in him in the
constitution? Is the vesting of executive power in the president a grant
of power? This is a different question from whether the legislature can
confer an executive function arising under a statute on persons or
agencies other than the president. Two opposing views are held upon
this question. It is asserted upon one view that 'the true view of
executive function is ... that the President can exercise no power
which cannot fairly and reasonably be traced to some *specific* grant
of power or justly implied and included within such express grant as
proper and necessary to its exercise. Such specific grant must be either

in the Constitution or in an act of Congress passed in pursuance thereof'.[36] It is argued that the clause vesting executive power in the President is not such a *specific* provision, and cannot therefore operate as a grant of power. Thus the United States Constitution, after declaring that the executive power shall be vested in the President, goes on to empower him to do specific things, such as the power of supreme command of the army, to reprieve offences, to take care that the laws be faithfully executed, and with the concurrence of the Senate to make treaties and appoint public servants. It is from these specific grants, and not from the general executive power clause, that the President derives whatever executive power he has under the Constitution. For if the general executive power clause were a grant of power, the specific enumerations in the subsequent clauses would be a mere surplusage, serving no purpose except perhaps as an emphasis. Thus Mr Webster, in a Senate debate in February 1835, expressed himself as follows:

> It is true that the Constitution declares that the executive power shall be vested in the President; but the first question which arises is, What is executive power? What is the degree, and what are the limitations? Executive power is not a thing so well known, and so accurately defined, as that the written Constitution of a limited government can be supposed to have conferred it in the lump. . . . I think it perfectly plain and manifest that, although the framers of the Constitution meant to confer executive power on the President, yet they meant to define and limit that power, and to confer no more than they did thus define and limit. When they say it shall be vested in a President, they mean that one magistrate, to be called a President, shall hold the executive authority; but they mean, further, that he shall hold this authority according to the grants and limitations of the Constitution itself.[37]

The Commonwealth African presidential constitutions contain no provision similar to the American, empowering the President to take care that the laws be faithfully executed, which means that, upon this view of the matter, the President cannot assume power to execute a law unless the same is specifically granted to him by that law.

The other school of thought holds that the clause vesting executive power in the President is a grant of power. This viewpoint has behind it the authority of the United States Supreme Court, for in 1926 it held that 'the vesting of the executive power in the President was essentially a grant of power to execute the laws'.[38] This view is clearly to be preferred as according more with a commonsense interpretation of the clause. What this means, therefore, is that once the legislature enacts a law authorising, say, the establishment of post offices, then — whether or not the law expressly vests him with the power in that behalf — the President can, by right of the vesting of the executive power in him by the Constitution, execute the postal law by building post offices, organising postal services and appointing the personnel to run them, provided of course an appropriation has been made therefor by the legislature.

REFERENCES

1. Allan Gledhill, *Pakistan: The Development of Its Laws and Constitution*, 2nd ed. (1967), p. 42.

2. *Humphrey* v. *United States* 295 U.S. 602 (1934).

3. *Myers* v. *United States* 272 U.S. 52.

4. 295 U.S. 602.

5. *ibid*. at p. 628.

6. at p. 629.

7. 272 U.S. 52.

8. Theodore Roosevelt, *Autobiography*, pp. 388–9

9. *Eshugbayi Eleko* v. *Government of Nigeria* [1931], A.C. 662, 670.

10. James Bryce, *The American Commonwealth*, Hacker (ed.) (1959), Vol. 1, p. 53.

11. Quoted in the judgment of Justice McReynolds in *Myers* v. *United States* 272 U.S. 52 at p. 237.

12. *ibid*. at p. 180.

13. See argument in *Kendall* v. *United States* 12 pet. 524 (1838). Also Hamilton in *Letters of Pacificus*.

14. Republic of Malawi (Constitution) Act, 1966; S.18 Zambia Independence Order, 1964; S.16 Constitution of Kenya (Amendment) Act, 1964; S.128, Constitution of Gambia, 1970.

15. Morris and Read, *Uganda: The Development of Its Laws and Constitution* (1966), p. 91, n. 14.

16. Ss. 7 and 8 Republic of Tanganyika (Consequential, Transitional and Temporary Provision) Act, 1962, Cap. 500.

17. Locke, *Two Treatises of Government* (Morley ed.), Bk.11, Ch.14, 159–66.

18. *Federation of Pakistan* v. *Shah* (1955) reported in Jennings, Constitutional Problems in Pakistan (1957) 353, 357 – per Muhammad Munir C. J.

19. *Lakanmi* v. *The A.-G. (West)* SC.58/69 of April 24, 1970 (Nigeria) – per Ademola C. J.

20. For more detailed discussion, see Nwabueze, *Constitionalism in the Emergent States* (1973), Ch. VII.

21. *Att.-Gen. of the Republic* v. *Mustafa Ibrahim and Others* (1964), Cyprus L. Rep. 195.

22. See *Att.-Gen.* v. *Eastern Railway* (1880) 5 App. Cas. 473; Gower, *Modern Company Law* (2nd ed. 1957), p. 82.

23. S.43(4), Gambia; S.44(1), Zambia; S.16(1), Kenya; S.33(1) Botswana; S.49(1), Malawi; S.13(2), Tanzania; *cf* art. 15(1), Ghana; art. 33(1), Uganda.

24. S.53, Gambia; S.56, Zambia; S.24, Kenya; S.57, Botswana; S.8(2), Malawi; S.21, Tanzania; art. 66, Uganda.

25. [1963] 1 W.L.R. 949.

26. *ibid.* at p. 961 per Lord Devlin delivering the judgment of the Privy Council; see to the same effect *Att.-Gen. for Commonwealth of Australia* v. *Colonial Sugar Refining Co. Ltd* [1911] A.C. 237 (P.C.).

27. *Cunningham* v. *Neagle* 135 U.S. 1 (1890), at p. 83 per Justice Lamar.

28. Art. 1, S.8.

29. *ibid.* at p. 83.

30. *ibid.* at p. 90.

31. Art. 11, S.1.

32. Edward S. Corwin, *The President: Office and Powers*, 4th ed. (1957), p. 63.

33. *Loc. cit.*

34. [1961] G.L.R. 523.

35. *ibid.* at p. 534 — per Korsah C. J. See below p. 301 for further discussion of the case.

36. William Taft, quoted in E. S. Corwin *op. cit.*

37. Quoted in Justice McReynolds' dissenting judgment in *Myers* v. *United States* 272 U.S. 52 at pp. 229–30.

38. *Myers* v. *United States, ibid.* at p. 117 — per Taft C. J. Chief Justice Taft had thus alternated between the two viewpoints.

CHAPTER II

THE NATURE OF THE EXECUTIVE IN THE PRESIDENTIAL SYSTEM

With the preceding analysis of the nature of executive power, we can now proceed to consider the nature of a presidential executive itself, its composition, the relations between its various agencies and with the other organs of government. It is these that determine the type of governmental system. Two main features characterise the executive in a presidential system. The executive consists of a single individual, and is independent of the legislature and the judiciary. These two features will now be discussed in turn.

1. *A Single Executive*

The composition of any institution has undoubtedly an important bearing upon its nature and character, and understandably, therefore, the framers of the first modern presidential constitution, the American, were much exercised by the question. Was the executive branch of the new government to consist of a single individual or of a plurality of persons? It is easy to see why the question should have provoked so much concern and discussion among the framers. For a people just emerging from a bloody armed confrontation with a monarchical government, monarchy or any other form of government by a single individual was apt to stir up sentiments of fear and even of hate. In the eyes of contemporary Americans it symbolised tyranny and oppression, and all the other evils of governmental absolutism. American reaction to this spectre of monarchy was already amply reflected in the constitutions adopted by many of the States after the successful conclusion of the war with Britain. The single executive was shunned like a plague. Yet, after lengthy discussions at the Constitutional Convention at Philadelphia of the various plans presented, the framers, unable to devise a more satisfactory alternative, settled for an executive of one man. Enacting this decision, the Constitution declares in Article II that 'the executive power shall be vested in *a* President of the United States of America'. What this implies, in terms of a specific requirement of the system, is the preclusion of a *concurrent* vesting of the executive power in two or more persons of *equal authority,* as in the case of the Roman consuls or the collegiate executive of the Swiss system. An arrangement whereby the executive power is vested concurrently in a plurality of persons of equal authority cannot therefore be presidential in the American sense.

The first question that arises upon the principle of a single executive is whether the vesting of executive power in a single person by the title of president requires that the President should be the sole repository of the entire executive authority of the state, and that no other executive function can exist independently of him or be exercised otherwise than under his direction and control? Or does the provision admit of other independent executive functions, but with the President's as the pre-eminent one, not in the sense of having an overriding force, but as being predominant in content and scope? If the preponderance of the executive functions of the state is vested in a single individual as president, is the system any the less presidential because a small proportion is also lodged elsewhere? Is not what the system requires that there should be, not a single executive, but a single *chief* executive? That is to say, a single individual in whom the bulk, the preponderant proportion, but not the entirety, of the executive functions of the state is vested. It is important, however, that the functions lodged elsewhere must not be so extensive as to rival (even if they do not equal) those of the President, as otherwise there would be two chief executives occupying two significant and mutually exclusive portions of the executive field.

William Anderson has argued against the idea of a chief executive. 'The Constitution', he wrote, 'does not say that the President is 'chief executive'. That would imply that there are other executives, of lesser power, associated with him. This vesting clause places the entire executive power of the United States Government in the hands of one man. It does so by constitutional provision, beyond the power of Congress or the Courts to take away'.[1] This position can hardly be maintained in the face of the Constitution itself which, while lodging the executive power in the President, also grants to other authorities functions which, under the monarchical system, are commonly treated as partaking of execution. Thus, the creation of offices, the declaration of war, and the raising of armies are lodged in Congress, and not in the President. And even the President's powers are subject to restrictions designed as part of a system of checks and balances, such as those affecting the power of appointment and of treaty-making, which are made dependent upon the concurrence of the Senate. Furthermore, as is pointed out in the preceding chapter, the executive power vested in the President does not embrace all functions that, by generally recognised governmental practice, are treated as executive, such as the function involved in the administration of a law, this being quasi-judicial or quasi-legislative in nature.[2] Not forming part of the President's executive power under the Constitution, such functions are at the disposal of Congress who may vest them in other persons than the President to be exercised by them independently of his control or direction.[3] As the Supreme Court observed, 'it would be an alarming doctrine that Congress cannot impose upon any executive officer any duty they may think proper, which is not repugnant to any rights secured and protected by the Constitution; and in such cases, the duty and responsibility grow out of and are subject to the control of the law, and not to the directive of the President. And this is emphatically the case where the duty enjoined is of a mere ministerial character.'[4]

There is also the question whether Congress cannot also competently confer away from the President functions of a strictly executive nature arising under its statutes. This was the question before the Supreme Court in the celebrated case of *Myers* v. *United States.*[5] By an act of Congress, postmasters of the first, second and third grades were to be appointed for a fixed term of four years, subject to earlier removal by the President with the consent of the Senate. Myers, a first-class postmaster, was removed from his office by the President without the consent of the Senate, and he sued for arrears of salary on the ground of wrongful dismissal. The Court by a majority held the part of the act making the Senate a party to the removal power to be void as an unconstitutional interference with the President's power to execute the laws. The reasoning was that the President could not execute the laws alone and unaided, and since he must needs have the assistance of subordinates, it followed that as part of his executive power he should have power to appoint these subordinates. The power to appoint attracted as a necessary incident the power of removal, for otherwise the President might be saddled, to the prejudice of his administration, with subordinates who could not be removed, notwithstanding that they were disloyal, incompetent or otherwise unfit. As part of the executive power granted to him, the appointing and removal power could only be limited or controlled by the Constitution or by Congress in accordance with the Constitution. As regards the appointing power, the Constitution contains express limitation (namely, concurrence of the Senate), but it neither restricts the removal power nor authorises Congress to do so. Congress's attempt to restrict it without constitutional authority was therefore, in the view of the majority, void as an unconstitutional interference with the President's executive power. The minority of the Court based their dissent on the ground that the removal power was not a necessary incident either of the general

executive power or of the power to take care to see that the laws be
faithfully executed, and was therefore not vested in the President by
virtue of the grant of these powers.

Whether the removal power is or is not a necessary incident of the
power to execute the laws, it is clear that the legislature cannot divest
the President of any functions properly belonging to him as part of his
power to execute the laws. This is in accord with the decisions of the
U.S. Supreme Court and of the Privy Council to the effect that the
vesting of the judicial power in the judiciary precludes the legislature
from either assuming it itself or transferring it to the executive. An Act
of the legislature which bars permanently from government employment certain *named* persons for alleged subversive activity[6] or which
condemns them to imprisonment or to a fine[7] or deprives them of their
property[8] is a legislative judgment, and therefore void as an unconstitutional encroachment upon the judical power.

It is well to note that there do in fact exist on the American statute
book a number of statutes conferring powers which pertain to the
President's executive power, but which are to be exercised independently of his control. There exists, too, at least one decision earlier than
Myers, which held invalid presidential attempt to instruct officers in the
exercise of such functions.[9] No doubt the constitutionality of these
enactments and decisions have become questionable in the light of
Myers, yet taken together with the decision in *Humphrey* v. *United
States* and the provisions of the Constitution lodging certain functions
of an executive nature in Congress, it seems clear that what the system
requires is a single chief executive, and not a single executive. Most
writers upon the American Constitution and Government accept this.[10]

A constitution may of course so distribute executive power between
the President and other executive agencies that it is not easy to say who
has the preponderant share of it. The Constitution of the French Fifth
Republic is a case in point.[11] It establishes a President with certain
significant executive powers — power to preserve and ensure the
integrity and continuance of the state[12] and, to this end, to take all
such actions as may be required for dealing with a grave and immediate
danger threatening the integrity of the state or its institutions and
authority;[13] power of the supreme command of the armed forces, of
pardon, of making appointments to the civil and military posts of the
state; the accreditation and reception of ambassadors and envoys
extraordinary, the negotiation and ratification of treaties.[14] Significantly, however, the power to execute the laws is vested, not in him,
but in a Premier. The Premier, the Constitution declares, is to direct the
operation of the government and ensure the execution of the laws. It is,
however, by no means conclusive as to wherein lies the preponderance
of executive functions under the Constitution. The crucial considera-

tion is whether, in the exercise of his power to ensure the execution of the laws, the Premier is subject to the control or direction of the President. It is to be noted, first, that the Premier is appointed by the President in his discretion. He can terminate 'the functions of the Premier when the latter presents the resignation of the Government', on its defeat in the legislature on a vote of no confidence, or on the rejection of the government's policy programme.[15] It seems clear that, apart from the occasion of the government's resignation when it is mandatory upon him to remove the Premier, the President can also remove him at any time in his discretion. The removal power effectively subordinates the person subject to it, to the will of its possessor. Between the President and the Premier, therefore, there can be no doubt as to who is boss or chief, even as regards the power to execute the laws. There is yet another source of control vested in the President. Although the President is conceived of as an impartial arbiter among politicians and the symbol of the continuity of the state, standing above and somewhat outside the Government, so that his tenure is unaffected by the resignation of the Government, he nevertheless presides over the Council of Ministers, the principal organ of the Government, in whom the responsiblitiy is vested for the determination and direction of policy. It has thus been said of the 1958 French Constitution that its chief drafter, Michel Debré, 'preferred the British system, which de Gaulle has perverted by widening the presidential powers until they formally exceed those of the American president, being less limited by the representative assembly, and not at all by either federal or judicially enforced constitutional restraints'.[16] The executive government under the French Constitution of 1958 may therefore be described without impropriety as essentially presidential in character, notwithstanding that it also contains features of the British parliamentary system.

In Commonwealth Africa no such difficulty arises, since all the presidential constitutions establish the paramountcy of the President in the executive field. Where a prime minister exists, as in Tanzania and in the one-party state constitution proposed for Zambia, he is completely under the President, with no independent executive power of his own. There is, however, a provision in all these constitutions, which would appear potentially to offer a serious threat to the paramountcy of the President. As in America, the President's executive power is subject to certain specific limitations, but the African constitutions provide additionally that the vesting of executive power in the President shall not prevent parliament from conferring functions on persons or authorities other than the President. The implication of this provision, which appears also in all the other Commonwealth African Constitutions with the exception of the Ghana Constitutions of 1960 and 1969, is not only to confirm and incorporate the principle of the U.S. Supreme Court decision in the *Humphrey* case as regards the power of the legislature to vest administrative functions of a quasi-judicial or quasi-legislative nature elsewhere than in the President, but also to jettison the rule in the *Myers* case. It means that, notwithstanding the vesting of executive power in the President, the legislature can, when it enacts a law, dispose in any manner it pleases of the power to execute it.

Arguing in favour of a limitation on the power of the legislature to vest executive functions independently of the President, Edward S. Corwin has said that to concede to Congress an unqualified power in this respect would be to make it possible for Congress, if it so wishes, to subvert and revolutionalise the system of executive government instituted by the constitution, by so dividing and sharing the executive power as to convert the government into a parliamentary system, with a nominal executive chief or president.[17] Even Congress' admitted power to dispose of administrative functions of a quasi-judicial or quasi-legislative nature can constitute quite a serious qualification upon the principle of a single chief executive, since such functions have become vastly important and extensive in recent years. The Committee on Administrative Management in the United States has thus been prompted to comment in 1937:

> The multiplication of these agencies [i.e. the independent commissions] cannot fail to obstruct the effective over-all management of the Executive Branch almost in geometric ratio to their number. At the present rate we shall have 40 to 50 of them within a decade. Every bit of executive and administrative authority which they enjoy means a relative weakening of the President, in whom, according to the Constitution, 'the executive Power shall be vested'. As they grow in number his stature is bound to diminish. He will no longer be in reality *the Executive,* but only one of many executives, threading his way around obstacles which he has no power to overcome.

The provision in the Commonwealth African constitutions empowering parliament to confer functions on persons or authorities other than the President, though of vast potentiality, is unlikely to assume great significance in actual practice. It seems to have been intended, not as a sword, but as a shield to guard against a situation where it could be argued that the legislature could not confer any functions under a statute, even of a purely administrative or ministerial type, upon persons or authorities who are independent of the President. It is improbable in Commonwealth Africa that the legislature might use the power to re-write the constitution and, in any case, the legislature is so subservient to the executive from which, after all, all legislative measures originate.

The principle of a single executive has another significant implication relating to the autonomy of the President within the executive branch. Perhaps we should first note what it does *not* imply in this connection. The fact of the President being the executive cannot possibly mean that, within his area of competence, he is to be the sole executive functionary, performing by himself personally and single-handedly all the functions embraced in the executive power vested in him. The presidential system imposes no such requirement, for the simple reason that it is impracticable, indeed absurd. As was ruled by the U.S. Supreme Court, although 'the President's duty in general requires his superintendence of the administration, yet this duty cannot require of him to become the administrative officer of every department and bureau, or to perform in person the numerous details incident to services which, nevertheless, he is, in a correct sense, by the Constitution and laws required and expected to perform. This cannot be; first, because, if it were practicable, its effect would be to absorb the duties and responsibilities of the various departments of the government in the personal action of one chief executive officer. It cannot be, for the stronger reason, that it is impracticable — nay, impossible.'[18] Expediency and practicability demands therefore that the President should be free to act through others. No express delegation is necessary except in cases where he is required to exercise a personal discretion; even then a general delegation suffices. Thus, where by statute the 'special direction' of the President was required for the advance of public money to the disbursing officers of the Government of the United States, the Supreme Court held the statute to have been complied with by a general authorisation given in writing by the President to the Secretary of the Treasury to make such advances from time to time to various classes of disbursing officers; the court rejected the argument that the statute required the President's authorisation in each individual case.[19] As the court ruled in another case, 'there can be no doubt that the President, in the exercise of his executive power under the Constitution, may act through the head of the appropriate executive department. The heads of the departments are his authorised assistants in the performance of his executive duties, and their official acts, promulgated in the regular course of business, are presumptively his acts'.[20] In Commonwealth Africa the question is covered by specific constitutional provision to the effect that the President may act either directly or through officers subordinate to him. Of course the constitution or other law may exceptionally create a duty which, by its terms or its nature, cannot be delegated.[21]

Invariably, therefore, the executive branch contains, besides the president, other functionaries or authorities established by the constitution or other laws or originating informally in governmental practice. The U.S. Constitution, for example, clearly envisages that the executive branch should be organised into departments headed by ministers, for it empowers the President, with the consent of the Senate, to appoint 'public ministers' and other public officers; and 'he may require the opinion, in writing, of the principal officer in each of the executive departments'.[22] The office of minister is directly established in the Commonwealth African constitutions to exercise such governmental responsibility, 'including the administration of any department of government', as the President may assign. These constitutions also establish or refer to certain other offices – attorney general, director of public prosecutions, auditor-general, commissioner of police, permanent secretary, ambassador, chairman and members of the Public Service Commission, etc.; they also empower the President to constitute and abolish other offices – subject, however, to any act of parliament.

The implication of the principle of a single executive in terms of the President's autonomy concerns his relationship to other executive functionaries or authorities. If within their respective departments or ministries, departmental heads or ministers have an independent authority, free of the President's control or direction, then the executive would have become a plural one. It is crucial to the principle of a single executive that, as regards functions properly within the executive power vested in the President, all other executive officers should have no independent authority. Their authority is merely a delegated one, and its exercise is subject to control by the President. A departmental head or minister is there only in the role of a subordinate to assist the President in the exercise of his executive power. He is not a co-beneficiary with the President of the executive power, and although he exercises initiative and personal discretion within his department, he does so only as a delegate. The appointment of a minister to be in charge of a department does not imply an abdication by the President of his power in and over that department. Constitutionally he always remains free to act directly in the department even without prior consultation with the departmental head or minister, and he may also overrule a decision or action taken by the minister within the department.[23]

The President's relationship to the departmental heads or ministers collectively as a body is equally crucial to the principle of a single executive. While the American Constitution clearly recognises the office of departmental head, as a collective body they (the departmental heads) have no existence whatever in the constitution. No obligation is cast upon the President to consult with them collectively as a cabinet with respect to the general programme or policy of the government.

The reference to writing in the provision empowering the President to require the written opinion of a departmental head suggests that the Constitution never contemplated a collective opinion or advice. However, collective consultation has developed informally in response to the demands and pressures of modern government. The interaction of many minds, it has been truly said, 'is usually more illuminating than the intuition of one. In a meeting representing different departments and diverse points of view, there is a greater likelihood of hearing alternatives, of exposing errors, and of challenging assumptions'.[24] Perhaps even more important is what has been described as the 'increased public confidence inspired by order and regularity and the increased *esprit de corps* of the participants'.[25] Modern government challenges the capacity of a single mind to deal with its many and complex problems. Crisis increases the intensity of this challenge, and modern government faces an ever-recurrent series of crises. The Cabinet in America as an institutionalised organ of government may be said indeed to have been the product of crisis. Before 1793 there was nothing that could be called a Cabinet. Although the first President, George Washington, occasionally called into collective consultation his departmental heads, of whom there were then only four (including the attorney-general), the meetings did not assume such frequency and regularity as to stamp them with an institutionalised character as an established machinery of the government. It was the diplomatic crisis of that year, arising out of the question whether or not America should adopt the position of neutrality in the war between England and France, that gave the Cabinet formal birth by impelling the President to meet his secretaries almost every day over the issue, the culmination being the meeting at which the decision was taken to proclaim American neurality in the war.

But the point that deserves to be noticed about the Cabinet in America is that, after nearly two centuries of existence as a definite institution of government, it has acquired no constitutional status by convention. There is no conventional obligation upon the President to consult it at regular intervals. How often he convenes the Cabinet is a matter entirely within the discretion of the President, and the practice has varied as between individual Presidents. Some hold meetings of the Cabinet fairly regularly; others, distrustful of meetings, consult their Cabinet at infrequent intervals, preferring informal consultations with various types of advisers. If there is no obligation to consult, much less is there is a duty to accept the Cabinet's advice. Again individual Presidents have differed as to the extent they defer to the advice of their Cabinet. Professor Sir Denis Brogan described the position accurately when he wrote: 'There is in American theory and practice no question of *primus inter pares*. The famous story of Lincoln consulting his

Cabinet and announcing, "Nos, 7: ayes, 1. The ayes have it" expresses perfectly the spirit of the American Constitution.'[26] The same President was reported to have said to his Cabinet on another occasion: 'I have gathered you together to hear what I have written down. I do not wish your advice about the main matter – that I have determined for myself.' And the matter in question was one indeed as momentous as the emancipation of slaves. Statements to similar effect are also credited to other Presidents of similarly strong personality, like Andrew Jackson, Theodore Roosevelt, Woodrow Wilson and Franklin Roosevelt.

The question that arises is whether it can be said to be a requirement of the principle of a single executive that the Cabinet should possess no recognition either in the constitution itself or in convention? This question is relevant because all the Commonwealth presidential constitutions establish a Cabinet. Is the formal establishment of a Cabinet in the constitution incompatible with a single executive? Provided that no obligation is imposed on the President to accept or act on the advice of the Cabinet, there can be no incompatibility. Admittedly such a formal recognition would clearly raise an obligation to consult. (In fact the Constitution of Botswana, 1966, expressly so provides.)[27] The establishment of a Cabinet in the constitution would be made pointless if the position were that the President is to be free to convene it or not as he wishes. Surely the intention must be to minimise as much as possible the possibilities of a personal government, such as occurred in America during the Civil War when consultations were for the most part with individual ministers only, with occasional Cabinet meetings now and again. Without question the authoritarianism of Lincoln owed much to the failure of the Constitution to provide for a Cabinet, and seemed to have vindicated those critics who at the time of the Constitution's adoption decried this omission as an open invitation to 'despotism', 'caprice, the intrigues of favourites and mistresses, etc'.[28] And according to Kenneth Kaunda, the establishment of a Cabinet in the Commonwealth African presidential constitutions was in order to ensure that, by subjecting him to the advice and influence of a Cabinet, the President 'would not be able to assume dictatorial powers'.[29] Individual consultation produces a different kind of effect from a collective one. It is less easy to ride roughshod over a determined opposition from a council than from an individual, and a President who does that faces a heavier responsibility in the event of failure or mistake; and he may also provoke the resignation of some ministers and a consequent undermining of the unity of his administration as well as a possible loss of public support and confidence. There can be no doubt therefore that an obligation to consult a Cabinet does operate to fetter the discretion of a President in the exercise of his powers.

Yet the true essence of presidential autonomy lies not so much in the absence of an obligation to consult the Cabinet nor in the power to override its advice, as in the fact that even the acceptance of an advice should be an act of choice or of will on the part of the President. His is the final decision, even if it be only a decision to accept advice. In practice, no American President is ever too eager to override his cabinet advisers, if for no other reason than to maintain their utility and credibility.[30] Secondly, for every such decision, the President must accept a personal responsibility, notwithstanding that it proceeded upon the advice of others. This is exactly the antithesis of a constitutional presidency or monarchy. A constitutional Head is bound to act on advice, whether or not he agrees with it. It is thus hardly necessary for him to bring his judgment or will to bear upon the content of an advice, for neither the decision nor the responsibility therefor is his. Provided therefore that a President has a freedom to accept or overrule the advice of his Cabinet, an obligation to consult regularly with it, though it fetters his autonomy somewhat, is nevertheless compatible with it.

2. *Executive Independence*

The second main characteristic of the executive in a presidential system is its independence from the control of the legislature. This is crucial to the system. The makers of the U.S. Constitution were conditioned as much by the tyranny of monarchy as by the excesses of an omnipotent legislature. The revolution against monarchy had led to the enthronement of the omnipotence of the legislature. For in the constitutions adopted by the States during the Revolution, the executive was reduced to virtual impotence, being at once the creature and a mere instrument of the legislature. And in the Articles of Confederation there was almost no executive at all, since much of the executive power of the Union was in the hands of Congress. At the time of the drafting of the Constitution therefore the prevailing view of the legislature was of a kind of octopus, drawing into its tentacles all the other governmental authorities. There was indeed a sorry record of excesses and abuse by state legislatures. The omnipotent legislature, which emerged as a reaction against executive despotism, had itself become despotic and therefore fallen out of favour. Contemporary Americans began now to look up to an independent executive as 'the guardian of the people, even of the lower classes, against legislative tyranny, against the great and the wealthy who in the course of things will necessarily compose the legislative body'.[31] Thus did executive independence come to be enshrined as a principle of the governmental system established by the Constitution.[32]

Executive independence requires freedom from control by the legislature as regards appointment and tenure. The American President is not chosen by Congress but independently of it — by the people at large, though the election is by an indirect method through popularly elected electoral colleges. If his choice were to be by Congress, he would be surbordinated to it through a desire to curry its favour in order to obtain re-election. A President chosen by the legislature can only be secured against subordination to the legislature if he is limited to just one term of office of fixed duration. The plan presented to the Constitutional Convention at Philadelphia to have the President chosen by Congress was thus accompanied by a proposal to limit him to one term of seven years.

The real significance of having the president elected by the people rather than by the legislature lies in the fact that it gives him an independent right to govern. The right flows directly from the people who elect him, and, arguably, is greater than the legislature's, because it is more nationally based. In the rather pointed words of McConnell:

> The President represents the nation as a whole, while the Congress represents it as a collection of states and congressional districts. . . . It would be comforting to assume that the many different positions that congressmen and senators take add up together to a position as national and as public-spirited as the President's. . . . The men of Capitol Hill represent different publics, different from each other's and from the President's. Their constituencies are vastly different, some consisting largely of farmers, some of large cities, some of working class districts, some of states where mining is overwhelmingly important, and so on; but the President's constituency consists of all the people. Because the smaller constituencies emphasise particular interests, the aggregate representation offered by Congress does not equal that of the presidency.[33]

An executive elected by the legislature owes its right to govern to the legislature. This is indeed the central feature of the parliamentary system. Government under the system is the rule of the legislature, hence it is called parliamentary government. What justifies this description is the fact that the right to govern flows through the legislature to the executive. There is only one popular election — that for members of the legislature. No separate popular election is held for the executive. Thus the only popular mandate for the government is that conferred by the votes that elected the members of parliament. Since that mandate is the only authority for government, the authority belongs to the legislature. However, because government by the entire members of the legislature is not practicable nor desirable under modern conditions, the legislature then delegates its authority to one or more of its members. The same reason that compels delegation to the legislature from the people also obliges a further delegation by the legislature to a more manageable body. An independent executive is thus antithetical to the parliamentary system.

Once elected, the President in the United States holds his office for four years unless he sooner dies or resigns. His tenure of office is independent of Congress and therefore free from the subordinating effect of the removal power. He is not responsible to Congress for his conduct of the government, and there is no question of his being under an obligation to resign because of an adverse vote in Congress. Though he needs the support of Congress for the effectuation of his programme and therefore for the success of his administration, he does not depend upon it for his continuance in office. He is not accountable to it, as is the executive under the Westminster system. The Constitution requires no more of him than simply to inform Congress, from time to time, of the state of the Union. He may of course be criticised or be denied congressional approval for his demands or for his legislative proposals. But that leaves his tenure unaffected. All this does not by any means make him an irresponsible executive; on the contrary he is fully responsible, but his responsibility is to the people by whom he is elected and to whom alone he is accountable for his stewardship.

The independence of the President from congressional control as regards appointment and tenure is also necessary for his departmental heads or ministers, who after all are only his agents appointed to exercise, in his name and on his behalf, functions relating to the departments entrusted to them. Their acts, as has been stated, are presumptively his. It follows that a power in the legislature to appoint or remove departmental heads or ministers would unquestionably be incompatible with executive independence.

The United States Constitution rigidly separates the personnel of the executive and the legislature. Neither the President nor his departmental heads are members of Congress. While this is a cardinal characteristic of American government, it cannot be said to be necessarily required by the principle of an independent executive. Its rationale lies elsewhere. It is designed as a limiting device to check a concentration of powers in the hands of the executive with the danger of tyranny to which that is prone. It may be that making the President a member of the legislature and subjecting him to questioning by its members may indirectly detract from his independence, but that would be nothing to the enhanced authority which it would bring to him. With respect to the departmental heads, even this indirect derogation would be hardly likely to result from their membership of the legislature. A departmental head loses nothing in prestige by his participation in the debates of the legislative houses. Of course it all depends on the consequences which the Constitution attaches to membership. If it carries with it an obligation to resign on a censure vote, then unquestionably membership will be incompatible with the independence of the executive. A leading authority on the American Constitution has however said that 'the creation of a Cabinet with legislative members would not amount to supplanting forthwith the 'presidential system' with the 'cabinet system'. The president would not become a prime minister, bound to resign when outvoted in Congress'. The Commonwealth African presidential constitutions require that ministers shall be members of the legislature.

(i) *Executive Independence and the System of Checks and Balances*

A further point arises concerning the system of checks and balances, and its relationship to the principle of independence. How does one reconcile one to the other, or are they mutually exclusive? Checks and balances are indeed a conspicuous feature even of the American Constitution. They are meant to reconcile the need for a strong executive with democracy. Thus, under the American Constitution, the President's power in regard to appointments and the making of treaties is 'checked' by the necessity for the Senate's approval, and he, the Vice-President and other civil officers are liable to impeachment before Congress for treason, bribery or other high crimes and misdemeanours, and, upon conviction, to automatic dismissal from office.

It has been suggested that these checks make the President dependent upon Congress, and that they contradict the principle of the separation of powers.[34] This seems to mistake the nature of the system of checks and balances. Its effect is not to subordinate the person checked to the authority exercising the check. For it neither divests him of discretion in the exercise of functions vested in him nor makes such functions a joint responsibility. And, far from being contradictory to the doctrine of the separation of powers, its purpose is to make the separation a more effective instrument of constitutionalism. The system rests on an open recognition that particular functions belong primarily to a given organ while at the same time superimposing a power of limited interference by another organ in order to ensure that the former does not exercise its acknowledged functions in an arbitrary and despotic manner. This is all that the system seeks to do.

Take, for instance, the interposition of the Senate in the matter of appointments under the American Constitution. The fact that appointments can only be validly made with the advice and consent of the Senate does not make appointments the joint responsibility of the Senate and the President. As the U.S. Supreme Court has held, the consent of the Senate does not make an appointment;[35] this still remains 'the act of the President, and is also a voluntary act'.[36] Alexander Hamilton put the matter quite lucidly in *The Federalist:*

> It will be the office of the president to *nominate,* and with the advice and consent of the senate to *appoint.* There will of course be no exertion of choice on the part of the senate. They may defeat one choice of the executive, and oblige him to make another; but they cannot themselves *choose* — they can only ratify or reject the choice of the President. They might even entertain a preference to some other person, at the very moment they were assenting to the one proposed; because there might be no positive ground for opposition to him; and they could not be sure, if they withheld their assent, that the subsequent nomination would fall upon their own favourite, or upon any other person in their estimation more meritorious than the one rejected.[37]

By contrast, if it be supposed that the Senate's consent were also requisite to removals, this would have imposed upon the President a limitation going beyond a mere check. 'A veto by the Senate . . . upon removal', said the Supreme Court, 'is a much greater limitation upon the executive branch and a much more serious blending of the legislative with the executive than a rejection of a proposed appointment.'[38] If a proposed appointment is vetoed by the Senate, this would not frustrate completely the President's discretion in respect of the appointment nor greatly embarrass the work of his administration. He can nominate another person of his choice, and he has a wide field from which to exercise his choice. A veto upon removal, on the other hand, will, whenever it is exercised, frustrate completely the President's discretion, thus making the Senate the final judge in the matter and so putting it above the President.[39] And by overriding him in favour of a subordinate, such a veto will greatly undermine not only his authority with his assistants but also the principle of dependence and responsibility upon which the unity of the whole administration rests. For it would impose upon the President subordinates whom he cannot discipline through the ultimate sanction of removal, although there may no longer be any confidence between him and them.

It also seems important that the true role of impeachment by Congress as a check should be appreciated. The power of impeachment is not meant to give Congress a control over the President's tenure. Impeachment, it has been aptly said, 'is not an "inquest of office", a political process for turning out a President whom a majority of the House and two-thirds of the Senate simply cannot abide. It is certainly not, nor was it ever intended to be, an extraordinary device for registering a vote of no confidence'.[40] If it were, then it would upset the balance of the American scheme of government, and destroy the independence of the executive, replacing it with the principle of executive responsibility to the legislature which characterises the parliamentary executive of the Westminster type. It is little wonder that, throughout the history of the American government, it has only once been called into use, and on that sole occasion the attempt failed. Its failure has served to re-affirm the intention behind its inclusion in the Constitution – that it is not to be a legislative censure device against the President's conduct of the government; and it has also served to consign impeachment to rustication as a mere blunderbuss. For it would seldom happen that a President of the United States would, while in office, indulge in acts of the kind for which impeachment is prescribed by the Constitution, namely treason, bribery or other high crimes or misdemeanours. The impeachment of President Johnson in 1868 – the one single occasion of the use of the power – was a disreputable perversion of power for purely partisan motive.[41] The ground of the impeachment was that the President had violated the Tenure of Office Act, 1867, by removing his Secretary of State without the consent of the Senate as was required by the Act. His conduct was certainly not treasonable or otherwise criminal, but at worst only an improper exercise of a power which, under the Constitution, belonged to him. Even its impropriety depended upon the constitutionality of the Act of Congress itself, and in the view of the President and his advisers the Act was a manifest contravention of the Constitution. It was upon this view of the Act that he acted in removing the Secretary of State, a view which half a century later the Supreme Court affirmed when it declared the Act unconstitutional and void.[42] In view of the Court's decision one may perhaps reflect what a great injury would have been done to the President and the entire American governmental system had the impeachment succeeded (it failed by only one vote).

Checks and balances are less a feature of the Commonwealth African presidential Constitutions than of the American. The power of impeachment does, however, exist in two of the Constitutions and is indeed wider than in America, since it is available in respect of any violation of the Constitution or any gross misconduct by the President, though as a safeguard against abuse of the power for partisan purposes there is interposed between the President and the legislature a judicial tribunal which must find against the President before the legislature can then convict him by motion supported by the appropriate majority.[43]

(ii) *Executive Independence and the Courts*

If the test of executive autonomy and independence is that the President should have discretion or judgment in the discharge of his functions under the constitution, then the independence, to be fully effective, must be enjoyed against not only the political agencies but the courts as well. Control of discretion by the courts is no less derogatory of executive independence than control by the legislature. Thus, although the cardinal principle of the American constitutional system is that the government is a government of laws and not of men, and that the courts as custodians of the Constitution and the laws have a duty to control all governmental acts to ensure their conformance to the law, yet the U.S. Supreme Court has disclaimed all power to control the exercise of their discretion by the political organs, both legislative and executive. For this purpose two distinctions need to be made. First between, on the one hand, compelling and restraining the exercise of a discretion and, on the other, determining the limits of a discretion, and whether it has been exceeded or otherwise properly exercised in any particular case. The functions of the President under the Constitution are for the most part discretionary; they are given to him to be exercised in his own judgment and discretion, and it would be 'an absurd and excessive extravagance' for the court to presume to compel or restrain their performance, except when a discretion is exercised in bad faith. 'The province of the court', said Chief Justice Marshall, 'is solely to decide on the rights of individuals, not to inquire how the executive, or executive officers, perform duties in which they have a discretion. Questions in their nature political or which are, by the Constitution and laws, submitted to the executive, can never be made in this court.'[44] The sanction is not judicial, but political, i.e. the political accountability of the executive and the legislature to the nation. Thus the court cannot by *mandamus* compel the legislature to enact a law or the President to execute a discretion conferred upon him by the Act. Equally it cannot by injunction restrain the one from enacting a law on the ground that the proposed law would be undesirable, harmful to society or even contrary to the Constitution, or the other from executing it after it has been enacted but before it has been pronounced unconstitutional in an appropriate proceeding. An action by the State of Mississippi seeking to restrain the President from executing certain acts of Congress – the Reconstruction Acts – before their constitutionality had been decided was accordingly dismissed by the Supreme Court.[45] Similarly in Australia the High Court unanimously rejected an application for an injunction to prevent a bill passed by the federal legislature from being presented for the Governor-General's assent, on the ground that the bill was beyond the powers of Parliament.[46] In his judgment in the case, Chief Justice Dixon rightly criticised as incorrect a decision of the Supreme Court of the State of New South Wales which expressed willingness to grant an injunction to restrain the presentation of a bill which had been passed by the State legislature but which was not submitted to a referendum as required by law.[47]

When once a discretion has been completely exercised, however, such act is, at the instance of any individual whose rights are violated or in danger of being violated, amenable to the process of the court for the purpose of testing its conformity to the law. If it is in excess of the discretion or otherwise improper, the court can strike it down. Its jurisdiction to do so is clearly implied in its duty as the sentinel of the individual's rights and liberties; the court cannot shy away from this duty any more than it can compel the exercise of political discretion. Executive autonomy or independence confers no immunity from judicial process in such a case, but equally is it not impaired thereby, since all the court does is to interpret, as an impartial umpire between the government and the individual, the meaning and scope of the discretion under the constitution and the laws. Once the discretion is held to exist and its proper scope is delimited, the court cannot, barring bad faith, substitute its own discretion for that of the executive. It can exercise no will in the matter. 'The so-called power of annulling an unconstitutional statute', Lord Bryce has said, 'is a duty rather than a power'.[48]

The second distinction which it is necessary to draw is between a discretionary power and a ministerial duty. While the functions of the executive under the constitution are largely discretionary, the law may cast upon individual officers specific duties of a purely ministerial character, that is to say, peremptory duties in which nothing is left to discretion. In regard to such a duty, the officer concerned is amenable to the law for his conduct. The court can compel its performance, as the U.S. Supreme Court did when it compelled the Secretary of State to exercise his statutory power to deliver to the plaintiff Marbury a commission, which had been duly signed by the President, appointing him to the office of justice of the peace;[49] the Postmaster-General was similarly ordered to perform his duty under a statute requiring him to credit a plaintiff with a sum which the solicitor of the Treasury had certified to be due to him.[50] The court can also restrain the exercise of a ministerial duty in violation of the law.

When an executive duty or power is properly controllable by the court, the exalted constitutional position of the President or minister cannot defeat the right of an individual injured by an act done thereunder. An action, in whatever *form* the law permits, will lie at the instance of such individual against the government. For, even under the monarchical system of Britain, the Queen herself is sued in the respectful form of a petition. The action may, in form, be against the state or against the individual officer who committed the act. 'If', said Chief Justice Marshall, 'one of the heads of departments commits any illegal act, under colour of his office, by which an individual sustains an injury, it cannot be pretended that his office alone exempts him from being sued in the ordinary mode of proceeding, and being compelled to obey the judgment of the law'.[51] Whether the President himself can *personally* be made so amenable in his capacity either as President or as an individual citizen raises, however, consideration affecting the dignity of the office, which is dealt with in a later chapter.[52]

REFERENCES

1. William Anderson, *National Government*.
2. *Humphrey* v. *United States*, 295 U.S. 602 (1934); *Kendall* v. *United States*, 12 Pet 524, at p. 610 (1838).
3. Above, Ch. I.
4. *Kendall* v. *United States*, 12 Pet. 524, 610 (1838) — per Justice Thompson delivering the opinion of the court.
5. 272 U.S. 52.
6. *United States* v. *Lovett* 328 U.S. 303 (1945).
7. *Liyanage* v. *R* [1967] 1 A.C. 259 (Privy Council Appeal from Ceylon).
8. *Lakanmi* v. *Att. Gen.* (West) Sc. 58/69 of April 24, 1970 (Supreme Court of Nigeria).
9. E. S. Corwin, *The President: Office and Powers*, 4th ed. 1957, pp. 372–3.
10. Professor Koenig even entitles his book *The Chief Executive*.
11. See also the constitution of Senegal 1960–3
12. Art. 5, Constitution, 1958.
13. Art. 16.
14. Arts. 13–17, and art. 52.
15. Art. 8.
16. Carl J. Friedrich, *Impact of American Constitutionalism Abroad* (1957), p. 20.
17. E. S. Corwin, *op. cit.*, pp. 80–1.
18. *Williams* v. *United States*, 1 How. 290 at p. 297 (1843).
19. *Williams* v. *United States*, ibid.
20. *Runkle* v. *United States*, 122 U.S. 543, at p. 557 (1886), and the host of other decisions there cited.
21. Such was the function in *Runkle* v. *United States*, ibid.
22. Art. II, Sect. 2.
23. See further, Ch. VII below.
24. Theodore C. Sorensen, *Decision-Making in the White House* (1963), p. 59.
25. Theodore C. Sorensen, *op. cit.*
26. 'The Possibilities of the Presidential System in Developing Countries' in *Parliament as an Export*, ed. Sir Alan Burns (1969), p. 195.

27. S.51(2).

28. Louis W. Koenig, *The Chief Executive*, revised ed. (1969), p. 20.

29. *Zambia, Independence and Beyond: The Speeches of Kenneth Kaunda*, ed. Colin Legum (1966), pp. 83–4.

30. See Theodore C. Sorensen, *op. cit.*

31. By a member of the Constitutional Convention at Philadelphia – quoted in E. S. Corwin, *op. cit.*, p. 12.

32. See Madison, *Federalist* No. 48.

33. McConnell, *The Modern Presidency* (1967), p. 35.

34. Koenig, *op. cit.*, pp. 22–3

35. *Myers* v. *United States*, 272 U.S. 52 (1926).

36. *Marbury* v. *Madison*, 1 Cranch 137, 155 (1803).

37. *Federalist*, No. 66.

38. *Myers* v. *United States*, 272 U.S. 52, 121 (1926).

39. On this ground perhaps Senate's concurrence in treaty-making is more than a mere check.

40. Clinton Rossiter, *The American Presidency*, 2nd ed. (1960), pp. 52–3.

41. For a full account, see Koenig, *op. cit.*, pp. 64–6; Corwin, *op. cit.*, pp. 64–6.

42. *Myers* v. *United States*, *ibid.*

43. See below, p. 133 for fuller discussion.

44. *Marbury* v. *Madison*, 1 Cranch 137, 170 (1803).

45. *Mississippi* v. *Johnson* 4 Wall 475 (1867).

46. *Hughes and Vale Pty Ltd.* v. *Gair* [1954] Argus L. R. 1094; S.28(5) Zambia.

47. *Trethowan* v. *Peden* (1930), 31 S.R. (N.S.W.) 183. For a review see Cowan, (1953) 71 L.Q.R. 376.

48. James Bryce, *The American Commonwealth*, Hacker, ed. (1959), Vol. 1, p. 59.

49. *Marbury* v. *Madison*, *ibid.*

50. *Kendall* v. *United States*, 12 Pet 527.

51. *Marbury* v. *Madison*, *ibid.* at p. 170.

52. Chap. V.

CHAPTER III

AFRICAN ADAPTATIONS OF PARLIAMENTARY TO PRESIDENTIAL GOVERNMENT

A remarkable feature of presidential government in Commonwealth Africa is the extent to which it incorporates elements of the Westminster parliamentary system. Indeed it may justifiably be said that vital elements from the latter system are the superstructure upon which presidentialism in Commonwealth Africa is built. Before examining the extent of the adaptation and whether it is such as to preclude the blended product being described as presidential, it is necessary to identify the essential features of parliamentary government. Perhaps its most apt and succinct definition is that it is 'the rule of the legislature through a committee of its own members, coupled with the irresponsibility of the permanent nominal head of the executive'.[1] Discounting the nominal head of the executive, whose position will be considered in the next chapter, this definition embodies three main characteristics, namely, the executive is parliamentary in composition; it consists of a plurality of persons who as a cabinet constitute the government; it is made by, and responsible to, the legislature. The adaptations and their implications for presidentialism will now be discussed.

1. Membership of Parliament as a Requirement for Executive Office

The principle of a parliamentary executive is not applied to the President in the Commonwealth African presidential constitutions. Except in Kenya, Botswana and (before 1971) Uganda, the President cannot be a member of the national assembly; he can of course address it, and in Malawi he can attend and take part in its proceedings as if he were a member but without a vote. In the three countries named above he must be a member. Quite apart from the right which he has as Head of State to address the assembly, his membership entitles him to 'attend all meetings of the Assembly and to take part in all proceedings thereof, and to vote on any question before the Assembly'.[2] By the Constitution of Botswana (Amendment) Act, 1972 the President's membership is now by virtue of his office, and not by election as a constituency member as in Kenya and Uganda.

In practice the President's parliamentary membership in Kenya, Botswana and Uganda is only nominal. He never in fact attends in that role. Participation as an ordinary member in the rough and tumble of parliamentary debates is not easily reconcilable with the dignity of the presidential office or with attendance in the assembly as Head of State. That dignity has to be maintained as much in the chamber of the assembly as outside it. When the President addresses the assembly as Head of State, the occasion is a ceremonial one of some solemnity, marked by great pomp. The President is received with great reverence as one representing the majesty of the state. This is a role that cannot easily be combined with participation in the verbal warfare of parliamentary debate, if the President is still to command the type of dignity and respect which his ceremonial attendance in the house demands. The reality of the matter must be accepted.

Thus we find that the President's role as an ordinary member has been allowed to fall into abeyance in Kenya and Botswana. On June 23, 1966, for example, the Kenyan President announced to the National Assembly, through his Finance Minister, his inability to discharge his responsibility as Leader of Government Business in the house, and the assignment of that responsibility to a minister of state in the President's office,[3] who since January 1968 has been replaced in that position by the Vice-President.[4] There is here a divergence between the theory and practice of the Constitution. Under the Constitution, the President as a member of the National Assembly is entitled, like any other member, to attend and participate in its proceedings and to vote; in practice, however, he never does. One wonders why the facade of the President's nominal membership was resorted to at all. The explanation given by the then Minister for Constitutional Affairs, Mr Tom Mboya, was that 'it is nonsense for any part of the Government to be outside Parliament. We believe it to be a true reflection of African thought and tradition that the chosen leader of the nation should have his home and his roots in a locality where, also, he is the chosen leader of his kinsmen and his neighbours. By this, Sir, we mean that we do not want to have as President a person who is unable to win an election in his own constitutuency or in the district from which he comes. We do not want to end up with a person rejected in his own district coming to govern over Kenya without the mandate of those who know him best, his close relatives, his neighbours, and we insist that the President − before he can become the President of this Republic − must first enjoy the confidence of the people among whom he lives, and be elected by them to the Parliament as an ordinary Member of this Parliament'.[5] It is indeed a strange analogy that seeks to justify the President's membership of the National Assembly by reference to African 'thought and tradition'. One would have thought that tradition is irrelevant to the question. There is nothing in tradition remotely relevant to the composition of the parliament of a modern state, a body without parallel in traditional society. The enjoyment by the President of the confidence of his kinsmen is an unnecessary addition to the requirement of citizenship, and would seem to be an encouragement to nepotism. If the confidence and support of his kinsmen is necessary to his election, then the President might be tempted to favour his kinsmen specially in the distribution of the patronage and amenities of the state in order to ensure that he keeps their confidence.

The principle of a parliamentary executive is fully incorporated with respect to the ministers, who are required everywhere to be members of the legislature. Even when an appointment is made during a dissolution, the appointee must have been a member immediately before the dissolution. In the interest of efficient administration, which may demand the inclusion in the government of an individual of proven or special ability but who has not won an election, it is *usually* not insisted (not so in Kenya) that a minister must be a member at the time of his first appointment. If, however, he is appointed from outside — and some constitutions, e.g., that of Botswana, limit the number that can be so appointed — then he must acquire membership within four (sometimes six) months of his appointment or lose office unless this period of grace expires at a time when the legislature is dissolved, in which case he is allowed to continue in office until the date of the first meeting of the legislature after the general election. A minister who has vacated office because of his inability to acquire a seat in the legislature within the period of grace cannot be reappointed during the life of that legislature, as otherwise the parliamentary basis of ministerial office may become stultified by seatless ministers being appointed and reappointed for successive periods of four (or six) months.

The character of a minister's membership, i.e. whether he is an elected or nominated member, has important bearing upon the parliamentary basis of the office. Here there is a wide variation in the provision contained in the relevant constitutions. In Botswana he must be an elected constituency member, while in Kenya, Zambia and Gambia he may be either an elected or a nominated member. (The Vice-President in Kenya and Gambia must be an elected member.) The number of nominated members is twelve in Kenya, five in Zambia and three in Gambia, and they are appointed by the President in his discretion. In Kenya therefore it is theoretically possible to have twelve ministers who are only nominated members of the legislature. In Malawi the President can appoint any number of ministers from outside, and such ministers become, by virtue of their appointment, members of the National Assembly.[6] The Malawian provision represents an extension of the favoured position accorded to the Attorney-General in all the countries, a concession which is perhaps justified by the special qualification prescribed for him. The Attorney-General is almost always *ex officio* a member of the legislature (not so in Zambia) though in Kenya he is without a vote.

It is a matter for argument whether or not the appointment of ministers from outside the elected constituency members is derogatory of the parliamentary principle. In recommending the appointment of a certain proportion of ministers from outside parliament, the Ghana Constitutional Commission (1969) expressed the view that 'the success of democracy depends not only on the political process but also on the efficiency of government. We believe that in present-day Ghana, when there is need to make use of the best available talents in all spheres, it is desirable to provide avenues for those persons who may not wish to submit themselves to the rough and tumble of party politics to serve in the Government'.[7] While not denying the democratic principle that government should be based on the consent and confidence of the people, the Commission believed that the appointment of a proportion of ministers from outside the house can be reconciled with the requirements of democracy by making the appointment of all ministers subject to approval by parliament, as in the United States.[8] The Commission no doubt exaggerated when it said that such approval amounted to 'a system of election by the highest representative body of the people',[9] for as previously stated[10] legislative approval of appointments involves no exercise of choice; the appointment remains that of the President, and the concurrence of the assembly is meant to be no more that a check upon the exercise of the appointing power by the President.

Membership of the legislature is necessary not only for the initial appointment of a minister but also for his continuance in office; his tenure of office as a minister is dependent upon his continuing membership of the legislature, so that he vacates his office if he ceases to be such a member otherwise than by reason of a dissolution. The dissolution of the legislature should in strictness cause a vacancy in the office of ministers. But this would be to sacrifice ordered government to a rigid adherence to principle. Society stands in no less need of government during a dissolution that during the life of parliament. For this reason ministers do not vacate their offices during a dissolution.

Whether the ministers' membership of the legislature is incompatible with presidential government depends, as previously stated,[11] on whether membership obliges a minister to resign upon a censure vote, a matter that will be considered below.[12]

2. *Establishment of the Cabinet in the Constitution*

Another important adaptation is the fact that unlike in the United States all the constitutions recognise the office of minister and also establish a cabinet. The critical question raised by this is as to the position of ministers and the cabinet *vis-à-vis* the President. The position of a minister can be stated very briefly. He has only such function as the President may assign to him, and this may or may not include responsibility for a department of government. Further, he is under the direction of the President in the exercise of functions assigned to him. And he may be removed at any time by the President.

The role of the cabinet is defined in four ways:

(*a*) Zambia, Malawi and Botswana represent one approach. The function of the cabinet is to 'advise the President with respect to the policies of the government and with respect to such other matters as may be referred to it by the President'.[13] But the President is not bound by such advice; he is to act in his 'own deliberate judgment' unfettered by anyone else's advice;[14] this is of course subject to any contrary provision in the constitution or (in Malawi) an act of parliament. The obligation of the President towards the cabinet is thus one of consultation only. This obligation is necessarily implied in the establishment of the cabinet by the constitution since, if the President were to be free to consult the cabinet or not as he liked, the provision that the cabinet shall be responsible for advising him might be stultified. The obligation to consult is in fact expressly imposed on the President in Botswana except in respect of the appointment or removal of the Vice-President, ministers, the dissolution of parliament, assignment of ministerial responsibilities and the exercise of the prerogative of money.[15]

(*b*) In Ghana (1960–6), Tanzania and Gambia, the cabinet is also advisory to the President, but except as may be otherwise provided by law, he is not bound by its advice and is free to act in his own deliberate judgment.[16] However, it is further provided that, subject to the powers of the President, the cabinet shall (in Ghana) have 'the general direction and control of the government',[17] and (in Tanzania and Gambia) be 'the principal instrument of policy'.[18] The Ghanaian provision would seem to be wider than the Tanzanian and Gambian, for it extends to the direction and control of the whole field of governmental activity. Read together with the clause vesting executive power in the President, the effect of the Ghanaian provision was that government was the concurrent responsibility of the President and the cabinet. The President could not claim responsibility for government to the exclusion of the cabinet; constitutionally the cabinet had an *independent* but concurrent responsibility for the general direction and control of the government, a position which at once ruled out any question of its being a mere instrument of the President. Since, however, the direction and control of the cabinet was declared to be subject to the powers of the President, the latter had the overriding voice. The significance of the Tanzanian and Gambian provision depends on whether the President's executive power embraces policy. If it does not, then the cabinet is, exclusively of the President personally, the *principal* instrument of policy. It seems that the President's executive power gives him a measure of control over policy. It is difficult to see how he can govern if he is not able to determine policy. The President's responsibility for policy is in fact clear from the Gambian provision. It declares that, subject to the powers of the President, the Cabinet shall be the instrument of policy and shall be responsible for advising the President with respect to the policy of the Government'.[19] Accepting therefore that the President's executive power embraces policy, the effect of the provision in Tanzania and Gambia must be to make policy the concurrent responsibility of the President and the cabinet, with the President having the overriding say.

The substantial independent function of the cabinet in these three countries is still compatible with the principle of a single executive, since the cabinet's independent function is limited in Tanzania and Gambia to policy only, leaving the President in sole control of the executive power, and in Ghana the President was also firmly in control of the executive power, which he could exercise unfettered by the cabinet's 'general direction and control'. The general direction and control of the cabinet was at the level of the government and not of the individual ministries. The ministers individually were under the direction of the President for the work of their respective ministries.

(c) In Kenya, unlike in Zambia, Malawi, Botswana, Ghana, Tanzania and Gambia, the position is left largely undefined. All the constitution says is that the function of the cabinet shall be to 'aid and advise the President in the government of Kenya'.[20] There is nothing on how the President is to exercise the executive power vested in him, whether he is to act in his own discretion or as advised by the cabinet. The relationship has then to be inferred from the provision that the cabinet is to 'aid and advise' the President. This is of course a phrase of imprecise import. What does advice imply? Does the provision mean that the President is bound by the advice of the cabinet, so that the cabinet, and not the President, has the ultimate responsibility for the government?

It is to be noted, first, that the provision is not even directed to the President; that is to say, it does not direct the President to seek the aid and advice of the cabinet. An aider or adviser can function only if and when his aid or advice is asked for. In all cases where an obligation is intended to be created, the usual device is to say that the President or other authority shall consult or obtain the advice of a person or body. The clause in the Kenya Constitution does not, *ipso facto,* impose an obligation on the President to seek the aid and advice of the cabinet. Nevertheless such obligation does in fact exist, but it exists not by virtue of the provision, but rather from the fact of the establishment of the cabinet in the constitution. For as previously stated, the constitution would not have established the cabinet if it were not meant thereby to cast upon the President an obligation to consult it. The obligation may also be said to arise by implication from the fact that the function of the cabinet to advise the President is specifically excluded in respect of certain matters. If cabinet advice is not mandatory at all, there would have been no need to exclude it with respect to any particular matters.

The crucial issue, however, is not whether the President is obliged to seek the advice of the cabinet, but whether he is bound by any advice given by the cabinet. A duty to seek advice cannot, by any accepted rule of construction, be interpreted to imply a duty to act on the advice. The expression 'aid and advise' is a familiar one in Commonwealth constitutions, but it is usually accompanied by specific provisions to the effect either that the President (or Governor) is to act in accordance with advice or in his own deliberate judgment. We may recall first the colonial precedent. The colonial Governor was the repository of the executive authority, endowed, as he was, with Her Majesty's powers and jurisdiction in the colony, which he originally exercised as an autocrat, subject only to directions from Her Majesty through a secretary of state. Later he was associated with an executive council of officials to 'aid and advise' him. The establishment of the executive council at this stage in no way diminished the Governor's powers; his remained the sole responsibility for government. In other words the function of the council to aid and advise the Governor did not result in the replacement of gubernatorial by cabinet rule. With the advance towards representative government came the appointment to the council of elected ministers and a corresponding change in its functions and relations to the Governor. Although the Governor might still sit and preside over it, the council was now declared the principal instrument of policy, acting by a majority, with the Governor having a casting vote. The Governor could no longer ordinarily act without the approval of the council or against its decision, though to maintain the subordination of the colony to the imperial authority, the Governor was equipped with reserve powers which he could use, when occasion demanded, to by-pass or override the council. Thus the colonial precedent clearly shows that the expression 'aid and advise' does not by itself imply a plural executive or cabinet government. The rule of the executive council was established by the provision in the constitution declaring it the principal instrument of policy. No such declaration is contained in the Kenya constitution.

Turning from the colonial to the independence constitutions, one also finds ample light on the interpretation of the words 'aid and advise'. Kenya's Independence Constitution of 1963 provided, in terms adopted by the present Constitution, that 'the function of the Cabinet shall be to advise the Governor-General in the government of Kenya'.[21] Had these words been enough to oblige the Governor-General to act on the advice of the cabinet, it would not have been necessary to provide in a subsequent section that, with certain exceptions, the Governor-General shall, in the exercise of his functions, 'act in accordance with the advice of the Cabinet or a Minister acting under the general authority of the cabinet'.[22] It is this latter stipulation, and not the former, which imposed upon the Governor-General the obligation to act only on advice. In all the other Commonwealth constitutions wherein the Head of State is assigned only a nominal role, the provision that the function of the cabinet is to advise the Head of State in the government of the country is accompanied by other provisions enjoining him to act only in accordance with the advice of the cabinet.

The framers of the Kenyan presidential Constitution seemed, however, to have entertained a different view of the meaning and effect of the words 'aid and advise'. Thus Tom Mboya, then Minister for Constitutional Affairs, said in the National Assembly during the debate on the draft Constitution that 'the expression "aid and advise" is an established legal formula for the constitutional convention by which the Head of State, in whom the executive power is legally vested, acts only as advised by a Prime Minister and a cabinet. In this case, as I have said, the President as Head of State will be advised by a cabinet which consists of the President as Head of Government, the Vice-President and the Ministers, and that, Sir, is exactly the same as we have today'.[23] He discounted the Opposition Leader's fears that the cabinet might be only a rubber stamp, saying with great emphasis that the government would be by the cabinet in the fullest sense of the term cabinet government.

It may be argued in support of Mr Mboya's interpretation that cabinet government is implied in the provision which makes the cabinet collectively responsible to the National Assembly for all things done by or under the authority of the President, or the Vice-President or any other Minister in the execution of his office,[24] since it does not seem very meaningful to make the cabinet collectively responsible to the assembly if the government is in law the sole responsibility of the President. The argument has on the face of it some force, but it is not well founded. Collective responsibility of ministers to the legislature is a concept distinct from the question as to who is entitled to exercise a power. It is intended to maintain the unity and strength of the government before the legislature. It is obvious that if ministers were to be free in the assembly to disagree among themselves on government decisions, this would not only discredit the government, but would also confuse and divide the party's parliamentary membership, thereby opening a breach in the government's ranks, which the opposition would be all too pleased to exploit in order to discredit the government with a view to its possible defeat. Collective responsibility does not bind only those who concurred in a decision or who are members of the cabinet; it obliges all ministers to support and defend the government's decisions or at least not to speak against them, notwithstanding that they opposed them at the cabinet meeting or that they were not present when they were taken; it binds non-cabinet ministers equally with their chiefs in the cabinet. The avenue open to a minister who feels his conscience violated by the obligation to support a government decision of which he disapproves, is to resign and not to oppose it from within the government. Clearly, therefore, collective responsibility *per se* does not import collective power for decision-taking.

A further point of some importance which deserves to be noted is that collective responsibility under Kenya's presidential Constitution relates to 'all things done by or under the authority of the President or the Vice-President or any other minister in the execution of his office'. The contrast with the Independence Constitution of 1963 is striking. As in other Commonwealth constitutions which establish cabinet government, the collective responsibility of the cabinet under Kenya's 1963 Independence Constitution was for *decisions of the cabinet* and for the acts of individual ministers;[25] a minister of course acted under the general authority of the cabinet.[26] This made it clear that government was the responsibility of the cabinet. The omission of any reference to cabinet decisions, or to 'advice given by or under the general authority of the cabinet', in the provision defining collective responsibility under the presidential Constitution suggests that the intention was not to make the cabinet the executive authority for the country. The omission is indeed significant. For under the cabinet system, important government decisions usually emanate from the cabinet, particularly when they require legislative action. It is therefore to the decisions of the cabinet as the principal instrument of policy that collective responsibility should relate. The fact that collective responsibility under Kenya's presidential Constitution relates only to 'things done by or under the authority of the President or the Vice-President or any other ministers' seem clearly to indicate the President as the ultimate organ for decision taking, since the Vice-President and the individual ministers are subject to his direction through his power to appoint and dismiss them and to assign responsibilities to them.

There is another provision which appears to lend support to Tom Mboya's interpretation. This is the provision which says that in respect of matters on which the President is not obliged to *seek* the advice of the cabinet,[27] an *acting* President must act 'in accordance with' a resolution of the cabinet.[28] This may be said to imply that with respect to matters not so excepted, an acting President, equally with the President himself, is bound to act on advice. While the argument is not without plausibility, a more persuasive inference would seem to be that this particular provision is intended to make it emphatically clear that an acting President is obliged to act on advice over certain matters, namely the appointment and removal of ministers and the assignment of responsibilities to them, and the prorogation and dissolution of parliament. These are indeed matters on which it is undesirable that an acting President should have a personal discretion unfettered by the advice of the cabinet, as he might otherwise be enabled to transform the whole government into his own image.

(*d*) Uganda represented the fourth pattern in the relationship of the President to his cabinet. The patterns existing respectively in 1966–7 and in 1967–71 were in fact different. During the former period, the function of the cabinet was to 'advise the President in the government of Uganda'[29] but, unlike in Kenya, the President was expressly required to 'act in accordance with the advice of the cabinet or a Minister acting under the general authority of the Cabinet' except where otherwise provided.[30] The cabinet was also collectively responsible to parliament for any advice given to the President by or under its general authority and for all things done by or under the authority of any minister in the execution of his office.[31] There could be no doubt here that the Constitution established cabinet government, and not presidential rule. But does it follow from this that the President was exactly like a Prime Minister? In terms of actual *formal* powers, their position might be equated, but not so in terms of authority. For the President is both the Head of State and Head of Government, and it is not right to conceive him as holding the two offices in two distinct, rigidly separated capacities as if he were two different persons – the President as chairman of the cabinet advising the President as Head of State. No such duality in the President's personality can reasonably be predicted upon the Constitution.

If we accept that the President could have but one capacity in relation to his functions, then the fact that he is bound by the advice of the cabinet would not equate him in *authority* with a Prime Minister. A chairman of the cabinet in whom also the executive authority is vested must possess greater authority than one who is not so endowed. He must be more than *primus inter pares*. The fact that the power which one exercises belongs legally to another cannot fail to have an inhibiting influence. Although the Queen in Britain cannot impose her will on the cabinet, yet she is not without influence. That influence the President brings with him into the cabinet. He comes to it therefore with an enhanced authority, the authority of Head of State who is also a Head of Government. All the dignity and respect attaching to the former office is there with him, and cannot but influence the attitude of his cabinet colleagues towards him. Obote as President under the 1966 Constitution must have been a different figure from Obote as Prime Minister under the previous constitution. He certainly was much more than *primus inter pares*.

The 1967 Constitution tilted the balance in favour of the President. There was no longer any reference to his being advised by the cabinet or his being bound by anyone's advice. However, the cabinet still retained quite significant functions. Although the President appointed ministers and assigned responsibilities to them, yet a minister's responsibility for the direction and control of a department assigned to him was to the cabinet.[32] He could of course be removed at any time by the President,[33] and was to that extent also responsible to him. The really significant function of the cabinet related to policy. It was provided that 'the functions of the cabinet shall be to formulate and implement the policy of the Government of Uganda.'[34] Its responsibility for policy was not stated to be subject to the powers of the President, and so must be taken to be exclusive of them. Its exclusive control over policy might be said to put the cabinet in a dominating position, for in government policy controls everything.[35]

3. *The Role of Parliament in the Election of the President*

In the parliamentary system it is the legislature that makes the government, in the sense that the support of a parliamentary majority determines the right to govern. The right to govern belongs to the legislature, and is delegated by it to the member or members controlling the votes of the majority of the house.[36] This principle has not been directly incorporated in the Commonwealth African presidential constitutions, but something of it is reflected in the system of presidential and parliamentary elections which it instituted. The central feature of this system is that the two elections are tied together, the object being to give presidential election a popular basis while at the same time relating it to a majority in parliament. Explaining this object in 1962 during the debates on the proposals for a republican, presidential constitution for Tanganyika, Nyerere said: 'our problem was to try and devise a method which puts the President and the National Assembly in the same relationship of confidence as the Prime Minister and the National Assembly. We did not have to think very much. We studied a number of constitutions and we found that Ghana had discovered an extremely ingenious but very simple method of doing this'.[37] A presidential election must take place at every general election for members of parliament. The actual method of election falls into two main types, discounting for the moment presidential elections which may occur in between general elections. (Tanzania and Malawi fall outside this system and must therefore be treated as an exception.)

Ghana, Uganda, Botswana and Gambia represent one type, which was substantially the same as that in Kenya between 1964 and 1968, and in Tanganyika between 1962 and 1965. The choice of a President during a general election is determined by preferences declared by persons returned to the assembly at the election. Each parliamentary candidate may declare beforehand the presidential candidate he is supporting. In Uganda (1967), Kenya between 1964 and 1968, and Botswana before 1969, but not in Ghana, Gambia, Botswana after 1969, and Tanganyika 1962–5,[38] it was mandatory for a parliamentary candidate to declare his preference, and failure to do so made his nomination null and void.[39] The presidential candidate who obtains the declared support of more than half the total number of elected members in the assembly becomes President. In Botswana before 1969, what was required for election was *not less than half* of the total membership.[40] In Uganda forty per cent sufficed; if more than one candidate obtained forty per cent, then the candidate sponsored by the party which had the greatest numerical strength in the national assembly at the immediately preceding general election became the winner. (In Kenya, the presidential candidate, in order to be elected, must himself be returned as a member from a constituency.) In form the election is for members of the legislature, and not for a President. The single vote cast by an elector is for the parliamentary candidate, so that the election of the President is, in form, the choice of prospective members of the legislature. Yet if we are to regard substance rather than form, it seems that the presidential preferences declared by the parliamentary candidates will be the decisive consideration in the election. The contest is more about the presidency. This is amply demonstrated by the fact that, in Uganda (1967), Kenya 1964–8 and Botswana before 1969 where a declaration of a preference was required, parliamentary candidates sometimes want to ride on the bandwagon of a popular presidential candidate by declaring support for him, although they are not of the same political persuasion as he is, or indeed belong to a different party. The necessity for the consent of the presidential candidate in Ghana, 1960–6, Gambia, Botswana after 1969, and Tanganyika 1962–5 was intended to check this. In any case, when parliamentary candidates declare their preferences they do so as private individuals, and not as members of the legislature, which as yet they are not. It seems therefore nearer the truth to regard the President as deriving his mandate from the people, rather than from the legislature.

The system in Zambia and (since 1968) Kenya is avowedly an election by the people, though for convenience and to avoid a duplication it is tied to the election of parliamentary members. The choice of the President is not dependent upon the declared support of the majority of persons elected as members of the national assembly. A presidential candidate is voted for specifically in each constituency, though only one vote is cast for him and for the parliamentary candidate supported by the same political party. Each party contesting a general election nominates one presidential candidate. If in constituency Z, party X is sponsoring A as President and B as parliamentary member, then A and B are paired together, and an elector casts only one vote for them both, which is credited to each of them separately. If the parliamentary seat is not contested, the vote goes to the presidential candidate alone. A presidential candidate who obtains a greater aggregate number of votes than any other presidential candidate(s) becomes President, provided in Kenya that he is also elected as a parliamentary member in his own constituency, since the President must be an elected member of the national assembly from a constituency. Under this system the President's right to govern is popularly conferred. However, unlike the former system, it does not always assure the President of a majority in parliament; the greatest aggregate number of votes may in fact represent a minority of the votes cast, and may, even when they represent a majority of the popular votes, carry only a minority in parliament.

In three cases, election of the President is by parliament instead of by the people: first, in Ghana and Gambia, where no presidential candidate obtains a majority of the declared preferences; secondly, in Zambia and Botswana, where a winning candidate dies before the result is announced or before his assumption of office; and thirdly, for elections taking place between general elections due to the death, resignation or incapacitation of the President or for any other reason – Ghana, Zambia,[41] Botswana, Gambia and (between 1964 and 1968) Kenya. In all three cases the election is determined by a majority of the national assembly voting by secret ballot. (In Uganda an election following the death or resignation of the President was by the party having the greatest numerical strength in the national assembly.) In Gambia the person to be elected in an election taking place between general elections must be an elected member, but on his assumption of office he automatically vacates his seat; in Botswana before 1972 he did not need be a member at the time, but if he was not, he could not continue in office after six months unless in the meantime he had become one; in Kenya before 1968 he had to be a member at the time.

Although election of the President by parliament is exceptional, its effect is that the mandate for government is more squarely based in the legislature than it is under the strict Westminster system. For under the latter, the party leadership largely predetermines the voting at the election and therefore the parliamentary majority that may emerge from it. But where a President is elected by the national assembly, the parliamentary majority that determines his choice might not have owed its own election to the leadership of the presidential candidate; this is particularly so where the election is ocasioned by the death, resignation or incapacitation of the popularly elected President. A President elected by the assembly is its choice alone, with hardly any influence by the people and their party loyalties. If independence is necessary in a presidential executive, then this may be said to constitute a negation of it. It was probably for this reason that election by the assembly was abolished in Kenya in 1968; a vacancy in the presidency occurring otherwise than by a dissolution is now filled by a new presidential election in each constituency.

Tanzania and Malawi use neither the single ballot system nor election by parliament, although a presidential election takes place whenever parliament is dissolved.[42] Whatever the occasion for a presidential election, whether it is the dissolution of parliament or the death, resignation or incapacitation of the President, a separate popular ballot is held for the presidency. A single ballot might have been considered unnecessary because only one presidential candidate is allowed. The election is determined by a simple majority vote.

4. *Dependence of Executive Tenure on Parliamentary Support*

Another area in which quite significant adaptation has taken place relates to the principle that parliamentary support is necessary for executive tenure. We may begin by noting a provision in the Constitution of Botswana which categorically rests executive tenure on parliamentary support. By this provision 'an Elected Member of the National Assembly may, in the event of there being one or more successful election petitions following a general election, move, at the first sitting of the Assembly after the resultant bye-elections have been decided and the members thereby elected have taken their seats, that the President does not enjoy the support of the majority of the Elected Members of the Assembly. . . . If it appears as a result of the voting on the question that the President does not enjoy the support of a majority of the Elected Members of the Assembly, the office of President shall become vacant'.[43] Once notice of an intention to move the motion is given to the President, he cannot dissolve the assembly until after the sitting at which the motion is to be voted on.[44]

Most of the Commonwealth African presidential constitutions — Uganda (1967), Kenya, Botswana, Malawi and Gambia, but not Ghana, Tanzania and Zambia — define the consequences of a parliamentary vote of no confidence in the government. The provisions exhibit three approaches. In Uganda the President was obliged to resign and parliament also stood dissolved whenever the national assembly passed a motion of no confidence in the government, provided that (i) at least fourteen days' notice in writing signed by not less than half of all the members of the national assembly had been given of the intention to move the motion; and (ii) the motion had been passed by the votes of not less than two-thirds of all members of the assembly.[45] (Under the 1966 Constitution no dissolution followed upon a motion of no confidence and the consequent resignation of the President.) The other constitutions do not require the President to resign nor, in Kenya and Botswana, need a dissolution always follow upon such a vote. In Malawi the President must dissolve parliament within three days of the vote,[46] while in Gambia it is not mandatory on him to dissolve, but if he does not within three days, then parliament stands automatically dissolved on the fourth day.[47] In Kenya and Botswana the President has a choice whether or not to resign.[48] If he chooses to resign, there is no dissolution, and the national assembly in Botswana will proceed to elect a new President in the manner described above; in Kenya a new presidential election takes place in the country. Should he choose not to resign, however, then he may dissolve parliament within three days, otherwise it stands automatically dissolved on the fourth day. It is necessary to emphasise the compulsory nature of dissolution in this connection. The President has power exercisable in his discretion to dissolve parliament at any time, but in the present context dissolution is imposed upon him by the constitution although he may not desire it.

All three approaches have much the same effect. Although the President in Uganda was required to resign, he did not in fact vacate office until someone else became President as a result of the election following on the dissolution.[49] In other words, he remained President during the critical election period. This is also the position in the other countries; for although a presidential election must take place following on a dissolution, the President remains in office until some other person is elected and assumes office. There is, however, one distinct advantage in the approach of Kenya and Botswana; it offers a chance for avoiding dissolution if the President should elect to resign — an unlikely event. The assembly would then have won a clear victory over the President by forcing him out of office without at the same time effacing itself.

Dissolution is not such an unmixed victory for the assembly. To the extent that it prematurely terminates the President's tenure at the instance of the assembly, it does demonstrate his dependence upon parliamentary support for his continuance in office. It is thus theoretically a parliamentary sanction against the President and his government, albeit one that may damage parliament as much as, if not more than, it does the executive. It is unlikely however to be much of a practical weapon partly because of the procedural restrictions on its use. Although Uganda's requirement of a two-thirds majority is not repeated in the other constitutions, they (with the exception of Malawi) all require an absolute majority (i.e. a majority of all the members entitled to vote, and not just those present and voting); and Kenya and Gambia also follow Uganda in requiring notice (not less than seven days) of the motion to be given. The notice and special majority are said to be necessary in order to prevent the government being overthrown on a snap vote by a minority. But the main reason why dissolution is not likely to be a practical weapon is that members of parliament, particularly in Africa, stand in great fear of an election, because of its cost and the danger of loss of seat with its perquisites. Naturally, therefore, M.P.s are quite disposed to agree to any compromise that would avert for them a financial commitment that might prove crippling. Regarding this situation as a show of strength, the assembly is likely to be the party to be worsted in the ensuing election contest. Julius Nyerere thinks, however, that it would be a rather poor bunch of M.P.s who, pitched against one single individual, albeit a President, would lose the contest.[50] A contest between the assembly and President, he argues, presupposes that the President has become alienated from the party, and cannot therefore use its platform in the contest. This is not necessarily so. It would depend on which side can more effectively mobilise the party's supporters outside the assembly. The M.P.s would no doubt want to present themselves to the people as the champions of their rights against an over-weening, power-drunk President, but there is the question how effectively they can put across that platform. It must be remembered that, while a dissolution automatically vacates a parliamentary seat. it leaves the President's tenure unaffected until the elections are concluded and result in some other person being elected. This at once gives the President a big advantage over the M.P.s. The latter have no effective means at their disposal for an appeal to the electorate against the President, whereas the President can mobilise in his own cause all the patronage and propaganda facilities of the state. By means of these, he may well succeed in persuading the electorate that the M.P.s are a group of obstructionists, trying to frustrate his well-intentioned efforts on the people's behalf.

The fact that no dissolution has ever taken place in any of these countries except upon a normal effluxion of the life of parliament does indicate its impotence as a practical parliamentary sanction against the executive. This is perhaps as well. A cardinal need of a developing country is stability, which demands that except at regular election times, the country should be spared the confusion, violence and the general unsettlement associated with elections in developing countries. One is not, of course, arguing against the formal existence of parliament's power to force a dissolution on the executive. It is indeed a useful weapon in parliament's control apparatus, which may, hopefully, induce in the executive a sense of restraint and a disinclination towards arbitrariness, arrogance and tyranny.

So far our discussion has been on dissolution as a legally mandatory procedure. But there are other circumstances in which the assembly may force a dissolution on the executive as a matter of political, though not legal, necessity, such as when it rejects important government measures, when it defeats a motion of confidence or when there is a stalemate between the two organs over a bill that has passed the assembly. None of these situations attracts dissolution as a mandatory procedure either by operation of law or by virtue of an obligation legally cast on the President to dissolve, but they may compel the exercise of his power to dissolve parliament at any time. Dissolution in these circumstances is no less restrictive of executive independence because it is at the discretion of the President. The exercise of the discretion is forced upon him by political necessity just as in the other case dissolution is imposed upon him by the terms of the constitution, and in both cases he has to face a premature election.

The really troublesome question concerns the consequences in this connection of a minister's membership of the national assembly. It may be argued that, since only by right of membership of the national assembly does a person qualify to be appointed minister, the confidence of the assembly should be an implied condition of ministerial tenure; accordingly, if the assembly passes a vote of censure against a minister, he should be obliged to resign. In other words, as far as a minister is concerned, his right to be in the government and to remain in it derives not only from presidential will but also from his membership of the assembly. The assembly may, arguably, determine his membership thereof by expulsion, which would *ipso facto* determine his appointment as minister. It ought also to be possible to accomplish the latter result by the device of a censure motion without also bringing about the further penalty of a loss of parliamentary membership. The effect would be that a minister is responsible for the proper discharge of his office both to the President whose authority he exercises and to the assembly from which his right of office derives.

Applied to all the ministers collectively, this view of the matter will enable the assembly to force the resignation of the entire cabinet. As used here, 'cabinet' is different from 'government'; it is used to refer to the ministers as a body, but excluding the President. Indeed the designation in some of the constitutions (e.g., Uganda and Malawi) is a *cabinet of ministers*. The designation excludes the President, who is not a minister. And in Tanzania, Zambia and Gambia the cabinet is defined as consisting of the Vice-President and the other ministers, though the President is empowered to summon and to preside at its meetings. The President is the government, and the cabinet is only one of his instruments for governing (this statement may need to be qualified in relation to Ghana, Tanzania, Gambia and possibly Kenya). A vote of no confidence in the cabinet is not therefore the same thing as a vote of no confidence in the government within the meaning of the provisions considered above, and should not necessarily involve the President unless he construes it as a censure on himself in which case he may decide to resign with his cabinet. If he decides not to resign with his ministers, he would have to appoint new ministers. He would then be expected to reverse the policy which called forth the parliamentary censure. It seems less likely that he would want to adopt this latter course, which means keeping himself in office at the expense of his entire cabinet. After all, the cabinet, as has just been stated, is nothing but the President's instrument for exercising the power which constitutionally belongs to him and for which he should be squarely responsible. What seems more likely is that in this kind of situation the President would dissolve parliament. Whatever course he adopts — whether he resigns with his cabinet, appoints a new one or dissolves parliament — the end-result would be to emphasise his dependence on parliamentary support for his tenure or for his policy. All this of course pertains to the theory of the constitution; its practice is another matter.

The power of the assembly to force the resignation of a minister or the cabinet may be forestalled by the ruling of the speaker of the Kenyan national assembly that the assembly cannot seize itself of a censure motion against a minister,[51] presumably because, since a censure motion is by the express terms of the constitution confined to the government, it must be taken to be excluded in regard to a minister. The ruling does not, apparently, deny the assembly's right of criticism. But once we admit the right of criticism, we are bound equally to admit the right to censure through a non-confidence motion which, after all, is only a formal method of criticism. It was unnecessary for the constitution to have provided specifically for a censure motion against a minister since such a motion is a necessary incident of a minister's membership of the house; it is a right which the constitution gives to the assembly by requiring ministers to be appointed from among its members and thereby enabling it to censure them without necessarily involving the President (i.e. the government) or precipitating a dissolution. With regard to the cabinet, the competence of the assembly to pass a censure motion against it may be inferred additionally from the provision which appears in the constitutions of Kenya, Botswana, Malawi and Gambia but not of Ghana, Zambia, Tanzania and Uganda, making the cabinet '*collectively* responsible to the National Assembly for all things done by or under the authority of the President or the Vice-President or any other minister in the execution of his office'.[52] (The collective responsibility of the cabinet to the assembly in Malawi is limited to acts of ministers, and does not extend to those of the President.) This responsibility must imply a right in the assembly not only to criticise but also to censure. The express mention of the cabinet's collective responsibility should not be taken to exclude a minister's individual responsibility to the assembly, which arises from the fact that his right to office derives from his membership thereof. On the contrary, collective responsibility presupposes a minister's individual responsibility, for it does not seem very sensible to make the cabinet responsible for the act of a minister if the minister is not himself responsible. The cabinet's collective responsibility for the act of a minister (the assumption is that the minister acted properly within the scope of his functions) may also be said to imply the responsibility of the minister to the cabinet, for it is again not intelligent to make the cabinet responsible for the act of a minister if it has no control over him. Persued to its logical end, the conclusion would also follow that the President is also responsible to the cabinet, since the latter's collective responsibility in Kenya, Botswana and Gambia extends to acts of the President. It seems that the real basis of the cabinet's collective responsibility for a minister's act is the latter's responsibility to the President, not his responsibility to the cabinet. If other ministers were to be free to disown the act of a minister properly done in the discharge of functions assigned to him by the President, then they would also in effect be disowning the President. However this may be, the important point here is that the cabinet's collective responsibility to the assembly for the acts of a minister does not exclude the latter's individual responsibility to the assembly for those acts; both entitle the assembly to censure ministers individually and collectively as a cabinet.

The Kenyan speaker's ruling also denies the right of the assembly to call into debate the conduct of the President except on a substantive motion. It could not have been the ground for this ruling that the express provision in the constitution for a vote of no confidence in the government altogether excludes debate on the President's conduct except on the occasion of such motion. If that were so, then ministers' conduct would also be entitled to immunity from parliamentary debate. No such immunity exists or has ever been claimed. Ministers are frequently questioned or criticised. The ground for the ruling would appear instead to be that it is unfair to discuss the President when he is not present in the assembly to defend himself. This is the ground stated by the speaker of the Zambian national assembly for his own ruling,[53] but it is hardly enough justification for a total ban on parliamentary debate on the President's conduct.[54]

The foregoing discussion reveals a considerable amount of blending of the principles of the two principal methods of organising executive government – presidential and parliamentary. If one had to classify the governmental system instituted by these constitutions, one might perhaps aptly call it parliamentary presidentialism. The executive government is organised around a single individual with the title of President, yet, not only are the principal functionaries and agency through which he conducts the government parliamentary in character, but parliament is also an important force influencing the President's election, his tenure and his policies. With the fore-going detailed analysis of the structure of the executive and its relationship to the legislative assembly, we will now proceed in the next chapter to the factors that account for the spread of presidentialism in Commonwealth Africa.

REFERENCES

1. James Bryce, *The American Commonwealth*, Hacker, ed. (1959) vol. 1, p. 122.
2. S.52 Constitution of Kenya, 1969.
3. House of Reps. Debates, Vol. IX, June 23, 1966, cols. 994–6.
4. *East African Standard*, Jan. 5, 1968.
5. House of Reps. Debates, Vol. VII Part III, 3 Nov., 1964, col. 4193..
6. S.50, as amended in 1971.
7. Report, para. 378.
8. *ibid.*, para. 379.
9. *ibid.*, para. 379.
10. above, Ch. II.
11. *supra* p. 300.
12. p. 53.
13. S.51(1) Zambia; S.53(2) Malawi; S.51(1) Botswana.
14. S.48(2) Zambia; S.8(3) Malawi; S.48(2) Botswana.
15. S.51(3).

16. Art. 8(4) Ghana; S.6(2) Tanzania; S.42(2) Gambia.
17. Art. 16(2).
18. S.17(2) Tanzania; S.49(2) Gambia.
19. S.49(2).
20. S.17(2) Constitution 1969.
21. S.76(2).
22. S.79(1).
23. Republic of Kenya, Official Report, House of Reps., vol. VII, Part III, 3 Nov., 1964, Col. 4193.
24. S.17(3).
25. S.76(2).
26. S.79(1).
27. S.17(4).
28. S.6(3).
29. S.43(2). Constitution 1966.
30. S.39(1), *ibid.*
31. S.43(2).
32. Art. 34.
33. Art. 33(2) (*e*).
34. Art. 37(2).
35. See below, p. 43.
36. Above, p. 28.
37. Constituent Assembly Deb., 28 June, 1962, col. 1109; also Govt. Paper No. 1 of 1962, p. 4.
38. Art.11(2) (*c*), Ghana; S.34(2) (*a*), Gambia; S.4(4) (*a*), Tanganyika; Constitution (Second) Amendment Act, 1969 Botswana.
39. Art.26(1) (*b*), Uganda; S.33(3) (*a*) Botswana; Constitution of Kenya (Amendment) Act, 1964.
40. The present position is prescribed by the Constitution (Second Amendment) Act, 1969.
41. In Zambia the Vice-President normally assumes the presidency in such a case, and an election by parliament is necessary only if the office of Vice-President is also vacant.
42. S.7 Interim Constitution, 1965 Tanzania; Presidential Elections Act, Cap.2:01 Laws of Malawi, 1969. President Banda of course holds the presidency for life.
43. S.33(8).
44. S.33(9).
45. Art.30(1), 8(2).
46. S.45(4).
47. S.85(3).
48. S.59(3) Kenya; S.93 Botswana.   49. Art.29(6).
50. Nat. Ass. Deb. on the Govt. Proposals for a Republic, June 28, 1962, cols. 1084 ff.
51. Nat. Ass. Deb., vol. XII Part II, July 6, 1967, col. 1853; July 19, 1967, col. 2410.
52. S.17(3) Kenya; S.51(1) Botswana; S.53(3) Malawi; S.50 Gambia.
53. Nat. Ass. Deb, Hansard No. 19, 7–17 Oct., 1969, col. 135.
54. See below, p. 123, for further discussion on this.

CHAPTER IV

THE ORIGINS AND SPREAD OF PRESIDENTIALISM IN COMMONWEALTH AFRICA

Indisputably, the dominant trend of post-Independence constitutional development in Commonwealth Africa is the change from a dual to a unified executive, the rejection of the dichotomy between the formal authority of a constitutional Head of State and the real authority of the Head of Government, and their unification in the same office. With only two exceptions — Zambia and Botswana — all Commonwealth African countries came into independent nationhood with this executive duality. Independence was granted on the Westminster system with the British Queen (or an indigenous monarch in Lesotho and Swaziland) as Head of the new state, occupying the same role of titular monarch as in Britain, while effective power lay in the hands of a cabinet headed by a Prime Minister. By 1973 all but one — Lesotho, a kingdom — had shed or at least suspended this system. (In Lesotho it was suspended for ten months in 1970.) Beginning with Ghana in 1960, the development has traversed West Africa (Gambia 1970, Sierra Leone 1971 and Nigeria through military intervention in 1966), Central Africa (Zambia 1964 and Malawi 1966), East Africa (Tanganyika 1962, Kenya 1964, Tanzania 1965 and Uganda 1966) and Southern Africa (Botswana 1966). Ironically the country (Ghana) in which the process was first inaugurated is also the place where the pendulum has swung back — in 1969, owing to a particularly sad experience with the system[1] — though the new Westminster-type government had again been brought to an abrupt end by the military take-over in January 1972.

A development of the dimension involved in the rejection of the Westminster system in favour of presidentialism in most of the Commonwealth could not be the result of one single factor. Constitutional developments are often the product of a complex of factors, and this is particularly so with the spread of presidentialism in Commonwealth Africa. Each country affected has its own peculiar experiences and circumstances which influenced the development to a greater or less extent, though certain factors are common to all, such as, for instance, the circumstance of a common background of colonialism and Africanism. It is proposed to examine these factors in some detail.

1. *Autochthony*

Presidentialism may be regarded as the culmination in the constitutional field of the nationalist struggle for emancipation from colonialism. Political freedom had been achieved with the grant of independence, yet this event, momentous though it was, could not obliterate in one stroke all the marks which a century or more of colonialism had left upon the social order of a former dependency. It is not being suggested that colonialism is an unmitigated evil, pernicious in all its effects. On the contrary, it has bequeathed to its subjects one pre-eminently beneficial heritage, which constitutes the foundation of the polity of the new nations.[2] Nonetheless it has to be admitted that aspects of this heritage are disturbingly reminiscent of the new nations' former status of dependence. It is a legitimate desire on the part of these nations that they should want, after independence, to remove from their political systems all those features that carry the taint of imperialism, and are thus incompatible with national sentiment. In the political development of a country just recently emancipated from colonialism, national sentiment has important significance, even in matters of pure form. A sentiment of national consciousness and identity has to be inculcated in the people in order to arouse them to a feeling of loyalty to the new state. Autochthony is therefore concerned with this quest for national identity, for the removal of the taint of imperialism from the country's social order; it expresses the desire of former colonial countries to give their political systems a distinct national character and form.[3]

From the constitutional standpoint autochthony has two aspects: it relates both to the source from which the constitution derives its authority as law, and to its contents, i.e. the frame of government which it establishes. The issue concerning the constitution's origin has been eloquently stated by Professor Wheare. 'For some members of the Commonwealth,' he writes, 'it is not enough to be able to say that they enjoy a system of government which is in no way subordinate to that of the United Kingdom. They wish to be able to say that their constitution has force of law and if necessary of supreme law within their territory through its own native authority and not because it was enacted or authorised by the parliament of the United Kingdom – that it is, so to speak, "home-grown", sprung from their own soil, and not imported from the United Kingdom'.[4] This issue is one stemming inevitably from the fact of colonialism. When independence was granted, it had to be upon the basis of a constitution made by the departing suzerain power, either as a specifically negotiated Independence Constitution or, as in the case of India and Pakistan, as a provisional constitution adapted from the pre-existing colonial constitution, pending the enactment of a suitable constitution by the legislature of the new state. Since the constitution is the foundation of the state, it is felt to be necessary for the consummation of full independent statehood that this foundation should be made locally, so as to remove any possible misunderstanding about the status of the country that might arise from the fact that its constitution was enacted by the former imperial power. It is unnecessary to pursue here the argument whether legal autochthony requires that the constitution should be enacted by virtue of an authority native to, or inherent in, the local enacting body, such as the people directly in a referendum or a Constituent Assembly, or whether it suffices that it is enacted by the state legislature created by the imperial authority.[5] In either case, legal autochthony, though it excites nationalistic sentiment and pride, is not desired for its own sake, but only as a means of effecting changes in the content of the constitution, with the object specifically of replacing the British Queen with an indigenous Head of State, either retaining the separation between him and the Head of Government or abolishing the separation altogether and merging the two offices into one. Thus the importance of constitutional autochthony relates more to the content rather than the origin of the constitution.

The retention of the British Queen as the Head of State of an African country after independence has an unmistakable taint of imperialism about it, both because the Queen is a foreigner so clearly set apart by her race and colour, and because no modern African country (with the exception of Lesotho and Swaziland) ever formed a single kingdom, while for many the institution of monarchy itself is altogether alien. But for its background of colonial subjugation, an African country could not possibly have a white monarch as its Queen and Head of State. The Queen is the very embodiment of British imperialism, and there could be no more telling and unmistakable reminder of the colonial misfortune than the continuation of her authority in the country after independence, however that authority might now be conceived. This has nothing to do with the sentiment towards the Queen as a person. She may be admired and loved by the people, yet her continued authority as Queen in an independent African country is hardly compatible with independence. It is perhaps not surprising that many foreign observers should have wondered how real was the independence after all, and whether somehow Britain did not retain some measure of control. What kind of independence was that which still made the country part of Her Majesty's dominions, thereby subjecting it to her sovereignty and its citizens to a duty of allegiance to her as sovereign? Except to the constitutional lawyer and other well-informed persons, it is no use saying that the Queen reigned, say in Ghana, by virtue, not of her British, but of her Ghanaian Crown. The Crown is nothing more than a symbol, and in the eyes of the Ghanaian masses, she is a British monarch and an embodiment of British imperial power, and it was by virtue of that power that she was still Queen in Ghana. The British Crown cannot, in any meaningful sense, become the common property of British, Asian and African peoples. It can have no place in African imagination, and the traditions and sentiments which give it meaning and sustenance cannot be shared by Africans. As regards African and Asian peoples, therefore, the whole talk of a common Crown is sheer fiction, and one that positively derogates from their personality. Thus, one of the impulses for autochthony has been, in Dr Nkrumah's words at the inauguration of Ghana's Republic in 1960, to give 'full expression to the African personality' by making the Head of State a native of the soil.

However, the replacement of the Queen by an indigenous Head of State is a separate issue from that involved in the system of separation between her and the Head of Government. As in Nigeria and Uganda in 1963, the Queen could be replaced by an indigenous President while leaving the separation unaffected. Does this, then, suggest that the separation is not considered as carrying any mark of colonialism about it? The issue raised here is whether the system was an inevitable consequence of the colonial experience. It might be argued, first, that the system was a positive imposition by the British, but this is difficult to establish, since we cannot probe the inner desires of the British Government in framing an independence constitution. The appearance is of a constitution negotiated and agreed upon by both the representatives of the British Government and of the colonial country; and the negotiations were often long and protracted, though invariably ending in what appeared as an agreed compromise. If an independence constitution was one freely agreed to by the representatives of the country concerned, then it can be said to have been autochthonous in content. But the question is whether a dependent people about to be granted independence could ever have a real choice in the framing of its independence constitution. The colonial power had a responsibility in the matter, which could not but limit the reality of choice. For often there was a lack of unanimity among the colonial people on the sort of constitution they wanted. The British Government was wont, perhaps justifiably, to construe its responsibility as requiring it not to agree to a constitution that did not guarantee reasonably adequate protection for tribal or racial minorities, which are present in all African countries to a greater or less degree. An important part of the institutional device for this protection was believed to be inherent in the diffusion, under the

Westminster system, of the executive authority between, on the one hand, the Head of State and the Head of Government, and, on the other, the individual members of the cabinet. The diffusion of power weakens it and thereby diminishes the dangers of dictatorship, while its concentration in a single person, such as under the American presidential system, might be thought to have a tendency to increase such dangers. The assumption on the part of the British representatives and those of the colonial country at the independence negotiations must then have been that the Westminster system was the only framework for the negotiations. Given a vocal tribally-based opposition party, such as existed in many of the African countries at the time of independence, and the sharp cleavage between it and the government party on the frame and safeguards of the independence constitution, it would have been idle for the latter to conceive, not to say propose, the American presidential system. If the Westminster system adopted at independence was not therefore exactly an imposition, neither can its choice be said to have been entirely real and unfettered.

Ghana was a notable case where a vocal tribal minority fiercely opposed the government party's proposals for an independence constitution, refusing to participate in the discussions on the matter or in any way to co-operate with the government. In the face of this opposition, the British Government announced that it would not agree to the Gold Coast (as Ghana was then called) becoming independent on the basis of the constitution proposed by the Gold Coast Government, although the proposals had been based upon the recommendations of an expert British adviser, Sir Frederick Bourne, and had been made an election issue, which the Government won with an overwhelming majority of 72 seats in the Legislative Assembly against the opposition parties' 32. In the event the country came to independence with a constitution that contained fettering provisions designed for the protection of the minorities but to which the majority was opposed. In a speech two years later, Prime Minister Nkrumah still recalled to the National Assembly that his 'Government accepted the Constitution as drawn up in the United Kingdom with the greatest misgivings. We were, however, faced with a situation where independence might well have been delayed had we refused to accept the text which was presented to us'.[6] And Geoffrey Bing has commented that 'if the British Government had been prepared to enact the Constitution as prepared by Dr Nkrumah's Government in 1956 ... it is possible that the pressures for a Republican Constitution would not have developed so early nor have been so insistent'.[7] The form of government proposed by Dr Nkrumah's Government was of course the Westminster system, but the Government must have felt itself precluded from proposing the presidential system. An executive presidency would have been no less, if not more, objectionable to the British Government than the proposals rejected, and would therefore have stood no better chance of acceptance.

The fact that, as in the Gold Coast (Ghana) in 1956, the nationalist leaders themselves proposed the Westminster system has been interpreted by some British writers and politicians to mean an unfettered choice on their part. This interpretation is clearly unwarranted. For, as has been stated, the assumption shared by the British and nationalist leaders alike was that the Westminster system was the one and only framework for an independence constitution. This assumption had been conditioned not only by a belief in its inherent suitability as a safeguard against dictatorship but also by the fact of long historical association with the system. It is the system of the 'mother' country itself, representing as it does the genius and wisdom of British political achievement, an achievement of which the British are justly proud, and which understandably they might wish to bequeath to all their former dependencies, if for no other reason than as a common heritage binding former ward and guardian together. The nationalist leaders themselves had also acquired a somewhat strong acquaintance with the system through a sojourn or visit in Britain or from actual experience in the modified form in which it operated during the brief self-government period of constitutional development in their own country. The past often exercises a powerful influence upon the present. Except for the radical-minded, it is a very natural inclination for people to want to perpetuate the established order of things, to maintain the *status quo*, and this is no less so in matters of government than in other areas of human activity. There were thus strong fetters upon the reality of the choice available to the nationalist leaders in the framing of the independence constitution. That they should within a matter of a year or so after independence repudiate the system raises a doubt whether its adoption in the first instance ever proceeded from an unfettered choice. In the case of Tanganyika indeed the repudiation came less than ten months after independence. Such an inconsistency is not to be lightly attributed to a mature politician of the calibre of Julius Nyerere. The truth must be acknowledged that the dual executive of the Westminster system was at least an inevitable heritage of colonialism.

In fairness to the British, it should also be acknowledged that they had seldom, if ever, sought to impose the dual executive against the unanimous or near-unanimous wishes of the various groups in the colony. Where such a unanimity or near-unanimity existed, the British Government had always appeared willing to respect and implement it. However, in Commonwealth Africa only two countries, Zambia and Botswana, appeared to have had the singular good fortune to be unanimous in this matter. Prime Minister Kenneth Kaunda had thus the profound satisfaction, not given to his counterparts in other countries, to announce at Northern Rhodesia's Constitutional Conference in May 1964 the unanimous agreement between his Government, the opposition parties and the chiefs that the country should become a republic directly on independence with a presidential form of government.[8] The idea was unprecedented in the history of the Commonwealth, apart from the special case of Cyprus in 1960 whose independence constitution establishing a republican presidential form of government was the product of an international agreement between Greece, Turkey and the two Cypriot communities, Greek and Turkish, with Britain more or less in the role of arbitrator. Despite the novelty of the Northern Rhodesian proposal, the British Government accepted and implemented it in the Constitution of independent Zambia, thus demonstrating that it would not press its undoubted preference for the Westminster system against a unanimous demand by the colonial representatives for the presidential form. The Zambian example was repeated two years later, in 1966, in Bechuanaland (Botswana). There the Government's proposals were opposed by the opposition party which had only three members in a Legislative Assembly of thirty-one members, but its opposition was not so much on the form of government proposed as because there had been inadequate consultation with the people of the country. In fact the proposals had been approved by both the House of Chiefs and the Legislative Assembly and by more than 150 public meetings held throughout the country.[9] There was thus a near-unanimity. It is of course possible that Britain's acquiescence in a presidential form of government for Zambia and Botswana was induced not so much by the unanimity among the politicians there as by the fact that by 1964 she herself might have lost faith in the suitability of the Westminster system for the emergent countries of Africa and Asia.

2. *Africanism*

The ground upon which the separation of the Head of State from the Head of Government has been more emphatically and uniformly repudiated is its incompatibility with African political experience. This is the aspect of autochthony that asserts that a constitution should accord with the people's traditional way of thinking about government and with their historical experience generally. For a formerly dependent people, the constitution should be an instrument of cultural revival, of 'national restatement', reflecting the people's choice of a frame of government as well as their traditional political concepts, if not specific institutions and procedures.[10]

A titular Head of State is said to be un-African. 'The historical process', said Tom Mboya, then Kenya's Minister for Constitutional Affairs, 'by which, in other lands, Heads of State, whether Kings or Presidents, have become figureheads, are no part of our African tradition'.[11] He described the arrangement as both illusory and foreign to the people of Kenya. Julius Nyerere of Tanganyika, in a letter to *The Observer* of London in July 1962 on his country's 1962 Republican Constitution, has made the same point in terms perhaps more intellectual and trenchant:

> Our constitution should fit in with the traditions of our people; it should be felt to belong to the country. Only then can it foster a sense of nationhood and inspire a sense of loyalty.
>
> First, as far as possible, the institutions of government must be able to be understood by the people. There must be no confusing outward forms which are meaningless in the light of our experience and history. This alone requires a republic, and one with an executive president.
>
> To us, honour and respect are accorded to a chief, monarch, or president not because of his symbolism, but because of the authority and responsibility he holds. We are not used to the division between real authority and formal authority.[12]

Thus, while a titular Head of State is denounced as meaningless in the light of African political experience and history, an executive presidency is extolled as being in accord with it. Speaking in the Legislative Assembly on May 27, 1964, on the executive presidency proposed for an independent Zambia, Prime Minister Kenneth Kaunda described it as 'in accord with our African way of life'.[13]

Can the argument based upon the Africanism of an executive presidency be substantiated, or is it merely an argument of convenience designed merely to arouse popular support for a case by showing it to be inspired by African traditions, a manifestation of what Ghai and McAuslan have called the 'phenomenon of liberation from the "cultural imperialism" of colonialism'?[14] It is as well that the true nature of the claim should be appreciated. It is not being suggested that the full range of functions of the executive president of a modern state and his overall position in the governmental structure have any parallel in African traditional political organisation. The claim asserts only a likeness in broad pattern. Beyond this, it must be admitted that African culture does not yield anything very relevant to the effective organisation of the government of a modern state. Secondly African political experience and history is not confined to traditional forms of political organisation. The colonial period certainly forms an important part of African political experience and history, of which account must be taken in determining what form of government can be understood by the people.

Now, an executive presidency is but a modern form of an ancient and once universal form of government, namely rule by a single person, which became formalised in the institution of kingship. Kingship, in whatever form, may be said to represent the natural frame of government in all ancient communities. 'The tendency of all people is to elevate a single person to the position of ruler. The idea is simple. It appeals to all orders of intellect. It can be understood by all. Around this centre all nationality and patriotism are grouped. A nation comes to know the characteristics and nature of an individual. It learns to believe in the man.'[15] Hence the universality of kingship in Europe until it was all but swept away by the revolutionary upsurge of republicanism which began with the American and French Revolutions. The king was the government, and originally an absolute one at that, combining in himself the executive power and the entire sovereignty of the state, which he exercised in his discretion as a personal ruler. The emergence of the legislature as a separate arm of government was a later development, dating only from the sixteenth century. But even after the legislative power had passed from him to the legislature, the king remained the sole executive.

Such was the universality of monarchy or rule by a single person that the first new experiment in government in America had to be modelled upon it. Strangely enough, indeed, the Americans, after successfully revolting against King George III of Great Britain for alleged tyranny and despotism, continued to hanker after monarchy as the only kind of executive government good enough for the country. Alexander Hamilton was the chief advocate of this. 'No good government', he told the Philadelphia Convention on a Constitution for the United States, 'could exist without a good executive, and no good executive could ever be established "on Republican principles". The hereditary monarch, endowed with great wealth, was above corruption from abroad and was "both sufficiently independent and sufficiently contented, to answer the purpose of the institution at home".'[16] Hamilton accordingly urged the Convention to establish a monarchy for the United States. Another delegate, John Dickinson of Delaware, also opined that 'a firm Executive could only exist in a limited monarchy'. Professor Koening, describing the proceedings of the Convention, tells the funny story that 'while the Convention analysed the monarchy, stories circulated in the world outside that the Fathers, in their love for that brand of executive, were bent upon importing a Hanoverian bishop to be King of the United States'.[17]

The idea of a single executive ruler or head is equally universal among Africans. The most widely prevalent form of political organisation in Africa is the chieftainship. The chief is the apex of the political system. Like the monarch in Europe, he was all three things at once — executive, judge and legislator — though his functions were more limited in scope owing to the primitive conditions of the society over which he ruled. Again like his European counterpart, his power might be absolute in some places, and limited in others. He might be obliged to exercise his powers in council with subordinate chiefs and other functionaries, but he never was a figurehead. He was a chieftain in a real sense, exercising powers of government as a personal ruler. Indeed the word 'chief' may be said to be an appellation invented by European colonisers to degrade the status of the African ruler so as to emphasise his inferiority *vis-à-vis* a king in Europe. In British Africa we have a clear example in Swaziland and Lesotho, each of which was, before British colonisation, ruled by a single monarch, who, with the establishment of British rule, was down-graded to the status of a Paramount Chief in order to underline his subordination to the British monarch. In 1967 Swaziland was elevated from a protectorate to a protected state, and with the renunciation of the sovereignty of the British monarch consequent upon this change, the way was clear for the restoration to the Swazi traditional ruler of his former dignities, rights and privileges as ruler, and he was formally recognised and confirmed as such with the title of King, instead of Paramount Chief;[18] this transition was re-enacted in the independence Constitution in 1968. So also the traditional ruler of Basutoland (now Lesotho), previously called the Paramount Chief by the British, was again recognised and confirmed as King in the independence Constitution, with the style of 'His Majesty'.[19]

Admittedly the powerful executive chieftain does not exist in all African communities, particularly in the so-called chiefless or acephalous societies beloved of anthropologists. It is erroneous to think of such societies as being without rulers. No human society can exist in peace and harmony without a leader. What distinguishes these societies from the chiefly ones is the fact that authority is fragmented and widely diffused. To begin with, the unit of political organisation, i.e. the political community, is small, often extending no wider than a village-group of a few thousand people. What is more, authority within this small group is diffused among various sectional heads, each village within the community, and each kindred or extended family within the village, having its own head. Yet, within their confined territory, these ward heads are no figureheads. On the contrary they rule their respective wards or villages somewhat in the manner of a *paterfamilias*, exercising control in a variety of matters affecting the social and spiritual well-being of the group, including particularly the settlement of disputes among the members. Together the ward heads constitute the governing council for the entire community, and in the council there is a well-recognised order of precedence among them, according to which the presidency of the council is determined. It is true that administration through the council is a 'massed' one in some places, in the sense that any adult male member is entitled to attend and to participate in the discussion, yet owing to the marked respect for age in these communities, the proceedings are dominated by the heads and other elders.

Traditional African political organisation has therefore its parallel both in the single executive or in an executive president associated with, and limited by, a council. There is thus ample evidence of tradition to justify the executive presidency in Commonwealth Africa. Of Kenya which belongs to the so-called chiefless societies, Tom Mboya has said: 'Our people have always governed their affairs by looking to a council of elders elected and headed by their own chosen leader, giving them strong and wise leadership. That tradition — which is an African-ism — will be preserved in this new Constitution.'[20]

The rejection of a constitutional in favour of an executive presidency may also be explained in terms of pan-Africanist attitudes. Outside the Commonwealth and the Republic of South Africa, which still retains its inherited British tradition in this regard, the executive presidency or monarchy is the usual form of government in Africa. At pan-African gatherings, leaders from Commonwealth African countries whose position was only that of Head of Government, must have experienced a certain sense of disappointment at being denied the honour and dignity accorded to their counterparts who were Heads of State in their own countries. A desire to conform to pan-African forms was accordingly a relevant consideration, though personal aspirations for the greater dignity and symbolism of a Head of State were also important.

The executive presidency also accords with African political experience during the colonial era. In that experience the Governor was the dominant political figure, epitomising the sort of strong, author-itarian, and irresponsible executive incarnated by the medieval European monarch. Commander-in-Chief, sole executive and legislator, he was empowered 'to exercise . . . all such power and jurisdiction as Her Majesty . . . had or may have within the territory, and to that end to take or cause to be taken all such measures and to do or cause to be done all such matters and things therein as are lawful and as in the interest of H.M.'s service he may think expedient'.[21] The executive Governor remained a feature of the colonial constitution up to the very end, though his powers diminished progressively as the colony advanced along the road to self-government; yet at no time did he shed his power completely to become a mere figurehead. He continued in some places to preside at meetings of the executive council right up to indepen-dence. In any case, the period of time during which most of his powers had been transferred to a Prime Minister and other ministers occupied altogether too brief a portion of the total colonial experience to have established any but a fleeting acquaintance with the British system of a constitutional Head of State. Moreover, as Geoffrey Bing has said, 'in fact an executive presidential type of Government was almost dictated by the nature of the civil service machine left behind by the departing British imperial authorities. Even to the last, the Gold Coast civil service administration had been centred around the Governor. From 1951 onwards, it is true, civil servants were distributed in theory to Ministries but the change was nominal rather than real. A centralised system of government was the colonial legacy. That Ghana should choose to adopt the same system as the individual British colonies of North America had chosen in view of similar institutions which they had been bequeathed was therefore in no way extraordinary'.[22]

3. *The Personality Factor*

Personality accounts for much in constitutional and political development. A Cromwell or a Hitler may take his country along the road to dictatorship and a Napoleon Bonaparte may have himself proclaimed emperor. So with the growth of presidentialism in Commonwealth Africa, the personality factor has been a dominant influence.

By the constitution and accepted convention, the Head of State has precedence over all other persons in the country. He is the first citizen, elevated in dignity and prestige above all else. He symbolises the state and its majesty and power; he represents it in the totality of its relations both within and without the country. This is a position which is naturally coveted — and ought indeed to be held — by the person who led the nationalist struggle for independence, and who is almost invariably the most outstanding and influential personality in the country, towering in stature above the rest of the community with an authority sanctioned in popular imagination and myth. Kwame Nkrumah in Ghana, Julius Nyerere in Tanganyika, Jomo Kenyata in Kenya, Kenneth Kaunda in Zambia, Kamuzu Banda in Malawi were all leaders of such dominating personality.

Given a separation between the Head of State and the Head of Government, such leaders will of course naturally go for the latter position which is the one carrying the effective power of government. But that at once creates a problem of finding another person as Head of State to whom the leader is expected to subordinate himself in point of precedence, though not of real power. The problem was easily evaded in the first year or two of independence by retaining the last British colonial Governor as Governor-General representing the Queen. Between the British Governor-General and the leader the issue of precedence had already been determined by their relations during the colonial period. The Governor-General enjoyed primacy because he once incarnated the imperial power and by virtue of the social pre-eminence that he had been accustomed to enjoy as colonial Governor. And so we find that the most cordial relations and mutual respect existed between the leader and his British Governor-General, between, for example, Nkrumah and the Earl of Listowel, and between Banda and Sir Glyn Jones, to mention only the two most masterful African leaders. So long as the British Governor-General remained, it was all right, but he had inevitably to be replaced by a native of the country. The prospect of his replacement lays bare at once the personality problem involved. To what Malawian could Dr Kamuzu Banda, for example, be expected to play a subordinate? The fact was frankly accepted as dominant in determining the form of government under the Malawi Republican Constitution. 'We cannot', said Kembo during the second reading of the Republic of Malawi (Constitution) Bill, 1966, 'help but relate the Constitution of the Republican Government of Malawi with the man who has moulded the nation'.[23]

Outside the kingdoms (Lesotho and Swaziland), only in Nigeria, Sierra Leone and Uganda was an indigenous constitutional Head of State found to replace the British monarch. That this had been possible at all was due however partly to the fact that in all three countries, with the exception of Sierra Leone, there was no undisputed leader of the nationalist struggle like Nkrumah or Banda. In Nigeria Dr Nnamdi Azikiwe was indisputably the outstanding figure of the nationalist movement though, owing to the size of the country and the tribal cleavages in that movement, his leadership was later renounced in many parts of the country, so that at independence his party drew its support only from the south, and more predominantly from his own tribal area (Ibo). Thus lacking support in the North with its overwhelming population, Azikiwe could not lead the government of independent Nigeria. The compromise that was eventually worked out was for a coalition government between his party and the northern party, under which he became the Head of State while headship of the government went to the deputy leader of the Northern party. The personality balance between Azikiwe and his Prime Minister, Sir Abubakar Tafawa Balewa, cannot easily be reproduced elsewhere, yet, as we shall see presently, it was not attended by exactly the sort of relationship envisaged by the British system of separation. In Sierra Leone an outstanding personality was also at hand, supplied by the sophisticated and elitist Creole community of Freetown, though the issue of elevating a tribal native to the headship of the state did not arise until after the death of the founder of the state, Sir Milton Margai. The problem presented in the regions of Nigeria was somewhat less troublesome, since the position of regional Governor was not comparable in dignity and symbolism to that of the Head of State; hence it was not too difficult there to fill the position with an outstanding personality from among older politicians or distinguished professional men like Sir Francis Ibiam in the then Eastern Nigeria.

The personality problem might also be solved by elevating a traditional ruler to the headship of the state. If there exists in the state a ruler with sufficient traditional authority over a wide area and with a high enough personal standing in the community, then there might be a chance that his headship of the state could be reconciled with the position of the leader. Unfortunately, rulers of such authority and stature are few in Commonwealth Africa. Moreover, the nationalist movement and the power politics of the modern state had seriously undermined the position of traditional rulers, removing much of their authority and influence, and subordinating them so thoroughly to the new rulers that at independence hardly any traditional ruler possessed social standing capable of matching that of the leader. Ghana, for example, has powerful and well-educated chiefs, but none has authority over even as much as one quarter of the country, and in national terms the personality and charisma of Nkrumah overshadowed them all. It is hardly conceivable that Nkrumah would have agreed to subordinate himself to any of them as his Head of State. This is even more inconceivable in the case of Kamuzu Banda, partly because Malawi has no such powerful and educated chiefs and partly because of Banda's over-weening personality which treats the rest of his countrymen, chiefs and commoners alike, as inferior beings.

Uganda comprises four kingdoms, one of which, Buganda, occupies over one-third of the country and was ruled by a Cambridge-educated king, the Kabaka, with the full trappings of modern government — a legislature, ministers, police, courts, etc. Furthermore there was no nationalist leader in Uganda of Nkrumah's or Banda's stature. In 1963, on the first anniversary of its independence, Uganda replaced the British Queen as its Head of State under an arrangement which enabled the traditional ruler of any of its four kingdoms (Buganda, Ankole, Bunyoro, and Toro), the ruler of Busoga and the constitutional heads of each of the ten districts to be elected President and Head of State by the National Assembly.[24] The Vice-President was also to be elected from among this class. Under this arrangement, the Kabaka of Buganda, Sir Edward Mutesa, and the Kyabazinga of Busoga, Sir Wilberforce Nadiope, were elected President and Vice-President respectively.

Lesotho and Swaziland did not present this personality problem, since each was a single kingdom whose monarch on independence simply stepped into the Queen's position as a constitutional Head of State.

When the first hurdle of finding a suitable native for the constitutional headship of the state has been surmounted, as it was in Nigeria, Sierra Leone, Uganda, Lesotho and Swaziland, then a problem of greater difficulty arises of establishing between him and the Head of Government the sort of relationship that makes the system work in Britain. The Queen's position in the British Constitution was the product of historical evolution. The monarch once embodied in himself the entire sovereign power of the state, which he exercised in his discretion as a personal ruler. The government was his in every sense of the word, and he was synonymous with the state. He possessed and exercised over his ministers, other public servants and subjects generally a power at once absolute and complete. Allegiance was owed to him personally, and he could destroy, elevate and honour whom he pleased. His person was invested with pomp, majesty and awe. This position of sovereign power and majesty had created a definite pattern of relationship between him and his ministers and between him and his subjects generally, a relationship which imposed upon the ministers conformity with certain norms of propriety in their behaviour towards him. These norms of court manners accorded him veneration, respect and courtesy. In the course of centuries of constitutional evolution, the monarch has lost his personal discretion in the exercise of his sovereignty. In law, sovereign power still reposes in him, the government is still his own, but he no longer governs personally, most of his powers having devolved upon a representative cabinet of ministers, yet these ministers still regard themselves, as of old, as the King's ministers, and the government which they administer is His Majesty's Government. This is no mere formality. The pattern of relationship has remained basically unchanged, and is still characterised by the same attitude of reverence, respect and personal allegiance. It would be unthinkable for a British Prime Minister or any other minister to conduct himself rudely or indecorously before the monarch, or to make insulting or derogatory remarks about him in public or to appear openly to defy his authority. If it happens that he should not share the government's view upon any policy matter, his views and warnings will be treated with the profoundest respect and consideration, and the Government will, so far as possible, try to accommodate them, though it is not bound to do so.

These, then, are the factors upon which the separation of the Head of State from the actual exercise of executive power is sanctioned in Britain; they operate to avoid or minimise conflict in the working of the system. They are, however, conditions not likely to be reproduced in a country lacking the historical background upon which the relation between the Head of State and the government is patterned. Ministers in Nigeria never regarded themselves as the President's ministers or the government as his own. If anything, the Prime Minister regarded himself as the President's superior and often behaved as such towards him. There was hardly any attitude of personal allegiance, of reverence or of courtesy towards him; he lacked the attribute of kingly majesty in the eyes of the people, much less so in the eyes of the ministers. They had been either colleagues or opponents in partisan politics, and the differences in tribal sentiment and loyalty intruded to make the cultivation of the right attitudes that should inform the relationship still more difficult. It is futile to try to reproduce what cannot be reproduced.

4. *Clash of Interest*

A constitutional Head of State is expected to be above party politics. That is one important underlying presupposition upon which the satisfactory working of the system depends. This condition is easily met in Britain. The Queen's upbringing within the seclusion of palaces, among a highly exclusive circle of people, and away from ordinary life has made it possible for her to maintain an impartiality, aloofness and serenity in relation to partisan politics. She belongs, not to any territorial segment of the community nor to any political party, but to the whole country. The British Governor-General as the Queen's representative in an independent African country could also be expected to maintain the same attitude and tradition of non-involvement in partisan politics, since he had no personal stake in the politics of the country. Like any human being he might have his own prejudices, but these normally fell far short of a personal commitment such as might be expected of a native, who will normally have personal interests and those of family, tribe or region to protect or promote.

When he became Governor-General of Nigeria in 1960 in succession to the outgoing British Governor-General, Sir James Robertson, Dr Nnamdi Azikiwe made it clear that he did not intend to follow in the tradition of keeping severely away from all forms of public political discussion. His article in 1961 caused many eyebrows to be raised because of the rather caustic tone of his political comments.[25] He had been a politician for much of his life, and a most volatile, articulate and explosive one at that, and so it was perhaps too much to expect him to cast off his colour so easily and completely. The gilded iron cage was bound to prove too confining for his expansive personality. He openly admonished the politicians for their nepotism, tribalism and perfidy, and did not hesitate to comment on the trend of political events in the country. His comments were interpreted in many quarters as showing partiality for his tribe and for the political party of which he was formerly the leader. The comments were apparently offered in the spirit of the father-of-the-nation, but, as Tansey and Kermode have said, 'the main difficulty was that mutual distrust between the main ethnic groupings in the country was and still is so great that few are willing to credit impartiality to a non-member of their own group'.[26] It cannot be claimed for Dr Azikiwe that he was entirely free of tribal bias. Perhaps no one could be, given the emotionally charged tribal atmosphere of Nigerian politics during those years. When the first major crisis broke out in 1964 over the conduct of the federal elections, it was obvious where Azikiwe's sympathy lay, and the charges made against him of involvement on the side of his former party the National Council of Nigerian Citizens (NCNC), which was now in alliance with the other major southern party (the Action Group), cannot be said to have been altogether unfounded. His effort to use his good offices to mediate in the crisis was therefore scorned by the other parties who refused to attend meetings called by him. By this time the symbolism associated with his office as the father of the nation had been seriously eroded.

More acute had been the clash of interest in Uganda between the Government of Prime Minister Milton Obote and the President, Sir Edward Mutesa, who was also the Kabaka (King) of Buganda. The interests of the two were diametrically at variance. It was much more than a conflict of personalities: it embraced the whole question of the relationship between the kingdom of Buganda and the Ugandan nation. It was essentially a clash between the forces of traditionalism and separatism personified by the Kabaka and those of radicalism and Ugandan nationalism represented by Milton Obote. A compromise had been worked out which guaranteed to Buganda autonomy over a wide list of matters under a federal arrangement, thus enabling the kingdom to preserve its separate identity and its traditional institutions within the Ugandan nation. The radical Obote and his followers acquiesced in this as a temporary expedient to stave off deadlock in the negotiations for independence, and even accepted an alliance with the specifically Baganda political party, the Kabaka Yekka ('Kabaka only').

It was this alliance that formed the coalition government that ushered the country into independence in 1962. But the alliance was one of convenience, for Obote and his party nursed aspirations of a Ugandan nation that would integrate the various tribes into a closely knit unity. The divergence in outlook and interests between the allies soon sparked off a series of clashes which rocked the coalition government, until its final break-up in August 1964. First was the quarrel over the central government's refusal to increase its grants to Buganda to finance the expansion of services taken over by Buganda under the terms of the 1962 Constitution, and the endorsement by the High Court of the government's action.[27] But the most embittering was the controversy over the so-called 'lost counties'. These were territories which traditionally belonged to Bunyoro but were transferred to Buganda by the British towards the end of the nineteenth century as a reward for Buganda's loyalty and support in the war against Bunyoro. These territories had since been administered as part of Buganda, though agitation for their return had continued unabated ever since. The 1962 Constitution provided for the holding of a referendum to ascertain the wishes of the people of the territories whether they wanted to be returned to Bunyoro or not. The Baganda were vehemently opposed to the referendum idea, but their opposition was ignored by the central government which, as a first step preparatory to the referendum, took over the administration of the two counties concerned. When the referendum was held, the result was an overwhelming victory for incorporation into Bunyoro. A court action by Buganda challenging the referendum was lost in the Ugandan courts and an appeal to the Privy Council in London also failed.[28] The last fatal blow had now been dealt to the coalition. In all this conflict between his obligation to his kingdom and to the central government of which he was also President, there was no doubt that the Kabaka's first duty was to his kingdom. So overriding indeed was his interest in his kingdom that he began plotting to overthrow the central government. It was this attempted coup that finally broke his relationship with the central government, and forced him into exile.

The situation in the kingdom of Lesotho had been no less disturbing, and provides perhaps the most glaring testimony of the incompatibility of a constitutional Head of State with the African traditional method of government. The problem was how to make an African king, accustomed by tradition to the exercise of executive authority, abide by the role of a constitutional monarch cast upon him by the constitution. From the beginning the King of Lesotho, Motlothlehi Moshoeshoe II, showed a disinclination to abide by this role, conceiving of himself and his chiefs as the real authorities of the country, just as of old. He engaged in various activities of a political nature which inevitably involved him in clashes with the government of Prime Minister Leabua Jonathan. His political activities were said to be the direct cause of the disturbances of December 27, 1966 (barely two and half months after independence), which resulted in bloodshed and loss of life. On account of this, he was, on January 5, 1967, made to sign an undertaking before both houses of parliament and the cabinet, promising to abide by the Constitution; not to convene or address any public meeting other than those convened on the advice of the government, and not to have political consultation with persons other than his ministers.[29] The undertaking ended with the declaration that 'if in the declared opinion of the Government it is evident that I have failed to carry out any of the terms of this undertaking and declaration, I freely and voluntarily agree that this declaration shall forthwith come into operation as a formal act and instrument of abdication by me of all my powers, rights, privileges and immunities as King of Lesotho without the necessity of any further act on my part'.[30]

These undertakings were of course not kept, as he (the King) continued his opposition to the Government. Under the Constitution he was entitled to nominate eleven members to the Senate. Of those so nominated by him, eight were from the opposition party. And when on April 29, 1966, five of his nominees voted with the government contrary to his wishes, he immediately dismissed and replaced them by other persons known to be opposed to the government. (The dismissal was later declared unlawful by the High Court.)[31] On the question whether Lesotho should align itself with South Africa or not, the King openly supported the opposition party's policy of non-fraternisation as against the government's increasing *entente* with that country. During the first post-independence election in 1970, the Prime Minister, Chief Leabua Jonathan, alleged that the King with his chiefs threatened the electors that if they did not vote for the opposition party they would be deprived of their lands, and that the King also addressed meetings of the chiefs urging them to ensure that their people voted for the opposition.[32] The elections were won by the opposition party, whereupon the Prime Minister declared a state of emergency, annulled the results of the elections, suspended the constitution, and had the King restricted, assuming to himself the entire executive authority of the country which, under the title of *Tona-Kholo*, he exercised in his own discretion, with the Council of Ministers acting only in a consultative capacity.[33] He too, jointly with the Council of Ministers, acts as the legislature.[34] (The King was restored on November 20, 1970, upon certain conditions.)[35] The moral of all this, as McAuslan has commented in relation to Uganda, 'seems to be that if "non-political" Heads of State are not already in existence, rules alone will not bring them into being'.[36]

In the other kingdom, Swaziland, a *modus vivendi* has been found in the conception of the ruler's position as involving a dual role:[37] as the Ngwenyama or traditional ruler of the Swazi nation, functions arising purely under Swazi law and custom, namely the offices of Ngwenyama and of the Queen Mother, appointment, revocation of appointment and suspension of chiefs, the composition of the Swazi National Council, the traditional *Ncwala* ceremony and the *Libutfo* (regimental) system were exercised by him in council with his chiefs and all adult male Swazi, i.e. the Swazi National Council. These matters continued to be regulated by Swazi law and custom, and were excluded from the legislative power of parliament; only with the written consent of the

Swazi National Council could parliament legislate upon them. Control of land and minerals was also vested in the Ngwenyama acting on the advice of his *Libandla* (council) and, in the case of minerals, after consultation with a Minerals Committee. In his capacity as king of the modern Swazi state, he was obliged to act on the advice of the cabinet; he could however delay action for seven days by requiring the advice to be reconsidered by the cabinet. The British Government had opposed the control of minerals by the Ngwenyama free of cabinet advice on the ground that it was undemocratic, and might result in a clash between him and the government.[38] Accordingly the internal self-government Constitution of 1967 vested the control of minerals and mineral oils in the King subject to the advice of the cabinet.[39] The requirement of cabinet advice was removed in the Independence Constitution on the insistence of the Swaziland Government itself, which argued that by Swazi law and custom 'the control of these assets should vest in the Ngwenyama as the head of the Swazi nation, and *ipso facto* the trustee of its property rather than in the King as a constitutional monarch, obliged to act in accordance with the decisions of the Government of the day'.[40] While regretting this departure from the arrangement of the internal self-government constitution which embodied what it considered 'a reasonable compromise between the responsibilities of a cabinet form of government in a modern state and recognition of Swazi respect for traditional authority',[41] the British Government had to acquiesce in the demand of the Swaziland Government and Parliament. In practice the King was the effective power behind the government even in non-traditional matters. The separation had little practical reality, as the King, by virtue of his age, prestige and powerful personality, overshadowed the Prime Minister (a member of the King's family) and other ministers. Even this nominal separation was abolished on April 12, 1973, when the King, upon a petition by parliament, abrogated the Constitution, and took over absolute powers of government.

5. *Conflict of Authority*

Conflict is to be expected in an arrangement whereby executive authority is vested in one person and exercised by another, especially where the two represent different interests. A constitutional Head of State has, it is true, only a formal authority; yet it is an authority that may become crucial in time of crisis. Most public acts are done in his name, and some require to be authenticated by him. He is required to act only as advised by the government. All this assumes the existence of normal relations between him and the government. The constitution usually provides no sanction for ensuring that the Head of State observes his obligation to act only as advised by the government. The normal legal sanction of a court action is clearly inappropriate for this purpose, and for that reason is expressly excluded by the constitution itself. Coercive sanction, such as the detention of the Head of State or his forcible ejection from office, would precipitate a revolution.

His removal in accordance with the terms of the constitution may be difficult depending upon the procedure prescribed therefor by the constitution. If it involves parliamentary action, the government may lack the necessary majority to bring it about. So what does the government do where, for example, the Head of State in defiance of advice refuses to assent to a government bill of which he personally disapproves, to dissolve parliament, or to authenticate some other government act? It is true he has sworn to observe the constitution, and that an oath imports a legal duty, but again he is as Head of State immune from legal process. Admittedly the occasions must be exceedingly rare when a Head of State will violate his oath and his constitutional duty in such a flagrant manner, yet this is not beyond the realm of possibility, and the possibility did in fact materialise on at least one occasion.

As we have seen, in 1964 the Central Government of Uganda decided to take over control of the administration of the counties of Buyaga and Bugangazzi, two of the 'lost counties', pending the holding of the referendum there to determine the question whether they should remain as part of Buganda or be returned to Bunyoro to which they traditionally belonged. The take-over had to be an act of the President, acting on the advice of the Prime Minister. Here was a case where, as already pointed out, the interest of Sir Edward Mutesa as ruler (Kabaka) of Buganda, which kingdom fiercely opposed the Government's action, conflicted with his duty as President of Uganda. As President he was obliged, on the advice of the Prime Minister, to sign the order transferring the control of the administration of the two counties to the Central Government, but he refused to comply with the advice, thus clearly allowing his interest to override his duty.[42] This situation had of course been anticipated in the Constitution. It was there provided that where the President was required by the Constitution to do any act in accordance with the advice of any person or authority, and the Prime Minister was satisfied that the President had neglected or declined to do so, the Prime Minister might inform the President that it was his intention to do that act himself after the expiration of a period to be specified by the Prime Minister, and if at the expiration of that period the President had not done that act the Prime Minister might do it himself; and the act, when so done by the Prime Minister, was deemed to have been done by the President and overrode any other inconsistent act by the President.[43] When, therefore, Sir Edward Mutesa refused to sign the order for the take-over, the provision was invoked to effect it.[44] Although this provision was adequate for the actual situation that arose, it would have been unavailing where the conflict of authority resulted from the President acting contrary to advice, and not merely refusing to act at all.

Lesotho, in its 1966 Independence Constitution, also adopted this provision. The King, as previously noted, was stripped of his functions after the Constitution was suspended during the emergency in January 1970, but was restored on November 20 of the same year by the Office of King Order which, while re-enacting the old provision,[45] also required the King to swear on oath that he will obey and observe the provision of the Order and all other laws of Lesotho, that he will discharge his duties in such manner as to preserve the character of the monarchy as a symbol of the unity of the Basotho nation, and will accordingly abstain from involving the monarchy in any way in politics, or with any political party or group.[46] The Prime Minister is empowered, in the event of the King violating his oath, to declare him as having abdicated his office, and such declaration operates from the date of its publication in the gazette to vacate the office and to render void any purported exercise of power by the ex-King.[47] In his press conference on January 31, 1970, Prime Minister Leabua Jonathan had described the independence Constitution as 'foreign and hybrid'; that he was prepared to restore the monarchy after his brief rule as sole executive may be attributed to the fact that, as a member of the Royal Family, he has a personal stake in its survival. As we shall see presently, Obote, after his encounter with Sir Edward Mutesa in 1966, abolished the Ugandan kingdoms.

We have so far assumed a situation in which the Head of State acts or refuses to act in violation of the constitution, a case of a clear abuse of office, motivated by tribal or other political interest. However, a constitutional Head of State is never without some executive discretion, restricted though it is. By the constitution he is empowered to act by his own deliberate judgment in a few cases. Such matters leave very little scope for a conflict of authority, except where, in a crisis, the government deliberately trespasses upon the Head of State's discretionary authority, a not altogether unlikely event. Apart from these, a genuine case of conflict of authority may arise from extraordinary situations which are either not contemplated by the constitution or are capable of conflicting constitutional interpretations. Two such cases may be instanced.

(i) *Authority to maintain and preserve the Constitution*

The maintenance of the constitution is the first function and duty implied in the executive authority vested in the Head of State. By his oath of office he swears 'to preserve, protect and defend the constitution'. What, then, is expected of him by his duty and oath when the provisions of the constitution are being perverted by the government contrary to the duty enjoined upon them by their own oath of office? Is he to sit by and acquiesce in the acts of perversion? He could of course warn, as did President Azikiwe of Nigeria when in his national broadcasts he told politicians that their 'tribalism, nepotism, perfidy, bribery and corruption' was disgracing the nation. But perversion might be carried to a point where mere warning is not enough. This was the point that appeared to have been reached during the 1964 federal election crisis in Nigeria. The election had been marked by blatant irregularities which even the supposedly independent Electoral Commission admitted. There had been widespread intimidation and violence, refusal by electoral officers to accept nomination papers from the supporters of opposition parties, abduction of prospective candidates or their sponsors, denial of freedom of campaigning and even of movement, use of illegal ballot papers and other kinds of perverted practices. The final culmination was the boycott of the election by the opposition parties on the ground of these well-attested irregularities. The election was a complete travesty of constitutional democracy. What was the constitutional duty of the President in the circumstances created by these acts of perversion? As he had good grounds to anticipate that the electoral system was going to be perverted, it has been suggested that the President should have acted in time to appoint a caretaker government to supervise the election.[48] That would certainly have altered nothing. For, although the President had unfettered power to dismiss the Prime Minister during a dissolution when no question of support in the lower house could arise, he could only appoint as a successor a member of the Cabinet.[49] A caretaker government might have been useful if a neutral, non-partisan person could have been appointed. But since the choice was limited to members of the Cabinet, there would have been no good ground for preferring one partisan minister to another. Moreover, 'it is hard to see how such a "caretaker" government could have enforced its will upon the regional civil servants conducting the election or upon the supposedly independent Electoral Commission'.[50]

The President could not therefore but allow the election to go on under the authority of the old government. To be sure, he did suggest that it should be postponed, but the Prime Minister insisted that it should go on, and his was constitutionally the overriding voice. When the results were announced and indicated that the government party had 'won' — a foregone conclusion — should the President then, consistent with his oath, ignore the well-attested irregularities and re-appoint the Prime Minister as the leader of the winning party? That was what the letter of the law of the constitution required of him. But was that in consonance with its spirit? The position of the President in this situation was a most unenviable one. He refused at first to re-appoint the Prime Minister, and from that refusal there ensued a crisis full of tension. It has been contended that in these circumstances the President could have dismissed the Prime Minister, and, there being nobody with a legitimate claim to be called upon to form a government on the basis of the irregular election, he could have assumed executive powers himself. The dismissal of the government and the absence of anyone else entitled to be called upon to form a government would have created a vacuum, leaving the President as the sole lawful functionary of the executive. With no Cabinet to advise him, the President, by the imperative necessity of avoiding an abeyance of government,[51] would have been justified in assuming the supreme function of policy formulation, and could have appointed ministers to assist him. By so doing, it was argued, the President would have been doing no more than discharge his oath to 'preserve, protect and defend' the Constitution. This contention might have had great plausibility and perhaps validity, had it not been based upon the false premise that a vacancy in the Premiership would have arisen after a general election by the President merely informing the Prime Minister that he was not going to re-appoint him. What the constitution actually provided was that the office of the Prime Minister should be vacated 'when, after any dissolution of the House of Representatives, the Prime Minister is informed by the President that the President is about to re-appoint him as Prime Minister or to appoint another person as Prime Minister'.[52] If an election was vitiated by irregularities so that nobody could legitimately be appointed Prime Minister on the basis of it, the President would have no ground to inform the Prime Minister that he was about to re-appoint him or to appoint someone else, from which it follows that the Prime Minister would have to continue in office until perhaps a fresh election had been held. During a dissolution the President could undoubtedly dismiss a Prime Minister, especially if he was believed to have been responsible for the irregularities in the election, simply by informing him that he was about to appoint someone else. Yet, having done that, he could not then assume executive functions himself; he would have been obliged to appoint a new Prime Minister who, as previously stated, would have to be a member of the outgoing Cabinet.

In a conflict between the clear letter of the Constitution and its spirit, the former should prevail, and the President was right in eventually adopting the course dictated by the law. But the crisis did shake the fabric of Nigerian government and society, and inflicted a wound from which the Republic never recovered. There was yet another aspect of it which provides a striking illustration of the conflict inherent in separating the Head of State from the Head of Government.

(ii) *The President as Commander-in-Chief*

So serious was the crisis provoked by the President's initial refusal to re-appoint the Prime Minister that both had openly to solicit the loyalty and support of the armed forces. The Constitution designated the President as Commander-in-Chief of the armed forces, and provided that his functions as such would be such as might be prescribed by Parliament. In the statutes governing the armed forces, however, no reference was made to the Commander-in-Chief. Under them overall responsibility for the operational use of the forces was vested in the Council of Ministers, though at the same time the Prime Minister was empowered to direct the commanders of the various units of the armed forces – the army, navy and air force – with respect to the operational use of the forces for the purpose of maintaining and securing public safety and public order, notwithstanding that the directions of the Council of Ministers had not been obtained. Was the implication of vesting the control of the operational use of the forces in the commanders subject to the direction of the Council of Ministers and the Prime Minister that the Commander-in-Chief had no functions or powers whatever in regard thereto? Was the President Commander-in-Chief just in name, and not in fact? The commanders of the army and the navy (the air force was still in the process of formation) had sought and obtained advice that that was in fact the true legal position and, on the basis of that advice, assured the Prime Minister of their loyalty and support for him as the rightful authority to dispose of the armed forces. The Commander of the Nigerian army, Major-General Welby-Everard, instructed his officers and men accordingly in a circular letter. Convinced as the General was of the correctness of the position he had adopted, the matter was not altogether free from doubt in the minds of some of his subordinates, to whom the idea of a Commander-in-Chief without powers of command was hardly intelligible. Ordinarily the Commander-in-Chief is a well-recognised position in the hierarchy of the armed forces, implying indeed the supreme command of the forces; he could directly command any unit or member of the armed forces, even over the head of the commander. The mere designation of the President in the Constitution as Commander-in-Chief attracted these powers; they followed inherently and necessarily from the name. The invidious question, then, was whether, if the Commander-in-Chief should command any member of the armed forces, such a member, trained as he had been to obey superior military orders without question, could properly refuse to obey. To him, it was irrelevant that the Armed Forces Act made no reference to the Commander-in-Chief. If there was a Commander-in-Chief designated by the supreme law of the land, his orders were lawful, superior orders which every member of the armed forces was duty-bound to obey. It was equally irrelevant to a soldier whether, in giving such orders, the Commander-in-Chief had received or acted in accordance with the advice of the Council of Ministers or the Prime Minister. These latter held no command positions in the armed forces. It is true that by law they could give direction to the commander of a unit of the armed forces, but such direction could only become a military order if re-issued by recognised command officers, of whom the Commander-in-Chief was the most superior. In view of these considerations, many of the officers of the army considered that the course of action best calculated to uphold the integrity and impartiality of the army lay in non-commitment to either side. Happily, in the event, the armed forces were saved the unpleasantness of a division in their ranks which a military intervention would have produced.

It has been said of the Ugandan crisis in 1966 that 'it was the purported exercise of other powers relating to the position of the President as Commander-in-Chief of the Armed Forces not thought about by the draftsman and his advisers which precipitated the final clash between the Kabaka and Mr Obote (as he then was)'.[53] Impelled by a sense of frustration over the defeat of his kingdom in its various contests with the central government, Sir Edward Mutesa nursed the idea that as President and Commander-in-Chief he was entitled to request military assistance from foreign countries ostensibly for curbing the depredations of Obote's soldiers in his kingdom. He admitted having approached the British High Commissioner for such assistance. Partly for this and partly for other reasons connected with the allegation that Obote and two of his ministers were involved in an alleged misappropriation of money (over $300,000) given to Uganda's Chief-of-Staff, Colonel Amin, to purchase supplies for rebel Congolese soldiers operating from Uganda (all the accused were later cleared in an inquiry conducted by the three Chief Justices of East Africa), Obote on February 22, 1966, seized absolute power, abrogated the Constitution, and dismissed Sir Edward as President. On April 15, a new Constitution was adopted in the National Assembly, which, among other things, abolished the constitutional presidency. The final showdown between Sir Edward and Obote came towards the end of May the same year. Fifty of the Kabaka's men, armed with guns issued to them from the royal palace, clashed with a unit of the national army, and there were also attacks upon national police posts in the kingdom. The army then besieged, shelled and reduced the mile-square palace on Mengo Hill, which was defended by a palace guard of 100 men.[54] The Kabaka escaped to neighbouring Burundi, whence he went to live as an exile in Britain. An observer has commented that 'if the Kabaka had been able to accept limited powers in Buganda and none in Uganda, perhaps there would have been no crisis'.[55]

6. *The Complexity and Uncertainty of Governmental Relations*

The separation of the Head of State from the actual exercise of executive power means that there exist in the executive branch two sets of relationship instead of one, that between the Head of State and the government, and between the Head of Government and the other ministers. This duality necessarily imports a certain amount of complexity in government. No doubt the fact that the authority of the Head of State is only a formal one minimises the complexity. As a constitutional head he can only act, by and large, as advised by the government. Yet, his very existence means that he cannot be excluded from all responsibility in respect to the appointment and dismissal of the government, or more precisely of the Prime Minister. In strict law the government is his, in the sense that the power which it exercises belongs to him by the terms of the constitution. It is true that by historical evolution the government has come to be a committee of the legislature from which its title to rule is derived, and that the emergence of the party system requires that the government should be drawn from the party having a majority support in the legislature. But practice has to be reconciled with law as much as possible, which means that the Head of State must be the instrument through which the appointment and dismissal are formally made. Situations of some complexity are capable of arising from this relationship. The election of an executive president, whether by the people or by the legislature, is usually a straightforward business; the candidate or candidates are known, and the result leaves no room for equivocation. But it may sometimes be a matter of some uncertainty which of several party leaders can command a majority in the legislature to entitle him to be called upon to form a government. An executive president is elected for a fixed term, and he may resign sooner, or dissolve the legislature and so bring his term to a premature end if his tenure is made co-terminous with the life of the legislature by the constitution, but there is no question of anyone exercising a discretion to dismiss him because he no longer enjoys the support of the legislature. On the other hand, since the Prime Minister, under the Westminster system, derives his right to rule from the legislature, he may be dismissed by the Head of State if, when he loses the legislature's support, he does not resign. He may of course, instead of resigning, ask for a dissolution. Herein lies another complexity, for the Head of State may refuse his request for a dissolution.

In Britain the relationship of the Head of State to the government is not defined by law. As far as the law is concerned, the Queen as Head of State is the executive, and the practice whereby she has ceased to exercise her executive power personally but rather through ministers is unrecognised by the strict letter of the law. The system is thus characterised by a divergence between the law of the Constitution, which recognises the Queen as the executive, and the practice of it. The practice rests entirely upon convention, which, being unwritten, is notoriously uncertain. When, if at all, may the Queen dismiss a Prime Minister, or refuse his request for a dissolution? These and similar other questions have continued to agitate constitutional lawyers and politicians in Britain. In Commonwealth Africa attempts to remove this uncertainty have been made through detailed specification of the relevant conventions in the constitution, thus imparting to them not only the quality of precision but also the sanctity of law. Yet this device has not, and cannot have, succeeded in removing all the incidence of uncertainty. Uncertainty is indeed inherent in a system of separation. And legal specification, by burdening the constitution with too much detail, increases its complexity and prolixity, making it difficult to read and to understand.

Take, for example, the question of the appointment of a Prime Minister. The usual provision is that he should be a member of the elected house who appears to the Head of State likely to command the support of the majority of members of the house. This provision leaves so much uncertain. It envisages a system in which, as in Britain, elections are largely a contest between two major parties, resulting in one of them winning a clear majority to be able to form a government. (The result is also influenced by the electoral system.) Where such is not the case and there is instead a multiciplicity of parties, it may be a matter of great difficulty and uncertainty to determine who can command majority support in the house. And how is the Head of State to determine this? No doubt consultation and the application of his personal knowledge of the standing of the parties and of their respective leaders may help in the determination, but the possibility of favouritism and other kinds of abuse is inherent in the discretion vested in the Head of State under this provision. Once there is no party with a majority, favouritism may determine the choice as between persons who are equally likely to command majority support, and may indeed induce a preference for a person who is less likely than others to command that support.

By amendments to its Constitution in 1963, Uganda had attempted even more detailed definition designed to restrict the Head of State's discretion and so minimise the uncertainty and abuse. The result of course was a complex and difficult section that covered two full pages of print.[56] The President was to appoint as Prime Minister the leader in the Assembly of the party having a majority of all the seats, and if none, then the leader of the party with the greatest numerical strength in the Assembly. If the government formed by such leader failed to command the support of the Assembly, then the leader of the party with the next largest numerical strength was to be appointed, and thereafter the leaders in turn of the largest parties which had at least twenty members in the house. In the event of equality in numerical strength between two parties, the President was to choose which was more likely to succeed in forming a government that would command support. In the last resort, if no government with legislative support could be formed, a 'caretaker' government was to be appointed for three months under the previous Prime Minister or, if he had ceased to be a member of the Assembly or it was otherwise impossible for him to act, then under the leader of the party with the greatest numerical strength in the house. The caretaker government needed no legislative support, though no legislative measures could be introduced, and parliament must be dissolved at the expiration of the three months, unless in the meantime a government with legislative support had been formed.

As will be noticed, this provision had not altogether eliminated uncertainty. First, the President was still left with a discretion to decide as between the leaders of two parties with equal numerical strength. Secondly, the question of leadership of a party might not be free from doubt, and upon this the Constitution offered no definition. A party may have no undisputed leader, or the recognised leader may not be in the house, as was the case with the leader of the Northern Peoples Congress (NPC), the largest party in the Nigerian federal parliament or the leader of the Democratic Party, the opposition party in Uganda. Should the President in such a case consult the constitution of the party, or ask the party to nominate or elect a parliamentary leader? Thirdly, the section stated that after the leader of the party with the largest numerical strength had been appointed Prime Minister, then, if his government failed to command the support of the Assembly, the President was to make another appointment. This again left uncertain what was to be the criterion of the Prime Minister's support in the Assembly. Was the defeat of a government measure to be a conclusive indication of lack of support? According to the Constitution, the President could remove a Prime Minister only upon a vote of no confidence, provided that three days had elapsed since the motion and the Prime Minister had not in the meantime resigned or asked for a dissolution.[57] This suggests that the only criterion of lack of support which would warrant the President removing a Prime Minister once he had been appointed was a vote of no confidence, though the provision relating to appointment would seem to imply something less.

The uncertainty about the President's source of information regarding the Prime Minister's support or lack of it has been raised in an acute form in relation to the power of dismissal. As with appointment, the old formula used to be that the President could remove a Prime Minister if it appeared to him that he (the Prime Minister) no longer enjoyed the majority support of the elected house. The question that had arisen upon this provision was whether the lack of support could so appear to the President only upon events on the floor of the house or also from sources outside it. Upon this question the courts in Nigeria were sharply divided in a case in 1962. Following a squabble within the ruling party in Western Nigeria, the regional Governor removed the Premier on the strength of a letter signed by sixty-six out of 117 members of the House of Assembly to the effect that they no longer had confidence in the Premier. The Supreme Court of Nigeria, by a majority, decided that the Governor was not entitled to act upon the strength of the letter.[58] It is easy enough to imagine how a power vested in a non-elected Head of State to dismiss an elected government on the evidence of events occurring outside the legislature can be put to a mischievous and arbitrary use. It was consciousness of this not too remote possibility that led the majority to the conclusion that the Governor's source of information as to the Premier's support or lack of it among the elected M.P.s must emanate from the house itself. 'Law and convention', said Chief Justice Ademola, 'cannot be replaced by party political moves outside the House'. While recognising the dangers of arbitrariness and abuse inherent in allowing the Head of State such a wide leeway, the Judicial Committee of the Privy Council held, upon a rather literal and legalistic approach, that the Governor was free to act on other than the testimony of recorded votes.[59]

A slight variation in wording led to a different result in Sarawak in 1966. There the Constitution provided that if the Chief Minister ceased to command the confidence of the majority of the Legislative Council, then, unless at his request the Governor dissolved the Assembly, the Chief Minister should tender the resignation of the government. Twenty-one out of the forty-two members of the Council had signed a letter to the Governor stating that they no longer had confidence in the Chief Minister. Upon the latter refusing to resign, the Governor purported to remove him. It was held, distinguishing the Nigerian case, that the words 'if the Chief Minister ceases to command' left no discretion in the Governor as to the source of his information, as did the words 'if it appears' in the Constitution of Western Nigeria, and that accordingly the Governor was not entitled to act otherwise than on the strength of events occurring on the floor of the house; and that, in any event, a refusal by the Chief Minister to resign after a vote of no confidence or defeat on a major issue, though in itself unconstitutional, gave the Governor no power to dismiss him in the absence of express provision to that effect.[60] One may also recall the dismissal of the Prime Minister of Pakistan in 1953 by the Governor-General. The Prime Minister, Nazimuddin, had previously been Governor-General, but on October 16, 1951, on the assassination of the then Prime Minister, Liaquat Ali Khan, he relinquished the office of Governor-General for the latter office. Between the new Governor-General and a Prime Minister who himself had once been Governor-General conflict was perhaps inevitable, as indeed proved to be the case, exacerbated no doubt by political developments in the country. Using his power under the provisional Constitution as contained in the Government of India Act, 1935, the Governor-General, Ghulam Mohammed, dismissed Nazimuddin as Prime Minister. This provoked the Constituent Assembly to amend the Act of 1935, abolishing the discretion of the Governor-General in the appointment and dismissal of the Prime Minister and making this dependent upon his support or lack of it in the Assembly. The Governor-General reacted by dissolving the Assembly and proclaiming a state of emergency under which he assumed power to rule by decree, and appointed a new ministry under Chaudhuri Mohamed Ali. (There were of course other reasons for the Governor-General's action.)

Such, therefore, is the uncertainty inherent in the relations of a constitutional Head of State to the government. What is even more undesirable is the effect of this uncertainty on government. In Western Nigeria the dismissed Premier, Chief Samuel Akintola, refused to accept his dismissal – quite unjustifiably, since it was not as if his dismissal was the act of an incompetent authority. He should, as did the Chief Minister in Sarawak, have retired to await the result of the court action which he instituted to test the legality of his dismissal. By refusing to abide by his dismissal, Chief Akintola thereby set himself up in competition with the newly-appointed Premier, throwing the civil service into uncertainty and confusion as to which of the rival Premiers to obey. A meeting of the Assembly, called to determine the question of support, erupted into great violence between the two factions, in which several members were injured, thereby inviting the intervention of the police, who then emptied and locked the house.[61] The Federal Government next stepped in, suspended the regional government and appointed an emergency administration in its place. In Sarawak the reinstatement of the dismissed Chief Minister following the court's decision triggered off a chain of events which culminated in the federal government of Malaysia (of which Sarawak is part) declaring a state of emergency in Sarawak and using its emergency powers to amend the state Constitution to empower the Governor to dismiss the Chief Minister.

The refusal of Chief Akintola to accept his dismissal meant that until the final decision of the Privy Council in the case – a space of more than a year – it remained uncertain who was the lawful Premier of Western Nigeria. Before the decision was handed down, however, Chief Akintola had been restored to power through the action of the Federal Government. And, now that the decision declared that his dismissal had been lawful after all, a constitutional amendment was rushed through, nullifying with retrospective effect the decision of the Privy Council by providing that the Governor could remove the Premier only in consequence of a vote of no confidence. The 1963 Republican Constitution abolished the power of removal altogether. Voluntary resignation or dissolution then became the only way by which a Premier who had lost legislative support could vacate office. If a government measure was rejected by the legislature, the government could ask for a dissolution, which the President might refuse if he considered that government could be carried on without a dissolution and that a dissolution would not be in the interest of the federation (or region).[62] Faced with such a refusal, the government might either resign or compromise with the legislature. In the case of a vote of no confidence, the government had again a choice between resignation and dissolution. If it chose to ask for dissolution, the President must dissolve. But if it resigned instead, the President could ask someone else to form a new government, unless he considered that nobody could be found to do so within a reasonable time, in which case he must again dissolve. He must also dissolve if the Premier would neither resign nor recommend a dissolution.

7. *The Needs of a Developing African Country*

A constitution should be adapted to the needs of the country and to the aspiration of its citizens. This has been one of the reasons for the rejection of the Westminster system in favour of presidentialism. 'The time has now come', said Dr Kwame Nkrumah in a speech in 1959 foreshadowing Ghana's switch to the presidential system, 'for the people of Ghana to devise for themselves a new constitution best suited to the needs of Ghana.'[63] The same point has been re-echoed by several other African leaders. The paramount need of an African country is for development. It wants to develop its economy, to modernise and integrate its society, to secure and promote stability in the community, and to safeguard civil liberty. Economic development and modernisation loom so large in discussions about development, but they are not enough nor even capable of achievement without national integration and social stability, which together provide the foundation for economic and social development. Progress can only be achieved within an ordered society, and order in turn presupposes unity among the people.

While it may be arguable whether presidentialism or the system of separation *per se* conduces more to economic and social development, the effect of the latter on national integration and social stability is positively detrimental. An account has already been given of the clashes of personalities and of interest, and the conflict of authority which the system of separation can engender. Such clashes and conflicts create instability in government and in society. The dismissal of the Premier of Western Nigeria by the Governor in 1962 and the refusal of the Premier to accept his dismissal plunged the region into an emergency which consumed the passion and energies of the people, and diverted attention from the vital needs of economic development; and the flames lit by it grew into a mighty conflagration in the arson, pillage, murder and other forms of violence which followed in the wake of the election fraud of 1965 by which the same Chief Akintola sought to maintain himself in power against the clear verdict of the people of Western Nigeria. The disagreement between the President of Nigeria, Dr Nnamdi Azikiwe, and the Prime Minister, Sir Abubaker Tafawa Balewa, over the conduct of the 1964 federal elections rocked the federation to its very foundation, and nearly precipitated a bloody civil war. Sir Edward Mutesa's conflict with the central government of Uganda headed by Milton Obote finally led him into an attempt at a *coup d'état*, the failure of which forced him into exile, and estranged his subjects, the Baganda, from the central government.

Not only social stability but also national unity suffered in all these conflicts. Any clash between the Head of State and the Premier necessarily divides the country into factions, based either on tribe or purely on party interests, or both. The faction supporting President Azikiwe of Nigeria in 1964 was partly tribal (most members of his own tribe, the Ibo, supported him) and partly party-political (his former party, the NCNC, the Action Group, the United Middle Belt Congress and the Northern Elements Progressive Union aligned with him). Sir Edward Mutesa was of course fighting for the interest of his own kingdom of Buganda. The system of separation clearly therefore fails to provide a clear focal point of loyalty, which is indispensable to national integration. Thus one of the reasons stated in the government white paper for the constitutional proposals for a presidential system in Tanganyika in 1962 was 'to devise a new constitutional form more appropriate for an independent African state and more capable of inspiring a sense of loyalty in the people of Tanganyika'.[64] There should be one national leader, who should symbolise the state and rally the people around himself in loyalty to the nation.

The single executive has also the merit of unity, energy and despatch. 'Energy in the executive', Alexander Hamilton said, 'is a leading character in the definition of good government. . . . That unity is conducive to energy will not be disputed. Decision, activity, secrecy, and dispatch will generally characterise the proceedings of one man, in a much more eminent degree, than the proceedings of any greater number; and in proportion as the number is increased, these qualities will be diminished.'[65] This is not, of course, to deny the virtue of collective discussion and consultation in bringing the views and experiences of different people to bear upon a problem or upon the determination of policy. Yet it is essential to effective leadership in government that there should be a single individual in the capacity of a chief executive who can decide and act promptly when despatch is demanded, and who can impose his will when differences of opinion among cabinet members threaten to paralyse the government. Blackstone has rightly said that many wills (where the executive power is placed in many hands and therefore subject to many wills) 'if disunited and drawing different ways, create weakness in a government; and to unite those several wills, and reduce them to one, is a work of more time and delay than the exigencies of state will afford.'[66]

Another demerit of the plural executive stressed by Alexander Hamilton is that it undermines responsibility. That it does in two ways: first, through the weakened authority of the Prime Minister to enforce collective responsibility, and secondly, by making it difficult to determine on whom the blame or punishment for misconduct should fall. One of the factors that has discredited cabinet government in the developing countries of the Commonwealth was the inability of the Prime Minister to control the actions of ministers and to enforce the requirements of collective responsibility. In Pakistan until 1958, when parliamentary government was finally abrogated, the situation was near-chaotic, with ministers openly disagreeing with each other and with cabinet decisions and the Prime Minister unable to enforce discipline and the unity of the government. The federal government of Nigeria before the army take-over in 1966 also exhibited much the same record of irresponsibility and indiscipline among ministers, and an inability on the part of the Prime Minister to control them, though this inability in his own case was accountable both to the attitude of independence bred in ministers by the system of a plural executive itself and to the unique circumstance that he was only the deputy leader of his party owing allegiance to the party leader outside the federal government, to whom also the other party members in the federal cabinet owed allegiance.

It is, therefore, as Professor Carl Friedrich has observed, 'precisely the need for vigorous and if necessary decisive action, unhampered by the need to consider parliamentary majorities, which has made constitution-makers in recent years look with increasing interest at the American presidency as a paradigm of how to organise effective executive government. Especially in the newly developing countries, in Africa and Asia, the efforts of British advisers to set up parliamentary systems have been crowned with anything but success, when their advice was accepted. In one after another of these states, a shaky parliamentary democracy has been superseded by some kind of military rule, and it may well be questioned whether these countries would not have been better off with some properly modified presidential system'.[67]

The Commonwealth African presidential constitutions are designed to implement this need through 'the creation of an office of President which contains a manifest potential for leadership and which functions as a centre of activity and initiative within the political system — one, that is, which is able to supply a positive source of direction *vis-à-vis* the course of governmental affairs and a unifying influence over the operations of the other institutions of government, and one which, accordingly, helps provide an overall cohering focus to the activities of government during period of normalcy and as well, a crucial ingredient of stability in times of domestic or foreign difficulty'.[68]

8. *The Backward Swing of the Pendulum in Ghana in 1969*

When the executive presidency is blended with features of the parliamentary system without adequate constitutional and other safeguards on the resultant power structure, the result might be dictatorship. This had been particularly the experience of Ghana under its presidential constitution in 1960–6. The executive president had progressively gathered to himself the supreme power in the state, erecting himself above the legislature and the party, and had then proceeded to use this absolute power to tyrannise and oppress the people by a systematic desecration of their civil liberties. It was perhaps natural that the people of Ghana should have developed a revulsion against a system that had played so much havoc with their freedom. This revulsion expressed itself quite emphatically in the memoranda and oral testimonies given to the Constitutional Commission appointed by the National Liberation Council after the overthrow of the Nkrumah regime on February 24, 1966. The opinion was practically unanimous throughout the country against presidentialism, and favouring a split executive as the only relevant alternative. This choice has therefore to be viewed against the background of the people's experience. It was a reaction against the tyranny and oppression which they suffered at the hands of President Nkrumah, and could hardly be considered a rejection of presidentialism on its intrinsic merits.

Influenced as it was by this revulsion, which its members shared no less than the public, the Commission was anything but dispassionate in its consideration of the matter or even in the language of its denunciation of Nkrumah. 'We entered upon our assignment', the Commission avowed in its Report, 'in the belief that with the experience of tyranny and oppression so fresh in the minds of the people of Ghana, Ghanaians were determined to ensure that never again would the political sovereignty of our country be allowed to reside so precariously in one man.'[69] Again, 'the recent history of tyranny in Ghana is well implanted in the minds of the people of Ghana. It is thus a great satisfaction to us that our people are almost unanimous both in their memorandum and oral evidence in asking for a ceremonial head of state who would be the father of the Nation'.[70] The preamble of the Constitution, as finally enacted in 1969, also recited the same fact: 'We the Chiefs and People of Ghana, Having experienced a regime of tyranny, Remembering with gratitude the heroic struggle against oppression, Having solemnly resolved never again to allow ourselves to be subjected to a like regime. . . .'

The Commission did of course consider the argument against a split executive, which was vigorously urged upon it by a small minority of people, but concluded that the fears expressed had been exaggerated. It argued:

> The clash of power *per se* is not an evil. Without such a clash freedom cannot be maintained; to maintain freedom it is necessary that power must be opposed to power. Never has freedom been won or maintained by approaching power with one's hands bound behind one. Whether the clash will endanger the security of the state or hamper development will depend upon two factors. It will depend, firstly, on what provisions are made for the resolution of such conflicts if and when they do in fact occur, Secondly, it will depend on how the powers are divided. We do not think that our proposals leave room for a clash or even confusion of powers between the President and the Cabinet or the Prime Minister. But should such a clash or confusion nevertheless occur the Supreme Court is the only legal body to resolve the conflict by interpreting the Constitution in such a way as to leave no confusion or conflict unresolved.[71]

The hope that any conflict will be resolved by the Supreme Court seems to border on the naïve. As experience in Nigeria, Uganda and other countries has amply shown, judicial guardianship of the constitution is, in such matters, like medicine after death, and, in any case, can seldom be obtained. The judicial determination of the legality of the

Governor's dismissal of the Premier of Western Nigeria came more than a year after the event, and resolved nothing. And was the Supreme Court not there in 1964 when Nigeria was dragged to the brink of disintegration as a result of the conflict between the President and the Prime Minister? Whether the President was constitutionally justified in refusing to re-appoint the Prime Minister because of the irregularities in the elections, and which of them was entitled to dispose of the armed forces were clearly justifiable issues, and yet no one ever thought, even remotely, of going to court over them. Surely the process of the court was most inexpedient in a crisis of that sort. However, it may be that the novel arrangement proposed by the Ghanaian Constitutional Commission would guarantee freedom and limited government generally, in which case it would have justified any conflict to which the separation might be prone, but it would be contrary to all experience to expect any system of separation to be entirely free of conflict. Conflict is not avoided merely by the Commission preaching to politicians to 'bear in mind that as office-holders they are but creatures of the law and that they must of necessity submit to it'.[72]

(i) *The Middle Way: A President with Limited Powers*

What the Commission did in fact propose for Ghana was not the ceremonial Head of State demanded by the people, but rather one with limited executive powers to enable him to act as a check upon the government of the day. The idea underlying this arrangement was to enable the President to exercise — free from ministerial advice — certain functions which are peculiarly liable to manipulation for political purposes, i.e. 'functions relating to institutions that are generally expected to be independent and whose independence is essential to good government and the maintenance of freedom'.[73] These proposals have been implemented in the 1969 Constitution of Ghana.

Following the usual Westminster pattern, the President was made the formal repository of the executive authority of Ghana, and was required in the performance of his functions under the Constitution to act in accordance with the advice of the Cabinet.[74] However, in a wide range of functions he was to act either in his own discretion or on the advice of, or in consultation with, some person or authority other than the Cabinet or a minister, the most important authority for this purpose being a Council of State composed of the Prime Minister, the Speaker of the National Assembly, the Leader of the Opposition in parliament, the President of the National House of Chiefs, four members appointed by the President in his discretion from among former Presidents, Chief Justices, Speakers and Prime Ministers, and eight other members, including two women and four chiefs, appointed by the President in his discretion.[75] Meetings of the Council were convened and presided over by the President. Thus the Council was largely an instrument of the President, to 'aid and counsel' him, and formed part of his office.[76]

Of the functions which the President was required to exercise on the advice of the Council of State the most important related to the creation or merger of regions or alteration of their boundaries,[77] the proclamation of an emergency (this would initially be by the President on the advice of the Cabinet but must then be approved by the Council of State within seventy-two hours),[78] the appointment and removal of the Electoral Commissioner (responsible for the conduct and super-vision of elections and referenda),[79] and the appointment and removal of the Chief of Defence Staff of the armed forces.[80] The making of electoral laws and regulations was vested, not in parliament, but in the Electoral Commissioner acting with the prior approval of the President, who himself must act on the advice of the Council of State in giving the approval.[81]

Only consultation was required for the exercise by the President of functions relating to the prerogative of mercy,[82] the appointment and removal of the Ombudsman, the Auditor-General, the chairman and members of the Audit Service Board (the removal of the Auditor-General required a separate procedure, and the members of the Audit Service Board could only be removed on the advice of the Council for inability or other good cause), the chairman and members of any commission established by the Constitution, such as the Public Service Commission, the Local Government Grants Commission (though in the case of the Grants Commission only the chairmen and two members were to be appointed in consultation with the Council, the remaining two members being appointed on the advice of the Prime Minister), the chairman and other members of the governing body of any corporation established by an act of Parliament, a statutory instrument, or out of public funds for wireless broadcasting, television, the press or other media for mass communication or information.[83] The Chief Justice was also to be appointed by the President in consultation with the Council, though his removal required a different procedure.

The President was also the authority to appoint and remove members of the public services, acting however on the advice of the Public Service Commission[84] or, in the case of members of the police and prisons services, on the advice of the Public Service Board.[85] (The Heads of the Police and Prison Service were, however, appointed and removable by the President on the advice of the Prime Minister.) In the case of officers and members of the armed forces (other than the Chief of Defence Staff) the President was to act on the advice of the Armed Forces Council, consisting of the Prime Minister as chairman, the

Ministers of Defence and the Interior, the Chief of Defence Staff and two other members appointed by the President on the advice of the Prime Minister. The Armed Forces Council also directed and controlled the Chief of Defence Staff in the operational control and administration of the armed forces.[86] This meant that the designation of the President as the Commander-in-Chief imported no command power.

The appointment of judges of the superior courts (other than the Chief Justice) was also insulated from political control and vested in the President acting on the advice of a Judicial Council comprised of the Chief Justice, the most senior justice respectively of the Supreme Court, the Court of Appeal and the High Court, and the Attorney-General.[87] And they (the superior judges) could only be removed by the President if so recommended by a tribunal of three judges appointed by the Judicial Council on the ground of inability or stated misbehaviour.[88] (This procedure must also be followed in the removal of the Auditor-General,[89] and members of the Public Services Commission.)[90] The tribunal to investigate the Chief Justice must consist of three justices of the Supreme Court and two other persons appointed by the President in consultation with the Council of State.[91] Inferior judicial officers – judges of inferior courts, magistrates, registrars, etc., were appointed by the Chief Justice on the advice of the Judicial Council and with the approval of the President.[92]

The emoluments of judges of the superior courts, the Auditor-General, the Electoral Commissioner, the members of the Public Services Commission and the Ombudsman were charged upon the Consolidated Fund, and were to be determined by the President on the recommendation of a committee appointed by him.[93] The President had to consult the Council of State in the appointment of the committee and in making the final determination. The President also fixed, in consultation with the Council of State, the salaries and allowances of ministers as well as the basic, sitting, travelling and rent allowance and gratuity of members of the National Assembly (members were not paid any salary as such).[94]

The functions which the President was to exercise entirely on his own discretion, without anyone else's advice or consultation, related mainly to his relationship with the government and the legislature. The provisions relating to the appointment of the Prime Minister sought, however, to confine his discretion within a narrow limit. If there was a party with an absolute majority in the National Assembly, then its leader was entitled to be appointed Prime Minister.[95] If no party had an absolute majority, the President was to nominate for election by the National Assembly a person who appeared to him most likely to command the support of the majority of all the members of the Assembly.[96] Should the person nominated by the President fail to get elected, the Assembly should within seven days elect a Prime Minister,[97] and failing that the President should dissolve the Assembly.[98] Election did not have the effect of an automatic appointment; this had still to be made formally by the President.[99] The President must be kept informed of Cabinet decisions, and might call for information concerning any matter, and might also require that any matter should be submitted for the consideration of the Cabinet.[100] He could not, however, remove the Prime Minister, though the latter was obliged to resign with his government if he sought a vote of confidence and lost it, or if the National Assembly passed a motion of no confidence in the government.[101] Subject to this, it was specifically provided that the defeat of the government on any measure in the Assembly should not oblige the government to resign.[102]

The President was of course a constituent part of the legislature,[103] and his assent was necessary before a bill could become law. He had power, exercisable on the advice of the Prime Minister, to dissolve or prorogue the Assembly. He might refuse to assent to a bill (other than a money bill) and return it to the Assembly for reconsideration, with recommendations for amendments, but if the bill was again passed by the Assembly, then he must assent to it.[104] There was thus no power of veto. What is not clear, however, is whether the power of the President to withhold his assent and return a bill to the Assembly for its reconsideration was exercisable in his discretion or on the advice of the government. The language of the provision would appear to suggest that the power was discretionary, and this accorded with the recommendation of the Constitutional Commission that he should have an 'absolute discretion to return any bill to the National Assembly without signing it and, instead, to recommend amendments to it'.[105] The Commission had also proposed that 'where the President feels that a bill sent to him for his assent borders on the unconstitutional, he shall withhold his assent and within seven days of so doing refer the bill to the Supreme Court. The Supreme Court within thirty days of receiving such a bill shall consider the matter and give its decision. If the Supreme Court finds that the act is constitutional, the President may give his assent. If on the other hand it finds that the act is unconstitutional, the President shall withhold his assent and the bill shall not be brought up in the National Assembly any more'.[106] This proposal was not, however, implemented in the Constitution as finally enacted.

It is clear that the President under the 1969 Ghana Constitution was much more than a constitutional or titular Head of State. But the extent to which his independent powers would assure constitutionalism depended upon his independence from the government, a point for which the Constitutional Commission showed full appreciation and concern. They proposed therefore and the Constitution enacted that he should not be appointed by the government of the day, but by an electoral college, consisting of all members of the National Assembly, three chiefs each elected by the regional Houses of Chiefs and fifteen members elected by the District Councils in each Region.[107] And he was to be removed only upon clearly defined grounds by an independent tribunal upon a notice signed by at least one-third of all the members of the National Assembly, demanding that the President be investigated on any of the specified grounds.[108] A preliminary investigation into the demand was first to be conducted by a judicial tribunal of three justices of the Supreme Court appointed by the Chief Justice. The removal tribunal consisted of the Chief Justice as chairman and four of the most senior justices of the Supreme Court other than those who conducted the preliminary investigation; three persons each appointed respectively by the Prime Minister, the Leader of the Opposition and the National House of Chiefs were to act as assessors to the tribunal.[109]

That this scheme was apt to engender conflict must be accepted. Of course, much would depend on the extent to which it hampered the ability of the government to govern effectively, especially in the area of economic and social development. The Constitutional Commission discounted any such fear, arguing that 'the power of the President cannot enable him to delay governmental proposals in the areas of taxation, acquisition of land and property generally, nationalisation, formulation of development plans and their execution, education, marriage, etc. — except where these are against the Constitution, and that too only where the exercise of legislative power is involved'.[110] The Commission also thought that the Council of State would provide a way of settling conflicts between the President and the Prime Minister without resort to legal process.[111] It might be said that the time was probably opportune in Ghana to assure the system the opportunity of a fair trial. With the ousting of Dr Nkrumah went the myth and charisma associated with the personality of the founder of the nation. No present-day leader in Ghana can assert a 'founder right' which might make unacceptable to him any form of subordination to any other person in the nation. The new Ghanaian system might well offer attraction to other Commonwealth African countries after their present Presidents, who are the founders of the nation, have departed from the scene. The system had been in operation in Ghana for more than two years (from August 22, 1969, to January 13, 1972, when the regime was overthrown by a military coup) without exciting any conflict between the President and the Prime Minister, though this might be nothing more than the result of a restraint imposed by the recent experience of tyranny and oppression which was still fresh in everyone's mind, and a natural desire on the part of the present leaders, who constituted the central core of the opposition force against Nkrumah, not to disappoint the expectations of their countrymen and of the rest of the world. Whether their performance would have been the same under different circumstances is anybody's guess. Politics in Africa has not acquired such a refined, mature and tolerant quality, and an ambitious Prime Minister, lacking the sobering experience of Dr Kofi Busia, might resent such a heavy limitation upon his powers and might therefore want to break away from it.

It is relevant to mention in this connection that at the Basutoland (now Lesotho) Independence Conference in 1966, the opposition parties had demanded that the King should not be a mere constitutional Head of State, but should be vested with residuary discretionary powers in regard to the public service, foreign affairs, defence and internal security. The British Government rejected this on the ground, *inter alia*, that it was 'fundamentally undemocratic and would lead to a division of responsibility and inevitable conflict in Basutoland'.[112]

Recently in Zambia the One-Party State Commission considered the matter. The Commission rejected the continuation of the *status quo* as well as the suggestion for the re-introduction of the ceremonial Head of State, the former on the ground that it concentrated 'too much work and power in the hands of the Chief Executive', and the latter because it was a 'luxury' in a developing country and might 'contain areas of conflict between the President and the Prime Minister'; the Commission came down in favour of 'an Executive President with specified powers supported by a Prime Minister who would be the Head of Government'.[113] The division of functions between the President and the Prime Minister was to follow upon the lines of the separation between policy and administration, with the President in control of the former. The specific functions to be assigned to the President were enumerated as follows: headship of the state and presidency of the party; supreme responsibility for national defence and security; the summoning, prorogation and dissolution of parliament in consultation with the Prime Minister; assenting to bills and promulgation of laws passed by the national assembly; appointment of the Prime Minister subject to the approval of the national assembly; appointment of the Secretary-General of the Party from among members of the central committee subject to the approval of the national council; appointment of such public officers as may be specified in the constitution or other law; the recognition of chiefs and the withdrawal of such recognition; conferment of national honours and awards; reception of foreign envoys; the prerogative of mercy; convening and presiding at extraordinary cabinet meetings. The Commission's proposal was rejected by the government in favour of a President with 'full executive powers', on the ground that the peculiar situation of the country, surrounded as it is by hostile white minority governments, required 'a unified command under an Executive President'.[114] The proposal about the creation of the office of Prime Minister was accepted, except that he is to be only assistant to, and under the direction of, the President.

REFERENCES

1. See below.

2. Gower, *Independent Africa: The Challenge of the Legal Profession* (1967).

3. Kenneth Robinson, 'Autochthony and the Transfer of Power'.

4. Wheare, *The Constitutional Structure of the Commonwealth* (1960), p. 89.

5. On this see Wheare, *op. cit.* Robinson, 'Constitutional Autochthony and the Transfer of Power', *op. cit.*; Roberts-Wray, *Commonwealth and Colonial Law* (1966), p. 289.

6. Parl. Deb., Official Report (1959), Vol. 12, p. 52.

7. Geoffrey Bing, *Reap the Whirlwind* (1968), p. 451.

8. See *Zambia, Independence and Beyond: The speeches of Kenneth Kaunda*, ed. Colin Legum (1966), p. 86.

9. Report of the Bechuanaland Independence Conference, 1966, Cmnd. 2929, p. 4.

10. See Mr Costello, Prime Minister of Ireland, speech to the Canadian Bar Association, Sept. 1, 1948, in Mansergh, *Documents and Speeches on British Commonwealth Affairs, 1931–52* (1953), pp. 798–801.

11. House of Reps. Debates, Vol. III, Part III, Oct. 1964, cols. 3881–3.

12. Reproduced in Africa Report Vol. 7, No. 7, July 1962, p. 7.

13. *Zambia, Independence and Beyond: The Speeches of Kenneth Kaunda*, ed. Colin Legum (1966), p. 87.

14. Ghai and McAuslan, *Public Law and Political Change in Kenya* (1970) pp. 217–18. For a similar cynicism, see Cole and Denison, *Tanganyika: The Development of Its Laws and Constitution* (1964), p. 25.

15. Henry C. Lockwood, *The Abolition of the Presidency* (1884), pp. 191–2, quoted from E. S. Corwin, *The President: Office and Powers*, 4th ed. (1957), pp. 25–6.

16. Koening, *The Chief Executive*, rev. ed. (1968), p. 17.

17. *op. cit.*, p. 18.

18. See Swaziland (Protected State) Agreement, 1967; Swaziland Constitutional Proposals 1966, Cmnd. 3119; and the Swaziland Constitution Order 1967; S.1 1967, No. 241.

19. Report of the Basutoland Independence Conference, 1966, Cmnd. 3038; the Lesotho Independence Order S.1 1966, No. 1172.

20. House of Reps. Debates, *op. cit.*

21. Art. 4, Nigeria Protectorate Order-in-Council, 1899, repeated in subsequent Orders-in-Council up to 1945. See Nwabueze, *Constitutional Law of the Nigerian Republic* (1964), pp. 43–51.

22. Geoffrey Bing, *Reap the Whirlwind* (1968), p. 278.

23. Assembly Debates, Official Reports (1966), p. 553.

24. S.36(1) Constitution of Uganda, 1962, as amended in 1963.

25. *Africa Report*, 1961.

26. 'The Westminster Model in Nigeria', *Parl. Affairs* (1968), p. 24.

27. C. Gertzel, 'Report from Kampala', *Africa Report*, Oct. 1964.

28. *The Kabaka's Government* v. *Attorney-General of Uganda*, Privy Council Appeal No. 56 of 1964. For a fuller account see, Morris and Read, *Uganda: The Development of Its Laws and Constitution* (1966), pp. 82–3.

29. See Reading in Bolewa, Govt. Select Documents on the Government and Politics of Botswana, Lesotho and Swaziland, Vol. 2, ed. J. A. Macartney (1971), pp. 195–6.

30. *ibid.*

31. *Molapo* v. *Seeiso* (1966) H.C.T.L.R. 150; discussed below, p. 281.

32. Transcript of press conference given by the Prime Minister on 31 January, 1970; see Macartney, *op. cit.*, pp. 133–42.

33. The Lesotho Order, Feb. 10, 1970, S.2 and 4.

34. *ibid.*, S.10.

35. See below, p. 79.

36. 'Parliamentary and Presidential System in the Commonwealth'.

37. S.62(2), 85, 94, 96, 135, and Schedule 3, Constitution, 1968.

38. Swaziland Constitutional Proposals 1966, Cmnd. 3110, para. 13.

39. S.91, Constitution of the Kingdom of Swaziland, 1967, S.1. No. 241.

40. Government White Paper on Independence Constitutional Proposals, 1968, p. 5.

41. *ibid.*

42. See Morris and Read, *op. cit.*, p. 100.

43. S.67(2), Constitution of Uganda 1962, as amended in 1963.

44. The Prime Minister was required to act by means of a Statutory instrument under the Presidential (Engagements) Act, 1963, Cap. 253.

45. S.11.

46. S.9 and Schedule.

47. S.10.

48. Ohonbamu, *The Nigerian Constitution and Its Review* (1965), pp. 20–1.

49. S.87(8) and (11), Constitution of the Federation, 1963.

50. Tansey and Kermode, *op. cit.*, p. 24.

51. See the Doctrine of Civil Necessity discussed below, Ch. X.

52. S.87(8) (*a*).

53. McAuslan, *op. cit.*

54. 'Unease in Uganda', by an East African correspondent, *Africa Today*, June 1966, Vol. XIII, No. 6, p. 5.

55. *ibid.*, p. 6.

56. S.62.

57. S.62(ii). A caretaker Prime Minister was not affected by a vote of confidence.

58. *Adegbenro* v. *Akintola* F.S.C. 187/1962.

59. [1963] A.C. 614.

60. *Ningkan* v. *Openg* (1966)2 M.L.J. 187. For a discussion of the case see Thio, *Dismissal of Chief Ministers* (1966), Malaya L. R. 283—91.

61. Similar violence in the East Pakistan Assembly in 1957 resulted in the death of the Deputy Speaker who was presiding.

62. This represents Lord Simon's view of the relevant convention under the British Constitution. Lord Chorley and others argued that the Queen should never under any circumstances refuse a Prime Minister's request for dissolution. See the letters to *The Times*, London, 24—27 April, 1950.

63. Parl. Deb., Official Report (1959), Vol. 17, pp. 637—8.

64. Govt. White Paper No. 1 of 1962.

65. *Federalist*, No. 70.

66. 1 Bl., Comm., p. 250.

67. Carl J. Friedrich, *The Impact of American Constitutionalism Abroad* (1966), p. 39.

68. R. A. Young, 'Zambia's Independence Constitution' (unpublished paper).

69. Report (1968), para. 3.

70. *ibid.*, para. 317.

71. *ibid.*, para. 340.

72. Para. 341.

73. Report, para. 353. There is really nothing novel about the idea of a President with limited executive powers. As far back as 1961 Dr Azikiwe had proposed it for Nigeria (see *Africa Report*, 1961).

74. Arts. 37 and 38(1).

75. Art. 53(1).

76. Art. 53(1) and (6).

77. Art. 4.

78. Art. 26(2). It must further be approved by the National Assembly within seven days.

79. Arts. 30 and 31.

80. Art. 151(1).

81. Art. 31(1).

82. Art. 50(1).

83. Art. 50.

84. Art. 140.

85. Arts. 143(3) and 147(3).

86. Art. 151.

87. Art. 119(1).

88. Art. 116(4).

89. Art. 135(12).

90. Art. 139(5).

91. Art. 116(5).

92. Art. 120.

93. Art. 52.

94. Art. 90, and see paras. 436—41 of the Constitutional Commission's Report.

95. Art. 60(2).

96. Art. 60(3).

97. Art. 60(4).

98. Art. 60(6).

99. Art. 61(9).

100. Art. 61(3).

101. Art. 66(3).

102. Art. 66(4).

103. Art. 69(1).

104. Art. 84(6)–(9).

105. Report, para. 359.

106. *ibid.*, para. 451.

107. Constitution 1969, art. 41(3).

108. Art. 47.

109. Art. 47(2).

110. Report, para. 342.

111. Para. 341.

112. Report of the Basutoland Independence Conference, 1966, Cmnd. 3038, para. 15.

113. Report of the National Commission on the Establishment of a One-Party Participatory Democracy in Zambia, Lusaka, Oct. 1972, para. 41.

114. Govt. White Paper on the Report of the National Commission, No. 1 of 1972, Govt. Printer, Lusaka, Nov. 1972, p. 4.

CHAPTER V

THE OFFICE OF PRESIDENT

1. *The Extent and the Reality of Presidential Power*

The most striking feature of the presidency in Africa is its tremendous powers. Its formal powers exceed those of its American prototype — not in nature, but in extent. The formal powers in both cases partake of the same nature, in the sense that the President in America and in Africa is the executive, and as such wields the executive power of the state as a personal ruler. Yet the mere vesting of executive power affords no conclusive indication of its actual extent, nor of its reality. Its extent has to be judged in relation to the entire constitutional system in which the presidency operates; that is to say, in the context of the restraints which the constitution imposes upon power. Viewed in that context, African presidentialism differs quite markedly from its American counterpart, so markedly indeed that the somewhat pejorative qualification 'African' has been applied to it. Professor Carl Friedrich has observed that 'it is part of the major perversion which accompanies the adaptation of American constitutional ideas in foreign lands that where one of the major institutions of American constitutionalism, such as the presidency, has been reproduced, federalism and judicial protection of human rights have not been';[1] he instanced in the next paragraph the separation of powers with its corollary, the independence of the legislature, which he described as 'a decisive feature of the American presidency'.[2]

The 'Africanness' of the presidency in Africa refers to the fact that it is largely free from such limiting constitutional devices, particularly those of a rigid separation of powers and federalism. It is the universal absence of such restraint mechanisms that is implied in the qualifying word 'African'. A feature of the presidency in Africa is what has been called 'democratic centralism'. From its inception in Ghana in 1960, centralism in the organisation of governmental powers, in the administration of government and in the organisation of politics has come to characterise every presidential regime in Commonwealth Africa.[3] Furthermore, one is deeply struck by the way in which almost every step in Ghana's post—independence constitutional development has been closely followed, almost in its precise sequence, in many of the other Commonwealth African countries.

Every kind of separation or division in governmental authority is rejected. Starting with the abolition – for good reason – of the separation of the Head of State from the Head of Government and the diffusion of executive power among cabinet members, the whole apparatus of power has been concentrated in the executive. The legislature is subordinated to the executive; bicameralism where it existed before is replaced by unicameralism, and federalism or regionalism by unitarism. The judiciary is subordinated to the executive as regards appointment, and sometimes even as regards dismissal too. All this is but a foundation for the emergence of that political monolith, the one-party state, which itself finally consummates the personalisation of rule – i.e. the centralisation, within the single party, of all power in the hands of the leader. In many cases the constitution still guarantees individual rights, but two countries in Commonwealth Africa, Tanzania and Malawi, have since followed the example of Ghana in rejecting a constitutional guarantee. The whole concept of 'checks and balances' is largely abandoned. 'Our Constitution', Julius Nyerere explained in an article on the 1962 constitutional proposals of Tanganyika, 'differs from the American system in that it avoids any blurring of the lines of responsibility, and enables the executive to function without being checked at every turn. For we recognise that the system of "checks and balances" is an admirable way of applying the brakes to social change. Our need is not for brakes – our lack of trained manpower and capital resources, and even our climate, act too effectively already. We need accelerators powerful enough to overcome the inertia bred of poverty, and the resistances which are inherent in all societies'.[4] Thus, for example, the power of the President to appoint ministers, judges and other public servants and to enter into treaties with foreign countries is not limited, as in America, by the necessity of obtaining the approval of the legislature. The departure from the system inherited at independence is even more marked. The President mostly replaces the various service commissions as the authority for the appointment, dismissal and disciplinary control of members of the civil and police services.[5]

But the constitution is only one of the sources of presidential power, though no doubt a supremely important one. The reality of power depends on other factors besides its formal structure as defined in the constitution. Two such factors of overwhelming importance are the character of the individual President and the circumstances of the country concerned, including social and political forces, conditions and events.[6] It may be said that the circumstances of Africa favour an authoritarian presidency. To begin with, there is the relative impotence of extra-constitutional sanctions against the abuse of power. The social values of the advanced democracies enshrine a national ethic which defines the limits of permissible action by the wielders of power. This national ethic is sanctified in deeply entrenched conventions operating as part of the rules of the game of politics. Thus, although an action may be well within the powers of the President under the constitution, still he cannot do it if it violates the moral sense of the nation, for he would risk calling down upon himself the wrath of public censure. The force of public opinion is sufficiently developed to act as a watchdog of the nation's ethic, and no action that seriously violates this ethic can hope to escape public condemnation. More than any constitutional restraints, perhaps, it is the ethic of the nation, its sense of right and wrong, and the capacity of the people to defend it, which provides the ultimate bulwark against tyranny.

Julius Nyerere of Tanzania has underscored the point: 'When the nation does not have the ethic which will enable the government to say: "We cannot do this, that is un-Tanganyikan" – or the people to say: "That we cannot tolerate, that is un-Tanganyikan" – if the people do not have that kind of ethic, it does not matter what kind of constitution you frame. They can always be victims of tyranny.'[7] Africa is yet to develop a strong moral sense in public affairs. Standards of public morality have not become deeply rooted, nor are they effectively articulated and enforced, partly because the instruments of public opinion are controlled by the very people to be checked. Because of this, an African President can get away with a lot of things which an American President dare not venture.

The traditional African attitude towards power is not of much assistance either. Tradition has inculcated in the people a certain amount of deference towards authority. The chief's authority is sanctioned in religion, and it is a sacrilege to flout it, except in cases of blatant and systematic oppression when the whole community might rise in revolt to destool, banish or even kill a tyrannical chief. Thus, while customary sanctions against extreme cases of abuse of power exist, there is also considerable toleration of arbitrariness by the chief. This attitude towards authority tends to be transferred to the modern political leader. The vast majority of the population, which of course is still illiterate and custom-bound, is not disposed to question the leader's authority, and indeed disapproves of those who are inclined to do so.

In a sense, therefore, the presidency in Africa is regarded by many in the light of the attitudes inculcated in them towards chiefly authority, and its power as the projection of chiefly authority into the national sphere. The President, in effect, is the *chief* of the new nation, and as such entitled to the authority and respect due by tradition to a chief.

This has not rested entirely on attitudes carried over from tradition. In places there has indeed been a conscious attempt to implant the attitude in the minds of the people, by, for example, publicly investing the President with the attributes of a chief. Thus, when he attended public rallies in Ghana, Nkrumah used to assume the style of a chief. He sat upon a 'chiefly throne under a resplendent umbrella, symbol of traditional rule', and he took 'chiefly titles meaningful to all major tribal units in Ghana: *Osagyefo, Katamanto, Kasapieko, Nufeno*, etc'.[8] His opening of parliament was also done in chiefly style. His approach was 'heralded by the beating of *fantomforom* (traditional drums). He was received by eight linguists representing the various Regions and each carrying a distinctive stick. A libation was poured and the President then entered the chamber to the sound of *mmenson* (the seven traditional horns)'.[9] Though this is explicable in part by Nkrumah's irredentist aspiration for the revival of the African cultural heritage, the political significance is obvious. It was intended to harness to the presidency the authority of tradition and the legitimacy which it confers. By aligning the presidency with the institution of chieftaincy in the public imagination, it is hoped to inspire public acceptance of the office and respect for its authority.

Similarly relevant to the reality of presidential power in Africa is the African's conception of authority. Authority in African traditional society is conceived as being personal, permanent, mystical and pervasive.[10] The chief is a personal ruler, and his office is held for life, which pervades all the other relations in the community, for he is both legislator, executive, judge, priest, medium, father, etc. These characteristics are reflected in the modern African presidency. The African President, as we have seen, is both the executive and the chief legislator. The office has tended to be an inheritance, which must be rendered secure by the liquidation of open and organised opposition. William Tubman of Liberia died in office after twenty-eight years as President. Kamuzu Banda has had himself installed as life President of Malawi, as had Bokassa of the Central African Republic before his overthrow by the military in 1972. Other African Presidents, like Kwame Nkrumah of Ghana and Kenneth Kaunda of Zambia, have rejected offers of a life presidency, just as Banda did for some time before finally succumbing to the pressure and the temptation. But all have said they would stay in office for as long as the people wanted them, which, given the indefinite eligibility for re-election, means in effect for life, the only difference being that every four years or so they will have to submit themselves to the ritual of an election. It was the ritualistic nature of the exercise perhaps that finally induced Banda, with his characteristic aversion to hypocrisy, to accept the life presidency. A life President, or one who has held office for twenty years, is a different kind of functionary from one who is limited to a maximum of two terms of four years each. His authority is bound to be greater, for after twenty years in office he is apt to become an institution himself, attracting loyalties of a personal nature. His authority tends to be all-pervading. The mysticism of religion in which the authority of the chief is sanctified is also sought to be transferred to the presidency. Even the attribute of divinity, which also characterises certain of the traditional chieftaincies, had been claimed for Nkrumah, a claim in which he apparently acquiesced.

The presidency in Africa is indeed clothed with a considerable amount of mystique which bestows upon it an authority transcending that of an ordinary Head of State. This mystical quality derives from the achievement of the present generation of African Presidents as the leaders of the nationalist movements which overthrew colonialism and established the new state. The leader incarnates the spirit of that struggle and the aspirations of those engaged in it. The realisation of those aspirations elevates him to the status of a deliverer, a messiah. The struggle against colonialism was in large measure a struggle to redeem the personality of the African from the indignities and degradations inflicted upon it by colonialism. The perpetuation of the inferiority of the African was central to the philosophy and technique of colonialism, and anyone who was able to challenge the myth of white superiority was considered a man of extraordinary qualities, and success in overthrowing it was a feat of miraculous proportions. All the awe and mystique associated with the white man is now transferred to the leader. The reality is brought home to the people by the spectacle of the leader occupying the former colonial governor's official residence, that symbol of the glory and glamour of empire. There he now sits, perhaps in the very chair used by the embodiment of white power, directing the affairs of the state, and giving instructions to all functionaries of the state, both white and black. The President thus incarnates power, indeed he is power himself, and Africans admire and respect a man of power. And so it is that the African President is revered. 'We are following Nkrumah', a Ghanaian minister once remarked, 'because his achievements are unexcelled in the country. He has done what the Ashantis were unable to do. He has been able to conquer the colonial power which the Ashantis failed to conquer by force of arms, even when the imperialists had not established themselves. . . . But now Nkrumah has been able to defeat the imperialists by word of mouth.'[11]

An attribute of mystique is charisma. No leader around whom such a fantastic myth has been built up can fail to arouse a charismatic appeal among the people. This, by and large, is the basis of the so-called charismatic authority of the present African leaders. It is due largely to their role in the nationalist movement, to the fervour and spontaneous popular enthusiasm which the movement generated. When the movement lost its fervour after having achieved its goal, the charisma remained, but was now sustained largely by manipulation and by the prestige of office. Unlike George Washington, who retired from the presidency after two terms against the exhortations of his countrymen and continued to be idolised in retirement, the office is indispensable to the charisma of African leaders, and the possibility of its loss arouses the fear of oblivion. Undeniably some, like Julius Nyerere of Tanzania, do possess a genuine charismatic appeal based partly on the myth of their achievement in the nationalist movement, and partly on personal charm and selfless, dedicated statesmanship. Yet, whatever its basis, the charisma of these leaders inspires tremendous personal loyalty among the population, which not only enhances their authority and prestige, but also enables the new state to win legitimacy. The charisma and mystique engender the belief that the leader is a kind of demi-god specially commissioned by Providence to deliver the people first from colonialism and now from the evils of poverty, ignorance and disease; a belief that Providence has endowed him with extraordinary power to divine what is good for the community, so that when he has so divined what should be done, there arises an implied obligation on the part of all to obey. Obedience is enjoined because the leader has ordered it.

An authority based on this kind of charisma needs constant nurture, since the myth on which it is based is liable to evaporate if exposed to public contact. The cult of personality is resorted to for the necessary nurture. A cult of infallibility and incorruptibility is accordingly built up around the leader. His name and his activities are kept tirelessly in the public view. His image is glorified in songs praising his achievments, in posters showing his photograph, in institutions and streets named after him, and in statues of him erected in the most conspicuous centres of the city. His head is engraved on postage stamps, coins and currency notes. The burden of mistakes or harsh decisions is made to fall upon lieutenants in order to create the feeling among the disaffected that the leader could not personally have permitted their plights to go unredressed.

These factors — tradition, mystique and charisma — are sources of power which are not easily accessible to a President in America and Europe. It has been said of the American presidency that its essential dimension today is how to 'generate sufficient authority for presidential action to match the needs of the nation'.[12] No modern American President, with the possible exception of Franklin D. Roosevelt, has been able to harness to the presidency a deep, widely-felt loyalty based upon charisma. This means that the authority of the American presidency in modern times is in no way comparable to that of its counterpart in Africa. Only George Washington, the first American President, seems to have inspired a loyalty comparable to that of the African President. But his too was a loyalty and authority based partly on the father-of-the-nation myth. Through his achievement in leading his countrymen to victory in the War of Independence against England, Washington became a legend. It is true that the wide loyalty which he attracted to himself owed also to his noble character, his humanity, uprightness and wisdom,[13] yet it seems that his elevation into a myth and a cult was more the result of his achievement as founder of the American nation.

The circumstances of underdevelopment is yet another source of presidential power in Africa. It is usual for Americans to classify their Presidents as either 'strong' or 'weak'. The strong President, writes Hirschfield, is one 'who regards government as the appropriate instrument for achieving progressive change in society and the presidency as the vital generating force in government. . . . His principal concern is not the administration of an inherited office, but the use of that office to bring about change in . . . society'.[14] Every African President is a strong President in this sense, for the condition of underdevelopment now prevailing on the continent makes imperative an interventionist policy based on socialism. Just as the economic depression of the early 1930s called forth Franklin Roosevelt's New Deal measure, which was perhaps the highest point presidential power has attained in peace-time in America, so also does the poverty of African societies aggregate power to the presidency. Given this poverty, and the illiteracy which contributed to it, the challenge and burden of development must rest first and foremost upon the state, since it alone has anything like the type of resources needed for development programmes in industry, commerce and agriculture. The nationalist struggle is an on-going struggle. Its political objective having been won, the next phase is in the economic field. The economic dependence of the new state upon the old colonial business interests must be brought to an end by nationalisation or by the state taking over majority shareholdings. Every African nationalist leader is therefore willy-nilly a socialist. Although all African Presidents rank as strong Presidents in this sense, some are stronger than others. While some are content with establishing new industries, commercial enterprises, agricultural projects and other nation-building schemes, leaving private enterprise virtually a free hand, others, notably Tanzania, have embarked upon a thorough-going nationalisation of the principal means of production and distribution.[15]

Nation-building is an objective to which all are committed. But it is a task that calls for total mobilisation of the nation if any impact is to be made upon it. An African President is therefore necessarily cast in the

role of popular leader. This again makes him a 'strong' President in
another sense of the American conception of the term. In this second
sense, American presidents have been rated as strong or weak according
to their ability to mobilise the nation. 'The greatest Presidents have all
ranked high on this scale, whatever their skills as administrators or
legislative managers. All have made themselves national symbols; in so
doing they have given substance and purpose to the nation itself'.[16]
But the popular leadership required of an African President is of a
much more personal and spiritual kind, for he has to be at once leader,
guide and teacher. The leader of a predominantly illiterate, poverty-
stricken community has not only to lead, but to guide as well. He has
to provide the light so that people may see the road in the first place,
and then guide and direct them along that road to the ultimate
destination of prosperity and progress. He may be likened to one who
leads a blind man. The leader of a blind man has to establish an
intimate personal identification with him. So it is with the leader of a
new nation. Having got the people on the difficult road to development, it is his duty 'to propose, to explain, and to persuade',[17] to
preach to them the need for hard work, for self-reliance, and for
integrity in order to maximise national productivity. Preaching has to
be accompanied by example: as, for example, the leader working
with the farmers in the field. 'There must be, among the leadership, a
desire and a determination to serve alongside, and in complete
identification with, the masses.'[18] Hence the title *Mwalimu* (Teacher)
given to President Nyerere. No other African President has more
devotedly discharged this teaching role. Reading his speeches and
writings one is deeply impressed by the fervour and dedication with
which he has gone about trying to inform and to educate his
countrymen on the needs and requirements of nation-building.

   Not the least of an African President's leadership role is that of a
showman. Whatever progress has been achieved needs to be advertised
to the people in order to keep up national morale and enthusiasm. The
President has therefore to perform the formal opening of completed
public projects, to launch shows that advertise the national effort, like
agricultural and commercial shows and trade fairs. All this is part of the
total mobilisation of the nation. It gives to presidential power in Africa
a reality that is usually lacking in advanced countries. The inadequacy
of the American presidency in providing this kind of leadership is often
a source of disillusionment among Americans. But the inadequacy
results, not from the personality of American Presidents, but from the
nature of American society as compared with the African.

   The African President's role of popular leadership is of course
greatly facilitated by the virtual state monopoly of the media of mass
information, perhaps the most crucial source of power in modern

government. The radio and television are always state-owned, as are the most influential newspapers, and a large part of the news items in all three media is taken up by news about the President, his speeches and other activities. The President is always in the news, perhaps inevitably so, since, as has been explained, the functions of government in Africa are all-pervading. Either he is laying the foundation stone of, or opening, a new factory, a new school or a new hospital, or he is touring different parts of the country, and preaching the need for unity, hard work or self-reliance. His being constantly in the news immensely enhances his legitimacy and authority. But the monopoly of the information media is significant also in determining popular consent in government. Whoever has it is put in a position where he can mobilise public opinion and the nation in support of himself and his policies and actions. Such a person can get away even with murder, for murder can be made to wear the appearance of a virtue or be represented as serving the best interests of the nation.

There is yet another respect in which the poverty of African societies is a source of power for the President. In a developing country where there is mass unemployment, where the state is the principal employer of labour and almost the sole provider of social amenities, and where a personal ambition for power and wealth and influence rather than principle determines political affiliations and alliances, power to dispense patronage is a very potent weapon in the hands of the President, enabling him to gain and maintain the loyalty of the people at various levels of society. Water installed in one area, industry sited in another, a school or hospital built in yet another may capture for the President the support and loyalty of the inhabitants of those areas. Scholarships, roads, government contracts, jobs, etc. – all these are crucial sources of power in Africa. Moreover, loyalty of the type secured by patronage can often border on subservience. It produces an attitude of dependence, a willingness to accept without question the wishes and dictates of the person dispensing the patronage. Patronage has therefore been one of the crucial means by which African leaders have secured the subordination of the legislature, the bureaucracy, the police and even the army.

Then there is the fact of the newness of the state, the heterogeneity of its society and the tensions of modernisation. The new state requires a legitimising force. The problem of legitimacy is peculiar to a new state, and is complicated by three factors. An artificial creation of colonialism, the state in Africa has no roots in the traditions or thoughts of the people. Their attitude towards it was that it was an instrument of the white man for the subjugation and exploitation of Africans. To the subject people, therefore, the state was not 'ours' but 'theirs', the white man's state. Such an attitude must be eradicated if the state is to be able to fulfil its purpose. And this requires the fostering among the people of a feeling of identity with the state. The second complicating factor is that the concept of state is a mere abstraction totally incomprehensible to the simple mind of a peasant. It needs therefore some visible, physical object to symbolise it in the eyes of the people, and no other object can be more readily comprehensible for this purpose than the personality of the President. The President thus assumes a symbolic role as the embodiment of the state. There is here a close parallel with the monarchical device of making the king the personification of the state, though the conception and the implications are different. Third is the fact that the state in Africa has an artificial and heterogeneous social composition, embracing a large variety of peoples of differing origin, culture, language and character. This heterogeneous collection needs to be integrated into a unity, infused with a sense of common destiny and common national aspirations. It is the role of the President as leader to serve as the focal point of unity around which this heterogeneous mass can be knit together.

This integrating role of an African President involves the exercise of power — power to prevent the inevitable cleavages of tribalism from destroying the state. Tribal conflicts create a condition of instability, which is made worse by the tensions of rapid change from a traditional to a modern economy. In the view of the African leaders the state of affairs is comparable to a state of emergency, and a state of emergency, even in the most advanced democracies, demands actions of an authoritarian type to preserve the peace and integrity of the state. The experience of the United States illustrates the great potency of a situation of emergency as a source of presidential power, for it is during such periods that the presidency has attained its zenith of power, as is 'illustrated by Lincoln's "dictatorial" regime during the Civil War, by Wilson's highly-centralised World War administration, and by Franklin Roosevelt's executive-dominated government during the emergencies of domestic depression and global conflict'.[19]

As we shall see in later chapters,[20] the preservation of the state against the insecurity inherent in tribal cleavage and the tensions of rapid social change is perhaps the greatest source of presidential power in Africa. Tribalism may also operate in other ways to put greater power in the hands of the President. For in the clash of interests between various tribes and their leaders, an atribal President may become a kind of counterpoise holding the balance of power in the state. President Kenneth Kaunda of Zambia was put in that role in 1968. The unbridled tribal bigotry which attended the elections within the ruling United National Independence Party (UNIP) in 1967 had virtually destroyed the credibility of the party's machinery in the eyes of the losing tribal faction in that contest, with the result that, when the time came for the parliamentary elections in 1968, that faction refused to accept the use of the party machinery for the nomination of candidates. In the event, President Kaunda, who is not identified with any particular tribe, became 'the fulcrum on which the contending political forces ... are balanced',[21] and was entrusted with sole power to nominate all party candidates.

Finally comes the personality of the individual Presidents. For, as Hirschfield has pointed out, 'while circumstances, and particularly crisis conditions, can make vast authority available to the President', yet they cannot by themselves 'guarantee an appropriate presidential response.... Only he can make the decision to use it'.[22] It is difficult to assess the part played by personality in the development of presidential power in Commonwealth Africa, since all the Presidents have responded in much the same way to basically similar situations. We have earlier remarked on the striking manner in which political responses in the presidential regimes have followed the pattern set by the first of Commonwealth Africa's Presidents, Kwame Nkrumah of Ghana. Most of the Presidents in Commonwealth Africa may fairly be described as moderate, not-too-assertive personalities – Jomo Kenyatta of Kenya, Kenneth Kaunda of Zambia, Julius Nyerere of Tanzania, Siaka Stevens of Sierra Leone, Seretse Khama of Botswana. Yet their methods can fairly be described as authoritarian and interventionist. Can it be, then, that circumstances alone have forced that posture upon them? As regards the policy of socialism, an affirmative answer must be returned to the question. Development through state action and state ownership is, as has been explained, an inevitable response to the poverty of African societies and to the economic domination of them by foreign business interests, and no President, however moderate, could remain passive and leave development entirely to individual enterprise. Julius Nyerere seems to be perhaps the most moderate of all, yet it is he who, under the compulsion of the circumstances of his country, has turned out the most thorough-going and radical socialist.

However, the authoritarian style of the African Presidents cannot be explained solely in terms of the pressure of circumstances. Personal ambition for power, and the wealth and prestige that go with it, are also decisively important. Of course a personal love of power has always been a prime motive in politics everywhere, but in underdeveloped countries power carries very high stakes indeed, and the stakes have an especial significance because of the general poverty of the society. In a society where money, jobs and social amenities are scarce, the ability to dispense them is eagerly sought after and, once achieved, is not easily relinquished. Again it may be argued that it is the circumstance of underdevelopment that has given the natural ambition for power its inordinate proportions in Africa, and that it is really nothing in-born in the African leaders; further, that the fact of having led the nationalist movement seemed to have predisposed the leaders to think that they have a right to rule and to defend that right against all those seeking to dislodge them. This is an argument of convenience. It would be a poor reflection on the moral character of the African to say that the general poverty of the society and the opportunity to dispense patronage would in every case dispose him to authoritarian methods to keep himself in power. The authoritarianism of the African Presidents must in part be attributed to their personalities. In the case of Nkrumah and Banda, at least, there can be no doubt that their personalities have a lot to do with their authoritarian style of rule. Both — and Banda perhaps more than Nkrumah — are inclined by nature to be domineering, egotistical and dictatorial; both have a predilection for personal rule and for the arbitrariness that is inseparable from it.

(i) *The Philosopher-President*

An African President has also to try to provide intellectual leadership for the new state. It is true that for the masses ideology has little relevance, their conception of government being in terms of the material benefits it can bring to them, peace and order, employment, medical services, water, etc. Yet the African President cannot neglect ideology completely. For a new nation has a great need for it. It needs a national ideology to act as an inspiration and guide for action. 'Unless we are so armed and inspired', Nkrumah once told his followers, 'we shall find ourselves rudderless. From the lowest members to the highest we must arm ourselves ideologically'.[23] Popular leadership in nation-building needs to be buttressed with an ideology if it is to infuse sufficient sense of purpose and direction in the people, especially the élite. And a sense of purpose and direction has virtue because of its unifying influence upon the actions of the members of the state. Ideology defines specific goals for society, prescribes the institutional forms and procedures for pursuing them, and by so doing seeks to direct and concert the efforts and actions of the people towards the achievement of those goals. In this way it seeks to unite the society into one people bound together by common attitudes, common institutions and procedures, and above all an acceptance of common social objectives and destiny. To quote Nkrumah again, 'the dominant ideology is that which in the light of circumstances decides what forms institutions shall take, and in what channels the common effort is to be directed'.[24] More succinctly but tellingly, Wole Soyinka has written: 'I think, after all, there is only one common definition for a people and a nation — a unit of humanity bound together by a common ideology'.[25] Explaining the need for an ideology, Julius Nyerere has said that, despite the many socialist measures launched by his government, 'it gradually became clear that the absence of a generally accepted and easily understood statement of philosophy and policy was allowing some government and party actions which were not consistent with the building of socialism, and which even encouraged the growth of non-socialist values and attitudes'.[26] It was to meet this need that the Arusha Declaration was issued in February 1967. As a statement of the country's national ideology, it 'provided the necessary sign-post of the direction in which the nation must travel to achieve its goals'.[27]

As leader and father of the nation, an African President feels it his peculiar duty to provide the new nation with the much-needed ideology. Hence his role of philosopher and theoretician. And there are other reasons why he has to assume this role. First, he is the leader of a revolution, and history shows leaders of great revolutions in politics as theorists — Lenin, Mao, Fidel Castro. It is natural that the African leader should see himself in the image of such great political leader-theorists. By so doing he is merely following in the footstep of history, and it is unfair to label him an imitator, lacking in originality.[28] The nationalist revolution in Africa and Asia may not have the world stature and impact of the communist revolution successfully launched in Russia by Lenin and in China by Mao, yet it comes close enough to the communist revolution as an epochal event in world history. It has added to international politics a third force. International politics, hitherto dominated by the struggle for ascendancy between East and West, has today to reckon with this third force, the non-aligned countries of Africa and Asia who constitute the third world. Like the authors of the first world revolution, the leaders of the third world have to expound, defend and consolidate their creation both within their national borders and at the international level. Among the nationalist leaders in Africa, Kwame Nkrumah's position approximated more closely to that of Lenin in the communist revolution. He it was who made black African independence a reality by the liberation of Ghana in 1957, and thereby created a haven for the intellectual protagonists of African independence as well as for the freedom fighters. He gave them both inspirational and material support. His unique position as the leader of the first black independent African country thrust upon him a special responsibility to expound and champion the nationalist revolution in Africa. His theorising may have lacked consistency and sufficient social relevance,[29] yet it cannot be denied that it gave inspiration and stimulated the pride and fervour of Africans in Ghana and elsewhere.

The objective of the nationalist movement did not end with the achievement of political independence. Africa's cultural past, so badly distorted by colonialism, must be rediscovered and revived. The nationalist movement is viewed as a kind of renaissance, 'a rebirth of ideas and actions' in Africa's cultural heritage. Yet this revival cannot be indiscriminate; it must take account of the cross-current of ideas and cultures in which modern Africa is caught. Thus, while preaching the revival of Africa's cultural past, the nationalist revolution has also got to try to reconcile that with the present – with the perhaps more paramount need for modernity. That too is a function of ideology. Part of the objective of this cultural revival is the restoration of the personality of the African which has been degraded by colonialism. In African society every individual had worth, and counted equally with any other individual. 'The only political ideology', Kofi Baako has said, 'which allows the maintenance of our own traditional beliefs and attitudes appears to be the socialist idea that all men are equal.'[30] Then there is the need to rationalise modern government in terms that would make it intelligible to the African masses. Modern government is impersonal, concerned as it is with roles and a variety of impersonal processes, whereas African traditional government has man as its central object, his needs, his relations with his family, friends and society generally. The ideas underlying modern government are foreign, creating therefore a necessity to try to relate and adapt them to African conditions in order to give them relevance and legitimacy. Thus it has been considered necessary to rationalise the form of government of the modern state in terms of African political organisation and procedures in order to make it understood by the people. The presidency is portrayed in the light of the chief in the traditional system, and the one-party state in the light of the consensus procedure of decision-taking in the traditional system. There is also the threat posed to the nationalist revolution by the machinations of imperialism and neo-colonialism, particularly economic imperialism which seeks to maintain its economic stranglehold on the African continent. These are the factors that have thrust the role of philosopher upon African Presidents. They have called forth the 'Humanism' of Kenneth Kaunda, the 'Neo-colonialism' and 'Consciencism' of Kwame Nkrumah, the 'Ujamaaism' of Julius Nyerere, and the 'African Socialism' of Jomo Kenyatta. Kamuzu Banda has stood outside this current. 'All these grey-haired professors or bald-headed professors at the University', he once exclaimed, 'making all this mysterious lingo, Socrates, Demosthenes, Solon, Edmund Burke and Rousseau, and all that. Talk about democracy, socialism, African socialism. What is African socialism? It makes me sick'.[31]

Banda's anti-intellectualism reflects the increasingly materialist role of political leadership in the advanced countries today. Political leaders have become too absorbed in the power struggle and in the practical job of government, which often induce a resort to a kind of hand-to-mouth attitude, characterised by a fondness for expediencies. They have thus tended to lose sight of the ideological function of political leadership. The necessity for a carefully formulated policy is of course acknowledged, but there is progressively less concern for the theoretical foundations of the policy. Intellectualism in politics has thus been submerged. The west in modern times has produced no political leaders who are also great political theorists of the calibre of Lenin and Mao.[32] The explanation for this seems to lie partly in the fact that the need for ideology in the politics and government of the western countries is perhaps somewhat less compelling than in the emergent states.

2. *Social Pre-eminence of the President*

Next to its tremendous power the other distinctive characteristic of the presidency in Africa is its social pre-eminence. The first modern presidency, the American, was modelled upon monarchy, and therefore inherited the pre-eminence and dignity of monarchy. 'I deny,' said a U.S. attorney-general, 'that there is a particle less dignity belonging to the office of President than to the office of King of Great Britain or of any other potentate on the face of the earth. He represents the majesty of the law and of the people as fully and as essentially, and with the same dignity, as does any absolute monarch or the head of any independent government in the world'.[33]

Of course monarchy and the presidency rest upon different political and legal conceptions, and have inspired different social attitudes. The former confers the title of sovereignty (the monarch is the sovereign), implying *dominium*. The monarch *owns* the government, and allegiance is owed to him personally, since he personifies the state in a real, and not merely in a symbolic, sense. He is indeed the state, a fact which is acknowledged in the national anthem ('God save the King') and in various other ways. Because of the personal identification with the state which the title of sovereignty implies, the sovereign attracts greater social pre-eminence. He is set apart from the rest of the community; as between him and them the relationship is one of sovereign lord and liege, a relationship that demands from the subject not only allegiance and obeisance but also a reverence that borders on obsequiousness. The monarch is 'fawned on in public and carped at in private'. He is 'majesty', which again expresses his claim to be the state. His style of living is equally majestic, since grace, pomp and splendour are indispensable to the dignity of a personal sovereign. He moves about in state, adorned with the full insignia of state and attended by uniformed guards. His person is inviolable. He can no more be made personally amenable to the process of the law than the state itself can. He is the fountain of justice. The courts are his courts, and administer justice in his name. It follows that it would be a manifest absurdity if he were to be triable by his own courts. What this means in fact is that he is above the law; 'the King can do no wrong' is a well-recognised maxim of law, which expresses the fact that his misdeeds are not cognisable by the courts. The only redress against an erring King is to force him to abdicate or to have him impeached and dethroned, but not to put him on trial in his own courts.

By comparison the American President has nothing of this majesty and pomp, and commands no such personal allegiance and obsequiousness. In the balanced words of Lord Bryce:

> The President is simply the first citizen of a free nation, depending for his dignity on no title, no official dress, no insignia of state. . . . To a European observer, weary of the slavish obsequiousness and lip-deep adulation with which the members of the reigning families are treated on the eastern side of the Atlantic, fawned on in public and carped at in private, the social relations of an American President to his people are eminently refreshing. There is a great respect for the office, and a corresponding respect for the man as the holder of the office, if he has done nothing to degrade it. There is no servility, no fictitious self-abasement on the part of the citizens, but a simple and hearty deference to one who represents the majesty of the nation. . . . He is followed about and fêted, and in every way treated as the first man in the company; but the spirit of equality which rules the country has sunk too deep into every American nature for him to be expected to be addressed with bated and whispering reverence. He has no military guard, no chamberlains or grooms-in-waiting; his everyday life is simple; . . . he is surrounded by no such pomp and enforces no such etiquette as that which belongs to the governors even of second-class English colonies, not to speak of the Viceroys of India and Ireland.[34]

Equality is thus a dominant characteristic of the social relations of an American President. It is even demanded that the President be amenable to the process of the court just like any other citizen. The Constitution, it is argued, grants him no immunity from suit, so that any concession of it would amount to placing him above the Constitution and thereby violating the cornerstone of American constitutionalism that the government is one of laws, and not of men. 'Under our system of government', said Chief Justice Bartley in granting a *mandamus* against a state Governor, 'no officer is placed above the restraining authority, which is truly said to be universal in its behests, all paying it homage, the least as feeling its care, and the greatest as not being exempt from its power'.[35] These observations, it is argued, should apply with equal, if not greater, force to the President of the United States. The argument was indeed accepted by Chief Justice Marshall when he sustained an application for a *subpoena duces tecum* against President Jefferson. Rejecting the President's contention that he could not be drawn from the discharge of his duties at the seat of government and made to attend the court sitting at Richmond, the Chief Justice drew a distinction between the President and the King of England, and held that all officers in the United States were subordinate to the law and must obey its mandate.

The social and legal relations of an African President are not characterised by anything like the same degree of equality. To begin with, there is no question of his being personally amenable to the process of the court while in office. That question is settled by the constitution itself. An incumbent President enjoys under the constitution immunity from suit or other process, both criminal and civil. However, the immunity prevails only during his incumbency. It is thus a procedural immunity only, and in no way removes his liability, which becomes enforceable again in the ordinary mode of proceeding at the end of his term of office, without any limitation as to time for the period covered by his incumbency. The President's immunity, limited though it is, came under heavy attack by members of the Kenya parliament during the debates on the presidential constitution in 1964, and the attack was only warded off by the Minister for Justice and Constitutional Affairs, Mr Tom Mboya, reminding members that they too enjoyed some immunity from legal process, no doubt more qualified than the President's but nevertheless proceeding from the same purpose, namely the protection of their office as M.P.s.[36]

It is for the office, and not for the man, that the special protection is needed. It is the majesty and dignity of the nation that is at stake. To drag an incumbent President to court and expose him to the process of examination and cross-examination cannot but degrade the office. The affront to the nation involved in this could be more easily perceived if it is imagined that a foreigner temporarily resident in the country were to take its President to court for, say, a breach of contract, and attempt to discredit him in cross-examination as a liar and a disreputable person. It should make no difference that the complainant is a national. The interest of the nation in the preservation of the integrity of its highest office should outweigh the inconvenience to the individual of the temporary postponement of his suit against the President. Where, however, the President holds office for life, there may be a real injustice, for the individual would have been deprived permanently of his suit. Even so the principle underlying the protection still demands that it should be maintained, though the situation does illustrate the undesirability of a life presidency. The immunity of the President covers only acts done in his private capacity in Zambia and Botswana, but acts done in his official capacity are also covered in Gambia and

Kenya. The appropriate defendant in cases of official wrong-doing is the attorney-general or the Republic, rather than the President personally.

There can, of course, be a compromise. Julius Nyerere of Tanzania, as always a modest leader with a strong belief in social equality, has devised an arrangement that seems nicely designed to accommodate the two conflicting objects of protecting the rights of individuals against an incumbent President as well as the dignity and integrity of the nation's highest office. Thus, under the Constitutions of 1962 and 1965, the President is amenable to civil (though understandably not criminal) action in his personal capacity.[37] However, a different procedure, designed to protect the dignity and integrity of the office, is instituted for an action against the President. This requires that at least thirty days' written notice of intention to bring an action, accompanied by a plaint which gives information about the nature of the proceedings, the cause of action, the name, description and place of residence of the plaintiff, should be served, not on the President personally, but on the permanent secretary, principal or private secretary to the President or sent by prepaid registered post to the permanent secretary at the State House.[38] Except by or under the direction of these officials, no legal process can be served or executed within the State House or, while he is resident therein, other official residences of the President, but, if a court so requests, the officials shall render all reasonable and necessary assistance to enable service or execution to be effected. The action has to be instituted in the High Court, and not in any other court. And, assuming the plaintiff to have been successful, the only form of relief that may be awarded at the conclusion of the proceedings is a declaration; no other kind of order, judgment, decree or relief can be given against the President while he is in office, though, should he fail to satisfy the court's declaration, then within 90 days of his ceasing to be President, the plaintiff may apply to have the declaration converted to a positive relief and the court shall act accordingly. Finally, no bar is imposed upon the right to apply to the court for process to require or compel the President to attend or appear personally in court or to produce any person or thing, but upon such application being made, the court is not in fact to issue process but should merely notify the President.

The immunity of the President from suit or legal process is, however, a different thing from saying that he should also be protected by law from insult or abuse beyond the protection afforded by the ordinary law of libel and sedition. Such a protection was conferred by an amendment to the Criminal Code in Ghana and Zambia in 1961 and 1965 respectively. It was made an offence to publish by writing, word of mouth or in any other manner any defamatory or insulting matter concerning the President with intent to bring him into hatred, ridicule or contempt.[39] The justification for this is questionable. The Ghanaian Minister of Justice, Mr Ofori Atta, had defended the provision on the ground that the 'Head of State of Ghana is a sacred person, irrespective of the party to which he belongs'.[40] Ideally, a Head of State should be above politics in order that his embodiment of the state and its majesty should attract maximum respect. But an apolitical Head of State is possible, if at all, only if he is a titular head. Such a head can be above partisan politics because he exercises no political function and belongs to no political party. An executive Head of State is in a different position. The exercise of executive powers necessarily invites criticism. One should not accept the office and refuse its price. That would be like eating one's cake and having it. Moreover, an executive President is not just the chief functionary of the government; he is the government itself. And to ban criticism of him is unduly to inhibit criticism of government. Where an executive President is a partisan leading a political party in a two- or multi-party system, as in Ghana or Zambia in 1961 and 1965, the protection becomes even more objectionable. Such a system necessarily implies political competition. The President should not be a partisan in politics and at the same time refuse to accept its price. Verbal attacks, sometimes of a very derogatory kind, are inseparable from political competition. Within reason it is legitimate for politicians to try to discredit each other as part of the effort to enhance one's standing and undermine that of opponents. The leader of the opposition in Kenya, Mr Ngala, put the point aptly when he said that, as a political head, the President is 'a person who throws mud at other fellow-politicians and mud can be thrown at him and he can have political fights with other leaders.'[41]

This should not, of course, be turned into a licence for vulgar insult against the Head of State, though the danger in prohibiting vulgar insult which is not an offence by the ordinary law of libel or sedition lies in the difficulty of drawing the line between it and permissible criticism. Nor does the use so far made of the prohibition in Ghana and Zambia lead one to believe that the law was aimed against vulgar abuse only. In Ghana a man who, in a conversation with a friend, said that Nkrumah's doctorate degree was an honorary one was prosecuted under the law; the prosecution was later withdrawn and the man detained instead.[42] The vituperation against President Kaunda of Zambia by the opposition M.P., Liso, was singularly vulgar, and his conviction under the provision was probably merited, but there was nothing vulgar in the other cases in respect of which prosecution had been threatened but not proceeded with; the criticisms might have been incautious and indiscreet but they were by no means vulgar.

The immunity of the President from verbal attack and criticism has also been made a rule of parliamentary procedure in some of the countries. In October 1969 during the debate in the Zambian National Assembly on an amendment to the Constitution, the Speaker repeatedly reminded Opposition M.P.s of his earlier ruling that the President should not be made the subject of debate. For, he said, 'a Head of State is a Head of State for everybody',[43] and is 'the nucleus of the pride of the nation, whether he be UNIP, Congress or otherwise'.[44] 'If', he continued, 'hon. Members wish to attack each other politically, there are many official Members here, Ministers, to attack, rather than attacking a person who is not connected with the debates of this House'.[45] The particular amendment under debate was that which sought to abolish the Barotseland Agreement. In opposing the abolition, an opposition member recalled President Kaunda's assurances to the chief and people of Barotseland on the eve of independence that the Agreement would be respected, and how the President had turned round in 1969 to denounce the Agreement at a UNIP meeting. This drew from the Speaker a warning that the member was violating his ruling not to involve the President's name in debate; upon which the member protested that the political activities of a President who is also the Secretary-General of the ruling party ought not to be above discussion in parliament. The Speaker then rose in anger and adjourned the house. The member was arraigned before the Standing Orders Committee, and found guilty of a most serious offence of a nature rendering him unfit to be a member of the house, and for which therefore a severe punishment was demanded. As, however, the offending member had only recently been discharged from hospital after an operation, the Committee felt disposed to be lenient with him, and accordingly imposed only an apology. Thus condemned, the member was ordered the following morning to stand at the bar of the house and 'register my sincere apology and say that I never intended to be disrespectful to His Excellency the President. My loyalty to His Excellency the President and Government is unquestionable'.[46] In discharging the member after this apology, the Speaker further warned that 'a time might arise in the future when I will not inconvenience the whole House by adjourning it, but I will be forced to mete out immediately some punishment to an hon. Member who does not heed the ruling of the Chair, like naming him'.[47] Was all this really warranted by what the member had said? The assurances given by the President in 1964 to the chief and people of Barotseland were very much relevant to the debate on the proposal to abrogate the Agreement, and it was legitimate, for the proper discharge of his duty to his constituents (the Barotse), that the member should criticise the President for denouncing what he had previously praised publicly and undertaken to respect.

Aside from his legal immunity from suit and from insult, equality is hardly apt to describe the social relations of an African President. Inequality is a necessary feature of an African society. It is an incident of the prevailing poverty and illiteracy. Equality expresses, by and large, the economic standing of a person in relation to another. But it is not so much economic power as the general economic condition that really determines equality in society. Britain and, even more, the United States still contain vast disparities of wealth – between the millionaire and the factory hand – yet it cannot be doubted that the social relations of the rich and poor are marked increasingly by an attitude of equality, quite unlike what used to be the case 100 or fifty years ago. This has resulted partly from political development, particularly the democratisation of government, but more perhaps from social redistribution measures, lower levels of unemployment and a consequent general improvement in living standards. Equality is basically an attitude of mind, which in turn is a product of social conditions. In comparison with the peasant farmer or urban labourer in Africa, the factory worker in Britain or the United States has a fairly good income and good living, medical, water, transport, electric and educational facilities. These amenities have improved his conditions of life to an extent where the gap between him and the upper classes has become somewhat narrowed. He can therefore afford to regard the latter with an attitude, if not of equality, then certainly not of servility. For he has no reason to feel humbled by any sense of inferiority. To him the President or Prime Minister is just another member of the community like himself, elevated no doubt by the power and perquisites of his office, but not basically different from himself. On the part of the President or Prime Minister too, there is little ground for that feeling of arrogance which social superiority induces in the human mind. The match of economic progress, which has almost obliterated the distinction between the haves and the have-nots, has sobered the arrogance of power, so that the President or Prime Minister does not now feel himself different from the rest of the community. Equally sobering is the realisation that his tenure of the office is temporary, and that sooner or later he will have to relinquish it and resume the life of an ordinary citizen.

On the other hand, the poverty and ignorance of the masses in Africa create in them a different kind of attitude. A modern, well-furnished house excites wonderment, and a car even more so; its owner is regarded with equal curiosity, as though he were a being from another planet. His world is indeed different from theirs, because of the fantastic gap in their respective standards of living. Poverty degrades the human personality and deprives it of its self-respect. Now, if we remember that the President represents the highest point in magnificent living in the society, the contrast between him and the masses becomes glaring, excluding at once any attitude of equality on either side. In these circumstances it can only border upon the ridiculous to speak at all of equality between them. The masses, sunk deep in poverty and never having experienced anything better or more elevating than life in a thatched hut, barren of any kind of furnishing, not to mention other modern comforts, can hardly be expected to develop any attitude of equality with the President. If anything, he is to them like a demi-god who occasionally comes down from his high pedestal to visit them during a tour of inspection or what is sometimes called a meet-the-people tour, in the course of which he addresses huge crowds, tells them nice, seductive things about what the government plans to do for them in the next planning period – promises which as often as not remain unfulfilled. Such meetings are an occasion for adulation and the display of slavish obsequiousness. The President is hailed, fêted and entertained with traditional dances, and showered with gifts. A modest President may take the opportunity of such meetings to demonstrate to the people that he is one of themselves, as President Kaunda of Zambia did when, during a tour of the southern province in 1971, he told the crowd that 'for anyone to say that President Kaunda is not a common man because he is President is rubbish. Kaunda is a common man just like you'.[48] On another occasion during a tour of the northern province he spoke of the equality of the masses with himself and his ministers. This is good politics, and coming from a professed humanist, it was probably sincerely meant. More than any African President with the exception of Julius Nyerere and perhaps Jomo Kenyatta, Kenneth Kaunda lives a life of Christian simplicity, without the kind of ostentatious display of wealth which characterises Presidents and ministers elsewhere. Yet, while this may mitigate, it cannot remove the stark reality of the economic and social gap between him and the huge peasant and labouring masses. The President's style of living, though simple, is none the less too far removed from their common experience for them to be able to regard him in terms of equality.

Splendour is indeed part of the social pre-eminence of African Presidents. 'Personifying the state', writes Arthur Lewis, 'they dress themselves up in uniforms, build themselves palaces, bring all other traffic to a standstill when they drive, hold fancy parades and generally demand to be treated like Egyptian Pharaohs'.[49] One is not of course condemning ceremony of any kind nor is there any suggestion that the president should move with the traffic on a busy street. Ceremony may indeed have quite a useful role in the life of a nation, provided that it is limited to appropriate state occasions and not made to attend the everyday life of the President. It gives expression to a nation's past and culture, and in Africa there is a special need for salvaging African traditional forms of ceremony from years of neglect and suppression under colonialism. It was this desire for cultural revival, a desire to demonstrate that the African has a past, that lay behind the elaborate and somewhat extravagant pomp and pageantry that marked ceremonial occasions in Ghana under Nkrumah. It was a desire to recreate in the institutions of the present the glory and splendour of ancient African kingdoms, like that of ancient Ghana, whose king was said, when holding audience, to sit 'in a pavilion around which stand his horses caparisoned in cloth of gold; behind him stand the pages holding shields and gold-mounted sword. . . .'[50] This is a desire in which every African should feel a nationalistic pride. George Washington too tried to create ceremony and pomp for the new American nation. For the state opening of Congress he drove to Capitol Hill in 'his coach and six, with outriders and footmen in livery'.[51] As it happened, however, his taste for ceremony and pomp on state occasions was not shared by his successors. And so, as Lord Bryce wrote, 'after oscillating between the ceremonious state of George Washington . . . and the ostentatious plainness of Citizen Jefferson, who rode up alone and hitched his horse to the post at the gate, the President has settled down into an attitude between that of the mayor of a great English town on a public occasion, and that of a European cabinet minister on a political tour.'[52] Yet, granted the need for ceremony, a desire for African cultural revival might be only a cover for indulging personal vanity and a desire to assume the style and attributes of a king. 'The adulation of ancient monarchs might overspill and help to create modern equivalents. Ancient kings and modern presidents are then forced to share royal characteristics.'[53] Some of the African presidents, Nkrumah in particular, cannot be acquitted of this charge.

One particular exception deserves to be specially noticed, namely President Julius Nyerere. An almost ascetic figure, he finds State House too much of a palace, and not easily compatible with his idea of equality which is a central theme in his philosophy of socialism. He prefers therefore to live in his own modest private house of four bedrooms. He has forbidden roads, buildings, etc., to be named after him, and has asked not be to addressed as 'Excellency' except on very formal occasions. He appears genuinely embarrassed by the gap in the standard of living between himself and the masses. But he passionately pleads that his extra comforts should be regarded as a necessary aid to the carrying out of his duties, as a 'tool' entrusted to him for the benefit of the people.[54]

3. *The Presidential Term of Office*

A vexed question in African presidential regimes is: How many terms of office should be permitted to a President? The different alternatives are a life presidency, indefinite eligibility for election with or without a break, and a constitutional limitation on permissible number of terms. A life presidency has not many advocates, not even among the leaders themselves, and is not instituted anywhere in Commonwealth Africa outside Malawi. A constitutional amendment in Malawi in 1970 provides that 'Ngwazi Dr Kamuzu Banda ... shall hold the office of President for his lifetime'.[55] In the rest of the Commonwealth African presidential regimes indefinite eligibility without a break is the accepted principle. This reflects the prevailing propensity among African leaders to perpetuate their rule indefinitely. The explanation involves a complex of factors, but a desire for power and its perquisites is at the root of it all. Once a President, a person feels it inconceivable that he can thereafter be anything else but a President. The power is so intoxicating, the adulation so flattering, and the prestige and grandeur of the office so dazzling as to be almost irreconcilable with a new life as an ordinary citizen. Hence the temptation to cling to the office for life.

This propensity to personalise rule and to perpetuate it indefinitely is perhaps the outstanding contrast between the politics of the emergent states and those of the established democracies, especially Britain and America. In Britain politics has attained a happy equilibrium in which the alternation of government at not too distant intervals between two parties has become a political norm. This is owing to the good sense not only of the electorate but of the politicians themselves. It is unthinkable that a party in power should want to rig an election in order to stay in power. But what is equally, if not more, remarkable is the frequent change in the personnel of the rulers within the governing party. A British politician would not normally want to remain Prime Minister for as long as his party continues to win elections. No law forbids him to do so, but there is a general acceptance that the talent for leadership is not the exclusive property of any one individual. Many would be satisfied with two terms, some indeed would prefer to retire before the expiration of their second term, as did Mr Macmillan; this may be due partly to health and other personal reasons, but there is no doubt also a desire to give others within the party a chance to succeed to the leadership. And from the point of view of the nation, a change in leadership may guarantee against sterility, complacency and the danger of the cult of personality. Change may enable a fresh vitality and a fresh approach to be brought to bear upon the problems of government. 'An untried President may be better than a tired one; a fresh approach better than a stale one.'[56] There is yet another striking feature of the system of rulership in Britain. It is not considered *infra dig.* for a person who has once been Prime Minister to serve as an ordinary minister under another leader. Each party has its own system of choosing its leader, and a previous appointment as Prime Minister carries with it no title to the continued leadership of the party in the future. A former Prime Minister who has lost in the contest for the party leadership would not necessarily feel embarrassment in serving as minister under a new party leader as Prime Minister, as happened in the case of Sir Alec Douglas-Home. The Prime Minister no doubt enjoys prestige and power, but he does not consider himself as uniquely set apart from the rest of the community.

In the United States the problem of succession to the rulership has received an equally happy solution, as a result again of the good sense of successive Presidents from the first downwards. Until 1951 the American Constitution imposed no restriction on the eligibility of a President to seek re-election indefinitely. At the time of the Constitution's adoption, most Americans wished indeed that George Washington, the first President, would remain President indefinitely, so profound was the confidence and love they had for him. As a matter of general political principle, quite apart from the personality of Washington, the question of indefinite eligibility had provoked a disagreement of views. Washington himself and Alexander Hamilton favoured it, while Jefferson opposed it. Hamilton, in *The Federalist*, argued that a limitation on the number of terms permitted to a President would stifle zeal and make the President indifferent to his duty; that a President, knowing he would be barred from the office for ever after, might be tempted to exploit for personal advantage the opportunities of the office while they lasted; that an ambitious President might be tempted to try to prolong his term by perverted means; that it would deprive the community of the advantage of the President's previous experience in the office; and that it would lead to a lack of continuity in policy, and consequently to instability in administration.

Washington did however retire after two terms, much against the wishes and expectations of his countrymen. His example was followed by Jefferson, also against appeals from eight state legislatures that he should continue in office. 'If', he argued, 'some termination to the services of the Chief Magistrate be not fixed by the Constitution, or supplied by practice, his office, normally four years, will in fact become for life, and history shows how easily that degenerates into an inheritance'.[57] Since then the tradition has stuck that no person should be President for more than two terms. Until 1940, this tradition has been consistently observed except when, taking advantage of the uncertainty as to whether two terms meant two consecutive terms, Theodore Roosevelt sought (but failed) to be elected in 1912 for a third term some years after his first two consecutive terms. Tradition was finally breached when Franklin Roosevelt was re-elected for a third consecutive term in 1940 and for a fourth in 1944. But this was in a period of grave emergency, that of the Second World War. It is such emergency situations that present the strongest argument in favour of indefinite eligibility. In such a situation the prestige and authority of the President's personality might be invaluable in saving the life of the nation. This was the consideration underlying the break with tradition of Franklin Roosevelt's third and fourth consecutive re-elections. Roosevelt himself professed a desire to adhere to the tradition, and to relinquish office in 1941 to a successor, if only he could do so with an assurance that 'I am at the same time turning over to him as President a nation intact, a nation at peace, a nation prosperous, a nation clear in its knowledge of what powers it has to serve its own citizens, a nation that is in a position to use those powers to the full in order to move forward steadily to meet the modern needs of humanity – a nation which has thus proved that the democratic form and methods of national government can and will succeed'.[58]

These are words which might be used by any African President to justify his rule in perpetuity, and it might even be more cogent and compelling in his case. As Corwin points out, this is just the 'indispensable man' argument. To accept it, he says, 'is next door to despairing of the country'.[59] In a temporary emergency, like a war, it might perhaps be condoned, but in the context of the sort of emergency created by the development crisis in the emergent states it is a positive evil. For since the development crisis is a continuing 'emergency', the argument is tantamount to making the presidency a life appointment. In any case, the Americans, after the Roosevelt experience, had to amend their Constitution in 1951 to give force of law to the tradition limiting the presidential office to two full elective terms or one full elective term plus more than one half of another term inherited from a previous President.[60]

The question of presidential term of office was considered recently in Zambia by the One-Party State Commission. A life presidency was rejected on the ground that it 'exposed the holder of the office and the country to many risks'.[61] What the Commission proposed represented a balance between indefinite eligibility and a limitation on terms. It recommended that a President should be eligible for an indefinite number of five-year terms provided that not more than two terms were to be held consecutively. After two consecutive terms, the President must step down, but after such a break he becomes eligible to stand again.[62] The object, as stated by the Commission, is to bring the office within 'reach of as many aspiring citizens as possible'.[63] In the view of the Government, however, 'there should be no limitation on how often a man or woman can serve his or her country in the office of President' – except, of course, the wishes of the people to whose verdict at elections the matter should be left.[64] It is pertinent to point out that the commission's recommendation is less restrictive than the system in Latin America whose circumstances of underdevelopment and the need for effective leadership are comparable to Africa's. There the break is after one term, not two, and in Costa Rica the duration of the break is even specified, the President being required to have been out of office for two terms to become eligible again.[65] Paraguay follows the United States in limiting the number of presidential terms to two, while in Mexico the limit is just one term.

(i) *The Related Question of a Successor*

It is relevant to the question of giving a chance to other aspirants to the office to mention that the Constitutions of Ghana and Malawi have no place at all for a second-in-command. The office of Vice-President is unrecognised. Neither is an acting President allowed. If the President is absent from the country or ill, his office is to be executed, not by an acting President, but by a presidential commission of three appointed by the President.[66] (Only cabinet ministers may be appointed in Malawi.) The President in Malawi is under no obligation to appoint a commission. On the other hand, the commission in Ghana was a permanent body with a constitutional right to act for the President during his absence abroad or illness; it also acted during any vacancy in the presidency, pending the election of a new President by the national assembly. A different body, a presidential council, acts during a vacancy or when the President is so incapacitated as to be unable to appoint a presidential commission in Malawi. The council consists of the secretary-general of the party, and two cabinet ministers who must be members of the national executive committee of the party. The two cabinet ministers are appointed by the national executive committee of the party and all cabinet ministers meeting jointly as a committee of appointment.[67]

All this is no doubt intended to prevent the emergence of a second-in-command who might become a serious rival to the President. When Mr Alake Banda, Malawi's Minister of Trade, Industry and Tourism, Transport and Communications, was reported to have claimed at a press interview during a visit to Zambia in 1973 that he was President Banda's right-hand man, the implication being that he was the President's likely successor, he was promptly suspended from the party and stripped of his ministerial office. His later public denial of the newspaper report does not appear to have restored him to the favour of the angry President.

In this connection Ghana and Malawi stand out as an exception to the rest of the Commonwealth African presidential regimes, where a Vice-President is recognised as the principal assistant of the President in the discharge of his executive functions and the leader of government business in the national assembly, his office being established directly by the constitution.[68] (The Vice-President was not so designated in Uganda, while his designation in Kenya is only as principal assistant of the President, though by presidential directive he deputises for the President as the leader of government business in the national assembly.)[69] Tanzania has two Vice-Presidents, the first being the principal assistant to the President in relation to Zanzibar under the style of President of Zanzibar and the head of the executive of Zanzibar, and the second being his principal assistant in relation to Tanganyika and leader of government business in the national assembly.[70] In addition to his independent functions, the Vice-President may be and usually is assigned ministerial responsibilities by the President. His status is that of a minister, and like other ministers, he is appointed by the President from among members of the national assembly. (He must be an elected constituency member in Gambia, Kenya, and Tanzania, but not in Uganda, Zambia and Botswana.) He is a member of the cabinet, and presides over it in the absence of the President.[71]

The most important independent function of the Vice-President under the constitution is to act as a stand-in for the President. For this purpose a vacancy in the presidency has to be distinguished from the absence abroad, illness or incapacity of the President. In the event of vacancy in the presidency occurring in Zambia and Gambia, the Vice-President is translated to the office. The constitution provides that he 'shall assume the office'; in other words he becomes President substantively, and not merely in an acting capacity.[72] If, however, there is no Vice-President, the functions of the President shall be performed by a minister appointed by the cabinet. In this latter case, the national assembly shall meet on the fourteenth day after the vacancy occurred to elect a new President.[73] Thus the constitution draws a clear distinction between assumption of the office of President by the Vice-President and the performance of the functions of the office by a minister appointed by the cabinet. (Under the one-party state constitution in Zambia the secretary-general is to act during a vacancy.) In Uganda (1967), Kenya, Botswana and Tanzania the Vice-President merely exercises the functions of the office during a vacancy – i.e. in the capacity of an acting President – pending the election of a new president.[74]

In the case of absence abroad, illness or incapacity, the Vice-President steps in automatically, without appointment by the President, to discharge the functions of the office in Uganda and Tanzania.[75] In Kenya, Zambia, Botswana and Gambia the functions do not become exercisable by the Vice-President by operation of law; he has to be authorised or appointed by the President, and his authority extends to only such functions as may be specified.[76] However, if in Zambia,

Botswana and Gambia the President is so incapacitated as to be unable to authorise the Vice-President to act, the latter is entitled to exercise the functions without the authorisation. It should be added that in the absence of the Vice-President during any of these occasions the presidency is to be exercised by a minister appointed by the cabinet.

It must not be supposed that this necessarily settles the question of succession in favour of the Vice-President. The Vice-President is not heir apparent to the leadership of the country. The identity of a successor will depend on a combination of forces in the community, not the least being that of tribe. The present Vice-President of Kenya, Mr Arap Moi, a non-Kikuyu, is not tipped as the most likely successor to President Kenyatta. In Zambia the vice-presidency has so far gone with the vice-presidency of the party. Each time there was a new Vice-President of the United National Independence Party following upon new party elections, a new Vice-President of the country was appointed, and the whole cabinet was reshuffled in the process. Owing to heavy tribal influence at the 1967 party elections which proved decisive, President Kaunda has indicated his unwillingness to allow the vice-presidency and other cabinet positions to be pre-empted by party offices.[77] The result of this practice is that Zambia has had three successive Vice-Presidents since independence, which makes it difficult to identify anyone as the number two to President Kaunda. Only in Tanzania is the Vice-President indisputably President Nyerere's number two, having been Vice-President since 1962 and Prime Minister for a brief period after Nyerere's resignation to reorganise the party.

4. *The President's Tenure of Office*

The indefinitude of the President's term of office is not even limited by age. No retiring age is prescribed for the office, as is the case with non-political public offices. An octogenarian President is thus not an uncommon phenomenon. This is not in itself objectionable so long as there is a limitation on the number of times a person, whether young or old, can stand for election to the presidency.

Resignation, forced upon a leader by defeat in parliament, by public scandal or by other similar circumstances, is firmly entrenched as part of the ethic of parliamentary government – in Britain, for example. The right to govern being in parliament and delegated by it to the leaders of the majority party, it follows that the latter should be obliged to resign when defeated on an issue of confidence. As already explained,[78] resignation on this ground is not constitutionally enjoined in the presidential system, because of the fact that the President is directly elected by the people to whom he therefore owes his right to rule and his responsibility for the government. When the assembly passes a vote of no confidence in the government, the President in Commonwealth Africa has a choice either to resign or to appeal to the people in a general election, an encounter from which he appears better placed to emerge victorious than the M.P.s.

Public scandal appears to affect a President's tenure of office less than it does the leader of a parliamentary government, either because no ethic of forced resignation has taken root or because continued confidence of parliament is not directly a determinant of presidential tenure. The Watergate scandal in the United States arising from the bugging of the Democratic Party headquarters by some members of the committee for the re-election of President Nixon in 1972 seems to bear this out. The established fact of the bugging itself and the scandal it generated would have been enough to force the resignation of a British Prime Minister regardless of his personal involvement or otherwise in the matter. But President Nixon has, up to the time of writing, indicated that he contemplates no resignation. It might be argued that, since heads of departments and other executive officers are only agents of the President, and not co-beneficiaries of the executive power as in a cabinet government, their misconduct should not involve the President to the same extent as in a cabinet government.

All this goes to underline the desirability, indeed the necessity, for a procedure for effecting the removal of a President in cases of gross misconduct where he does not resign of his own volition. For this purpose as we have seen, the U.S. Constitution institutes proceedings by way of impeachment before the Senate under the chairmanship of the Chief Justice, with the House of Representatives as the accuser. But the kind of misconduct triable by impeachment is limited by the Constitution to treason, bribery or other high crimes or mis-demeanours.[79] It is another of the characteristics of African pres-identialism that no such procedure is available in the Commonwealth African presidential regimes except Zambia and Gambia. Once elected, a President is practically irremovable, however much he misconducts himself. A President in Zambia and Gambia may be removed from office for violating the constitution or for gross misconduct in accordance with a somewhat self-stultifying procedure.[80] It requires that a written notice of motion, signed by one-half (one-third in Zambia) of all national assembly members, should be given to the Speaker, alleging that the President has committed a violation of the constitution or gross misconduct (particulars of which must be specified) and proposing that a tribunal of investigation be appointed. The motion is then voted on without debate by the assembly, and if passed by two-thirds majority of all members, the chief justice shall appoint a tribunal of three judges (present or former judges), which shall then investigate and report to the assembly. The President has a right of audience and of representation before the tribunal. A finding by the tribunal in favour of the President terminates all further proceedings on the allegation. If, on the other hand, the tribunal finds the allegation to have been substantiated, the assembly may then by resolution supported by three-quarters majority (two-thirds in Gambia) of all members pronounce the President guilty accordingly. The resolution operates to vacate the office of the President on the third day of its passage, unless before that the President has dissolved Parliament. This is the self-stultifying aspect of the procedure. What is the purpose of going through this stiff procedure if, at the end of it all, the President can forestall his removal by dissolving parliament? In any case the procedure is so stiff as to make the chances of a President being successfully removed by means of it very slight.

It is also desirable and necessary to have a procedure for removing a President who will not resign although, owing to illness, he has become incapable of performing the functions of his office. The prospect of an ailing and incapacitated President hanging on to the office for a long time is not a remote one. Again there is a conspicuous absence of a procedure for this in the Commonwealth African presidential regimes, except in Uganda (1967), Kenya, Zambia and Gambia. The procedure in all four countries is at the instance of the cabinet who, by a majority of its members, may resolve that the mental or physical capacity of the President to discharge the functions of his office should be investigated.[81] Upon information or request to him by the cabinet (through the speaker of the national assembly in Kenya), the Chief Justice shall appoint an investigating board or tribunal of five qualified medical practitioners (three in Zambia and Gambia) which, after investigation, shall report to him whether, in its opinion, the President is, by reason of infirmity of body or mind, incapable of discharging the function of his office. If the report confirms the President's incapacity, the Chief Justice shall certify accordingly. (From the time of the cabinet's resolution, the President shall not exercise his functions until the tribunal or board reports that he is not incapable.) The certificate of the Chief Justice has the effect of automatically vacating the office of President in Zambia and Gambia, but in Kenya the vacation takes effect at the end of three months and only if within that period the Chief Justice has not again certified, following another report of the medical board or tribunal, that the President has recovered his capacity. The Chief Justice's certificate in Uganda was only a basis for action by the national assembly which unless the President has resigned on being informed of the adverse medical report, might remove him by resolution; the cabinet could act in a like manner when parliament was dissolved. In Tanzania incapacity to discharge the functions of the office on the ground of physical or mental infirmity, certified by the

Chief Justice in his own discretion after being so requested by a resolution of the cabinet and after considering medical evidence, does not vacate the office but only suspends the President until the time when he recovers his capacity.[82] This was also the effect of incapacity in Ghana (1960), though it was the Speaker of the national assembly, rather than the Chief Justice, who, in pursuance of a resolution of the assembly and after considering medical evidence, had to declare the President incapable; the President remained suspended until the Speaker, acting on a similar resolution, withdrew his declaration.[83]

The President's salary, pension, gratuity and allowances provide no channel through which pressure may be exerted to force his resignation. They are determined by the national assembly, but so long as there is an incumbent President, the salary and allowances cannot be reduced without his consent.[84] Moreover, they (including pension and gratuity) are, by the constitution, charged upon the Consolidated Fund, and so are not subject to debate in the national assembly or to its power to withhold appropriation. The President is also exempt from personal taxation.

We will proceed in the next four chapters to discuss the features of African presidentialism mentioned in the opening paragraphs of this chapter, namely centralism in the organisation of governmental powers, in the administration of government, and in the organisation of politics, and the subordination of the legislature.

REFERENCES

1. Carl J. Friedrich, *The Impact of American Constitutionalism Abroad* (1966), p. 8.

2. *ibid.*, p. 19.

3. See below, Chs. VI, VII and VIII.

4. Julius Nyerere, 'How much Power for a Leader', *Africa Report*, vol. 7, No. 7, July 1962, p. 7.

5. See below, ch. VII.

6. R. S. Hirschfield, 'The Reality of Presidential Power', *Parl. Affairs*, 1967/8, vol. xxi, p. 375.

7. Nat. Ass. Deb., 1962, col. 1104.

8. H. L. Bretton, *The Rise and Fall of Kwame Nkrumah* (1966), p. 80.

9. Bennion, *Constitutional Law of Ghana* (1962), p. 110.

10. Alvin W. Wolfe, 'African Conceptions of Authority', unpublished paper (1965); cited by K. W. Grundy and M. Weinstein, 'The Political Uses of Imagination' (1966), *Transition* 31, p. 5.

11. Parl. Deb. 23 April—12 July, 1957, cols. 438—39.

12. Grant McConnell, *The Modern Presidency* (1967), p. 15.

13. See a portrait of him by one of his biographers in Marcus Cunliffe, *George Washington, Man and Monument* (1960), pp. 20–1.

14. R. S. Hirschfield, 'The Reality of Presidential Power', *op. cit.* pp. 379–80.

15. Below chap. XII.

16. Grant McConnell, *op. cit.*, p. 15.

17. Julius K. Nyerere, *Ujamaa – Essays on Socialism* (1968), p. 90.

18. Julius K. Nyerere, *op. cit.*, p. 89.

19. R. S. Hirschfield, *op. cit.*, p. 382.

20. Below, chs. X and XI.

21. R. I. Rotberg, 'Tribalism and Politics in Zambia', *Africa Report*, Dec. 1967, p. 34.

22. *op. cit.*, p. 381.

23. *Evening News*, Accra, 14 June 1959, address by Nkrumah.

24. Kwame Nkrumah, *Consciencism* (1964), p. 57.

25. Wole Soyinka, *The Man Died* (1972), p. 183.

26. Julius Nyerere, *Ujamaa – Essays on Socialism* (1968), Preface.

27. *ibid.*

28. See the provocative article by Ali Mazrui, 'Nkrumah: the Leninist Czar' (1966), *Transition* 26, p. 9, and the great controversy which it provoked in subsequent issues of the same journal, nos. 27, 29, 30 and 31.

29. H. L. Bretton, *Rise and Fall of Kwame Nkrumah* (1966), p. 135.

30. Kofi Baako, Speech delivered to the conference of Ghana's envoys, Jan. 1962, reproduced in T. P. Omari, *Kwame Nkrumah: the Anatomy of an African Dictatorship* (1970) pp. 192–3.

31. Parl. Debate, April 1966, p. 563 (Malawi).

32. Professor Ali Mazrui laments this 'anti-intellectual tradition in Western politics' in his article, 'Tanzaphilia: a Diagnosis', *Transition* 30, p. 21.

33. *Mississippi* v. *Johnson* 4 Wall 475 (1867).

34. Bryce, *The American Commonwealth*, Vol. 1, Hacker ed., (1959), pp. 25–6.

35. *State of Ohio* v. *Salmon P. Chase, Governor*, 5 Ohio St. 529.

36. Parl. Deb., Oct. 27, 1964, cols. 3893–4.

37. S.9, Constitution 1962; S.11, Constitution 1965.

38. Presidential Affairs Act, 1962, Cap. 502.

39. S.183A Ghana; S.69 Zambia.

40. Nat. Ass. Deb., 1961.

41. House of Reps Deb., Oct. 27, 1964, col. 3910.

42. H. L. Bretton, *The Rise and Fall of Kwame Nkrumah* (1966), p. 58.

43. *Zambia Hansard* No. 19, 7–17 October, 1969, col. 135.

44. *ibid.*, col. 144.

45. Col. 135.

46. *ibid.*, col. 143 (personal statement by the Member for Mongu, Mr Mumbuna).

47. *ibid.*, col. 145.

48. *Times of Zambia*, October 13, 1971.

49. Arthur Lewis, *Politics in West Africa* (1965), p. 31.

50. Stephen Dzirasa, *Political Thought of Dr Kwame Nkrumah* (Accra, Guinea Press Ltd.), pp. 19–20.

51. James Bryce, *op. cit.*, p. 26.

52. *Loc. cit.*

53. Ali Mazrui, 'Nkrumah: the Leninist Czar' (1966), *Transition* 26, p. 16.

54. Julius Nyerere, *Ujamaa: Essays on Socialism* (1968), p. 4.

55. S.9, Constitution 1966.

56. E. S. Corwin, *The President: Office and Powers*, 4th ed., p. 37.

57. Quoted from E. S. Corwin, *op. cit.*, p. 332.

58. Quoted from E. S. Corwin, *op. cit.*, p. 336.

59. *ibid.*, p. 37.

60. XXII Amendment.

61. Report of the National Commission on the Establishment of a One-Party Participatory Democracy in Zambia, Lusaka, Oct. 1972, para. 41.

62. Report, *op. cit.*, para. 48.

63. *ibid.*, para. 47.

64. Govt. White Paper on Commission's Report, No. 1 of 1972, Govt. Printer, Lusaka, 1972, p. 5.

65. Martin Needler, 'Cabinet Responsibility in a Presidential System: the Case of Peru', *Parl. Affairs*, Vol. XVIII, p. 156.

66. Art. 18, Ghana (1960); S.15, Malawi.

67. SS.13 and 14.

68. Art. 32, Uganda (1967); S.15, Kenya; SS.41 and 50, Zambia; SS.40 and 50, Botswana; S.43, Gambia.

69. Above, ch. III.

70. S.13.

71. Arts. 37 and 38, Uganda; S.17, Kenya; S.45, Zambia; S.45, Botswana; S.49, Gambia.

72. S.37, Zambia; S.39, Gambia.

73. Report, National Commission on the Establishment of a One-Party Participatory Democracy in Zambia, Lusaka, 1972, para. 50.

74. Art. 79, Uganda; S.6(2), Kenya; S.36, Botswana; S.9, Tanzania.

75. Art. 79, Uganda; S.9, Tanzania.

76. S.11, Kenya; S.38, Zambia; S.37, Botswana; S.39, Gambia.

77. R. I. Rotberg, 'Tribalism and Politics in Zambia', *Africa Report*, Dec. 1967, p. 34.

78. Above, ch. III.

79. Above, ch. II.

80. S.36, Zambia; S.38, Gambia.

81. Art. 31, Uganda; S.12, Kenya; S.35, Zambia; S.37, Gambia.

82. S.9.

83. Art. 18.

84. Art. 19, Ghana; S.10, Tanzania; S.13, Kenya; S.42, Zambia; S.40, Gambia; S.41, Botswana; S.16, Malawi.

CHAPTER VI

CENTRALISM IN THE ORGANISATION OF GOVERNMENTAL POWERS

The organisation of governmental powers in the Commonwealth African presidential regimes has involved three main issues — whether the organisation should be federal or unitary, the relations of the central government to local administration and to the chiefs. These will now be considered in turn.

1. *The Unitary State*

British colonial government had a bias for a unitary system of government as against federalism. Government was conceived of in terms of a centralised authority flowing from the imperial power to a single governor as the sole representative of the monarch for the exercise of the entirety of her powers and jurisdiction within the dependency. Thus the conception upon which the office of governor rests is at once incompatible with the division of powers among co-ordinate territorial units of government. Being therefore antithetical to gubernatorial rule, federalism had little place in the organisation of British colonial governments in Africa. Unitarism was the accepted structure, and it was established regardless of the size and social composition of the countries concerned. In spite of vast differences in territory, population and social structure, Nigeria, Ghana, Sierra Leone and Gambia in West Africa were governed as unitary states, so were Tanganyika, Kenya, Uganda and Zanzibar in East Africa, the Rhodesias and Malawi in Central Africa, and Botswana, Lesotho and Swaziland in the South. So long as government was by the colonial governor and his officials, unitarism worked and was acquiesced in by the local population. The centralism of the colonial system of administration no doubt had its own advantages. It meant uniformity of laws and institutions, which in turn served as a foundation upon which national unity might in time be nurtured. Moreover, for a colonial government, handicapped by an acute shortage of trained staff and of money, unitarism was economically expedient, because it avoided the expensive duplication of offices. Yet whatever its advantages, its continued use was bound to come increasingly under challenge as political power began gradually to be handed over to the local people. As the process was accelerated and more and more power was handed over, the challenge was intensified. The approach of independence made it a burning issue. Nationalist politics came to be dominated by the controversy of unitarism v. federalism (or regionalism). Was the power of the departing British to be devolved upon a single group or was it to be divided among several territorial groupings? This was a pre-occupation of the politics of the period, a pre-occupation which tended sometimes to overshadow, and even to jeopardise, the nationalist goal of independence.

The British were sympathetic to this challenge to a system which, under their own practice, had become firmly established and been accepted. They viewed the issue as no longer merely concerned with administrative expediency. Far weightier considerations were now involved — the stability, and indeed the very survival of the state itself. The colonial government was a regime of subjugation, resting upon superior force for the maintenance and enforcement of its authority. Now that this enforced *pax* was about to be withdrawn it became urgent to devise a suitable political arrangement that could secure to the young state the loyalty of its diverse elements. The question was easily answered in favour of federalism or regionalism, because of the opportunity which it afforded for each tribal group to manage its own internal affairs within the unity of the whole. Arthur Lewis has stated the case rather cogently. The basic explanation of politics in the plural societies of Africa, he writes, is that 'a society which has very wide geographical differences can live together at peace only in a federal framework'; such a society, he adds, 'needs to give its provinces the opportunity to look after their own affairs, if they are to feel content with the political union'.[1]

It was these considerations that made Britain, in its withdrawal from Africa, a convert to federalism or regionalism, and so took steps to entrench it in the independence constitutions of Ghana, Nigeria, Kenya and Uganda. It had been forced to dissolve the ill-assorted federation of Rhodesia and Nyasaland, and to grant independence to Northern Rhodesia and Nyasaland as separate unitary states; yet it sought to accord to Barotseland a special place in the unitary constitution of Zambia (Northern Rhodesia). In every one of these places (except Nigeria) federalism or regionalism was imposed in the face of opposition from the dominant party. British concern for its responsibility towards tribal and other political minorities was made to prevail over the wishes of the majority represented by the dominant or ruling party. Naturally this rankled with the ruling party and its leaders, particularly Kwame Nkrumah of Ghana, whose ruling Convention

People's Party (CPP) had had, on the insistence of the British Government, to fight a premature general election on the eve of independence to obtain popular approval for its unitarist platform. In view of the CPP's overwhelming victory at the elections, British insistence on writing regionalism into the constitution as a condition for the grant of independence became therefore a source of intense resentment to Nkrumah, who questioned the moral and political basis of British solicitude for the interests of minorities against those of the majority. Independence, Nkrumah argued, 'involved the right of the local population alone to determine the nature of the laws, regulations and procedures of their State'.[2] He protested vigorously the ability of his government to 'safeguard the rights of our own people', arguing that 'if my Government could be suspected of ulterior intentions towards our political opponents, we were equally open to the suspicion that we might abrogate the imposed constitution on the morrow of British departure'.[3] In order, however, not to delay the date for independence, the CPP government accepted the constitution but determined to dismantle it when the time was considered opportune. Nkrumah's resentment at the regional scheme of Ghana's independence constitution and his plans for dismantling it were shared by the dominant party in Kenya and Uganda. But perhaps at this juncture it may be as well to consider the grounds on which the opposition to federation or regionalism was based.

Was the desire for unitarism part of the aim to achieve concentrated power under a presidential system? A federal arrangement would unquestionably operate to limit presidential power, and that is why federalism has proved an effective cornerstone of American constitutionalism. Its limitation is quite a severe one, going beyond that of the separation of legislative, executive and judicial powers. For it involves a division of powers that is both functional and territorial. Instead of just one national government exercising the entirety of governmental functions and powers over the whole territory and its inhabitants, under federalism the country is divided into two or more territorial units under separate, independent governments co-existing with the national government, with which they share functions and powers of government in a manner that allows to each an exclusive jurisdiction over certain fields of governmental activity wide and significant enough to give it a meaningful independent existence. Independence of the component governments, both national and regional, from each other is of the very essence of the federal arrangement. Within its field of competence, each government must, by and large, be independent of control from outside. Within their respective spheres of power, however these may be demarcated, the national government and a regional government are co-ordinate, in the sense that neither can dictate to the other. A regional government owes its powers, not to the national government, but to the constitution, and exercises it over persons and property within its territory. The national government also operates directly on persons and property within all the regions, but, unlike in a unitary state, its operation is limited to the extent of its constitutional powers and functions. Its claim on the obedience and loyalty of the people is similarly limited by the range of its powers and functions. While reserving an exclusive sphere of authority to each government, a federal scheme of division may of course make certain functions common or concurrent to all, giving to either the national government or the regional governments an overriding voice in case of conflict. So long as the area of exclusive power is wide and significant enough to make each government's independence meaningful, the technique of concurrent powers is perfectly consistent with the federal principle, and is indeed commonly instituted.

Federalism involves yet a further limitation upon power at the centre. This arises from the demands of co-operation and co-existence, which lie at the root of the federal concept. Federalism is an exercise in co-operative living and mutual tolerance. It envisages that the powers lodged at the centre should be exercised with the willing co-operation of the component regions. The principle of co-operation demands the representation of the regions in the various organs of the national government. This at once operates as a limitation on the manner in which that government is to be conducted. It requires that due account be taken of the various major interests existing in the state, and an effort made to balance them in order to maintain the equilibrium which the federal arrangement is supposed to embody. The principle of co-operation demands further that in the exercise of concurrent powers, the national government should consult with the regional governments in accordance with a procedure that should be written into the constitution.

It is to be expected that a leader with ambition for centralised power might be impatient with such a scheme of division and the restraints which it imposes. While, however, personal ambitions for power might have been a relevant and important factor, the argument was based on other grounds. It was argued that federalism or regionalism would impede development. 'In communications, for example', Nkrumah argued, 'the Government might decide on a trunk road that would pass through several Regions. Opposition by the Regional Assembly of one affected Region could hold up the project indefinitely. As part of its national health scheme, the Government might determine the sites on which hospitals and clinics should be built. The Regional Assemblies could object to and obstruct these plans, in keeping with their constitutional authority over the regional health and medical services. . . . Extend this to education, public works, housing, agricultural and industrial development, and it can be accepted that the central Government would have been in the position of possessing merely token sovereignty. Our hands and feet would be virtually bound the moment we attempted to govern'.[4]

Next it was argued that federalism or regionalism undermined national unity by providing an institutional base for tribal politics and by fostering all the cleavages and conflicts inherent in a plural society. From their base of power in the regions, tribal political parties are enabled to pursue their opposition to the central government with greater effect than would otherwise have been possible. And they are able to harness not only the power and influence of a regional government but also the financial and other resources available in the region, particularly the moral authority of the chiefs. Then there was the old argument about the expense of running a federal government, which in a new state, facing an acute shortfall of trained personnel and money, might constitute a serious inroad into the resources needed to finance development. The effect of having to share resources might be to weaken the ability of both the central and regional governments to discharge their functions effectively.

These arguments must not be taken as conclusive in favour of unitarism as against federalism. More should depend on the peculiar circumstances of each country, its territorial size, population, resources, and the nature and extent of the differences between its constituent groups. In the context of Ghana, the arguments against federalism seemed pretty compelling. The country is small in territory and population, and the differences between the component tribes are not nearly so great as those dividing the Muslim North from the southern population of Nigeria. In Nigeria, unlike in Ghana, the differences are not just those of tribe, but of peoples – the Hamites and Negroid peoples.

Granted that there are compelling arguments against federalism in Ghana, the validity of Nkrumah's opposition should more appropriately be considered in the context of the actual scheme instituted by the constitution. Did it in fact restrict the power of the central government in the way and to the extent claimed by Nkrumah? The first thing to notice is that the Ghanaian scheme was not a thorough-going federal set-up. Under the constitution the country was divided into five regions, but, apart from establishing a house of chiefs for each region with a Head to be elected by the house of chiefs (in the Ashanti Region the Asantehene was specifically named as Head) the constitution left the form, organisation, powers and functions of the regional government very largely to the discretion of parliament.

Parliament did not of course have an entirely free hand. It was mandatory upon it to establish a regional assembly for each region.[5] And, when so established, the regional assembly 'shall have and exercise authority, functions and powers to such extent as may be prescribed by Act of Parliament relating to (*a*) local government; (*b*) agriculture, animal health and forestry; (*c*) education; (*d*) communication; (*e*) medical and health services; (*f*) public works; (*g*) town and country planning; (*h*) housing; (*i*) police; (*j*) and other such matters as Parliament may from time to time determine'.[6] A regional assembly was by this provision entitled to exercise authority and powers in every one of these fields, and the discretion given to parliament was merely to determine the extent of such authority or powers, but not to say that in respect of any of these fields a regional assembly was to have no function at all. Nor was it open to parliament to refuse to enact an implementing legislation prescribing the extent of the functions and powers of regional assemblies, although no time-limit was set for it to do so. To have refused to implement the regional scheme would clearly have been contrary to the declared intention of the constitution which was to fulfil 'the need for a body at the regional level with effective powers in specified fields'.[7]

From the reference to 'effective powers' it seems also to have been the intention that within the specified fields the regions were to be given both legislative and executive powers. This comes out more clearly from the provision for the appointment of a regional constitutional commission to enquire into and report on the devolution of functions and powers to the regional assemblies, and to recommend the 'composition of each Regional Assembly, the executive, legislative, financial and advisory powers to be exercised by it, the funds required to meet the capital and recurrent expenditure. . . .'[8] Although it was for parliament to prescribe the functions and powers of the regional assemblies within the specified fields, once it had done so, the functions and powers so prescribed became incorporated into the constitution as part thereof, and could only be revoked or diminished by an entrenched procedure for the amendment of the constitution.[9]

The scheme, as intended, might appropriately be described as a quasi-federal one. The regions were to have substantial functions in the fields specified, but their powers in those fields were not to be exclusive of those of the central government; they were to be concurrent, with the central government having the overriding authority. A quasi-federal scheme of this kind might well still have impinged upon the sovereignty of the central government as Nkrumah contended. Yet the constitutional provisions were flexible enough to have enabled parliament to curtail drastically the powers of the regions, and so reduce to the minimum their impingement on the activity of the central government. It is not quite clear how far parliament could have gone in this. The farthest extreme would be to say that, within the specified fields, a regional assembly should have only advisory powers; a purely advisory regional assembly would not seem, however, to be in conformity with the terms of the constitution. It does violence to language to say that a purely advisory assembly *has and exercises authority, functions and powers*. Nor, clearly, would such an assembly be within the spirit and intention of the constitution. Yet that was what in fact the regional assemblies in Ghana were made to be. The implementing legislation — the Regional Assemblies Act, 1958 — devolved neither legislative nor executive powers on the regional assemblies, merely making them advisory to the central government ministers in specified areas. The government had rejected the recommendations of the regional constitutional commission that regional assemblies should be given executive and subordinate legislative powers, but with no power to tax; they were to be financed entirely from grants-in-aid from the central government and from precepts issued on local government authorities.[10]

In terms of actual powers of government, therefore, the regional assemblies, as implemented in the Regional Assemblies Act, 1958, were in no way derogatory of the authority of the central government. Nkrumah's claim in 1963 that they would obstruct a planned and integrated development of the country as a united nation was not supported by the scheme as it actually existed. However, aside from actual powers of government, the regional assemblies had a vital function in regard to the amendment of the constitution. Any legislation amending or repealing entrenched provisions of the constitution, such as those relating to the principal organs of government, the public service, chieftaincy, the regional organisations and their functions and powers, needed to be referred to all regional assemblies and approved by two-thirds of them, including those whose functions and powers were affected by the legislation. This requirement was additional to the two-thirds majority in parliament required for every amendment of the constitution. If a bill affecting the functions or powers of a regional assembly was rejected by the assembly, its objection could be got rid of only by means of a referendum conducted for the purpose in the region, at which the majority of the registered voters voted in favour. Nkrumah and his CPP government took strong objection to this, castigating it as the worst demonstration of 'imperialist arrogance', an affront to the sovereignty of the new state, and a perversion of the democratic principle.[11] This is the argument of a dictator. It is a repudiation of the very concept of limited government, i.e. of constitutionalism. A constitution is not an instrument of a narrow majority, but of the nation as a whole. In Ghana, as indeed in most other countries, it was the product of a compromise between competing interests in the nation, and its objective was to design a frame of government that could hold the loyalty of all the constituent groups. If its amendment were to be a matter solely for a narrow majority in parliament, then it would have ceased to serve the purposes of constitutionalism.

The second factor that tainted the regional scheme in the eyes of Nkrumah and his government was that, although the regional assemblies had no powers of government, they nevertheless boosted the position and effectiveness of opposition parties in the country. All opposition in Ghana, as elsewhere in Africa, had its base in the tribe, and tribe in Ghana was co-extensive with the most powerful and important region, the Ashanti Region. It was in this region that the main opposition party, the National Liberation Movement (NLM) had its home, sponsored as it was by the traditional King of Ashanti, the Asantehene, who was also the constitutionally-designated Head of the Ashanti Region. The Asantehene had thrown in the authority and influence of his office and its immense wealth behind the NLM. Nkrumah charged that the designation of the Asantehene in the constitution as the Head of the Ashanti Region had entrenched 'the greatest focal point of disintegration within our new state'. This, he asserted, was 'a most dangerous situation and limitation upon our power as a fully independent Government that we could not accept. It would have amounted to the exclusion of Ashanti from the sphere of Ghana's sovereignty. It was unthinkable we should lay ourselves open to this possibility and so endanger the future of the country'.[12] Nkrumah's dislike of the regional scheme was accentuated by the politics of the opposition parties; it was a politics of destruction, obstruction and non-co-operation as expressed in boycotts, organised violence, calumny and demands for secession.[13] The abolition of regionalism was considered necessary if the opposition parties were ever to adopt a responsible and constructive attitude towards politics.

Thus Nkrumah and his government set about dismantling the regional structure. Having won virtually all the seats in all five regional assemblies through the opposition boycott of the regional elections, it took the initial step in December 1958, two months after the regional elections, of repealing the constitutional amendment procedure.[14] The repeal strictly complied with the procedure laid down. With the government's overwhelming majority in the national assembly and its control of all five regional assemblies, this was easy enough. By this repeal all that was now needed for constitutional amendments was a simple majority in the national assembly. Early in 1959, using the new procedure, the regional assemblies were dissolved and the establishing act repealed.[15] When the republican constitution was enacted in 1960, unitarism was confirmed, and power to provide for a form of government other than a unitary republic was reserved to the people.[16]

The regions were retained but only as administrative sub-divisions of the central government.

Unlike the Ghanaian, the Independence Constitution of Uganda established a supposedly federal system, in which power was divided between a central government and five federal states, four of which were traditional kingdoms. With a population of about seven million (1962) and an area of 240,000 square km., the country might be considered not really large enough for a federal structure. But the problem of federalism in Uganda was not so much one of size as of the fact that the federal states were identified with the traditional kingdoms, whose authority was thus enshrined in the Constitution. The state government was the Kabaka's government in Buganda, the Omugade's government in Ankole, the Omukama's government in Bunyoro and the Omukama's government in Toro; the executive council included the Katikkiro (Prime Minister), the Omulamuzi, and the Omuwanika in Buganda, the Enganzi and the Omubiki in Ankole, the Katikiro and Omukeeto in Bunyoro, the Omuhikirwa in Toro and the Katukiro in Busoga; and the legislative assembly was the Lukiko in Buganda, the Eishengyero in Ankole, the Rukurato in Bunyoro and Toro, and the Lukiko in Busoga.[17] Moreover, many government processes were conducted according to traditional forms and procedures. The entrenchment of traditional kingdoms, with all their institutions, forms and procedures, as a basis for federal government in a modern state was bound to intensify competition between the centre and the regions for the loyalty of the citizens.

The Kingdom of Buganda, with its special and privileged position under the Constitution, was the focal point of this problem. The competition between tribe and state for the loyalty of the people is disturbing enough for the stability, unity and progress of a new nation, but when tribal loyalty is institutionalised in an organised traditional government system enshrined in the Constitution itself, then the challenge it poses to the new state is infinitely more disturbing. To build a regional structure of government upon the foundation of a traditional government was to give added vigour to this challenge. This was the problem that Uganda faced under its federal Independence Constitution. Buganda was the most populous and developed unit in the country, with a strong and sophisticated tradition of kingship and government, a tradition that has imbued the Baganda with a strong attachment and loyalty to the Kabaka (king) and his government. Such loyalty could not easily be subordinated to loyalty to the new Ugandan state. The conflict of loyalty inherent in this situation was easily contained so long as power was in the hands of the British, but it was well calculated to bedevil the stability and unity of a self-governing Ugandan state. The recognition of the Kabaka and his traditional government as the base for a regional government under the constitution simply aggravated the conflict. For his claim on the loyalty of the Baganda was no longer based on tradition alone but also on the authority of a regional government under the Constitution. Such loyalty was apt to be stronger than loyalty to the Ugandan state. Only if the central government was controlled by the Kabaka's men, with himself as Head of State, could the Bagandas' loyalty to the Ugandan state be expected to transcend their loyalty to their kingdom. Thus it was that pre-independence politics came to be dominated by the question of the personality of the Head of State and the control of the central government. The question was temporarily resolved by making the Kabaka the constitutional President and Head of State, and by the joint control of the central government by his party, the Kabaka Yekka ('Kabaka only') and Milton Obote's Uganda People's Congress. Yet the dominance of the UPC in the coalition and Prime Minister Obote's anti-traditionalism had produced in the Kabaka and his subjects a mood of disaffection, which was expressed in acts of subversion after Obote terminated the coalition in August 1964. Thereupon the conflict of loyalty erupted in a violent form. In Obote's words, the issue in post-independence Uganda under its federal Constitution was whether a Ugandan nation or its constituent parts should carry the banner of independence.[18] A 'crisis of loyalty' held the young nation in its strangulating grip.

As between the centre and Buganda the crisis was fuelled by the special position accorded to the latter under the so-called federal arrangement. This favouritism manifested itself in three main ways. First, only Buganda among the five federal states had a separate formal constitution scheduled to the national Constitution; separate special provisions were also scheduled for the other federal states, but they were not referred to as 'constitution', the implication being that their status was less than that of a constitution. In point of content, however, there was hardly anything to justify this discrimination in nomenclature. Both the Constitution of Buganda and the special provisions for the other federal states provided for a frame of government – the kingship (or constitutional head in Busogo), ministers, legislature, public service, chiefs, etc. And, the provisions followed an almost identical order of arrangement, with a two-part division and corresponding section numbering and headings.

The reason for the discriminatory nomenclature was to be found in the far wider powers reserved to Buganda *vis-à-vis* the other federal states. Contrary to the requirements of true federalism, the division of powers under the Constitution was not between equal-ranking states on the one hand and the centre on the other. Buganda was treated quite differently from the other federal states in terms of the principle of division; in other words different principles of division were applied between the centre and Buganda, and between the centre and the other federal states, necessitating the use of different schedules for the lists of enumerated matters within the exclusive competences of Buganda and the other federal states.

Within Buganda there were two lists, one exclusive to the Bugandan legislature and the other exclusive to parliament, while the residue belonged to both.[19] And, although parliament enjoyed supremacy within the residual field, any of its enactments that altered or replaced the Buganda Courts Ordinance, Public Lands Ordinance, mailo land tenure system or the local government system could not take effect within Buganda without the consent of the Lukiko. The matters exclusive to the Bugandan legislature were few and, in terms of social control and development, relatively unimportant — the Kabakaship, Bugandan ministers, public service, the Lukiko, public debt, public holidays and festivals, traditional and customary matters, and taxation matters agreed to between Buganda and the centre. The national assembly might add to Buganda's exclusive competence by designating any other matters (other than a matter exclusive to the centre) as being exclusive Bugandan matters on the ground that they were primarily of domestic concern to Buganda. Central exclusive legislative competence, on the other hand, covered the whole area of foreign affairs, defence, internal security, the creation and punishment of offences, administration of justice (other than courts dealing with Bugandan clan cases), currency, banking, taxation and the whole field of finance, medical, health and veterinary services, civil aviation, foreign trade, and trade between Buganda and the rest of the country. Perhaps more significant than the relative unimportance of Buganda's exclusive legislative competence *vis-à-vis* the centre's was the fact that it shared the whole of the residual field with the centre, and in that field lay the power over economic development — roads, agriculture, industries, etc. Executive power followed the legislative, but in addition Buganda's executive authority was specifically extended to the maintenance of public order and public safety within the Kingdom.[20] Finally, Buganda was granted special financial relations with the centre, which imposed upon the latter an obligation not only to contribute 50 per cent of Buganda's general revenue but also to assign to Buganda 50 per cent of certain revenue raised in Buganda (mainly petrol and diesel duty and stamp duty on mailo transfers), with guaranteed minimum yield.[21]

In contrast to the extensive powers and ample financial provisions granted to Buganda, the powers reserved to the other federal states justified neither that name ('federal states') nor the impressive paraphernalia of government created for them — ministers, legislature, public service, etc. They had authority (legislative as well as executive) only over the office of ruler, state public holidays and festivals, and traditional and customary matters.[22] For the rest their powers depended either upon agreement with the centre or delegation from it. They possessed no independent concurrent power with the centre over the vast residue of matter left over from the utterly scanty allocation to them. Federalism presupposes that the centre and the regions should, in terms of powers, stand to each other in some relation, not necessarily of equality, but at least of meaningful independence resting upon a balanced division of powers and resources. Each must have powers and resources sufficient to support the structure of functioning government able to stand on its own against the other. As between the centre and the federal states (other than Buganda) the system was clearly not federal. And, since federal relationship could not meaningfully exist between the centre and a single region, the façade of a federal structure was resorted to in order to enable Buganda to govern itself free of central interference. Buganda's overwhelming power *vis-à-vis* the other federal states must have contributed in large measure to its arrogance.

The third element in Buganda's favoured position was that the national assembly members from Buganda (twenty-one) were elected, not directly to represent individual constituencies, as was the case in the rest of the country, but by the Lukiko, only provided that the latter contained at least sixty-eight directly elected members at the time of the national elections.[23] (With the exception of the ministers, not exceeding six, and four members appointed by the Kabaka, only directly elected members of the Lukiko could vote or otherwise take part in any proceedings connected with the election.) Separate provisions were annexed to the national Constitution in a separate schedule (Schedule 6) to regulate the conduct of the election by the Lukiko. As might be expected, this indirect method of election greatly enhanced the influence of the Kabaka and his government at the centre, as the attitude of the Lukiko as well as of the twenty-one Baganda members seemed to indicate that the latter were regarded as mere delegates, and often themselves behaved as though they were such. In truth, although they were not delegates of the Lukiko, they were equally not representatives of individual constituencies with separate interests; they represented the Kingdom. This accounted for the united Bugandan front which they championed in the national assembly.

In Uganda, therefore, federalism posed a threat of disintegration of the state, and its abolition was considered an imperative step if Uganda was to survive as a single, stable and prosperous country.[24] The desired abolition could not be brought about by constitutional means, as in Ghana. For a two-thirds majority in the national assembly was necessary, and in addition the consent (given by a two-thirds majority) of the legislative assembly of Buganda and each of the other federal states had to be obtained before the federal and other vital provisions of the Constitution could be altered.[25] Obote was not, as Nkrumah was, in the fortunate position of controlling overwhelming majorities in both the national assembly and the regional ones. (Actually, the Constitution could have been constitutionally abolished by a simple majority in the national assembly, since only a simple majority was required for the alteration of Section 3 of the Independence Order in Council which established the Constitution.[26] Yet, considering the adverse vote against Obote in February 1966, even a simple majority might have been difficult to muster for this purpose.) In the circumstances a coup seemed the only alternative. Accordingly on February 22, 1966, Obote unilaterally abrogated the Constitution.

But he did not immediatly abolish the Kingdoms and the federal structure built upon them. The Kingdoms were preserved, and with them the powers, dignities, status and privileges of their rulers.[27] A revolutionary Constitution, promulgated on April 15, again preserved the kingdoms, and the federal structure though radically modified in relation to Buganda. Each of the other federal states was not treated alike with Buganda in terms not only of powers but also of the use of the word 'constitution' to refer to the scheduled provisions that constituted a frame of government for them. Buganda was stripped of the wider powers and financial resources it had enjoyed under the 1962 Constitution. There was now only one legislative list for all the federal states (including Buganda), which was the same in content as the scanty allocation made to the federal states (other than Buganda) in 1962 (Sixth Schedule). Although this Schedule described matters enumerated there as exclusive to the states, the main text of the Constitution did not exclude the centre therefrom, and it was provided that a law made by parliament should override a state law in the event of inconsistency between them.[28] In any case, even assuming these matters to be exclusive to the states, their utter insignificance made the arrangement more unitary than federal. The indirect election by the Lukiko of the national assembly members from Buganda was also abolished. Obote was of course only biding his time. The following year (1967) he took the final step in the dismantling process. By the Constitution of that year, the Kingdoms were altogether abolished,[29] and what was left of the federal features of the Independence Constitution was erased. Thus Uganda emerged as a full-fledged unitary state.[30]

The conversion of the state in Kenya from a federal to a unitary one was more a part of the centralising design of presidentialism than anything else. There was certainly less justification for it in Kenya than in Uganda or in Ghana. Kenya's land area is more than double that of Ghana (224,900 square miles as against 92,000 square miles), and its population about half as large again (an estimated 12 million as against

7.1 million). Like Ghana and Uganda, it has wide ethnic diversity, but this is not complicated by the existence of powerful chiefdoms or kingdoms exercising a strong hold upon the loyalty of their subjects, as did the Asantehene in Ashanti and the Kabaka in Buganda. Chiefs in Kenya are indeed only minor administrative officials deriving whatever power they have from their appointment by the government, and not from customary law.

The main charge against *majimbo* (i.e. the regional scheme of the Independence Constitution) was that the functions devolved upon the regions and the fixed share of national revenue assigned to them had no proper regard to their ability to discharge those functions. The division of powers between the centre and the regions under the Constitution followed upon the familiar scheme of enumerated and residual powers but it had also some unusual and complicating features. For purposes of legislation, there were two lists of subjects, one exclusive to the regions, and the other concurrent to both the regions and the centre; the residue belonged to the centre.[31] The matters that were exclusive to the regions were largely of purely local concern – for example, primary, intermediate and secondary education (including technical and trade schools) other than certain specified institutions, aspects of agriculture, housing, community development, markets and fairs, common minerals, pawnbrokers, second-hand dealers and moneylenders, places of public entertainment or recreation, wash-houses and laundries, barbers and hairdressers, public lavatories, refuse and effluent disposal, etc. The concurrent list included matters of greater importance to development and nation-building-aspects of education: co-operative societies, economic development (but not light, heat, power or transport), land settlement, medical research and training, national plans for social development, public health, public safety and public order (but not immigration, emigration, deportation, extradition or fugitive offenders), etc. The exclusiveness of regional competence in respect of any matters at all was, of course, subject to the power of the centre to make laws on all matters during an emergency to an extent appearing to parliament to be necessary or expedient for maintaining or securing peace, order and good government, and to its power to make laws on any matter whatever for a region subverting the central government.[32]

The division of executive power, however, departed from the general rule of making executive power follow the legislative, i.e. of enabling each governmental unit to execute its own laws. The executive authority of the regions was made exclusive of the centre in respect of both matters on the exclusive and concurrent legislative lists.[33] In other words, a law made by the central parliament on a concurrent matter was to be executed not by the central executive, but by the regional executives (except in the area of Nairobi, the capital, which came under exclusive central authority in all fields). Further, there was a third list of matters outside exclusive or concurrent regional legislative competence but to which the executive authority of the regions was nevertheless extended to the exclusion of the centre. The list included, for example, town and country planning, rent control, probation services, registration of births, deaths and marriages, children and young persons, adulteration of food, etc.

But then came the feature that complicated the scheme, for superimposed on the above formula of division and overriding it were certain 'special provisions relating to legislative and executive powers of the centre and the regions'.[34] In these provisions certain aspects of matters otherwise exclusive to the regions, or concurrent to both the centre and the regions or exclusive to the centre as being residual, were singled out and redistributed differently, the effect of which was sometimes to diminish and sometimes to increase the powers of the regions. Thus, although economic development, co-operative societies, civil aerodromes, marketing of agricultural produce, antiquities and museums were on the concurrent list, and should therefore have come under exclusive regional executive authority, central executive authority was extended to them under these special provisions, thereby making regional and central executive authority concurrent in respect thereof. The question of standards at all levels of education was detached from primary, intermediate and secondary education otherwise within exclusive regional competence, and it was provided that parliament might, and a regional assembly might not, make laws with respect thereto, and also with respect to terms of service of teachers at any level of education; and the executive authority of the centre was extended to terms of service of teachers (exclusively), to public examinations and the maintenance of educational standards at any level of education (concurrent). This kind of arrangement (which was also applied to other areas, e.g., agricultural and veterinary education up to the diploma level, ordinarily exclusive to the regions) whereby one authority controlled education at a certain level, and another determined standards at that level must have been a source of confusion and friction, although the intention, which was to maintain uniformity throughout the country, was unquestionably desirable. The attendant confusion might have contributed to the blurring of the lines of responsibility between the centre and the regions.

The aspects of the 'special provisions' that increased the powers of the regions were those aimed at securing consultation and co-operation between them and the centre — as, for example, the establishment of a central land settlement board and a central agricultural board containing regional representatives, the function of the latter board being to advise the centre and the regions on questions relating to agriculture that were of common concern.

The machinery for the government of the region was hardly well-suited to an effective discharge of its vast functions. Government was by committees of the regional legislative assembly, and not through ministers exercising individual responsibility over specific subjects or departments. The committee in whom the executive authority was vested was a Finance and Establishments Committee, but its actual responsibility was limited to finance and establishments.[35] The regional assembly was required to establish other committees to deal with its other executive functions.[36] Lacking the initiative, drive and sense of purpose of an individual, the committees, it was alleged, proved incapable of living up to the demands and challenges of development in the regions. People in the regions and even the regional assemblies themselves began then to look to the central government to provide the services which were the responsibility of the regional executive but which they were incapable of providing. Since, however, the functions lay outside its competence, the central government was itself powerless to do anything. The result was that nothing got done; in industry, agriculture and elsewhere, development was held up. No one could be saddled with responsibility for this failure: the central government disclaimed responsibility on the ground that the functions belonged to the regional authorities, while in the regions responsibility for executive government was diffused in various committees that no one could be held accountable for anything.

The central government further claimed that co-operation between the centre and the regions was made difficult because of the obstructionist attitude and tribal bigotry of some presidents of regional assemblies and chairmen of regional committees; this made it impossible for the centre and the regions controlled by such presidents and chairmen to collaborate in development efforts. Development projects requiring the joint enterprise of the centre and the regions were thus frustrated by the unco-operative action of regional authorities, by their refusal to give the approvals necessary for the implementation of projects and by their insistence on prior consultation with them before any development scheme, however beneficial, could be initiated.[37]

Now that the regional governments had proved incapable of discharging their functions under the Constitution, the central government argued that the assumption on which a sizeable portion of the nation's revenue was assigned to the regions had been falsified, and that it was undesirable to continue to hold back from the central government valuable funds that would otherwise have been available for vital development projects.

This was the crux of the central government's case against *majimbo*. It was, however, strenuously denied by the protagonists of *majimbo*. They argued that it was the central government's policy of deliberate strangulation that incapacitated the regions from effectively discharging their constitutional functions. They claimed, first, that the region's constitutional share of revenue was not in fact made available to them but was sat upon by the central treasury whose administrative practice was used to block the release of the money. And without the money flowing from the centre to the regions as the constitution envisaged, the regional governments could not develop their regions. In the view of the regional authorities therefore it was disingenuous for the central government to charge them with inability to discharge their functions when it was its own action that was responsible for that state of affairs. It was a case of giving a dog a bad name in order to hang it. Had the central government 'allowed the constitutional funds to flow to the regions', argued the opposition leader, Mr Ngala, in October 1964, 'then we would be in a position to carry out the various plans that we have in the regions. ... It is, in my opinion, the Government which is at fault, because the Government has not given the money to the regions. It has withheld the money, sat on the money, and the money has not been issued. If I told any hon. Member to go to Mombasa, and yet refuse to give him money to buy petrol, he would have to go on foot, which would take him about six months. ... The same thing applies to these regions. If the Government sits on the money, how can they expect development to take place in the regions?'[38] The central government's denial of this charge seemed somewhat feeble, and consisted of a mere assertion by the minister for finance that it was not true that he had been sitting on the money, and that he knew of 'regions who have presented their budgets with deficits and which the Central Government according to the Constitution as it now stands could not possibly support. We have no power and therefore we have to leave these regions to themselves to try and find the money necessary. In many cases today the story is upsetting, that the money is not being collected'.[39] It is not clear to what class of revenue the allegation of a lapse in collection related. Under the Constitution each region had an independent power to levy income, poll and entertainment tax on persons resident in the region, and also to levy rates on land or buildings and royalties on *common* minerals extracted in the region.[40] But the constitutional revenue to which the regions were entitled from the central government related to the whole or a fixed proportion of revenue from excise, sale or purchase tax and import duty, and from motor licences and mineral royalties.[41] If the alleged lapse in collection referred to the constitutional revenue, then the responsibility for it must clearly be laid on the central government, since the Constitution contemplated it as the collecting authority.

There was yet another way in which the central government tried to stifle the regional governments. This was through its control of the public service. The Constitution had established one public service for the whole country under one public service commission though both the centre and the regions had power to determine their respective establishments. However, coming into existence only six months before independence in December 1963, the regions in Kenya, unlike those in Nigeria, for example, had not had the opportunity to build up their own establishment under British supervision, and had therefore to rely on officers seconded from the central government for the initial nucleus of civil servants needed to launch them into operation. For the central government, this was an opportunity to demonstrate in a practical and effective way its opposition to *majimbo*. A seconded officer owes his first loyalty to the seconding government, who after all holds the power of recall, transfer and dismissal. This power was exploited by the central government to undermine the authority and activity of the regional governments. Ministers of the central government often by-passed the presidents of the regional assemblies to give directives direct to civil servants in the regions.[42]

It is clear therefore that the abolition of *majimbo* would be very much in the forefront of the central government's plan for a presidential republican constitution. But the abolition could not be accomplished in one sweep, since certain aspects of regionalism were specially entrenched, requiring for their amendment a three-fourths majority in the house of representatives and nine-tenths in the senate. At the material time (October 1964) the government's strength in both houses was up to the three-fourths majority required for ordinary amendment, but it fell short of nine-tenths in the senate, which therefore put the specially entrenched provisions beyond its power to repeal. The aspects of regionalism that were specially entrenched were the provisions establishing the regions, their organs and their legislative and financial procedures. Also specially entrenched was the formal principle of division of powers in the body of the Constitution but curiously enough neither the lists in Schedule 1 which enumerated the matters to which the power extended, nor 'the special provisions relating to legislative and executive powers' with their supporting schedule (Schedule 2), nor the financial relations between the centre and the regions were specially entrenched. This provided the central government with the loophole it needed. Taking advantage of this, it abolished the obnoxious 'special provisions' with their schedule, the financial apportionment provisions and the lists in Schedule 1. A new list was substituted, which limited regional legislative and executive competence to only 'those matters which, under the specially entrench- ed provisions of this Constitution, may be provided for by a law made by a Regional Assembly', and any other 'matter which, under any provision of this Constitution . . . may be provided for by a law made by a Regional Assembly'.[43] The resulting position was something of a farce. The text of the Constitution itself still instituted a formal federal structure with all the characteristics of true federalism – exclusive regional and central powers and concurrent power. But the regional power in both its exclusive and concurrent aspects had been practically emptied of any content. The structure had been stripped bare, leaving only the skeleton framework. The only matters which, under the specially entrenched provisions, might be provided for by a law made by a regional assembly were regional appropriation, trust land, compulsory acquisition of land for regional purposes, control over transactions in agricultural land, and alteration of regional boundaries. And there were scarcely any other matters of substance affecting a power of government, which 'under any provisions of the Constitution . . . might be provided for by a law made by a Regional Assembly'. This was particularly so because of the excision of local government from the Constitution. The executive functions of the regional authority in relation to the police were also abolished, as was the greater part of the revenue apportionment provisions.

On November 10, 1964, occurred a momentous development in the politics of Kenya. The opposition Kenya African Democratic Party (KADU) dissolved itself and joined the government party, thus making the country a *de facto* one-party state and so removing the obstacle that earlier in October had stood in the way of the central government with regard to the specially entrenched provisions. A second amendment passed later that month (November) renamed the president of a regional assembly 'chairman', abolished separate regional establishments, the financial procedures of regional assemblies, the remaining parts of the revenue apportionment procedure, and regional power in relation to the alteration of regional boundaries.[44]

The process of dismantling was carried much further in 1965.[45] The framework of division of powers, already stripped bare of substance, was itself abolished in both the legislative and executive fields. The legislative power of the centre was now extended to all matters, so that its power was concurrent with that of a regional assembly (now renamed provincial council) in respect of the few and insignificant matters within provincial legislative competence. It was provided that, 'subject to the provisions of this Constitution, a Provincial Council shall have power to make laws for the Province or any part thereof with respect to such matters as may be specified in this Constitution and such further matters as may be specified by Act of Parliament', and that 'an Act of Parliament conferring power on a Provincial Council to make laws may be general or specific, may be given for an indefinite period or for a specific period and may be subject to such conditions or restrictions as may be specified in the Act'. As in fact almost no legislative powers were left to the provinces in the Constitution, it followed that whatever power they had to make law derived from delegation by the centre. The President was given power for six months (i.e. from June to December 1965) to repeal any law made by a regional assembly before December 12, 1964, if it appeared to him necessary or expedient to do so in consequence of these amendments. Subject to this, all existing laws made by a regional assembly before December 12, 1964, should from that date have effect as if they had been made by parliament but with their operation restricted to the respective provinces for which they were made. The changes in the executive field were more drastic, as the separate regional executive authority was completely abolished. The regions (or rather provinces) still, of course, remained formally established in the Constitution, but, there being no longer a separate regional finance or establishments, their principal executive organ, the Finance and Establishment Committee, was now renamed a General Purposes Committee. With these changes in the regional structure disappeared the *raison d'être* for the senate, which was then abolished in 1967.[46] The continued existence of the provinces in the Constitution was now largely nominal; they had become 'at best a glorified system of local government'.[47] In 1968 this nominal existence was finally abolished by the Constitution of Kenya (Amendment) Act, which repealed the provisions establishing the provinces, their organs and functions, and all other other provisions relating or referring to the provinces; all laws made by the provincial councils or the former regional assemblies, other than those which by virtue of the 1965 amendment have effect as if they had been made by parliament, were repealed. It is necessary to explain that what was abolished was the existence of the provinces as entities under the Constitution; they remain as part of the ordinary law of Kenya for purely local government and administrative purposes.

An East African Federation was announced on June 5, 1963, by the leaders of Kenya, Tanganyika and Uganda. It was to be inaugurated by the end of that year, and a working party was appointed to prepare a draft constitution to be submitted to the leaders for discussion in August. As it happened, the federation never materialised, in spite of favourable centripetal circumstances at the time — 'a customs union, a common currency, tariff, and income tax system; such common services as railways and harbours, airways, ports and telegraphs, and research; and an arrangement for fiscal redistribution which attempts to compensate for the unequal effects of the custom union. Capital goods and labour move with considerable freedom throughout the area.'[48] As in Uganda and Kenya, political interests were largely responsible for its failure. The economic advantages of federation were never in doubt, and were generally acknowledged. But, as Donald Rothschild has said, 'just as men can want peace and go to war, they can want the advantages of federation while opposing every progressive step to this end'.[49] No doubt, the advantages would have been unequal between the three states, yet 'the crucial issue for a country to determine is whether its national interest is served by an inter-territorial arrangement, not whether some other partner benefits more'.[50]

The political interests involved were personal, tribal and national. There was the personal interest in retaining cherished positions within the governmental structure of each state, the fear of being reduced to 'nonentities'[51] through the loss of those positions, and the headship of the new federal state. As always, the role of personal interest in such matters is difficult to assess, but it is ever present in the background, intruding from time to time to condition the attitude of the actors. It unquestionably had much to do with Uganda's opposition. While the Tanganyikan and Kenyan leaders might have been unaffected by it in June 1963, Kenyan independence in December of that year appeared to have fostered a personal stake in newly-acquired positions among some of her leaders, which undermined their initial enthusiasm and support for federation. Some testimony to this was provided by Kenyatta's opposition to a motion in the Kenyan house of representatives calling upon the government to present instruments of federation for ratification by August 15, 1964 — the motion was carried against the government — as well as his failure to support, as did Nyerere,[52] the initiative of a meeting of the backbenchers of the Kenya and Tanzania parliaments which had adopted a resolution urging an immediate federation and followed it up with delegations to the three heads of government.

Opposition by tribal interest came mainly from Buganda, prompted by a concern that federation might spell the loss of its individuality and powers. When it withdrew from a position of outright rejection of federation, it was only to demand a place for itself as a constituent unit, or alternatively that whatever powers should be surrendered to the federation should not affect its own powers under the Ugandan Constitution but should come from those of the Ugandan government. In Kenya, the opposition Kenya African Democratic Union (KADU) had similarly demanded that the regions, rather than Kenya as an entity, should be made constituent units, but KADU appeared willing to compromise if the attainment of federation would thereby be facilitated.

Buganda's opposition and demands were a factor in the Ugandan government's attitude towards federation. Whatever his personal position might have been, Obote was unwilling to risk the break-up of his coalition government, in which Buganda's Kabaka Yekka (KY) was a partner. In any case, without Buganda's co-operation, he lacked the necessary majority for the amendments to the Uganda Constitution which federation would have entailed. However, quite apart from the Buganda problem, the Ugandan government had serious reservations of its own as to whether federation was feasible at that time. Its reservations stemmed from its apprehension about Uganda's position as the smallest of the federating states. It therefore demanded 'the location of the federal capital in their country, the right of secession from the proposed federation, the authority to conduct their own foreign affairs and to control their labour unions, restrictions on freedom of movement within the federation, continuance of territorial (as opposed to East African) citizenship',[53] the creation of a strong senate in which the states will be equally represented, and a weak central government with the minimum alteration in existing state constitutions. These demands represented a big gulf on fundamentals between Uganda on the one hand and her partners on the other. There were of course other points of divergence relating, for example, to distribution of revenue, location of industries, etc., but these did not touch upon fundamentals.[54]

2. *The Central Government in Relation to Functions of Local Government*

Power of local government is not a qualification upon the constitutional powers of the central government in a unitary state. Subject only to the constitution, the authority of the central government is entire and undivided over the whole country and over its constituent local units. How it chooses to exercise its sovereign power in the local communities is a matter of practical administration resting upon considerations of expediency and efficiency, and in no way affects the nature or status of the central government itself. It may choose to exercise the *entirety* of its power directly in each local community. There is nothing improper or 'unconstitutional' about the direct administration of the local communities by the central government. It was indeed the method of French colonial administration. And the British too, enamoured as they were of the indirect method, had sometimes used the direct method in the early period of their administration of some fragmentary societies in Africa with no executive chiefs, such as those of the east of Nigeria before 1925. The district officer representing the central government was the local authority in place of the absent chief. In the context of a modern, independent African state, direct administration would clearly be out of tune with the current of thought. Democracy was an essential element in the nationalist protest against colonial rule. It was the central principle upon which the struggle was fought and won, and it would have been a betrayal of that principle to have refused after independence to apply it in the administration of the local communities. Participatory democracy in both national and local government is thus a principle to which even the presidential regimes in Commonwealth Africa subscribe, in spite of their predilection for centralised power. And participatory democracy at the local level demands that the local people should participate in making decisions affecting their own life and welfare. Local self-government has the advantage that it enables such decisions to be taken by persons whose close touch with conditions in the local community enables them to understand better the needs of the people.

Granted that power of local government has to be devolved upon local bodies, how much of it has in fact been so delegated in the presidential regimes of Commonwealth Africa and what degree of local autonomy is allowed? The British colonial administration in Africa was, as has been noted, unitary and centralised in structure, but it also allowed considerable decentralisation. Indeed, the native authorities might quite properly be described as the main support of the colonial administrative structure. Over a wide range of matters which included law and order, education, health, agriculture, town and country planning, etc., they were permitted to exercise both subordinate legislative and executive powers. They also administered justice among the local population as part of their function for law and order. The control of the central government was however never abandoned; it was effectively maintained through the administrative officers stationed in the provinces and districts, who supervised the native authorities, often themselves initiating and executing some of the functions of local government.

It was not to be expected that this system of local government would be acceptable to the nationalist governments. Their objection to it stemmed from a variety of reasons. The degree of decentralisation permitted by the system was considered excessive. Indeed some of the bigger native authorities were more like regional governments than local authorities. Secondly, native authorities belonged to the *political* arm of government, and it was objectionable that they should be supervised by resident civil servants doubling up as both administrative and political officers. These officers were allowed too much discretion to take administrative and political decisions on the spot, which meant that the capital had only remote control, exercised through the normal civil service procedures with all their restrictive effects. Further, in many of the countries the bulk of the field officers remained British many years after independence, and the phenomenon of British officers continuing to control a vital aspect of the political government of an independent African country was not one that would commend itself to any true nationalist. And, not only were administrative officers performing political functions, but the system also mixed political and judicial functions. Perhaps the greatest source of objection was the position accorded to the chief under the system. The chief was the central figure around whom the system was built. Its object was to put at the chief's disposal the methods and machinery of the modern state in order to make his administration more effective and efficient. This required that the authority and powers of his office under customary law should be recognised and supported. He was to be encouraged to assume and exercise responsibility and leadership. It was for these reasons that the system was abolished and replaced by a conciliar system, with elected councillors exercising political powers of local government on behalf of the people of the district or province. Their powers are smaller than those of the native authorities, and they enjoy less autonomy than the latter. They come under the responsibility of a minister for local government, and are supervised by him through ministry officials acting in his name and by his authority.

The abolition of the native authority system did not mean the end of chiefly authority in the local communities, for the office of chief is one that exists independently of the statutes of the central government. What was to be the relation of the central government to this source of power within the state became a matter of considerable concern, especially to the presidential regimes.

3. *The Central Government and Chiefly Power*

It is easy to see why the power of the chief should be a matter of concern to the government. The combination of traditional and statutory functions under the native authority system of local administration had so bolstered up the chief's position as to have made him a rival source of power and influence within the state, competing with the central government for the loyalty of the people, and in some places even displacing it. What was more, some of the more powerful chiefs, like the Asantehene of Ashanti in Ghana and the Kabaka of Buganda in Uganda, became the rallying point of opposition politics within their respective chiefdoms or kingdoms, supporting the opposition parties with the moral and spiritual authority of their office and with the vast resources of money at their disposal. There would seem to be some incompatibility between an executive President embodying the power and majesty of the state, and a king or chief commanding vast power within the state became a matter of considerable concern, accords to the President primacy and precedence, whereas by custom the king or chief is both pre-eminent and divine within his domain. This contradiction even found sanction in the Independence Constitution of Uganda, 1962. The President was accorded precedence, but within a kingdom he took second place to the king on traditional occasions.[55] President Kaunda of Zambia was also reported to have placed himself second to the Litunga of Barotseland in a traditional Lozi ceremony.[56] Such a contradiction, with its divisive effect on the loyalty of the people, was intolerable to the more radical leaders like Nkrumah, Nyerere and Obote.

The first line of assault on chiefly power was to exclude the chiefs from the new local government councils. Initially exclusion was partial in some of the countries. In Ghana, for example, the new councils originally comprised both elected and traditional elements with the traditional members in a minority of one to two in local and urban councils, one to three in the district councils, and one to six in the municipal councils, but by 1959 the new upsurge of elective democracy had carried everything in its tide. The chiefs were completely swept away. This is now the position in nearly all the countries, though in Zambia the minister has power to add to the membership of a council by appointment, and a chief may be so appointed.

Next to be attacked was the chief's power under customary law, much of which had survived even after his exclusion from statutory local government. The chief remained very much the focal point of local affairs in the districts and villages. One cannot conceive of the administration of local affairs in terms only of statutory local government. The traditional aspect of life forms an essential aspect of it. And so long as the traditional pattern of life persists, the chief will continue to have vital functions in it. One can no more abolish the chiefly function in traditional life than one can abolish traditional life itself by legislation. His place in traditional life was still one of considerable power and influence such as no government could afford to ignore. Understandably, therefore, the nationalist governments took steps to control this power too. The method used had differed. The most extreme was the abolition of the institution of chieftaincy or kingship. Tanzania adopted this extreme approach in 1963 when it repealed[57] the African Chiefs Ordinance,[58] which had been the source of chiefly authority within any area designated as a chiefdom. By this repeal, the appointment and tenure of all chiefs of chiefdoms became *ipso facto* terminated. A second Act was passed barring any right to compensation for loss of office; no existing judgment for such compensation could be enforced except with the consent of the President and subject to such conditions as he might impose.[59] The background to this later Act was a case in which 919,000 shillings were awarded to a Chagga chief for loss of office.[60] The repeal of the African Chiefs Ordinance did not fully accomplish the object intended, namely the abolition of the institution. It abolished the statutory basis of a chief's authority, but not his functions as they pre-existed in customary law. Another Act, the African Chiefs Act, had therefore to be enacted in 1969. This abolished the traditional or customary law powers and functions of a chief, and prohibited, under heavy penalty, any exercise or attempted exercise thereof by any person; any rule of customary law conferring such powers and functions was declared invalid. Although the abolition applies only to the chief of a chiefdom, he was the only politically important traditional ruler in the country deserving the title chief.

As we have seen, the five kingdoms of Uganda were abolished by the Republican Constitution enacted in 1967 by Milton Obote's government. In spite of its desire to discredit Obote and to carry the support of the Baganda, the military government of General Amin has rejected repeated demands to restore the kingdoms. On this at least, if on nothing else, it shares a common outlook with Obote's government. The abolition of the kingdoms has not, however, affected the office of lesser chiefs. County, divisional and parish chiefs still remain as important arms of government within their respective areas of jurisdiction, exercising functions in regard to the maintenance of law and order and good government. But they are only agents of the government, and are under a duty to implement government policy, to ensure the observance of any by-laws made by the administration, and to obey and execute all lawful orders issued to them by a competent authority.[61]

Recognising the essential place of chiefs in the traditional life of the people, Nkrumah preferred to preserve the institution while at the same time asserting the supremacy of the government over them so as not to allow them to become mini-states within the state, as they might be if their appointment, powers and revenue were to continue to be governed by customary law with the government having no say at all in them. It was considered an affront to the supremacy of the government that any person within the state should be able to accede to such a position of power and influence entirely through the processes of custom and with no power of intervention by the government. The British themselves had not been unmindful of this affront, and had in many cases assumed power to determine who should enjoy the status of a chief, and also power to depose or suspend chiefs. In the Gold Coast, this power was assumed in Ashanti from 1935, and in regard to head or paramount chiefs in the colony area from 1925. Moved by the political involvement of some chiefs on the side of the opposition parties, Nkrumah's government in 1959 extended the requirement of government recognition generally to all classes of chief throughout the country. By the Chiefs (Recognition) Act, 1959, recognition by the government was superimposed upon the customary procedures for the selection and installation of chiefs. The Act does not give the government power to appoint; selection and installation have still to be in accordance with customary law, and the installation is not to take effect so as to enable the person installed to exercise the traditional functions and powers of the chieftaincy until he has been recognised by the government, and the government can take action against anyone purporting to exercise such function without the necessary recognition. A chief is therefore a person who '(*a*) has been nominated, elected and installed as a Chief in accordance with customary law, and (*b*) is recognised as a Chief by the Minister responsible for Local Government'.[62] Recognition, when granted, can be withdrawn whenever the government 'considers it to be in the public interest'.[63] Thus, in the words of William Harvey, 'the legal tool of a modern state has operated so effectively on the institution of chieftaincy that one may accurately say that the chief in Ghana today achieves and retains his office only by the sufferance of the national government'.[64] By the use of this power, 'every pro-NLM chief in Ashanti was removed from office with the exception of the Asantehene who was spared only after he had made a public declaration of support for the "government of the day".'[65] The subordination of the chiefs to the government had been accomplished not only in Ashanti but also throughout the country.

The chiefs' functions under customary law also came under severe government scrutiny and control. The traditional functions that most attracted government control were those described as 'matters of a constitutional nature', namely the election, installation, deposition or abdication of a chief, the right of any person to take part in such procedures, the recovery or delivery of stool property and the political relations between chiefs. Their jurisdiction in these matters was curtailed. No longer was it exclusive or final. Cases involving paramount chiefs could not only be determined by a judicial commissioner, to whom the minister also might refer any case whatsoever, notwithstanding that it was already pending before a traditional council of chiefs. Further, any decision rendered by a council of chiefs on a 'constitutional matter' was made reviewable by a judicial commissioner whose findings might be confirmed, varied or rejected by the President. A traditional council of chiefs had power conferred by statute to make a declaration or modification of customary law. This function was now reduced to that of merely making recommendation to the minister who might approve, reject or amend it on the ground of repugnance to statute, natural justice, equity or good conscience.[66]

The chiefs had been assigned some definite role under the Independence Constitution. That Constitution had guaranteed the office of chiefs, and provided for the establishment, within twelve months of independence, of a house of chiefs for each region, which was to elect the Head of the region (except in the Ashanti Region

where the Asantehene was specifically designated as Head).[67] Either
the national assembly or a minister might refer any matter to the
houses of chiefs for advice and report,[68] but in the case of a bill for the
amendment of the specially entrenched provisions of the constitution
reference to them was mandatory.[69] A bill affecting the traditional
functions or privileges of a chief must be referred to the house of chiefs
of the region in which the chief exercised his function, and could not
be proceeded with further until three months from the date it was first
introduced in the national assembly.[70] The views of the houses of
chiefs on any matter referred to them were, however, not binding on
anyone, their role in such cases being purely advisory. Nkrumah's
government had considered it derogatory that there should be a
mandatory reference of any matter to the houses of chiefs. This was
therefore abolished in 1958 along with other restrictive provisions by
the Constitution (Repeal of Restrictions) Act of that year. The
Republican Constitution of 1960 did away with the guarantee of
chieftaincy; in place of the guarantee the President had merely to declare
at his inauguration that 'chieftaincy in Ghana should be guaranteed and
preserved'.[71]

The main support of chiefly authority and influence in the politics
of modern Ghana was perhaps the vast financial resources of the bigger
chieftaincies. It was this that enabled them to give financial sponsorship
to opposition parties. These resources consisted mostly of revenue from
stool lands and mining and timber concessions. In 1951, as part of the
local government reforms of that year, the collection and management
of revenue from stool lands had been transferred to the new local and
urban councils which had replaced the native authorities as statutory
local authorities. As control by local authorities proved ineffective, the
government took it over itself. The minister of local government was
empowered in his absolute discretion to apportion part of the revenue
from stool property to local authorities and to use the balance to
support the chiefs and their stools as well as any projects beneficial to
the people of the stool. This meant that chiefs no longer had any say in
the application of revenue from their chieftaincies. However, ownership
of chieftaincy property still remained formally vested in the chief as
'trustee' for his stool. This, of course, was of very little practical
significance as a source of chiefly authority and influence. Yet the
chief's formal title of ownership was not without concern to the
government. Accordingly, in Ashanti the ownership of Kumasi town
lands was divested from the Asantehene and vested in the President,
who was also given power to declare any stool land anywhere in the
country to be vested in him if he thought that to be in the public
interest.[72] The considerable use that had been made of his power had
resulted in numerous stool lands now being vested in the government.

Concessions too had been brought under the firm control of the government. Commenting on the effect of all these measures, William Harvey has observed that government control had 'struck directly to the heart of the institution of chieftaincy itself, to the conception of the chief not as a secular leader but as the priest whose ritual functions preserved a desirable relation of the living to the dead and of the human to the divine. Today, his status in Ghana is reduced to that of a stipendiary of the central government, dependent in fact for office on official recognition. . . .'[73]

This also describes quite aptly the position of the chief in Zambia. He too owes his office to government recognition, which the President may withdraw at any time if he thinks it necessary in the interest of peace, order and good government.[74] With the establishment of the elected councils as local authorities in place of the native authorities, his functions are now under customary law. Specific functions may of course be conferred upon him by statute, and in this connection the Chiefs Act requires him to preserve public peace in his area and to take reasonable measures to quell riots and affrays.[75] The President may however strip him of his functions and transfer them to a deputy chief appointed by himself (*i.e.* the President), though his traditional functions can be so transferred only to the extent that such functions may competently be discharged under customary law by a person who is not a chief.[76] There is one interesting respect in which the relations of a chief to the President in Zambia differ from what they were in Ghana. Apart from withdrawal of recognition and removal of a chief from his area of jurisdiction when his presence is considered prejudicial to the maintenance of public order, the President in Zambia possesses no power of deposition. Chiefs in Zambia are associated in national government through the house of chiefs, which is established by the Constitution, not as a second legislative chamber but merely as an advisory body to discuss any matter, including a bill, referred to it or approved by the President.[77] When a matter is referred to it, its resolution thereon, if any, must be laid before the national assembly by the President. The house is entirely an instrument of the President meeting only when called by him and transacting only such business as he authorises.[78]

It is necessary to notice the special position of the Litunga (paramount chief) of Barotseland (now renamed the Western Province). The traditional government of the territory, of which the Litunga is head, has evolved a fairly sophisticated organisation, with a legislative and an executive body, very much like that in the Kingdom of Buganda (Uganda). The territory had special treaty relations with Britain in that the 'constitutional power or authority' of the Litunga as chief was expressly preserved. When Britain assumed full powers of government over Barotseland in 1899 and later merged it with the rest of Northern Rhodesia in one protectorate, the order-in-council which constituted the government of the protectorate enjoined that nothing in the provision conferring power to regulate the conduct of natives 'shall be deemed to limit or affect the exercise by the Chief of the Barotse of his authority in tribal matters'.[79] Other reservations in the concession treaties with the British South Africa Company were also confirmed.[80] The special position thus bestowed on Barotseland was continued by all the successive orders-in-council and other legislation down to the time of independence. Thus, when the first Native Authority Ordinance was enacted in 1929 giving the Governor of Northern Rhodesia power to constitute the chiefs as statutory native authorities for their respective areas, it was expressly provided that the Governor's power to appoint and remove chiefs and to institute an inquiry into disputed succession to chieftainship should not apply to Barotseland. The separateness of Barotseland was pushed a stage further when in 1936 its native administration was established under a completely separate legislation, namely the Barotse Native Authority Ordinance, 1936, and the Barotse Native Courts Ordinance, 1936. Barotse autonomy became a bedevilling issue at the independence negotiations, as the Lozis were not willing to remain in an independent republic of Zambia unless they were guaranteed their autonomy and separateness. The matter was finally resolved in a formal agreement — the Barotseland Agreement, 1964 — concluded between Dr Kenneth Kaunda on behalf of the Government of Northern Rhodesia of the one part and the Litunga, council, chiefs and people of Barotseland of the other part. It was signed by the British Secretary of State for Commonwealth Relations and Colonies to signify the approval of the British Government. The Agreement was meant to take the place of the earlier treaties with the British and to preserve to Barotseland the special position it had enjoyed under the British. It was the price for Barotseland coming into the new republic, and thereby enabling the country to emerge into independent statehood as one united nation.

The Agreement in Paragraph 2 stipulated that 'the Constitution of the Republic of Zambia shall include the provisions agreed upon for inclusion therein at the constitutional conference held in London in May 1964 relating to (a) the protection of human rights and fundamental freedoms of the individual; (b) the judiciary; and (c) the public services, and these provisions shall have full force and effect in Barotseland'. Paragraph 3 imposed an obligation not to discriminate against the people of Barotseland as regards rights of access to the courts of Zambia, and stipulated for regular circuit sessions in Barotseland by judges of the High Court. By Paragraph 4 recognition was to be accorded to 'the person who is for the time being the Litunga of Barotseland under customary law'; and 'the Litunga of Barotseland, acting after consultation with his council as constituted for the time being under the customary law of Barotseland shall be the principal local authority for the government and administration of Barotseland', and 'shall be authorised and empowered to make laws for Barotseland' in relation to certain enumerated matters. Paragraph 5 preserved the powers of the Litunga in land matters under customary law, and the land jurisdiction of Barotse statutory native courts. Paragraph 7 imposed upon the government an obligation to treat Barotseland alike with other parts of Zambia in the provision of financial support for administration and economic development. And by Paragraph 8 the government undertook to 'take such steps as may be necessary to ensure that laws for the time being in force in the Republic are not inconsistent with the provisions of this agreement'. By Paragraph 9 the government might and, if so requested by the Litunga, shall refer to the High Court any question concerning the interpretation of the Agreement.

Addressing the Litunga, Sir Mwanawina Lewanika, the Royal Family and other members of the Barotse Government on August 6, 1964, Dr Kenneth Kaunda, then Prime Minister of Northern Rhodesia, assured them that 'it is the Government's full intention that the Barotseland Agreement will be honoured fully after independence. I believe that the Agreement reached in London was an honourable Agreement from the point of view of both the Central Government and the Barotseland Government. I am very glad that the basis of the Agreement is that Barotseland is an integral part of Zambia, and I can assure you, Sir Mwanawina, and all members of the Barotse Royal Family and of the Barotse Government, that the Goverment has no wish to interfere with the day-to-day running of the internal affairs of Barotseland. This is the responsibility of the Barotse Government and the intention of the Central Government will be no more than to give to the Barotse Government its maximum assistance and co-operation'.[81]

This appeared to be one of those political assurances which it is expedient to make but which are not meant to be honoured, because their implementation would be at variance with vital policies or interests of the government. The Barotseland Agreement had been breached or disregarded in many important respects by the time it was finally abrogated in 1969. Taking, first, the question of recognition of the Litunga. Although the Chiefs Act provides specifically for the recognition of the Litunga, recognition might be withdrawn under the Act if the President, after due inquiry, was satisfied that this was necessary in the interests of peace, order and good government,[82] whereas the Agreement contemplated that the only ground upon which recognition might be withdrawn was if an incumbent Litunga ceased to be entitled to the office under customary law. The stipulation of the Agreement that the Litunga should be 'the principal local authority for the government and administration of Barotseland' would run counter to the prevailing policy of local democracy which has swept through the whole of Africa. Its implementation would have meant continuing in force the Barotse Native Authority Ordinance and the Barotse Native Courts Ordinance. It would have meant having two different systems of local government, one for Barotseland based on the Native Authority Ordinance, and another for the rest of the country based on elected councils.

In the event the government rejected this. The Barotse Native Authority Ordinance and the Barotse Native Court Ordinance were repealed by the Local Government Act 1965,[83] and the Local Courts Act, 1966.[84] Statutory functions of local government in Barotseland, as in other parts of the country, are now the responsibility of elected councils, and the Local Government Act, 1965 provides that its provisions 'shall apply in Barotseland and the powers contained herein may be exercised in relation to Barotseland, notwithstanding anything to the contrary contained in any other written law or in the Barotseland Agreement, 1964'.[85] Like any other chief, the Litunga's functions under customary law are confirmed to him by the Chiefs Act, though only to the extent that the discharge of such functions is not contrary to the constitution or any written law and is not repugnant to natural justice or morality.[86] Under the Act too, he has functions for the preservation of public peace in Barotseland. Yet without his functions and powers under the Barotse Native Authority Ordinance, the Litunga's functions under customary law and his function for the preservation of public peace under the Chiefs Act can hardly be said to satisfy the stipulation of the Agreement that he was to be 'the principal local authority for the government and administration of Barotseland'.

The stipulation that the Litunga 'shall be authorised and empowered to make laws for Barotseland' in respect of certain enumerated matters did not purport to invest him with power to make law on those matters. Unless he already had the power under customary law, the stipulation would seem to have contemplated an implementing legislation authorising and empowering him in that behalf. No such legislation has been passed. A constitutional amendment of 1970 authorises legislation for compulsory acquisition of property for the purpose of its administration or disposition by the President in implementation of a comprehensive land policy or of a policy designed to ensure that the statute law, the common law and the doctrines of equity relating to or affecting the interests in or rights over land or any other interests or rights enjoyed by chiefs shall apply with substantial uniformity throughout Zambia.[87] This was obviously aimed against the Litunga's special land powers in Barotseland. His mineral rights in certain lands reserved under the agreement with the British South Africa Company were divested in 1970 and transferred to the state.[88]

The Agreement itself was abrogated in its entirety in 1969 by a constitutional amendment,[89] which provided that the 'Barotseland Agreement, 1964 shall cease to have effect and all rights (whether vested or otherwise), liabilities and obligations thereunder shall lapse'. It was necessary to adopt the procedure of a constitutional amendment in abrogating the Agreement, because the Agreement was recognised by the Independence Order, 1964. The Independence Order provided that:

> All rights, liabilities and obligations of –
> (a) Her Majesty in respect of the Government of Northern Rhodesia; and
> (b) the Governor of Northern Rhodesia or the holder of any other office under the crown in respect of the Government of Northern Rhodesia on behalf of that Government,
> shall, from the commencement of this Order, be rights, liabilities and obligations of the President on behalf of the Government of Zambia and, subject to the provisions of any law, shall be enforceable by or against the President accordingly.[90]

The confirmation of the obligations arising under the Agreement by the Independence Order did not give them the character of constitutional limitations on the legislative power of parliament. The Agreement was an ordinary contract,[91] and not an engagement between two sovereign governments, since on May 18, 1964, when it was signed, the Government of Northern Rhodesia had full powers of internal government in Barotseland, subject to the ultimate authority of Britain. The confirmation of the government's obligation arising under the Agreement did not change its legal character. It remained a contract. As such it could not affect the legal relations of persons who were not parties to it. It could neither confer rights nor impose duties upon them. More important, it was subject to the sovereign power in the state. A contract to which the state is a party cannot operate to limit or fetter its sovereign power of government. However morally reprehensible this may be, it can always legislate to annul its obligations under the contract.[92] An act of the parliament of Zambia alleged to be inconsistent with any of the obligations of the Agreement could not therefore be invalid on that ground, whether it was enacted as a constitutional amendment or not.

The object of confirming the Agreement in the Independence Order was merely to enable its obligations to be transferred from the Queen to the President. This conclusion would still hold even if the Agreement were to be regarded as a public engagement, for, so regarded, it would be subject to both the prerogative power of act of state and the sovereign power of the new Republic of Zambia. The prerogative power of an act of state derives its sanction from the common law. When the Queen ceased to be the monarch of Northern Rhodesia, some at least of her prerogatives, including that of an act of state, enured to the President. For it is provided that 'where under any law in force in Northern Rhodesia immediately before the commencement of this Order any prerogatives or privileges are vested in Her Majesty those prerogatives or privileges shall, from the commencement of this Order, vest in the President'.[93] The legality of any violation by the Queen of treaty obligations under the prerogatives has been held to be beyond question by the courts.[94]

In 1970 Barotseland was renamed Western Province by a further amendment to the Constitution.[95] Provisions in the Constitution relating specially to Barotseland, such as the provision that the chiefs representing the province in the house of chiefs should be appointed by the Litunga and Council, were expunged.

The office of chief in Malawi has become entirely a government post. It is established by statute,[96] and the incumbent is appointed by the President, though an appointee must be a person who is entitled to hold the office under customary law and who has the support of the majority of the people of the chieftaincy.[97] The President may also remove a chief if, after due enquiry, he is satisfied that the person has ceased to be entitled under customary law to the office, or has lost the confidence of the majority of the people in his area, or that the removal is necessary in the interests of peace, order and good government.[98] When a chief is removed or suspended, the President may order him removed from any specified area if he (the President) is satisfied that his presence would be prejudicial to the maintenance of public order.[99] The functions of a chief are (a) to preserve the public peace; (b) to carry out the traditional functions of his office under customary law in so far as the discharge of such functions is not contrary to the Constitution or any written law and is not repugnant to natural justice or morality; (c) to assist in the collection of taxes; (d) to assist in the general administration of his district in accordance with the directions of the district commissioner.[100] These functions pertain to a chief or sub-chief. A paramount chief has only such functions as the President may specify in the instrument of appointment.[101]

REFERENCES

1. Arthur Lewis, *Politics in West Africa* (1965), p. 55.
2. Kwame Nkrumah, *Africa Must Unite* (1963), pp. 59–60.
3. *loc. cit.*
4. Kwame Nkrumah, *Africa Must Unite* (1965), p. 62.

5. S.64(1).

6. S.64(2).

7. S.64(1).

8. S.85.

9. S.32.

10. W. B. Harvey, *Law and Social Change in Ghana* (1966), pp. 134–50.

11. Kwame Nkrumah, *Africa Must Unite* (1963), pp. 60–1.

12. *ibid.*, pp. 63–4.

13. *ibid.*, pp. 66–71; Harvey, *op. cit.*, pp. 139–41; Dennis Austin, *Politics in Ghana, 1946–60* (1964).

14. Constitution (Repeal of Restrictions) Act, 1958.

15. Constitution (Amendment) Act, 1959.

16. Art. 4(1).

17. See the constitutions of the Federal States in Schedules 1, 2, 3, 4 and 5 of the Constitution, 1962.

18. Milton Obote, Uganda National Assembly Debate, 22 June, 1967, p. 301.

19. S.74 and 7th Schedule.

20. S.77.

21. S.107 and 9th Schedule.

22. S.75 and 8th Schedule.

23. S.43.

24. Obote. Nat. Ass. Deb. 22 June, 1967, p. 301.

25. S.5. See further, ch. 1, XIV below.

26. S.30 Uganda (Independence) Order in Council, 1962.

27. Declaration by the Government, Feb. 24 1966, reproduced as Schedule 9 to the 1966 Constitution.

28. SS.74–6.

29. S.118, Constitution 1967.

30. SS.63 and 65, *ibid.*

31. SS.66, 102 and Schedule 1.

32. SS.69, 70, and 106.

33. SS.72, 74, 106.

34. Ch. VII, S.118, 119 and Second Schedule.

35. S.105, *ibid.*

36. S.113.

37. Kibaki, House of Reps. Deb., 27 Oct., 1964, col. 3975.

38. House of Reps. Deb., October 1964, cols. 3908–13.

39. *ibid.*, col. 3926.

40. S.142, Constitution 1963.

41. SS.137–40, *ibid.*

42. Ngala, House of Reps. Deb., Oct. 27, 1964, col. 3909.

43. Constitution of Kenya (Amendment) Act, 1964.

44. Constitution of Kenya (Amendment) (No. 2) Act, 1964.

45. Constitution of Kenya (Amendment) Act, 1965.

46. Constitution of Kenya (Amendment) (No. 4) Act, 1966 (operative from 1967).

47. Ghai and McAuslan, *Public Law and Policital Change in Kenya* (1970), p. 213.

48. D. Rothchild, 'East African Federation', *Transition* 111 (Jan.–Feb. 1964), p. 38.

49. D. Rothchild, *Toward Unity in Africa: A Study of Federalism in British Africa* (1960), p. 15.

50. D. Rothchild, 'East African Federation', *op. cit*, p. 40.

51. J. Nye, *Pan-Africanism and East African Integration* (1961), p. 188.

52. Nyerere, *Freedom and Unity* (1966), pp. 295–7 (speech welcoming the delegation).

53. D. Rothchild and M. Rogin '*National Unity and Regionalism*' in G. Carter, *Eight African States*, p. 433.

54. D. Rothchild and M. Rogin, *op. cit.* For more details as well as for the influence of pan-Africanist arguments, see J. Nye, *op. cit.*, pp. 183–210. On the history of the federation movement, see Rothchild, *Toward Unity in Africa* (1960).

55. S.123.

56. *Times of Zambia*, 27 August, 1969.

57. African Chiefs Ordinance (Repeal) Act, 1963.

58. Cap. 331.

59. Chiefs (Abolition of Office: Consequential Provisions) Act, 1963.

60. *Marealle* v. *Kilimanjaro District Council*, High Court at Arusha, Civil Case No. 44 of 1961.

61. The Local Administration Act, 1967, SS.39–44.

62. Chieftaincy Act, 1961, S.1(1).

63. S.1(2)(*b*), Act of 1961.

64. W. B. Harvey, *Law and Social Change in Ghana* (1960), p. 87.

65. Dennis Austin, *Politics in Ghana 1946–60* (1964), p. 378.

66. See Harvey, *op. cit.*, pp. 94–104, for details.

67. S.63(2).

68. S.67.

69. S.32(2).

70. S.35.

71. Article 13(1), Constitution 1960. For the effect of the declaration, see below, Ch. X.

72. Stool Lands Act, 1960, S.27.

73. William Harvey, *op. cit.*, p. 121.

74. Chiefs Act, cap. 479, Laws of Zambia, 1972, SS.3, 4, 8.

75. S.11(1).

76. *ibid.*, S.6.

77. SS.85–96, Constitution 1964

78. House of Chiefs, Rules of Procedure, Sch. IV, Constitution of Zambia.

79. Northern Rhodesia Order-in-Council, 1911, S.44.

80. *ibid.*, S.40.

81. Colin Legum, ed., *Zambia: Independence and Beyond, The Speeches of Kenneth Kaunda* (1966), pp. 98–102.
82. S.4(1).
83. S.115.
84. S.71.
85. S.113. See also S.70. Local Courts Act, 1966.
86. S.10(1) Chiefs Act.
87. Constitution (Amendment) Act, 1970.
88. Mines and Minerals Act, 1969
89. Constitution (Amendment)(No. 5) Act, 1969.
90. S.20(1).
91. Compare the Privy Council in *Re. Southern Rhodesia* [1919] A.C. 211, at pp. 235–6 – per Lord Sumner.
92. Cp. *Burmah Oil Co.* v. *Lord Advocate* [1965] A.C. 75 (H.L.); the War Damage Act, 1965 (Britain).
93. S.18. Independence Order, 1964.
94. *Nyali Ltd* v. *Attorney-General* [1956] 1 Q.B.1; *Sobhuza II* v. *Miller* [1926] A.C. 518.
95. Constitution (Amendment) Act, 1970.
96. Chiefs Act, cap. 22:03 Laws of Malawi, 1969, S.3.
97. *ibid.*, S.4.
98. *ibid.*, S.8.
99. S.15.
100. S.7.
101. S.6.

CHAPTER VII

CENTRALISM IN RELATION TO THE PRESIDENT'S ROLE IN THE ADMINISTRATION OF GOVERNMENT

It is perhaps as well to begin by emphasising that we are here concerned not with the formal constitutional position of the President, but with his *actual* role in the administration of government.

The divergence between practice and the strict letter of the law is perhaps nowhere better exemplified than in the realm of government. By the strict letter of the presidential constitutions of Commonwealth Africa as we have seen, the President is the government. His responsibility for it is entire and undivided. The executive power is vested in him alone, and in the exercise of it he is bound by no one else's advice. With him too lies the ultimate responsibility for policy. Although the constitution contemplates that the President should appoint ministers and consult with them in his administration of the government, he has an unfettered discretion what functions to assign to them. There is no obligation on him to assign specific portfolios or departments to them. He can use them for general duties as ministers without portfolio, while keeping all the departments directly under his control. Whatever functions he assigns to them, he can direct them as he likes as to their exercise. The ministers have no independent authority with regard to such functions; they are merely agents of the President.

With respect also to policy, their role is merely that of adviser, whose advice may or may not be sought, and when it is sought, may be accepted or rejected. When he does assign portfolios to ministers this is not required to be by a formal act. The most that is required – in Uganda (1967), Kenya and Malawi[1] – is that it shall be in writing; in the rest of the countries – Ghana (1960), Tanzania, Zambia, Botswana and Gambia[2] – not even writing is required. The absence of formality is significant. It means that the President can legally move ministers about or re-shuffle the whole government as and when he pleases without being inhibited by any formalities. 'There was a time', comments a *Times of Zambia* editorial, 'when ministers, heads of para-statal bodies and top civil servants lived in constant fear of pending re-shuffles. Indeed the frequency of the re-shuffles was such that at times people were driving to their new destinations only to hear they had again been posted to yet another place'.[3] This cannot but increase the President's power over the ministers. In practice allocation of ministerial responsibilities is published as a notice in the government gazette.

There can be no doubt that the legal structure of power just described manifests a high degree of centralism. But it is equally clear that the same degree of centralism is hardly practicable in the actual administration of government. The President cannot be his own minister for every department of state. Of necessity he must assign responsibility in respect of specific departments to ministers. Nor, within such departments, can he, as a practical matter, direct them with respect to every point of policy or administration.

It will have become apparent from what has been said that the role of the President in the actual administration of government depends largely on three things, viz. the extent of his direct ministerial responsibility, the extent of control or direction which he exercises over the ministers within their respective ministries, and the role of the cabinet in the co-ordination of the activities of the various ministries and in the determination of policy affecting the government as distinct from purely departmental policy which, subject or not to presidential direction, is determined within each ministry by the responsible minister. It is these three factors that condition the actual relations of the President to his ministers. The powers of a minister depend upon the degree of autonomy he enjoys within his ministry, while his standing in relation to the President depends on the extent and nature of the latter's direct ministerial responsibilities and the role allowed to the cabinet. A concentration of direct ministerial responsibilities in the hands of the President, coupled with his specific powers under the constitution and the statutes, will create such an imbalance between him and the ministers as cannot but diminish the status of the latter. Such a concentration is bound to emphasise the ministers' inferiority and subordination to the President.

The role of the President in the administration of government must of course be viewed against the background of the immediate past. In every case presidentialism in Commonwealth Africa was preceded by a period of parliamentary government headed by a Prime Minister, who was the same person as subsequently became President. During this period of parliamentary government, certain administrative practices had been built up, upon which the relationship of the Prime Minister and his ministerial colleagues was patterned'. Did the establishment of the presidential system of government involve a complete change in these practices and in the pattern of relationship? On the whole, it can be said that it did not. It is not reasonably to be expected that a person who had been heading a government as Prime Minister would alter so radically the practices that had governed his relationship with his colleagues, merely because he is now President, more especially when the ministers have remained the same persons as before. This is not to underrate the influence of power. Consciousness of the vastly enhanced power and authority of an executive President *vis-à-vis* that of a Prime Minister may well incline the incumbent to a greater assertiveness and authoritarianism. In practice, with the exception of Ghana, and to a lesser extent Tanzania, the relationship between the President and the ministers has remained substantially as it was before the establishment of the presidential system. Ministers have retained much the same powers and status in relation to the President as they had before. There have, no doubt, been changes in the allocation of ministerial responsibilities, but these by themselves have not resulted in any undue concentration of responsibilities in the hands of the President such as would alter the pre-existing relationship to that of total subordination. The enhancement in the powers of the President has resulted not so much from increased ministerial responsibilities as from powers conferred by statute, much of which had been inherited from the Governor-General who had previously exercised them on the advice of the cabinet or sometimes of the Prime Minister alone.

1. *The President's Ministerial Responsibilities*

It is necessary to state at the outset that when it is said that the President or a minister has responsibility for a particular portfolio, this does not mean that he personally handles every function connected with it. He must necessarily act through others in respect of certain matters. Although the function belongs to him constitutionally, in practice much of it is exercised on his behalf by his civil service advisers, subject to his control or direction. The acts of the civil service experts are presumptively his, for which therefore he must accept political responsibility. The degree of reliance on civil servants varies of course from individual to individual. Policy, although often initiated by civil servants, must usually have ministerial approval before it can be implemented, and the President or minister can, and often does, modify the policy proposals put forward by the civil service experts.

In the allocation of ministerial responsibilities, there are two portfolios that are almost invariably retained by the President, namely central establishment and regional or provincial administration. The importance of these portfolios lies in the fact that they give him overall control over all areas of government activity, especially in the districts.

(i) *Central Establishment*

The public service is the bedrock of the administration, responsible for advising the President and his ministers on policy and for executing those policies. It is therefore upon it that the effectiveness and success of the government depends to a very large extent. The President is the political head of the public service. As Head of State and chief executive he has power to constitute and abolish offices in the public service subject of course to the constitution and other laws.[4] It is however his specific responsibility for establishment that enables him to direct the civil service machinery of government. It is, however, important to emphasise that his power of direction through establishment control is not directed to individual civil servants but rather to civil service policy and administration generally. Normally he does not direct civil servants in their day-to-day work. Within each ministry civil servants are responsible to the minister in charge, and the minister enforces this responsibility through the civil service head of the ministry, the permanent or principal secretary. The President is not supposed, and normally does not, by-pass the minister to give direction directly to civil servants within a ministry. Excepting those employed in his own office or in a ministry or department under his portfolio who are directly responsible to him through the permanent or principal secretary in the President's office, presidential direction of the individual civil servants in their day-to-day work is indirectly through the ministers. But it is he who, through his control of establishments, determines the policy governing the entire civil service and its administration.[5] Every civil servant is bound by his directives in this respect and it is within these directives and general orders that the civil service functions. This is an aspect of the practice of government in Commonwealth Africa that distinguishes it from the parent Whitehall model. For in Whitehall practice it was until recently the Treasury rather than the Prime Minister's office that had responsibility for establishment controls. But it is argued that in a young country, at a transitional stage of political and institutional development, establishment control needs to be backed up with the authority of the Head of Government if it is to be effective. (As a result of the Fulton Report, this appears now to be the position in Britain.) The Treasury in Commonwealth Africa does, however, share with the President part of establishment control; such matters as terms and conditions of service, staff complements and gradings, salaries, and allowances are normally delegated to the Minister of Finance.

The President's function of establishment control is exercised through the Ministry of Establishment, or the Directorate of Personnel as it is called in Kenya, which may be located within the President's office as an integral part thereof, as in Kenya, or may exist as a separate ministry but still under the President. It is headed by a permanent secretary who is responsible, through the permanent secretary in the President's office, to the President himself.

A crucial, and unquestionably the most sensitive, function of establishment control relates to the appointment, promotion, dismissal and disciplinary control of the civil service. It is the ultimate sanction of all establishment control, since a power over a man's means of livelihood operates to render him amenable to the will of the person wielding the power. The policy of the British in handing over power to nationalist governments has been to remove this power from political control and to vest it in an independent commission(s) established directly by the constitution. The object was to ensure that merit rather than political considerations should be the criterion for appointment and promotion, that dismissals and disciplinary control were not to be used as an instrument of political victimisation, and that the political neutrality of the civil service, that cornerstone of the British civil service system, would not be jeopardised. The device was also part of the total scheme of institutional safeguards for political and tribal minorities.

As was to be expected, the arrangement has excited the criticism and resentment of the independent governments. It was considered a serious derogation from the power of the government to govern. The civil service, as has been stated, is the bedrock of the government, providing not only the expert advice on the basis of which policy is determined but also the machinery for the execution of such policy. It seems both logical and fair that government should have power to appoint and dismiss the people who are to advise it and execute its measures. To deny it that power is indeed to cut off perhaps the most critical and decisive part of the executive power vested in it for the government of the nation. If the government is to be able to govern effectively it must be free to choose those who are to work for and with it, and to fire them if they prove incompetent or disloyal. Without a legal power to appoint, 'ministers must – and do – use unconstitutional pressure to get into their offices men with whom they can work'; the government's right of appointment should therefore be legally recognised in order that the law should accord with the facts.[6] The affront was, understandably, felt most keenly in the context of an executive presidency. A President with the executive power of the state, yet lacking power to appoint or dismiss his executive officers, might well be considered a contradiction in terms.

Nor were the nationalist governments easily persuaded by the argument about the need for a politically neutral civil service. This to them is nothing but a 'fiction' which, 'if carried to its logical conclusion, would in fact deprive the civil servant of his basic democratic right to vote. For in casting his vote, he exercises a choice in favour of one political party and thereby demonstrates a bias'.[7] They argued that the need for dedication and loyalty far outweighs any advantages of maintaining the political neutrality of the civil service. And maximum dedication and loyalty in the civil service can only be ensured if civil servants share the government's outlook. For, although their training has conditioned them to be able to subordinate their own personal political views to their duty of loyalty to the government of the day, yet the pull of conscience may occasionally prove so strong as to override the civil servant's sense of loyalty.[8] Enthusiasm in the civil servant's application to his work, said Julius Nyerere of Tanzania, 'is a most important national asset. We cannot afford the luxury of administrators who are neutral'.[9] It is this same concern for loyalty and enthusiasm in the civil service that prompted the statement from President Kaunda: 'When I next appoint a senior civil servant it's because he is a loyal party man. All appointments I will make are going to be political, I am afraid.'[10] Even in Britain the 'neutralism' of the civil service is gradually being eroded by the practice, which seems to have been gaining ground from the 1960s onwards, of a newly-elected government appointing, on an *ad hoc* basis, 'political' civil servants in the role of 'advisers'. This attained quite a substantial scale under the Wilson administration of 1964–70, and continued under Heath.

In any case, Nyerere has further argued, the reason for enforcing political neutrality upon civil servants has no application in a one-party state, where there is no opposition party claiming to be an alternative government. 'Once you begin to think in terms of a single national movement instead of a number of rival factional parties, it becomes absurd to exclude a whole group of the most intelligent and able members of the community from participation in the discussion of policy, simply because they happen to be civil servants.'[11] Nyerere had accordingly abrogated the rules which prohibited civil servants, members of the police and military forces from participating in politics; these officers have since been enrolling in TANU in large numbers, a development which the presidential commission on the one-party state in 1964 wholeheartedly endorsed.[12] In Zambia, President Kaunda has also appointed senior civil servants to the UNIP National Council. The report of the recent Commission on a one-party state constitution for Zambia envisages a fairly thorough politicisation of the public service, the police and the armed forces. The commission recommended, and the government accepted, that civil servants and members of the police and armed forces should be free to belong to the party as ordinary members without office, and also to stand for parliamentary elections, resigning their appointment only if elected.[13] The commission had also proposed the institutional representation of the civil service and the security forces in parliament and the policy-making organs of the party, but this was rejected by the government.[14]

In fairness, it should be said that British policy on this matter conceded that there are certain categories of public servant whose appointment and removal could not be removed from the control of the government. A permanent secretary, for example, represents the government within his ministry. The strategic importance of his position makes him so much part of the government that loyalty must be a pre-eminent consideration in his appointment. If he is ill-disposed towards the government, this may affect not only the advice he gives to it but also the way he conducts the affairs of his ministry. The same consideration should also apply, perhaps with greater force, to the country's principal representatives abroad. The auditor-general, the comissioner of police and the director of prisons also come under this category. With respect to the extent of independence to be accorded to the public service commission, a concession was also made. The primary concern was that the commission should, without control by the government, have and exercise original power (i.e. power conferred directly by the constitution) to appoint, remove and discipline public servants. A power conferred by the constitution is believed to enhance the commission's independence because the constitution is supposed to have greater sanctity and permanence than an ordinary law. At the same time it was recognised that the appointment and removal of members of the commission should be a function of the government. From the standpoint of government the office of a public service commissioner is almost as strategic as that of a permanent secretary, so that similar consideration should apply in his appointment. The power was therefore vested in the government in all the independence constitutions, subject to certain safeguards as regards the removal power. The British approach involved a somewhat delicate balance of interests. Through its power to appoint members of the commission, the government might be able to influence — though not control — the appointment, removal and disciplinary control of public servants. Once appointed, however, a public service commissioner was given considerable security of tenure. His term of office was fixed by the constitution and secured against premature termination except for incompetence or misbehaviour and in accordance with a constitutionally laid down procedure; his salary was made a charge on the public revenue, and protected against reduction during his tenure of office.

The revolt against the British policy towards the power of appointment, removal and disciplinary control of the public service has not been universally espoused in the presidential constitutions of Commonwealth Africa. Both the new and the old approaches have their adherents: Ghana (1960), Tanganyika (1962), Uganda (1967), Tanzania and Malawi adhere to the former; Kenya, Botswana and Gambia to the latter; while Zambia pursues a middle course. In the first group of countries – Ghana (1960), Tanganyika (1962), Uganda (1967), Tanzania and Malawi, the power is now lodged in the President, and not in a public service commission.[15] However, there is a difference of mechanics between these countries. While the public service commission disappeared completely from the constitutions of Ghana, Tanganyika and Tanzania and was reconstituted in an ordinary act of parliament, it remains in those of Malawi and Uganda. Yet, apart from this difference in the method and form of its establishment, the function of the commission is basically the same in all four countries, namely to advise the President, and to exercise such powers as may be delegated to it by the President. A delegation cannot however be made in respect of the appointment of a permanent secretary, auditor-general, inspector-general of police, ambassador, high commissioner or other principal representative abroad. The commission has lost its independent power and become a mere delegate of the President. Only in Malawi does it still retain some independent power, and that is in respect of disciplinary control otherwise than by removal, though this again is subject to the general or special directions of the President and to the public service regulations and general orders.

It is necessary to explain the categories of public officers included in the President's power in the present context. The power embraces not only civil servants in the ministries and departments but also members of the police, prison service and teachers employed and paid by the government. Also included in the public service are servants of the local government authorities. Their appointment, removal and disciplinary control are, however, a local concern, sometimes with the approval of the minister for local government in the case of the top officials, like the town clerk, medical officer of health, etc.

There is a growing practice to have a separate commission for each of the services in the public service – civil, police, prison and teaching. Malawi established a separate police service commission in 1966, and Uganda a separate teaching service commission in 1967, with the same functions and status as the public service commission. The 1969 Constitution of Ghana established a public services commission, a police council and a prison services board.

The appointment and removal of members of the service commissions remain, as in the past, a prerogative of the President, with the same safeguards regarding removal. The removal power of the President in Malawi is not, however, limited to removal on grounds only of inability or misbehaviour.

In the group of countries where the old British procedure still applies — Kenya, Botswana (before July 1970) and Gambia — the power is/was vested in a public service commission established by the constitution.[16] The independence of the commission is guaranteed by an express stipulation that, in the exercise of its functions, it shall not be subject to the direction or control of any person or authority. The security of tenure bestowed by a fixed term of office and by the requirement that removal shall be only on grounds of inability or misbehaviour is now strengthened by a new procedure for removal which requires that the matter should first be enquired into and reported upon by a tribunal composed of judges or former judges appointed by the President, and that a removal can only be effected if the tribunal so recommends.[17] The President's power of appointment of members of the commission is similarly subject to qualification designed to secure public confidence in the commission. In addition to the familiar requirement that a member of the commission must not be an M.P., a public officer or a member of a local government council, the republican constitutions of Kenya and Gambia require further that he should at no time have been nominated as a candidate for election to parliament or a regional assembly or have been the holder of an office in an organisation that sponsors or otherwise supports, or has at any time sponsored or otherwise supported, a candidate for election to parliament or a regional assembly. (In Gambia the disqualification relates to a period of two years immediately prior to the appointment.) In Botswana a person cannot be appointed a member of the commission if, within the two years immediately preceding his appointment, he is or has been actively engaged in politics.

Although what is important here are the qualifications on the powers of the commission in favour of the President, it should be mentioned that the appointment, removal and disciplinary control of members of the police force are shared between the commission and the commissioner of police, all officers of the rank of sub-inspector or above in Kenya, and above the rank of chief inspector in Gambia and assistant superintendent in Botswana (before July 1970) coming under the commission and the rest under the commissioner of police, but the commission may delegate any of its powers to the commissioner. This arrangement is also applied to the prison service in Botswana, the dividing line being, as in the case of the police, the rank of assistant superintendent of prisons. However the qualification operates in Botswana only to the extent that the commissioner of police or the director of prisons is actually empowered by law to exercise the power.

Turning now to the qualifications on the powers of the commission in favour of the President — first, appointment to an office on the President's personal staff can only be made with his concurrence. More important, the President, and not the commission, is the authority to appoint, remove and discipline the following categories of public servants: permanent secretary, commissioner of police, ambassador, high commissioner or other principal representative abroad. In Kenya the President does not have power to remove and discipline a permanent secretary, secretary to the cabinet, director of personnel or commissioner of police, this being also vested in the commission. And in Botswana, before July 1970, he was required to consult the commission before exercising his powers in respect of these categories of public servants. The appointment, removal and disciplinary control of the auditor-general are dealt with differently between the three countries. He is/was appointed in Kenya by the President, in Gambia by the President acting in accordance with the advice of the public service commission, and in Botswana, before July 1970, by the public service commission.[18] He may be removed by the President in Kenya or by the national assembly in Gambia and Botswana, but only on grounds of inability or misbehaviour and after considering a report by a tribunal of inquiry composed of judges or former judges. The initiation of the process of inquiry and the appointment of the members of the tribunal are by the President in Kenya and by the national assembly in Gambia and Botswana. The recommendation of the tribunal that the auditor-general should not be removed is binding on the president in Kenya but not on the national assembly in Gambia and Botswana. The national assembly in both countries is only required to consider the tribunal's report, and may, upon such consideration, by resolution remove him. The functions and powers of the auditor-general are spelt out in all the countries (including those in the first group above – Ghana, Tanzania, Malawi and Uganda),[19] and it is provided (except in Ghana) that he shall not be subject to the direction or control of any other person or authority in the exercise of those functions and powers.

In Botswana before July 1970 the President was vested with a supervisory power by means of a review on appeal. A person who had been removed from office or otherwise subjected to some other disciplinary punishment might appeal to the President, who might dismiss the appeal or set up a tribunal to hear it.[20] After hearing, the tribunal, which must be chaired by a person who holds or has held high judicial office or is qualified to be appointed as a judge of the High Court, advised the President whether or not the appeal should be allowed either wholly or in part, and the President shall then act accordingly.

The changes that have taken place in Botswana since July 10, 1970, must now be noted. Before that, indeed, the power of the commission had on August 18, 1969, been made subject to such general directions as the President might consider necessary to give;[21] then on July 10, 1970, it was stripped of all executive powers, acting now only as an appeal body in cases of removal and other punishment.[22] Its decision, in so far as it allows an appeal in full, is final, but where it dismisses an appeal or allows it in part only, then a further appeal is possible to the President, his appellate function being exercisable in exactly the same way as before July 1970. The appointments of existing members of the public service commission were statutorily terminated on July 9, 1970, but without prejudice to their eligibility for reappointment.[23] The executive powers of the commission were transferred to such person or persons as might be prescribed by act of parliament, except in respect of such superscale officers (other than ambassadors, high commissioners or other overseas representatives, secretary to the cabinet, attorney-general, permanent secretaries, commissioner of police, court registrars, magistrates and other inferior court judges) as might be prescribed by an act of parliament, which were transferred to the President. In other words, the commission's executive functions are now shared between the President and other authorities designated by parliament. The President, of course, retains his power in relation to ambassadors, high commissioners or other overseas representatives, secretary to the cabinet, attorney-general, permanent secretaries, and commissioner of police, and is no longer obliged to consult anyone else before exercising it. (The attorney-general was added to the list in 1969.) Court registrars, magistrates and judges of other inferior courts continue to be appointed by the President on the advice of the judicial service commission. Subject to these changes, the old provisions discussed above remain in force.

As already noted, Zambia in its 1964 Constitution adopted a compromise approach. The power of appointment, removal and disciplinary control of the public service is vested in the President, but exercised on his behalf and in his name by a public service commission or, in the case of government teachers, by a teaching service commission, established directly by the Constitution.[24] (The teaching service commission was established in 1970 by a constitutional amendment act.)[25] The Zambian approach follows the Westminster device of separating the formal vesting of power from its actual exercise. The powers of the commissions thus derive, not from delegation by the President as in Ghana (1960), Uganda (1967), Tanzania and Malawi, but directly from the Constitution. However, unlike in Kenya, Gambia and Botswana, its powers are not exclusive in respect of any class of public officers. For not only can the President give it general direction with respect to the exercise of its functions, but he may also require it to refer any matter relating to its functions to him.[26] Upon such reference the President may himself exercise the power in question.

In a recent case which arose upon these provisions,[27] a government teacher, Mr Kang'ombe, was dismissed by the permanent secretary of the Ministry of Education on the orders of the President. The permanent secretary had earlier recommended to the commission that the teacher be dismissed. Finding no 'justifiable cause for dismissal', the commission directed that Mr Kang'ombe be 'restored to his substantive rank but posted to a Boys' School as Head in the same grade'. Alternatively, if no such vacancy was immediately available, then he should be 'seconded to the ministry headquarters for administrative and/or personnel duties in his capacity as Head'. In response to a request by the permanent secretary that the commission reconsider its decision, the commission reiterated that it could find no justifiable cause for dismissal, and suggested that if Mr Kang'ombe were no longer acceptable in the Ministry of Education, 'arrangements should be made to transfer him to another ministry'. On the recommendation of the secretary-general to the government, the President intervened and directed that Mr Kang'ombe be discharged 'with immediate effect', a decision which the permanent secretary, Ministry of Education, conveyed to Mr Kang'ombe in a letter. The High Court held the dismissal to be unconstitutional and void, on the ground that under the relevant provision of the Constitution, the President can himself exercise the powers vested in him to appoint, dismiss and discipline public servants *only*, and *only* if he first required the public service or the teaching service commission to refer to him a case still *under consideration* by the commission. If a commission has given a decision in a case, then it is no longer under consideration. Its decision finally disposes of the case, and there is no power in anyone else other than the courts to review that decision. The power given to the President under the constitutional provision is not a power to review the commission's decision; it is not concurrent or cumulative. 'Either the President exercises the said power when the matter is still under consideration . . . or the commission itself exercises them in the name of and on behalf of the President. There is no power for the President to set aside a decision of the . . . commission.' Under the regulations governing the service commissions, a responsible officer (i.e. permanent secretary) may require a commission to reconsider its decision. This provision might have saved the situation if the President's intervention had taken place after the permanent secretary had asked the commission to reconsider its decision but before it made a further decision. The dismissal would seem also to be invalid on the ground that the President became seized of the case without first requiring the commission to refer it to him. He appeared to have acted entirely at the instance of the secretary-general.

As in the other countries, a permanent secretary, commissioner of police, ambassador, high commissioner or other principal representative of Zambia abroad is outside the commission's power, but in accordance with the country's compromise approach in this matter, the President, as the responsible authority, is required to consult the commission before exercising his power. Concerning the auditor-general the position is exactly the same as in Botswana,[28] while the police force and the prison service are the shared responsibility of the commission and the commissioner of police or, as the case may be, commissioner of prisons, the dividing rank being, as in Botswana, that of assistant superintendent. A separate police service commission is to be established in the new one-party state constitution.[29] The one-party state commission had recommended the merging of all the service commissions into a single common services commission,[30] but this was rejected by the government on the ground that 'it would be difficult to devise a *modus operandi* for a common services commission'.[31]

Subject therefore to the power of the President to give general directions, and to require it to refer to him a case under consideration, a service commission in Zambia has independence; it cannot be directed or controlled by any person or authority in the exercise of its functions. Its members have a fixed term of office which is not determinable except on grounds of incompetence or misbehaviour.

A function that vitally affects not only the public welfare but also the freedom of the individual is public prosecutions, i.e. the institution, conduct, take-over and discontinuance of criminal prosecutions. Their control follows upon two different lines in the Commonwealth African presidential constitutions. In one – Kenya, Zambia and Botswana[32] – they are insulated from political control. The power is vested in a public officer (attorney-general in Kenya and Botswana, and director of public prosecutions in Zambia) and its exercise is guaranteed against direction or control by any other person or authority. In Zambia the attorney-general (a minister) may direct the director of public prosecutions in any case involving general considerations of public policy, but the power of the attorney-general in this regard is not subject to the direction or control of any other person or authority. The attorney-general is appointed by the President in Kenya and Zambia; in Botswana before July 1970 it was by the public service commission in consultation with the President and since July 1970 it has been by the President. He is removable in Zambia by the President in the same manner as any other minister, and in Kenya and Botswana by the President but only if a tribunal composed of judges or former judges so recommends on grounds of incompetence or misbehaviour. The director of public prosecutions in Zambia is appointed by the public service commission, and his removal can only be effected on the same grounds and by the same procedure as in the case of the attorney-general in Kenya or Botswana.

In the rest of the countries, public prosecutions are politically controlled – by the attorney-general (a minister) assisted by the director of public prosecutions (a public officer) in Gambia, by the director of public prosecutions (a public officer) in Uganda (1967) and Malawi but subject to the direction and control of the attorney-general (a minister).[33] The attorney-general may be either a minister or a public officer in Malawi, but where he is not a minister, then the minister responsible for administration of justice (the President holds this responsibility at present) may at any time require any case or class of case to be submitted to him for the purpose of giving a direction as to whether or not criminal proceedings should be instituted or discontinued. In Ghana (1960) the attorney-general, who might be a minister or other person appointed by the President, had responsibility for public prosecutions – subject, however, to the directions of the President.[34] Neither the office of attorney-general nor that of director of public prosecutions is specifically established in the Interim Constitution of Tanzania but they exist in fact as public offices, apparently from the 1962 Constitution which established them. The President could of course have created them in pursuance of his power to constitute offices.[35] Political control of public prosecutions is not *per se* objectionable. As a Tanganyikan government paper on the proposal for a republican constitution explained in 1962, 'the even-handed administration of criminal justice manifestly requires that in normal circumstances decisions relating to prosecutions should be taken impartially, without regard to persons. However, it is generally recognised that there are occasionally cases in which it is not only proper but necessary for the director of public prosecutions to consider questions relating to the public interest before deciding whether to prosecute. ... The Government therefore considers that, in order to provide for the exceptional case where the public interest is of overriding importance, the President should be invested with power to give directions to the director of public prosecutions.'[36]

In parenthesis, the varying status of the attorney-general in these countries deserves to be noted. He is a public officer in Kenya and Botswana, a minister in Zambia, Uganda and Gambia, and he may be a minister or a public officer in Malawi, Ghana and Tanzania.

(ii) *Provincial Administration*

Like central establishment, regional or provincial administration – which, as stated above, is usually preserved in the President's portfolio – is strategic from the point of view of the President's overall control of the activities of government. Just as his responsibility for establishments gives him control over the civil service machinery in the capital, so does provincial administration enable him to control the work of the ministries in the districts and provinces. Government is not administered merely by the simple device of formulating policies and issuing directives from the capital. The implementation of these policies and directives in the districts where the overwhelming majority of the people live is perhaps the most crucial part of governmental administration. The supervision and co-ordination of the activities of the personnel of the various ministries engaged in this task of implementation in the districts, and maintenance of the law and order necessary for their proper functioning, are the work of regional or provincial administration. It is therefore on the regional or provincial administration that the government relies for the welfare, development and general progress of the districts, the maintenance of peace and good government, and the proper working of the machinery of government in conformity with the policy laid down by the government. President Kaunda of Zambia has summed up these functions admirably in his Directives of 19 June, 1966:

(*a*) to be the chief government co-ordinating officers in their provinces or districts with particular reference to the work of economic development;
(*b*) to maintain the morale and well-being of the civil service;
(*c*) to ensure that government policies and procedures are understood by the people;
(*d*) to ensure that the presence of the government is felt throughout the provinces and districts;
(*e*) to supervise generally the functioning of other government departments within their provinces or districts.

The work of regional or provincial administration is thus both political and administrative. It acts as a link between the government and the people, explaining government policies to the people and relaying the mood of the people to the government, while at the same time maintaining law and order as well as supervising and co-ordinating the work of the other government departments in the field. During the colonial period both the political and administrative aspects of provincial administration were performed by civil servants. The use of civil servants in a political capacity did not commend itself to the nationalist governments especially as many of the civil servants were expatriates, and control of their work had to follow established civil service routine and procedures. This led eventually to a separation in personnel, corresponding to that between a minister and his civil service advisers in the ministries at the capital. Political functionaries variously designated as commissioners, ministers or governors are now placed at the head of the districts and provinces, advised by administrative officers. No doubt the appointment of politicians to head the provinces and districts facilitates control, since the relationship of a political provincial commissioner or minister to the President is not governed by any formal code as in the case of civil servants. Yet, as the experience of Kenya shows, the rigidities of civil service procedures and approach have not proved that civil servants are any less competent than politicians to perform political functions or less amenable to political control. There the provincial and district commissioners are still civil servants.

The head of the provincial administration, whether a politician or a civil servant, is there as the personal representative and agent of the President. It follows, therefore, that the President, through his responsibility for provincial administration, has overall charge of government activities in the districts and provinces. Again this does not mean that, through the provincial commissioners or ministers, he normally directs the field departmental officers. The relationship between the provincial administration and the departmental officers is rather a complex one which sometimes gives rise to conflict. It has been defined as being that, although departmental officers in the districts are responsible for the implementation of their minister's policies, the provincial commissioner, as the principal executive officer of the government within the limits of his province, with a duty to supervise and co-ordinate the activities of all public officers to ensure efficiency, is entitled to direct them.[37] He is, of course, not supposed to interfere actively in purely departmental or technical questions; nevertheless, in cases of emergency, of which he is the sole judge, he may intervene and issue orders, which must be carried out. With respect to law and order, the provincial administration's responsibility is concurrent with that of the police, which therefore imposes a necessity for close consultation and co-operation between them, though in the event of difference of opinion at a time of emergency, which permits no time for reference of the disputed point to their respective superiors, the overriding voice is that of the provincial administration. As regards detection of crime and criminal prosecutions, however, the police are independent of the administration, and are responsible only to the law and to the attorney-general; nonetheless, in so far as the function of criminal investigations and prosecutions is likely in any particular case to have repercussions on peace and order within the province or district, as where the relations of two communities are involved, the police should act in consultation with the administration.

The conflict inherent in this relationship has, unfortunately, been somewhat accentuated by a certain over-zealousness with which some of the new political heads of provinces and districts have approached their functions. This has been particularly the case with the heads of the districts in Zambia, called district governors. Under the reforms of

1969, the country was divided into eight provinces and fifty-three districts. Each province is in charge of a resident cabinet minister, serviced by a provincial permanent secretary. In his relationship to the President, the provincial cabinet minister is quite unlike his colleague in charge of a ministry in the capital. He does not have the latter's autonomy from presidential direction. He is the agent of, and therefore directly responsible to, the President for the administration of his province. He comes directly under the Provincial and District Government Division in the President's office. At the head of each district is a district governor who, under the provincial cabinet minister, administers the district as agent of the President, combining both political and civil service functions to an extent that makes it difficult to say whether he is a civil servant or a politician. Many of them have presumed to meddle in practically every aspect of government activity and every aspect of life generally in their districts with hardly any regard to the constitutionality or propriety of their actions, and in the result have provoked widespread resentment and hatred.

(iii) *Foreign Relations*

The relations of a country with other countries are another of the vital and crucial functions of modern government, with which a President must inevitably be involved, though the extent of his involvement will vary according as he is his own minister of foreign affairs.

Except in Malawi, Botswana and (before 1971) Zambia it was usual and convenient for the foreign affairs portfolio to be assigned to a minister. But such an assignment only minimises the President's involvement. The conduct of foreign affairs requires close and constant liaison between the minister and the President to an extent that makes the former's autonomy much less than that of the other ministers. Furthermore, there are aspects of foreign relations that are inextricably bound up with the President's headship of the state, and for which he has direct personal responsibility. His position as head of state is expressly affirmed and recognised in all the constitutions, unlike in the United States. The significance of this position lies in the nature of a state as a mere legal abstraction, which therefore needs a human person to act as its *alter ego* in its relations with other states. The President as Head of State is thus cast in the role of representative. He represents the state in the totality of its international relations. As such a representative he is its sole channel of communication with other states.

Certain of the functions implied in this position are of a personal kind. These are usually performed by the President in person or at least require his personal authority, namely the reception and accreditation of diplomatic agents (ambassadors, high commissioners, consuls, etc.);

the making of war, peace, treaties and alliances; and the cession or acquisition of territory or jurisdiction. In the British constitutional system these powers are sanctioned to the Queen by the royal prerogatives, the prerogative power of act of state. When the Queen was succeeded by an indigenous President in the headship of the new states in Commonwealth Africa, the prerogatives were usually preserved to the President by express constitutional provision. The provision is perhaps worth citing here again. 'Where under any law in force in . . . immediately before the commencement of this Constitution any prerogatives or privileges are vested in Her Majesty, those prerogatives or privileges shall, from the commencement of this Constitution [or Order], vest in the President.'[38]

The critical nature of these powers hardly needs any emphasis. Even the reception or accreditation of diplomatic agents is not always a ceremonial or formal act, as it may sometimes raise considerations of policy regarding recognition. Critical policy issues are also implicated in war, peace, treaties, alliances and the cession or acquisition of territory or jurisdiction. And, since policy is involved, the decision is usually that of the cabinet, as in other matters of foreign policy. In some cases the approval or ratification of the legislative body may also be necessary. Under the 1967 Constitution of Uganda, the treaty-making power of the President was expressly qualified in favour of the cabinet and the national assembly. Any treaty, convention, agreement or other engagement made by the President was required to be in terms approved by the cabinet and, insofar as it related to armistice, neutrality or peace, by a resolution of the national assembly.[39] In all the countries the power to declare war is similarly qualified by the necessity for approval by the national assembly within a prescribed time. This qualification must be taken to relate to a formal declaration of war, and not to the making of war generally. For a country may be at war without a formal declaration, such as when it is attacked by another country and is obliged to defend itself.

Of these powers, those that have featured prominently in the foreign relations of the Commonwealth African countries are the reception and accreditation of diplomatic agents and the making of treaties or other agreements. All of course belong to the United Nations Organisation and its agencies, to the Conimonwealth itself and to the Organisation for African Unity, of which the highest organ is the Heads of States Meeting with a rotating chairman. A meeting of Commonwealth Heads of Government also takes place every year. The only regional organisation of any importance to which any of the Commonwealth African countries belongs is the East African Community, which comprises Kenya, Tanzania and Uganda. Replacing the former East African Common Services Organisation, the Community was established by the Treaty for East African Co-operation of June 6, 1967, certain of whose provisions have been given force of law within each member-country by its own enactment. The Community's principal executive organ is the East African Authority, composed of the Heads of State of the three countries.[40] Political union among African countries has been more a matter of slogan than of reality, as each country clings jealously to its sovereignty. An East African Federation comprising Kenya, Tanganyika and Uganda had once seemed a distinct possibility, but is now dead and forgotten. Even the efforts of Kwame Nkrumah, the great champion of a union of African states, achieved no lasting results. The Ghana-Guinea Union which he and Sekou Touré formed in 1958 and which in 1960 was re-named the Union of African States, with the addition of a third member, Mali, never attained more than a formal existence, its only practical manifestation being the exchange of resident ministers and occasional meetings between the three Heads of States. Nkrumah had also negotiated a union between Ghana and Togo in 1960, which was frustrated by the sudden withdrawal of his partner, Sylvanus Olympio. In the same year he actually signed an agreement with Patrice Lumumba for a Ghana-Congo Union.[41] The union of Tanganyika and Zanzibar into a United Republic of Tanzania stands out as the only on-going political union in Africa. Military alliances have played an even less active part in the foreign relations of Commonwealth African countries, owing mainly to their commitment to a policy of non-alignment. Nonetheless Britain maintains a strong military presence in Kenya. Nor have they been involved in war, except for the clashes between Uganda and Tanzania in 1972. Military seizures of government and the late Nigerian Civil War have called forth the exercise of the power of recognition.

(iv) *National Defence*

This is yet another of the basic functions of government — the defence of the nation against enemies both internal and external. Reference has already been made to the war-making power of the President in the context of foreign relations. More important than the formal power to make war, however, is the organisation, support, command and control of the means of war. An organised armed force is a necessary armoury in the apparatus of any state, being the primary instrument for its defence, which may also be called in aid of the civil authorities for the preservation of public order and for relief in cases of emergency. The powers and functions of the President in regard to it are therefore crucial.

The armed forces in the Commonwealth occupy a rather special status in that they are not normally classified as part of the public service. They are a distinct unit of the state apparatus, governed by their own special code of relationships. In regard to the civil service, for example, the President, as we have seen,[42] has power under the Constitution to constitute offices and to abolish them. He possesses no similar power to raise an armed force, this being a cardinal principle of the inherited British constitutional system, won after a long-drawn-out contest between King and Parliament. The principle is specifically enshrined in the Constitutions of Ghana (1960) and Tanzania: 'No person' — or, in the more specific words of the Ghana Constitution, 'neither the President nor any other person' — 'shall raise any armed force except under the authority of an Act of Parliament'.[43] An armed force exists in all the countries, but does so only by the express authority of an act of parliament.[44] However, the maximum strength of such force or forces is left to the President to determine, except in Uganda where it is fixed by parliament. The President is also given power to determine the formations, units and other elements into which the armed forces shall be divided. But their primary division into, say, an army, air force and navy, and the division of each of these into, say, a regular force, a territorial force, a reserve or auxiliary force is by act of parliament. The membership of a force is divided into officers and men. In nearly all the countries, the power to commission officers is vested in the President, and is exercisable only by him.

Apart from its establishment and maintenance, the two other most important powers affecting the armed forces are those of command and operational use. By the Constitution the President is invariably proclaimed Commander-in-Chief.[45] Most of the constitutions — Ghana (1960), Uganda (1967), Tanzania, Malawi, Zambia and Botswana — go on to spell out the powers implied in this position. (Kenya's does not, while Gambia's merely says that the functions shall be such as may be prescribed by parliament.)[46] The provision vests supreme command in the President, and defines his powers in that respect as including control and direction of the operational use of the armed forces, and the appointment and dismissal of their members.[47] (The command powers of the President in Botswana are only formal, as there is as yet no army. Thus, the police, which includes a para-military unit, assume great importance as the country's only organised force, and for this reason are placed under the President's portfolio.) At the same time parliament is given power to regulate the exercise of the power. By his power over their operational use, the President may order the armed forces to be used outside the country, as Ghana did when it contributed a contingent to the United Nations peace-keeping force in the Congo (now Zaire) in 1960. The power to engage the armed forces outside the country is sanctioned by express enactment in some of the countries, e.g., Malawi and Zambia.

As the President cannot command the armed forces alone, provision is made by the governing enactments for a commander of each of the primary units (army, air force and navy) who is to be appointed by the President, and who, subject to the President's supreme command, is to have command of the unit under him. In addition to the commanders of the army and air force, both Tanzania and Uganda have also a chief of defence staff exercising overall command of the combined forces, subject again to the President's supreme command. A defence council is almost invariably established to advise the President with respect to his power of supreme command, and to policy and other matters affecting the discipline and administration of the armed forces. Responsibility for armed forces policy and administration may also be assigned to a minister, who in that case becomes chairman of the defence council. Or the President may choose to retain the defence portfolio himself, as in Malawi and (until 1970) Zambia. (In Malawi the secretary to the President is the chairman of the defence council.) The one-party state commission in Zambia recommended that the President should resume the defence portfolio.[48] This being a matter entirely within the President's discretion, the government white paper on the commission's report made no comment on the recommendation,[49] but the President may well be influenced by this when he next re-shuffles his cabinet. At the commission's recommendation, the government agreed to study the possibility of bringing the two units of the Zambian armed forces (the army and air force) under a unified command.

Discipline of the armed force, other than by dismissal, is regulated by detailed statutory provisions which define military offences and prescribe the punishment and trial procedures for them.

The armed forces in Africa have in recent years become a danger to the government whose instrument they are supposed to be. There have been seven military coups in Commonwealth African since 1966 and at least two attempted coups, not to mention still-born plots. Earlier, in 1964, there had been a mutiny among the armies of the three East African countries of Kenya, Tanzania and Uganda, though the motivation there was not the seizure of the government but redress for army grievances mainly over pay, africanisation of command positions and promotions generally. Such military actions against the government itself have necessitated the importation of outside military aid in Tanzania and in Sierra Leone. In 1964 President Nyerere brought in British troops to quell the mutiny among his own soldiers, who voluntarily surrendered to the visiting British troops without any resistance. Later the British troops were replaced by Nigerian troops in consonance with Nyerere's Africanist outlook, and with O.A.U. policy in such matters. It was with the aid of troops from neighbouring Guinea that President Siaka Stevens of Sierra Leone was able to put down the attempt by some of his own troops to oust him in 1971. It might have been thought that the importation of foreign troops violated the prohibition against the raising of an armed force other than one authorised by an act of parliament. There exists, however, in nearly all the Commonwealth African countries a statutory authority for the President, whenever he considers it appropriate so to do, to declare, by notice in the gazette, the military, naval or air forces of any other country to be forces acting in *co-operation* with the national defence forces.[50] The troops that may be invited in this way may, under the law of some of the countries, be restricted to troops of the United Kingdom or Commonwealth countries.[51] Even without express statutory authorisation, importation of foreign troops in these circumstances may be justified on the basis of necessity.

The army mutiny in Tanzania has led to the politicisation of the armed forces there. 'As a direct consequence of the mutiny,' writes William Tordoff, '. . . a new army recruiting procedure was devised, which shifted the criterion for selection from physical fitness to loyalty and political affiliation. The basic qualification for entry to the armed services is now membership of TANU, the Afro-Shirazi Party (ASP) of Zanzibar, or the young wings of these organisations. Further, it is intended that entry to the forces shall no longer be direct but through the national service, which was introduced in 1963 in order to provide education and training for the country's youth. . . . All military personnel – those already serving, as well as new recruits – can now belong to TANU (or the ASP) and they have in fact joined in large numbers. . . . Other measures taken by the Government to ensure the political loyalty of the armed forces include the appointment of Mr S. J. Kitundu, the Coast regional commissioner, as political commissar of the Tanzania Defence Forces with the honorary rank of colonel,[52] and the appointment of each company commander as head of the TANU committee established in his company. Moreover, the informal arrangements by which members of TANU and the TANU Youth League assisted the police force have been regularised by the creation of a reserve force for national defence.'[53] Many of the other countries, e.g., Zambia and Malawi, have followed the example of Tanzania in establishing a reserve force and national service, and in politicising the regular forces. Under Zambia's one-party system members of the armed forces are eligible and free to belong to the party, and to stand for parliamentary elections. By extending the party's control machinery to the armed forces the President's authority over them is enhanced.

(v) *Other Ministerial Responsibilities of the President*

The President has usually other ministerial responsibilities besides those already mentioned. These vary from time to time, and from country to country. Examples drawn from one or two countries might help to create a more rounded picture of the President's role in the administration of government.

In May 1969, the President in Zambia had responsibility for the President's office, cabinet office, establishment, defence, trade, industry and mines, provincial and local government, technical and vocational education, and legal affairs.[54] It cannot be denied that, in comparison with a minister's portfolio, the President's was quite extensive. His functions and powers in respect of these matters were largely contained in relevant statutes, of which there were 127 at the time, ranging from the National Flag and Armorial Ensigns Act to the Civil Service Act, the Defence Act, the Town and Country Planning Act, the Local Government Act, the penal code, the mining companies, Zambia Railways, Zambia Airways Corporation and the National Coal Board of Zambia acts.[55] As the minister responsible for these, the President has responsibility for administering the provisions of these statutes. These are of course exclusive of enactments which confer functions and powers upon him specifically as President, such, for instance, as the Preservation of Public Security Act; these latter are by far the most crucial sources of presidential power. To assist him in the discharge of those functions were one special assistant, five ministers of state, four district governors, four permanent secretaries, the solicitor-general and the attorney-general (the provincial ministers with their ministers of state, district governors and permanent secretaries were not counted). In October 1969, the President dropped the portfolios of provincial and local government (as distinct from provincial administration), and of trade, industry and mines, and took on instead those of foreign affairs, and state participation (which included vital functions previously located in the ministry of trade, industry and mines such as mining, pioneer industries, the National Coal Board of Zambia, Zambia Railways, Zambia Airways Corporation, and the Tanzania-Zambia Railways Authority).[56] In 1970 he shed defence,[57] and in 1971 foreign affairs.[58]

In Malawi the portfolios under the President's direct ministerial responsibility include justice, agriculture and natural resources, external affairs, works and supplies, the office of the President and the Cabinet. Again this is quite extensive compared with the portfolios assigned to ministers, e.g., education, health, labour or finance, each of which is under a separate minister. Local government, community development and social welfare are under one minister, and trade, industry and tourism, transport and communications are under another. Two ministers are without portfolio. Then there is a minister in charge of each of the country's three regions, Northern, Southern and Central.

2. *Directing of Ministers*

Here it can be said straight away that there is no significant difference between the practice now and in the period of parliamentary government. Ministers have continued to run their ministries with almost complete autonomy, subject of course to the control imposed by finance and the need for co-ordination and for integrated policy. In purely departmental policy and administration the minister's autonomy is uncontrolled. If a policy affects only his ministry and does not need enabling legislation, it may be initiated and decided finally within the ministry without any interference by the President. If, however, it affects other ministries or requires legislation to implement it, the minister can initiate but cannot decide it finally. It is here that the function of co-ordination arises to impinge upon the minister's autonomy.

3. *The Function of Co-ordination*

Co-ordination is exercised, as in pre-republican days, by the President's office (formerly the Prime Minister's office), by the cabinet or by one of its committees. The cabinet performs its co-ordinating function largely through the cabinet secretariat. When the President issues directives or the cabinet takes a decision, it is the job of the President's office to convey them to the service or to the particular department concerned, and to ensure that they are carried out. But the President's office is greatly handicapped in this task by the small establishment available in it. Both before and after the creation of the republic, the establishment in this office has consisted only of a handful of officers. At the head of it is a permanent or principal secretary, whose pre-eminent authority as secretary to the President and the cabinet puts him in a position of leadership of the entire civil service. He is often designated as such. In Zambia since 1969, he has been redesignated Secretary-General to the government, and he need no longer be a civil servant;[59] indeed since the change all the incumbents have been politicians with the status of a minister, the idea being to have someone at the very centre of the government's machinery to co-ordinate the various departments and activities of the government.[60] But the secretary-general remains directly responsible to the President.

It might have been thought that after the establishment of the presidency in these countries, the President's office would be considerably expanded in terms of personnel and physical facilities. This has not been the case. If anything, the staff needs of the office have sometimes been sacrificed to those of the ministries. The result is that it lacks the capacity to co-ordinate the activities of the ministries effectively.

Indeed it is often the Treasury more than the President's office that does a good deal of the co-ordination. In consequence therefore the ministers' autonomy has not suffered greatly from the President's role of co-ordination.

Although constitutionally only an advisory body, the cabinet is far from being a mere sounding board for the President; most policy decisions emanate from it. Two questions are relevant concerning the status of the cabinet. The first is the method by which decisions are arrived at. It can perhaps be said with some assurance that decisions are not taken by vote, but by consensus after full discussion. Voting at cabinet meetings, except when desired by the President himself, would be clearly incompatible with the position of the cabinet as an advisory body and with that of the President as the executive and the authority over policy, since it would enable it to override the President when he happens to take a position different from that of the majority. Admittedly consensus may, on its part, enable the President to pre-determine the decision by indicating at the outset of the discussions the direction he wants them to take. It is perhaps reasonable to expect this to happen now and again on matters on which the President has strong feelings. But then the Prime Minister could not have been free from this. Like the President, he was the creator and the chairman of the cabinet. And decision-taking by unanimity or consensus was as much a feature of the earlier period as it is now. In general, it may be said that cabinet decisions are genuinely the product of the collective views of its members expressed quite independently. There seem to have been no cases of the President imposing a decision against the views of the majority, or unilaterally reversing a cabinet decision because he later thought it wrong or inexpedient.

It is, of course, not enough that when a matter is brought before the cabinet, its members are free to express independent views upon it and that the final decision is based upon a consensus of such views. Equally important is the question whether the cabinet is in fact consulted upon all major policy matters, or is sometimes by-passed by the President in the determination of such matters. Now, a Prime Minister could not really afford to do that, as otherwise he would incur the accusation of wanting to subvert the Constitution, since he has a joint responsibility with the other ministers for government and its policies. As the executive with unshared responsibility for policy, the President is strictly within his constitutional rights to by-pass the cabinet. In practice, however, he usually does not, at least in normal times. Meetings of the cabinet are held regularly and frequently, either weekly as in Tanzania and Botswana or fortnightly as in Kenya or monthly as in Zambia since 1968. (Before 1968 in Zambia the cabinet used to meet weekly.) As far as legislation is concerned, the cabinet has always been consulted upon it. All government legislative proposals, from whichever ministry they originate, are considered either by the full cabinet or first by the legislation committee of the cabinet, whence they go to the full cabinet. And since most policies need to be implemented by legislation, this ensures that the cabinet must be consulted on them and its approval obtained. The system of cabinet committees is pretty well developed in some of the countries, notably Kenya, which has three such committees, one for manpower and training, another for foreign affairs, and the third for economic development; each of the committees is chaired by the minister in whose portfolio the subject falls.[61] The President does not sit in any of the cabinet committees, not even the legislation committee where it exists.

4. *The President in Ghana and Tanzania*

Ghana and Tanzania, as has earlier been observed, do not conform to the picture just presented. Presidentialism in Tanganyika began indeed with the President holding very little ministerial responsibility. On the establishment of the republic in 1962, the President divested himself of many of the responsibilities which he had previously held as Prime Minister, preferring instead to concentrate upon general policy and party matters including the party's local organisations and its links with the people in the districts. Central establishment, regional administration, finance, printing and information services, previously in the Prime Minister's office, were transferred to the office of the Vice-President, a new office created by the republican Constitution. Soon after, in March 1963, development planning was also transferred to the newly-created Ministry of Development Planning, and external affairs and defence to the Ministry of External Affairs and Defence, each under a separate minister. Even co-ordination of the work of the ministries was left largely in the hands of the Vice-President, whose office, rather than that of the President, became therefore 'the nerve-centre of the Administration'.[62] The only matters for which the President retained direct responsibility were the cabinet secretariat and civil service policy.

The army mutiny of January 1964 changed all this. It precipitated a re-organisation in the allocation of ministerial responsibilities, which was characterised by an increasing concentration of functions in the hands of the President. First regional administration and central establishment, then development planning, and in October 1965 local government and external affairs were taken back to the President's office. However, at the same time as the President assumed responsibility for external affairs, regional administration and local government were given over to a new minister for regional administration, while development planning was returned to a minister for economic affairs and development planning. This process of decentralisation has been consolidated by the establishment of the office of Prime Minister which was announced on February 25, 1972.[63] In the re-allocation of ministerial responsibilities which followed upon this,[64] the President assigned to himself the following matters — co-ordination of government business, cabinet secretariat, civil service policy, establishments, the Institute of Development Management, secretariat training, the East African Affairs Bureau, the East African Authority, and the Permanent Commission of Enquiry. To the Prime Minister (who is also the Second Vice-President) he assigned justice, the judiciary, the attorney-general's chambers, the national assembly, regional administration, rural development, local government, etc. President Nyerere explained the creation of the office of Prime Minister as resting on the need to share leadership. 'As a result of there being no Prime Minister,' he explained, 'the only leader of Government outside Parliament is the President himself. . . . Outside Parliament each minister has to see the President himself on any matter where he needs discussion or needs guidance. Similarly, if any two ministers have a difficulty among themselves which they cannot settle without help, they have no alternative but to take it to the President. And similarly, it is the President, and only the President, who can push ministers and their ministries about the implementation of decisions made by the cabinet. For working purposes, this is not a good system. Therefore, for the first time, I have chosen the ministers and also a leader for them — that is a Prime Minister. My choosing to appoint a Prime Minister does not involve a change in our Constitution. The executive responsibilities of the President remain exactly the same as they were before. . . .' Tanzania has thus reverted to the position at the inauguration of presidentialism there. The period of concentration of ministerial responsibilities in the President had been a short one, lasting from January to October 1965. Yet while it lasted, and as the President accumulated more and more functions, the status of the ministers correspondingly diminished. So did the functions and status of the cabinet, as the President took certain major decisions without consulting it, such as the union with Zanzibar and the break of diplomatic relations with Britain over the Rhodesian independence issue in 1965. We may here note in parenthesis the decision of the Zambia Government that there will be, in a one-party state Constitution proposed for the country, an office of Prime Minister on the same lines as in Tanzania.[65]

Republican Ghana under Nkrumah epitomised the extreme of concentration of ministerial responsibilities in the President. A different technique was applied here in the allocation of ministerial responsibilities between the President and the ministers. There was a full complement of ministries to which were appointed separate ministers, but the critical aspects of the functions of most of them were detached from the minister and vested in the President, for example, armed forces were detached from defence, commerce from trade, banking and foreign exchange from finance, major contracting from all departments, police from interior, development expenditure from all departments, radio and television from information and broadcasting, and higher education and research from education.[66] The President also had responsibility over a wide range of other matters: regional organisation including regional and district commissioner, local authorities, regional party organisations and propaganda; establishment, auditor-general's department; African affairs; development planning and certain development projects; all state enterprises such as Ghana National Trading corporation, Ghana National Construction Corporation, Ghana Aluminium Product, State Cocoa Marketing Board, State Tele-Communication Corporation, and Guinea Press. The full list was quite formidable.[67] For many of these functions and others appropriate secretariats were organised, all responsible to the President, e.g., publicity secretariat, African affairs secretariat, establishment secretariat, state enterprises secretariat, etc.

Denuded of the vital aspects of their functions, the ministries were left as mere 'hollow shells'.[68] The minister was deprived of initiative and autonomy, which necessarily followed from the transfer to the President's office of the vital functions of the ministry. Since the function so transferred must impinge on the work of the ministry, very little scope was left for independent action by the minster. He could hardly initiate policy entirely on his own. By their nature and importance, the functions vested in the President were bound to be the factors controlling policy, which meant therefore that the President was to be the source of initiative in departmental policy as well as in general policy. Without the power to initiate policy for his ministry, a minister can be little more than an administrator concerned in the main to ensure that policy decided elsewhere is properly executed.

Nor was he allowed a free hand even in matters of pure administration. Here too the minister in Nkrumahist Ghana was under the thumb of the President. By law the President could, by legislative instrument, amend a statute so as to transfer to himself, to another minister or to a public officer, any functions conferred upon a minister by that statute.[69] The description of Dr Lee that ministers in Ghana under Nkrumah were 'little more than presidential secretaries who represent the leader in departments of state'[70] therefore seemed apt. With obvious exaggeration Henry Bretton also described them as 'no more than highly paid messengers who drove beflagged automobiles to and from the President's office, carried orders, made enquiries, and sought to resolve impasses stemming from the ambiguities surrounding their own positions and the apparatus of government in general'.[71]

The President's office was, of course, well equipped for its extensive functions. Flagstaff House, as it was called, was a vast establishment, staffed by skilled, hand-picked officers chosen both for their ability and for their loyalty to the President.

5. *A Presidential Watchdog of the Administration: Tanzania's Permanent Commission of Inquiry and Zambia's Commission for Investigations*

The foregoing account leaves no doubt that the President is the executive in name as well as in fact. The administration of government is very much centralised in him – not of course in the sense that he personally performs all the functions of government, for this is clearly impracticable. His direct ministerial responsibilities and his non-ministerial powers under specific statutes are quite vast. His formal power of control over other functions of government that are exercised on his behalf by others are consummate, varying in form with the different categories of officers, the control mechanisms being, for ministers, the power to appoint and remove them, to assign responsibilities to them, to re-shuffle and to direct them, to co-ordinate their activities, and to determine general policy affecting the overall conduct and operations of the government; for the public service, the power over the responsible ministers, the power over civil service policy and administration, and the power to appoint, remove and discipline its members; for the armed forces, the power over their operational use, the power to commission officers and command them, to make war and peace; for the entire governmental structure, the consummating power to constitute offices (ministerial or otherwise) and to abolish them.

This is a formidable array of powers, reaching into almost every aspect of government administration. How effectively they are employed in practice is, however, a matter that depends upon a variety of factors of which perhaps the most important are the channels of feedback. The activation of the power of removal, for example, from its formal existence into a potent weapon of control depends upon the means by which the President can inform himself of the occurrence of acts or omissions calling for the exercise of this power. Many serious derelictions of duty, abuses of power and other administrative lapses and malpractices, for which the exercise of the power would have been warranted, go on unnoticed all the time in the various branches of the government. What is needed to give reality to the formal power is a system of feedback, channels of communication to the President and other disciplinary authorities in cases of maladministration — in short, a watchdog over the conduct of administration.

No doubt many cases of maladministration get spotted by the administration itself and dealt with, but these often concern the doings or omissions of officers low down the hierarchy, while those of ministers, permanent secretaries and other top officials are largely immune against scrutiny and exposure. Questions to ministers by M.P.s in African parliaments seldom probe into matters of administration, being mostly concerned with roads, scholarships, water supply and similar services. Moreover, most African M.P.s maintain only ephemeral and fleeting contact with their constituents, they have neither the courage nor the inclination to probe complaints of maladministration, and the minister may just gloss over such questions about the administration as get asked at all, especially if they concern his own act or one to which he is personally privy; he (the minister) may, in the words of the Whyatt Report in Britain, just 'dig in his heels and refuse to disclose information'.[72] Thus, as a machinery for highlighting abuses of power and administrative lapses, and for securing corrective measures, parliamentary questions to ministers have little value in Africa.

If a person affected feels sufficiently aggrieved to initiate court action, then there is a good chance that the publicity of judicial proceedings may bring the matter to the attention of the President or other disciplinary authority. But this machinery also suffers from serious limitations. Its publicity is not really designed to serve as a channel of communication calculated to induce disciplinary action by the President. On the contrary, court proceeding against an administrative official is usually viewed as a contest in which the administration as an organisation, its honour and integrity in relation to the public, is involved, and which therefore calls for solidarity on its part in order to safeguard the principle of responsibility by which its unity and strength are sustained. No organisation ever takes kindly to having its dirty linen washed in public, thereby exposing its failings. The administration is no exception in this. It is seldom therefore that a court proceeding reveals the enormity of administrative malpractices, at least not to anything like their full extent. In any case, the opportunity for litigation is greatly limited by the fact that a case of maladministration may not be redressible by court action, either because it is not justiciable at all or, if it is, it cannot easily be proved by legal evidence, or because the aggrieved person, for fear of victimisation, lack of funds or just sheer ignorance of his rights, fails to take action. These impediments are aggravated because the judicial remedies available against the administration, the prerogative writs and orders with their limiting requirements, can only be obtained in the High Court, which therefore puts them 'economically and logistically beyond the reach of most [Africans]'.[73] This is especially so as the court's procedure does not allow it to seize itself of any matter except at the instance of a complainant. The very formality of that procedure, and its pre-occupation with legality rather than with the moral merit of an action or with negotiated settlement, makes it all the more unappealing to many an aggrieved person.

The President can, of course, order an inquiry into 'the conduct of any officer ... or the conduct or management of any department of the public service or of any public or local institution or into any matter in which an inquiry would be for the public welfare'.[74] Such an inquiry has to be public, unless the President otherwise directs,[75] and there is a right of representation by counsel.[76] It seems obvious that this kind of inquiry is unsuited for present purposes and that it is not intended to suit them. The President has to be moved to appoint an inquiry, just as the High Court has to be moved by a complainant, and it is more difficult to bring a complaint to the notice of the President and to move him to institute an inquiry than it is to invoke the jurisdiction of the court. Ordinarily the conduct of an officer or the management of a department of the public service is not likely to be considered by the President a fit subject for this kind of inquiry. Only if the political interests of the government itself are involved and it is considered necessary to obtain public vindication for it and safeguard its image and integrity will a public inquiry be instituted into the management of a government department or the conduct of one of its officers. The Doyle Commission in 1967 into the allegations of corruption in the administration of the funds of two statutory corporations in Zambia was for just this purpose. A commission may also be appointed ostensibly as a corrective measure by a 'reformist' revolutionary military government; such were the Ollennu Commission into alleged malpractice in the issue of import licences in Ghana, and the numerous commissions of inquiry appointed by the military government of Nigeria in 1966–7. Or its purpose may be to discredit an opposition regional government in a federation, as witness the Coker Commission of Inquiry of 1962 into the Action Group-administered statutory corporations in Western Nigeria,[77] or simply to discredit a particular minister. Apart from such cases, the publicity of an *ad hoc* commission of inquiry into administrative malpractices will be some-what too self-destructive ever to be resorted to by any government, and its procedure too elaborate for isolated acts of maladministration. What seems to have been primarily intended is an inquiry into proposals for the introduction of new political or administrative forms or procedures, such as the one-party state commissions in Tanzania and Zambia, or an inquiry into the activities of subordinate public authorities, like local government councils, marketing boards, etc., or the activities of registered public companies or other private organisations alleged to affect the public interest. It could not have been without reason that Zambia removed reference to 'the conduct of an officer ... or the conduct or management of any department of the public service' in its Inquiries Act of 1967, which simply authorises the President to order an inquiry into any matter in which an inquiry would, in his opinion, be for the public welfare.[78]

Nevertheless, a commission of inquiry provides a model that can be adapted to suit the need for a watchdog of the administration. The adaptation needed is simply to put it on a permanent footing and endow it with initiative to conduct inquiry in private into administrative malpractices, and to report its findings and recommendations; in other words a private, confidential investigating machinery that would be effective in checking on administrative malpractices without publicly discrediting and thereby antagonising the administration. It was this that provided the basis for Tanzania's permanent commission of inquiry, which was established in 1965 by the Interim Constitution.[79] The commission is to inquire into allegations of misconduct or abuse of office by persons in the service of the United Republic, the Party, local government authority, and such commissions, statutory corporations, public authorities or boards as may be specified by an act of parliament; the only public officers exempted from the jurisdiction of the commission are the President himself, the chief executive for Zanzibar, a judge, magistrate or registrar or a member of a tribunal in his judicial (but not administrative) capacity.[80] Without waiting for a formal complaint by an aggrieved person, as in the case of a court, the commission can, unless otherwise directed by the President, inquire into any alleged misconduct or abuse of office entirely on its own initiative or if so directed by the President.[81] The commission operates informally and in private, with no hearings, no rigid rules of evidence and no legal representation, its method of investigation being entirely at its own discretion, except that it must give hearing to any person, department or organisation that may be adversely affected by its report.[82] Easy accessibility, informality and flexibility are thus among the characteristics of the commission.[83]

The character of the commission as a presidential instrument needs to be emphasised at the outset in order to underline the difference between it and an ombudsman. Its members are appointed by the President, and also removable by him though only for incompetence or misbehaviour.[84] The President may direct it to hold or not to hold an inquiry. Its responsibility is entirely to the President, to whom it must report after each inquiry,[85] and without whose permission the contents of its report cannot be disclosed to anyone else.[86] The President decides what action, if any, is to be taken on the findings and recommendations of the commission, and in this he is free from outside pressures, either from parliament or the public at large, since the commission's findings and recommendations are private and confidential. Thus, without the force of public opinion to back up its recommendations, the commission is largely dependent on the President for its authority and prestige with the public. The only connection it has with parliament is through an annual report on its operation and activities, which the President is to cause to be prepared and laid before the national assembly for its information only, and not for debate or action.[87] The annual report to the national assembly does not impinge upon the confidentiality of the reports to the President on individual cases, since the report is not to disclose the identity, or contain any comment which may give an indication as to the identity, of persons into whose conduct the commission inquired.

The difference between the commission and an ombudsman strictly so-called is thus clearly marked, for the latter is a parliamentary, not a presidential, commissioner, responsible to, and relying upon the backing of, parliament, which provides the ultimate sanction for his authority and prestige. 'Continued disregard of the ombudsman's recommendations and suggestions will lead to a clash between the administration and the ombudsman's superior, parliament'[88] and with the public over whose rights the ombudsman exists to watch. Their functions are of course the same, and indeed in Sweden and Finland, the birthplace of the institution, an ombudsman exists side by side with a *justitiekansler* (or chancellor of justice corresponding to Tanzania's permanent commission) 'carrying out the same task in the same way and doing so equally successfully from the citizen's point of view. There is no evident demarcation between them and cases seem to be referred by the public rather haphazardly to one or the other. Close personal co-operation between them prevents any wasteful overlapping in practice'.[89] So long as the objective of effective control and supervision of the administration with a view to making it just, honest and efficient is achieved, it seems not to matter very much whether this is done through a parliamentary or presidential agent.

Given the undoubted need for a feedback to the President on the conduct of public officers, there can be no doubt that Tanzania's permanent commission of inquiry is well designed to, and does in fact, meet that need. The first step was to educate the public, on whom after all the commission must largely depend for information (the press provides a secondary source) about administrative malpractices. To this end, the commission, after its inauguration in July 1966, spent seven months touring all parts of the country, covering 16,096 miles in the course of which it addressed 64,065 people.[90] Realising that an insistence on complaints being made in person might make its machinery inaccessible to the vast majority of Tanzanians living in the rural areas, the commission very prudently allowed complaints to be made by letter, which became the most popular method.[91] Within one year of its operation, it had received 1,966 complaints, of which 1,060 were declined – 439 for lack of jurisdiction, and 621 because an appropriate and adequate alternative machinery, e.g., the courts, tribunals, the ministry's machinery, etc., was available, the commission acting in such cases merely as adviser to direct the complainant to the appropriate authority. This left 906 cases as the number actually investigated and upon which a report was made to the President. These cases involved nearly every ministry and department, and therefore provide information that might enable the President to supervise the public services more effectively. Although it is true that in roughly half these cases, the ministry or department complained against was vindicated by the commission, nonetheless the facts had been made available to the President.

The operations of the commission could not have failed to emphasise and to enhance the authority of the President *vis-à-vis* the ministers and the public service. The fear of being adversely reported upon must have a subordinating effect upon them. The commission testified to this fear when it wrote in its report that 'some leaders on hearing the approach of the Permanent Commission of Enquiry had unnecessary fevers, in some cases leaders were so apprehensive of what the . . . Commission . . . was doing in their areas that they planted some informers to report back to them what we were doing'.[92]

It seems clear too that the President's control on the public service would have gained in effectiveness. The mere reporting by the commission of cases of misuse of government property, shortages, dereliction of duty, arbitrariness, improper use of discretionary power, and sheer or malicious abuse of power by officers, such as unlawful detentions by area or regional commissioners or divisional officers, or politicians ordering a magistrate to convict an individual or otherwise interfering with the course of justice in the subordinate courts,[93] must have exercised a corrective and sobering influence on the officers concerned. But the report of the commission in such cases is invariably accompanied by a recommendation for action which may be a warning, dismissal, transfer, demotion, etc., for the official concerned, and for the complainant a reversal or cancellation of the decision or order complained against, release from detention, compensation, restoration of property wrongfully taken, reinstatement in job, etc.[94] The commission asserts that 'its effectiveness is beginning to leave its mark in the public services' as evidenced by the reduced incidence of improper exercise of powers.[95]

By thus ensuring compliance with established rules and procedures, and by reducing the incidence of abuse and corruption without destroying the credibility of the administration, the commission may be said to have enhanced the quality of public administration, and to have promoted confidence and friendly relations between it and the public, especially through its role in negotiating a settlement in cases where the action of the administration is otherwise legally unimpeachable.[96] The existence of a body, able and willing to take up its complaints against the administration and to investigate them impartially, must give psychological satisfaction to the public, while for the administration itself the rejection of unjustified complaints must be satisfying as a vote of confidence. More, of course, will depend on the extent to which the commission's recommendations are implemented by the President, which must in turn depend upon his own desire for a just, honest and efficient administration. Although no information is available on this, the President is unlikely to disregard or be indifferent to the commission's recommendations; the fear that political considerations or pressures might lead to the President interfering with the work of the commission[97] seemed not to have been borne out by experience so far. The President has proved himself to be imbued with a genuine desire to ensure justice, honesty and efficiency in the administration of government.[98]

Zambia's one-party state Constitution is to establish a four-man commission for investigations on the same lines as the Tanzanian permanent commission of inquiry, with the same functions and jurisdiction and the same relationship to the President and national assembly, the only difference being that the removal of the chairman of the commission, to be styled investigator-general, will require a resolution of the national assembly supported by a two-thirds majority, followed by an affirmative recommendation by an investigating tribunal of three persons appointed by the Chief Justice. The chairman and one other member of the tribunal must be present or former superior court judges. The recommendations of the one-party state commission, which were based on the ombudsman provisions of the Ghana Constitution of 1969, seemed to have envisaged a commission somewhat more independent of the President than the Tanzanian P.C.E. Actually there was no express indication of this in the commission's report, and it is only an inference from the fact that, under the Ghanaian scheme, the ombudsman's recommendations for action in individual cases were directed to the minister or department concerned, and were to be made public. All the commission's reports said was that the investigator-general was to submit an annual report to the President and to the national assembly, which should contain a summary of the matters investigated and the action taken or recommended by him.[99] But no indication was given as to who was to take the action or to whom the recommendation was to be made – parliament, the President, minister or other responsible authority.

It has been argued that an ombudsman strictly so-called, i.e. an agent of parliament, is 'strangely out of place' in a one-party state, on the ground that his success depends on the existence of a strong parliament which, backed up by 'an alert, intelligent, independent, well-informed and vocal electorate' reflects the 'real locus of power'.[100] While it is true that the sanction of an independent parliament and public opinion would import greater efficacy to the work of an ombudsman, it must be equally true that, given an equal desire for a just, honest and efficient administration, a parliamentary commissioner in a one-party state should be expected to be more effective than Tanzania's presidential commissioners by the mere fact that his findings and recommendations are made public, and so likely to provoke public demand for action on them.[101] Public opinion in African one-party states is not as dormant or indifferent as this argument seems to imply.

As previously noted, the Zambian one-party state commission's recommendations regarding the functions and jurisdiction of the ombudsman were based on the provisions of the Ghana Constitution, 1969. Under that Constitution, an act of parliament was to provide for the appointment of an ombudsman.[102] The Act was duly passed in August 1970, but no ombudsman had in fact been appointed when in January 1972 the Constitution was abrogated by a military coup.[103]

REFERENCES

1. Uganda (1967) Art. 34(1); Kenya S.18; Malawi S.54.

2. Ghana (1960) Art. 15(1); Tanzania S.13(3); Zambia S.51(2) and (3); Botswana S.51(4); Gambia S.50.

3. *Times of Zambia*, April 9, 1973.

4. S.8(2) Malawi; S.21 Tanzania; Art. 66 Uganda; S.53 Gambia; S.57 Botswana; S.56 Zambia; S.24 Kenya.

5. C. Gertzel and others, *Govt. and Politics in Kenya* (1969), p. 345.

6. Julius Nyerere, 'How much Power for a Leader?' *Africa Report*, 1962 Vol. 7, No. 71, p. 7.

7. Kwame Nkrumah, *Africa Must Unite* (1963), p. 89.

8. Nkrumah, *op. cit.*, pp. 89–90.

9. Julius Nyerere 'How much Power for a Leader?', *Africa Report* (1962), Vol. 7. No. 7, p. 7.

10. *Times of Zambia*, 3 December, 1968.

11. Julius Nyerere, *Democracy and the Party System* (1963).

12. Report (1964), p. 69.

13. Report of the National Commission on the Establishment of a One-Party Participatory Democracy in Zambia, Lusaka, October 1972, paras. 103–12; Govt. White Paper on the Report of the Commission, No. 1 of 1972, Govt. Printer, Lusaka, Nov. 1972, p. 7, 14–16.

14. *op. cit.*

15. S.51 Ghana; S.18 Tanganyika; S.21 Tanzania; S.87 Malawi; S.104 Uganda.

16. S.107 Kenya; S.111 Botswana; S.111 Gambia.

17. The provisions relating to the membership of the public service commission are contained in S.106 Kenya; S.110 Botswana; S.110 Gambia.

18. S.110 Kenya; S.112 Gambia; SS.111 and 116 Botswana.

19. S.105 Kenya; S.109 Gambia; S.126 Botswana; Art. 38 Ghana; S.78 Tanzania; S.85 Malawi; Art. 99 Uganda.

20. SS.112 and 113.

21. Constitution (Amendment and Supplementary Provisions) Act, 1969.

22. Constitution (Amendment) Act, 1970.

23. S.11 Constitution (Amendment) Act, 1970.

24. SS.114, 115, 115A, 115B, 116, 117, 119.

25. Constitution (Amendment) Act, 1970.

26. S.114(*a*) and (10).

27. *Kang'ombe* v. *Att.-Gen.* 1972/HP/511 of 1 Nov., 1972.

28. Supra p. 184.

29. Govt. White on the Report of the One-Party State Commission, No. 1 of 1972, Govt. Printer, Lusaka, 1972 p. 14.

30. Report, Lusaka, Oct. 1972 paras. 100 and 101.

31. Govt. White, *loc. cit.*

32. SS.26 and 109 Kenya; SS.53 and 118 Zambia; SS.52 and 115 Botswana.

33. SS.47 and 48 Gambia; S.35 71 Uganda; SS.56 and 88 Malawi.

34. Art. 47.

35. SS.13(2) and 20.

36. Govt. Paper No. 1 of 1962.

37. 'Relationship in Districts between Administration and Departmental Officers', Kenyan Chief Secretary's Circular No. 12 of 1960; reproduced in *Journal of African Administration*, Jan. 1961.

38. S.18 Zambia Independence Order; S.10 Republic of Malawi (Constitution) Act, 1966; S.16 Constitution of Kenya (Amendment) Act, 1964; S.128 Constitution of the Republic of the Gambia, 1970.

39. Art. 76.

40. Articles 46 and 47 of Treaty.

41. T. P. Omari, *Kwame Nkrumah: The Anatomy of an African Dictatorship* (1970), pp. 132–3.

42. Above, p. 178.

43. Art. 53(1) Ghana; S.80 Tanzania.

44. S.8 National Defence Act, 1966 (Tanzania); S.4 Army Act. cap. 12:01 (Malawi); S.1 Armed Forces Act, cap. 295 (Uganda); S.4(1) Defence Act, cap. 131 (Zambia).

45. Ghana (1960) Art. 54(1); Uganda (1967) Art. 24(1); Tanzania S.6(1); Zambia S.49(1); Kenya S.4; Malawi S.8(1); Botswana S.49(1); Gambia, S.3.

46. S.133(15)(*c*), Gambia.

47. Ghana Art. 54; Tanzania S.81; Uganda Art. 78; Zambia S.49; Malawi S.48; Botswana S.49.

48. Report, Lusaka, Oct., 1972, para. 110.

49. Govt. Paper No. 1 of 1972, Govt. Printer, Lusaka, p. 15.

50. See, e.g., S.25 National Defence Act, 1966 (Tanzania).

51. See, e.g., S.181(2), Army Act, cap. 12:01 (Malawi).

52. The idea for this originated with Ghana under Nkrumah.

53. William Tordoff, *Government and Politics in Tanzania* (1967), p. 164.

54. Gazette Notice No. 766 of 1969.

55. *ibid.*

56. Gazette Notice No. 1663 of 1969.

57. Gazette Notice Nos. 80 and 81 of 1970 (Jan.).

58. Gazette Notice No. 802 of 1971.

59. Constitution (Amendment) Act, 1969.

60. Nat. Ass. Deb. No. 17, 21–23 April, 1969, col. 62.

61. Gertzel *et al.*, *Government and Politics in Kenya* (1969), p. 313.

62. W. Tordoff, *Government and Politics in Tanzania* (1967), p. 66.

63. Govt. Notice No. 41/1972 of 25 February, 1972, made under S.13 of the Constitution. By this the President de-established all existing offices of ministers and established in their place the office of prime minister and six other offices of ministers.

64. Ministers (Assignment of Ministerial Responsibilities) Notice, GN 40/72, replacing GN 263/1971.

65. Govt. White Paper on the Report of the National Commission on the Establishment of a One-Party Participatory Democracy in Zambia, Govt. Printer, Lusaka, 1972, p. 6.

66. H. L. Bretton, *The Rise and Fall of Kwame Nkrumah* (1968), p. 183.

67. Bretton, *op. cit.*, pp. 180–2; Rubin and Murray, *The Constitution and Government of Ghana* (1961), Appendix 5, pp. 273–83.

68. Bretton, *op. cit.*, p. 183.

69. The Presidential Affairs (Amendment) Act, 1965, S.4.

70. J. M. Lee, 'Parliament in Republican Ghana', *Parl. Affairs* (1962–3) Vol. XVI, p. 382.

71. Bretton, *op. cit.*, pp. 97–8.

72. Whyatt Report, *The Citizen and the Administration*, Oct. 1961.

73. Robert Martin, 'Tanzania, Permanent Commission of Enquiry, Annual Report 1966–67' (1969), 7, *Journal of Modern African Studies*, p. 178.

74. S.2 Commission of Inquiry Act, 1914 (as amended), cap. 56, Laws of Uganda (1964), and the Inquiry Acts of the other countries.

75. S.2(3).

76. S.13.

77. The Doyle, Coker and Ollennu Commissions are described in detail in T. Ocran, 'Law in Aid of Development', Ch. XII (not yet published).

78. S.2.

79. S.67(1); see Report of the Presidential Commission on a One-Party State (1965), paras 106–7.

80. S.67(4) and (5).

81. S.67(2).

82. S.10 Permanent Commission of Enquiry Act, 1966.

83. Y. P. Ghai, 'Ombudsman and Others' (1969), 7, *East African Journal*, pp. 34ff. For a detailed account of the structure, powers and procedure of the P.C.E. see T. Ocran, *op. cit.*, ch. X.

84. S.68(1) and (5) Constitution.

85. S.67(3) Constitution.

86. S.16 P.C.E. Act, 1966.

87. S.17(1) P.C.E. Act.

88. E. V. Mittlebeeler, 'The Ombudsman in Africa', Correspondence to Editor, [1965] 9 *J.A.L.* 184. Also T. Sargant, 'The Ombudsman and One-Party States in Africa', Correspondence to Editor, [1964] 8 *J.A.L.* 195. See generally D. C. Rowat, ed., *The Ombudsman* (1965), and the bibliography, pp. 293–9.

89. N. H. Hunnings, 'The Ombudsman in Africa', Correspondence to Editor [1966] 10 *J.A.L.* 138.

90. Annual Report, 1966–7, Govt. Printer, Dar es Salaam, 1968, para. 6.

91. *ibid.*, paras. 12–14.

92. Report, *op. cit.*, para. 10.

93. Annual Report, 1967–8, Govt. Printer, Dar es Salaam, 1969, paras. 14–33; also E. A. M. Mang'anya, The Permanent Commission of Enquiry (Ombudsman), Govt. Printer, Dar es Salaam (1970).

94. Annual Report 1966–7, para. 33.

95. Annual Report 1967–8, para. 50.

96. Y. P. Ghai, 'Ombudsman and Others', (1969) 7, *East Africa Journal*, pp. 34ff.

97. McAuslan and Ghai, 'Constitutional Innovation and Political Stability in Tanzania', (1966) 4, *Journal of Modern African Studies*, pp. 501ff.

98. Nyerere, Address to the Nat. Ass., 8 June, 1965, introducing the one-party state constitutional proposals; Kawawa, Nat. Ass. Deb., 22 Feb., 1966, introducing the P.C.E. Bill.

99. Report, 1972, paras 128 and 129.

100. E. V. Mittlebeeler, *op. cit.*; H. Kjekshus, 'The Ombudsman in the Tanzanian One-Party System', *The African Review*, Vol. 1, No. 2, Sept. 1971, p. 19.

101. Cf. T. Sargant's view that even in a one-party state the ombudsman 'might provide at least a transitional answer to Africa's problems of how to reconcile dynamic and purposeful government with

respect for administrative justice and the rights of the individual', *op. cit.*, p. 196; see also N. M. Hunnings, *op. cit.*

102. SS.100 and 101; see Constitutional Commission Report, 1968, pp. 125–36.

103. T. Ocran, *op. cit.*, for a detailed description of the Ghanaian model; J. Hagan, 'Whatever happened to Ghana's Ombudsman?', *Transition* 8 (1971), p. 29.

CHAPTER VIII

CENTRALISM IN THE ORGANISATION OF POLITICS: THE ONE-PARTY STATE

Of the nine presidential regimes in Commonwealth Africa, six — Tanzania, Kenya, Malawi, Zambia, Ghana and Uganda (the last two are now ruled by the military) — are one-party states. Recently rumblings of it have been heard in Sierra Leone, the newest of the presidential regimes.

It is certainly remarkable that as many as six of the nine presidential regimes are one-party states. They account indeed for the total number of one-party states in Commonwealth Africa. Outside the presidential regimes, the two- or multi-party system still holds the stage, except that Nigeria is at present under military rule, and Lesotho, ruled since Prime Minister Leabua Jonathan's coup in 1970 by a civilian revolutionary government without parliament, is seriously contemplating a 'no-party government'. As with unitarism, the question is also prompted as to the reasons for the increasing predominance of the one-party system in the presidential regimes. Is the phenomenon attributable to the centralising propensity of an executive presidency in Africa, or is it dictated by the genuine needs of the countries concerned?

1. *Origins of the One-party System in the Presidential Regimes*

For an insight into the motivations for the introduction of the one-party system in these countries, it is necessary to examine the circumstances of its origin, with a view particularly to seeing to what extent it can be said to rest upon the voluntary choice of the people. Ghana perhaps came nearest to a one-party state founded upon the choice of the electorate. It must be said to the credit of Nkrumah and his CPP government that no resort was ever made to outright proscription of opposition parties. No doubt they were subjected to various forms of repression, both subtle and blatant, which took quite a heavy toll of their following in the country and in parliament. Thus, of the thirty-three opposition members elected to parliament in 1956 (as against seventy-one CPP), only seven were left by the end of 1963, the rest having either joined the CPP, been detained under the Preventive Detention Act or left the country and thereby vacated their seats under the disqualifications introduced in 1959.[1] 'By 1960', writes Dennis Austin, 'the effect of the combination of threats and blandishments was plain to see: of the thirty-two opposition members at independence, three were being held in detention, one was in exile, and twelve had crossed to the government side. A number more were to take the same road under the republic, some to prison, some abroad, and others to the sanctuary of the ruling party'.[2] Yet the fact remains that opposition parties were not then proscribed or prohibited. The nearest that Ghana came to that was the ban on tribally-based parties imposed by the Avoidance of Discrimination Act of 1957. The object of the Act, as declared in its preamble, was to 'prohibit organisations using or engaging in tribal, regional, racial or religious propaganda to the detriment of any other community or securing the election of persons on account of their tribal, regional, or religious affiliations and for other purposes connected therewith'. The prohibition took a somewhat subtle form. It was made an offence for 'any organisation whose membership is substantially limited to one community or religious faith to have as one of its objects the exposure of any other organisation however constituted or of any part of the community, to hatred, contempt or ridicule on account of their community or religion'. This provision, though ostensibly aimed against the practice of tribal, racial or religious discrimination, had a restrictive implication for the opposition parties, all of which were based in tribes or regions. It made it impossible for them to appeal to tribal sentiment in their opposition to the CPP, such as by accusing the CPP of being an instrument of the coastal people for the domination of the rest of the country, a fear which had conditioned Ashanti's opposition to the CPP.[3] Secondly, the Act prohibited any organisation, 'established substantially for the direct or indirect benefit or advancement of the interests of any particular community or operating for the purposes of engaging in any election', and empowered the President to declare it illegal. The prohibitions of the Act were forestalled by the opposition parties merging into a single United Party just before it was enacted. The Act must have operated also to prevent the formation of new tribally or regionally based parties.

In January 1964 Ghana formally became a one-party state. This had, however, come about as the result of a referendum organised in terms of the 1960 Republican Constitution. Was the referendum a genuine expression of the people's choice? William Harvey thinks not. He writes: 'While there was no organised opposition to the proposals, the nearly unanimous approval[4] does not seem likely or even possible in a free election. In Ashanti, for example, where opposition to the CPP had traditionally been strongest, not a single "No" vote was reported. Opportunities for voter intimidation were ample; each ballot was marked with the voter's serial number as recorded in the electoral register. The Party press warned voters that they could not hide behind the so-called secrecy of the polling booth. Observers reported that in many polling places no box for "No" votes was available or the slot in this box was sealed. The high percentage of the electorate voting may be in part attributable to warnings in the Party press against staying at home and promises that "the people's wrath is apt to descend without mercy upon those who are not with us".[5]

Following the referendum, the Constitution was amended to provide that 'there shall be one National Party' which 'shall be the Convention People's Party'.[6] Strictly interpreted, this provision would seem to admit of the possibility of other parties existing otherwise than on a national basis. A party exclusively of professionals or of workers is not a national party, if by that is meant a party that represents the nation as a whole; such a party would, therefore, not be in conflict with the status accorded to the CPP as the one national party, though one based on tribal or religious affiliations would be caught by the prohibition in the Avoidance of Discrimination Act. The point is, of course, purely academic for, since every association with any political influence, such as trade unions, farmers' associations, etc., was affiliated to the CPP, the practical effect of the amendment was to bestow exclusiveness upon the CPP. In the result, the opposition parties, having been forced by the Avoidance of Discrimination Act to merge into a single nation-wide party, were now forced out of existence as a national party. The opposition in Ghana had been extremely destructive, but in 1964 Nkrumah had really nothing to fear from it. In the circumstances it is difficult to resist the conclusion that the one-party state was proclaimed because, as Dennis Austin has said,[7] Nkrumah could not be content with the role of leader of a dominant party which had still to contend with an opposition, feeble though its strength in the country and parliament might be. Nkrumah, Dennis Austin says, 'liked to take a unique view of himself and his place in history'.[8] For such a man the role of leader of a dominant party in a two-party state could hardly be satisfying.

Next to Ghana comes Kenya in the degree of voluntariness of its one-party system. This voluntariness of the Kenyan one-party system rests upon two bases; it originated in a voluntary merger of existing parties, and it has never been formally established by law. On the eve of independence Kenya had three main political parties, the Kenya African National Union (KANU), the Kenya African Democratic Union (KADU) and the African People's Party (APP), with sixty-four, thirty-two and eight members respectively in the house of representatives. In September 1963, the APP, which originated as a splinter group from KANU, dissolved itself and returned to the fold. There followed in the same year two isolated defections from KADU to KANU. The defections were accentuated in 1964 through a concerted campaign by the government to woo away opposition members in an effort to secure the majority which it needed to effect certain changes in the Constitution. There being no question of the opposition as a party supporting the proposed changes, which in part sought to cut off its main bases of support and power (i.e. regionalism), the government was faced with the alternatives of either wooing over enough opposition members to give it the required nine-tenths majority in the senate or going to the people in a referendum. The former seemed the less difficult and expensive.

The wooing campaign was launched by President Kenyatta himself in meetings with the chiefs and elders in some of the opposition strongholds. The aim was to get those chiefs and elders to use their influence with the opposition members. The chiefs and elders duly played their part, and there then followed mass defections from KADU to KANU, which gave the latter the necessary nine-tenths majority in the senate. In the light of this development the KADU executive met and decided that the most honourable course for the party was to cross over *en masse* to the government party before the votes on the constitutional changes could be taken in the senate.[9] Accordingly on November 10, its leader, Mr Ngala, in the house of representatives announced that 'in the interests of Kenya, I have full mandate to declare today that the Official Opposition is dissolved, and Kadu joins the Government under the leadership of *Mzee* Kenyatta. . . . I have taken Kadu into the Government fully aware of the challenges that are facing us in Kenya and East Africa today and in future'.[9a] He urged M.P.s of both parties in the spirit of nation-building to forget the past inter-party hostilities, and the members outside parliament to regard themselves as one and to work together to build a united country. 'The reunion of old 1952 and 1957 members', he continued, 'is a great joy to us. This is an historic moment when we have to overlook our personal political dignity, gains or losses in favour of the Kenya cause, and the presentation of a united front to the world. Tribal and racial conflicts must cease and should have no meaning to us in order to build a united nation'. Welcoming the former KADU members into KANU, the Prime Minister described the event as a great victory for Kenya. The Speaker then ordered the serjeants-at-arms to complete the process of transformation by removing the arms that divided the members on his left (i.e. former KADU members). Thus was born the one-party state in Kenya.

Was the merger really voluntary? Clearly, it was forced upon KADU by the mass defection of many of its parliamentary members. KADU was forced into it as a face-saving device, not out of a free choice. Nor were the defections voluntary. They were procured by pressure exerted on the members by the chiefs and elders. The pressure here was more direct and openly avowed than is generally the case in Africa. Floor-crossing from the opposition to the government party has been perhaps the most decisive single factor undermining the position of opposition parties in Africa. The technique has been to make life as intolerable as possible for the opposition members by various forms of discrimination and victimisation ranging from denial of amenities or rights to physical molestation, and even lynching and death, until, their will broken, they are obliged to join the ruling party.

Admittedly part of the motivation is sheer opportunism on the part of opposition members, a desire to share in the spoils of office. Yet, even this opportunistic desire to share in the spoils of office is not, in the African context, without an extenuating aspect. Ruling parties in Africa are mostly dominant parties who, not content with their overwhelming predominance, often resort to repression and perverted methods to perpetuate their rule and so exclude the opposition from ever coming into power. The prospect of being a permanent opposition, with the hazards involved, naturally creates despondency among opposition members, forcing the not deeply committed or not so highly principled to seek the security of membership of the ruling party. For the diehards it is either continuing the vain effort of trying to swim against the tide or taking to unconstitutional means of obtaining power. The latter course invariably provokes greater repressive measures from the government, resulting in more and more defections as the weight of these measures press more and more heavily upon demoralised opposition members. In so far, therefore, as a one-party state originates in defections from the opposition party, the presumption in the context of our experience of politics in Africa is that it is not voluntary.

In any case, whatever claim Kenya's one-party system has to being voluntary was destroyed by subsequent events in the country. Soon after its birth, the new one-party state began to experience internal dissension. The dissolution of KADU had meant that all political discussions and opposition were now directed inwards within KANU. When the conflicts and clashes could no longer be contained within the party, a split occurred in 1966. The Vice-President of the party and of the country, Mr Oginga Odinga, leading a faction in the dispute, broke away to form his own party, the Kenya People's Union (KPU). It looked as if the drain on the government's support in parliament was going to be much heavier than the initial publicly-announced resignations. To halt this the government, as a first measure, introduced a constitutional amendment, which forfeited the parliamentary seats of the defectors.[10] It worked. Thirteen of the defectors, 'faced with the loss of perquisites, applied for readmission to KANU and publicly reaffirmed their loyalty to Mr Kenyatta. They helped to get the constitutional amendment passed by the two Houses. But in spite of their renewed declarations of allegiance to the party, the dissidents were told that they too would have to stand for re-election under the new law. On hearing this, ten of the penitents crossed the floor again – and rejoined the KPU.[11]

When the elections – the Little General Election – were held, only nine of the KPU members retained their seats. With its members in the house so drastically reduced, the party failed to qualify as the official opposition party within the meaning of the amended standing orders, which defined an official opposition party as an opposition party or coalition of opposition parties consisting of not less than thirty members.[12] Consequently, the recognition previously accorded to the KPU by the Speaker as an official opposition was withdrawn, and with it the privileges that go with that status. A further amendment to the Constitution and to the Preservation of Public Security Act enabled the President to order the detention of persons at any time without parliamentary approval.[13] Thereupon thirteen officials of the KPU were detained. In 1969, Odinga himself was detained and the KPU banned. Kenya was again restored to the cherished status of a *de facto* one-party state, not by the voluntary choice of the people, but by the exercise of sheer political power.

Uganda shared with Kenya the characteristic that its one-party system was not formally established by law. It was a product of a combination of defections to the ruling party and of proscription. At independence in 1962 the three parties in the country – the Uganda People's Congress (UPC), the Kabaka Yekka (KY) and the Democratic Party (DP) – were represented in the national assembly in the proportion of forty-four, twenty-four and twenty-four. The first two teamed up to form a coalition government, with the latter in opposition. By the end of 1964 the majority of the DP M.P.s, including its parliamentary leader, Mr Bataringaya, had crossed the floor to the UPC. The Prime Minister, Milton Obote, then withdrew recognition from it as the official opposition. Here, however, the defections appeared to have been more the result of disagreements within the DP itself than of victimisation by the government or the opportunistic desire for the perquisites of office. The DP was in the awkward position of having its leader outside parliament. As is usually the case, the attempt by a leader outside parliament to rule the conduct of the members in parliament led to clashes between him and the parliamentary leader. The members became disenchanted with the party, and began to cross over to the UPC. At the same time, some KY members, dissatisfied with the conservatism of the party leadership, especially the Kabaka and his chiefs, had also crossed over to the UPC. In August 1964, when a total of ten KY members had defected to the UPC, Obote dropped the KY from the government. In July 1965 six of the remaining KY members crossed over to the UPC. However, these latest defections were purposely organised in order to internalise opposition to Obote within the UPC.[14] The strategy succeeded, for on February 4, 1966, Obote's government was defeated on a motion calling for a commission of inquiry into an alleged misappropriation in which Obote was said to be implicated. But the success was turned against the KY itself by Obote, since in the manoeuvres following upon this event, what was left of its parliamentary membership disappeared. Returning from a tour of the north where he was at the time of the vote, Obote had the Constitution suspended and a new one promulgated in its place. When the remaining KY members refused to take the oath of allegiance to the new Constitution, their seats were promptly declared vacated; no by-elections were held to fill them. In 1969 the DP and a number of other smaller parties were proscribed, so that Uganda thereby became a *de facto* one-party state.

Tanzania would have been the classic example of a one-party state based on the voluntary choice of the people but for two factors which tainted its standing in this matter. In the 1960 parliamentary elections just on the eve of independence, the Tanganyika African National Union (TANU) won all but one of the seventy-one constituencies. This might be considered a proof that *at that time* the electorate desired no other party. But that vote was certainly not a decision to bar for ever the formation of new parties. These are two widely different things. The same electorate that voted almost unanimously for TANU might have recoiled if asked to vote on whether TANU should be established as the one and only party. That was not the issue before them in 1960: the choice that they expressed then was for TANU as the government of the day.

In 1962 the People's Democratic Party was founded by Tumbo, former leader of the Railway Union, and lately Tanganyikan High Commissioner in London. Subsequently the party was proscribed and Tumbo detained.[15] In view of what has just been said, this action cannot be justified by reference to the vote in the 1960 election. In 1964, TANU was formally established as the only political party in the country, under whose auspices all political activities have to be conducted.[16] The decision was taken by the national executive committee of TANU, and announced by President Nyerere on January 28, 1964. The people were not consulted upon it either in a referendum or otherwise. Again, the vote in the 1960 election cannot be taken as a mandate for it. A presidential commission was appointed to consider 'the changes in the Constitution of Tanganyika and the Constitution of the Tanganyika African National Union, and in the practice of Government that might be necessary to bring into effect a democratic One-Party State in Tanganyika'. In other words, the principle of a one-party state was decided, and was therefore not open to discussion either by the commission or by the people. Thus, although the commission consulted widely on the form of the new Constitution, not a word was said for or against the principle of a one-party state itself during the consultations.

This was also the method used in Zambia. On February 25, 1972, President Kaunda announced at a press conference the decision of his government that Zambia was to become a one-party participatory democracy, and that a commission would be set up to advise on the form this should take. The commission was duly appointed on March 1, 1972. As in Tanganyika earlier in 1964, it was to consider, not the case for or against a one-party state, but only the 'changes in (a) the Constitution of the Republic of Zambia; (b) the practices and procedures of the Government of the Republic; and (c) the Constitution of the United National Independence Party, necessary to bring about and establish One-Party Participatory Democracy in Zambia'. The commission was thus precluded from entertaining submissions for or against the principle of a one-party state. As it stated in its report: 'A number of petitioners did not confine themselves strictly to the terms of reference regarding the form of the One-Party Democracy as such and discussed matters relating to the pros and cons of its establishment. We, however, insisted that our task was not to listen to petitioners who gave reasons for or against the establishment of the One-Party System'.[17]

The United National Independence Party (UNIP) could not even, like its counterpart in Tanganyika, rely on an almost unanimous electoral verdict in support of the government's decision. At independence there were three parties competing for power, UNIP with fifty-six elected members in parliament, the African National Congress (ANC) eight, and the National Progressive Party (NPP), a European organisation, with ten members elected on the reserved European roll. When the special European roll was abolished in 1968,[18] the NPP quickly dissolved itself. In the same year a new party, the United Party (UP), a splinter group from UNIP, emerged under the leadership of the former UNIP Minister of Commerce, Mr Nalumino Mundia, but was banned not long after and its leaders detained, because of violent clashes with the UNIP Youth Brigade. Its members then joined the ANC.

Nineteen hundred and sixty-eight happened also to be an election year. With the dissolution of the NPP and the banning of the UP, the election became a straight fight between UNIP and ANC. From the contest the two parties emerged with eighty-one and twenty-three elected members respectively. (To the eighty-one UNIP elected members must of course be added the five members nominated by the President.) On this result the Speaker of the new national assembly ruled that the ANC was not entitled to recognition as an official opposition, since its strength in the house was less than the 25 per cent (twenty-eight members) required 'to form a quorum to run the business of the House or in the absence of UNIP to be able to form a government'.[19] Thus, as in Kenya in 1966, the party lost the privileges attached to the status of an official opposition, such as the right of access for its leader to certain official information, to government departments and to ministers, and the right to an annual salary and to official accommodation.

In 1970 the Speaker sought to deny the party recognition as a parliamentary party at all. In accordance with the provisions of a 1966 constitutional amendment, the leader of the party, Mr Harry Nkumbula, had given notice to the Speaker seeking to unseat two of its parliamentary members who, having been elected on the party's platform at the 1968 election, had subsequently crossed the floor to UNIP. The procedure for this required notice in writing to be given to the Speaker, signed by a member of the national assembly recognised by the Speaker as the leader in the assembly of a particular political party, alleging that an M.P. who conducted his election campaign as a member of the party had since ceased to be such member.[20] The Speaker, after informing the house of the allegation, was then required to send a copy of the notice to the chief justice for inquiry to determine the truth of the allegation. The Speaker in this case refused to act on Mr Nkumbula's notice, on the ground that he did not recognise him as leader of a political party in the national assembly. As, however, the Hansard contained several instances where the Speaker, while refusing to recognise Nkumbula as leader of the *official opposition*, had referred to him as leader of the ANC in parliament, the court, in an application by Nkumbula, held that these references amounted to an unequivocal recognition; and that accordingly it was mandatory on the Speaker to take the further actions prescribed by the constitutional provisions.[21]

The ANC has faced other hazards which, as previously stated, are the lot of any opposition in Africa. Many of its parliamentary members, therefore, had to cross the floor to UNIP, so that of the twenty-three returned at the 1968 general elections, only fourteen remained by December 1971. It is significant that at a by-election in 1971, the ANC was able to win back five of the seats vacated by its members who crossed the floor to UNIP.

In 1971 another split occurred in the UNIP, leading to the formation of a new splinter party, the United Progressive Party (UPP) led by a former UNIP Vice-President, Mr Simon Kapwepwe. As with Mundia's United Party, the new party was short-lived. It was banned on February 4, 1972, and its leaders were again detained. The departure of Kapwepwe and his followers from UNIP brought no additional parliamentary members to the opposition benches, since under the 1966 constitutional amendment referred to above, such of Kapwepwe's followers as were M.P.s were subsequently unseated, and in the by-election that followed in December 1971, only Kapwepwe was re-elected. Part of the reason for the party's poor showing at the election might have been that, with the exception of Kapwepwe himself, the rest of its parliamentary members were in detention and so became, by the terms of a 1969 constitutional amendment, disqualified to stand as candidates at the election.[22] By the same amendment, the seat of a member is vacated if he has been in detention or restriction for a continuous period of six months. Under this provision, Kapwepwe, who was detained in January and remained in detention until his release in December, 1972, lost his seat.

This, then, was how Zambia came to be what has been described as a quasi-one-party state.[23] The government's decision to make Zambia a full-fledged one-party state has now been implemented by an amendment to the Constitution.[24] The amendment establishes UNIP as the 'one and only political party in Zambia', and prohibits the formation of other political parties or organisations as well as any expression of opinion or other activity in sympathy with such political parties or organisations. Membership of the party becomes a necessary qualification for election to, and membership of, parliament, but the tenure of existing M.P.s who are not members of UNIP continues unaffected until December 31, 1973, or until the dissolution of parliament, whichever is earlier.

In March 1964, President Kaunda assured the nation that 'any disappearance of the Parliamentary Opposition in this country and the introduction of one-party system would not be, and I emphasise, would not be an act of the government, but would only be according to the wishes of the people of this country . . . as expressed at the polls in any future election'.[25] The actual establishment of the one-party system by an act of the government without the verdict of the electorate at the polls was clearly a departure from this assurance. But President Kaunda insists that the government's decision was in accordance with the wishes of the people, because, 'since Independence there has been a constant demand for the establishment of a one-party state in Zambia. The demands have increasingly become more and more widespread in all corners of Zambia. In recent months I have received hundreds of messages and letters from organisations and individuals appealing to me to take concrete steps to bring about a one-party system of government. In the resolutions passed by almost every conference, whether political or non-political, unequivocal demands have been made for government to introduce a one-party system of government. Chiefs last year joined the chorus of the overwhelming majority of the people. Indeed, the UNIP National Council sitting in Mulungushi Hall between 1 and 3 October last year charged the central committee of the ruling party to work towards the achievement of a one-party democracy....'[26]

These demands were made by UNIP partisans, and should not be taken as conclusive of the wishes of the Zambian people as a whole. The procedure of a national commission is certainly a more reliable method of ascertaining the wishes of the people than the resolutions of UNIP conferences and partisan messages to the President by individuals and organisations. Even if popular consultation by the commission would only have confirmed what the government already believed, still it would have given the decision the stamp of popular approval and thereby strengthened the position of the government. The refusal to let the commission enquire into this has created the impression that the government was afraid of the result of a popular opinion poll. Or was it a fear that those testifying before the commission might not be truly representative of the people? If so, the commission should not have been set up at all. The government should then have used the more popular procedure of a referendum. That the referendum has been abolished as a specific procedure for constitutional amendment in Zambia does not affect its general legitimacy as a means of popular consultation on matters of government. Ideally, quite apart from any specific procedure for constitutional amendment, a government should not alter the fundamental structure or system of government without popular consultation, by whatever method it is conducted. It seems that the fear that further eruptions of the Mundia and Kapwepwe sort of episode might destroy UNIP was an operative factor in the decision to establish the one-party state. The motivation was more that of self-preservation than of national unity.

It is relevant finally to note that the ANC never acquiesced in what was done. Its president, Mr Harry Nkumbula, and his deputy, Mr Mundia, were put on the one-party state commission but declined to serve, thereby demonstrating in concrete form their opposition to the establishment of the one-party state. Mr Nkumbula had gone further and instituted a court action in which he challenged the government's decision to establish a one-party state.[27] The case is sufficiently important to justify a somewhat extended discussion. The claim was that the government's decision was 'likely' to infringe rights guaranteed to the petitioner by the Constitution as it existed at that time, that is to say, the right to assemble freely and associate with other persons and in particular to form political association,[28] the right to express and receive opinions,[29] and freedom from discrimination on the ground of political opinion.[30] The grounds for the claim were that these rights could not exist or be enjoyed unhindered under a one-party system, because of the incompatibility between them and the system. A one-party state, the argument asserted, was manifestly 'contrary to the spirit of the Constitution' as reflected in its bill of rights.

It is necessary at the outset to appreciate the nature of the claim. It was not contended that the government lacked the power to amend the Constitution for the purpose of establishing a one-party state or that such an amendment would be unconstitutional and void. The power of the government, by the prescribed majority in parliament, to amend the Constitution for any purpose could not well be doubted, and the petitioner acknowledged it by implication. The claim related entirely to the petitioner's rights in the period before an amendment would have been effected. Herein lay the insuperable difficulty confronting the claim. The government's decision imported no more than a declaration of intention to introduce legislation in parliament to amend the Constitution for this purpose. How can a mere declaration of intention to introduce legislation be said to be likely to infringe rights under the Constitution, especially where the proposed legislation was to amend the Constitution itself? There is something of a contradiction here. If the government possessed the right and power to amend the Constitution for any purpose, how can the prior announcement of an intention to exercise that right and power be an infringement of rights under the Constitution? When the power had been exercised, and a one-party system had thereby been established, the petitioner's rights to form and belong to political parties other than the constitutionally recognised one, and to express and receive opinions against the latter party, would have ceased to exist.

It seems absurdly contradictory to argue, as counsel for the petitioner did, that it was sufficient for the petitioner to show that the introduction in the future of a 'one-party democracy will infringe his rights under the Constitution in its present form', without having to show that after the new system had been lawfully and constitutionally introduced, those rights would be likely to be contravened. If there was no likelihood of the rights being infringed by the constitutional amendment establishing the new system, it seems utterly meaningless to say that the mere proposal to introduce it would infringe them. To admit the petitioner's argument would amount to saying that the court could, by order or declaration, prevent the carrying into effect of an intention to amend the Constitution in a perfectly lawful manner.

A different point might have arisen if the government's decision had been to introduce a one-party system by unlawful and unconstitutional means (e.g., by ordinary legislation not passed with the requisite majority), for it could then be argued that rights guaranteed by the Constitution would be likely to be infringed, and that any person likely to be affected thereby would be entitled to invoke the jurisdiction of the High Court under S.28(1) of the Constitution, which provides:

(1) ... if any person alleges that any of the provisions of Sections 13 to 26 (inclusive) of this Constitution has been, is being or is *likely* to by contravened in relation to him, then, without prejudice to any other action with respect to the same matter which is lawfully available, that person may apply to the High Court for redress.

However, the right of recourse to the High Court under this section is limited by a later provision of the same section to the effect that 'no application shall be brought under Subsection (1) of this section on the grounds that the provisions of SS.13 to 26 (inclusive) of this Constitution are likely to be contravened by reason of proposals contained in any bill which, at the date of the application, has not become a law'.[31] Counsel for Nkumbula argued that this limitation had no application where what was involved was not a bill, but an authoritative pronouncement or step taken by the government indicating an intention to introduce legislation. In the case of such an authoritative pronouncement, he submitted that it was open to any interested party to go to court for a declaration. It seems startling to suggest that the limitation should apply to a bill, but not to a declaration of intention to introduce a bill. In the words of Judge President Baron, delivering the judgment of the Court of Appeal, 'it is ... absurd to suggest that the legislature intended the courts to be vested with the power to pronounce in advance that if the government pursued an expressed intention, legislation on the lines of that expressed intention would be *ultra vires* the Constitution. This would involve all manner of debate as to which expressions of intention were authoritative and which were not to be regarded as expressing government policy. The consequences of such a construction would be truly chaotic'.

Mr Nkumbula's claim should more meaningfully have been based, not on the mere declaration of intention to introduce a one-party system, but on actions taken or threatened by the government in furtherance or pursuance of its decision, if it could be shown that such actions would be likely to infringe his rights under the Constitution before its amendment. There cannot be any doubt, as Chief Justice Doyle said at first instance, that if, before an amendment, 'the

Government of Zambia did take steps to prohibit the expression of opinion against the introduction of a one-party state, that would be a contravention of Section 22 of the Constitution [guaranteeing freedom of expression], and the petitioner would be entitled to redress'. Were any such steps in fact taken by the government? The petitioner alleged two such steps. One was a statement by the district governor for Lusaka, Mr Justin Kabwe, that 'UNIP was ready to crush anyone who opposed the formation of a one-party state', and that 'whether people liked it or not, the one-party democracy had come to stay in Zambia'. While deprecating the 'somewhat extravagant language' in which Mr Kabwe's statement was couched, the High Court held that 'an isolated statement by a comparatively junior official' cannot be said to be official government policy; on the contrary, the evidence showed that the government had neither taken nor contemplated any step to prohibit the expression of opinion against a one-party state. This finding was conceded on behalf of the petitioner during the appeal before the Court of Appeal.

The other action of the government that was challenged was the setting up of a commission on a constitution for the proposed one-party state. It was contended on behalf of the petitioner that, since the terms of reference of the commission precluded it from considering argument supporting or opposing the principle of a one-party system, and since, in accordance with this, the commission had publicly announced its intention not to listen to such argument, the setting up of the commission infringed the petitioner's freedom of expression, and freedom from discrimination, and was therefore unconstitutional. Obviously, as the High Court held and the petitioner's counsel conceded on appeal, there could be no infringement of these rights simply because a commission set up to examine a particular question declined to hear his views on some other question falling outside its terms of reference. The evidence showed that, after the setting up of the commission, the petitioner freely expressed his opinion against a one-party state, not only privately but also on television and at a public rally in Lusaka.

It was further contended on behalf of the petitioner that the setting up of the commission with the intention of making a material constitutional change inconsistent with the then existing Constitution was seditious, but, as the High Court held, there was nothing in the sections dealing with either treason or sedition which prohibits an expression of opinion to alter the Constitution by lawful means. On appeal the point was put in different form. The argument now was that the setting up of the commission could not be 'for the public welfare' within the meaning of the Inquiries Act[32] under which the Commission was appointed, because 'it cannot in law be for the public welfare to prepare to deprive a citizen of any of the fundamental rights protected by the existing Constitution'. The Inquiries Act empowers the President to set up a commission to inquire into any matter in which an inquiry would, in his opinion, be 'for the public welfare'.[33] This clearly makes the matter one for the subjective decision of the President, unimpeachable by the courts in the absence of evidence showing that the President acted in bad faith or from improper motives or on extraneous considerations or under a view of the facts or the law which could not reasonably be entertained.[34]

Whether in setting up the commission the President acted on a view of the facts or the law which could not reasonably be entertained may depend on how one defines 'public welfare'. In the view of the petitioner's counsel, 'public welfare' meant the welfare of the individuals comprising the public, so that to derogate from individual rights and freedoms could not be for their welfare. Rejecting this view, the Appeal Court held that 'the public' in the context of the Inquiries Act means 'the community in general, as an aggregate, the people as a whole'. The court then concluded: 'What is in the public interest or for the public benefit is a question of balance; the interests of the society at large must be balanced against the interests of the particular section of society or of the individual whose rights or interests are in issue, and if the interests of the society at large are regarded as sufficiently important to override the individual interests then the action in question must be held to be in the public interest or for the public benefit.' Accordingly it held that the setting up of the commission was *intra vires* the powers of the President under the Inquiries Act, and therefore lawful.

The Appeal Court rightly questioned whether a declaration that the setting up of the commission was unlawful and void would have availed the petitioner anything in practical terms, since the decision to introduce a one-party system was that of the government, and since the commission was, by its terms of reference, forbidden to inquire into that aspect of the matter. A court declaration that the commission was unlawful would not affect that decision nor prevent its effectuation. Even if the decision had been based on the commission's recommendation, declaring the commission unlawful would still not be effective to prevent the introduction of a one-party system.

As to the origins of the one-party state in Malawi. Malawi has always had only one political party, the Malawi Congress Party (MCP). The party was established as the national party in the Republican Constitution of 1966, which was enacted by parliament without consultation with the people.

(i) *Other alleged Motivations*

Since, as Arthur Lewis has observed, no politician will ever admit that he suppresses opponents primarily because he wants to stay in power, other reasons have been advanced to justify this preference for a one-party state. Of the most forceful is the argument based on national unity, stability and economic development, admittedly the most imperative needs of all developing countries. It is argued that in a new nation, riven by tribal or racial divisions and conflicts, the unity of a single political party is necessary for stability and economic development. The task of development is said to be a most challenging one for a variety of reasons: first, because, unlike in the advanced countries where the pressure on the government is for more social services for a society already at an advanced stage of development, in which most of its members possess and enjoy the basic necessities for a decent life, in a new nation even those basic necessities are either non-existent or minimal for the vast majority of the population. Development in these circumstances requires that the whole population should team up together as one people in a concerted effort. Inter-party bickering only undermines the ability of the nation to organise the supreme efforts called for. Moreover, the task is an urgent one, since upon it depends the very survival of the nation itself. The masses had been led to expect that independence would bring about an immediate improvement in their conditions, and the non-realisation of these expectations had in turn bred a mood of impatience. Unless, therefore, improvement could be effected as speedily as possible, this mood of impatience might explode into violent hostility — to endanger, if not destroy, the state itself. The urgency of the task, it is argued, admits of no diffusion of energies in an unbridled competition for power.

Secondly, political unity is necessary to fight neo-colonialist forces trying to subvert the newly-won independence. Having taken a forced exit, the imperial powers are suspected of wanting to exploit the inexperience and poverty of the new nation in order to perpetuate their economic stranglehold or to discredit it as incapable of self-government. Neo-colonialism is represented as an insidious evil, working through paid agents among the disgruntled elements in the state, and as such is perhaps even more sinister than colonialism. Only by imposing unity through the medium of a single party can the government check or neutralise those prone to fall prey to the machinations of neo-colonialism. Thirdly, political unity is posited as necessary to contain the turbulence and tension following in the wake of change engendered by economic development. Free competition for political power would enable the opposition to cash in on this turbulence and tension to discredit the government with a view to displacing it.

The objectives stated in these arguments are of course not in dispute. No one ever disputes the need for economic development. Modernisation is indeed a matter upon which all are agreed. The need for national integration is equally not in dispute. It is the ruling party's insistence that unity must be equated with political unity – that is, the forcible fusion of all political parties and groups into a common mould – that is challenged. No doubt, a national party aggregating diverse elements in a plural society can perform an integrating role, but must it then for that reason be erected into an exclusive, monolithic organisation, to which all other associations, groups and individuals must be compelled to belong on pain of being suppressed? Is the need for unity so compelling that the individual's freedom of choice and expression should be sacrificed, and his freedom to associate with others in the pursuit of common desires and aspirations be taken away?

The plain truth, which deserves to be recognised, is that in a plural society an attempt to erase tribal or racial loyalties by political fiat is futile. The ban on parties does not abolish the differences between the various social groupings in the state or the jealousies and conflicts generated thereby. It merely prevents them from being exploited by rival political parties. Yet, with the suppression of opposition parties, these jealousies and conflicts are directed inwards within the single party. As the experience of Kenya shows, such intra-party clashes have all the intensity of inter-party conflicts, and may be just as much disruptive of nation-building and stability. Unity can only be achieved through the evolutionary process of education, and through social intercourse in trade, intermarriage and other social and cultural relationships, professional and business life, a functional realignment of people cutting across tribal or racial divisions, and a shared community life generally. The claim that the one-party state conduces more to economic development is not borne out by experience. It has indeed fared worse than the two- or multi-party state.[35]

In his well-argued book, *Africa: The Politics of Independence*, Immanuel Wallerstein appears to have shown a somewhat excessive indulgence towards African one-party governments. For him, the one-party system is indispensable to national integration. 'The party', he argues, 'should run the government, not vice versa, because the party, not the government, is the emanation of the people, that is, holds their loyalty and ties them to the state. The party integrates the nation and allows the integration to be accomplished by a method that maximises the opportunity of every citizen to participate on a regular and meaningful basis in the decision-making process'.[36] Few would quarrel with the system if in fact it maximises the opportunity for popular participation in government in a meaningful way. Experience of the actual working of the system shows, however, that popular participation is far from being maximised. And, in any case, can participation be really meaningful where there is only a minimal scope for dissent and where organised dissent is not permitted at all? Can debate conducted on the basis of only one set of programmes lead to a really meaningful consent? It is easy to imagine that a mass meeting, which after debate approves a policy presented to it by the leaders, could easily be swayed to a different viewpoint if a different group of leaders were given the chance to present its case. Clearly the meaningfulness of consent presupposes the possibility of a choice between alternative views or policies presented by different groups. And, as Professor Busia remarked, 'even where there is agreement on objectives, the differences on methods and priorities by which to achieve the objectives can be very important and fundamental'.[37]

Wallerstein's next point is that 'entry of the opposition into the government and the machinery of the governing party not only serves the interests of unity, but usually, though not always, helps to maintain within the dominant party openness of discussion and the necessary pressures for arriving at a consensus that takes into account all interests'.[38] But cannot this advantage be better achieved through the opposition entering into the government without also being absorbed into 'the machinery of the governing party'? There seems to be here an inability to distinguish a coalition from a one-party government. A coalition government which enables all the parties in a plural society to co-operate in the task of national integration and reconstruction while retaining their separate identities may indeed be the most desirable way in which the problems confronting such societies can best be solved within the framework of constitutional democracy. The case for it has been very ably presented by one of the most unsparing critics of the one-party system, Arthur Lewis. Coalition, he says, accords with the primary meaning of democracy, which is that all those affected by a decision should participate in making it. In a plural society, majority rule, implying government by and for one class of persons at the expense of others, is not only antithetical to this primary meaning of democracy, but is also immoral. The consolation of majority rule that the opposition may have its chance next time has no meaning in a plural society, for the minority may never have a chance of forming a government. And even if it had, this conception of democracy is inappropriate in Africa where an elector in casting his vote is mainly interested, not in the ideology of the party to which his representative belongs, but in what the representative can achieve for his district in terms of material benefits. He expects that his representative, in order to be able to secure benefits for his district, will play a full part in decision-making. For him (the elector) 'these basic needs and expectations remain the same whether the representative is in the winning or the losing party. This is especially the case if the elector belongs to a community (e.g., religious or tribal) which has no chance of winning an election and forming the Government, and to which therefore the game of ins and outs is completely irrelevant'.[39] Professor Lewis then concludes:

> The democratic problem in a plural society is to create political institutions which give all the various groups the opportunity to participate in decision-making, since only thus can they feel that they are full members of a nation, respected by their more numerous brethren, and owing equal respect to the national bond which holds them together. In such a society a slogan that the will of the minority should prevail would make better sense than the slogan that the will of the majority should prevail; but neither slogan is appropriate. It is necessary to get right away from the idea that somebody is to prevail over somebody else. . . . Group hostility and political warfare are precisely what must be eradicated if the political problem is to be solved; in their place we have to create an atmosphere of mutual toleration and compromise.[40]

But he maintains that this argument points, not to a one-party government, but to a coalition, because 'the single party imprisons those who oppose or criticise its policy, whereas a free coalition respects the rule of law and the right of free criticism, leaving individuals and parties free to oppose if they so desire'.[41]

Wallerstein finally postulates the one-party system as the only alternative to anarchy or military regimes in Africa. 'The choice', he writes, 'has not been between one-party and multi-party states; it has been between one-party states and either anarchy or military regimes or various combinations of the two'.[42] Surely, it is the authoritarianism of the ruling oligarchs and their determination to perpetuate their rule that are the root causes of military coups in developing countries. As new generations of the élite come of age, they naturally develop their own aspiration for power and leadership. Finding their elders firmly entrenched in power and unwilling to retire in the foreseeable future, the young élite becomes restless and impatient, and their impatience tends to find an outlet in radicalism and subversion. Collaborating with their mates in the army, with whom they share this mood of radicalism born of frustration, they contrive to effect a coup, toppling the old guards. Nor has the point about anarchy any more validity. African opposition parties may be irresponsible and their tactics destructive of the security of the state, yet it must not be forgotten that it is the attempt by the ruling parties to impose political unanimity by force, to perpetuate their rule by the suppression of the opposition, that drives the opposition to extremism. An opposition denied of any say in government except at the cost of self-effacement, or which cannot get redress for its grievances by constitutional means, may well be morally justified to revolt.

It has also been argued that the task of fighting poverty, disease and illiteracy creates a continuing state of emergency, justifying the authoritarian methods of the one-party government. Advocates of the one-party system point to the fact that even developed constitutional systems recognise that under the stress of crisis the regular procedures are suspended and the country lives under a system of constitutional dictatorship. The point has been argued with some force by President Nyerere in defending the case for the one-party system for his country. But the analogy is wholly untenable. An emergency in this context is a state of affairs such as war or other kind of public disorder, which threatens the physical security of the state. Furthermore, even when such a state of affairs has arisen, it seldom leads in the developed democracies to a complete suspension of the machinery of constitutional government. Even conceding that the task of national integration and modernisation can be regarded as constituting some kind of 'emergency', its solution certainly does not require the institution of what has been called a 'development dictatorship'.[43] And what guarantee is there that when the assumed emergency condition is over, the ruling oligarchs will be disposed to shed their authoritarian posture? After having tasted the intoxication of personalised power and the flattering adulation of hero worship, and given the corrupting influence of authoritarian power, it would be too much, indeed contrary to the nature of man and to all human experience, to expect them to do so.

Tradition is the next argument that has been advanced in justification of the one-party system. It is said that the idea of an organised opposition is foreign to the African concept of government. Whatever the nature of the political organisation in any given African country, whether government is by a chief in council, or by a council of elders or by the whole mass of the village peasantry, the process of decision-making is through lengthy and unhurried discussion among those present, during which all shades of opinion are given full expression until a consensus emerges. No votes are ever taken and so there is no question of a majority or a minority or of government and opposition organised as mutually competing and warring groups.[44] While this is generally an accurate picture of the African system of government, it is wrong to suppose that factionalism is entirely absent at such meetings. The factions may represent family or other kinship groups. If they are not effectively organised, it is simply because the matters at issue are of relatively minor importance. It is, in any case, misconceived to attempt to justify the processes of a modern, complex state, embracing peoples of different tribal or racial origins, with widely differing interests, by reference to those of a small face-to-face community in which kinship and various other kinds of intimate relationships operate to limit disagreements, in which authority is diffused or is not backed up by organised coercive forces, and in which the functions of government and therefore the possible areas of conflict are severely limited. The conditions and sanctions which make a 'consensus democracy' possible in the traditional set-up are not present in the modern state. If organised opposition is alien to African conceptions, so is the modern state itself. Its functions, procedures, and institutions and the coercive powers at its disposal have no parallel in African traditional communities. The things at stake are incomparably weightier, and are thus well calculated to provoke a conflict of interest of a type that can never arise in the traditional community. The modern state is a large-scale organisation, and from this arises the necessity that those who compete to control its power should similary organise themselves on a large scale. If we accept the modern state as a beneficial organisation for the development of the African continent, we will also be obliged to accept that its politics cannot be confined within the frontiers of tradition. The argument is not that tradition has no relevance to the government of the modern state, but rather that it can provide no justification for one-party rule. Indeed given a government based upon a free coalition, African consensus democracy can have great value in promoting greater harmony. Decision-taking by means of the vote has obvious disadvantages. As Professor Grey has observed:

> When issue between opposing parties are decided ultimately by parliamentary vote, it leaves the outvoted minority with its will or desire unsatisfied. A whole society must exist for indefinite periods of time knowing that some of its members, who may represent a substantial proportion, do not favour the political action being pursued, but have only agreed to restrain their active opposition for the time being. . . . The usual procedure of parliamentary voting makes it inevitable that at all times, part of the society will remain in unsatisfied opposition to important decisions effecting the whole society.[45]

The one-party system has been described as a kind of 'tutelary democracy', as a transitional phase to prepare the ground by creating the conditions needed for the evolution of full democracy at a later stage. These conditions are said to be a relatively high standard of living, mass education, a substantial middle class, industrialisation and urbanisation.[46] While these are undeniably predisposing factors for the stability of democratic institutions, they cannot by themselves create democracy if the democratic tradition has not been sufficiently nurtured among the people. The democratic tradition requires a spirit of tolerance and of respect for differing opinions, which in turn depends upon the existence of a broad consensus on fundamentals.[47] Democracy cannot thrive in a country where 'the contenders for power disagree so sharply on matters which they consider fundamental that they are not willing to allow their opponents to govern, whatever the ballot box may say.'[48] Although the disagreement among the politicians in emergent countries is not about fundamentals, the democratic spirit is badly lacking. But Arthur Lewis is not without hope for the future. He believes that, since the single party is incapable of containing the degree of tension which rapid change inevitably produces, the chances are that it will sooner or later split into separate groups, which may then come together again in free coalition. Such a development could be the beginning of the democratic road, whence a spirit of compromise and mutual tolerance may gradually be nurtured.[49]

(ii) *Why the Conversion of an existing* de facto *into a* de jure *one-party state?*

A further insight into motivation in this matter may be gleaned from the fact that in two of the countries, Tanzania and Malawi, a one-party state already existed *de facto* before it became formally established. If the reason for wanting only one party is solely a concern for the welfare of the nation – its unity and progress – then a one-party state existing on a *de facto* basis ought to meet the need, and there should be no need to give it a legal sanction. For a *de facto* one-party state is not open to the cardinal vice of the system on which all the objections to it hinge. It leaves the door open for the formation of a rival political organisation when disagreements can no longer be contained within the single party. A *de jure* one-party state, on the other hand, 'while it can allow free discussion, perhaps within fairly broad limits, ... cannot countenance free association *outside* the single party system. Those who disagree fundamentally with the ruling party are not free to form a rival political association in order to promote their own views. They must either keep quiet and conform or seek to promote their cause by resorting to unconstitutional action'.[50]

The prohibition of rival parties may involve a total exclusion from organised politics for some people, because they either do not wish or are not allowed to join the single party. The possibility of total exclusion which may follow from the prohibition of rival parties makes the right to join the party and to remain in it a very vital one, deserving to be specially protected by the constitution. For to exclude a person against his wish from organised politics is pretty tyrannical, especially as membership of the party is usually made a legal requirement for the holding of certain constitutional offices, such as those of President, minister, M.P., etc. And the chances of such exclusion are quite real. It is easily conceivable that after the formal establishment of a one-party system in what was hitherto a multi-party state, certain leaders of the defunct opposition parties might be denied admission into the single party because of their past record of opposition. This is clearly tyranny. For this reason the conditions of admission into, and expulsion from from, the single party become a matter of vital importance. Two rights and here in conflict — the right of an interested individual not to be excluded from participation in politics within the single party, and the right of any organisation to determine who to admit as member and the conditions of such membership. An organisation which is open to all and sundry, notwithstanding that they may be disloyal or hostile to the aims and objectives of the association, or which has no power to expel those guilty of flagrant breaches of its rules or other serious misconduct, can hardly be expected to be able to maintain its authority.

What, then, should be the approach to this conflict? The approach in Tanzania's Interim Constitution is to say that 'every citizen of Tanzania who has attained the age of eighteen years and who subscribes to the beliefs, aims and objects of the Party as expressed in the constitution of the Party shall, on payment of the fees and subscriptions provided for in the constitution of the Party, be entitled to be a member of the Party'.[51] It is argued that if membership of the party is automatic by right of citizenship alone and with no commitment to the beliefs, aims and objectives of the party, then the party would have become co-extensive with the nation, and thereby cease to function as a political party in any serious sense.[52] The Tanzanian Presidential Commission thinks that it should not be objectionable to require adherence to the beliefs, aims and objectives of the party, because the principles expressed therein are not based upon any narrow ideology. To insist on 'a narrow ideological conformity', the commission admits, 'would clearly be inconsistent with the mass participation in the affairs of the party which we regard as essential'. It asserts that 'the principles of TANU ... do not contain any narrow ideological formulations which might change with time and circumstances. They are a broad statement of political faith. We believe they carry the support of the vast majority of the people of Tanganyika, and must strike a responsive chord in men of goodwill in every civilised country in the world. A party based on these principles and requiring adherence to them as a condition of membership would he open to all but an insignificant minority of our citizens and would, we believe, be a truly national movement'.[53]

It may be conceded that adherence to the beliefs, aims and objectives of the party and payment of subscriptions are perhaps the minimum that may be required. The provision in the Tanzanian

Constitution not only guarantees the right to be admitted to membership but also gives protection against arbitrary expulsion. Under it, a person may be expelled only on ground of disloyalty to, or violation of, the beliefs, aims and objectives of the party or default in payment of fees and subscriptions, but not because he is critical of, or opposed to, the leadership.

It is possible that the Tanzanian approach gives insufficient recognition to the interests of the party. Membership of a party involves more than a simple adherence to its aims and objectives, and payment of subscriptions. On this view, it may be argued that the right of the party to regulate terms and conditions of membership should be fully recognised, subject to the proviso that no one is to be denied admission solely on the ground of his past activity as a member of a defunct opposition party or be expelled without just cause. Alternatively, the conditions of admission and expulsion should be spelt out specifically in the constitution, which will make them unalterable except by the procedure for constitutional amendment.

It is regrettable that this compromise approach has been found unacceptable in Zambia. The argument for some kind of constitutional protection of the right to belong to, and remain in, the party was finally lost. The draft one-party state constitution, as published, contains no protective provisions at all. The matter is thus left entirely to the discretion of the party in accordance with its constitution.

The annexing of the party constitution as a schedule to the national constitution is no protection. The precedent set by Tanzania of annexing the party constitution to the national constitution has been followed in Zambia. Tanzania's Interim Constitution, 1965, provides that 'the constitution set out in the First Schedule to this Constitution shall be the constitution of the Tanganyika African National Union, and such constitution may be amended from time to time ... in accordance with the provisions in that behalf in that constitution'.[54] Although this is unique among one-party state constitutions which do not normally contain the party constitution, its effect is not to establish or incorporate the party constitution as part of the national Constitution; in other words, mere annexation gives to the party constitution no force of law beyond whatever legal force it has in contract. It is true that the Independence Constitutions of Commonwealth African countries are scheduled to an order-in-council, but they are also expressly given legal effect. The formula is that 'the Constitution set out in Schedule ... shall come into effect in' the country concerned.[55] If it is intended that a document scheduled to an Act shall have force of law, then that should be said in the terms. For example, the two documents annexed as a schedule to the Independence Constitution of Cyprus, 1960 — the treaty between Cyprus,

Greece, Turkey and the United Kingdom guaranteeing the independence, territorial integrity and constitution of the state of Cyprus, and the treaty of alliance between Cyprus, Greece and Turkey providing for the stationing in Cyprus of Greek and Turkish military contingents for the defence of the island republic — were expressly given force of law by the Constitution.[56] In any case it is not actually desirable that the party constitution should have force of law as part of the national constitution. To give it force of law will make its provisions binding on all persons, members and non-members alike. This may be undesirable in view of the fact that there are persons who cannot be members of the party either because they are not citizens or because they hold offices (e.g., judges) which enjoin on them non-involvement in politics.

Besides the denial of the right to form rival political parties, and of the right to belong to, and remain a member of, the one permitted party, a *de jure* one-party system imposes other restrictions on individual rights. It may be said to be incompatible with the whole idea of a bill of rights. The rejection of a bill of rights in Ghana (1960), Tanzania (1965) and Malawi (1966)[57] may thus have been due in part to the formal establishment of the one-party system there. What is certain is that a bill of rights cannot co-exist with a *de jure* one-party state without serious modifications and qualifications. A guarantee of freedom of speech and assembly, and freedom from discrimination on the ground of political opinions, will necessarily have to be qualified. Thus, although the guidelines given by President Kaunda to the one-party state commission in Zambia emphatically enjoined that the 'fundamental rights and freedom of the individual shall be protected as now provided under Chapter 3 of the Constitution of the Republic of Zambia',[58] it was clear that the establishment of the one-party system would involve modifications in the bill of rights.[59] And so, as we have seen, it is enacted in the implementing legislation that 'nothing contained in this Constitution shall be so construed as to entitle any person to lawfully form or attempt to form any political party or organisation other than the Party or to belong to or assemble, associate, express opinion or do any other thing in sympathy with such political party or organisation'.[60] All this would have been unnecessary in a *de facto* one-party state. Kenya has not had to qualify its bill of rights in this way because it is a *de facto* one-party state.

The question, then, is whether a one-party system on a *de facto* basis is less effective than a *de jure* one for securing the alleged advantages of the system. If the claim that the system promotes rapid economic development, nation-building and stability is valid, there should be no reason why a *de facto* one-party system should be less effective for securing these objectives, provided every effort is made to maintain the appeal of the party. It must be admitted that a *de facto* one-party state is fraught with the possibility of the Odinga, Kapwepwe and Mundia sort of split, with its undermining effect on stability. Yet, while a *de jure* one-party state is free of instability arising from the formation of splinter groups, it does not guarantee against instability in other forms. For when the inevitable political disagreements can no longer be contained within the one party, then people will seek other avenues for their grievances if the avenue of a rival political party is legally barred. The alternative consists of coups, assassinations and other unconstitutional methods of removing a government. No doubt experience has shown that a *de facto* one-party system can be maintained only at the cost of proscribing or suppressing any new parties that may be formed, and detaining their leaders, as happened in Kenya, Zambia and Tanzania before 1965. The price is high, but it seems well worth paying in order to assert the individual's right to organise in opposition to an unacceptable government. In Zambia the United Progressive Party (UPP) of Simon Kapwepwe was banned and its leaders were detained. The constitutional right to organise in opposition to the government remained, however; and no sooner were some of the detained leaders released than they asserted that right and formed another opposition party, calling it by a name with the same initials, United People's Party (UPP). The sponsors were immediately re-detained, and the party, though not specifically banned, disappeared with the formal establishment of the one-party state. This experience illustrates that, for the citizen, proscription and detention, as the price to be paid for the freedom to organise in opposition to the government, are a more acceptable evil than a complete ban on that freedom. In all ages the maintenance of freedom has always involved great sacrifices. For the government, of course, the preference is clearly the other way. It was the unexpected emergence of the United People's Party, perhaps, that prompted the Zambian Government to rush in a constitutional amendment bill for the establishment of a one-party state, before the report of the national commission could be published and before the new constitution that would implement the recommendations of the commission could be drafted.

A different and more persuasive case for converting an existing *de facto* one-party state into a *de jure* one has been argued by the Tanzanian presidential commission as follows:

> One-party government operating within the context of a constitu-tion intended for two or more parties inevitably results in the disenfranchisement of the voter. So long as the law permits the establishment of alternative parties T.A.N.U. must continue to fight elections, both national and local, on a party basis. This means putting forward a single candidate in each constituency or ward. In Tanganyika in most cases such candidates have been unopposed and

the people have, in consequence, the right to vote but no opportunity to do so. In the rare cases where a candidate has stood in opposition to T.A.N.U. his chance of succeeding at the polls has been so meagre that the election itself has been a matter of small significance. The real choice has been made at an earlier stage when T.A.N.U. adopted its candidate. By a paradox the more support the people have given to T.A.N.U. as a party the more they have reduced their participation in the process of government.[61]

The commission also argued that, unless it is formally established by law, a *de facto* one-party state has still to maintain the traditional methods of party discipline with their undesirably inhibiting effect on freedom of discussion within the party and in parliament, notwithstanding that they are wholly inappropriate in the context of a single national political movement.[62] The risks to the single party of permitting free discussion in parliament can only be removed if the party is formally established by law as the only national political party.

As will presently be shown, the claim that discussions in parliament would become freer when the one-party is formally established has not been borne out by experience so far. The inclination has been to withdraw critical discussions from the public forum in parliament to the privacy of the party. The other argument advanced by the Tanzanian commission is more difficult to refute. The formal establishment of the one-party state has certainly enabled Tanzania to improve its electoral process to secure fuller participation by the people in the choice of representatives,[63] though the experience in the other one-party states has been the exact opposite.[64] It should not however be impossible to devise appropriate procedures which would enable such fuller participation to be secured in a *de facto* one-party state. The danger actually comes, not from a non-existent opposition party (if an opposition party exists, then the system cannot be a *de facto* one-party one), but from independents who might be contesting in competition with the party candidates. This danger can be removed by barring independents altogether, as is done in Kenya — i.e. by saying that only candidates sponsored by a political party can stand. Admittedly this is undemocratic, but it is less so than the ban on rival parties imposed by the formal establishment of the one-party system. In any case independents have a rather doubtful value; they are more a nuisance than anything else.

2. *The Dominating Position of the Executive in a One-party State*

The position of the executive is unquestionably more dominating in a one-party system than in a multi-party one. We will consider the matter in relation to (i) the control of the legislature, and (ii) the control of non-political organisations.

(i) *Subservience of the Legislature in a One-Party State*

In a strenuous and impressive argument, Julius Nyerere has set out to show that it is the two- or multi-party system that has brought the legislature in Africa to its present position of subservience. Party discipline in parliament, he says, has been made so stringent because of 'the need to avoid giving accidental support or encouragement to the rival party by any lack of unity between the leaders and their backbench supporters'.[65] In a one-party system, on the other hand, no such need for unity exists, and so party discipline and its restrictions on an M.P.'s freedom of debate and of voting become unnecessary.[66] With the exception of Tanzania and Kenya, actual experience shows the legislature in the one-party state to be much less independent than in a two-party system.

Perhaps the first thing to notice is that the theory of the one-party state which identifies the party with the nation serves to underline the primacy of the executive more forcefully than in a two-party system. By this theory *the party* is the people's party, or, in the words of the Ghanaian Constitution, 'the leading core of all organisations of the People'.[67] The conception therefore is that the party embodies the whole people, and not just a section of it. As the embodiment of the nation, the party is (according to the conception) above the organs of government, since government is only an instrument or agent and not an embodiment, of the people; and an agent must necessarily be subordinate to his principal. Given this conceptual primacy of the party in a one-party state, it becomes crucial whether the party is in fact independent of the executive and the legislature, since only if it is could it assert its primacy effectively against those organs. Otherwise the primacy of the party would simply enure to that organ which directs and so controls it.

In the Soviet Union and the East European countries, the primacy of the party has reality, because the party has independence. The practice of the one-party system in Africa is different. There does exist, of course, the formal structure of an independent party organisation – the central committee or the national executive committee, the national council or delegates' conference, and so on. Nonetheless, the real power within the party is the chairman/secretary-general, who invariably is also the chief executive/Head of State. It is in him therefore that the powers of the party and its primacy are lodged, and the concentration of functions serves to subordinate the legislature and the other organs of the party to him. Most of the ministers too are in the policy-making organs of the party to strengthen the government's voice. And so the primacy which the executive ordinarily enjoys over the legislature receives a formal recognition in the constitution through the medium of the party. The one-party state commission in Zambia has tried to give reality to the independence of the party by recommending that its secretary-general should be a functionary different from its president; that, except for the Prime Minister, no minister should be a member of the central committee; and that the central committee and the cabinet should be separate bodies but should meet in joint sessions when need arises to resolve common problems.[68] The central committee is to be responsible for policy, and the cabinet for the administration of government. Although the president of the party/president of the country is to be a member of the central committee, the commission recommends that the secretary-general of the party shall have power to convene and preside over administrative meetings of the central committee, to appoint chairmen of sub-committees of the central committee in consultation with the President, and to act for or succeed the President in the event of his absence, inability, resignation or death. It is gratifying that the Zambian Government has accepted these recommendations.[69]

In relation to the legislature, the position of the executive in a one-party system is further strengthened in a number of ways. First, party candidates for election to the national assembly are nominated by the central committee, in effect by the chairman/secretary-general/chief executive, and not by the local constituency organisations. Secondly, only one candidate is so nominated for each constituency — independents, of course, being disallowed. Since the real choice is exercised by the party leaders and not by the electors, the elections become a ritual, thereby losing their value in sanctioning the political responsibility of the government. The one-party elections in Ghana in 1965 illustrated the farcical character of the exercise in a most telling manner. All the candidates nominated by the central committee of the Convention People's Party (CPP) were declared to have been elected unopposed. Surely an M.P. who owes his nomination and election entirely to the party leaders cannot afford to be too independent of them.

In a one-party state the actual legislative process iteslf tends increasingly to submerge parliament. Legislative proposals are first taken to the central organs of the party. There they are discussed in detail; and because the proceedings are in private, the discussions can be freer and more critical without offending a government's natural sensitivity to criticism conducted in the view and hearing of the public. It must not be supposed that the discussions within the party organs are entirely free. The extent of freedom allowed must necessarily vary according as the outlook of the leaders is authoritarian or not. When the matter reaches parliament, the proceedings there are reduced to a mere formality. There is no need to go again over the ground covered during the discussions in the central party organs. Most M.P.s would have had an opportunity to express their views during the discussions in the central party organs of which they are also members. Only the barest minimum of discussion is therefore necessary in parliament. Indeed, the attitude is that it is a waste of time re-discussing matters, and any attempt on the part of any member to indulge his power of oratory in the assembly would incur the displeasure of the leaders. Yet however free the discussions in the central party organs may be, they do not adequately meet the needs of democracy. Although they may serve to check and temper the government, the sanction of publicity is lacking. The absence of publicity ensures that the public is not made fully aware of the mistakes and shortcomings of the government. And, shielded from public exposure, the government need not fear loss of confidence with the people, which might result in its eventual defeat at the polls. The political responsibility of the government to the people is again stultified almost as effectively as it is by the denial of a choice in the nomination of candidates.

These are the subordinating aspects of the position of the legislature in a one-party state, which President Julius Nyerere has determined to remedy in order to make good his claim that a *de jure* one-party system can maximise popular participation in government more than a two-party one. First, he has tried to preserve the element of popular choice in the nomination of candidates. Under Tanzania's one-party state Constitution of 1965, it is the electors in each constituency who, in the first instance, nominate the candidates. Provided a nomination is sponsored by at least twenty-five registered electors, any number of candidates may be nominated in a constituency.[70] The elector's nominations have, however, to be approved by the national executive committee of the party (TANU), which is a mere formality where only one or two candidates are nominated. In that case the nomination of the electors is final and binding upon the national executive committee. Only where more than two candidates are nominated does the party become involved in deciding which two of them are to stand in accordance with the provision limiting the number of candidates in a constituency to two.

The involvement of the party is at two levels. A list of nominated candidates in each constituency is first voted on by the annual district conference of the party for the district in which the constituency is situated. With the votes of the district conference the list is submitted to the national executive committee. Although constitutionally the committee is not bound by the preferences indicated by the votes of the district conference,[71] in practice it normally endorses them, except where two persons tied in second place or where either of the winning candidates had a poor party record or had sought to gain an unfair advantage at an earlier stage of the election proceedings.[72] Except for six ministers who were returned unopposed, all the constituencies in Tanzania's 1965 elections were contested, four at the actual election stage and the rest at both the nomination and election stages. It is a measure of the reality of the people's participation that the results were not always in favour of the candidates who came first in the district conference voting or in the national executive committee rating. The most significant result was, perhaps, the defeat of the Minister for Finance, Mr Paul Bomani. He had topped the district conference poll with forty-four votes, the second and third candidates scoring five and three votes respectively; two candidates came fourth with one vote each. The national executive committee dropped the second and third candidates because of poor party records, and chose one of the fourth candidates in a tie. It was this candidate who won with 14,146 votes against Bomani's 9,639 votes. There were several other instances of the electorate refusing to endorse changes made by the national executive committee, and forty-four cases in which it reversed the choice of the district conference. Also significant was the fact that one other minister, six junior ministers and nine backbenchers lost their seats, while three junior ministers and ten backbenchers were not selected by the party to contest, added to which the twenty-seven other backbenchers did not stand at all. The number of new constituency members in the assembly came to eighty-six out of 107.[73]

Two comments need, however, to be made on the reality of popular participation in Tanzania's one-party elections of 1965. The first concerns the exclusion of non-party members from the contest.[74] This is, of course, in line with the tradition in other African one-party states.[75] The Tanzanian Constitution requires that a member of the national assembly must be a Tanzanian citizen of the age of twenty-one years or over, who is a member of the party.[76] Is the effect of the membership requirement not to undermine the reality of the electorate's choice? The Tanzanian presidential commission has defended this on the ground that a one-party government is government by the one constitutionally recognised party, and that, accordingly, no one who is not a member of the party should be in any of the organs of the government.[77] The commission argued further that if non-party members were allowed to stand for election to parliament, separate organisations to support and finance them might grow up and become a nucleus for new opposition parties.[78] The implication of the membership qualification is of course that an M.P. vacates his seat on ceasing to be a member of the party either by resignation or expulsion.[79]

The second comment concerns the procedure for the election of the

President. The Constitution allows for only one candidate to be selected by an electoral conference of the party.[80] Although the candidate so nominated cannot become President and cannot be re-nominated in the same election if he fails to win the majority of votes cast, this procedure leaves little choice to the people, since it is almost unthinkable that an only presidential candidate selected by the party would fail to win a simple majority of the votes cast. In the 1965 presidential election, the only candidate, President Nyerere, won 2,519,866 out of the 2,612,225 votes cast.[81] This was no doubt a reflection of Nyerere's personal popularity, but an adverse vote could hardly have been expected in the circumstances.

Apart from the electoral process, another objective of the reforms in Tanzania was directed towards making parliament a more effective forum of discussion. The overlap between it and the central party organs had made parliament almost redundant. Under the reforms, the party organs are now limited to the discussion and formulation of broad lines of policy, leaving details of specific legislation for discussion and final enactment by parliament. The body which in the past had threatened to eclipse the assembly completely was the TANU Parliamentary Group, whose membership was identical with that of the national assembly itself. Because discussions in the Parliamentary Group were in private, the tendency had been for most of the debate on government bills to take place there, with the result that when the matter got to parliament, hardly any points would remain undebated. The Parliamentary Group has now been abolished and with it the threat of total eclipse which it had posed to parliament. But there still remains the problem whether Nyerere and his government can overcome the natural preference of all governments for private, closed-door discussions where criticisms and conflicts can be kept away from public view. William Tordoff's finding is that, despite the removal of the whips and the disappearance of the Parliamentary Group, and notwithstanding that Nyerere is less sensitive to criticism than Nkrumah, 'opinions were certainly expressed more vigorously in the various organs of the party than in the national legislature'.[82]

Events in 1968 were to bear out the truth of what William Tordoff had written in 1967. The session, July to October 1968, has been described as the liveliest in the history of the Tanzanian national assembly.[83] A private member's motion had been successfully carried criticising the government's plan to pay ministers and regional and area commissioners a gratuity based on 25 per cent of their salary; the motion called upon the government to drop the proposal. Although the proposal was dropped in deference to this criticism, the assembly's more ambitious attempt to carry criticism into the sphere of general policy, as by members' criticism of the exclusiveness of the party in the one-party system and its increasing dominance in national life, and their assertion of the supremacy of parliament over the party, met with stern disciplinary action by the party leaders. Five M.P.s who spearheaded the criticism were expelled from the party by the national executive committee on the ground of gross violation of the party creed. Two other M.P.s from the West Lake Region, who had criticised the regional commissioner for using autocratic methods to carry out an *ujamaa* village programme, were also expelled on the same ground after a committee of investigation appointed by the national executive committee had found the allegation to have been unfounded.

The expulsion of Oscar Kambona and Anangisye at this time also followed on the same grounds, though for different reasons. These expulsions underlined the significance of a 1967 amendment to the party constitution, which transferred the power of expulsion from the national conference to the national executive committee. It is needless to repeat that expulsion from the party meant loss of his parliamentary seat for the individual affected. Commenting on the limitations on M.P.s' critical function in the light of these expulsions, Robert Martin writes: 'They [i.e. M.P.s] may not criticise government policy on principle, only on practical grounds, they may not criticise a policy decision of the National Executive Committee; they may not be contemptuous of party principles and party ideology; they may not speak with cynicism of Tanzania's socialist goals; they may not question whether TANU should have authority over them.'[84]

For a striking illustration of candour and vigour in a one-party legislature in Africa it is to Kenya rather than Tanzania that we have to turn. During the period before the emergence of the Kenya People's Union in 1966, and to a lesser extent after its suppression in 1969, the Kenyan parliament had been a scene of vigorous debates characterised by independent and fierce criticism of nearly all aspects of governmental activity to a degree unknown anywhere else in Commonwealth Africa. 'The House of Representatives has been the scene of some memorable occasions when M.P.s and ministers have clashed both over specific executive actions as well as over the larger policy issues that face the country.'[85] Although the total impact on government policy of all this fierce criticism had been small, it had nevertheless achieved a concrete result in securing amendments to bills and in a few cases even the withdrawal or abandonment of important measures.[86] But the most important result was that it had produced in the government a distinct disinclination to take the assembly for granted.

However, the fierce independence of the Kenyan parliament was not so much an achievement of its one-party system as an accident of history. The wish of both the ministers and the M.P.s would have been to confine all the conflicts and clashes within the privacy of the party organs. As it happened, parliament was forced to assume this role by the absence of effective party organs which could provide a forum for the discussion and criticism of government policies.[87] As elsewhere, the party had a national executive committee and a national conference but these had never met since independence. Without a functioning party machinery capable of pressing party views upon the government, parliament felt itself obliged to fill the vacuum. Again, a Parliamentary Group, created at independence under the chairmanship of the Prime Minister with the intention of bringing ministers and M.P.s together on a common meeting ground to discuss government policies and legislative proposals, failed to function, because ministers would not attend its meetings. This had created a feeling among M.P.s that the ministers were purposely ignoring them in order to rule without parliament. Imbued by a sense of what they conceived to be their duty as representatives of the people and a determination to perform that duty, the M.P.s took on a mood of revolt.

Granted that a one-party parliament can be as independent as the Kenyan assembly has been, the question still remains whether the fullest effect of independent criticism can ever be realised in the absence of an opposition party seeking by means of it to supplant the government in the good opinion of the electorate. Can a government which has no rival to contend with be as responsive to criticism as one which has? Embarrassed certainly it would be by the criticism, but fear of embarrassment alone is of little consequence if there is no risk of losing power to an opposition which might cash in on it. Yet, notwithstanding that in one-party system there would be no question of 'the overthrowing of one-party government by a rival party', Julius Nyerere has nevertheless asserted that the government could still be 'removed by the people at any time; there would be no need for a statutory period of so many years to elapse before an unsatisfactory leader could be replaced by them. In this way the government of the country would be truly in the hands of the electorate at all times. It would no longer be a mere matter of their casting votes for or against a "party" at intervals of four or five years. And anybody who continued to occupy a position of leadership, under such conditions, would do so because the people were satisfied with him; not because he was protected by a law which made it impossible for them to replace him until the next general election'.[88]

How this result would be brought about was not explained. By what means could the people remove the President from office before the next presidential election? Under the Interim Constitution of Tanzania, the office of President can only be vacated by the dissolution of parliament, death or resignation of the President or by inability certified by the Chief Justice.[89]

(ii) *Integration of non-political Organisations*

The one-party state in Africa has tended to confirm the statement that absolute, centralised power is by its nature indivisible. It does not tolerate pockets of power within the state, even when their purpose is not political. It seeks to integrate every organisation of any public significance like trade unions, co-operative societies, farmers' associations, women's and youth associations, etc. Kwame Nkrumah likened his Convention People's Party to 'a mighty tree with many branches. The Convention People's Party constitutes the root and the trunk, and its branches include such organisations as the United Ghana Farmers' Council, the Trades Union Congress, the Co-operative Movement, the Ex-servicemen, Women's Organisations, the Kwame Nkrumah Kurye Kuw, the National Associations of Socialist Students' Organisation, the League of Ghana Patriots and other patriotic organisations which in their various ways are giving support to our Party. . . .'[90]

Integration in Ghana meant not merely affiliation but a complete merger. It meant the abolition of separate membership cards for the integral organisations. 'In all Regional Headquarters,' Nkrumah announced in his Dawn Broadcast of April 8, 1961, 'provision will be made for the Central Party and these integral organisations to be housed in the same buildings. . . . Also the separate flags used by these organisations will be abolished and replaced by the flag of the Convention People's Party. . . .' In Accra, the capital, the common housing arrangement had been in existence since 1960. In Tanzania, although integration has not been carried as far as in Ghana, the trade union movement and women's and youth organisations are affiliated to TANU. The League of Malawi Women and the League of Malawi Youth are also affiliates of the Malawi Congress Party. Interestingly, trade unions in Malawi have been left to continue their separate existence.[91] Before its formal establishment as the one and only party in Zambia, the United National Independence Party (UNIP) had the Zambia Congress of Trade Unions and a number of other organisations as affiliated members. Such organisations will retain their affiliated status under the one-party system, provided they re-apply for affiliation.[92] A National Council for Youth and a National Women's Council are to be created and affiliated to the party. In addition, the one-party state commission listed farmers' organisations, the co-operative movement and professional societies among organisations to be affiliated to the party.[93]

Integration or affiliation involves control by the party and the government. In Ghana the voluntary federation of trade unions, known as the Ghana Trade Union Congress, was dissolved and replaced by a statutory body, the Trade Union Congress, which was to be the only representative of the trade union movement in the country, comprising twenty-four different unions.[94] It was under the control of the Minister of Labour as regards its management and finance. The President could make the congress virtually defunct by directing all its assets to be transferred and vested in a receiver appointed by him, if it appeared to him, among other things, that the Congress had taken any action which was not conducive to the public good.

Government control goes farther in Tanzania. As in Ghana, the voluntary Tanganyika Federation of Labour (TFL) and its member-unions were dissolved by statute[95] and replaced by a single statutory organisation, the National Union of Tanganyika Workers' Union (NUTA), which is affiliated to TANU, and is obliged by law to 'do everything in its power to promote the policies of TANU' and to encourage its members to join TANU. The formerly individual unions which federated to form TFL became only industrial sections of NUTA. NUTA cannot dissolve itself but may be dissolved by the President if he is satisfied that it has failed adequately to carry out its objects, and upon such dissolution the President may establish some other body representative of employees. The President appoints and dismisses the general-secretary and the deputy general-secretary. He has appointed the minister of labour to be the first general-secretary. It is in the general-secretary that the control of the union is firmly lodged. He is the chief executive officer and chief spokesman of the union, responsible for its overall supervision and management, and for the appointment and dismissal of the other general officers after consultation with the general council. He is the union's spokesman at all conferences and general and executive council meetings. The first executive council was in fact appointed by him. He engages all executive staff. The minister of labour/general-secretary is thus NUTA. The government's control could not have been more complete.

It is not suggested that the Commonwealth African presidential regimes have become totalitarian; that is to say, a form of rule that tries to integrate 'so many aspects of human existence: family life, friendship, work, leisure, production, exchange, worship, art, manners, travel, dress — even that final assertion of human privacy, death'.[96] The individual is not regimented in his life, he is free to choose his occupation, to indulge in as much leisure as he can afford, to form friendships and business associations. There is quite ample scope for the enjoyment of personal and organisational autonomy in non-political matters.[97]

REFERENCES

1. J. M. Lee, 'Parliament in Republican Ghana', *Parl. Affairs*, 1962–3, vol. xvi, p. 376; W. B. Harvey, *Law and Social Change in Ghana* (1966), p. 323; Dennis Austin, *Politics in Ghana 1946–60* (1964), p. 386.

2. Dennis Austin, *loc. cit.*

3. Harvey, *op. cit.*, p. 306.

4. Out of a registered electorate of 2,988,598, 2,773,920 votes were cast in favour, and 2,452 against, giving thus a 99.9 per cent 'yes' vote.

5. Harvey, *op. cit.*, p. 325.

6. Art. 1A.

7. Dennis Austin, 'Opposition in Ghana, 1947–67', in *Govt. and Opposition*, vol. 2, no. 4, July/October 1967, p. 539.

8. *Ibid.*, p. 555.

9. G. F. Engholm and Ali Mazrui, 'Crossing the Floor and the Tensions of Representation in East Africa', *Parl. Affairs* (1967/8), vol. xxi, p. 187.

9a. House of Reps. Deb., 10 Nov, 1964, col. 4415.

10. For fuller discussion of this amendment, see below, ch. IX.

11. Engholm and Mazrui, *op. cit.*, p. 149.

12. Standing Orders of the National Assembly, Nairobi, 1968.

13. See below, Ch. IX, for details.

14. Engholm and Mazrui, *op. cit.*, on which this account is largely based.

15. See below, ch. XI, for further detail.

16. S.3 Interim Constitution.

17. Report of the National Commission on the Establishment of a One-Party Participatory Democracy in Zambia, Lusaka, Oct. 1972, para. 13.

18. Constitution (Amendment) (No. 3) Act, 1968.

19. Nat. Ass. Deb., 22 Jan., 1969, cols. 28–9.

20. Constitution (Amendment) (No. 2) Act, 1966.

21. *The People* v. *The Speaker of the National Assembly, The Hon R. M. Nabulyato, ex parte Harry Nkumbula, HP/4/1970* of 24 Dec., 1970.

22. Constitution (Amendment) (No. 5) Act, 1969; discussed more fully below, ch. IX.

23. Mubako, 'The Presidential System in the Zambian Constitution', unpublished thesis for M.Phil. degree, University of London (1970), p. 344.

24. Constitution (Amendment) (No. 5) Act, 1972.

25. Leg. Ass. Debates, 20 March, 1964, col. 420; also speech at Chifubu on 17 Jan., 1965, quoted in Colin Legum, ed., *Zambia: Independence and Beyond* (1966), pp. 108–9.

26. Press conference on Feb. 25, 1972; quoted in the Report of the One-Party state Commission, para. 2 (1972).

27. *Nkumbula* v. *Att.-Gen. for Zambia* HP/CONST/REF/1/1972 of 6 April, 1972. For the judgment on appeal see Appeal No. 6 of 1972.

28. S.23 Constitution.

29. S.22, *ibid.*

30. S.25.

31. S.28(5).

32. Cap. 181 Laws of Zambia, 1972 ed.

33. S.2(1).

34. See per Lord Denning M.R. in *Secretary of State for Employment* v. *A.S.L.E.F. (No. 2)* [1972] 2 W.L.R. 1370.

35. S. E. Finer, 'The One-Party regimes in Africa: Reconsiderations', in *Government and Opposition* (1970), p. 491.

36. At pp. 97–8.

37. *Africa in Search of Democracy* (1967), p. 140.

38. *Op. cit.*, p. 165.

39. *Politics in West Africa* (1965), p. 75.

40. *Ibid.*, pp. 66–7.

41. P. 81.

42. *Op. cit.*, pp. 96, 163.

43. See Carl Friedrich, *Constitutionalism for Emergent Political Orders*, p. 25.

44. See Cowan, *The Dilemmas of African Independence* (1964), pp. 11–12. Emerson *op. cit.*, p. 284; Fletcher-Cooke, in Alan Burns, ed., *Parliament as an Export* (1966), pp. 145 *et seq.*

45. 'Political Parties in New African Nations: An Anthropological View', *Comparative Studies in Society and History*, IV., No. 4 (July 19, 1963), p. 456, quoted in Cowan, *op. cit.*, p. 12.

46. Lipset, 'Some Social Requisite of Democracy: Economic Development and Political Legitimacy', *American Pol. Sc. Rev.* (1959), Vol. III, pp. 69–105.

47. C. F. Zolberg, One-Party Government in the Ivory Coast, Revised ed. (1969), pp. 338–9; Emerson, *From Empire to Nation* (1962), pp. 278–80.

48. Arthur Lewis, *op. cit.*, p. 37.

49. *Ibid.*, p. 88.

50. W. Tordoff, *Government and Politics in Tanzania* (1967), p. xvii.

51. S.5.

52. Presidential Commission Report. 1965, para. 37. CP Report of the One-Party State Commission of Zambia, para. 155 – 'Automatic membership was tantamount to a partyless state'.

53. Report, *op. cit.*, paras. 37 and 38.

54. S.3(4).

55. See, e.g., S.3, The Zambia Independence Order 1964.

56. Art. 181.

57. For the rejection of the bill of rights in these countries, see below, ch. X.

58. See Report of the Commission.

59. *Nkumbula* v. *The Att.-Gen. for the Republic of Zambia,* HP/CONST/REF/1/1972 of 6/4/72.

60. Constitution (Amendment) (No. 5) Act, 1972.

61. Report (1964), para. 32.

62. Report *op. cit.,* para 33.

63. See below, p. 244.

64. Below, p. 243.

65. Julius Nyerere, *Democracy and the Party System* (1962) p. 6.

66. *Ibid.,* p. 6.

67. Art. 1A; added by the Constitution (Amendment) Act, 1964.

68. Report, Oct. 1972, paras. 144–9.

69. White Paper on Report, Govt. Printer, Lusaka (1972), pp. 22–5.

70. S.28, Interim Constitution, 1965.

71. S.28.

72. W. Tordoff, *Government and Politics in Tanzania* (1967), p. 34.

73. Tordoff, *op. cit.,* p. 39.

74. S.27(1).

75. E.g., Ghana, Malawi and Zambia.

76. S.27(1)

77. Report 1965, para. 37.

78. *Ibid.,* para. 46.

79. SS.27(1) and 35(1)(*a*), Interim Constitution of Tanzania.

80. S.7(3), (4) 8(5).

81. Tordoff, *op. cit.,* p. 38.

82. *Ibid.,* p. xiv.

83. R. Martin, 'Personal Freedom and the Law in Tanzania', p. 8 (not yet published).

84. *Op. cit.,* p. 80. See also Cliffe, 'Democracy in a One-Party State: 'The Tanzanian Experience', *The Parliamentarian* (1968), Vol. 2, 206; Hopkins, 'The Role of the M.P. in Tanzania', *American Pol. Sc. Rev.* 1970, Vol. LXIV, No. 3, p. 754.

85. C. Gertzel, *The Politics of Independent Kenya* (1970), pp. 131–2; Engholm and Mazrui, 'Crossing the Floor and the Tensions of Representation in East Africa', *Parl. Affairs* (1967/68), vol. xxi, 137, 148.

86. Ghai and McAuslan, *Public Law and Political Change in Kenya* (1970), pp. 336–7.

87. C. Gertzel, *loc. cit.*

88. Julius Nyerere, *Democracy and the Party System* (1962), pp. 25–6.

89. S.7(2).

90. Prime Minister's speech to 10th annual Delegates' Conference, *Evening News,* 3 Aug., 1959.

91. See Trade Unions Act, cap. 54:01, Laws of Malawi 1969.

92. White Paper on the Report of the One-Party State Commission (1972), p. 28.

93. Report (1972), para. 163.

94. Industrial Relations Act, 1958.

95. National Union of Tanganyika Workers (Establishment) Act, 1964.

96. Eckstein and Apter, Ed., 'Democracy and Totalitarianism', in *Comparative Politics* (1965).

97. This may need to be qualified in relation to Tanzania. The control which President Banda exercises over dress and manners in Malawi is almost totalitarian.

CHAPTER IX

SUBORDINATION OF THE LEGISLATURE

1. *The Importance of an Independent Legislature*

A co-ordinated machinery of government under the leadership of a President or Prime Minister, such as exists under the parliamentary system, necessarily accords primacy to the executive. The President co-ordinates, and therefore dominates, both the executive and legislative processes of government. Thus even the government of Britain, universally acknowledged to be perhaps the most liberal constitutionalist regime, accords a 'genuine' primacy to the executive,[1] or what Sir Kenneth Wheare calls the 'supremacy of the executive'.[2] The problem which the primacy of the executive under this kind of system poses to constitutionalism is one of how to safeguard and maintain the independence of the legislature in the face of it. How is the control implied in the executive's co-ordinating role to be prevented from becoming so complete as to reduce the legislature to utter impotence? How, in other words, is co-ordinated leadership to be secured without sacrificing the independence of the legislature? The primacy of the executive is sometimes represented as if it necessarily implies that it can never co-exist with an independent legislature. This is clearly an exaggerated picture, as the example of England itself shows. There 'the primacy of the executive remains, but it is tempered by a reasonable balance of democratic usage,'[3] which guarantees to the legislature a reasonable amount of independence consistent with the demands and exigencies of a co-ordinated, modern government.

The importance of an independent legislature needs no special emphasis. Unless parliament is in fact independent of the executive, then the sovereignty of parliament, to which African leaders are fond of constantly referring, means simply the sovereignty of the executive. An executive possessed of the legal sovereignty of the state (i.e. power to legislate) is unquestionably a danger to liberty and democracy. It may be conceded that, in the interests of governmental efficiency and effectiveness, the executive should have control of policy and therefore of the legislative initiative. But the final process by which policy is legislated into law binding on the community must not only be separated from, but needs also to be independent of, the executive. For it is in this that the real essence of liberty lies. Liberty is not secured by a constitutional guarantee of rights alone. No constitution, however strongly entrenched, can be guaranteed against the temptations of power on the part of the executive, unless there is an independent legislature to act as a counterpoise against such temptations, and unless there is a strong national ethic against executive pretensions. In a young, largely illiterate country where public opinion is under-developed and slow to form and to articulate, an independent legislature can be the rallying force of the people against incipient tyranny. Its members, by virtue of their education and standing in society, are eminently well placed to act as the articulators and guardians of the nation's ethic, and the assembly provides them with an excellent platform from which to try to mobilise public opinion against abuse of power by the executive.

The importance of legislation in the governmental process lies in the fact that it is the means by which the life of the nation is regulated, and from which, therefore, the authority of the government to govern derives. In the light of this, the danger to liberty of an executive endowed with an independent power of legislation becomes apparent. It is not just that he can pass tyrannical laws and then execute them tyrannically; he can also act arbitrarily in flagrant disregard of the limits of his power and then proceed to legalise his action by retrospective legislation. Opposition under such circumstances becomes both futile and dangerous. The individual has virtually no rights against the government, because its powers are, for practical purposes, unlimited.

2. *Elements and Extent of the Legislature's Subservience*

Dr Lee has characterised the parliaments of the presidential regimes of Africa by the word 'passivity'. Adopting the language of Walter Bagehot, he describes the executive as the 'efficient' and parliament as the 'decorative' organ.[4] This description may well be criticised as somewhat exaggerated. The Kenyan parliament, as we have seen,[5] is known to be fiercely independent, and both the Tanzanian and Ugandan parliaments, while lacking the fierceness of their Kenyan counterpart, have also had a record of independent criticism and action. Yet, as a general description, it is true that parliaments in Africa are largely decorative, serving mostly to rubber-stamp decisions taken by the executive. The extent of this subordination may perhaps be best perceived by considering how the powers and functions involved in legislation are shared between the legislature and the executive. Legislation comprises three main powers and functions, namely the formal legislative power, the legislative initiative, and the actual enactment of legislative proposals into law. Each of these will now be considered in turn.

3. *The Legislative Power*

A legislature cannot be said to be completely sovereign if it does not possess the entirety of the legislative power of the state. The sovereignty of parliament demands that it alone shall have the power of legislation, and that no other body can legislate except by its authority and with its consent. Any sharing of the legislative power between the legislature and the executive, whereby a part of that power is vested in the executive exclusively and independently of the legislature, would therefore be a serious derogation of the sovereignty and independence of the legislature.

The distribution of political powers in the presidential constitutions in Commonwealth Africa follows the general principle of making parliament the sole repository of the legislative power. Generally speaking, the executive has no independent legislative power; under the constitution there is only one legislative authority, namely parliament, from which it follows that whatever power the executive possesses to make law is a derivative or delegated one, and therefore subordinate to parliament's supreme legislative authority under the constitution. A delegated power implies that the delegation may be revoked at any time by the donor, and that, while it lasts, the exercise of the power must be strictly within the terms of the delegation.

This general statement must be taken with serious qualifications and exceptions. First, all that is meant by it is that the legislative power is not divided between parliament and the executive as two co-ordinate organs, each controlling its assigned sphere of legislative competence independently of the other. It does not mean that this undivided legislative power is vested completely away from the executive (i.e. the president). For the entity, called parliament, in which the constitution vests this undivided legislative power, is not the legislative assembly alone, but rather the legislative assembly and the President together. The President is as much a constituent part of parliament as the assembly; their title to the legislative power is both joint and equal in the sense that, in the absence of a contrary provision in the constitution, the concurrence of both is indispensable to its exercise.

Subject to the constitution, neither the one nor the other alone can exercise the power. This must be accounted a serious qualification upon the autonomy of the legislature, a qualification which it is difficult to justify in a republican constitution. It is a relic of monarchy, and is explicable only in that context. It is an attempt to reconcile monarchy with popular sovereignty. The monarch is the sovereign, and the cardinal essence of sovereignty in the legal sense is the power to make laws. Time was indeed when the monarch, as sovereign, possessed and exercised an unfettered power of law-making. But then he had to bow to the forces of representative democracy, and to concede legislative power to the people's representatives in parliament. Yet, while monarchy remains the framework of government, the monarch's title of sovereignty must needs be given cognisance in the distribution of power to the representative organs of government. The device of making him a constituent part of the legislature seeks therefore to accommodate his title of sovereignty with the popular sovereignty of the people which the assembly represents.

Such a device should have no place in a republic. It has none indeed in the first modern republic, the United States of America. The American Constitution vests legislative power in Congress alone; i.e. the Senate and the House of Representatives. Undoubtedly, the framers' pre-occupation with the doctrine of separation of powers greatly influenced the provision, but the principles of republicanism were also a crucial factor. The point at issue here should not be confused with the question of authentication. No doubt, legislation, being a solemn and authoritative act of state, would need to be authenticated by the state functionary who personifies the authority and majesty of the state. The President's signature is necessary to bestow the seal of authority of the state upon a law passed by the assembly. But the fact that his signature is necessary to the efficacy of a law does not by itself make him a co-beneficiary of the legislative power. His signature stands on the same footing as the requirement that a company's corporate seal is essential to the validity of certain of its acts. The authority to do the act is something distinct from the act of appending a signature or affixing a seal.

That the significance of this is purely formal is illustrated by the fact that, whereas in British constitutional theory and practice the concurrence of the monarch to legislation cannot be dispensed with under any circumstances, under the American Constitution a bill passed by Congress can become law without the President's signature if he fails to return it within ten days of its being presented to him, or if he refuses to sign it at all and Congress then repasses it with a two-thirds majority. The power of an American President to withhold his signature from a bill operates by way of a veto (a qualified veto) in the strict sense of the word, since it operates to block the effectuation of the decision of an otherwise competent authority. Had the Constitution not required a bill to be signed by the President, passage of a bill through Congress would have been enough to give it the force of law since the legislative power is vested in Congress alone. It would be otherwise had the President been made a constituent part of the legislature. His consent, however it is to be expressed, would then have been integrally involved in the legislative power; so that the withholding of it would not strictly be a veto, since a veto implies that the power of decision-taking is elsewhere than in the person exercising the veto. A member of a body may be enabled to veto the decision of that body, but that is because the decision-taking power is for all practical purposes in the majority.

It has been noted that the fact that the President is a constituent part of parliament means that his consent to legislation cannot be dispensed with. No bill passed by the assembly can become law without the President's assent. This means that, in the event of conflict between him and the assembly, either the bill is killed completely by the President withholding his assent from it, or he would be obliged to assent to it against his wishes. Alternatively, he may be given the choice of either assenting or dissolving parliament. In Ghana (1960), if the President refused his assent to a bill or part of a bill, then that was the end of the bill or the part of it so 'vetoed'.[6] In Uganda (1967), he must assent to every bill passed by the assembly and presented to him.[7] In Tanzania, Zambia, Malawi, Botswana and Gambia he has the choice of either assenting or dissolving provided that the bill, after having been refused assent by the President, is passed again within six months by a two-thirds majority (or a simple majority in Malawi and Botswana); the President must then assent within twenty-one days unless before that he has exercised his choice of dissolution.[8]

The provision in the Kenyan Constitution seems to suggest that a bill can become law without the assent of the President. First, whereas the provision in the other constitutions is that the legislative power of parliament is to be exercised by bills passed by the assembly and assented to by the President (Tanzania and Gambia even stress that a bill shall not become law unless it is so passed and assented to), in Kenya it is to be exercised by bills passed by the national assembly.[9] Further, 'upon a bill that has been passed by the National Assembly being presented to the President for assent, it shall become law and shall thereupon be published in the Kenya Gazette as a law.'[10] These provisions are somewhat curious in so far as they suggest that presentation alone and not actual assent is all that is required for a bill to become law; this is hardly consistent with an earlier provision making the President a constituent part of parliament.[11] During the debate on the Constitution Bill in 1964, the Minister for Justice and Constitutional Affairs, Mr Tom Mboya, explained that 'the assent of the President will be a formality. We have decided not to retain or preserve the "royal veto". ... Only Parliament can pass laws and the President will have no power to veto any law passed by Parliament.'[12] This seems to suggest that presidential assent is legally necessary but must be given as a matter of course.

The main exceptions to the statement that parliament is the sole repository of the legislative power must now be noticed. There are four of these in Commonwealth Africa.

(i) *The Special Powers of the First President in Ghana and of the President in Uganda*

Part X of the Republican Constitution of Ghana, 1960, entitled 'Special Powers for First President', empowered the first President, Dr Nkrumah, whenever he considered it to be in the national interest, to give directions by legislative instrument which would override any enactment other than the Constitution.[13] This comes as something of a paradox, for the Constitution had in an earlier article provided that 'no person or body other than Parliament shall have power to make provisions having the force of law except under authority conferred by Act of Parliament.'[14] The special powers of the first President were however declared to have effect notwithstanding this affirmation of parliament's exclusive legislative authority. But the paradox is accounted for by the manner in which the special power of the first President found its way into the Constitution. It did so as it were by the side door. It was not in the original draft of the Constitution presented to parliament. That draft was already in its second reading stage when a member, perhaps over-enthused with the role of constitution-maker, suddenly proposed the addition of the special power for the first President, which, he said, was necessary to deal with a situation of impasse between the President and the assembly, leading to a breakdown of the normal legislative machinery.[15] The government at first opposed the proposal, but later changed its stand and adopted it in a modified form during the committee stage. In this modified form the amendment passed by sixty-three votes to seven to disfigure an otherwise good piece of work.

To the Attorney-General, Geoffrey Bing, one of the chief architects of the Constitution, this was a monstrous excrescence; it had outraged him to the point that he contemplated resignation – the only time he ever did so. 'This seemed to me,' he commented some years after, 'to undermine the whole principle of the Constitution which had been so carefully elaborated and explained. At one stroke it appeared that the delicate balance between the powers of parliament and of the President, so laboriously examined in cabinet after cabinet and, after much alteration in detail to meet every point of view, finally agreed, was suddenly to be abandoned to meet the whim of a notoriously irresponsible parliament.'[16] The power was of course never used, yet the mere fact of its existence at once subordinated parliament to the first President.

It was principally for this reason that it was rejected in Tanganyika in 1962. 'The government,' explained the government white paper introducing the proposals for a republican constitution, 'has studied the provisions of a number of constitutions which, to a greater or lesser extent, invest an executive President with power to legislate without recourse to parliament. The government considers that such provisions, although they may have the advantage of strengthening executive authority, by their very nature subvert democratic principles and inevitably lead to abuse. It is not, therefore, proposed to confer on the President any power to legislate otherwise than by, or under, the authority of an Act of Parliament.'[17] The power was very much reminiscent of the power of the imperial government under the colonial constitution to disallow legislation of the colonial legislature, and to legislate over its head. It is fair to mention that the requirement of the national interest placed a limit upon the President's power in Ghana. Its use must be warranted by the national interest, which might perhaps be why it was never invoked at all.

Under the 1967 Constitution of Uganda, the President might exercise the legislative power of the country in two situations:[18] (a) When the national assembly was not sitting, either because it was in recess or had been prorogued or dissolved, and the cabinet advised that exceptional circumstances existed which made it necessary for the President to take immediate action, then he might promulgate such ordinances as the circumstances appeared to him to require. (b) When the national assembly was dissolved and the ensuing general election was nullified because no party had a majority of up to 40 per cent or more, he might promulgate such ordinances as circumstances required for the effective government of Uganda during such period. Such an ordinance had the same force and effect as an act of parliament, and continued in force until six weeks after the assembly reassembled, unless earlier repealed by the President or parliament. It must, however, be laid before the national assembly immediately on the first meeting following its promulgation.

This power of the President in Ghana and Uganda was concurrent with that of parliament, which was not thereby excluded from any sphere of legislation. It was not therefore as derogatory of the authority and independence of parliament as an arrangement whereby only specifically enumerated matters are reserved to parliament while the residue is made the subject of rule-making by the executive. This is the scheme of the Constitution of the French Fifth Republic and the ex-French African Republics. Under this arrangement, not only is the rule-making power of the executive independent of the legislature, but it also covers quite a considerable range of matters. A law enacted by parliament on a matter which is properly the subject of the rule-making power of the executive may be modified or annulled by an executive decree. What is more, should parliament fail to pass a finance bill within seventy days, the government may put it into effect by ordinance. It may also, with parliamentary authorisation, issue ordinances during a limited period of time on matters reserved to the legislature, in order to implement its programme. Although such an ordinance has to be ratified by an act of parliament, yet this is more than a subordinate legislation as it is understood under the British system, since subordinate legislation presupposes that the legislature has legislated on the matter, leaving only certain points of detailed administration to be regulated by rules or regulations made by the executive.

(ii) *Defence and Security Appropriation in Zambia*

Appropriation of money for public expenditure is an important part of the legislative power vested in parliament. Public expenditure has to be authorised by parliament in an appropriation act, except in the case of an expenditure charged upon the general revenue of the country by the constitution itself or by some other law,[19] such as the public debt and the salaries of the President, judges, director of public prosecutions and auditor-general.[20] In 1970 the Constitution of Zambia was amended to make unnecessary an appropriation act in the case of defence and security expenditure; in place of an appropriation act authorising such expenditure, the amendment makes a warrant issued by the President sufficient.[21] For the sake of completeness it may be noted that the amendment also makes it unnecessary for any expenditure charged on the general revenue by the Constitution or other law (including defence and security expenditure) to appear in the financial report which the Minister for Finance is to prepare and lay before the national assembly showing the total government revenue and expenditure for each financial year. Further, the auditor-general is no longer to report to the national assembly on such expenditure, but only to the President.

Defence and security expenditure occupies a large proportion of total government expenditure. The heads of expenditure comprised therein are not known and identified like the public debt or the salaries of the president, judges, etc. The substitution of a presidential warrant in place of an appropriation act has the effect therefore of a sharing of appropriation legislation between the executive and parliament. Surprisingly, the opposition in parliament acquiesced in this, only questioning the provision of the amendment which removed from the purview of the house both the financial report and the auditor-general's report on the expenditures in question. In so far as they questioned the main provision of the amendment it was only to demand that it should be limited to defence, and not include 'security', because of the elastic meaning of that term. The government's explanation was that this rather far-reaching power was warranted by the need for keeping the country's defence and security expenditure secret from its hostile neighbours. The amendment was passed by seventy-seven votes at the second reading — four votes more than the required two-thirds majority. It was lost, however, at the third reading, with only sixty-eight votes cast in favour.[22] Nine of the government M.P.s who took part in the division on the second reading were not present at the division on the third reading, but it was not clear whether they deliberately absented themselves, because they had had second thoughts about the amendment. However that might be, the opposition hailed it as a defeat for the government, and called upon it to resign. But the third reading was re-opened five days later, this having been made possible by a motion suspending a standing order which would have precluded further proceeding on the amendment after its previous defeat.[23]

It is questionable, however, whether this procedure was strictly in conformity with other provisions of the standing orders. The opposition had contended that the standing order applicable to the occasion was not the one actually suspended, but that which says that 'when a bill has passed or has been rejected, no bill of the same substance shall be introduced again during the current session'.[24] This contemplates that the bill should be introduced afresh as a new bill. In the view of the government, however, it was not the bill itself, but the motion for its third reading, that had been rejected; accordingly the standing order just quoted did not apply, and it was enough merely to suspend Standing Order 36 which provides that 'no motion or amendment shall be moved which is the same in substance as any motion or amendment which during the current session has been resolved in the affirmative or negative, unless the order, resolution or vote on such motion or amendment has been rescinded'. It is regrettable that no ruling on the point in dispute was made by the Speaker. The government got its way, and on the renewed third reading the amendment bill was passed by eighty votes. (The opposition abstained completely from voting.)

(iii) *Transitional Legislation after Adoption of a new Constitution*

A change of constitution creates a necessity for adapting existing laws to the new constitution. Such adaptation is an exercise of legislative power by way of amendment of existing laws in order to bring them into conformity with the new constitution, and so facilitate an orderly transition to the new order. In the Commonwealth it has become the invariable practice to give this power to the Head of State, i.e. the executive. This is both expedient and desirable. For not only are the necessary adaptations often extensive, involving the whole body of existing legislation, but they are also very minute, like changing names, titles and designations, substituting appropriate functionaries, and various other amendments of a purely verbal nature. The power partakes therefore of a clerical character, and cannot be used to bring in changes of substance in the law. It is also limited in time, seldom extending for more than one year from the date of the new constitution. Further, it is not a power to amend the constitution itself, but merely to enable other laws to be brought into conformity with the constitution. Exceptionally, power to adapt the constitution itself may be given, but even so it still remains a power of adaptive, and not of substantive, legislation.

The 1962 Constitution of Pakistan, for example, empowered the President to 'direct by order that the provisions of the constitution shall have effect subject to such adaptations ... as he may deem necessary and expedient'.[25] Under the Constitution, a member of the national assembly vacated his seat if he was appointed a minister. The President found this inexpedient in the case of two members of the assembly whom he wanted to appoint as ministers; accordingly, he used his adaptive power to amend the provision, which then made it possible for the two members to retain their seats after being appointed ministers. The amendment was held to be *ultra vires*, as being outside the scope of adaptation, since otherwise the President would have been enabled to alter fundamental provisions of the constitution 'without resorting to the special and massive machinery of amendment'.[26]

In one particular instance in Commonwealth Africa, the President's power of transitional legislation exceeds what has just been described, but there was perhaps some justification for this in the peculiar circumstances of that case. When the union of Tanganyika and Zanzibar was formed in 1964, there was not immediately a constituent assembly or other body to exercise the constituent powers of the union which would enable full effect to be given to the union. The Articles of Union did of course authorise the appointment of a constitutional commission and the summoning of a constituent assembly, which was to consider the proposals of the commission and adopt a constitution for the united republic.[27] Until that was done, they (i.e. the Articles of Union) provided that the Parliament of Tanganyika and the Revolutionary Council of Zanzibar, in conjunction with the cabinet of ministers thereof, were to enact laws to provide for the government of the united republic and of Zanzibar.[28] The laws so enacted provided that for an interim period until a constituent assembly could be summoned to adopt a permanent constitution, the united republic was to be governed by the Constitution of Tanganyika, but they also empowered the union President to amend that Constitution by decree in order to provide for the following: the reservation of certain matters exclusively to the union parliament and executive, a separate legislature and executive for Zanzibar with exclusive authority in matters other than those reserved exclusively to the union, the appointment of two Vice-Presidents, the representation of Zanzibar in the union parliament, and such other matters as might be expedient or desirable to give effect to the union and to the Articles of Union.[29] The parliament of Tanganyika, with the Zanzibari representatives added, was therefore to become the parliament of the union for the interim period. But even after a union parliament had been so constituted, the President still has other legislative powers which are not merely of an adaptive kind. He may during the interim period, by decree—

(*a*) extend any existing law of Tanganyika on matters within the exclusive competence of the union to Zanzibar as part of the law thereof and repeal or revoke any law of Zanzibar corresponding to, or inconsistent with, any law so extended;

(*b*) make such transitional, consequential and temporary provision in respect of matters within the exclusive competence of the union or in relation to the existing laws of Tanganyika, as may appear to him to be necessary or expedient for giving effect to the union.[30]

These are of course additional to his power of adaptive legislation.[31] A decree made by the President is to have effect as if enacted in the enabling act itself, and may provide for the making of rules and for the delegation of powers.[32] Although a presidential decree is required to be laid before the interim parliament, this is not to affect its operation prior to its being so laid.

These are quite significant powers, especially as they include vital constituent powers. President Nyerere has refused to exercise them, because, he says, they are '*per se* subversive of democratic principles and inevitably lead to abuse'.[33] The Interim Constitution is not in fact the constitution of Tankanyika as modified by the President in the manner stated above, but an entirely new constitution enacted by the parliament of the united republic. The President has left it to parliament to enact all the necessary transitional legislation. Tanzania is still governed by an interim constitution, so that the President's powers of transitional legislation still remain in theory.

Under the republican constitution of Kenya, 1964, the President also had powers which went somewhat beyond that of mere adaptive legislation. His power to amend existing laws during the normal transitional twelve months' period extended not only to amendments appearing to him necessary or expedient for bringing such existing laws into conformity with the new Constitution, but also to any changes that he otherwise considered necessary or expedient in consequence of the new Constitution. In particular, he might repeal any enactment of a regional assembly.[34]

(iv) *Emergency Legislation by the President*

In practice this is perhaps the most potent qualification upon the exclusiveness of parliament's legislative authority. The principle of executive legislation during an emergency is universal throughout the Commonwealth. Its normal scope and purpose is to enable the executive to make such regulations as appear to him necessary or expedient during an emergency for securing the public safety, the defence of the state, the maintenance of public order and the suppression of mutiny, rebellion and riot, and for maintaining supplies and services essential to the life of the community. There is perhaps nothing exceptionable in giving this power to the executive in times of dire emergency threatening the life of the nation — subject, however, to strict parliamentary control. The difference in Commonwealth Africa is in the wider scope and overriding force of emergency powers, the inadequacy of parliamentary control, the frequency of emergencies, and the fact that the declaration is often in the sole discretion of the executive. It is these that tend to make emergency powers in Africa objectionable.

The President in Africa has power, outside the normal scope of emergency powers in the advanced democracies, to make regulations for the detention of persons or the restriction of their movements — both citizens and non-citizens — and for any other thing that appears to him strictly required by the exigencies of the situation in the country.[35] As Chief Justice Tregold observed, the power is thus virtually 'co-extensive with the ordinary legislative authority of the Territory'.[36] It is also overriding, for the President can by regulation amend any enactment, suspend its operation or apply its provisions with or without modification. A presidential emergency regulation overrides an inconsistent parliamentary enactment which is thus rendered ineffective to the extent of such inconsistency.

By law, of course, emergency regulations need to be approved by parliament either before they take effect or within a period of, say, three months thereafter. In practice the approval is given as a matter of course with little or no critical discussion of the necessity for the extent of powers claimed. It is ironical that it is at such times as this when the possibility of abuse is greatest, that parliamentary control is at its lowest and most ineffective, with parliament virtually abandoning the field to the executive. This might be considered a tragedy, especially when it is remembered that, apart from war, an emergency is whatever else the leaders regard as such, there being no definition in the constitution of the sort of situation that should constitute an emergency.

The opportunity for abuse inherent in this lack of precise definition has not been missed in Commonwealth Africa, as witness the action of the government during the so-called emergency in Western Nigeria in 1962.[37] The tragedy of the situation is further heightened by the fact that in practically all the presidential regimes in Commonwealth Africa, the authority to declare an emergency belongs in the first instance to the President alone; parliamentary approval comes only after the initial declaration by the President, and is then given again as a matter of course. A useful safeguard is that a declaration remains in force only for six months unless it is extended by parliament for further periods of six months at a time. Again, extensions are granted without question if only they are asked for by the President. Indeed in Zambia since 1969, a declaration now continues in force indefinitely until revoked by either the President or the national assembly, or unless there is a new President, when it lapses within seven days of his assumption of office.[38] By means of this and of earlier parliamentary extensions, the declaration made in July 1964 has been continued in force in Zambia up to the time of writing, a period of more than eight years later. During this period the President could, had he so wished, have become the sole legislator for Zambia on a wide range of matters.

Perhaps the widest emergency powers were those given to the President of Kenya in the North-Eastern Province and contiguous districts of the country, where a war of secession, begun just before independence in 1963, had continued until 1971. The power was unlimited both as to scope and time. The President was to make any regulations that appeared to him necessary or expedient for the purpose of ensuring effective government in the area, and the regulations might make any temporary adaptations, modifications or qualifications of, or exceptions to, the Constitution or any other law.[39] It was an original power, conferred by the Constitution itself, and not by the legislature as in the other cases. Nor were regulations made in pursuance of it dependent upon parliamentary approval.

4. *The Legislative Initiative*

In theory every M.P. has the right to initiate bills, motions and questions in parliament quite independently of the government and without its prior approval. There are, of course, both legal and practical qualifications upon this right. It does not exist in respect of financial matters involving the raising and expenditure of public funds. Such matters can only be initiated by the government through the Vice-President or a minister. The reason for this is said to be that good and orderly government requires that only those who administer the government and therefore have an intimate connection with it, should propose national expenditure, and how the money needed for it can be raised;[40] and that there would be financial chaos if every member were to be free to propose expenditure, since members would then be competing among themselves to secure as much of the public funds as possible for the constituencies or interests which they represent.[41]

Desirable as this qualification may be, its effect is undoubtedly to increase the monopoly of the executive over policy. For finance and policy are intricately interwoven. Finance is the lever that links all activities of government, from which it follows that the organ controlling it is also given an overview of the entire functions of government, including policy.

A member's right of initiative is also limited by the opportunities available for its exercise. First, how frequently parliament should meet is determined by the government. It is the President who summons a session of parliament and brings it to an end by prorogation, though he is constitutionally bound to call a session once every year at intervals of less than twelve months.[42] Within a session, the assembly (in effect, the government) determines the sittings; the President can, of course, summon a meeting at any time.[43] In Africa, meetings of the assembly are too few to provide the members ample opportunity to discharge their functions adequately and effectively. In any case, it is just not practicable that every member in a house of, say, 100 members should have the chance to initiate a bill or motion, unless the assembly is to sit round the clock throughout the year. And the greater the number, the less the chances. Inevitably, therefore, the chance can come to only a fraction of the members during any session. It is usual to settle the competing claims of members by ballot. However, it is the demands of government business more than the competitive claims of other members that impose the severest limitations upon the opportunities available to a member to initiate measures. The government's responsibility to govern gives it a first claim on the time of the assembly, since without the approval of the assembly, in the form of legislation or otherwise, the government cannot implement its policies and programme. It is probably proper, therefore, that government business should have priority over that of private members. In practice, much of the assembly's time is taken up by government business, and because of this it is reasonable that the leader of government business in the assembly should have control over the whole agenda of the assembly. This has become a prerogative of the government under the British parliamentary system, and it is a feature that distinguishes it from the American, where there are no government ministers and *ipso facto* no leader of government business in Congress.

But the right of the government to determine the business of the assembly under the Westminster parliamentary system has to be exercised within the framework of the standing orders and any relevant conventions. In Britain the business of the House of Commons is by convention arranged informally between the Prime Minister and the Leader of the Opposition, and a significant amount of parliamentary time must be devoted to debate upon topics chosen by the opposition.[44] This is not the case in Commonwealth Africa. No doubt the standing orders provide for private members' participation, and try to balance this with the demands of government business. Thus they provide for question time at the beginning of every meeting, for private members' motions during the adjournment debate, and for motions to introduce bills; there are also other opportunities during the debate on the budget and on the presidential address.

While, however, the opportunity for questions appears fairly ample and is fully utilised,[45] that for initiating motions and bills is not. The adjournment debate is limited to only thirty minutes, and the debates on the budget and the presidential address take place only once in a session. Moreover, except for one day in the week, called private members' day, government business takes precedence over private members' business on all other days. This operates in practice to limit private members' business to just one day in the week, and much of that may be, and often is, appropriated by the government to meet the pressure of government business. The opportunities for a private members' bill are further restricted. For while a motion requires only notice to the house and success in the ballot where that is necessary, a bill additionally requires leave of the house. And unless the bill has the support of the government which controls the majority vote, the application for leave stands little chance of success. Generally, too, a private member is inhibited by the work and expense of promoting a bill, since the facilities of the government, such as the services of the government legal draftsman, are not available to him for this purpose, not even, it appears, on terms of payment. It is only in respect of private bills (to be distinguished from a private member's bill) that government facilities can be used on terms of payment. A private bill is one intended to affect or benefit some particular person, association or corporate body rather than the public generally; it is brought to the assembly by means of petition, and its promoters must pay a prescribed fee as well as the expenses, such as drafting and printing costs, incidental to the passing of the bill.

These are the factors that have made the legislative initiative a monopoly of the government in Africa. So complete has this monopoly become in practice that most M.P.s are not even aware that they have a right to initiate legislation.[46] With only one private member's bill introduced in 1966, the Kenyan parliament stands out as the only parliament in Commonwealth Africa in which a private member's bill has ever been introduced – and passed. (The bill dealt with hire-purchase.) However, executive monopoly of the legislative initiative cannot really be said to be such a subordinating factor. The question is whether the initiation of legislation, with all its policy implications, is essentially a function of the government or of the legislature. To put it differently, is legislative initiative an integral part of the legislative power, so as to make it, like the latter, the prerogative of the legislature? It would be out of tune with the realities of modern government to regard the legislative initiative as belonging exclusively to the legislature as an integral part of the legislative power. In a recent report, the Study of Parliament Group in Britain has sought to dispel the popular misconception on this point. 'Legislation today', the Group affirms, 'is pre-eminently a function of government. It is largely by means of legislation that administrations implement party programmes, react to the need for basic changes in the economic, social and political structure of the country, and bring the law into conformity with current standards of what is acceptable or tolerable. That being so, it is misleading to regard the legislative process as something in principle separable from government, still less to see it as beginning and ending in parliament'.[47]

This statement underlines the change that has taken place in the character and content of modern legislation. In the days before the emergence of the positive welfare state, the matters that needed to be regulated by legislation were few and simple — domestic relations, land, criminal offences, etc. These were easily within the initiative of individual M.P.s. The concern of the government was mainly with foreign relations, the maintenance of law and order, and execution generally. Modern government has an infinitely wider concern, involving active intervention in the life of society with a view to improving its quality. This, as has just been observed, requires legislation, and legislation with high policy content. But policy is essentially an executive function;[48] it is implicit in the right to govern, a fact which most Commonwealth African presidential constitutions recognise in the provision vesting the responsibility for policy in the President.

There is another reason why high policy legislation must be a function of the government. Much of it is of an extremely complex and technical nature, with wide-ranging ramifications, which at once put it beyond the capacity of an individual M.P. to manage or even to comprehend. The dimension of the issues with which it deals may be beyond his vision; they may be issues arising in the administration of the departments or other institutions of state and about which only someone inside the government can have knowledge and experience; such are questions of fiscal policy, social reform, economic development and even pure administration. Their complexity and technical nature require special expertise. Thus we find that, because of this, the introduction of such legislation in parliament is usually preceded by a long and protracted period of gestation during which it is put through an elaborate process of consultation and discussion among various interested groups — the party, the sponsoring department, the cabinet and its committees, and other interested sections of the community, like trade unions, trade associations, etc. When at last the policy aspects have been thrashed out, then comes the drafting stage. Even this may be a complex and complicated matter. Sir Courtney Ilbert has described what is involved in this seemingly simple work. 'The first crude sketch', he wrote, 'will be generally elaborated. There will be daily conferences with the minister, or with the permanent head of the department, or with both. There will be interviews and correspondence with experts in various branches of the subject with which the measure deals. Notes will have to be written tracing the history of previous legislation or attempts at legislation, and explaining the reasons for and effect of the several proposals embodied in the draft bill, and stating the arguments which may be advanced for and against them, and these will soon grow into a formidable literature of commentaries'.[49]

In Africa, admittedly, the process is seldom, if ever, as elaborate as this, consultation with interested groups being rare and never exhaustive, while the drafting process is not nearly so thorough. Indeed the whole process may begin and end with a few individuals, the minister, his permanent secretary, the attorney-general's chamber and the cabinet. Yet the fact still remains that no individual M.P. can alone muster the facilities needed. Furthermore, modern government is constantly beset with crises of various types such as war, economic depression, and industrial disputes. These create a situation which may call for a legislative leadership of a kind which only the executive, with its greater capacity for action, can provide.[50]

These, then, are the factors which have placed the legislative initiative largely in the hands of the government, rather than of the legislature. In Britain the reality of the matter had been recognised since at least the middle of the eighteenth century. Most bills in Britain, estimated at 85 per cent, are government bills.[51] America, too, is gradually coming round to this recognition — gradually, since Congress still regards legislative initiative as its prerogative by virtue of the separation of powers in the Constitution. Congress (or rather, its leaders) exercises the final discretion as to which bills should be introduced. It is these leaders who determine and control the business of Congress; no government ministers are in Congress anyway. Naturally these legislative leaders are quite jealous of their own and their colleagues' right of initiative, which is therefore allowed a far wider scope than in Britain. And there exist in Congress facilities to assist members in the preparation and drafting of bills; of which the committee system and the legislative expertise which it has developed are perhaps the most helpful. Furthermore, there is no such restriction as exists in the Commonwealth on members' right of initiative with respect to financial matters. Yet, while private members' bills account for a substantial proportion, estimated at half or perhaps even more,[52] of all bills introduced in the houses, Congress is coming increasingly to yield legislative leadership to the executive, because of its superior resources and greater capacity for action. The process has been accentuated by the budgetary reform of 1921, which entrusted to the President the responsibility for the preparation of an annual budget to be presented to Congress, thereby enabling him to 'work out a general and integrated plan of government programmes and operations, which hitherto had been lacking'.[53] The present position is summed up thus by McConnell:

> The relationship between the President and Congress is considerably different from that formally drawn in the great scheme of the constitution. The separation of powers between these two branches has not indeed been removed; a vast gap separates the two. Nevertheless, the increasing complexities of modern political life have required an increasing role for the President, and the presidency has become increasingly institutionalised. Correlatively, the legislative branch has become less and less capable of mastering the daily flow of events of which policy is so largely composed; it is compelled to leave much to the executive branch. If present trends were to be projected into the future, we could envision a government system in which the President with the whole executive branch under his effective control governs, and Congress checks and criticises. Already, this picture accords with what happens in some areas of policy, military and foreign affairs for example.[54]

We must conclude therefore that legislative initiative is not indispensable to the independence of the legislature under modern government. What seems of greater importance is not that the assembly should control the initiation of legislation, but rather that legislation introduced by the government, as the organ better able to do so, should be thoroughly scrutinised and discussed in the assembly. It is this scrutinising and critical function that should form the chief concern of parliament. How free and effective are African parliaments in discharging this function?

5. *The Enacting or Approving Function*

Perhaps the most crucial criterion of an independent legislature is the freedom that it has when approving, whether by means of legislation or otherwise, measures introduced before it by the government. This raises the question of the degree of freedom which a legislature should be able to apply to this function before it can be said to possess real independence. Must it be such a degree of freedom as gives it unfettered discretion to reject government measures if and when it pleases, or is what is needed essentially freedom to criticise? The dangers of unfettered legislative discretion, such as is a characteristic of the American Congress, will be touched on in a later chapter.[55] It has the unfortunate consequence of impairing executive-legislature relations, because of the jealousy with which Congress guards its legislative prerogative, and the control over policy which this is supposed to give it. The result is that its relations with the President are marked by antipathy and antagonism, instead of by regular, healthy co-operation, which is what governmental effectiveness demands. What co-operation there is, is of a somewhat 'intermittent and haphazard' type, rather than 'regular and predictable'.[56] Now and again, though not too often, the antagonism precipitates a stalemate, which paralyses the government, leaving the nation without a clear, co-ordinated leadership. Even without such a breakdown, the policy that results from such a system of executive-legislature antagonism is seldom an integral whole, but rather a patchwork, with vital pieces cut off by a Congress jealously asserting its power, regardless of the true needs of the nation.

The lesson of this is that if we must have a co-ordinated governmental process, the freedom of the legislature in relation to government measures cannot be unfettered. The legislature should not be free, at its own whim and pleasure, to reject government measures; otherwise it would be assuming the function of the cabinet and the ministers. The government of a modern state cannot be run effectively in parliament. Even if all the expert advice and information available to the cabinet were to be laid before parliament, its numbers alone make it singularly unsuited to undertake the determination and formulation of policy. It is a function that requires the mental concentration of an individual or a small committee of men who can analyse and co-ordinate the various aspects of the policy in an atmosphere of detachment, free from the emotion and heat of parliamentary debate. It would be difficult to have an effective government if M.P.s were to be free to substitute their own policy for that of the government. It would only lead to chaos if every government measure, which might have occupied the time, mind and skill of ministers and their expert advisers for many months, were to be subjected to the free *vote* of M.P.s who in all probability might have had only a few days to reflect upon its purport, if they are at all in a position to appreciate it.

Ability to reject government measures should not therefore be the criterion of independence in a legislature, except as an ultimate sanction. Independence should be judged instead by the degree of freedom which the legislature has to discuss and criticise, or what is known as the critical function. The point was made long ago by John Stuart Mill. A legislature, he wrote, should not attempt to govern. Its proper office is 'to watch and control the government; to throw the light of publicity on its acts, to compel a full exposition and justification of all of them which anyone considers questionable, and, if the men who compose the government abuse their trust, or fulfil it in a manner which conflicts with the deliberate sense of the nation, to expel them from office. . . .'[57] If effectively discharged, parliament's critical function would produce an attitude of responsibility and restraint in the government, which would oblige it to reckon with the possible reaction of the house in framing policy proposals, and to consult with interested groups in the country. This is a cardinal value of parliament's critical function. But, as stated in the last chapter, this value can only be fully realised if there is an opposition party seeking by it to supplant the government in the favour of the electorate. A government which has no rival cannot be expected to be as responsive to criticism as one which has. The fear of losing office to a rival is necessary to the efficacy of the critical function. A virile opposition may therefore be posited as essential to real independence in a legislature. An opposition 'does not have the *legal* power to obstruct government action, but it has the political power to force the government to act responsibly or suffer disastrously with the electorate'.[58]

If the government is being really outrageous, the opposition may indeed be able to inspire enough 'rebels' among the government M.P.s to vote against it and so bring about its defeat in parliament. It is against an irresponsible government that the ultimate power of rejection is meant to be a sanction. That the power is seldom used is perhaps evidence of the restraint which the fear of its use imposes on the government. Nowadays one frequently hears cries in Britain of the passing of parliament, but inasmuch as the British parliament still discharges its critical function in quite a vigorous manner, spearheaded and inspired by an active and alert opposition, the cries seem somewhat exaggerated. Parliament in Britain can clearly not be said to have lost its independence in the sense just explained. The same can hardly be said of parliaments in Africa. An attempt will now be made to identify the factors responsible for the subservience of the legislature in Africa.

(i) *The Conduct and Atmosphere of Debates in Parliament*

We will begin with the conduct of proceedings in the assembly, since how effectively the assembly discharges its critical function may depend to some extent on the way the proceedings are conducted, particularly on the character and outlook of the person presiding. A dictatorial chairman or Speaker can be a serious obstacle to freedom of discussion, especially if he is partisan and over-zealous in his support of the government.

The chairman of a legislative assembly has very wide powers to interpret the standing orders of the assembly, to rule on the relevance of a member's contribution and on other points of order, to ensure orderly debate and generally to enforce order and discipline in the house. A written constitution gives even greater interpretative power to a Speaker. He has to rule on the meaning and requirements of the constitution so far as it is relevant to the proceedings of the house, for example, what majorities are required for various actions, when a member can move a vote of confidence against the government or a minister, etc. To challenge or flout the Speaker's authority is to invite the risk of reprimand, exclusion, suspension or, in Ghana, even expulsion. A partisan and dictatorial Speaker may get impatient of criticism of the government or condone unnecessary interruptions of a critical speech.

Thus the most important quality required of a Speaker is impartiality. It is his paramount duty to hold the balance even between the competing elements in the house, and to 'ensure that the voice of the minority is always given a fair hearing'.[59] He is there to guard the dignity and independence of the house, and not to reflect the wishes of the government or to carry out its directives on the conduct of parliamentary business or the interpretation of relevant points of law. Should the government try to invade the autonomy of the assembly, he should not allow his loyalty to the government as his sponsors to the office to override his duty to the house. His duty as chairman demands that he should apply his own independent judgment in resolving points of dispute in the house with the assistance, where necessary, of independent expert advice, and not merely act on the opinion of the attorney-general, however learned. With perhaps the exception of Ghana under Nkrumah, it has not been known for any government in Commonwealth Africa to want to use the Speaker as an instrument to control the assembly. Nkrumah was alleged on one or two occasions to have directed the Speaker on what ruling to give, and the Leader of the House had sometimes given a ruling over the Speaker's head.[60] On the part of the Speakers themselves, while most have been remarkably impartial, quite a number have displayed some over-zealousness in their support of the government, and have thereby undermined opposition members' freedom of criticism.

The political atmosphere and mood in the house also affects the freedom and quality of debates. The reports of debates in the two-party legislatures leave a distinct impression of intense antagonism, amounting almost to a feud in which the paramount consideration is to place every conceivable obstacle in the way of the other side by interruptions and numerous but frivolous points of order, while giving every conceivable encouragement and support to one's own side by cheers, even when what is said amounts to very little.[61] Twenty or thirty interruptions in the course of one short speech are by no means unusual, with the result that the reports often make incoherent and disjointed reading. Members on both sides seem engaged in a competition to see who will interrupt the other more, completely disregarding the injunctions of the standing orders. In an atmosphere in which debate is regarded as a kind of feud between two opposing sides, it is obvious that the subject-matter of the debate cannot receive dispassionate and reasoned consideration, and that government M.P.s would refrain from voicing any criticism against the measure lest they should thereby give advantage to the opposition. To criticise a government measure in those circumstances is to betray the interests of the party, to be a traitor to the cause, and members would rather keep silent than run the risk of being so branded. And so one finds in Ghana and Zambia, for example, that government M.P.s seldom spoke against a government measure.

(ii) *Patronage*[62]

The inhibitions of party loyalty are reinforced by those of patronage, for many government M.P.s hold government appointments as ministers, commissioners, district governors, chairmen or members of public corporations; many others hold government contracts, agencies or other types of patronage. The subordinating influence of patronage is so obvious as not perhaps to require special comment. Throughout history, it has maintained its sway as perhaps the most potent instrument used by the executive, whether hereditary or elected, to ensure that the legislature remains compliant to its will and wishes. Even in Britain today, with the education and high standard of living of its M.P.s, patronage has continued to be a powerful armour in the control apparatus of the government, a fact which, it is said, has unbalanced the constitution by making parliament subservient to the will of the executive, in much the same way as during the heyday of Crown patronage under George III. 'With over a hundred members of the ruling party holding ministerial positions', laments one commentator, 'Mr Wilson has assuredly dispensed patronage with a liberality at which even George III or Lord North might have blushed'.[63] The figure of 100 ministers in parliament represents less than *one-sixth* of the total membership of the British House of Commons. In many parts of Commonwealth Africa, on the other hand, the proportion of M.P.s enjoying government patronage of one kind or another may be as high as *half or more*, and in the most notorious case (Western Nigeria in 1965) there were as many as forty-nine ministers (not to mention other patronage-holders) in a house of ninety-four. Zambia comes close behind, with fifty-three ministers (excluding district governors) in a house of 109.[64] The number of ministers in the Kenyan parliament on May 20, 1969, stood at fifty-two in a house of 171.

Needless to say, a minister is bound by the obligations of collective responsibility not to oppose or criticise a government measure in the house. One who did so was instantly dismissed by President Milton Obote in 1967, and in Kenya one received a warning letter from President Jomo Kenyatta in 1966. An assembly, half of whose members are ministers or other government functionaries, is a negation of the doctrine of separation in the personnel of the two primary political organs. The partial fusion of personnel which the Westminster system entails can only be defended if the proportion of government ministers to the total membership of the house is kept low. Where it is as much as half, the position becomes quite indefensible, since the assembly would then have become an extension of the executive, and would thus be incapable of fulfilling the role of watchdog of the nation's liberties against the pretensions of power on the part of the executive. It is desirable that the constitution itself should limit the number of ministers to be appointed, and not leave it entirely to the discretion of the President, as is the case in Tanzania, Gambia and Uganda. The limitation should not, of course, be by way of a fixed number, but rather by reference to a number to be determined by parliament from time to time. This is the arrangement in Zambia, Kenya, Malawi and Botswana, except that in default of parliamentary determination the President has authority under the constitution to appoint any number of ministers that he likes. Originally the Constitution of Zambia prescribed a ceiling of fourteen ministers (not including junior ministers), later increased to sixteen, then to nineteen, and finally abolished altogether on the ground that a constitutionally-determined ceiling is undesirable in a fast developing country.

In this connection the rules of disqualification for parliamentary membership become rather important, since they may operate to limit the number of government patronage-holders in parliament. Apart from ministers and other office-holders required to be appointed from among the members of the assembly, the general rule is that an office of emolument under the state disqualifies from membership. Civil servants and members of the judiciary, police and armed forces are thus generally disqualified. However, it is only in Kenya and Botswana that disqualification on this ground is imposed by the Constitution directly. In the rest of the presidential regimes the matter is left to be prescribed by parliament, which has in fact imposed the same disqualifications, subject however to any exceptions which it may see fit to prescribe. A more difficult point concerns disqualification on the ground of membership of statutory corporations and other parastatal bodies. The earlier approach to the problem in the Westminster-made African Constitutions, such as that of Nigeria, 1960, was not to treat membership of a statutory corporation as an office of emolument under the state and consequently as not disqualifying from membership; while at the same time declaring that membership of such a corporation or body shall be vacated automatically upon election or appointment as an M.P. None of the presidential constitutions in Commonwealth Africa directly imposes a disqualification on this ground, nor do they require that membership of a statutory corporation shall be vacated on election or appointment as an M.P.; these constitutions merely authorise parliament to prescribe the offices the holding of which shall disqualify from membership of parliament. (In Tanzania, while it is still for parliament to prescribe disqualifications on the ground of office-holding under the state, a 1967 amendment has added a whole new list of disqualifications not based on office-holding but designed to reflect the country's socialist policy.) No such power is conferred on parliament in Kenya or Botswana, from which it follows that, since the public service in these two countries is not defined as including an office in a statutory corporation or other parastatal body, a member or even an employee of such a body (other than an employee of a local authority in Kenya) is not disqualified.

Leaving the matter to be prescribed by parliament has the merit of flexibility. It enables parliament to fix and vary the disqualifications according to the prevailing needs and outlook of the society, without going through the slow and difficult process of a constitutional amendment, whose rigidity may be inexpedient in a young nation facing a shortage of educated and experienced people.

Only three constitutions – Tanzania, Kenya and Botswana – make reference to an interest in a government contract as a possible disqualifying factor, but they only empower parliament to impose such disqualification, subject to such exceptions and limitations as it may prescribe.

To be classified with ministers, commissioners, district governors, members of statutory corporations and government contractors in the assembly are government-nominated members. All the presidential constitutions in Commonwealth Africa, with the exception of Ghana (1960) and Botswana, empower the President to nominate members to the national assembly – three in Gambia, five (to be increased to ten in the one-party state Constitution) in Zambia, twelve in Kenya, fifteen in Malawi, and sixty-two in Tanzania (of whom fifty-two were to be from Zanzibar, where conditions are considered not yet ripe for general elections). The original draft of the 1967 Constitution of Uganda proposed to give the President power to nominate up to one-third of the membership of the national assembly. This was, however, later withdrawn in deference to the concerted attack by the opposition, but the substituted arrangement was for the party with the greatest numerical strength of elected members in the national assembly to elect such number of members as would give it a majority of ten in the assembly.[65]

The survival of nominated members in the independence and post-independence constitutions of Commonwealth Africa is somewhat ironical, in view of the fact that it was one of the main targets of nationalist attack on earlier colonial constitutions. The colonial nominated member was denounced as a stooge of the colonial government, as indeed in many cases he unquestionably was. Yet there was a plausible reason for the use of nominated members at that stage of colonial development. Except in the few urban centres, popular election was considered premature at the time, because of the mass illiteracy and poverty of the society, difficulties of communication, and a shortfall of trained personnel to conduct and supervise elections. Nomination seemed the next best method of providing representation to the people outside the main administrative and commercial centres. When elections became possible with the march of education and urbanisation, nomination was retained to cater for deserving interests, for which election would provide no representation, such as the professions, commerce, labour, the teaching profession and chiefly elements. It is also this last purpose that provides the main argument for the retention of nominated members several years after independence. The power of nomination, it is claimed, is necessary in order that the house might be given the benefit of the service of persons of experience and proven ability who might not wish to subject themselves to the ordeal of an election, and also to provide representation to racial minorities in the multi-racial communities of East and Central Africa. Coming from the very same opponents of the power of nomination in the colonial constitutions, the argument is somewhat disingenuous, and looks like a disguise to mask the real motive, which is the desire of the government to increase its support in the assembly. The government spokesman in the debates on the 1967 Ugandan Constitution admitted this when he explained, as the reason for the proposal that the President should nominate up to one-third of the assembly's total membership, that they did not want to have a government with a majority of, say, one, adding that a comfortable majority was necessary to governmental stability.[66] A similar admission was made on behalf of the government of Kenya in 1968.[67] Even where a government already has a comfortable majority, the extra support from five or so nominated members adds to its confidence, and of course arrogance, and also facilitates the progress to the eventual reduction of the opposition.

The motive of partisan support is of course inapplicable as an explanation of the survival of the nominated member in the *de jure* legislature of Tanzania and Malawi. Here it may be accepted as genuine that the primary purpose is to bring into the house the services of persons of experience and proven ability as well as to provide representation to special interests; nonetheless, a motive of personal power is not to be discounted, for it must be satisfying to the ego and private interests of the President to be able to nominate people to parliament. The Tanzanian presidential commission asserted, in support of its view in favour of the retention of the power, that 'nominated members have already proved their worth, and we believe that the case for retaining them is greatly strengthened by the recommendations we make later in this report for the participation of civil servants in politics'.[68] While rejecting the demand for the abolition of nominated members, on the ground that 'the Head of State should be left with some discretion to bring to Parliament special talent,' the Zambian one-party state commission thought that the need would be partly met by the institutional representation of chiefs (to be represented by eight members), the churches (1), the civil service (1), the National Council of Commerce and Industry (1), the National Women's Council (1), professional organisations (1), security forces (1), the University of Zambia (1), the Youth Council of Zambia (1), and the Zambia Congress of Trade Unions (1); accordingly, it recommended that the number of nominated members should be reduced from five to three, and that no one defeated in an election to parliament should be nominated to that parliament.[69] The government turned down the proposal about institutional representation, preferring instead to increase the number of nominated members to ten.[70] The inference to be drawn from this increase must be that nominated members are to be used to serve the purpose of representation for institutional and special interests.

It is worthy of note that Tanzania combines something of institutional or special representation with nominated members. Under the Interim Constitution, implementing a recommendation of the presidential commission, there are fifteen M.P.s elected by the national assembly from among persons approved by the national executive committee from a list nominated by institutions designated by the President as national institutions.[71] The procedure is that the President designates institutions which he considers to be of national character, e.g. the National Union of Tanganyika Workers, the co-operative movement, the Association of Chambers of Commerce, the University of Dar es Salaam, etc. Each designated institution nominates five persons, not necessarily members of the institution. Indeed the presidential commission expressed the hope that nominations would be made from all walks of life in the country.[72] A list of all nominees is submitted to the national executive committee of the party for approval, and those so approved are then presented to the national assembly for election. This ought to cater for the need for special talent in the assembly and for institutional representation, leaving only the interest of racial minorities as the one requiring to be represented through presidential nomination. In Tanzania, therefore, the use of nominated members for any other purpose than the representation of racial minorities is hardly justified.

Even assuming that nomination is intended primarily to secure special talent or special representation, and not partisan or personal interests, the crucial question is whether a nominated member has the same degree of security of tenure — and of the independence that goes with it — as an elected member. Or does he hold his seat as a mere agent of the President, and therefore at the latter's will and pleasure? This question assumed the character of a great constitutional issue in Lesotho in *Molapo* v. *Seeiso*.[73] The Constitution of the country provided for a senate consisting of twenty-two chiefs and eleven other members nominated in his absolute discretion by the King, Moshoeshoe II, whose politics were aligned to those of the opposition party and against those of the government of Prime Minister Leabua Jonathan. On April 29, 1966, five of the King's nominees in the senate voted with the government contrary to the wishes of the king, who thereupon purported to revoke their appointment, and to appoint others in their place. In this action brought by the five dismissed senators, it was argued on behalf of the King that, as he had no nominees in the national assembly, his power of nomination to the senate was intended to enable him to exert his influence on parliament through the senate, and that, accordingly, the nominated senators were there as his agents to look after his interests, to express his views and to represent his wishes. But the court considered the argument to be subversive of democratic government, because it 'strikes at the whole principle of the right of free speech of a member of Parliament in either house, and indeed at the right of freedom of expression in Section 11 of the Constitution'; moreover, where a nominated senator is a member of the cabinet, it is also 'incompatible with the concept of collective responsibility of the cabinet enshrined in Section 67(2) of the Constitution'.[74]

The actual decision of the court invalidating the purported revocation of the plaintiffs' appointment was based on the fact that the Constitution contained no express provision for the power claimed. Although there is a general rule of interpretation, enacted in the Interpretation Proclamation, that power to appoint imports a power to revoke the appointment, this general rule is inapplicable when there is a contrary intention to be gathered either from express provision or from necessary implication. In this case the Constitution specifically provided that a nominated senator would vacate his seat at the next dissolution of parliament or if, before such dissolution, he ceased to be a citizen of Lesotho or if any circumstances arose which would have disqualified him from being nominated in the first place. This provision manifests an intention to be all-embracing on the conditions of tenure

of a nominated senator, thus excluding the general rule of interpretation which would otherwise have applied if no provision had been
made at all as to when he was to vacate his seat. Had it been the
intention that a nominated senator was to hold his seat at the pleasure
of the King, then the legislature, having once embarked upon a
definition of the conditions of his tenure, would reasonably have been
expected to have added a further condition to that effect, namely 'if his
nomination is revoked by the king'. Reinforcing this conclusion is the
fact that, although the section on the discretionary powers of the King
referred to the appointment of senators, and the appointment of the
Prime Minister and *his removal*, reference was only to the appointment
of senators, and not to their removal. The omission to refer to this
power in a section dealing specifically with the King's discretionary
power of appointment and removal is significant as pointing to the
conclusion that it was not intended that he should have the power.

This decision is excluded in Zambia, Malawi and Tanzania by the
provision that a nominated member shall vacate his seat if his
appointment is revoked by the President.[75] Now, independence of will
can hardly be expected of a member subject to removal at the pleasure
of the President. With the risk of removal hanging over him, and
anxious to remain in the President's favour in order to assure his
re-nomination, a nominated member in Zambia, Malawi and Tanzania
can ill afford to be too independent of the government, at all events not
to the extent of voting against it. He is therefore as much a stooge of
the government as was his colonial predecessor.

(iii) *The Party Whip*

All government M.P.s, both office-holders and non-office-holders,
are subject to the party whip. Party discipline is necessary in any
system of government based upon organised party or parties. Where
there is the duality of a government and an opposition party, there is
the need to maintain the unity of one against the other. For the
government this is of far greater consequence because of the need to
avoid the risk of defeat, and possible dismissal from office which this
may entail. But discipline is necessary for effective government whether
the system is a two-party or a one-party one. In a one-party system, the
absence of an opposition party against whom it is necessary to unite
means that the government *can* allow its M.P.s greater freedom of
debate and criticism, but it certainly does not mean that parliament will
be allowed unfettered freedom not only to criticise but also to modify
or reject government measures at its whim and pleasure.[76] Clearly
restrictions on M.P.s' freedom of *voting* do not, as Julius Nyerere
claims, become unnecessary under a one-party system.[77]

While admitting the necessity for party discipline in parliament, the whip has unfortunately been applied in Africa so stringently as to become a negation of parliamentary independence. The reason is because party unity is interpreted as demanding that an M.P. must never speak, much less vote, against the government. Politics is viewed as a feud between opposing groups, and a feud calls for far greater unity than an ordinary competition. In the developed democracies, rivalry between the parties is kept within the bounds of ordinary competition, conducted with due regard to principle and conscience. When, however, political rivalry goes beyond ordinary competition and assumes the character of a feud, then the unity called for must be of a type that demands that nothing should be done, not a word uttered, that might open even the smallest hole in the party defences. No quarter of any sort should be given to the enemy. It is in this atmosphere of a feud that the whip operates in Africa. Its effect is to impose a total ban on deviation, by word or vote, from the party line. Government M.P.s must toe the party line mechanically like robots, or else be branded as traitors. This attitude towards politics is perhaps characteristic of the African, but it may also have been a carry-over from the colonial days when it was considered traitorous for an indigene to support the imperialists against the nationalist party. Now the nationalist party has become the government in place of the imperialists, the old attitude still persists that to oppose the party is to be a traitor to the cause.

In Britain, for example, the whip does not operate in exactly the same way with respect to speech and to voting. Within reasonable limits a government M.P. may speak against a government measure, though having done so, he is expected not to vote against it. However, he may feel so strongly about the matter as to feel obliged on the ground of conscience to abstain from voting or even to vote against. Occasionally the government may withdraw the whip and allow its members to vote freely according to their conscience, and it has been suggested that a free vote should be allowed with greater liberality than is the case at the moment. 'It is hard to see why a voluntary loosening of conventional practices on a minor scale by a government with a safe majority, or an extension of the number of occasions a free vote is permitted, must be incompatible with the principles of the parliamentary system.'[78] But for the rather primitive attitude among African politicians that 'whoever is not with me is an enemy', to whom no support or encouragement of any kind should be given, African presidential regimes have less reason than the government in Britain for a stringent application of the whip, since a defeat in parliament does not oblige the government to resign. Admittedly, this does not remove all the danger of party disunity in parliament. There is still the long-term danger of losing to the enemy at the next general elections, which demands that unity in parliament should be maintained in order to prevent the party's supporters outside parliament from falling away to the enemy. Even so, it is the attitude to opposition as amounting to enmity which is largely responsible for the stringent use of the whip. It is argued that one must recognise this attitude as a reality of African life, and that, accordingly, if one wanted to do away with the whip or to relax it, one must first abolish political competition among two or more parties, since it is this which induces an attitude to government as a feud between mutually antagonistic groups. It is on this ground among others that the advocates of the one-party system in Africa have based their case.[79]

(iv) *Forfeiture of Seat*

The demands of party unity have imposed further restriction on an M.P.'s freedom of action, of a type not known in the Western democracies. In Britain an M.P. who feels on grounds of conscience that he can no longer support his party may resign or be expelled from the party without losing his parliamentary seat. Expulsion from the party is the severest punishment the party can inflict on a rebellious member who flouts the party whip, though the flouting must, it seems, be persistent to merit the admittedly harsh punishment of expulsion. But expulsion or resignation from the party leaves the member's seat in parliament unaffected. In Africa, on the other hand, it now attracts the further consequence of loss of the member's seat in parliament. This new sanction, like so many other such devices, had its origin in Nkrumah's Ghana; a power to recall a member who had abused the confidence reposed in him at the election was in 1965 bestowed upon the party and the electorate. From Ghana it was transported in a modified form to Kenya, Zambia and Malawi in 1966. In the form which it takes in Kenya and Malawi, it is not really a power of recall, since a power of recall is discretionary and not self-operating. For example, in the American states in which it exists, the procedure is for a specified number of electors to demand the recall of a member; a vote is then held in the member's constituency, and if it goes against him, his seat is declared vacated. In Kenya and Malawi resignation from the party operates by itself to vacate the member's seat. The forfeiture is self-operating, requiring no further action by anyone.

However, in Kenya its operation is postponed until the expiration of the current session, or, if parliament is not then in session, at the expiration of the session next following.[80] The party from which the member resigned must be a parliamentary party both at the time of resignation and at the time when the forfeiture is to take effect, and any question regarding this is to be determined by the Speaker, whose certificate shall be final. The member must have stood election with the support of, or as a supporter of, the party or, in the case of a nominated member if he accepted appointment as a member of the party. If the party had in the meantime been dissolved, and the member joined another party, which still exists as a parliamentary party, then resignation from the latter party also vacates the member's seat. It is otherwise if the member contested an election or accepted appointment as an independent and later joined a parliamentary party; in that case his seat is not vacated when he resigns from the party. The question whether a member in fact stood for election with the support or as a member of a political party or accepted an appointment as such a member is left at large, and it may be presumed that it is to be determined by the court. So is the question whether the member has in fact resigned or what constitutes resignation. It should finally be noted that only resignation, *and not expulsion*, attracts the sanction of forfeiture of seat under this provision (i.e. Kenya).

Under the Malawian provisions all that is needed in the case of an elected member is a notice in writing from the secretary-general of the party to the Speaker that the member has ceased to be a member of the party, whether by resignation or expulsion; thereupon the member's seat in the assembly is automatically vacated.[81] This does not apply in the case of a nominated member, but he loses his seat anyway if the President so directs.[82] More interesting is the provision forfeiting a member's seat for voting against the President in a motion of confidence if in the last parliamentary election he had declared his support for the President as the presidential candidate.[83] Parliament may provide that a member shall vacate his seat if he has lost the confidence and support of a majority of the voters in his constituency.[84] This last provision caused considerable apprehension among members during the debate on the Constitution, because of its susceptibility to abuse by those who might want to use it to fabricate false reports of loss of confidence against opponents, but Dr Banda assured members that the provision would not be invoked without thorough investigation, and cited instances of two such cases investigated by a commission of inquiry on a petition to him by the chiefs and people of the constituencies concerned. The commission found the complaints to have been well-founded, whereupon he fired the M.P.s in question. This, he boasted, was evidence that Malawi was a democracy, because 'people in this country can get rid of their member of parliament much more easily than they can in Britain. I have never heard of constituents in Britain petitioning the Speaker to get rid of their member of parliament. ... I have never heard of it in America either, but it has happened here — twice! So if that is not democracy I do not know what your definition of democracy is.'[85]

The Zambian provision is different from both the Kenyan and Malawian ones, in that it was not self-operating; its operation was conditional upon the party from which the member resigned or was expelled, taking the initiative to unseat him. The procedure for this contained some safeguards for the member concerned.[86] The parliamentary leader of the party had to give notice in writing, signed by himself, to the Speaker, alleging that the member named conducted his election campaign as a member of the party and had since ceased to be a member of it. The Speaker would then report the allegation to the assembly, and forward a copy of the notice to the chief justice for investigation either by himself or by another judge of the High Court nominated by him. After the investigation, at which the member had a right to appear and to be represented, the investigating judge would report to the Speaker whether he found the allegation to have been substantiated. If it was found to be true, the Speaker would so report to the assembly and call on the member to vacate his seat. With the formal establishment of the one-party state in Zambia on December 13, 1972, the provision was repealed, but its effect has been re-enacted, in that membership of the one constitutionally recognised party (UNIP) is a condition for election to and continued membership of the national assembly; so that resignation or expulsion from the party still operates to vacate a member's seat. This is also the position in Tanzania.[87]

The origin of this device in Kenya and Zambia is interesting as showing the motivation for it. In both countries it originated as an amendment to the Constitution. The occasion was the resignation of a number of influential leaders from the ruling party following on a split. In Zambia the Minister of Commerce, Mr Mundia, and his followers had broken with the ruling UNIP in 1966 to form a new party, the United Party. And in Kenya, the Vice-President of the country and of the ruling party, Mr Oginga Odinga, two assistant ministers and eighteen other M.P.s had resigned from the ruling KANU and formed their own Kenya Peoples' Union on April 14, 1966; they were followed later by the Minister of Information. There was a strong indication that many more were to follow. A *de facto* government since 1964, when the opposition Kenya African Democractic Union (KADU) dissolved itself, the KANU government was put into a state of panic by the prospect that the trickle of resignations might become a flood. It was to stem this that the amendment was passed. The national assembly was called into a special emergency meeting, and the amendment rushed through in one day after getting the relevant standing order suspended so as to make this possible.[88] The amendment had the desired effect of stemming the tide of resignation. More significant, perhaps, was the 'reduced candour in public debate and reduced effectiveness in challenging government',[89] which followed in its wake. If criticising the government or voting against it might lead to expulsion and loss of seat, many M.P.s would prefer to follow the party line without question. And few would ever contemplate resignation even on the grounds of conscience, knowing that this would mean loss of membership.

The government in both Kenya and Zambia had of course been at pains to justify the amendment and the consequent unseating of the rebels. Their concern stemmed, no doubt, from the admittedly restrictive effect of the amendment upon M.P.s' freedom of action in parliament. The leader of the defectors in Zambia, Mr Mundia, had described it as a 'curse' and a violation of members' consciences.[90] The justification pleaded by the Kenyan government was that members (independents excepted) are elected to the assembly not so much on their individual standing as because they are sponsored by a political party with a defined ideology and policy under a certain leadership. Such a member is thus not a completely free agent. He is, of course, free to disagree with the party, but should disagreement be carried to the point of deserting the party, then it is necessary that this decision to change horses should be referred to his constituents for ratification. Since it is they who voted the member to parliament, the constituents, it is argued, have a right to be consulted. In the developed democracies this consultation has become almost a matter of convention. The member will of his own free will go to his constituents, explain his position, and offer to resign. It is then for the constituents to endorse his stand or otherwise accept his offer of resignation. In Africa no such practice has developed. Accordingly, 'in the absence of the kind of public opinion that exercises the checks that we find in other developed democracies, and in the absence of a strong individual conscience to act according to established practices upon which parliamentary democracy thrives, the Government was left with no alternative but to protect the interests of the voters in every part of Kenya',[91] by requiring a defecting member to go back to his constituents in a by-election and obtain a renewal of his mandate.

The opposition KPU accepted that a member who has abandoned the policy to which he had pledged himself at election should resign his seat, but argued that it was the government, and not they, who had been guilty of this; further, that their resignation from the ruling party was a protest against the government's betrayal of its pledges to the electorate. It was therefore for the government to resign or dissolve the assembly.

As a purely theoretical argument, it seems that the government has the better of the argument. Electors in Africa are clearly more interested in the party label of a candidate than in the policy programme of the party. They vote for who should govern, not so much on what policies the party has pledged itself to pursue. They attach far greater importance to the personality of the leader than to ideologies or policies. And, in any case the argument that the government had betrayed its election pledges was really a matter of personal opinion. A government usually makes a number of promises at election, and it is for it to define its priorities and the order in which it is going to pursue them within the limits of the resources available to it. More often than not a government in a developing country finds that, because of limitation in resources, it is unable to achieve more than a fraction of what it has set itself to do.

However the fact that the vote for an M.P. was based on his party affiliation does not necessarily conclude the issue in favour of the government. The question is whether the vote is revoked or nullified by the member's resignation from the party. Is his continued membership of the party a condition of the vote, so that the vote is revoked whenever the condition is broken? This, it must be explained, is a different argument from that upon which the power of recall is claimed. The latter proceeds upon the premise that the member being recalled has lost the confidence of his electors. Resignation or expulsion from the party may perhaps raise a presumption of loss of confidence, but it is certainly not conclusive of it, as is demonstrated by the fact that nine of the 'carpet crossers' in Kenya were voted back to the house. But the government's case would perhaps be that the only way to rebut the *prima facie* presumption of loss of confidence is to have a fresh recourse to the electors. The government also admitted that an M.P. is not a delegate, bound to act according to the directives of his constituents, but a representative. Its case was therefore not that the defectors had failed to carry out any specific directives from their electors, but simply that they had deserted the party on whose ticket they were elected.

The whole question is rather intricate. Although the vote for an M.P. is largely based upon his party affiliation and less upon his individual personality, it would be difficult to maintain that the electors, when they gave their vote, intended that it should be a condition that the member should continue to be a member of the party for the whole period for which he is elected. Furthermore it is difficult to determine to what degrees party affiliation and the individual personality of an M.P. has respectively contributed towards his election in every case. It is conceivable that in some cases individual personality may have predominated. In any case, the Kenya government was on a weak moral ground in this matter. The defectors and at least one government member, Mr Shikuku, rightly pointed to the event in 1964 when the entire opposition (i.e. the Kenya African Democratic Union) crossed over to the government, and no forfeiture of seats was enforced upon them. Perhaps it might be argued that the dissolution of the party itself released the members from their obligation to it. But the implied condition of the vote which sent them to the house had been broken, nonetheless, without permission from the electors. It is better probably to admit that what was sought to be protected was the interest not of the electors but of the party in keeping the support of those elected on its ticket.

This is further exemplified by the fact that the Kenya amendment does not vacate the seat of an expelled member, but expulsion affects the implied condition no less than resignation. If the party is competent to waive the breach in the case of expulsion, does that not prove that it is the interest of the party that was sought to be protected? No doubt 'carpet-crossing' has become a disturbing phenomenon in African politics. It has lost its original purpose as an avenue of escape from a member's genuine pangs of conscience, and become a vehicle of opportunism enabling him to change his political affiliation according to which way the political wind happens to be blowing at any particular time.[92] Yet forfeiture of a member's parliamentary seat hardly seems the right answer to the problem. It is unethical that the genuine, conscientious 'carpet-crosser' should be penalised for the sake of the opportunistic 'political acrobat'; better that ten guilty people should escape than that one innocent man should be incarcerated. More objectionable, perhaps, is the practice among some political parties (e.g., the NCNC in Nigeria) of requiring party M.P.s to sign in advance undated letters of resignation from parliament, which could then be dated and submitted whenever the party so decides, either upon the resignation or expulsion of the M.P. from the party.

Opposition can be and sometimes is demonstrated in the form of a boycott or walk-out. It is a dramatic form of protest, and has a publicity value insofar as it attracts public attention to the matter at issue. As a form of political protest, however, it has been needlessly indulged in Africa, almost to the point of childishness and irresponsibility, and has often done more harm than good to those engaging in it. An opposition party boycott of an election invariably hands over an easy and, it may be, unmerited victory to the government. The opposition in Ghana had been particularly guilty of this — boycotting constitutional conferences, elections and meetings of parliament. Nkrumah sought to put a lever on them by imposing forfeiture of seat upon any M.P. who, in the course of a meeting and in the hearing of the Speaker or other person presiding, made a public declaration of intention to be absent systematically from meetings of the house.[93] It is not clear when a boycott becomes a systematic absence. Irresponsible as these boycotts may have been, the idea of suppressing this form of protest by a compulsory forfeiture of a member's seat seems too harsh and undemocratic. Now and again, as has been pointed out, a boycott or walk-out may have a real value in dramatising a tyrannical measure or some other type of abuse of power. The argument of the Ghana

Government that it is derogatory of the prestige and dignity of the assembly for a member to declare publicly before the Speaker and in his hearing that he intended to boycott its meetings[93a] does not justify the repressive implication of the law. Happily Ghana stood alone as the only presidential regime in Commonwealth Africa which has attached forfeiture of seat to a boycott of meetings of parliament.

But absence from meetings for a specified period is a ground of forfeiture in most of the countries – Ghana,[94] Tanzania,[95] Kenya,[96] Malawi,[97] Botswana[98] and Uganda.[99] While in Ghana the prescribed period of absence was twenty consecutive *sittings*, in Tanzania it is three consecutive meetings, and in Kenya eight consecutive days in any session. Of the three, the Kenyan provision is certainly the most restrictive, but Tanzania's may be more or less restrictive than Ghana's, depending on the number of sittings comprised in each of the three consecutive meetings at which the member was absent. (A meeting is any period, which may consist of one or of several days, when the assembly sits before adjourning *sine die*.) The Malawian, Ugandan and Gambian provisions merely refer to absence for 'such period and in such circumstances as may be prescribed in the rules of procedure of the Assembly'.

There seems to be nothing intrinsically reprehensible in penalising repeated and unauthorised absences from meetings by means of forfeiture of seat. Such a penalty is not uncommon in the rules governing even purely social and cultural associations, and whatever justification there is for it in that case must be more in the case of members of a national assembly entrusted with such weighty responsibility as the government of the nation. The nation ought not to pay for an M.P. who does not bother to attend meetings. Yet the origin of the law in Ghana – where it was first adopted – seemed to have had a political motivation, being designed as part of a whole network of repression, of which preventive detention was the hob. To escape the dragnet of the PDA, many opposition M.P.s and one or two government M.P.s, like Gbedemah, had been forced to flee the country. The aim seemed to have been to complement the effect of the Act by visiting loss of seat upon the exiles. Every hole was plugged in a way that left no avenue of escape: if an opponent stayed in the country he might be detained and thereby lose his seat; if he fled the country he lost his seat just the same. But we must now examine more closely the impact of the PDA on M.P.s.

(v) *Impact of the Power of Preventive Detention*

Preventive detention has had a very restrictive effect on M.P.s' freedom of debate and criticism. The mere thought of prison is apt to inhibit freedom of speech. An M.P., of course, enjoys immunity from criminal and civil process for anything he says in parliament; the immunity is considered essential to the effective exercise of his freedom of speech and action in parliament. Seizing a member by means of a criminal process while he is in the house or on his way to it is as derogatory of his freedom of speech as prosecution for a critical speech; the former may indeed be more derogatory, since it prevents him from delivering the speech at all. Immunity, therefore, extends to a member while he is in the house or while he is proceeding to or from it. It is a collective privilege of the house, which a member enjoys by virtue of his membership of the house. The immunity is specifically enacted in all the presidential regimes in Commonwealth Africa. The Ghana enactment, for example, declares that 'there shall be freedom of speech, debate and proceedings in the Assembly, and that freedom shall not be impeached or questioned in any court or *place* out of the Assembly,'[100] and then goes on to prohibit the institution of any civil or criminal proceedings against a member in respect of anything said by him in the assembly or any matter or thing brought by him before it by petition, bill, motion or otherwise, and the service or execution on a member of any civil or criminal process issuing from any court or *place* outside the assembly while he is in the house or within its precincts or on his way to, attending at or returning from any proceeding of the assembly.[101]

These immunities are unquestionably very wide, but the question is whether they avail a member against the power of preventive detention which exists in one form or another in nearly all the presidential regimes. It should perhaps be noted that the Privileges and Immunities Act of the other countries is not so widely phrased as the Ghanaian act. If a member can be detained or restricted under the PDA while he is in the assembly or going to or returning from its meetings, or for something said in it, will this not amount to questioning the member's freedom of speech in a 'place out of the assembly'? And is not a detention or restriction order a process issuing from a 'place out of the assembly'? The rule of interpretation in cases of conflict between two statutes, one of which is general and the other special, is that the latter constitutes an exception to the former. The PDA is a general statute relating to persons generally, while the Privileges and Immunities Act is a special Act affecting only M.P.s. Accordingly, in a conflict between them, the Privileges and Immunities Act will prevail, notwithstanding that it is earlier in time. This, however, is not likely to be of any avail to a member, since it would be almost impossible to prove that he was being detained or restricted for something he said in parliament, and any reasons which the government might state as ground for the detention would be of such a general nature as not to refer specifically to things said in debate in parliament; nor can the courts compel it to particularise the reasons for the order. If the case is that a member was arrested for purposes of detention or restriction under the PDA while he was in the house or on his way to or from it, there would be no room for equivocation that a contravention of the Privileges and Immunities Act had been committed. In Kenya this would still be of no avail to a detained member, because the Kenyan version of the PDA (the Preservation of Public Security Act) overrides anything inconsistent with it in any other law (except the Constitution).[102]

If, therefore, a member may be detained under the PDA for what he has said in the assembly, this cannot but be a deterrent to criticism. It would require uncommon courage in a member to expose the weaknesses and malpractices of the government when he knows that he might be picked up later and clamped into detention as a security risk. No member, whether of the opposition or the government, can afford to speak or act in disregard of this power; anything can be construed as prejudicial to the security of the state — which, of course, includes the security of the President's tenure of office. It is gratifying that in Kenya the Vice-President had, on behalf of the government, given an assurance during the parliamentary debate on a motion to continue in force the order authorising preventive detentions,[103] that 'Government recognises the principle that no Member of Parliament may be detained on account of anything said by him in this House.'[104] But the assurance is qualified by the fact, as announced by the Speaker, that 'in the unfortunate event of any Hon. Member being detained and a question arising as to whether such detention is on account of his utterances in this House, Hon. Members will have to be satisfied simply by a Ministerial assurance that the detention is not on that account, without further inquiry.'[105] There is no evidence, happily, of any M.P. in any of these countries having been detained on account of what he has said in parliament.

But, of course, many members have been detained for other things than their utterances in parliament. The effect of such detention may be to divest a member of his seat in parliament. Ghana was again the first to give to preventive detention this rather drastic consequence. In 1959 it made preventive detention or restriction not only a ground for automatic forfeiture of a member's seat, but also a disqualification for election to parliament where the detention or restriction occurred within the five years immediately preceding the date of the election.[106] Backdated to 1958, the Act enabled Nkrumah to unseat those members of parliament, mostly opposition members, against whom preventive detention orders had been made since the passing of the PDA in 1958. The impact of this both in parliament and in the country must have been to inhibit public criticism of the President and the government. From that date on, debate in the Ghana National Assembly became, in the words of an opposition M.P., Joe Appiah, more of a 'ritual dance',[107] in which the government M.P.s, like gagged captives, merely nodded their assent to every government measure, raising their voices only to interrupt opposition speakers who, it must be said, appeared not to have been unduly repressed by either the PDA or the Disqualification Act. The justification proffered for the disqualification was that it would be 'unfair in the extreme to the constituents'[108] for them to be without representation during the period of a member's detention, which might extend to five years or more.

Following in the footsteps of Ghana, Tanzania in 1965[109] and Zambia in 1969[110] made preventive detention or restriction a disqualification for election as well as a ground for automatic forfeiture of a member's seat, provided that, for the latter consequence, the detention or restriction has lasted for six months. There is a further difference from the Ghanaian provision: in Tanzania and Zambia, detention or restriction is a disqualification for election only while it lasts, but not after it has been lifted. The Government of Zambia must have been embarrassed when in 1968 Mundia, formerly a UNIP minister before his defection in 1966, was elected to parliament while in detention. The 1969 amendment removed the occasion for such embarrassment.

(vi) *Extra-Legal Factors*

Our discussion so far has centred on what may be called, in Harvey's words, the 'legal tools of political monopoly'.[111] But the extra-legal tools are no less telling.

It has been observed that an opposition is essential to the effectiveness of parliament's critical function. And the ruling parties know it, hence their desire to liquidate the opposition. It has also been observed that the government's arrogance towards the legislature increases with the strength of its parliamentary majority. (The position of the legislature in the one-party states was discussed in the last chapter.) Without proscribing opposition parties or formally establishing themselves as the one and only party, ruling parties in Africa have used the perversion of the electoral process as a tool for enlarging their majority at the expense of the opposition.

Nigeria, in the closing years of its first republic, affords perhaps the most notorious example of this. The technique of electoral perversion might be said to have attained its highest point of perfection there. It had taken a variety of forms — wholesale use of illegal ballot papers; the massive list of government candidates returned unopposed through the abduction, imprisonment or even murder of opposition candidates or their nominators, or through returning officers illegally cancelling opposition candidates' nomination papers or refusing to accept them at all on some flimsy technicality; denial of the basic freedoms indispensable to free elections; and, perhaps most brazen of all, the reversal of constituency results by the government, using its monopoly of radio and television services to announce losing government party candidates as the winners. It should perhaps be said that such perverted practices on the part of ruling parties have generally been absent in East and Central Africa. But voter intimidation by party thugs or other strong-arm men is a common phenomenon of elections all over Africa, varying in extent and intensity from country to country.

Strong-arm treatment of the opposition does not, of course, end with the elections. It is an on-going regime. Leading opposition politicians, especially those who managed to get into parliament in spite of the rigging, are victimised and harassed in many ways — unwarranted prosecutions, often on trumped-up charges, destruction of property or business, beating or lynching, denial of facilities for business activities, etc. — the aim being to make life as intolerable as possible for them, and thereby to subdue their will to oppose and criticise.

REFERENCES

1. D. C. M. Yardley, 'The Primacy of the Executive', *Parl. Affairs* (1967/8), Vol. xxi, p. 155.

2. K. C. Wheare, *Legislatures*, 2nd ed., 1968, p. 93.

3. D. C. M. Yardley, *op. cit.*, p. 165.

4. J. M. Lee, 'Parliament in Ghana', *Parl. Affairs* (1962/3), Vol. 16, p. 376.

5. Above, ch. VIII.

6. Art. 24.

7. Art. 58.

8. Tanzania S.50; Zambia S.71; Malawi S.35; Botswana S.88; Gambia S.71.

9. S.46(1).

10. S.46(2).

11. S.30.

12. House of Rep. Deb., 27 Oct., 1964, col. 3895.

13. Art. 55.

14. Art. 20(5).

15. Kwaku Boateng, *Proceedings of the Constituent Assembly* (1960), p. 194.

16. Geoffrey Bing, *Reap the Whirlwind* (1968), p. 311.

17. Government Paper No. 1 of 1962, p. 6; also Govt. Paper No. 162 of 1964, p. 6.

18. Art. 64.

19. See, e.g., S.109, Constitution of Zambia.

20. SS.111 and 112, *ibid*.

21. Constitution (Amendment) (No. 6) Act, 1969 (No. 12 of 1970).

22. Nat. Ass. Deb. 1970, cols. 383–409, 448–57, 524–6, 634–5.

23. Nat. Ass. Deb. 1970, cols. 587–633.

24. Standing Order 96.

25. Art. 224(3).

26. *Hague* v. *Chowdhury, Times* Law Report, 22 Nov., 1963.

27. Art. vii.

28. Art. viii.

29. Union of Tanganyika and Zanzibar Act, 1964, S.5.

30. *Ibid.*, S.8(2)(*a*) and (*c*).

31. *Ibid.*, S.8(2)(*b*).

32. S.10(1).

33. Government Paper No. 162 of 1964, p. 6.

34. The Constitution of Kenya (Amendment) Act, 1964, SS.14(4) and (5).

35. See Emergency Powers Act, and the Preservation of Public Security Act of Zambia, Uganda, Kenya and Malawi.

36. *Attorney-General for Northern Rhodesia* v. *Mungoni* 1958, R and N. 710 (F.S.C.)

37. Below, p. 317.

38. Constitution (Amendment) (No. 5) Act, 1969.

39. S.127 Constitution of Kenya, 1969.

40. Walter Bagehot, *The English Constitution*, p. 154.

41. Wade and Phillips, *Constitutional Law* (1958), p. 108.

42. See, e.g., S.82, Constitution of Zambia.

43. S.84 Zambia.

44. D. C. M. Yardley, 'The Primacy of the Executive', *Parl. Affairs* (1967/8), Vol. xxi, p. 455.

45. C. Gertzel records that in the session December 1963 to October 1965, members of the Kenya Parliament asked 1,617 questions, of which 1,533 were answered; 320 motions were tabled in the house of representatives in 1965, of which 68 were debated; see *The Politics of Independent Kenya* (1970), p. 130.

46. C. Gertzel, *loc. cit.*

47. *Parl. Affairs* (1969), vol. xxii, p. 210.

48. Above, p. 2.

49. C. P. Ilbert, *Legislative Methods and Forms* (1901), p. 228; also J. A. G. Griffith, 'The Place of Parliament in the Legislative Process' (1951), 14 *M.L.R.*, 279.

50. Grant McConnell, *The Modern Presidency* (1967), pp. 34–51.

51. K. C. Wheare, *Legislatures*, 2nd ed. (1968), p. 102.

52. K. C. Wheare, *op. cit.*, p. 103.

53. Grant McConnell, *loc. cit.*

54. *Op. cit.*, pp. 50–1.

55. Below, ch. XIV.

56. Q. L. Quade, 'Presidential Leadership: Paralysed or Irresponsible', *Parliamentary Affairs* (1963–4), Vol. xvii, p. 66.

57. J. S. Mill, *Representative Government*.

58. Q. L. Quade, *op. cit.*, p. 66.

59. Speaker, Kenya House of Reps, Debates Vol. 1, June 7, 1963, col. 2.

60. H. L. Bretton, *The Rise and Fall of Kwame Nkrumah*; T. P. Omari, *Kwame Nkrumah: The Anatomy of an African Dictatorship*.

61. A. Gupta, 'The Zambian National Assembly: a Study of an African Legislature', *Parl. Affairs* (1965–6), Vol. xix.

62. On patronage as a source of presidential power generally, see p. 112 above.

63. Richard Middleton, 'The Problems and Consequences of Parliamentary Government: A Historical View', *Parl. Affairs* (1969–70), Vol. xxiii, p. 55.

64. Position as on Jan. 7, 1970; Hansard.

65. Arts. 40(*b*) and 49.

66. *Transition* 33, Oct./Nov. 1967, Vol. 7, p. 43.

67. Nat. Ass. Deb., Vol. XV, May 1968, col. 90.

68. Report 1965, para. 43.

69. Report 1972, paras 60 and 61.

70. Govt. White Paper No. 1 of 1972, p. 7.

71. S.30.

72. Report, *op. cit.*, para. 45.

73. (1966) SS.150.

74. *Ibid.* at p. 166.

75. Zambia S.65(7); Malawi S.28(2)(*i*); Tanzania S.35(1)(*d*).

76. See above, p. 246.

77. J. Nyerere, *Democracy and the Party System* (1963), p. 7.

78. Marshall and Moodie, *Some Problems of the Constitution* (1961), p. 74.

79. J. Nyerere, *Democracy and the Party System* (1963).

80. S.40 Constitution of Kenya, 1969.

81. S.29(2)(*h*).

82. S.28(2)(*i*).

83. S.28(2)(*f*).

84. S.28(2)(*g*).

85. Parl. Deb. 1966, p. 551.

86. S.65(2)(*e*), and subsections (4) (5) and (6).

87. S.27(1); S.35(1)(*a*), Interim Constitution, 1965.

88. House of Reps, April 28, 196, cols. 1994ff.

89. Engholm and Mazrui, 'Crossing the Floor and the Tensions of Representation in East Africa', *Parl. Affairs* (1967–8), Vol. xxi, 137, 149.

90. Nat. Ass. Deb., Sept. 7, 1966, col. 1650.

91. Tom Mboya, House of Reps, Deb., Vol. viii, April 28, 1966, cols. 2018–61.

92. Engholm and Mazrui, *op. cit.*

93. National Assembly Act, 1961, S.2(1)(*e*) – consolidating earlier Acts on the matter.

93*a*. Nat. Ass. Deb., March 17, 1959, col. 359.

94. National Assembly Act, 1961.

95. S.35(1)(*c*), Constitution.

96. S.39(1)(*c*), Constitution.

97. S.28(2)(*c*).

98. S.69(1)(*b*).

99. S.50(2)(*b*).

100. National Assembly Act, 1965, S.18; italics supplied.

101. *Ibid.*, SS.19 and 20.

102. J. P. McAuslan, *East African Standard*, June 2, 1967; reprinted in C. Gertzel *et al., Government and Politics in Kenya* (1969), p. 221.

103. Constitution (Public Security) Order, 1966.

104. Nat. Ass. Deb., Nov. 21, 1967, cols. 2175–6.

105. *Ibid.*

106. National Assembly (Disqualification) Act, 1959.

107. Nat. Ass. Deb., July 14, 1958, col. 457.

108. Nat. Ass. Deb., March 17, 1959, cols. 357 ff. – per Kojo Botsio, Minister of External Affairs.

109. S.35(1)(*a*) Interim Constitution.

110. Constitution (Amendment) (No. 5) Act, 1969.

111. W. B. Harvey, *Law and Social Change in Ghana.*

CHAPTER X

HUMAN RIGHTS *VERSUS* NATIONAL SECURITY

The question here is whether a strong, centralised government, such as characterises the presidential regimes in Africa, permits of adequate enjoyment of human rights. The record in Africa would seem to indicate a negative answer. It is very significant, for example, that the instances in Commonwealth Africa of a preventive detention law outside declared emergency are found only in the presidential regimes. Equally significant is the fact that three of these regimes, Ghana, Tanzania and Malawi, have rejected a bill of rights.

It can hardly be disputed that the presidential regimes are more sensitive about national security than the prime ministerial ones. All these seem to point to a negative answer to the question whether a strong, centralised government permits of adequate enjoyment of human rights. Concentrated power is very sensitive to criticism and very jealous and suspicious of rivals or competitors. Hence the increasing predominance of the one-party system in the presidential regimes. The President is a personal ruler; he is indeed the government, and as such is identified with the state. National security is thus given a personal dimension too. It involves not only the security of the state and its institutions, but also the security of the President's tenure of office. Anything that threatens the security of his continuance in office is also a threat to the security of the nation. He is the symbol of the nation, and the instrument through which this personal identification is achieved is the single or dominant party. A threat to the security of the party is therefore viewed as a threat to the security of the nation. Herein, therefore, lies the underlying reason for the sensitive concern for national security in the presidential regimes. The power given to the President for the preservation of the nation is perhaps his greatest source of power and authority in the whole machinery of government. The foundation for that power has been laid by the rejection of a bill of rights in three of the presidential regimes – Ghana, Tanzania and Malawi – and we should perhaps first notice that development.

1. *Rejection of Constitutional Guarantee of Rights*

With the exception of Tanganyika in 1961, all the presidential regimes in Commonwealth Africa came to independence with some constitutional guarantee of rights in one form or another. Ghana's (1957) was the least ample, guaranteeing only freedom from racial discrimination, freedom of conscience or religion, property and the franchise.[1] But then Ghana, as the first British black African territory to become independent, was a pioneer. At that time (1957) the bill of rights, as a deliberate constitutional technique for limiting governmental power, had not quite come into its own in the Commonwealth, having still to overcome the resistance of Anglo-American scepticism.[2] Outside Africa, India was the first innovator in 1950, but its Constitution originated not in Westminster but in New Delhi.

It was Nigeria in 1960 that launched the bill of rights as a thoroughgoing feature of Westminster-made independence constitutions; it was thoroughgoing both in the range of rights guaranteed and in the formulation of them. Subsequent independence constitutions have adopted and in some respects improved upon the Nigerian model, the most noteworthy innovation being that the protection of rights by specific prohibitions is now preceded by a clause in which the rights are positively and expressly affirmed or conferred. The Nigerian model contains only specific prohibitions — 'no person shall be deprived of his personal liberty' — the presupposition being that the rights already existed, and that the concern of the bill of rights was not to affirm or confer them anew, but merely to protect them. The neo-Nigerian bills of rights, on the other hand, begin with an express recital of the rights, going on thereafter to protect them by means of specific prohibitions. The recital is in a preambulary form, as follows:

> Whereas every person in [the country concerned] is entitled to the fundamental rights and freedoms of the individual, that is to say the right, whatever his race, place of origin, political opinions, colour, creed or sex, *but subject to respect for the rights and freedoms of others and for the public interest* to each and all of the following, namely —
> (*a*) life, liberty, security of the person and the protection of the law;
> (*b*) freedom of conscience, of expression and of assembly and association; and
> (*c*) protection for the privacy of home and other property and from deprivation of property without compensation;
> the provisions of this Chapter shall have effect for the purpose of affording protection to those rights and freedoms subject to such limitations of that protection as are contained in those provisions,

being limitations designed to ensure that the enjoyment of the said rights and freedoms by any individual does not prejudice the rights and freedoms of others or the public interest.[3]

Like the Nigerian bill of rights, this provision takes it for granted that the individual already has these rights, apparently under the common law – certainly not by the law of nature.[4] The rights cannot, therefore, be said to exist by virtue of the Constitution, though, whatever the source for their existence as legal rights, they are given protection by the Constitution by means of specific prohibitions against their violation, subject to defined limitations. Although only a recital, the provision errs in saying that the rights are 'subject to respect for the rights and freedoms of others and for the public interest'. This proviso goes beyond the limitations attached to the protective prohibitions, since under the latter not all the rights are protected subject to respect for the rights and freedoms of others or to the public interest – the protection of the right to personal liberty, protection from slavery and forced labour and from inhuman treatment, the right to a fair trial in criminal prosecutions by an independent and impartial tribunal, and protection from discriminatory laws are certainly not subject to the rights and freedoms of others. Nor is public interest, where it is recognised as a limitation on a protected right, admitted without qualification. It is thus incorrect and derogatory of the rights to say, as does the recital, that each and every one of them is, even at common law, always 'subject to respect for the rights and freedoms of others and for the public interest'. Nonetheless, the recital is useful in emphasising that the purpose of the chapter is primarily to afford protection not to qualifications but to the rights; in other words, that liberty is the rule and restraint the exception, that the bill is a bill of rights, not a bill of exceptions. This emphasis was used in a recent Zambian case in fixing upon the state the onus of proving that a derogation from a protected right on the ground of public security is reasonably required in that interest.[5]

Uganda's Constitution of 1967 took the innovation further by positively conferring these rights and then protecting them by means of specific prohibitions, thereby giving them positive constitutional existence. It was provided that 'every person in Uganda shall enjoy the fundamental rights and freedoms of the individual, that is to say, the right to each and all of the following, namely, (*a*) life, liberty, security of the person and the protection of the law; (*b*) freedom of conscience, of expression and of assembly and association; and (*c*) protection for the privacy of his home and other property and from deprivation of property without compensation.'[6] Although it was also provided that in the enjoyment of the rights 'no person shall prejudice the rights and freedoms of others or the public interest',[7] yet this proviso, as well as the conferment of the rights, was to 'have effect subject to the limitations contained in this chapter';[8] in other words the qualification of the conferred rights in favour of the rights of others or the public interest was to be only in terms of, and to the extent defined by, the chapter. Ghana in its 1969 Constitution has followed in Uganda's footsteps, by providing that 'every person in Ghana shall be entitled to the fundamental rights and freedoms of the individual' as therein enumerated, but like the preambulatory recital in the earlier neo-Nigerian bills, it erred in making the conferment 'subject to respect for the rights and freedoms of others and for the public interest' in every case.[9] This error is avoided in Zambia's one-party state Constitution, 1973, though the provision here takes the form of a declaration: 'It is recognised and declared that every person in Zambia has been and shall continue to be entitled to the fundamental rights and freedoms of the individual' as therein enumerated, 'but subject to the limitations contained in Article 4 [establishing the one-party system] and in this Part'.[10]

In the light of these gratifying improvements in the quality of constitutional guarantee of human rights, Ghana's rejection of a bill of rights in its 1960 Republican Constitution must appear unfortunate. It has been followed in this by Tanzania in its Independence, Republican and One-party state Constitutions of 1961, 1962 and 1965 respectively. Malawi did the same in its one-party state, Republican Constitution of 1966. Ghana's and Malawi's former guarantees were replaced by a declaration of directive principles of government, with the difference (apart from difference in content) that in Ghana the declaration was to be made by the President on assumption of office, though in terms prescribed by the Constitution,[11] while in Malawi the principles were declared in the Constitution.[12] The Tanzanian Constitutions of 1961, 1962 and 1965 confined all reference to human rights to a preamble which recited as 'inalienable' and as 'the foundation of freedom, justice and peace', life, liberty, security of the person, property, the protection of the person, freedom of conscience, expression, assembly, association, and privacy of family life. It seems clear that neither the presidential or the constitutional declaration of fundamental principles in Ghana and Malawi, nor the recital of rights in the Tanzanian preamble, has the effect of a constitutional guarantee of rights.

As regards the presidential declaration in Ghana, the point has been emphatically decided on the highest judicial authority in the country. In an action impugning the Preventive Detention Act 1958 on the ground that it was repugnant to the fundamental principles embodied in the presidential declaration, it was argued that by reciting the principles and enjoining the President to declare his adherence to them, the Constitution had conferred upon them the character of legally enforceable rights operating to limit the powers of parliament; alternatively, if they only imposed an obligation on the President personally, he was thereby precluded from assenting to a bill which derogated from any of the principles, since that would be a violation of his solemn declaration.[13] The supreme court likened the solemn declaration to the Queen's coronation oath, and held that 'neither the oath nor the declaration can be said to have a statutory effect. . . . The suggestion that the declaration . . . constitute(s) a "Bill of Rights" . . . is therefore untenable'.[14] The court then went on to explain:

> It will be observed that Article 13(1) is in the form of a personal declaration by the President and is in no way part of the general law of Ghana. In the other parts of the Constitution where a duty is imposed the word 'shall' is used, but throughout the declaration the word used is 'should'. In our view the declaration merely represents the goals to which every President must pledge himself to attempt to achieve. It does not represent a legal requirement which can be enforced by the courts.
>
> On examination of the said declaration with a view to finding out how any could be enforced we are satisfied that the provisions of Article 13(1) do not create legal obligations enforceable by a court of law. The declarations, however, impose on every President a moral obligation, and provide a political yardstick by which the conduct of the Head of State can be measured by the electorate. The people's remedy for any departure from the principles of the declaration is through the use of the ballot box, and not through the courts.[15]

The Malawian provision is perhaps more difficult to interpret, both because, unlike the Ghanaian one, it is not a personal declaration of the President, and because it is in part mandatory in its terms. 'The Government of the Republic *shall*', it declares, 'be founded upon the following principles.'[16] Six principles are so declared, but of the six, three are of special relevance: 'the Government and the people of Malawi *shall* continue to recognise the sanctity of the personal liberties enshrined in the United Nations Universal Declaration of Human Rights, and of adherence to the Law of Nations', no person *should* be deprived of his property without payment of fair compensation, and only where the public interest so requires', 'all persons regardless of colour, race or creed *should* enjoy equal rights and freedoms'. An amendment of 1968 adds that 'nothing contained in or done under the authority of any law shall be held to be inconsistent with or in contravention of [the declaration] to the extent that the law in question is reasonably required in the interests of defence, public safety, public order or the national economy'.[17]

This seems clearly to suggest that the declaration has legal effect, but the difficulty is to determine precisely the extent of this effect.

First, the 1968 amendment does not necessarily imply that a law or an executive act which contravenes the declaration and which is not reasonably required in the interests of defence, etc., is void. In the absence of a specific provision to that effect in the Constitution, a judgment that a law or an executive act contravenes the Constitution does not *ipso facto* invalidate the law or act, though the courts are entitled to refuse to give effect to it. Thus, in some of the European constitutions, for example the Italian, the function of judicial review is limited to the making of a bare declaration that an impugned law or executive act is or is not inconsistent with the Constitution but without any effect on the legal validity of the law or act itself. Secondly, as was stated by the Ghana supreme court in *Re Akoto*, the use of the word 'should' imports no mandatory duty. Thus, the statement that the government of the republic shall be founded upon the declared principles merely means that the practice of government should conform to them; but, because of the use of the word 'should', no specific duty, enforceable at the instance of a subject, is imposed upon the legislature not to deprive him of his property without compensation or not to discriminate against him on the ground of colour, race or creed. Thirdly, although 'shall' is used in the recognition of the sanctity of personal liberty, the duty is imposed on the 'Government' – defined as the 'authority' for the time being, in which is vested the executive power of the Republic'.[18] In so far as the recognition of the sanctity of personal liberty applies only to the executive, it is merely declaratory of the common law whose continued application in Malawi is affirmed by the Republic of Malawi (Constitution) Act,[19] to which the Constitution is scheduled. The common law guarantees human rights, including personal liberty and property, against the executive, though not against the legislature. In conclusion, therefore, it may be said that the declaration of fundamental principles of government in the Malawian Constitution is not a constitutional guarantee of rights enforceable by the individual.

No such interpretative problem arises in connection with the recital in the preamble to the Tanzanian Constitution, which does not purport to be a guarantee of rights at all, irrespective of whether or not a preamble is legally effective for that purpose. With France and some of her former dependencies – the Central African Republic, Chad, the Malagasy Republic and Mali – the preamble is the place for an affirmation of rights in the form of a full and detailed definition of all the rights of the individual and the conditions for their enjoyment. The preamble to the Constitution of the Central African Republic, for example, runs into three pages of print. It is difficult to see how this can operate as a legally enforceable guarantee. A preamble, at least in the British conception, forms no part of a statute, and so can create no legal rights or obligations, though its spirit may be a guide in the interpretation of the substantive provisions. Whatever effect the recital in the Tanzanian preamble has can therefore only be a moral and an educative one. This is in fact all the effect its framers intended that it should have — a way of trying to 'entrench the national ethic in the moral imagination of the people'.[20]

In that role, it may well be more useful than the detailed guarantees of a bill of rights. Thomas Franck at least thinks so. 'The broad declaration of principle in the preamble to the Tanzanian Constitution', he writes, 'perhaps conveys a more meaningful description of a democracy to the average citizen than the rather legalistic Nigerian provisions.'[21] However, the framers of the Tanzanian Constitution recognised that mere recital in a preamble is not enough, and that in addition 'everything possible should be done to win for these principles a strong commitment from the citizens'.[22] The reasons for the framers' preference for a preambulary recital rather than a justiciable guarantee will be explained in a later chapter.[23]

2. *Powers of the President for the Preservation of the Nation*

It cannot be denied that the state must take sufficient power to preserve itself. *Salus populi est suprema lex* — the safety of the nation is the supreme law. The rights of the individual, it has been said, 'depend for their very existence and implementation upon the continuance of the organised political society — that is the ordered society — established by the Constitution. The continuance of that society itself depends upon national security, for without security any society is in danger of collapse or overthrow. National security is thus paramount not only in the interests of the state but also in the interests of each individual member of the state; and measures designed to achieve and maintain that security must come first; and, subject to the provisions of the Constitution, must override, if need be, the interests of individuals and of minorities with which they conflict'.[24] The point of controversy is, however: In what circumstances and subject to what safeguards should individual rights yield to the claim of extra-ordinary powers by the government to preserve the nation? Should every threat to the peace and security of the state, whether real or imaginary, justify encroachment upon the rights of the individual?

(i) *The American Legacy*

This is undoubtedly among the most critical problems of government in the newly-independent states in Africa and Asia. But the problem is not new, nor is it even peculiar to the emergent states. The older-established nations face exactly the same conflict of human rights *versus* state security. It is said, however, that their approach to the problem is irrelevant to the conditions of a new nation which 'has neither the long tradition of nationhood, nor the strong physical means of national security, which older countries take for granted'.[25] This is true if we view these older countries in their present state of maturity and advancement, and ignore their past history, when conditions then prevailing within them were fairly comparable with those in the new states of today. When the strongest and most advanced of these nations, the United States of America, emerged into independent statehood in 1783, it too had to grapple with the usual teething problems of infancy, problems of state security and of unity, and the means then available to it for dealing with these problems could hardly be said to have been 'stronger' or better organised than those at the disposal of the new states today. The American approach to the conflict of state security *versus* individual liberty is therefore relevant, both because America had undergone a similar experience of colonial rule and of independence, and also because it is governed under a written Constitution. That approach, significantly, remains basically the same today as when the American nation was formed in 1787 with the adoption of the Constitution. It was maintained, even during the dark days of the greatest civil war known to history, and through the several smaller insurrections of which American history is replete, such as the Dorr insurrection in Rhode Island in 1849.

The keynote in the American approach is contained in the following words of the U.S. Supreme Court in the great civil war case of *ex parte Milligan* in 1866:[26]

> The Constitution of the United States is a law for rulers and people, equally in war and peace, and covers with the shield of its protection all classes of men, at all times, and under any circumstances. No doctrine, involving more pernicious consequences, was ever invented by the wit of man than that any of its provisions can be suspended during any of the great exigencies of government. Such a doctrine leads directly to anarchy or despotism, but the theory of necessity on which it is based is false; for the government, within the Constitution, has all the powers granted to it which are necessary to preserve its existence. . . .[27]

These words were again re-echoed by the same court in another great constitutional case arising from the Great War of 1939–45.[28] We may here also recall the similar words of Lord Atkin in his famous dissenting judgment in another Second World War case, *Liversige* v. *Anderson*.[29] 'In England, amidst the clash of arms', he said, 'the laws are not silent. They may be changed, but they speak the same language in war as in peace'. In the view of the U.S. Supreme Court in the

Milligan case, it is just at times of grave exigency that liberty requires to be protected against the pretensions and abuses of unlimited power; in any case, the court observed, a nation preserved at the sacrifice of the cardinal principles of liberty is not worth the cost of preservation.

The court was not, of course, denying any form of extraordinary power for the government to deal with an exigency endangering the peace or security of the nation. But an exigency, such as will justify interference with individual liberty, must not only be real but also grave and immediate. The most obvious situation is war, either foreign or domestic. Other situations of civil strife short of war may also justify interference, but it must be such as amounts to or is comparable with an insurrection, as where striking workers engage in acts defiant of the government or disruptive of public peace.[30] The extent of justifiable interference would of course vary with the gravity of the exigency. In the case of a mere insurrection resulting from, say, a strike, its suppression justifies the use of force by the executive. In the application of such force, the executive is entitled to kill and, *a fortiori*, to detain anyone resisting, such detention being by way, not of punishment, but of precaution, to prevent the exercise of hostile power, provided it is not continued after the insurrection has been put down.[31]

A war creates an extreme situation calling for sterner measures, such as a general suspension of the writ of *habeas corpus*, 'that greatest of all muniments of Anglo-American liberty'.[32] The U.S. Constitution itself authorises the suspension of the writ in an invasion or rebellion, if the public safety requires it.[33] Whether public safety requires a general suspension of the writ is, apparently, an exclusively executive decision not subject to review by the courts, yet it seems that the courts will assume to decide whether there had in fact been an 'invasion or rebellion' within the meaning of the Constitution. The executive power to decide what the public safety requires arises only if an invasion or rebellion actually exists as a judicially ascertainable fact. An equally important question is as to what act is actually authorised by the suspension of the writ. The U.S. Supreme Court in *ex parte Milligan* has laid it down that 'the suspension of the writ does not authorise the arrest of anyone, but simply denies to one arrested the privilege of this writ in order to obtain his liberty';[34] a minority of the court, dissenting from this view, took the contrary position that 'where the writ of *habeas corpus* is suspended, the Executive is authorised to arrest as well as detain'.[35]

The question is not, of course, whether the person to be detained can be arrested at all — for how otherwise can his detention be effected? — but rather whether the suspension of the writ authorises arbitrary detention as well as *arbitrary* arrest, i.e. arrest effected summarily without compliance with the law prescribing the conditions for a lawful arrest. These conditions require the authority of a warrant of arrest issued by a magistrate or judge, on a sworn information of the commission of a criminal offence, and which specifies both the person to be arrested and the offence alleged to have been committed by him, the warrant being shown or read to the person arrested at the time of the arrest or a reasonable time thereafter, so that he may know the reason why he is being deprived of his liberty. Only in exceptional cases may an arrest lawfully be made without warrant, but just as a warrant must specify the offence, so also must a person arresting without warrant inform the person arrested of the ground for it, and failure so to do makes the arrest unlawful.[36]

It seems, too, though the point is disputed, that suspension requires congressional authorisation. Although the two executive suspensions in 1861 and 1862 by Lincoln were without prior congressional authority, Congress, by an Act of 1863, did assert the power to authorise it, and in doing so imposed severe limitations on the President's power of detention. First, a list of all persons detained in pursuance of the suspension in any state where the administration of the law had continued unimpaired in the federal courts should be furnished to the judges of these courts. If, while the grand jury for the district was in session, any person named in the list was not brought before it charged with an offence, then after the closure of the session, he was entitled to his discharge; and it was the duty of the judge of the court to order him brought forward to be discharged subject or not to such condition as to good behaviour or future appearance in court as the judge might impose. Secondly, if the list were not furnished within twenty days of the arrest then, after the termination of the session of the grand jury without indictment, any citizen might, on behalf of the person detained, petition the judge and thereby obtain the discharge of the prisoner subject or not to the same conditions regarding good behaviour and appearance. Thus a person detained had the benefit either of trial by the grand jury while it was sitting or of discharge under the writ of *habeas corpus* after the session of the jury. Only where the administration of the law by the ordinary federal courts had been obstructed, or in the case of prisoners-of-war, would a person be held in detention without these safeguards. What is particularly remarkable was that these provisions were applied to order the release of persons alleged to have been giving aid and comfort to the rebels during the American Civil War.[37]

In the face of that devastating war the court also refused to sacrifice to the exigency of public safety the individual's right not to be deprived of his liberty or life in pursuance of the judgment of a military court. It rejected the argument that in time of war state necessity justifies the assumption by a military commander of absolute power to suspend all civil rights and their remedies, and to subject civilians as well as soldiers to the rule of his will. In pursuance of this alleged power, one Milligan had been tried, convicted and sentenced to death by a military commission, with the approval of the President, for alleged conspiracy against the government in giving aid and comfort to the rebels while in the loyal state of Indiana, whose citizen and resident he had been for twenty years. The court held unanimously that the trial, conviction and sentence were illegal as being unauthorised by the Constitution and the laws. The majority rested its decision on the ground that trial of civilians by a military court cannot be authorised, whether by the President or Congress, except when, as a result of military operations, the ordinary courts have ceased to function or can no longer function. But so long as they continue to function, then, notwithstanding the existence of war, the independent and impartial administration of the law by them with the assistance of an impartial jury cannot be suspended or superseded, not even by the authority of an Act of Congress. The court observed:

> Martial law cannot arise from a threatened invasion. The necessity must be actual and present; the invasion real, such as effectually closes the courts and deposes the civil administration. . . . If, in foreign invasion or civil war, the courts are actually closed, and it is impossible to administer criminal justice according to law, then, on the theatre of actual military operations where war really prevails, there is a necessity to furnish a substitute for the civil authority, thus overthrown, to preserve the safety of the army and society; and as no power is left but the military, it is allowed to govern by martial rule until the laws can have their free course. As necessity creates the rule, so it limits its duration; for if this government is continued after the courts are reinstated, it is a gross usurpation of power. Martial law can never exist where the courts are open, and in the proper and unobstructed exercise of their jurisdiction.[38]

The implication of the view taken by the majority is that since Congress could not have authorised the trial of Milligan by the military tribunal, it could not indemnify the tribunal's members from the legal consequences of the illegal trial. A minority of the court took the view that only the power of the President to declare martial law was limited in the way suggested. As far as Congress was concerned, however, it was competent, by virtue of its power to provide for the government of the national forces, to declare war and to provide for its prosecution, to authorise martial law in districts where the threat of invasion was such as to justify it. The fact that the ordinary courts are open might have been sufficient reason for its not exercising the power, but could not affect its existence.

The 'open court' rule of the majority was substantially affirmed by the court in 1945 in a series of cases arising out of the Second World War.[39] After the surprise Japanese air attack on Pearl Harbor, the Governor of Hawaii, with the approval of the President, placed the territory under martial law and handed over the entire administration to the military authorities. The military government then closed down all the civil courts and established military tribunals in their place. The two appellants in this case were respectively convicted of embezzlement and assault by the military tribunals seven months and two-and-a-half years after the attack on Pearl Harbor, at a time when any threat of further attack or invasion had completely disappeared. The court held that, in view of the fact that the Constitution has the same force and effect in Hawaii as in other parts of the United States, the provision of the Territory's Organic Act authorising the Governor, with the approval of the President, to declare martial law 'in case of rebellion or invasion or imminent danger thereof, when the public safety requires it', did not include power to supplant civilian laws and courts by military orders and tribunals where conditions were not such as to prevent the enforcement of the laws by the civilian courts; the provision was only intended to authorise the military to act vigorously for the maintenance of an orderly civil government and for the defence of the Territory against actual or threatened rebellion or invasion. The court reiterated what it had said in the earlier case of *ex parte Milligan*[40] that 'civil liberty and this kind of martial law cannot endure together; the antagonism is irreconcilable; and, in the conflict, one or the other must perish'.[41] It rejected the argument that, however adequate the 'open court' rule might have been in 1864, it was distinctly unsuited to modern warfare conditions where all the territories of a warring nation might be in combat zones or imminently threatened by long-range attack even while civil courts were operating. The trials were accordingly declared illegal as an unjustified interference with the constitutional guarantee of a fair trial. 'Those who founded this nation,' said Justice Murphy, 'knew full well that the arbitrary power of conviction and punishment for pretended offences is the hallmark of despotism. ... From time immemorial despots have used real or imagined threats to the public welfare as an excuse for needlessly abrogating human rights. That excuse is no less unworthy of our traditions when used in this day of atomic warfare or at a future time when other types of warfare may be devised. ... There must be some overpowering factor that makes a recognition of those rights incompatible with the public safety before we should consent to their temporary suspension.'[42]

The fact that martial law has been validly declared does not therefore by itself confer unlimited power on the executive. It may enable it to do no more than to effect summary arrests and detentions and the forcible entry and searching of private houses. Thus, when a revolutionary group, dissatisfied with the old charter government of the State of Rhode Island, established a new constitution and government, and raised an army which attempted by force to seize possession of the state arsenal, the Supreme Court held that the legislature of the old government was, in the circumstances, entitled to declare martial law, and to use extraordinary powers of arbitrary arrest and detention and the forcible entry into private houses of persons reasonably believed to be engaged in the insurrection, in order to maintain itself and overcome the unlawful and armed opposition.[43] The decision, as the court explained in the subsequent cases,[44] did no more than approve the specific action taken in that case, namely forcible entry into the plaintiff's house for the purpose of effecting his arrest. But it did not decide that every lawful declaration of martial law, by the fact of having been lawfully made, authorises any conceivable kind of power. The extent of power it justifies depends upon the gravity of the situation, and in particular upon whether the civil authorities have been incapacitated by military operations.[45]

A decision in 1972 of the Pakistan Supreme Court follows on the same principle. The court held that the martial law declared in March 1959 did not justify the military in assuming complete power to govern by military decrees and ordinances, and that the military regime so established from 1959 to 1971 was illegal, with the consequence that all the laws made by that regime were void except to the extent that any of them might be saved under the doctrine of necessity.[46]

(ii) *The Colonial Legacy*

It also seems relevant to consider human rights *vis-à-vis* public security in the new states of Africa against the background of the immediate colonial past, in order to determine how much of the security laws of today is an inheritance from that past, and whether that inheritance has been added to or mitigated in stringency.

A principal preoccupation of the colonial government was with public order and security. Based upon force and the subjugation of the subject people, it was always apprehensive of any kind of challenge to its authority; and was therefore disposed to subordinate the rights of the individual to public security whenever both should happen to be in conflict. This over-zealous concern for public security underlines all colonial security legislation. Three different types of such legislation may be here noticed — those applicable during (*a*) a declared or proclaimed emergency, (*b*) an undeclared or unproclaimed emergency, and (*c*) normal times. The difference between the three categories is that (*a*) and (*b*) require a situation out of the ordinary. The degree of seriousness of that situation provides the distinguishing mark between (*a*) and (*b*), since only serious situations will justify a declaration or proclamation. For brevity, situation (*a*) will be referred to throughout as 'emergency', and (*b*) as 'semi-emergency'.

The principal emergency legislation was the Emergency Powers Orders-in-Council 1939–61, which formed part of the constitutional framework of every British dependency in Africa and Asia. It was also part of the constitutional arrangement for independence to continue their provisions in force for some time after independence. They authorised the governor, if he was satisfied that a public emergency existed, to declare by formal proclamation that the provisions of the order-in-council shold come into operation in the whole or part only of the country concerned.[47] The governor thus had an unchallengeable discretion to say when a public emergency existed such as to justify the invocation of the wide powers conferred by the order, since all that was needed was the governor's subjective satisfaction that a public emergency existed.[48] Having by proclamation brought the order into operation, he could then make any kind of regulations appearing to him necessary or expedient for securing public safety, the defence of the territory, the maintenance of public order and the suppression of mutiny, rebellion and riot, and for maintaining supplies and services essential to the life of the community. In particular, the regulations might authorise the detention of persons without trial, the acquisition or taking of possession of property, and the apprehension, trial and punishment of persons offending against the regulations. The trial of persons by military courts was, however, expressly forbidden and excluded from the governor's regulation-making power. Once brought into force, these extraordinary powers were not specifically limited in duration; they continued in operation until the governor, by another proclamation, directed that they should cease to have effect.

The powers conferred by the orders-in-council had been quite widely used. Between 1946 and 1960 there had been twenty-nine proclamations of emergency in different parts of the British dependent empire, varying in duration from a few days to months or several years.[49] The regulations made by the governors had also varied in severity according to the way each governor viewed the situation with which he had to deal. In every case, however, the regulations had authorised arbitrary arrests and detentions, though always with a right of representation both to the governor and to a review panel whose role was invariably purely advisory. The manner in which an emergency and its regulations were executed is, of course, extremely important, and might make the difference between a 'police state' and a liberal one. In this connection perhaps the most notorious was the emergency proclaimed in Nyasaland from March 1959 to 1960. So widely was the detention dragnet spread, and so arbitrary and harsh were the methods used by the police, that the British Government had to send all the way from Britain a commission of enquiry under a distinguished English High Court judge to investigate the matter. The commission found that within just two-and-a-half months of the emergency, about 1,000 persons had been detained, most of them on mere suspicion of subversive behaviour; that the detentions were effected by means of arbitrary and unlawful arrests, often involving the use of more force than necessary and the denial of the right to be informed of the reason for the arrest; and that, on the whole, the administration of the emergency made the territory very much a 'police state'.[50]

It should perhaps be reiterated again that these extraordinary powers of the governor under the orders-in-council were available only during a full-scale emergency, though the governor was made the sole judge as to its existence. Powers for dealing with a semi-emergency were more limited. A situation of semi-emergency might arise as an aftermath of a full emergency or as a prelude to it, requiring in the former case mopping-up measures, and in the latter measures to nip the threat in the bud. Thus, when the emergency proclaimed in Kenya on March 10, 1952, was terminated on November 10, 1959, the colonial government took on powers of a semi-emergency kind under two statutes. By the Preservation of Public Security Ordinance, 1959,[51] the governor was empowered to make regulations for the control of publications and assemblies, or, if he considered the situation serious enough to warrant sterner measures, for the detention of persons. No regulations were in fact made for the detention of persons under the Ordinance. The Detained and Restricted Persons (Special Provisions) Ordinance, 1959, authorised him to make regulations for the detention or restriction of persons against whom a detention or restriction order had been in force immediately prior to the commencement of the ordinance, or persons outside the country whom it would be necessary to control if they entered it. In 1957 the Governor of Northern Rhodesia was also given power to make regulations to deal with a situation which, though not amounting to an emergency, was nevertheless calculated to create or lead to it, if allowed to continue unchecked.[52] On March 11, 1959, the Governor invoked this power. He first declared that the circumstances required by the enabling enactment existed, and then issued regulations authorising the *restriction* (but not detention) of persons in certain circumstances, which were then executed on the leaders of the Zambia National Congress.[53] In this category also was Nyasaland's Preservation of Public Security Ordinance of 1960 which empowered the Governor, if he was satisfied that it was necessary for the preservation of public security, to declare by gazette notice that the provisions of the ordinance should come into operation, and to make regulations; among the provisions of such regulations were the detention or restriction of persons and the rendering of forced labour. That the provisions of the ordinance needed to be brought into operation only when and if a necessity arose shows that it contemplated a situation out of the ordinary, i.e. a semi-emergency. The provisions were not in fact brought into operation up to the time of independence, as no such situation arose.

In normal times, when no situation of emergency or semi-emergency existed, security measures under the British colonial government cannot really be said to have been unduly restrictive of individual rights – at least, of the individual right of personal liberty. In accordance with the regime's preoccupation with security, the governor was, of course, equipped with certain extraordinary security powers, such as the power to 'deport' from one part of the country to another a person found conducting himself in a manner dangerous to peace and good order, or endeavouring to excite enmity between the people and the government, or otherwise intriguing against the authority of the government;[54] he also had the power to expel aliens convicted of criminal offences or whose presence in the country was otherwise not conducive to the public good.[55] The individual was not, however, without certain safeguards against these powers. For example, deportation in Uganda could only be ordered on the report of a judge appointed to inquire into the matter. The deportee must be informed in writing before the inquiry of the grounds on which it was proposed to deport him, and be required to show cause, before the investigating judge, why he should not be deported. At the inquiry he was entitled to be present and to be represented by an advocate, though no appeal lay from an order of deportation. A warrant of arrest issued by a magistrate was, however, necessary before he could be taken into custody in execution of the order. These safeguards were absent in the Tanganyikan Deportation Ordinance, but its Expulsion of Undesirables Ordinance required that, if the would-be expellee showed cause why the order should not be enforced against him, then judicial enquiry was to be held, at which the expellee was entitled to be represented by counsel. The report of the enquiry was not however to prejudice the power to expel on the ground that it was deemed to be 'conducive to the public good'.[56]

It is particularly significant nevertheless that, outside periods of emergency or semi-emergency, the colonial security legislation conferred no general power of preventive detention without trial. (Cyprus and Singapore excepted.)[57] The only example of what approached a power of preventive detention or restriction was in Nyasaland and Kenya. In Nyasaland the Restriction and Security Orders Ordinance of 1954 empowered the Governor in Council, if he thought fit, to issue a *restriction* (not detention) order against a person, being a British subject, British-protected person or citizen of the Republic of Ireland, 'who is or has been conducting himself so as to be dangerous to peace, order, good government or public morals, who is or has been attempting or conducting himself in a manner calculated to raise discontent or disaffection amongst Her Majesty's subjects or the inhabitants of the Protectorate or to promote feelings of ill-will and hostility between different races or classes of the population of the Protectorate'. No restriction order was, however, to be made except on the report of a judge enquiring into the case and unless the Governor in Council was satisfied, having regard to the findings of fact and any conclusions of law as stated in the report, that such an order might lawfully be made. The order, when made, must then be reported forthwith to the secretary of state. The Political Removal and Detention of Africans Ordinance, 1909 (Nyasaland), also empowered a district commissioner in the interests of peace, order and good government to detain any African in his district, if it were proved to his satisfaction by evidence on oath that such African was conducting himself so as to be dangerous to peace, order and good government or was intriguing against the Crown's power and authority in the country. The detention must be reported to the Governor who might revoke or confirm it, in which latter event he must in turn report to the secretary of state. Under the Native Courts Regulations of 1899 (Kenya), the Commissioner for the East African Protectorate might detain or restrict any African who was disaffected towards the government, was about to commit an offence against the Regulations, or was otherwise conducting himself so as to be dangerous to peace and good government.[58]

This, then, was the colonial legacy on this matter, and the question now is whether the independent governments have exceeded this either in the way of new powers, or by removing the safeguards on pre-existing powers or through a more extensive use of them.

3. *Security Powers Under the Independent Governments*

Taking Ghana first, at independence in 1957, the Emergency Powers Orders-in-Council, 1939—56, were continued in force for one year. Under the Constitution, the authority to proclaim an emergency was vested in the Governor-General acting on the advice of the cabinet, but regulations issued in pursuance of such a proclamation must be laid before parliament and approved by it by resolution within twenty-eight days, or else cease to have effect. Later in the same year (1957) the Emergency Powers Orders-in-Council, 1939—56, which conferred the regulation-making power, were repealed and replaced by the Emergency Powers Act, which was in turn repealed and replaced by the Emergency Powers Act, 1961. In the meantime, of course, the country had become a republic under a constitution that contained neither a bill of rights nor provisions limiting the executive's security powers. The 1961 Act empowered the President to proclaim an emergency on the advice of the cabinet. Significantly it abolished the requirement for emergency regulations to be approved by a resolution of parliament within twenty-eight days; laying before parliament was all that was required.

The Act may thus be said to have reverted Ghana to the position before independence when the authority of the colonial government to make emergency regulations was not fettered by the controlling discretion of an elected parliament. Without the constitutional limitations imposed by a bill of rights, the post-independence years saw a vast increase in the security powers of the government. The Criminal Code (Amendment) Act, 1960, authorised the President to impose press censorship whenever he was of the opinion that there was in any newspaper, book or document which was published periodically a systematic publication of matter calculated to prejudice public order or safety, or the maintenance of the public services or the economy or that any person was likely to publish individual documents containing such matter.[59] The Sedition Act, 1959, made it an offence 'falsely to accuse any public officer of misconduct in the exercise of his official duties, knowing the accusation to be false or reckless whether it be true or false'.[60] False communications of any kind (except when made in proceedings in court or parliament), which were likely to injure the credit or reputation of Ghana or the Government of Ghana, were made an offence if the person making them knew or had reason to believe them to be false, unless he proved that before making them he took reasonable measure to verify their accuracy.[61]

It was in the area of personal liberty that these new powers had the greatest impact. By the Deportation Act, 1957, re-enacting the existing colonial statute, the Governor-General (later the President) was authorised to deport aliens if, among other grounds, their presence was not conducive to the public good. The Criminal Procedure Code, 1962, authorised the police to detain persons arrested without warrants for twenty-eight days or such longer period as the Attorney-General might determine. Finally there was the Preventive Detention Act of 1958, the most drastic of all, under which the Governor-General (later the President) could detain persons in both normal and emergency times alike. As originally enacted, the Act was to expire after five years, but it was later established on a permanent basis, becoming thereby a normal feature of life in Ghana until it was repealed after the army coup in February 1966.

Tanganyika came to independence in June 1961 without a bill of rights, thus permitting not only the colonial security legislation to continue in force but also new legislation to be enacted by the new sovereign legislature. Both the Deportation Ordinance, 1921, and the Expulsion of Undesirables Ordinance, 1930, therefore remained. In 1961, following in the footsteps of Ghana, a Preventive Detention Act was enacted on a permanent basis. On the establishment of the republic in 1962, the Emergency Powers Orders-in-Council, 1939–61, which were continued in force for one year at independence, were adopted as part of the law of the country.[62]

The rest of the presidential regimes – Sierra Leone, Uganda, Kenya, Malawi, Zambia, Botswana and Gambia – were in a different position in that they all came to independence with a bill of rights. The bill of rights was not, however, at the expense of public order and security. The approach to the conflict between them followed three different lines. For this purpose rights guaranteed in the constitution might be grouped into three classes.

First, there were those guaranteed subject at all times to public security – freedom of conscience, of expression, assembly, association, movement, freedom from arbitrary search or entry, and the right of property. The old colonial security restrictions on these rights were thus largely unaffected by the bill of rights, although Uganda's Deportation Ordinance was held to have been invalidated by it, because it authorised the deportation of individuals, whereas the bill of rights permitted restrictions on freedom of movement only if the restriction was imposed on persons generally or any class of persons.[63] It follows that detention pending deportation under the ordinance was unlawful, notwithstanding that the constitution authorised detention in execution of a lawful deportation order.

Then there was the second class of rights which could be derogated from in the interest of public security, etc., only during an emergency – personal liberty, freedom from forced labour, and freedom from discriminatory treatment. The inclusion of personal liberty in this class meant that detention without trial in normal times or during a semi- (i.e. undeclared) emergency situation, was forbidden. Existing colonial laws which allowed it, such as Nyasaland's Preservation of Public Security Ordinance or the Political Removal and Detention of Africans Ordinance, therefore became invalidated. In Zambia, however, derogation was permitted during a semi-emergency situation (i.e. threatened emergency), but as a safeguard a proclamation was then to be made just as in an *actual* emergency. Existing emergency laws were either continued in force with or without amendment or were replaced by new ones. For example, Zambia enacted a new Emergency Powers Act in 1964 to replace both the Emergency Powers Orders-in-Council and the Emergency Powers Ordinance, 1948, while continuing in force with amendments the Preservation of Public Security Ordinance, 1960, which applies during a threatened (semi- but declared) emergency.

Uganda too enacted a new Emergency Powers Act in 1963. It is remarkable that, apart from war, what is to constitute an emergency is, lamentably, left undefined in these constitutions, thus leaving the door wide open to abuse, as happened in Nigeria in 1962 when the federal government declared an emergency in the western region of the country merely on the strength of fighting among M.P.s within the chamber of the region's legislative assembly. In circumstances similar to those in Western Nigeria, the federal government of Malaysia had also used its power to declare an emergency in Sarawak. In its ordinary meaning, 'emergency' presupposes some event, usually of a violent nature, endangering or threatening public order or public safety. Thus, the Constitution of Cyprus, 1960, authorises the proclamation of an emergency only 'in the case of war or other public danger threatening the life of the Republic',[64] and the constitutions of the ex-French African countries, following in the manner of the Constitution of the Fifth French Republic itself, define an emergency as 'a clear and present danger', threatening the institutions or independence of the nation, the integrity of its territory, or the carrying out of its international undertakings, or any other situation 'when the regular functioning of governmental authorities is interrupted'.[65]

The third class of rights were those which were not subject at all to derogation in the interests of public security whether in normal times or during an emergency – the right to life (except during a war, riot, insurrection or mutiny), freedom from inhuman treatment and slavery, and the right to a fair trial in criminal prosecution by an independent and impartial court – though a law may, in the interests of defence, public safety or public order, authorise the proceedings to be held in private. The fact that the right to fair trial in criminal prosecutions is not subject to derogation at any time deserves to be specially noticed, because it means that trial by military tribunals could not be authorised at all, except when the ordinary courts had been made incapable of functioning owing to actual military operations, when the necessity of the situation thus created would justify trial by military tribunals as the only alternative to the incapacitated civil courts. The effect was, of course, that the 'open court' rule of the U.S. Supreme Court became incorporated by implication into the independence constitutions of Commonwealth Africa.

It is perhaps necessary to explain at this point that the terms 'public security' or 'national security' are not used in any of the bills of rights. The expression used is 'defence, public safety, public order'. These three categories touch upon aspects of public security, though they are by no means mutually exclusive. However, whether public or national security is wider or narrower than, or co-extensive with, defence, public safety and public order, it is being used here as a compendious expression to cover all three or any of them, depending on the context. Indeed, 'public security' is given the widest connotation in the Preservation of Public Security Acts of Zambia, Kenya and Malawi as including 'the safety of persons and property, the maintenance of supplies and services essential to the life of the community, the prevention and suppression of violence, intimidation, disorder and crime, the prevention and suppression of mutiny, rebellion, and concerted defiance of and disobedience to the law and lawful authority, and the maintenance of the administration of justice'.[66]

It must not be supposed from what has been said that any derogation from a constitutionally guaranteed right that is required by public security is permitted. Far from it. The importance accorded to public security is not that overriding. No *carte blanche* is given to the government to do whatever public security requires. However much public security may require an act in derogation of a guaranteed right, it still cannot be lawfully done unless the act is authorised by a law. Only by the authority of an enabling law may a derogation be made. This is a recognition of the cardinal principle noted in an earlier chapter,[67] that the executive cannot interfere with private rights unless it can justify such interference on the basis of a law. The authority often takes the form of a statute enacted by the legislature, but 'law' in this context is not confined to acts of parliament. It includes regulations or other statutory instruments made by the executive under statutory power,[68] the most far-reaching of these being the security regulations made under emergency or other security statutes. Also included in the term 'law' are the unwritten rules of the common law, in so far as they are applicable in Africa, and the law of necessity which, as previously stated,[69] is implied in the constitution of every civilised community so as to qualify, though not to abrogate, the express provisions thereof. By this law of necessity the executive can, whenever the safety of the state or of society is imperilled, interfere with private rights without the authority of an enabling legislation, in order to safeguard law and order and preserve the state and society. It may, for example, take possession of a citizen's property[70] even without payment of compensation,[71] or restrict the movement of persons (e.g. by curfew) or their residence.[72]

However, the necessity which will justify such interference must be an imperative one arising from an imminent and extreme danger to the safety of the state or society, which makes it necessary for the executive to act without statutory authorisation. And the act of interference must (*a*) be inevitable in the sense of being the only remedy; (*b*) be proportionate to the necessity, i.e. it must be reasonably warranted by the danger which it was intended to avert; and (*c*) be of a temporary character, limited to the duration of the exceptional circumstance. The power of the executive under the law of necessity is independent of its powers during an emergency declared in terms of the constitution; in other words it can be invoked although no emergency has been declared under the constitution. It seems, however, that a more imperative situation is needed for it than for an emergency under the constitution; imperative, that is to say, in the sense of the danger of disruption in the life of society though not necessarily in terms of physical violence. As may be recalled,[73] the Pakistan Supreme Court in 1972 declared the martial law administration of the country from 1959–71 to have been illegal. It had then to decide which of the acts and legislative measures of the illegal regime could be saved under the doctrine of necessity. It held that the presidential orders under which the applicants in the case had been detained were not among the measures so saved; accordingly their detention was illegal and they were ordered to be released.[74]

Even given an enabling law, a derogation on the ground of public security is still not permitted under the exceptions to the bill of rights unless, in the case of rights in the first class noted above — freedom of conscience, expression, assembly, association, movement, and from arbitrary search or entry (property is considered in the next chapter) — the law or the action taken thereunder is both (a) reasonably required in the interests of public security, and (b) reasonably justifiable in a democratic society. For rights in the second class, i.e. those that could be derogated from only during a situation of emergency (or semi-emergency) — personal liberty, freedom from forced labour and freedom from discriminatory treatment — the derogation must be reasonably justifiable for the purpose of dealing with the situation (Kenya abolished this requirement in 1966).

The approach in the bills of rights of the independence constitutions seems to strike perhaps a fair balance which, if interpreted liberally by the courts,[75] might allow quite ample scope for the enjoyment of individual liberties and freedoms. But how far has this approach been maintained under the presidential regimes? The answer, happily, is that, except in Uganda, Kenya and Malawi, presidentialism has not brought about any departure from this approach. There have of course been changes affecting conditions of detention and restriction, but these have not altered the broad approach to the conflict between human rights and public security described above.

Turning now to the depatures in Uganda, Kenya and Malawi, the Republican Constitution of Uganda 1967 made the guarantee of personal liberty subject to any law authorising the detention of persons without trial.[76] In pursuance of this, the Public Order and Security Act, 1967, was enacted, authorising the President, as a permanent measure and in terms similar to Tanganyika's Preventive Detention Act,

1961, to detain or restrict people without trial. The guarantee of freedom of movement was modified to permit the imposition of restrictions, not only on persons generally or on any class of persons, but also on any person, thus salvaging the Deportation Act from the decision declaring it unconstitutional and void.[77]

Kenya's Preservation of Public Security Ordinance was clearly *ultra vires* the Constitution, and void in so far as it authorised detention without trial or forced labour outside a full-scale emergency. In 1966 the Constitution was amended to make it conform to the provisions of the Security Act. The amendment provided that 'nothing contained in or done under the authority of any provision of ... the Preservation of Public Security Act shall be held to be inconsistent with or in contravention' of the guarantee of personal liberty, freedom of movement or freedom from discriminatory treatment.[78] These rights and freedoms can now be derogated from in the interests of public security at all times, notwithstanding that no emergency, in the strict sense of the word, exists; all that is necessary is for the President, by notice in the gazette, to bring the provisions of the security act into operation.[79] The definition of an emergency in the Constitution was also abolished.[80] At the same time the Security Act itself was amended. Previously the harsher measures of detention and restriction could be authorised only if the situation was 'so grave' that the milder powers conferred by S.3 of the Act would be inadequate to deal with it. Thus when the Act was brought into force in 1960, only the milder powers were used, the situation not being so grave.[81] The requirement that the situation must be so grave before detention or restriction could be authorised was removed by the 1966 amendment. By a gazette notice the President can bring the whole or any part of the Act into force at any time, whether the situation is grave or not.

Do these amendments make Kenya's Preservation of Public Security Act a preventive detention law? On behalf of the government, it was strenuously argued that they did not.[82] It seems that the government is right to the extent that the coming into operation of the Act needs action by the President as well as a *situation* out of the ordinary (i.e. a semi-emergency), whereas a preventive detention law is in operation all the time by its own authority, and not by a presidential order or notice. Yet the departure from the independence scheme is quite serious. For not only is derogation from the right to personal liberty now permitted during a semi-emergency, but the situation deemed to constitute the semi-emergency, and so warranting the use of the harsher powers under the Act (restriction and detention of persons), need not be serious or so grave. In this respect therefore the amendment in Kenya goes further than the colonial precedent, and further still from the position in Zambia, both of which make it a condition for the exercise of the power of restriction and detention that the situation must be 'so grave'. And the requirement of a proclamation in Zambia for a situation of threatened (or semi-) emergency as for an emergency provides yet another safeguard. There is a significant difference between a Head of State declaring that a situation of threatened emergency exists and simply publishing a gazette notice to bring the provisions of an Act into force. Barring the possibility of a deliberate abuse of power, a Head of State would not normally lie by solemnly declaring that a threatened emergency exists when in fact it does not. But he makes no such solemn averment when he publishes a gazette notice. Further, although a proclamation is necessary under the Constitution[83] for both, Zambia still distinguishes a threatened emergency (governed by the Preservation of Public Security Act, 1960) from an emergency (governed by the Emergency Powers Act, 1964); both Acts, of course, confer virtually the same amplitude of powers, which explains why it has not been necessary to use the latter act. The Kenyan Government had tried to justify the abolition of the safeguards of a formal declaration of an emergency on the ground that an emergency 'has for us the most distasteful associations of memory';[84] further, that 'it gives a misleading picture of a country, it gives a bad image of a country, and it gives too many sweeping powers that might not really be necessary in dealing with a localised situation.'[85]

Malawi, as already stated,[86] has, in its Republican Constitution, done away with the bill of rights given to it at independence, thus removing any question of inconsistency between the Constitution and the Preservation of Public Security Act. With the abolition of the constitutional guarantee of the right to fair trial, the way might have been open to authorise military trials under the Act. Happily, the Act itself provides that nothing contained therein 'shall authorise the making of any regulations providing for the trial of persons by military courts'.[87] The Malawian Preservation of Public Security Act may be brought into force at any time, and is not, like the Kenyan Act, divided into parts according to the severity of the measures it authorises to be taken. In spite of this, the Malawian Act is not a preventive detention law; for, like the Kenyan Act, it envisages a situation out of the ordinary; it differs from the Ghanaian, Tanzanian or Ugandan preventive detention laws in the sense that, although it is permanently on the statute book, it needs, like the Kenyan Act, to be brought into operation by notice in the gazette as and when it is required, but there are no limiting conditions on when it may be brought into force. All that is required is for the minister to be satisfied that it is necessary for the preservation of public security to bring it into operation. No use was made of the Act by the colonial government, and it was first brought into operation after independence.[88] The regulations made under it in

1965[89] were much more severe and repressive than those in Kenya or Zambia or, in some respects, even the security legislation of Nkrumahist Ghana. Not only do they authorise detention or restriction of persons, but they also authorise any authorised officer, pending the decision of the minister, to detain or restrict for twenty-eight days any person of whom he has reason to believe that there are grounds which would justify his detention.

The provisions peculiar to Malawi relate to the prohibition of any act or publication, written or oral, likely (a) to be prejudicial to public security; (b) to undermine the authority of, or the public confidence in, the government; (c) to promote feelings of ill-will or hostility between any sections or classes or races of the inhabitants of the country; or (d) to promote industrial unrest in any industry in which the person concerned has not been *bona fide* engaged for at least the previous two years. The minister is empowered to declare any district a special area, upon which any person in the area becomes liable to arbitrary search and to be shot if he resists; seven districts were declared special areas in 1965.[90] Power is also given to disconnect telephones, or to require any person to furnish or produce any information, article, book or document in his possession or power which is considered necessary for the preservation of public security. It is made an offence, punishable by seven years imprisonment, to consort with or harbour (for example, by giving shelter, food, drink, money, clothing, medicine or any other valuable commodity or giving any other kind of assistance) a person intending or about to act or who has recently acted in a manner prejudicial to the preservation of public order. Any building, hut or other structure which an authorised officer reasonably suspects is being used or intended to be used for the purpose of harbouring such a person may be dismantled or destroyed. Independent Malawi has clearly surpassed in the severity of its security measures anything that the colonial government had done anywhere in Africa when no emergency had been declared.

REFERENCES

1. SS.31, 34 and 69, Constitution, 1957.
2. S. A. de Smith, *The New Commonwealth and its Constitutions* (1964).
3. S.13, Zambia; S.70, Kenya; S.13, Gambia; S.3, Botswana; S.11, Malawi (1964); S.17, Uganda (1963 and 1966). Italics supplied.
4. *Liyanage* v. *R* [1967] 1 A.C. 259 (P.C. Appeal from Ceylon).
5. *Patel* v. *Att.-Gen. of Zambia* 1968 S.J.Z.1.
6. Art. 8(2).
7. Art. 8(5).

8. Art. 8(6).

9. Art. 12.

10. Art. 13.

11. Art. 13.

12. S.2.

13. *Re Akoto* [1961]G.L.R. 523. The form of the argument was not in the report of the case.

14. *Ibid.*, at p. 534 — per Korsah C. J.

15. *Ibid.*, at p. 535.

16. S.2(i); italics supplied.

17. S.2(2).

18. S.98.

19. S.15.

20. Presidential Commission Report (1964), para. 105.

21. Thomas Franck, *Comparative Constitutional Process* (1968), p. 8.

22. Report, *op. cit.*, para. 105.

23. Post, ch. XII.

24. *Kachasu* v. *Att.-Gen. of Zambia* 1967/HP/273 — per Blagden C. J. Cf. Justice Holmes in *Moyer* v. *Peabody* 212 U.S. 78, at p. 85 (1909).

25. Julius Nyerere, 'Development and State Power' (speech inaugurating the University College, Dar es Salaam, 1964), reprinted in *Freedom and Unity* (1966), p. 305.

26. 4 Wall 2 (1966).

27. At pp. 120—1.

28. *Duncan* v. *Kahanamoku* 327 U.S. 304 (1945); particularly the concurring judgment of Justice Murphy, pp. 325—35.

29. [1942] A.C. 206.

30. *Moyer* v. *Peabody* 212 U.S. 78 (1909).

31. *Moyer* v. *Peabody, ibid.*

32. Edward S. Corwin, *The President: Office and Powers* (1957), p. 144.

33. Art. 1, S.9.

34. 4 Wall 2 at p. 115; Justice Woodbury expressed himself to the same effect in *Lurther* v. *Borden* 7 How at p. 62 (1849).

35. At p. 137.

36. *Christie* v. *Leachinsky* [1947] A.C. 573.

37. *Ex parte Milligan, ibid.*

38. *Ibid.* at p. 127.

39. *Duncan* v. *Kahanamoku* 327 U.S. 304.

40. 4 Wall 2 at p. 124.

41. 327 U.S. 304 at p. 324.

42. At p. 325, p. 330.

43. *Lurther* v. *Borden* 7 How 1 (1849).

44. *Ex parte Milligan, ibid.*

45. Cf. the dissenting judgment of Justice Woodbury where the learned justice wrongfully assumed that every declaration of martial law authorises not only summary arrests and detentions and the forcible

entry into private houses, but also arbitrary trials by court-martials. 'By it', he said, 'every citizen, instead of reposing under the shield of known and fixed laws as to liberty, property, and life, exists with a rope round his neck, subject to being hung up by a military despot at the next lamp post, under the sentence of some drumhead court-martial.' *Lurther* v. *Borden* 7 How 1, p. 62.

46. *Malik Ghulan Jilami and Alter Gauhar* v. *The Province of Sind and Others*, Cr. Appeals Nos. 19 and K2 of 20 April, 1972.

47. S.3, as amended in 1956.

48. The wording of the old S.3 of the original 1939 Order did not in terms confer such a discretion; it merely provided that in case of any public emergency, the Governor might by proclamation bring its provisions into operation.

49. See D. C. Holland, 'Emergency Legislation in the Commonwealth' (1960), 13 C.L.P. 138.

50. The Devlin Report, Cmnd. 814, 1959; Holland, *op. cit.*

51. This repealed and replaced the Emergency Powers Ordinance, 1948, which was in terms similar to the U.K. Emergency Powers Act, 1920.

52. S.4A(1) Emergency Powers Ordinance, 1948, as amended in 1957.

53. Holland, *op. cit.*

54. Deportation Ordinance, 1908 (Uganda), Deportation Ordinance, 1921 (Tanganyika).

55. Expulsion of Undesirables Ordinance, 1930 (Tanganyika); Deportation Ordinance (Ghana). For comparable enactments in Kenya, see Ghai and McAuslan, *Public Law and Political Change in Kenya* (1970), pp. 407–10.

56. See McAuslan, 'The Republican Constitution of Tanganyika' (1964), 13 *I.C.L.Q.*, pp. 561–6.

57. Detention of Persons Law, 1955 (Cyprus); Preservation of Public Security Ordinance, 1955 (Singapore). See Holland, 'Personal Liberty in the Commonwealth' (1958), *C,L.P.* 151.

58. Ghai and McAuslan, *op. cit.*, pp. 407–8.

59. Now S.183(2) Criminal Code.

60. Now S.183(1) Criminal Code.

61. Offences Against the State (False Reports) Act, 1959.

62. S.28, Republic of Tanganyika (Constitutional, Transitional and Temporary Provisions) Act, 1962, cap. 500.

63. *Grace Stuart Ibingira* v. *Uganda* [1966] E.A. 306.

64. Art. 183.1.

65. See, e.g., Cameroon 1961, art. 15; Central African Republic 1960, art. 12; Chad, 1962, art. 14; Congo Brazzaville 1963, art. 37; Dahomey, 1964, art 27; Gabon, 1961, art. 19; Ivory Coast 1960, art. 19; Senegal 1960, art. 47.

66. S.2 Zambia, 1960; S.2 Kenya, 1962; S.2 Malawi, 1960.

67. Above, ch. II.

68. *Patel* v. *Att.-Gen. for Zambia* 1968 S.J.Z.1.

69. Above, ch. II.

70. *Burmah Oil Co* v. *Lord Advocate* [1965] A.C. 75 (H.L.).

71. *Att.-Gen.* v. *De Keyser's Royal Hotel* [1920] A.C. 508 (H.L.).

72. See the Japanese-American cases of *Hirabayashi* v. *U.S.; Yasui* v. *U.S.* 320 U.S. 81 and 115 (1943); *Korematsu* v. *U.S.* 323 U.S. 214; *ex parte Endo* 323 U.S. 283.

73. Above, p. 310.

74. *Malik Ghulam Jilani and Altaf Gauhar* v. *The Province of Sind*, Cr. Appeal Nos. 19 and K2 of 20 April 1972, noted in International Commission of Jurists No. 8, June 1972, pp. 64–5.

75. See, e.g., *Patel* v. *Att.-Gen. of Zambia* 1968 S.J.Z.1; but contrast *Kachasu* v. *Att.-Gen. for Zambia* 1967/HP/273; *Arzika* v. *Governor, Northern Region of Nigeria* (1961), all N.L.R.379; *Cheranci* v. *Cheranci* 1960 N.R.N.L.R. 24 (Nigeria).

76. Art. 10(1)(*j*).

77. *Grace Stuart Ibingira* v. *Uganda, ibid.*

78. S.83(1), Constitution 1969.

79. S.85(1).

80. See above.

81. LN. 13/1960.

82. House of Reps. Deb., 2 June, 1966, cols 273–326.

83. S.29 Constitution of Zambia, 1964.

84. House of Reps. Deb. 2 June, 1966, col. 279 – per Att.-Gen. Njonjo.

85. *Ibid.*, col. 286 – Tom Mboya, Minister for Economic Planning.

86. Above, p. 301.

87. S.4 proviso. This proviso is also contained in the Zambian and Kenyan Acts.

88. GN. 70/1964.

89. GN. 43/1965; 70/1965; 127/1965, and 38/1966.

90. GN. 55/1965; 251/1965.

CHAPTER XI

THE REALITY OF SECURITY POWERS

1. *The Formal Nature of Security Powers*

Security powers in Africa have a frightful reality. They are formally very wide and drastic both in and out of an emergency. As noted in the last chapter, the Constitution leaves undefined what constitutes an emergency, war apart. Not only that, but there is also insufficient check on the power to declare it. The authority to declare an emergency is, in fact, defined in three different ways in the independence constitutions of Commonwealth Africa. Zambia, Uganda, Malawi and Botswana represented one approach. There, the authority to declare an emergency (or semi-emergency) was vested in the Governor-General or President as in colonial times, but it had to be approved by parliament by resolution within five days (seven days in Botswana) if in session, or within twenty-one days (fifteen days in Uganda) if it is not in session; otherwise the declaration ceased to have effect after the expiration of that period.[1] In Kenya the declaration was also to be made by the Governor-General (later the President), but only with the *prior* approval of one of the legislative houses (the approving resolution must be supported by 65 per cent of all the members), and it had then to be approved within five days by the other house by the same majority; otherwise it lapsed.[2] The prior approval of a legislative house was dispensed with when parliament was adjourned, prorogued or dissolved; in that case the declaration lapsed after seven days unless in the meantime it had been approved, in case of a declaration made during an adjournment or prorogation, by both houses by 65 per cent majority, or, in the case of a declaration made during a dissolution, by 65 per cent majority of the senate. The third approach was represented by Sierra Leone and Nigeria; only parliament could declare an emergency with a two-thirds majority of all its members.[3]

These safeguards still remain in the constitutions of all the presidential regimes except those of Kenya and Malawi. In both countries nothing like a formal declaration of emergency is recognised any longer, the full amplitude of the emergency regulation-making power being available whenever the President considers it necessary for the preservation of public security. However, in Kenya an order of the

President bringing the Preservation of Public Security Act into operation must be approved by a resolution of the national assembly within twenty-eight days, any period when parliament is dissolved being discounted. Uganda had retained the safeguard of a parliamentary approval in its 1967 republican Constitution, while at the same time extending the period within which a declaration must be so approved to fourteen days if parliament is in session and thirty days if it is not.[4] (There has of course been no parliament since the army coup of January 1971.) Zambia too has extended the period to twenty-eight days, exclusive of any time during which parliament is dissolved.[5]

It is perhaps on personal liberty that security powers have impinged most. The power of detention and restriction is extensive. The ordinary legal limitations on arrest are usually dispensed with. It is a precondition of a lawful detention that the arrest must have been effected in accordance with the requirements of law. The courts 'will not allow any individual to procure the imprisonment of another, unless he takes care to follow with extreme precision every form and every step in the process which is to procure that imprisonment'.[6] As already stated, except in certain specific situations, the law requires an arrest to be made by warrant. The preventive detention laws of Ghana, Tanzania and Uganda all authorise arbitrary arrest for this purpose. In anticipation of the sort of question that has arisen in the U.S. Supreme Court,[7] they provide that 'a detention order shall constitute an authority to any police officer to arrest the person in respect of whom it is made and for any police or prison officer to detain such person as a civil prisoner'. The regulations under all the emergency and security statutes make a similar provision. The effect of this is thus to dispense with the ordinary requirements for a lawful arrest; no warrant of arrest is necessary, nor need the person be informed of the reason for the arrest. As the form of a detention order or its content is not prescribed by law, it may be oral; the detaining authority can simply order orally that a person be detained, and he can ratify days later an arrest and detention made initially by the police without prior order. If the order is in writing, it need not name the person to be detained; this can be communicated orally or in a list or schedule attached to the order.[8] If it names the person to be detained simply by his surname without any other description, such as his first names, business and address, this is not necessarily fatal if his identity is otherwise known to the police.[9] Nor need the order recite the Act by authority of which the detention is ordered.[10]

As regards its length, if detention or restriction is in pursuance of a declaration of an emergency or semi-emergency, then it can last only so long as the declaration is in force. In the independence constitutions the maximum permitted period was six months (two months in Kenya, and twelve in Sierra Leone), subject to extension for further periods of six months at a time (two months in Kenya and twelve in Sierra Leone). An extension, however, can only be authorised by resolution of parliament, and not by the President. Either the President or parliament can of course revoke a declaration at any time. This position has no longer obtained in Zambia since 1969; a declaration now continues in force indefinitely until revoked by either the President or the national assembly, or unless there is a new President when it lapses within seven days of his assumption of office.[11] Malawi and Kenya, as has been noted, have abolished formal declarations of emergency, but an order of the President in Kenya bringing the Preservation of Public Security Act into operation still requires to be approved by the national assembly within twenty-eight days; when it has been so approved, it continues in force indefinitely until revoked by either the President or the national assembly; it lapses within seven days of a new President taking office.[12] In Malawi it is entirely at the discretion of the minister when to terminate the operation of the Preservation of Public Security Act after it has been brought into operation by gazette notice.

The preventive detention laws of Ghana, Tanzania and Uganda are independent of any emergency declaration or gazette notice. In Uganda, a detention or restriction in pursuance of a declaration of emergency may, on the termination of the emergency, be continued under the Preventive Detention Act if the President is satisfied that it is necessary in the interests of public security. The duration of a detention or restriction under both the Tanzanian and Ugandan Acts is entirely at the discretion of the President. Under the Ghanaian Act, the maximum permitted period was five years renewable for further five-year periods. The original Act of 1958 did not authorise renewal after the initial five years except on grounds of activities carried on since the order of detention, though if a person against whom an order had been made tried to evade its execution, he might be detained for ten years. The power of successive renewals was conferred by an amendment of 1962.

Perhaps the most critical feature of the power of detention and restriction is that it permits little scope for challenge in the court. It is necessary at the outset to distinguish between the legality of the order of detention and the question whether the actual detention complies with the requirements of the law. On the first question, the authority to issue a detention order is in all cases, both under the emergency legislation and under the preventive detention laws, an absolutely discretionary one, requiring only that the President or other detaining authority should be satisfied in a subjective sense about the necessity for the order. Neither the reasonableness of the President's satisfaction nor the truth of the facts providing the grounds for the order can therefore be enquired into by the court, for otherwise the court might be substituting its own subjective satisfaction for that of the President.[13] The detaining authory must, however, have acted in good faith.[14] This requires, first, that he must apply his mind to the necessity alleged for the detention. In other words, he must actually have been 'satisfied'; thus, where the detaining authority (the Governor of Northern Rhodesia) delegated the *power* to make a detention order but not the *duty* to be satisfied, and the delegate made detention orders against fifty-four persons, the orders were held unlawful without proof that the Governor had himself been satisfied about the necessity for the detentions.[15] (The decision was overruled on the ground that the duty to be satisfied is ancillary to, and inextricably interwoven with, the power to detain, so that the delegation of the one necessarily included the other; the satisfaction of the delegate was therefore sufficient without the personal satisfaction of the governor himself.[16]) Secondly, there must be some basis of fact giving rise to the necessity. Necessity presupposes a certain state of fact or conduct; it cannot arise out of the blue, as it were; the facts need not be sufficient nor need the conclusion based upon them be reasonable, yet there must be some facts on which the necessity is predicated. The absence of a factual basis for detention is a clear evidence of bad faith. However the facts needed to support a detention need not amount to an offence or to dangerous conduct, for, as the Ghana Supreme Court explained, the object of such detention is 'to prevent the commission of acts which may endanger public order and the security of the State'.[17] Thus, detention may be ordered as much on actual conduct dangerous to public security as in order to prevent such conduct. It is not for the detaining authority to prove that he acted in good faith, as the court will presume good faith on the part of high officers of state in the discharge of their duties.[18] The onus is on persons alleging bad faith to prove it. Both the Tanzanian and Ugandan Preventive Detention Acts provide that no order made thereunder shall be questioned in any court;[19] thus the possibility of challenge on grounds of bad faith is ruled out.

(i) *Safeguards available to a Detained or Restricted Person*

Wide as is the power of detention or restriction, a detained or restricted person is not without some safeguards. The conditions for a lawful detention or restriction are indeed spelled out in all the bills of rights, except in Sierra Leone. A person detained '*shall*, as soon as reasonably practicable and in any case not more that five days after the commencement of his detention, be furnished with a statement in writing in a language that he understands specifying in detail the grounds upon which he is detained'. Within fourteen days of it, the detention must be published in the gazette with particulars of the provision of law authorising it. These conditions have disappeared in the 1966 Malawian Republican Constitution, which guarantees no rights, but they remain in the others (Uganda, Kenya, Zambia,[20] Botswana and Gambia), except that the time for furnishing grounds and for publication in the gazette has been extended from five and fourteen days respectively to two months and twenty-eight days respectively in Uganda (1967), fourteen days and one month in Zambia (1969), seven days (the time for the gazette notification remains at fourteen days) in Gambia. Both Ghana's and Tanzania's Preventive Detention Acts provide that within five days (fifteen days in Tanzania) of detention, a detainee shall be informed of the grounds for his detention; the 1967 Uganda Constitution also requires grounds to be furnished within twenty-eight days to a detainee under Uganda's preventive detention law. No publication in the gazette is, however, required for the purposes of the Act in all three countries. The Malawian Preservation of Public Security Act requires neither the furnishing of grounds nor publication in the gazette.

These requirements are mandatory, and non-compliance or compliance even one day late, is not a mere procedural defect which can be cured by appropriate remedy, but one that renders the detention unlawful[21] and the state liable to pay compensation[22] from the expiration of the time prescribed. The detainee is then entitled to be discharged forthwith, subject to the right of the state to make a fresh detention order. It is perhaps necessary to emphasise that the detention order is not made unlawful and void from the beginning; only further detention under it becomes unlawful. It might have been thought that publication in the gazette is only directory, and so remediable in case of non-compliance by, say, *mandamus*. But it has been held to be as necessary for the protection of the individual's right of personal liberty as the furnishing of grounds. Failure to comply with one or the other would detract from the ability of a detainee to secure his release, and, in particular, publication in the gazette would guarantee against the possibility, remote though it might be, of a person being whisked away in secret and held incommunicado for an indefinite period. If this were possible, and the state could, after any period of time, such as when news of the detention may have leaked out, remedy the matter by a tardy publication before action is instituted, then publication would have ceased to be a useful safeguard.[23]

The requirement that the grounds must be furnished in detail raises some difficulty as to the exact nature of the detail that must be furnished. It has been suggested on one view that the grounds must be at least as particularised as they would have to be in a pleading in an ordinary action,[24] and, on another, that grounds, however detailed, are merely conclusions drawn from facts and not a detailed specification of those facts;[25] 'grounds are simply reasons. . . . While some factual basis for those reasons must be shown . . . the detaining authority is [not] under the same obligations as a civil litigant'.[26] On this latter view, the reference to 'detail' in the constitutional provisions merely requires that the grounds must be more than a general ground which merely states, for example, that the detention is necessary for the purpose of preserving public security or that the detained person's activities had been prejudicial to the security of the state.

A useful test that has been suggested is that, as the furnishing of grounds is to enable the person detained to make representation, the detail required must be such as would be adequate to enable him, in making representation, to answer the allegations on which the detention was based, with a view to persuading the detaining authority to release him.[27] What is clear is that if the grounds furnished lack the sort of detail envisaged by the constitution, however that may be defined, the detention becomes unlawful from that time; in other words, insufficiency of detail, like failure to furnish grounds at all, is not a mere matter of procedure; each has the same effect of invalidating further detention.[28] If several grounds are given, and one or more of them fail to give the necessary detail, the fact that the others are sufficiently detailed to support the detention might not save the detention from invalidity.[29] If, however, the grounds all give the necessary detail, then mere vagueness does not invalidate the detention.[30] The right to make representation to the detaining authority or to a review tribunal or to both is usually expressly conferred, but even without an express grant a detained person can always make a representation to the detaining authority.

The opportunities for the making of representation are an important condition for a lawful detention under the bills of rights. As has just been stated, a detainee has an inherent right to make representation to the detaining authority. The bills of rights in the independence constitutions invariably provided for a review tribunal, and for a right of automatic review by the tribunal within one month of detention and thereafter at six-monthly intervals (three-monthly in Kenya). In Sierra Leone only review on request by the detainee was guaranteed. The tribunal was required to be an independent and impartial one established by law and presided over by a person (a lawyer in some countries) appointed by the Chief Justice. The detainee was entitled to the services of a lawyer of his own choice (at his own expense) both for the purpose of making representation and also at the hearing of his case by the tribunal, and he must be afforded reasonable facilities to consult with the lawyer. The choice of a lawyer is, of course, restricted to lawyers who are properly qualified, have a right of audience before the courts and, in the case of non-citizens, have been permitted by the authorities to enter or to remain in the country under the relevant immigration law.[31] The role of the tribunal was merely to make recommendations to the detaining authority concerning the necessity or expediency of continuing the detention, but the latter was not bound to act in accordance with the recommendation.

The right of automatic review still remains in the Republican Constitutions of Kenya, Uganda, Botswana and Gambia, although in Uganda the time for the first review was extended from one month to three, and in Kenya the chairman of the review tribunal is now to be appointed by the President, and not by the Chief Justice. Zambia, by a constitutional amendment in 1969, abolished automatic review, substituting a review on request, and extended the time for the first such review to one year, with yearly intervals thereafter.[32] When the Constitution was amended in 1969, there was no corresponding amendment to the regulations under the Preservation of Public Security Act, which continued to speak of automatic review within one month and thereafter at six-monthly intervals. The question thus arose whether the two provisions were cumulative: i.e. was the 1969 amendment to be regarded as setting out only the minimum rights to which the subject was entitled, and which could be supplemented by other legislation, without any risk of a conflict with the constitution? Rejecting this view, the Court of Appeal for Zambia held that the 1969 amendment was not merely setting out general limits of permissible derogation but did in fact prescribe the limits of a detainee's rights.[33]

In the case of a restricted person, review on request within six months of restriction and at six-monthly intervals thereafter (three months in both cases in Kenya and Gambia) was guaranteed by all the bills of rights at independence, and has remained so under the republican bills of rights. The 1969 amendment in Zambia assimilated detention and restriction for this purpose, so that the one year prescribed for detention now applies also to restriction; also a restricted person in Zambia has now all the rights, which a detained person has, to be furnished with grounds, to have his restriction published in the gazette, and to have the services of a lawyer – rights which are not available to him in any of the other countries, as they were not in Zambia before 1969.

What is the effect of a denial of these rights? Are the provisions guaranteeing them mandatory like those relating to the furnishing of grounds and publication in the gazette, with the consequence that denial of them, e.g., failure or refusal to carry out a review, also invalidates the detention or restriction? Both sets of provisions use the word 'shall', and unquestionably confer constitutional rights; moreover, they appear in the same section. This is, of course, not conclusive, since an apparently mandatory provision may be interpreted so as to have only a directory effect if the context so requires.[34] A more important consideration, however, is that all the safeguards have the same object in view, namely to enable the detained person to obtain his release. The furnishing of grounds is to enable him to make representation with a view to his release, and the purpose of a review is to enable the tribunal to make recommendation concerning the necessity or expediency of continuing the detention or restriction. Can the tribunal's recommendation be said to be less important for this purpose? *Prima facie* it can be said that the tribunal's recommendation would carry a much greater weight with the detaining authority than the detainee's representation. Although the detaining authority is not bound by the tribunal's recommendation, yet it would be reasonable to expect that the former would not lightly disregard a strong recommendation by the tribunal for the detainee's release. While the detainee's representation may be regarded with scepticism as being biased in his own interest, the report of an independent and impartial tribunal cannot but be treated with great consideration. And the services of a lawyer may enable the case of the detainee to be put more cogently and forcefully before the tribunal, and so persuade it to come to a decision favourable to the detainee. One is inclined to say, therefore, that all the safeguards are mandatory, and that violation of any one of them would make further detention unlawful.[35] It is of interest to note that in India under its Preventive Detention Act the report of an advisory board in favour of a detainee's release is binding and conclusive on the detaining authority.

Both Ghana's and Tanzania's preventive detention laws provide that a detained or restricted person shall be afforded opportunity to make representations in writing to the President. Tanzania's, but not Ghana's, law provides for review within twelve months of detention if no representation has been made, or, where a representation has been made, then as soon after the representation as may be, and thereafter at yearly intervals. The review is by an advisory committee of five, three of whom, including the chairman, are to be appointed by the President, the remaining two by the Chief Justice. The quorum is three – the chairman and one member each appointed by the President and Chief Justice. The committee is to be furnished with the grounds of detention, the detainee's representation, if any, and any other relevant information, and is to be afforded the opportunity of interviewing the detainee. It may advise that the detention be continued, rescinded or suspended, but the President is not bound by such advice. All this is subject to the provision that a detention or restriction order cannot be questioned in any court. Malawi provides for review within six months of detention or restriction, and thereafter at six-monthly intervals, but the order is reviewed by the detaining authority himself, and so is no safeguard at all.

In its report published in 1972, the one-party state commission in Zambia recommended the following safeguards:[36]

(i) that there be no detention without trial except during a state of emergency;

(ii) that a detainee or restrictee be furnished with a written statement specifying the grounds for his detention or restriction within ten days;

(iii) that the notification of detention or restriction be published in the Government Gazette within fourteen days of such detention or restriction;

(iv) that a tribunal be established to review the detention or restriction within three months and that its decision be binding on the authority;

(v) that the membership of the tribunal be a chairman and two other persons (one lawyer and one other person) to be appointed by the Chief Justice in consultation with the President;

(vi) that detainees be free to communicate with their lawyers and relatives and not be incommunicado;

(vii) that whenever a state of emergency is declared while parliament is not in session or after its dissolution, the national assembly be summoned within twenty-eight days of the date of proclamation for approval; and

(viii) that a declaration of a state of emergency ceases after a period of six months from the date of the proclamation unless the national assembly approves its continuation.

The government rejected the suggested safeguards, arguing that 'at this stage in the nation's development and in view of Zambia's geo-political position in Southern Africa these recommendations could not be implemented without detriment to Zambia's security and sovereignty'.[37] The present position is therefore to remain.

2. *Extent and Manner of Use*

The reality of power lies more in the manner and extent of its use rather than in its formal existence. A repressive law is in itself objectionable, even if it may not be used at all, but when it is used extensively and oppressively, then tyranny is created. As has already been shown, security laws in Africa are quite repressive of individual rights. It is, however, the rather extensive and oppressive use made of them that has given them a fearful reality. The record of the independent governments in the use of security powers is perhaps no better than that of their colonial predecessors; in some respects it is certainly worse. In the countries with which we are concerned there had, during the immediately preceding colonial period, been two emergencies in the Gold Coast (Ghana), two in Kenya, three in Northern Rhodesia (Zambia), one in Nyasaland (Malawi), one in Tanganyika, one in Zanzibar, and two in Uganda.[38]

Within five years of independence the Ghana government exceeded the colonial record. There had been five local emergencies between 1957 and 1962 – Accra (1957), Kumasi municipality (1957), Dormaa State (1958), Sekondi-Takoradi (1961), Accra and Tema (1962).[39] The measures that first attracted world attention were those taken under the Deportation Act of 1957. In August 1957 deportation orders were, on the grounds of national security, issued against the two leaders of the Muslim Community in Kumasi, the Zerikin Zongo, Alhaji Amadu Buba, and Alhaji Othman Larden, both of whom had been born and lived all their lives in Ghana. Neither they nor those with whom they lived ever thought of them as having any other nationality than Ghanaian. But while their claim that they were Ghanaian citizens was pending in the High Court, the government brought in a special bill, the Deportation (Othman Larden and Abadu Buba) Bill, which specifically authorised the deportation of the two men. The argument was that the threat of violence by supporters of the two deportees had made it impossible for the court proceedings to go on. The Minister of Justice, Mr Ofori Atta, invited the House to accept the judgment of the Government that the presence of these two men was prejudicial to the peace and security of Ghana. Yet as the leader of the opposition, Dr Kofi Busia, passionately pleaded, the question was not whether the Government should have the power to deport undesirable non-citizens, but whether it should be allowed to use that power to deprive a person of his right of access to the court to determine his citizenship. To the Minister of Justice, however, it was 'illogical to say that if the Government can always exercise their power in regard to persons not Ghana citizens the Government may never exercise the same powers in relation to citizens of Ghana'.[40]

This was a startling assertion, but more startling was the boast by the Minister for the Interior, Mr Krobo Edusei, that 'there is nothing in the country of Ghana that the Government cannot do, except to change a man into woman and a woman into man'.[41] The government M.P.s made no demur to these wild claims. The bill was rushed through all its stages in one day (August 23). Again no government M.P. spoke or voted against it, and any suggestion that the government was being arbitrary and dictatorial was cried down with shouts of 'nonsense'. The following day (August 24) the two Alhajis were deported to Nigeria. It seemed not to have mattered to the Ghanaian authorities what the fate of the two men would have been if Nigeria had refused to take them on the ground that they were not Nigerians. 'Presumably deportation would have involved them in travelling the high seas until death released them'.[42] In the event no such problem arose as Nigeria voluntarily accepted them.

Dr Busia had indeed touched upon what might be considered a more sinister aspect of the case. It is not just that the government had interfered with the process of the courts; it had impinged upon the normal protection afforded by the courts against deprivation of right without trial. Deportation in this case was a double penalty; it deprived the individuals concerned of both their freedom of residence and the right to have their claim to Ghanaian citizenship determined by the courts. The special deportation act was thus clearly an *ad hominem* law, and objectionable as such.[43] This is what makes such laws a danger to liberty. If one may recall the familiar dictum of Montesquieu, 'there is no liberty yet, if the power to judge is not separated from the legislative and executive power'. The U.S. Supreme Court re-echoed this view when it held unconstitutional and void a statute which permanently debarred certain *named* persons from employment in the government: 'When our Constitution and Bill of Rights were written, our ancestors had ample reason to know that legislative trials and punishments were too dangerous to liberty to exist in the nation of free men they envisioned.'[44]

Further deprecatory use of the power of deportation was still to come. On 20 December, 1958, the Government deported four men when, to the knowledge of the Minister for the Interior, Mr Krobo Edusei, and the Commissioner of Police, Mr Maditey, a *habeas corpus* proceeding filed by the deportees was already before the court. For this action, the Minister and the police chief were on 23 December committed for contempt of court, though a stay of execution was ordered until the following morning. On December 24, parliament was suddenly recalled from its Christmas recess to approve a special bill, the Deportation (Indemnity) Bill, to indemnify the culprits. Parliament was asked to pass the bill because, as the new Minister for the Interior, Mr Kofi Baako, put it, 'it is obviously most undesirable that the man who heads the country's police force and on whom the government of the country relies for peace and order should be questioned by anybody in this country for carrying out lawful instructions from a lawful minister as directed by a lawful cabinet. ... If we allow this thing to happen, in fact, what we shall be saying is that the whole cabinet has committed a contempt of court'.[45] The bill passed through all its stages in just twenty-five minutes to find its way into the statute book. A total of sixty-two persons were deported in 1957, 161 in 1958 and seventy-seven in 1959.

The Preventive Detention Act was passed in August 1958, and in

November the first wave of detentions under it took place; forty persons alleged to be the organisers of violence and terrorism were involved. From terrorists, it was next the plotters of coups, then the top leadership of the opposition party and finally the members and ministers of the ruling party. In August 1962, for example, the Minister of Information and Broadcasting Mr Tawia Adamafio, the Minister of Foreign Affairs Mr Ako Adjei, and the General Secretary of the C.P.P. Mr H. H. Cofie-Crabbe, were detained for their alleged involvement in the attempt on Nkrumah's life at Kulungugu while he was returning from a state visit to Upper Volta. The Minister of Finance, Mr Gbedemah, narrowly escaped detention by fleeing the country. It has been estimated that from August 1958, when the P.D.A. came into force, over 1,000 Ghanaians were detained under it for periods ranging up to ten years in conditions of severity worse than those laid down by law and accorded to convict prisoners.[46] This was of course exclusive of the large numbers detained by the police on a short-term basis under the 1962 amendment to the Criminal Procedure Code.

The first three years of independence in Uganda (October 1962 to February 1966) might be described as a golden era of liberalism in the country. There were no emergencies and no preventive detentions. But the curtain was brought down on that period on February 22, 1966, when, following the defeat of the government on a critical motion in the national assembly the Prime Minister, Milton Obote, suspended the Constitution. On the same day five ministers were arrested with a view to their deportation under the colonial Deportation Ordinance. They were still held in detention on March 14 without an order of deportation having been made. Their detention was subsequently (July 14) declared unlawful by the Court of Appeal for East Africa on the ground that the Deportation Ordinance was *ultra vires* the Constitution and void.[47] The case was accordingly remitted to the High Court with a direction that it should order the release of the detainees. The High Court at Entebbe ordered accordingly on July 15, but without ordering that the bodies of the detainees be first produced before the court, as the court practice required.

It is necessary at this point to refer to an intervening event which materially affected the subsequent development of the case. On May 23 the government declared a state of emergency over the whole of Buganda (Entebbe is within its territory), and issued emergency regulations which applied to Entebbe as to other parts of Buganda. Before the High Court order was given, the detained ministers were held in various places of detention outside Buganda, but they were flown to Entebbe on the same day. It appeared that three of them were already in Entebbe at the time of the court order, but the remaining two did not arrive there until well on in the afternoon, having been delayed on the way by bad weather which prevented the plane carrying them from taking off after a stop-over. Brought together at Entebbe airport that afternoon, they were informed of the court order and asked to go, but only to be re-arrested outside the airport building under a detention order made pursuant to the Emergency Powers (Detention) Regulations, 1966, then in force in Buganda.

Was the second arrest and detention a *bona fide* exercise of the government's emergency powers? The detainees argued that the government had acted in bad faith in bringing them against their will within the emergency area, instead of releasing them at their various places of detention as the order of the High Court in terms directed. In the view of the court, however, it was proper that the government should take all necessary action to produce the bodies of the detainees before the court in anticipation of what should have been the proper order of the court; bad faith was therefore negatived, and would not indeed have arisen had it not been that the aeroplane carrying two of the detainees had been delayed on the way by bad weather.[48] The facts would seem to support the court's conclusion. It was only the detainees' misfortune that the court happened to have been in an area where they would be reached by the government's emergency power.

But the arrest and detention was attacked on another, more subtle ground. It was argued that, the initial detention being unlawful, the act of bringing the detainees to Entebbe was similarly unlawful, and no lawful exercise of the emergency power of detention could be based on it; it was as if they had been kidnapped into Buganda for the purpose of enabling the emergency power of detention to be exercised over them. Rejecting this second argument, the court held that, while it was true that the initial detention was unlawful, that unlawful detention was not initiated in order to create a right of further detention, nor was their being brought into Buganda meant primarily for that purpose, but rather for the purpose of complying with what was properly assumed would be an order of the court.

The detention of a certain Matovu followed a similar method. He was first arrested and detained under the Deportation Act outside Buganda, was later (but before the declaration of emergency) transferred to Buganda, then released and immediately re-arrested and detained under the emergency regulations.[49]

Altogether eight ministers – G. S. Ibingira, B. K. Kirya, M. M. Ngobi, E. S. Lumu, C. B. K. Magezi, L. Sebanakita, M. Matovu and J. Lutaya — were 'deported' at the time, and a special act, the Deportation (Validation) Act, 1966, was passed to regularise the government's action. The act indemnifies and exonerates the government or minister, or any person acting on the authority of the government or minister, from any liability for damages, costs or otherwise for the detention of the eight ministers.

The emergency declared in Buganda was extended throughout the country in 1969,[50] and remained in force until March 1971 when it was revoked by the military which had ousted the government of Milton Obote earlier in the year.[51] During the period of the emergency all political organisations other than the ruling party – the Democratic Party, Uganda National Union, Uganda Farmers Voice, Uganda Conservative Party, Uganda National Socialist Party and Uganda Vietnam Socialist Party – were proscribed under the Penal Code Act[52] as being dangerous to peace and order.[53] The leader of the Democratic Party (the main opposition party) was detained. The exact number of detainees is not known, but considering the widespread disaffection among the Baganda against Obote's government, the detainees are likely to have numbered several hundreds. Among them were seventy-eight non-Ugandan citizens (twenty-six Gambian, fourteen Mali, eleven Mauritanian, eight Senegalese, six Sierra Leonian, four Nigerian, four Congolese, one Liberian, one Guinean, one Burundi and one Ivorian) detained on allegation of smuggling. Although these persons were arrested on June 16, 1969, not until July 4, 1969, was an order of detention under the emergency regulations made and served upon them.[54] Apart from the detentions and the proscription of opposition political parties, the powers assumed by the government for the purpose of dealing with what is regarded as a rebellion by Buganda were quite plenary. These emergency measures reached their climax in the bombardment of the Kabaka's palace on Mengo Hill, which was defended by the palace guards armed with mounted guns and other types of weapons. The palace was taken after severe fighting. The Kabaka escaped by climbing over the palace wall and eventually made his way to Britain. It may be recalled that in 1967 the government took additional powers under the preventive detention act of that year, but in view of the extension of the emergency throughout the country the power of detention and restriction under the Act was never used.

The year 1966 was a bad one for liberalism not only in Uganda but also in Kenya. In July that year, hardly a month after both the Constitution and the Preservation of Public Security Act had been amended to enable the President, without prior parliamentary approval, to bring the Act into operation whenever he thought fit, regardless of whether the situation was grave or not, the Act was brought into operation. The President issued regulations authorising the detention and restriction of persons,[55] and then proceeded to detain eight leaders of the newly-formed opposition Kenya Peoples Union (KPU). With five more detentions the total reached thirteen in March 1968, although five had been released up to that date.[56] The opposition party leader, Mr Oginga Odinga, was spared for a time, but eventually in 1969 he too was detained (he was released only in 1971) and the party was banned.

In Zambia the Preservation of Public Security Act was brought into operation on July 27, 1964, just on the eve of independence, and has continued ever since. The purpose of its being brought into operation was to deal with the menace of the Lumpa Church led by the prophetess Alice Lenshina. The sect had launched a regime of violence and arson in the Chinsali district. Pursuant to regulations made under the Act, the government banned meetings and assemblies within the affected area; movement generally was controlled and a curfew was imposed. The whole of the Northern Province and the Lundazi district were declared 'prescribed areas', which made them amenable to the special power of the police to prohibit meetings and processions. The power to detain or restrict people was exercised with great moderation, and on the whole only about five persons (the prophetess Lenshina, her husband, who was a deacon of the church, and other relatives) were detained. Lenshina is still in restriction, having refused to renounce her faith in the church, which was a condition for her release. The church itself was banned.

The proclamation of July 27 bringing the Act into operation was continued in force until April 24, 1965, by the Independence Order-in-Council,[57] which provided that the proclamation should be deemed a declaration by the President duly approved by the national assembly in terms of the Constitution. The relevant provision of the Constitution, as may be recalled, empowers the President to declare that 'a situation exists which, if it is allowed to continue, may lead to a state of public emergency';[58] upon such a declaration he could then issue regulations under the Preservation of Public Security Act to deal with the situation. The declaration had then to be approved by the national assembly within five days, and might be continued in force for sucessive periods of six months by the assembly. This procedure was used to extend the declaration of July 27 from April 24, 1965, until 1969 when the Constitution (Amendment) (No. 5) Act of that year made it unnecessary. For by this amendment a declaration continues in force until revoked by either the President or the national assembly. The declaration has remained in force until the present. This means that the whole of Zambia has, since July 27, 1964, been subject to the emergency regulations made by the President, and indeed the whole country has been declared a prescribed area. Since 1968 the detention and restriction power under the regulations has been extensively used, often against political opponents for political reasons. Between March 16, 1971, and February 1972 alone, about 338 persons had been detained, and about fiften restricted.[59] In 1968 and 1972 respectively two opposition parties formed by splinter groups from the ruling United National Independence Party (UNIP) – Mundia's United Party (UP) and Simon Kapwepwe's United Progressive Party (UPP) – had been banned in the interest of public security, not of course under the emergency regulations but under the Societies Act.[60]

It is fair to say that, apart from the detentions and restrictions, the other powers of the President under the regulations have not been much used. Of course public processions are controlled and – in the case of students' processions – banned, but such is the air of normality that prevails that it is generally not realised that the country has been living under a state of semi-emergency for more than eight years. The crisis in the University in July 1971 served to bring home to that section of the community the reality of the President's emergency powers. The University was closed down for one month, the students were sent away, and ten of their leaders were expelled – all this being done over the heads of the University authorities, apparently by virtue of the President's emergency powers.

The power to deport non-citizens of Zambia in the interests *inter alia* of public security has also been extensively used, sometimes with hardly any regard to humanity or even in clear disregard of the law. The deportation in November of one Paton, a resident farmer of fifteen years' standing, is a case in point. He was given only twenty-four hours notice, expiring on a Sunday. It turned out later that his deportation had been unlawful, as he was not a person liable to be declared a prohibited immigrant. He then returned to the country on the advice of his lawyer, but was picked up at the airport by the immigration authorities, and, without even the opportunity of a telephone conversation with his lawyer, was driven to the border and told to walk across the bridge to Southern Rhodesia. The evidence showed that the immigration authorites knew at the time that Paton was not a prohibited immigrant and could not be deported, because they were aware of a law that had been introduced, but not yet passed, in the legislature to enable him to be deported. Their action had thus been castigated by the court as a 'flagrant and disgraceful disregard of the law and of common decency' and as 'clearly oppressive and arbitrary'.[61]

Quite ample use has been made of Tanzania's Preventive Detention Act. Its main victims have been trade unionists. For example, the former leader of the Railway Union, and founder of the People's Democratic Party, Mr Tumbo, had to flee the country in 1962 out of fear that he might be detained under the Act. He established his base in Mombasa, Kenya. Tumbo's fears soon proved real, for towards the end of the year (1962) the Act was executed on the president of the Tanganyika Federation of Labour/General-Secretary of the Plantation Workers Union, Victor Mkello, and that union's organising secretary. In 1964, after the army mutiny, over 500 people were arrested and detained under the Act; it was estimated that more than half of these, including Mkello, were trade unionists. Tumbo himself, having been taken to the border by the Kenyan police and handed over to the Tanzanian police, was also detained.

It must be said for the use made of the power of preventive detention in Tanzania, that the detentions have usually been for short periods. This is an aspect of security measures in Tanzania that contrasts sharply with the excessively long periods of detention in Ghana. Although the 1965 amnesty revealed that, of those detained between 1962 and 1964 thirty-six, including Mkello and Tumbo, were still in detention and remained in detention until September 1966 when they were finally released, leaving only military personnel, yet the normal period of detention had not been more than a couple of months. There have of course been further detentions since 1966, notably the detention of the leaders of the coups inspired by Oscar Kambona in 1967 and 1969, the four Patel brothers for corrupt practices in 1969, and the thirty-nine persons arrested in November 1969, also for corrupt practices.

Malawi has achieved notoriety in this matter. Brought into operation soon after independence in 1964, the Preservation of Public Security Act, together with the regulations made under it in 1965, is still in operation. Statistics of those detained or restricted are not available, but the number must be considerable. Deportation of non-citizens has been frequent and often arbitrary, depending sometimes on nothing more than the whim or fancy of President Kamuzu Banda. The five ministers who dared challenge the President's power in 1964 were hounded out of the country and are still in exile today.

3. *Justification*

It is tempting to condemn out of hand the independent African governments for their extensive and oppressive use of security powers. But it might be that the situations with which they had to deal have been graver and more dangerous than those which faced the colonial governments. No one, of course, including the leaders themselves, questions that these measures, particularly that of detention without trial, are extremely dangerous to freedom and the rule of law. 'It means [in the rather telling words of President Nyerere, speaking of detention without trial] that you are imprisoning a man when he has not broken any written law, when you cannot be sure of proving beyond reasonable doubt that he has done so. You are restricting his liberty, and making him suffer materially and spiritually, for what you think he intends to do, or is trying to do, or for what you believe he has done. Few things are more dangerous to the freedom of a society than that. For freedom is indivisible, and with such an opportunity open to the Government of the day, the freedom of every citizen is reduced. To suspend the Rule of Law under any circumstances is to leave open the possibility of the grossest injustices being perpetrated.'[62] In somewhat oratorical style, an editorial in the Kenya *Daily Nation* had said: 'A Preventive Detention Act, by its very nature, degenerates into a sordid instrument of tyranny. It destroys the judiciary. It destroys the freedom of the press and academic freedom. It turns citizens into spies for the administration — it destroys their morals; and it might be used by some citizens to blackmail others. It corrupts the morals of the whole nation.'[63] Preventive detention, it is said, has a tendency to spread discontent. 'To detain one man meant to detain six, because his friends and family would become discontented.'[64]

Yet it is argued that the peculiar exigencies of a new state with the inherent insecurity arising from tribal or racial divisions, from the newness of the state and the immaturity and divisive politics of its leaders, and from the tensions of rapid change, justify these extraordinary measures. Freedom, the argument asserts, 'cannot exist, nor can the courts function, under a threat of violence and lawlessness or in a situation in which civil strife or war is threatened. In order to preserve the due process of law, it may on occasion be unfortunately necessary to take special powers'. That was Kwame Nkrumah, as Prime Minister, introducing the Preventive Detention Bill in the Ghana National Assembly on July 14, 1957.[65] It becomes necessary therefore to enquire into the exact incidence of this threat of violence, lawlessness, civil strife or war, and whether it was really such as to justify the extent and severity of the measures taken.

Ghana seemed to have had the worst of this experience. There the impending withdrawal of the British unleashed a recrudescence of old tribal jealousies and divisions, now aggravated by those of the politics of a modern state. The Ewe of Togoland, backed by the Togoland Congress, threatened to secede from Ghana into a great Republic of Togo; the Ga, the owners of the land of the capital, again backed by an organised modern political party, the Ga Shifimo Kpee, organised activities aimed at driving out of Accra all those who were not of Ga origin. The opposition parties in other parts of the country quickly allied themselves with these aspirations and activities, and gave them encouragement, thus assuming a posture that was both tribal and regionalist as well as unco-operative and destructive. They deliberately provoked an all-out struggle with the government party, using as its weapon organised violence, conspiracy, defiance of the law and non-cooperation: they refused to participate in discussions of proposals for an independence constitution, or to confer with the constitutional adviser, Sir Frederick Bourne, sponsored to Ghana by the British Government; they boycotted the All-Party Achimota Conference on the constitution, national assembly meetings, and the regional assembly elections. It is thus not without some truth that the government charged them of being 'violent, waspish and malignant'.

Independent Ghana truly simmered with unrest, and attempted coups, strikes and attempts on the life of the Prime Minister (later

President) Nkrumah were the order of the day. The actions of the government must therefore be viewed in the context of an all-out contest with its opponents, in which no holds were barred on either side. The government side in this contest was pushed to harness all the powers of the modern state in order to counter those of the opposition and of the traditional authorities, whch were put at the disposal of the opposition parties in the disaffected areas, particularly Ashanti and the State of Akin Abuakwa.[66]

Yet, provocative and dangerous as the situation was, it seems that the government overstepped the bounds of reason in its determination to answer force with force. In this, it sacrificed completely the wider interests of the community and abandoned its obligation to act with a statesmanlike spirit of tolerance and self-restraint; instead, it succumbed to the promptings of vindictiveness, and acted in an arbitrary and authoritarian way. As is usual with unrestrained power, it became difficult, once the battle was joined, to maintain a clear line between friend and foe, as the net of detention was spread out ever wider and wider. Even in the circumstances then prevailing in Ghana, there could be no justification for detaining a person for more than ten years without any opportunity of a review by an independent and impartial tribunal. Nor was the government justified in abandoning faith in the ordinary process of the criminal law, in preference for arbitrary detention without trial. The fact that many of the prosecutions instituted by the government against suspected terrorists and plotters of treason, assassination and coups failed was no justification. The procedural safeguards of the common law method of criminal justice — such as the rule against self-incrimination, the presumption of in-nocence and the requirement that the prosecution must prove its case beyond reasonable doubt — may well be said, in Ghana's peculiar circumstances, and given the inadequacy of the security forces to cope with the task of investigation and proof, to have been unduly solicitous for the protection of the freedom of the individual accused of a crime. If so, a relaxation of these safeguards in cases involving the security of the state might have been more tolerable than arbitrary detentions without any kind of judicial process.

The stringent security measures instituted in Uganda from 1966 were also in response to alleged attempts to change the government by violence and other unconstitutional means or to break up the state itself. But it was the action of Prime Minister Milton Obote himself that provoked these attempts. Whatever its motivation, the vote passed against him in the national assembly on February 4, 1966, was perfectly constitutional, and he should have complied with its terms by appointing a commission to enquire into the matter raised. Instead he chose to suspend the Constitution, taking over the executive authority of the country and forcibly ejecting the President, Sir Edward Mutesa, from State House – all this allegedly in the 'interest of national stability and public security and tranquillity', and in furtherance of 'the wishes of the people of this country for peace, order and prosperity'.[67] The specific threat to public security was, according to the Prime Minister, that, while he was away on a tour of the Northern Region, an attempt was made to overthrow the government by the use of foreign troops, and that certain members of the government had requested a foreign mission for military assistance in arms and troops to be used in invading the country and overthrowing the government.[68] A month after he had seized the government, the Prime Minister on April 13 promulgated a new Constitution through the national assembly, which not only confirmed him as President with executive powers, in place of the deposed Sir Edward Mutesa, who was also the King (Kabaka) of Buganda, but also abolished the special federal relations of that kingdom to the rest of the country, and the right of its legislature, the Lukiko, to act as an electoral college for the election of Buganda's representatives in the national assembly.

These 'drastic measures' touched the most sensitive area of the Buganda polity. Much as one might disapprove of the scheme of the Independence Constitution, was it really expected that Buganda should take lying down this unilateral and violent abrogation of an arrangement which had taken the best efforts of all concerned to arrive at? The expected reply from Buganda came in an equally provacative form. On May 20, the Lukiko adopted a resolution demanding that the Ugandan Government quit Bugandan soil immediately. (Both Kampala, the capital, and Entebbe are on Bugandan soil.) Obote and his new revolutionary government construed this as tantamount to a declaration of secession, and accordingly on May 23 declared a state of emergency over Buganda. In a statement to the national assembly on his action, he repeated the allegations he had made on February 24 soon after seizing the government.[69] Specifically he accused Sir Edward Mutesa of organising action to further Buganda's rebellion by soliciting, by letter and through personal emissaries, the support of foreign countries for Buganda as a separate, sovereign state, by addressing a letter to the Secretary-General of the United Nations, and by organising violence against central government officers in Buganda which resulted in the killing of eight policemen in the course of their duty in the preservation of law and order and of two Europeans employed by the government – the killing of the two Europeans being, he alleged, intended to provide an excuse for foreign governments to intervene to protect their own nationals on the ground that the Ugandan government had lost the capacity to provide such protection. He further claimed that the preparations for the rebellion had been going on for a long time before 1966 and were only intensified after the failure of the attempt to unseat him through the motion in the national assembly in February.

It might be argued that, a situation of emergency having arisen, it was no longer immediately important who was to blame for it, and that what mattered first and foremost was a vigorous action to deal with it. But that necessity existed only within Buganda and not outside it. It is thus difficult to see what the justification was for extending the emergency throughout the country, and for continuing it in operation three years after the trouble was supposed to have been over.

The Lumpa Church affair in Zambia created a truly grave situation, one indeed that challenged the power of the government. For the Lumpas were not only an 'anti-social' group, who preferred a segregationist life in a separate community of their own in open antagonism with the communities around them, but they were also 'anti-society' and anti-government. Violent killing and arson were to them a legitimate weapon against those who were not of their persuasion. And so they went burning the houses of the neighbouring villagers together with their inmates. Unwilling to accept the authority of the government, they began training themselves in anticipation of a confrontation with the government.[70] When the confrontation came, they proved defiant and uncompromising, involving the nation in the loss of about 650 lives. Surely no government could tolerate the activities of such a group within its territory. No doubt a lot of provocation was offered to the Lumpas by the UNIP, but thereafter they spurned all opportunities for reconciliation. The situation therefore justified the measures taken.

If the proclamation of July 27, 1964, was justified by the situation then existing, its continuation up to the time before the present border crisis was a completely different proposition. Certainly, by April 1965 the Lumpa menace had effectively been brought under control, and could no longer justify the extension of the proclamation. The government considered, however, that an independent Zambia faces a continuing threat from the white minority regimes in the south — Rhodesia, Angola, Mozambique and Namibia, with all of whom Zambia has common boundaries. In November 1965 the threat from Rhodesia took a concrete form when Rhodesia unilaterally proclaimed itself independent, and then threatened to cut off Zambia's main source of electricity supply at Kariba, to hold up supplies of petroleum and other vital commodities passing through its territory to Zambia, and to disrupt lines of communication, particularly the railway. Rhodesian troops were reported to be massing along the border with Zambia, and there was evidence of other warlike preparations.[71] Perhaps in these circumstances there was necessity for maximum security precautions in

Zambia, which justified the extension of the proclamation. But once U.D.I. in Rhodesia was several years old, could it really be said that Zambia was still in any *real and immediate* danger of invasion or of economic strangulation from the Rhodesian regime, such as to justify the continued application of the emergency powers? Of course the border crisis which began early in 1973 completely altered the situation to one of an emergency, with all the disruption to supplies caused by the border closure, and with Rhodesian-planted land mines exploding continually at the border and killing numerous innocent people. There is in this situation ample justification for the use of emergency powers; but it cannot be said that the possibility of this kind of situation arising also justified the use of those powers between 1967 and 1972. Whatever threat might be said to have faced Zambia from Rhodesia during that period can hardly constitute a grave situation of semi-emergency.

Assuming that the somewhat distant threat existing between 1967 and 1972 justified the continued application of the emergency powers, another question arises: does it justify the detention of opposition politicians and the banning of their parties for reasons seemingly unconnected with the Rhodesian threat? To put the question differently supposing there had been no U.D.I. in Rhodesia, would the split in the ruling United National Independence Party in 1968 and 1971 and the clashes that followed in its wake have been sufficient for continuing the proclamation in force? Could the situation thus created by the split be described as 'so grave', within the meaning of the Preservation of Public Security Act, as to enable the President to take on powers of detention under the Act? It might, of course, be said that the justification lies in the fact that, in the face of the threat from the south, distant though it may have become, Zambia cannot afford internal disharmony, that violent clashes between members of the parent and splinter parties would undermine the ability of the country to maintain the vigilance called for by that threat. One is left, nonetheless, with a strong feeling that the detentions of opposition politicians were motivated by political considerations and had little to do with state security. In one of the cases the detention was challenged on this ground, but this was rejected on the ground that at that time the leader of the new splinter party, Simon Kapwepwe, had not been detained, and that among the detainees were also some UNIP partisans.[72] However, Kapwepwe had since been detained. There is a parallel here with Kenya where the leader of the splinter party, Oginga Odinga, was also allowed to be at liberty for a long time while his subordinates were in detention.

It might provide some insight into the motivation for the detentions to examine the grounds stated for them in order to see what connection there was between them and the threat from the south. Although the stated grounds varied from case to case, those in respect of Simon Kapwepwe and Elias Mwamba Kaenga might be taken as fairly representative.[73] The grounds for Kapwepwe's detention were that during the months of December 1971, January and February 1972 he and other members of the UPP conspired to engage in activities to endanger the safety of persons and property, in consequence of which eighteen named persons were assaulted and threatened with death and the property of twenty-three named persons was damaged; also, that during those months he likewise conspired to be defiant of and disobedient to the law and lawful authority and to publish, by word of mouth and by way of circulars, statements defamatory and contemptuous of the Head of State and Government. Kaenga was alleged to have conspired between August 1970 and September 1971 with others to publish circulars which were subversive, and which among other things claimed that duly elected members of the Government including His Excellency the President were not Zambian nationals; secondly, that during the same period he had been actively engaged in organising the UPP in a manner designed to create tribal conflict; and thirdly, that he had conspired and assisted others, or that his activities in furthering the aims of the UPP, knowingly or unknowingly, had assisted in obtaining from governments hostile to Zambia materials including firearms and the training of Zambian nationals with the intention to dislodge by unlawful means the legally constituted government. It is thus only the last ground in respect of Kaenga's detention that might possibly connect him or the UPP with the white minority regimes in the south. The charge of bringing arms into the country from hostile governments had previously been made orally against Kapwepwe by the President, who promised, on Kapwepwe's protestation of innocence, to produce proof. This proof had not so far been forthcoming.

More serious allegations were published, under the heading 'UPP "Army" Trained in Angola, Defector reveals' in the *Times of Zambia* for November 11, 1971. It was there reported that 'revelations of alleged subversive activities against the Government were made in Luanshya yesterday by a former UPP organiser who has defected to UNIP. He is Mr Mukango Liyoka, 23, ex-acting Copperbelt UPP provincial president, and a former University of Zambia law student. Mr Liyoka told Luanshya district governor, Jonathan Ntambo, that UPP leader Mr Simon Kapwepwe had sent between 200 and 300 Zambians to Angola for training in guerrilla warfare. 'Mr Kapwepwe has been sending people to Angola for the past one and a half years. I personally have seen the entry point where these people cross into the Angolan jungle. I went there on August 16 in the company of several other UPP officials,' Mr Likoya said. He also claimed that Mr Kapwepwe sent between 60 and 70 Zambian students to East Germany between 1969 and 1971. In a libel action by Kapwepwe on this report,[74] the *Times* admitted liability and, having been condemned to pay K20,000 damages, is now claiming a contribution from the government, on the ground that it was from the government that it obtained the information in the newspaper report.

It seems clear from the stated grounds for the detentions that the connection between the detentions and the threat from the south is pretty tenuous. If the declaration of the semi-emergency is to continue in force for as long as there are white minority regimes in the south, then the Preservation of Public Security Act would have become a permanent preventive detention law and Zambia a permanent emergency state.

In Malawi and Kenya, as may be recalled,[75] a Preservation of Public Security Act has been in operation since 1964 and 1966 respectively. And the event that necessitated its being brought into operation was in each case a split within the ruling party — the Malawi Congress Party (MCP) and the Kenya African National Union (KANU). In Kenya, but not in Malawi, the split led to the formation of a break-away party, the Kenya People's Union (KPU). The emergence of an opposition party in what had been a *de facto* one-party state must have looked to the President a threat to his leadership. Yet that alone could not justify either the bringing into operation of the Act or the detentions. Was there, then, in the split a real and immediate threat to public security?

An important fact to notice in both cases was that the split was not really tribal. It was essentially ideological in Kenya, and in Malawi the clash was a revolt against Banda's increasing dictatorial style of rule and his policy of accommodation towards the minority regimes in Southern Africa. The first violent tribal display attributable to the split in Kenya occurred only in 1969 during President Kenyatta's visit to Odinga's tribal area — that is, three years after the first wave of detentions. No tribal violence ever followed in Malawi at all. The conclusion thus seems inescapable that in both Kenya and Malawi the detentions and other security measures taken under the Preservation of Public Security Act were motivated largely by a desire to maintain, through the instrumentality of the Act, the political monopoly of the ruling party and its leader.

This conclusion is perhaps even more true of Tanganyika which has always been free, relatively at least, from the destructive effects of deep-rooted tribal divisions. Until the army mutiny of 1964 the government in Tanganyika faced no real and immediate threat to state security, at least not such as to warrant a preventive detention law. The government took excessive alarm at the formation of the People's

Democratic Party by Tumbo in 1962 after he had resigned his appointment as the country's High Commissioner in London. He had been a thorn in the flesh for the government. There was also the fear of industrial unrest, which the trade unionists were believed to be helping to foment. Then came the army mutiny in 1964, and the widespread rumours about the country's stability which the mutiny engendered.

Recently new grounds for detention under the Act have been added, such as practising racial discrimination against Africans, mixing religion with politics, acting as spies for Southern African governments against refugees in Tanzania, or subverting the economy through corrupt and other practices.[76] These hardly seem sufficiently powerful reasons to detain people without the benefit of impartial judicial trial. The President has defended the use of preventive detention for this purpose on the ground that proof of such practices by legal evidence is difficult, and because the suspects, if left at liberty, are prone to want to interfere with police investigations. In the case of non-citizens, however, detention is only a temporary measure pending appropriate adminstrative action after investigations shall have been completed. Thus on April 21, 1970, the non-Tanzanians among the thirty-nine persons detained in November 1969 on this ground were expelled from the country and had their property confiscated; naturalised persons were first divested of their citizenship and then dealt with in the same way. But the citizens among them were kept in detention.[77]

Equally unjustifiable is the use of preventive detention to enforce the implementation of *ujamaa*. For example, fourteen peasants in Ukerewe District who refused to surrender their land for use as a site for a *ujamaa* village were arrested and held in detention for one year.

REFERENCES

1. Zambia, S.29; Uganda, S.30; Malawi, S.26; Botswana, S.17.
2. S.29.
3. S.25 Sierra Leone; S.70(3) Nigeria — a simple majority sufficed in Nigeria.
4. S.21.
5. Constitution (Amendment) (No. 5) Act, 1969.
6. *Dale's Case* (1881)6 Q.B.D. 376, at p. 463 per Brett, L. J.
7. *ex parte Milligan, ibid.*
8. *Re Ibrahim and others*, High Court, Uganda, Miscellaneous Cause No. 26 of 1969; *Re Akoto, ibid.*
9. *In the Matter of K. S. Patel's Application for a Writ of Habeas Corpus*, 1971/HN/1032 of 8 October 1972.
10. *Ibid.*
11. Constitution (Amendment) (No. 5) Act, 1969.

12. S.85. The 1969 amendment in Zambia was borrowed from Kenya.

13. *Liversidge* v. *Anderson* [1941]3 All E.R. 338 (H.L.); *R.* v. *Home Secretary, ex parte Greene* [1941]3 All E.R. 104 (C.A.); *R.* v. *Home Secretary, ex parte Budd* [1942]1 All E.R. 373 (C.A.); *Re Akoto* [1961]G.L.R. 523.

14. *Bhardwaj* v. *The State of Delhi* 1953 S.C.R. 708 – reprinted in Franck, *Comparative Constitutional Process* (1967) p. 220.

15. *Stewart* v. *Chief Secretary of Northern Rhodesia* 1956 R. and N. 617.

16. *Att.-Gen. for Northern Rhodesia* v. *Mungoni* 1958 R. and N. 710 (Fed.S.C.).

17. *Re Akoto, op. cit,* p. 531.

18. *Re Akoto, ibid.*

19. It is difficult to square this provision with certain of the guarantees in Uganda's Constitution of 1967.

20. In Zambia since 1969 the conditions apply also to restriction.

21. *Chipango* v. *Att.-Gen. of Zambia*, 1970 S.J.Z. 179 (grounds furnished and gazette notice published 2 days and 3 weeks out of time respectively); *Mundia* v. *Att.-Gen. for Zambia* HP/902/70 of 1 August, 1971 (grounds furnished 5 days and gazette notice published 19 days out of time).

22. *Chipango* v. *Att.-Gen.*, High Court, Lusaka 1971/HP/931 of 2 August, 1972.

23. *Att.-Gen. of Zambia* v. *Chipango*, Court of Appeal Judgment No. 2, 1971.

24. Per Magnus J. in Chipango's Case 1970 S.J.Z. 179.

25. *Naresh Chanda* v. *The State of West Bengal* (1959) 46 A.I.R. 1335.

26. Per Scott J. in *In the Matter of Simon Kapwepwe* 1972/HP/307 of 7 July 1972.

27. *Bhardwaj* v. *The State of Delhi, ibid.*

28. *Attorney-General for Zambia* v. *Chipango, ibid*; contrast *Uganda* v. *Commissioner of Prisons, ex parte Matovu* (1966) E.A. 514, where the High Court of Uganda held that 'insufficiency of the statement of grounds of detention served on the applicant is a mere matter of procedure'. See also *Greene* v. *Home Secretary* [1941] 3 All E.R. 388 (H.L.)

29. *Bhardwaj* v. *The State of Delhi, ibid.*

30. *Ujagar Singh* v. *The State of the Punjab* (1952) S.C.R. 756; reprinted in Franck, *Comparative Constitutional Process* (1967), p. 224.

31. *S. B. Patel* v. *Attorney-General for Zambia* 1969/Const/REF/HP/8 of 24 June, 1969; *Awolowo* v. *Fed. Minister of Internal Affairs (Nigeria)* 1962 L.L.R. 177.

32. Constitution (Amendment) (No. 5) Act, 1969. Whereas before any person might be appointed chairman by the Chief Justice, under the 1969 amendment he has to be a person qualified to be a judge of the High Court.

33. *Sinkamba* v. *Doyle*, Court of Appeal for Zambia, No. 16 of 23 June, 1972, affirming the judgment of the High Court: *Sinkamba* v. *Doyle* HN/1971/2111 of 16 December, 1971.

34. *Att.-Gen. of Zambia* v. *Chipango, ibid.*, where this question was left undecided.

35. Cf Justice Magnus in *Chipango* v. *Att.-Gen. for Zambia, ibid.* The application in *Sinkamba* v. *Doyle, ibid.*, was however only for an order of *mandamus* to compel the Chief Justice to appoint a chairman of a tribunal, and there was no claim that the detention had become unlawful because of failure to have a review in accordance with the terms of the Constitution.

36. Report (1972), para. 33.

37. White Paper on Report (1972), p. 3.

38. See D. C. Holland, 'Emergency Legislation in the Commonwealth' (1961), 13 *C.L.P.* 148, for dates.

39. For details of regulations made during these emergencies, see Harvey, *Law and Social Change in Ghana* (1966), pp. 303—4.

40. Parliamentary Debates, Official Report, 23 August, 1957, ed. 102.

41. *Ibid.*, 3 March, 1959, Col. 169.

42. D. C. Holland, 'Personal Liberty in the Commonwealth' (1950), *C.L.P.* 151, 160.

43. Acts authorising the deportation of particular individuals, mostly chiefs, were not, however, unknown during the colonial period.

44. *U.S.* v. *Lovett* (1945), 328 U.S. 303 at p. 318.

45. Parl. Debates, Official Report, December 24, 1958, Cols. 3—4.

46. International Commission of Jurists Report; quoted in Busia, *Africa in Search of Democracy* (1967), p. 129. According to Harvey, *op.cit.*, p. 285, 'estimates range from a few hundred to thousands'.

47. *Grace Stuart Ibingira and others* v. *Uganda* [1966] E.A. 306.

48. *Grace Stuart Ibingira and others* v. *Uganda* [1966] E.A. 445.

49. *Uganda* v. *Commissioner of Prisons, ex parte Matovu* [1966] E.A. 514.

50. The Constitution (State of Public Emergency) Proclamation, 1969.

51. The Constitution (State of Public Emergency) Revocation Decree, 1971.

52. S.54(2)(*c*).

53. The Penal (Unlawful Societies) (No. 2) Order, 1969.

54. *Re Ibrahim and others*, Miscellaneous Clause No. 26 of 1969.

55. The Public Security (Detained and Restricted Persons) Regulation, 1966, LN212 of July 25, 1966.

56. C. Gertzel and others (ed.), *Government and Politics in Kenya* (1969), p. 241.

57. S.7.

58. S.29(1)(*b*).

59. See the Gazette notices.

60. S.1. 80/1968; S.1. 30/1972.

61. *Paton* v. *Att.-Gen. of Zambia* 1969 S.J.Z. 10; see also *Att.-Gen.* v. *Thixton* 1967 S.J.Z. 1.

62. 'Development and State Power', speech inaugurating the University College, Dar Es Salaam, Reprinted in Thomas Franck, *Comparative Constitutional Process* (1968), p. 231.

63. *Daily Nation*, editorial, May 26, 1966; reprinted in Gertzel and others, *op.cit.*, pp. 238—9.

64. A. A. Nekyon, Constituent Assembly Debate on the proposal for a Ugandan Constitution, 1967; see Nelson Kasfir, in *Transition* 33, p. 52 (1967).

65. Parliamentary Debates, Official Report, July 14, 1958, Col. 410. Nkrumah was merely re-echoing views he had early expressed in his Autobiography (1957). He in turn was re-echoed by the Tanzanian Presidential Commission when it said: 'Democratic government cannot be practised nor individual rights protected in a society torn by internal disorder.' Report (1964), para. 100.

66. For a detailed account, see Dennis Austin, *Politics in Ghana 1946—60* (1964), Ch. 8; Harvey, *Law and Social Change in Ghana* (1966) pp. 325—42. Statement by the Government on the Report of the Commission Appointed to Enquire into the Matters Disclosed at the Trial of Captain Benjamin Awhaitey before a Court Martial and surrounding circumstances, W.P. 10/59 of 1959.

67. 'Statement to the Nation by the Prime Minister', February 22, 1966.

68. 'Statement to the Nation by the Prime Minister', February 24, 1966.

69. 'Declaration of Emergency in Buganda: Statement by President Obote', May 25, 1966, Ugandan National Assembly Debates, May 25—27, 1966, pp. 52—60.

70. *Zambia: Independence and Beyond, The Speeches of Kenneth Kaunda*, ed. Colin Legum (1966), pp. 104—9.

71. *Zambia: Independence and Beyond, op. cit.*, pp. 217—44.

72. *In the matter of K. S. Patel's Application for Habeas Corpus*, 1971/HN/1032 or S/10/71.

73. See *In the Matter of Simon Kapwepwe and Elias Mwamba Kaenga*, from which the statement following is reproduced.

74. *Simon Kapwepwe* v. *Times Newspapers Zambia, Ltd.*, 1972/HP/38.

75. Above, p. 319.

76. McAuslan, Reproduced in Franck, *Comparative Constitutional Process* (1966), p. 235.

77. *The Standard*, April 22, 1970; R. Martin, 'Personal Liberty in Tanzania', pp. 146—7 (not yet published).

CHAPTER XII

HUMAN RIGHTS *VERSUS* ECONOMIC DEVELOPMENT

Economic development and national security are the two components in a two-pronged assault on human rights in developing countries. An inherent antagonism is posited between them. The primary need of a young, developing nation, it is said, is to combat ignorance, disease and poverty by securing to the individual the minimum basic requirements for human existence – food and clothing, water, housing, education, and medical and sanitary services – since only in the context of a decent life can the enjoyment of political rights be meaningful. At present, for the overwhelming majority of the people, living in squalor and poverty, political rights have no meaning at all. The needed improvement in their condition of life cannot be brought about without revolutionary changes in the economic structure on a dynamic socialist programme of development, which must necessarily involve a somewhat drastic measure of re-distribution of the national wealth, and other forms of interference with individual rights. A bill of rights, the argument continues, would unduly fetter the implementation of such a dynamic programme of development, because of the danger that highly desirable development projects might be defeated by the courts at the instance of individuals alleging that a right guaranteed to them by the constitution had been or was thereby likely to be violated. This would be to involve the courts in a conflict with the government, because 'decisions concerning the extent to which individual rights must give way to the wider considerations of social progress are not properly judicial decisions. They are political decisions best taken by political leaders responsible to the electorate.'[1]

Although this argument is perhaps valid to some extent, it has definitely over-stated the case. The view that the conditions for a decent life – food and clothing, housing, education, etc. – are more important than civil liberties to the realisation of an individual's personality and dignity is not one that is universally shared. A starving peasant may indeed be the envy of a well-fed prisoner. The comparison is, of course, irrelevant. The truth is that liberty and material comfort are both necessary for a happy life. There should be no question of having one and not the other. Both must need co-exist, and the co-existence can be achieve in a bill of rights framed so as not to impose undue fetter upon social progress.

Among the objectives of economic development, three in particular pose a conflict with individual rights. These are economic independence, social equality, and increased national productivity and income.

1. *Economic Independence*

Economic independence is a primary nationalistic aspiration of the emergent African nations.[2] Without it, political independence is considered incomplete, almost futile. Fenner Brockway has expressed in rather eloquent language the African's sentiment on this matter. 'Africans', he writes, 'resent alien economic control as much as they resent alien political control. They are frustrated by alien ownership of mines, plantations and factories, and by the racial inequality of alien managements, alien skilled craftsmen, alien workers paid more than African workers on similar jobs. They are humiliated by the social superiority and segregation which these privileges involve. They resent the way in which white settlers and financial corporations have taken possession of their best land in many parts of Africa. They regard themselves as living under an economic occupation and identify their economic masters with colonialism against which they are in revolt.'[3]

Every African leader therefore feels a sense of commitment to the emancipation of his country from the economic domination of the old colonial interests, and he sees in socialism perhaps the only effective method of achieving this emancipation. His nationalism thus leads him instinctively to socialism. This is why, as Fenner Brockway says, 'nearly every politically alert African nationalist regards himself as a socialist.'[4] The old colonial business interests that dominate the economy must be bought out, and the intervention of the state is a necessity for this purpose. With respect to the big businesses, this intervention must take the form of direct take-over by the state itself, since, owing to lack of adequate private capital, only the state can muster anything like the kind of resources, in money and organisational skill, necessary for the take-over.

Apart from the nationalistic motivation, there is a more distinctly economic consideration in the desire to terminate alien economic domination. 'It is evident', Professor Ann Seidman has written, '. . . that to leave critical investment decisions entirely to private enterprise motivated by the search for profits was to leave the economy essentially as it was inherited from the colonial era; a dual economy hinged through the export enclave to the uncertainties of the world market. If the structure of the economy was to become more internally integrated, geared to increasing productivity to raise the levels of living of the entire population, it was necessary for the state to intervene to ensure the implementation of a meaningful development strategy'.[5]

Nationalisation or state take-over is obviously in conflict with individual rights. In the strict sense of the word, nationalisation involves the prohibition of private enterprise, and thus the creation of state monopoly in a particular line of business. And, of course, existing private enterprises have first to be bought out. Now, to compel an owner against his wish to sell his property, even at the best price possible, is a denial of his freedom of choice and action, since emotionally, and even materially, money may not have the same value for him as the property taken over. In the conflict, it cannot be disputed that the interests of economic development must prevail, subject to certain safeguards. The protection of property rights, vital though it is to the individual, must be qualified by the power of the state to acquire property compulsorily on terms of payment of compensation. Yet the reality of the qualification depends upon the conditions for the exercise of the power — upon whether the conditions are such as to make compulsory acquisition a practical proposition in a new nation faced with an acute shortfall of capital. Given the necessity for a considerable amount of state ownership in the new African states, any constitutional protection of private property which makes it impossible, as by an absolute prohibition, or which makes it unduly difficult, for the state to acquire property compulsorily must be considered an undesirable fetter on development. One of the charges frequently urged against a bill of rights is that it entrenches private property at the expense of economic development. It is relevant to examine to what extent the protection of property rights in the bills of rights in Commonwealth Africa confirms this charge.

A preliminary point to notice is that, in all these bills of rights, compulsory acquisition is permitted only if it is *necessary* in the interests of defence, public safety, public order, public morality, public health, town and country planning, land settlement, or the development or utilisation of property for a purpose beneficial to the community. In Malawi (before 1966), Zambia (before 1969) and Botswana, it is/was enough if the acquisition is either necessary or merely *expedient* in the specified interests. Expedient in this context has been judicially defined as 'conducive to the purpose in hand' or 'suitable to the circumstances of the case'; manifestly, therefore, it is less restrictive than 'necessary' or 'reasonably required'.[6] However, the necessity or expediency of the acquisition must be proved objectively. An acquisition which is not in the specified interests at all, or which is otherwise not necessary or expedient in those interests, is invalid. The seizure, under statutory powers, of postal packets containing currency notes which were being illegally exported out of the country was held to be expedient for a scheme of exchange control designed to secure the development of the country's financial resources for a purpose beneficial to the community.[7] In Uganda, Kenya, and Sierra Leone it has further to be shown that the necessity is such as to afford reasonable justification for the causing of any hardship that may result to any person having an interest in the property acquired.

(i) *Compulsory Acquisition without Compensation*

The first condition governing compulsory acquisition in the Commonwealth African bills of rights is that confiscation is virtually prohibited. Only very limited recognition is given to it — limited, that is, to circumstances in which it would have been acceptable in the advanced democracies, such as where property is taken (*a*) in satisfaction of a tax, rate or due; (*b* in execution of a judgment; (*c*) by way of penalty for breach of some law; (*d*) as an incident of a lease, mortgage or charge; (*e*) in circumstances where it is reasonably necessary to do so because the property is in a dangerous state or injurious to the health of human beings, animals or plants; (*f*) in consequence of any law with respect to the limitation of actions; (*g*) for so long as may be necessary for the purposes of any examination, investigation, trial or inquiry or, in the case of land, for the purpose of carrying out on it work of conservation of soil or other natural resources, or work relating to agricultural development or improvement that the owner or occupier of the land has been required, and has without reasonable excuse refused or failed, to carry out. In every one of these cases it is required that the law authorising the deprivation of property, as well as any action taken under it, must be reasonably justifiable in a democratic society.

It can be said that none of these situations amounts strictly to confiscation. The deprivation involved in a statute of limitation, for example, results, not from a positive act of confiscation, but from the failure of the owner to assert his right in time; it is, as the Judicial Committee of the Privy Council has observed, thanks to his own inaction.[8] When property is taken in execution of a court judgment or as an incident of a lease, mortgage or charge, it is again thanks to the failure of the owner to honour obligations freely entered into; there is nothing at all of confiscation about that. The same might be said of a deprivation resulting from failure to pay taxes or rates, or from the breach of some law. It can therefore be said that confiscation is absolutely prohibited in the Commonwealth African bills of rights.

No one, ordinarily, would quarrel with this, for confiscation is the very antithesis of a bill of rights. Property is generally the fruit of legitimate labour or of speculative venture, and it is unjust, and repugnant to all accepted codes of morality, to take it away without compensation. This assumes, however, that there had been no immorality in the acquisition of the property, for morality is relative to circumstances. Clearly no morality would be violated by making a person disgorge property improperly or corruptly obtained, as where, for example, stolen property found in the possession of a thief is taken away from him and restored to the true owner. Far from reprobating it, morality indeed sanctions the deprivation.

No doubt there are gradations of immorality that may be involved in the acquisition of property. Allowing, therefore, for the fact that modern business methods are by no means morally beyond reproach, it may nevertheless be questioned whether some of the acquisitions by foreign business interests operating in Africa during the colonial era were not so immoral as not to deserve protection from confiscation. They were part of colonialism's web of exploitation, but one should not expropriate them without compensation on that ground alone, however aggrieved one might feel about the vast exploitation perpetrated upon the colonial peoples by these foreign business interests. But some acquisitions, like the mineral rights, were patently immoral on other considerations. The morality of any individual or company claiming to own the mineral wealth of the country is questionable. In the African situation the transaction by which foreign companies, such as the British South Africa Company in Northern Rhodesia (now Zambia), acquired rights over virtually the entire mineral wealth of the country was highly colourable. They were concessions from unknowing African rulers in return for paltry sums. None of the rulers concerned can be said to have entered into the transaction in a commercial sense, with anything like a full understanding of its true significance, even assuming they had the power to make those concessions. In any case, after more than half a century of lucrative exploitation of their concessions, it would seem somewhat immoral that these companies should claim to continue to own in perpetuity rights acquired under such colourable circumstances. Yet that is the practical effect of the prohibition of confiscation in the African bills of rights. Fenner Brockway has rightly remarked that 'capitalism in Africa *is* the ownership of minerals. One cannot think of an Africa which is socialist without the transference of its mineral resources and wealth to the people'. He laments the fact that lack of capital to pay compensation to the foreign mining companies might make 'the realisation of mineral socialism difficult and perhaps distant'.[9]

The pinch and affront of this situation weighed perhaps more heavily on Zambia than on any other Commonwealth African country, because the backbone of her economy, copper, was owned by a foreign company, the British South Africa Company. The extraordinary extent of the country's dependence upon copper — it accounts for 40 per cent of the GDP, 34 per cent of the GNP, 93 per cent of exports, 68 per cent of revenue and 15 per cent of employment[10] — coupled with the colourableness of the transaction by which the company acquired its title to the minerals, made its ownership intolerable to the nationalist government which took office in 1963. The British plan of prohibiting confiscation in the constitution proposed for an independent republic of Zambia would have entrenched the rights of the company at the expense of the proper development of the country's mineral resources for the benefit of the community as a whole. Understandably, therefore, the nationalist government threatened that if the company persisted in its refusal to transfer its rights to the state under terms of settlement acceptable to the government, the constitution would be amended immediately after independence to enable these rights to be taken over without compensation. In the event, the possibility was averted by the company agreeing to be bought over for £4 million, half being paid by the British Government and the other half by the Zambian Government after deduction of appropriate Zambian tax.

Yet the prohibition of expropriation without compensation in Zambia's Independence Constitution was still to impede the utilisation of its mineral resources for the development of the country. For apart from ownership of the title to the minerals, the rights of prospecting, exploration and mining over roughtly 70 per cent of the country were held exclusively by two companies, in some cases in perpetuity under special grants by the British South Africa Company. It seemed morally indefensible that these rights should be protected against expropriation except on terms of payment of compensation. Accordingly, in 1969 the Zambian Government amended the Constitution to permit their acquisition by the state without compensation.[11] The amendment greatly extended the permitted scope of confiscation beyond that stipulated in the original Constitution. Confiscation may now be authorised not only by a law which vests in the President rights of ownership, searching for, mining and disposal of minerals, and which empowers him to revoke grants of prospecting, exploration or mining licences on failure to comply with the conditions of such licences. It may also be authorised by any law relating to the following: (*a*) exchange control; (*b*) abandoned, unoccupied, unutilised or un-developed land; (*c*) absent or non-resident owners; (*d*) the acquisition of shares or a class of shares, in a corporate body on terms agreed to by the holders of not less than nine-tenths in value of those shares or that class thereof; (*e*) the forfeiture or confiscation of the property of a person who has left Zambia for the purpose, or apparent purpose, of defeating the ends of justice; and (*f*) the administration or disposal of property by the President in implementation of a comprehensive land policy or of a policy designed to ensure that the statute law, the common law and the doctrines of equity relating to or affecting the interests in property enjoyed by chiefs shall apply with substantial uniformity throughout Zambia.

The amendment was immediately implemented by two pieces of legislation in 1970 – the Mines and Minerals Act, 1969 (effective January 1, 1970) and the Lands Acquisition Act, 1970. The latter denies the right of compensation in respect of undeveloped or unutilised land as defined therein except for unexhausted improvements. Even for unexhausted improvements, no compensation is payable if the land is unutilised land belonging to an absent owner, i.e. a person not ordinarily resident in Zambia. The Mines and Minerals Act vests all minerals in the President. The bulk of the country's minerals, already vested in the President when the British South Africa Company, was bought out at independence in October 1964. By this Act, minerals not included in the company's rights, such as those in lands reserved to the Paramount Chief of Barotseland (now Western Province) under the concession agreements with the company, now pass to the state. Any areas over which the company had made prospecting and exploration grants in perpetuity (special grants) revert to the state if no prospecting had taken place in them since independence; other special grants were converted to ordinary prospecting and exploration licences valid for periods prescribed by the Act. All existing mining rights were extinguished and converted to mining licences valid for six months, renewable for further periods of twenty-five years provided that the holder can show that ore reserves remain to be exploited and submits a satisfactory programme. These provisions enabled the areas previously held by the two major mining companies, the Anglo-American and Roan Selection Trust, under exclusive licences or special grants to be reduced to 12 per cent of their former extent, this making it possible for vast areas hitherto tied up and unexploited under the special grant system to become available for prospecting by other companies.

There seems also to have been ample justification for the expropriation of unutilised land belonging to absentee or non-resident owners. According to the report of the Monckton Commission in 1960, the white settlers in the two Rhodesias, Northern and Southern, who were numbered only in thousands, had grabbed most of the agricultural land in the territory – 48 million acres, as against 41 million acres occupied by the Africal millions. Those lands were granted virtually gratis. But it is the fact of abandonment that provided the real ground for forfeiting them. For, after U.D.I. in Southern Rhodesia in 1965, many of the white settlers in Zambia fled south, maintaining only a remote control of their farms as absentee owners. Part of the declared objective of the 1969 constitutional amendment was therefore to enable the government to take over the farms of these absentee owners without compensation. Today most of the former white farms are owned either by the government or by Zambians to whom they had been sold by the government.

(ii) *Compulsory Purchase*

By the prohibition of expropriation without compensation, therefore, the system of compulsory acquisition instituted by the Commonwealth African bills of rights is that of compulsory purchase. The idea underlying compulsory purchase is that the owner receives for the property so acquired its equivalent in money, so that the property is not diminished in amount, but is only compulsorily changed in form. In accordance with this underlying idea, the bills of rights require *adequate* compensation to be paid, and paid *promptly*, for property compulsorily acquired, whether the acquisition relates to ownership or to possession only. The word, *adequate*, emphasises the nature of the acquisition as a purchase, albeit a compulsory one. It entitles the owner to be paid the full market value of the property; that is to say, the price he would have bargained for if he were a willing seller selling in the open market.[12] The Kenyan bill of rights makes this clear by stipulating a 'full compensation'. Where, therefore, a Compulsory Acquisition Act provides for the payment of compensation on the basis of a *fair* market value, its constitutionality was questioned on the ground that a fair market value is something less than adequate compensation.[13] It cannot be disputed that a fair market value may be, and often is, less than a full market value. Happily, however, the court in this case refused to allow the statute to be voided on this ground, because, as the court reasoned, a willing seller in the market does not always get the full market value. If he gets a fair market value – and he usually does get it – he is happy and contented; accordingly, compensation based on a fair market value is adequate compensation within the meaning of the constitutional provision, for though not an exact or full equivalent in money, it is a *just* equivalent.

This case illustrates at once the undesirability of stipulating in the constitution that compensation must be adequate. Its undesirability is accentuated when the goodwill of a business forms a substantial part of the value of the property in question. Is the 'fair price' of the property in such a case to be assessed on the book value, share value or future discounted profits of the business? It has been said that 'no such thing as a "fair" price exists,' because neither the book value nor the share value nor the future discounted profits of a business are objectively determinable, and that, accordingly 'an underdeveloped country should pay as much and no more than will buy what it wants, whether it be management goodwill or investor goodwill.'[14] While the constitutional stipulation may be appropriate to land or chattel, it is clearly not so in cases of property of which a large parts consists of business goodwill. And it is with respect to these that compulsory acquisition is vitally needed in the developing economies. To insist on adequate compensation, meaning full market value, in such cases is to give an unfair advantage to the foreign business interests in the emergent states, and to put it beyond their power to terminate the foreign economic stranglehold on their economies.

Along with this is the fact that compensation is required to be paid *promptly*. The requirement of prompt payment is perhaps even more inhibiting to the capacity of a new nation to launch development along the lines of state ownership. It is a drag on development, because a new state, desirous of pursuing a programme of public ownership in both the industrial and commercial sectors, may lack the capital to pay prompt compensation for taking over privately-owned industries, banks, building societies, insurance companies and other commercial enterprises. What is objected to here is not the principle of compensation as such, for, as already conceded, it is proper that, in the ordinary case, the state should pay compensation for depriving a person of the legitimate fruit of his labour or investment. But the principle of compensation should have been satisfied by the state accepting the liability to compensate, without being obliged to do so promptly. Instead of prompt payment, the value of the property could be treated as a loan to be paid out of the profits of the business over a period of years. To insist on prompt payment may amount in practice to a prohibition on desirable schemes of nationalisation, thereby blocking development along those lines, which, as previously stated, seem to be a matter of political and economic necessity in the new states, given the control of development policy by foreign business interests. The cost of the acquisition will be all the more telling on the financial resources of the new state by reason of the right guaranteed to an expropriated owner in Kenya, Botswana, Zambia (before 1969) and Malawi (before 1966) to remit the whole of the compensation money to any country of his choice. This means that the money is not to be re-invested in the country (though re-investment may create a new problem of alien economic domination), but has to be paid out of its meagre foreign reserves, so vitally needed to finance schemes of industrialisation.

All the independence bills of rights guarantee access to the High Court to an owner for the determination not only of the legality of an acquisition and his right to compensation but also of the amount of such compensation. The appropriateness of employing the machinery of the courts for determining the legality of an acquisition and a person's right to compensation cannot be disputed, but its appropriateness for the assessment of compensation is another matter. It may be argued, on the one hand, that the court is ill-qualified for the task, where what is concerned is the acquisition of a big business enterprise a large part of the value of which consists of goodwill and profit prospects. It is not just a matter of the taking of account, in which the court can rely on the services of experts. It is rather a matter of straight bargaining in which policy and other considerations pre-dominate. As Charles Harvey has rightly observed, 'how much to pay depends fundamentally on whom the country is trying to satisfy' — the existing shareholders or their compatriots, investors in other capitalist countries, or socialist countries. He continues: 'The scale should really be two-dimensional, with the second dimension being time. Thus, a payment that succeeds in not scaring off capitalist investors in time should generally satisfy investors from countries where previous shareholders live. The other oddity of the scale is that the more a country rejects capitalist criteria for compensation, the more likely it is that the socialist countries will be pleased and thus willing to supply technical expertise.'[15] These are some of the considerations that operate in such cases, and they are considerations into which a court of law cannot be expected to enter.

On the other hand, it may be argued that a court judgment affirming an owner's entitlement to compensation may be largely stultified if its amount is to be fixed by some other body, which may then so under-assess it as to make the right meaningless. It may also be said that its daily work and experience in the quantification of monetary values in all sorts of cases involving, say, personal injury and the value of buildings, businesses, patents, copyrights, etc., eminently qualify a court to undertake the assessment in this kind of case too. And its task may be facilitated by the use of expert valuation, preferably three sets of valuation, one made on behalf of the government, another on behalf of the business being acquired, and the third independent of both.

The prohibitive effect on socialist development programmes of the guarantee of property in terms of prompt payment of adequate compensation is amply illustrated by the experience of some of the countries. Kenya, for example, has rejected nationalisation as a technique of development. An important consideration for this was the cost of compensation which, under its bill of rights, it would have had to pay to the owners of the businesses to be taken over, a cost that would have needed to be met largely out of the country's small foreign reserves. No doubt other factors, such as the possible effect of nationalisation as a disincentive on individual enterprise and its discouragement of private investment, entered into the decision. Nonetheless it appears that the crucial consideration was the cost of compensation, which in the eyes of the government made nationalisa-tion a matter of last resort to be applied when other less costly means of control were not available or effective, or when national security was threatened, productive resources were being wasted or where a service was vital to the people and had to be provided by the government as part of its responsibility to the nation.[16] One such area is agriculture. The Kenyan Government is at present buying up large areas of former white farmlands for the settlement of Africans.

Neighbouring Tanzania, on the other hand, which is uninhibited by a bill of rights, has been able to carry through an extensive programme of nationalisation.[17] Under the nationalisation Acts – the National Bank of Commerce (Establishment and Vesting of Assets and Liabilities) Act, 1967, the State Trading Corporation (Establishment and Vesting of Interests) Act, 1967, the National Agricultural Products Board (Vesting of Interests) Act, 1967, and the Insurance (Vesting of Interests and Regulation) Act, 1967 – the state acquired full ownership of all the businesses scheduled to the Acts.[18] Industrial concerns were not nationalised, but provision was made under the Industrial Shares (Acquisition) Act, 1967, enabling the state, by a ministerial order, to acquire a majority shareholding, not exceeding 60 per cent, in scheduled industrial concerns. All five Acts provide for the payment of 'full and fair compensation in respect of the net value of the assets taken over ... after taking into account the liabilities also taken over'. How and by whom this full and fair compensation is to be assessed is not stated, from which it may be implied that, in default of agreement, recourse may be had to the court. However, the amount of compensation, when determined, is made a charge on, and is to be paid out of, the consolidated fund, though payment is to be in such manner and in such instalments as the Minister of Finance, after consultation with the person entitled, shall determine. The determination of the minister is that the compensation money, estimated in 1968 to be of the order of £11.5 million, representing 20 per cent of the total national debt, is to be treated as a loan (at 7–7½ per cent interest) to the government.

The effect of the take-overs is aptly summarised by Ann Seidman:

> Through its control of the commercial banks, the Government sought to direct the volume and kind of credit in a way which would ensure the agricultural and industrial growth required to achieve economic reconstruction. Through the State Trading Corporation, it hoped to attain a sufficient degree of national control of export–import and internal wholesale trade to direct the pattern of trade to contribute more effectively to restructuring the national economy. By acquiring a majority share of ownership of several of the largest private industrial firms in the country through the National Development Corporation, the Government sought to ensure the implementation of an industrialisation programme directed to increasing productivity throughout the economy.[19]

Zambia presents a more depressing picture of the way in which the huge cost of compensation to foreign business interests may inhibit public ownership when that is manifestly a desirable line along which to pursue development. Government take-over of the country's minerals has always been accepted as necessary even by the British Government. The idea was considered as far back as 1948 and dropped, because, without assistance from the British exchequer, the fair purchase price, estimated at £20 million, was clearly beyond the means of the Northern Rhodesian Government.[20] As the next best alternative, the government accepted an arrangement which guaranteed the British South Africa Company's right to the country's mineral wealth up till October 1, 1986, in return for the company assigning to the government 20 per cent of mineral royalties received after October 1, 1949. Although this arrangement increased the revenue available to the government for the development of the country, the perpetuation of the company's ownership up till 1986 was undoubtedly to the detriment of the development of Northern Rhodesia, since the company had shown itself loath to invest any part of its profits in the development of the country. In 1963 it was proposed to the company that it surrender its ownership for the price of £35 million to be paid in 22½ annual payments. This the company rejected, 'because of the uncertainty of receiving annual payments over such a long period of years, particularly after independence when both the composition and policies of future governments could not be foreseen'.[21] And so matters remained until on the eve of independence the company was induced by threat of expropriation without compensation to agree to surrender its rights for the price of £4 million paid in equal parts by the British and Zambian Governments. In 1969, as we have seen, the government took over the remaining mineral rights — prospecting, exploration and mining — held by private companies under licences granted by the British South Africa Company.

The take-over of mineral rights in 1969 was only part of a wider programme of economic reforms, first announced by President Kaunda in a speech at Lusaka in April 1968. This involved a 51 per cent government take-over of twenty-seven selected companies in the construction industry, the transport sector, the retail/wholesale sector — including all five retail chain stores, the brewing industry, and a few miscellaneous enterprises. The main consideration here was to make available to the state a share of the large profits from these businesses, to give it control over loan and investment policies and to check inflation. The agency used by the government for participation in private business was the Industrial Development Corporation (INDECO). In announcing the reforms the President said: 'There is no such thing as business goodwill in paying for future profits as far as I am concerned.' The owners of the businesses taken over proved amenable to negotiation on the question of compensation, and accepted an assessment based on 'fair value represented by the book value', which, because it excluded goodwill and future profits, was clearly less than the *adequate* compenstion stipulated for in the Constitution. What was perhaps more important, they agreed to be paid out of future profits. Had they insisted on their rights under the Constitution, the reforms might have been held up, since the government would have been hard put to find the large sums of money that would have been needed to compensate the owners; or it might have had to resort to the ultimate power of amending the Constitution. There were, of course, extra benefits which contributed to induce the ready acceptance by the owners of the terms offered by the government. For although the state became the majority shareholder in those businesses, operational control still remained in many cases in the hands of the former owners under the management/consultant agreements. Furthermore, by virtue of the state having a 51 per cent interest in them, the companies became exempt from the exchange control regulation which restricted the amount of remittable profit to 50 per cent. So attractive were the fringe benefits that other companies voluntarily invited government participation in their businesses.

The take-over of the mining companies followed in 1969. Here the amount of money involved was such that it seemed imprudent for the government to trust that the companies would accept its terms. As a prelude, and in anticipation of a possible disagreement, the Constitution was amended in that year (1969).[22] As will be recalled, the amendment enabled the government to acquire without compensation mineral rights still held by individuals and private companies. But its main importance in the present connection is that it abolished the requirement that compulsory acquisition had to be necessary or expedient in the interests of defence, public safety, public order, public morality, public health, town and country planning, land settlement or the development or utilisation of property for a purpose beneficial to the community; and that compensation had to be adequate and paid promptly. Also abolished was the guarantee of the owner's right to remit the compensation money to any country of his choice, and his right of access to the court for the determination of the amount of compensation. The only constitutional condition now for compulsory acquisition is that the acquisition must be authorised by an act of parliament, and that, unless the parties otherwise agree, compensation has to be paid in money. In place of the courts, the amendment makes the national assembly the authority to determine the amount of compensation in default of agreement, and puts its determination beyond challenge in a court of law. Implementing the amendment, the

Lands Acquisition Act, 1970, empowers the President, whenever he considers it desirable or expedient in the interests of the Republic, to acquire compulsorily *property of any description*, paying the owner such compensation as may be agreed, or as may, in default of agreement be determined by the national assembly acting through a select committee. Compensation is to be assessed on the basis of the fair market value. The Act preserves the right of access to the court in cases of dispute not involving the amount of compensation.

Thus armed legally against the eventuality of a default of agreement on the amount of compensation and the terms of payment, the President on August 11, 1969, announced the government's intention to acquire a 51 per cent participation in the mining companies. The companies were those in the Anglo-American and Roan Selection Trust Groups. The President reminded them of the advantages to them of government participation, such as the benefits of the management/consultancy agreements and exemption from exchange control regulations mentioned above. Regarding compensation, he said: 'This year again I intend to leave it to INDECO to negotiate the value and terms of payment, but again I want to make it clear that what INDECO will pay is a fair value represented by the book value. At the same time I want to make it clear that Government has no money to pay as a deposit against these shares. ... INDECO will, therefore, have to negotiate payment out of future dividends bearing in mind the advantage the shareholders will derive from associating with the state.'

On the basis of book value proposed by President Kaunda and accepted by the mining companies, the total compensation came to US \$296.4 million, of which \$178.6 million was due to the Anglo-American Group and \$117.8 million to the RST Group. Had the assessment been based on the full market value of the business, which would then have included the value represented by goodwill and future profits, the amount of compensation would have been considerably higher. Relatively wealthy as it is, Zambia might have found the take-over impossible if it had had to pay the whole of the compensation in a single lump sum, especially as the money, whether paid in local or foreign currency, would ultimately have to come out of the country's foreign reserves (now, incidentally, standing at less than the value of the compensation). In the event, the arrangement agreed between the parties enabled the take-over to proceed without the government having to draw on its foreign reserves or from its general tax revenue at the expense of the economy as a whole. Payment was to be made in US dollars from the government's share of the profits by instalments every six months over a period of twelve years in the case of Anglo-American, and eight years in the case of RST, at an interest of 6 per cent. In entering into these arrangements the government acted through the agency of a state corporation, the Zambia Industrial and Mining Corporation (ZIMCO). ZIMCO's obligation in respect of the compensation payments was given a commercial character by the issue of negotiable 6 per cent loan stock to Anglo-American and 6 per cent bonds to RST.

It should be stated that, though the acceptance of these terms by the mining companies enabled the government's take-over objective to be achieved without impairing the economy, the acceptance was bought at quite a high price. The government unconditionally guaranteed the payment of all due instalments, even though no profits have been earned or the profits are insufficient to cover the payment. On the other hand, if two-thirds of ZIMCO's share of profits exceed the amount of the annual compensation, the excess over the two-thirds must be applied to accelerate payment of compensation, but such accelerated payment cannot be used as a set-off in any instalment period when profits are not earned or are insufficient. What is perhaps more crucial is that the deferred payment termes were used to secure the due performance by the government of the other stipulations of the take-over arrangement. There were, for example, agreements entitling Anglo-American and RST to act as management contractors for the new government mining companies until the loan stocks and bonds are repaid; to veto any financial policy which they consider inimical to their interests or those of the minority shareholders they represent; and to externalise substantial sums of money free of exchange control.

Under other agreements, the government undertook, so long as the loan stock and bonds remain outstanding, not to increase mineral tax, and to exempt all payments of interest, capital redemption and dividends from taxation and exchange control. For breach of any of these agreements as well as for default in the payment of capital or interest, all the ZIMCO stock and bonds become immediately due and payable. The agreements provide that any dispute between the parties is to be arbitrated by the International Centre for the Settlement of Investment Disputes (ICSID). It seems obvious that, were any of the agreements to be broken now, the government cannot, in the present state of its foreign exchange reserves, find the money to pay the instalments at once. However, as Bostock and Harvey have remarked, the provisions about immediate payment in the event of breach and about reference of disputes to arbitration by ICSID are important, in order to 'ensure that any dispute between the Zambian Government and the private shareholders, or their representatives the management companies, is not a private affair that can be ignored by the rest of the world. Whether such a· dispute concerned non-financial or financial matters, the whole financial world would immediately be made aware of it because the Zimco bonds would be declared due and the dispute would be taken to the ICSID.'[22] And since ICSID is affiliated with the World Bank and has a wide international membership, 'other investors in Zambia — including the World Bank itself and the IMF — whose money could very well be needed to bridge a period of low copper prices, would be unlikely to ignore any refusal by Zambia to abide by a ruling of ICSID. In other words, the mining companies have successfully ensured that their own private agreement is an inseparable part of the whole complex of Zambia's international financial relations.'[23]

An option in favour of the government to participate in any new mine to the extent of 51 per cent is now written into all prospecting licences as a condition thereof. If the option is exercised, the government must bear a proportionate cost of prospecting, exploration and production. The government's 51 per cent take-over programme has since November 1970 been extended to banks and building societies. From January 1972 too, insurance has become an exclusive state concern, conducted through the agency of the State Insurance Corporation.

The government's take-over of the big commercial, financial, industrial and mining concerns would still have left the bulk of the small retail business in the hands of foreigners. Accordingly, at the same time as the take-over of the twenty-seven selected companies in 1968, it was announced that all non-Zambians would be refused retail trading licences from the following January, except in the main town centres, and that no credit would be granted to any non-Zambian individual or company (i.e. any company less than 100 per cent — 50 per cent from August 1969 — Zambian-owned) without the permission of the Bank of Zambia. From January 1972 the ban on retail trading licences to non-Zambians was extended to the main town centres.

The stated objective of this ban was of course to compel non-Zambian owners to sell their retail businesses to Zambians. Ostensibly, the purchase was to be a private contractual transaction resting upon agreement, yet the reality of the matter was that the non-Zambian owners were made to sell under compulsion exercised through the use of the government's power over the granting or denial of trading licences. The important point is that, being voluntary contractual transactions, the transfers were not affected by the constitutional protection of property rights. But was the denial of retail trading licences not a violation of the constitutional protection against discrimination? Discrimination under a law or by a person acting by virtue of any written law, or in the performance of the function of any public office or any public authority, is prohibited if it involves treatment whereby persons of a particular race, tribe, place of origin, political opinions, colour or creed are subjected to disabilities or restrictions to which others are not subjected or are accorded privileges or advantages which others are not accorded.[24] A law discriminatory of non-citizens is not, however, affected by this prohibition, nor is a discriminatory act done under such law.[25] The law governing the issue of trading licences, the Trades Licensing Act, 1968, authorises a licensing authority to refuse an application for a licence if satisfied that its issue would be against the public interest, and the minister can direct the authority on what appears to him to affect the public interest.[26] Since the subjective satisfaction of the licensing authority suffices, it seems that a denial of trading licences to non-citizens on the ground that it is against the public interest is lawful under the Act. The economic independence of any country must be reckoned an important public interest, and the control of its wholesale or retail trade by foreigners is clearly against that interest.

In the Common Man's Charter adopted on December 18, 1969, the Annual Delegates' Conference of the ruling Uganda Peoples' Congress adopted, as the broad basic policy of the party and government, 'the realisation of the real meaning of independence, namely, that the resources of the country, material and human, be exploited for the benefit of all the people of Unganda in accordance with the principle of Socialism'.[27] It affirmed that 'the guiding economic principle will be that the means of production and distribution must be in the hands of the people as a whole. The fulfilment of this principle may involve nationalisation of the enterprise privately owned'.[28] The obstacle posed to the realisation of the nationalisation stipulation of the charter by the constitutional requirement about 'prompt payment of adequate compensation'[29] had first to be removed.

By the Constitution (First Amendment) Act, 1970, the references to 'prompt' and 'adequate' were deleted; thereafter the obligation was only 'the payment of reasonable compensation'. The constitutional amendment was enacted on January 1, 1970, and in May an Act was passed transferring to the government, with effect from the close of business on April 30, 60 per cent of the issued share capital of 84 listed companies and also authorising it to acquire 60 per cent of any future issue of shares in the companies concerned.[30] Power was given to the responsible minister to add to, or subtract from, the list of affected companies. Until the appointment of government nominated directors, the companies listed were forbidden, on penalty of a fine, to dismiss or engage staff, sell its assets including stocks and shares, to declare dividends, take on new liabilities, issue new shares, change its assets, change the salaries or terms of employment of staff, cancel existing insurance policies or allow them to lapse, go into voluntary liquidation or otherwise stop business or appoint new directors, or in any way vary the conditions and terms of service of the directors or their remuneration. Compensation was to be based on a valuation made by valuers appointed by the minister, with a right of appeal to a tribunal appointed by the minister, and from there to the High Court. Payment was to be from the government's share of profit within a maximum of fifteen years.

At the same time the import and export trade was nationalised, becoming the sole monopoly of a government corporation, the Export and Import Corporation.[31] All existing import licences were cancelled, but without prejudice to goods already in transit. And for the purposes of its import or export business the government or the corporation was empowered to take possession compulsorily of any premises, fixtures, fittings or any ancillary equipment used by a former importer or exporter in the course of his business, paying such compensation as might be assessed by valuers appointed by the minister and on the same terms as in the case of the listed companies.

The military government of General Idi Amin, unfettered by any constitutional restraints, has carried the indigenisation of the economy further, but the method used was the rather crude one of expelling all non-citizen Asians from the country, thereby making their businesses available for purchase by the government and by Uganda's African nationals. Among the businesses now open for purchase by Ugandan Africans is the giant Madhvani group, the biggest industrial enterprise in East Africa, which operated a steel factory, a sugar works, a brewery, a textile mill, a match factory and tea estates, with a capital of K36 million, a turnover of nearly K55 million, and a labour force of 20,000. In an interview on November 3, 1972, President Amin complained that, though the banks had plenty of money to lend, Ugandans were not coming forward to borrow it for investment in the purchase of the businesses of the expelled non-citizen Asians. It should really not be surprising if people with no experience of the management of big business feel reluctant to accept the burden of indebtedness in order to buy a business worth nearly K40 million.

Amin's expulsion policy has attracted adverse world notice because the ninety days' notice given to the Asians to quit the country was grossly inadequate to enable them to wind up their affairs, and in particular to negotiate prices and terms of payment for the sale of their businesses. As it is, the government is assuming to act as seller; it is not known whether, and if so how, the government intends that the money should be remitted to the owners. It is, of course, expected that Britain, whose nationals the expelled Asians are, will eventually take the matter up with the Uganda Government in the ordinary course of diplomatic pressure. The sheer size of the numbers involved, an estimated 40,000, and the fact that the people have made their homes in Uganda, have given to the expulsions a particularly abhorrent flavour and made them a matter for international concern. To uproot 40,000 people suddenly from their homes and sources of livelihood without adequate notice seems terrible, and to have gone beyond what the economic independence of Uganda could reasonably be said to require. That objective could be achieved by less brutal means of control at the disposal of the government, such as the denial of trading licences to foreigners – the method used in Zambia. The announcement that the expulsion order was being extended to Asians of Ugandan citizenship confounded an already inhuman situation. While the expulsion of non-citizens might be supported as a legally legitimate, if inhuman, exercise of the government's power to determine the conditions of residence of foreigners, the expulsion of citizens, even naturalised citizens, would be a flagrant violation of the moral basis of government whose first duty is the protection of all its nationals, irrespective of race, tribe, place of origin, political opinions, colour or creed. The Ugandan Constitution of 1967, like the other bills of rights in Commonwealth Africa, did indeed enjoin discriminatory treatment of nationals on any of these grounds. Although the expulsion order against Ugandan Asians was later withdrawn, its initial announcement seemed to have done immeasurable damage to Amin's standing in this whole unpleasant business. His latest move is an order that the Ugandan Asians should leave the towns for the rural areas in order to mix with fellow-Ugandans there, and help develop those areas. This again is a violation of the moral obligation of government, as enshrined in the 1967 Constitution of Uganda,[32] to permit every national to move about freely throughout the country, and to reside in any part of it. However, this latest order is less abhorrent than the earlier order of expulsion. Indeed, if the choice of moving to the rural areas had been offered to the non-citizen Asians, it is conceivable that, repressive as it undoubtedly is, many might have preferred to remain in the country even under such conditions, and in doing so help to bring development to the rural areas. Amin's Asian policy simply illustrates the dangers of absolute power unlimited by a judicially enforceable bill of rights.

The commercial exploitation of minerals in Botswana has prompted a constitutional amendment in August 1969 somewhat similar to that in Zambia and Uganda.[33] The amendment did two things. First, although under the existing provisions compulsory acquisition is permitted if it is necessary or expedient in order to secure the development or utilisation of property for a purpose beneficial to the community, the amendment specifically extended this authority to the development or utilisation of the mineral resources of Botswana. Secondly, it provides that the stipulation about 'prompt payment of adequate compensation' shall be 'deemed to be satisfied in relation to any law applicable to the taking of possession of minerals or the acquisition of rights to minerals if that law makes provision for the payment at reasonable intervals of adequate royalties'.

(iii) *Social Equality*

Social inequality is a firmly entrenched phenomenon of the emergent African nations. Like alien economic domination, it is a product of colonialism. Apart from the chiefs, the pre-colonial African society was a classless one, a subsistence economy in which everyone lived at much the same level, with no industries or other large-scale methods of production. Such wealth as existed was of an impermanent kind that could not be passed on from generation to generation.

Colonialism introduced Europeans into the societies of Africa as bureaucrats, traders and missionaries with a monopoly of all the good things provided by the modern state. They had good incomes, lived in decent houses equipped with modern amenities, and generally enjoyed a standard of living altogether different from and superior to that of the indigenous population. With the transformation of the state from a colonial to an independent one, the privileges of the European functionaries were inherited by Africans in the capacity of ministers, legislators, judges, permanent secretaries, directors of departments, chairmen and general managers of public corporations, etc. In the churches and universities and the private sector generally, a similar development took place, as indigenous bishops and clergy, professors and lecturers, company directors and managers gradually replaced expatriates. This development was accompanied by an expansion in the services provided by the government — education, health, water, roads, electricity, commerce and industry, building societies and other credit facilities, etc. These activities had opened up additional employment opportunities as well as new avenues for the acquisition of wealth by indigenous businessmen in such capacities as contractors, government agents, industrialists, transporters and traders.

Unfortunately the benefits of this progress were not evenly distributed among the population. Much of it is concentrated in the hands of a few people — the ministers, other top politicians and their associates in business, top state officials and the company directors — while the real income, and, consequently, the standard of living of the ordinary clerk, artisan or peasant farmer have remained substantially as they were before. In the event, four social classes have emerged: 'the huge mass of family farmers, living like the English peasant of the middle centuries, illiterate, superstitious, handling very little money, their world bounded by the family or clan; wage-earners and urban proletariat, living like their counterparts in nineteenth-century Britain, semi-literate, underpaid, badly housed, but beginning to understand their rights and to feel their power; the growing middle class of traders, teachers and officials, whose styles and standards of living approximate to those of the privileged classes of the twentieth century; and the top professional and businessmen, whose material and often professional standards equal or exceed those of the western world'.[34]

The inequity and unfairness of this situation has created a genuine disquiet among African leaders. For social inequality implies not only a grossly inequitable distribution of the nation's wealth, but also the exploitation of one class of the population by another. The rich become so by exploiting the poor, and their enjoyment of this wealth is inevitably at the expense of the poor, since the luxuries and other things that they need will have to be imported, or produced locally at high cost. The import of such goods has to be paid for largely out of the produce of the farmers and labouring classes. Local industrial production is also dictated by the needs of the rich, and is carried on at a cost that places its products beyond the reach of the poor. President Milton Obote stated the matter admirably when he wrote: 'The crucial point here is that inequitable distribution of income leads directly to non-development of resources which could cater for the consumption needs of the poor, since the masses cannot afford to pay for the goods which would be produced, and instead the economy becomes dependent on exports of primary commodities in order to pay for imports of luxurious goods for the rich. The end result is a constant problem of unfavourable balance of payments and external debts, and a neglect of the welfare of the Common Man.'[35]

Increased national productivity can have little meaning therefore unless it brings to the masses a rise in their own real income which would enable them to enjoy a good standard of living. This demands a somewhat drastic re-distribution of income and the diversification of the economy, which in turn may involve interference with individual rights. Three classes of right have been particularly affected, namely the right of workers to strike, the right of property, and freedom of enterprise. The right to strike and freedom of enterprise are not, of course, protected by the constitution, but they are nonetheless important to the individual.

Many African governments have passed legislation to regulate strikes by public servants, either prohibiting them or subjecting them to rather stringent conditions. In Uganda, for example, strikes in essential services are prohibited; outside the essential services, it is illegal for a public servant to take part in any strike unless the negotiating machinery provided for in the regulating act has broken down, a report of this has been made to the responsible minister, and a specified period of time has elapsed since the report without the dispute having been resolved.[36] The Tanzanian legislation is to a similar effect.[37] The rationale of these restrictions is that, quite apart from the loss of man-hours involved, workers' demands for wage increases can only be met at the expense of farmers and other self-employed persons who account for the overwhelming majority of the population, and would widen the income gap between the two classes.

President Léopold Senghor has stated the argument thus: 'In Black Africa, civil servants and white collar workers, even manual workers, are bourgeois by comparison with the peasants, herdsmen, fishermen and labourers. It is a swindle to call the former the proletariat. . . . Salaries will not be lowered, but they will be blocked. . . . This will make it possible to use the savings realised for productive investment in agriculture, building, fisheries, and crafts'.[38] Equally cogently, President Julius Nyerere has argued: 'It is one of the purposes of trade unions to ensure for the workers a fair share of the profits of their labour. But a "fair" share must be fair in relation to the whole society. If it is greater than the country can afford without having to penalise some other section of society, then it is *not* a fair share'.[39] A libertarian might deplore this invasion of the right of workers to withhold their labour, as does Fenner Brockway, on the ground that democracy ought to begin from the grass roots – in the workshop. Yet freedom of industrial action should not become a licence for industrial anarchy. The emergent nations of Africa cannot afford this in their present stage of development. Even the United States and Britain have recently had to restrict this right.

Among countries in Commonwealth Africa perhaps Tanzania is foremost in the theory and practice of socialism, particularly with regard to the elimination of social inequality. The interim constitution of the country affirms in a preamble that it is the duty of the government to 'conduct the affairs of the state so that its resources are preserved, developed and enjoyed for the benefit of its citizens as a whole and so as to prevent the exploitation of one man by another'.[40] The Arusha Declaration of February 5, 1967, also affirms that 'every individual has the right to receive a just return for his labour;' and that 'it is the responsibility of the state to intervene actively in the economic life of the nation so as to ensure the well-being of all citizens, and so as to prevent the exploitation of one person by another or one group by another, and so as to prevent the accumulation of wealth to an extent which is inconsistent with the existence of a classless society'. These objectives have been further explained and elaborated in the writings of President Julius Nyerere, for whom socialism, being essentially distributive, is the only answer to social inequality and exploitation.

The first target in the socialist solution thus prescribed is land. This is because of the tendency of private ownership of land towards social inequality. It is argued that the idea of free marketability of land implicit in private ownership encourages land speculation with all the exploitation that it engenders. The village peasantry would be induced by the attractions of cash to sell its land to the speculator, becoming a landless class or a 'rural proletariat', to use Julius Nyerere's expression.[41] The speculator often does not care to develop the land but waits until its value has been enhanced through the activities of the government or those of other private owners, and then re-sells it at an inflated price, reaping thereby much unearned income at the expense of the community. Or, instead of re-selling, he may choose to remain the landlord, even an absentee one, taking exorbitant rent from those who actually need and use it. The inflation of land prices means that only the well-to-do can afford to buy land, and it may conceivably impede its development since the purchaser could be left after the purchase with insufficient capital to develop it. Land ownership by the state, on the other hand, ensures against these dangers.

In making grants of land, the state would try to observe the principle of social justice by ensuring that no one gets more land than he actually needs, and by making continued use a condition of the grant. Prices would be kept down and brought within the reach of the average citizen; and income from land sales and rents would enure to the whole community, instead of to private individuals. There is no doubt that state ownership would enable the nation's wealth represented by its land to be equitably distributed, and the exploitation of landlordism to be eliminated or checked.

However, the argument in favour of it seems to assume that social equality is the only objective of economic development, or at least an overriding one. It is doubtful whether state ownership of land serves the interests of social progress better than private ownership. It seems that progress can be more effectively pursued under a system which permits free, though regulated, individual enterprise and initiative in regard to land. There is little virtue in allocating land to a person who has no money to develop it or withholding it from a person who can, merely on the ground that the latter has a plot already. If an individual is able through his initiative and enterprise to establish two or more plantations or farms or to build two or more houses and thereby make more food, employment or accommodation available to the community, the state should not stand in his way in the name of social equality. Ability to develop, rather than any doctrinaire adherence to the principle of social justice, should be the criterion for the allocation of land. But this is provided that the method of allocation is fair and equitable as between all those who possess this ability, and that land racketeering, profiteering and other forms of abuse are not tolerated.

There are various control mechanisms that can be used to check the evils of landlordism, among which may be mentioned land tax, price and rent control, agricultural development conditions, and various other devices for protecting the tenant against the landlord. 'Owner-ship', says a Kenyan Sessional Paper, 'is not an absolute indivisible right subject only to complete control or none. Practical systems have demonstrated that the resources of society are best guided into proper uses by a range of sensitive controls each specifically designed for the task to be performed'.[42]

Wherever the balance of advantage in this argument lies, Tanzania has chosen the path of nationalisation. In July 1, 1963, all freehold titles were extinguished in favour of the state, and converted to leaseholds for not more than ninety-nine years, so that the former owners become thereafter rent-paying tenants of the state, losing thereby the reversion on the ninety-nine-year term.[43] For this loss they received no compensation, the argument being that it is immoral for anyone to claim to own land allodially; it is God's gift to society, and should not be commercialised into a marketable commodity commanding a price, except for unexhausted improvements made on it. Many of the freehold owners had bought their lands at high prices not long before the conversion; it is difficult to understand the kind of morality that would justify expropriating them of their investment in the circumstances of the case. There were, of course, others whose titles originated in grants by either the German or the British colonial authorities in circumstances that amounted to cheating the previous African owners out of their lands, sometimes with no compensation at all. For such owners, the 1963 expropriation is perhaps not so reprehensible. The small concession made to the new government lessees under the conversion act was that they were not required to pay economic rent for their occupation of the land, but only a nominal one, and were in many cases, though not all, subject to no development conditions. Even this concession was revoked in 1969 when the government leaseholds were statutorily extinguished and converted to mere rights of occupancy under which the holders become obliged to pay economic rent and to observe the development requirements prescribed in the Land Ordinance — all this again without compensa-tion.[44]

All lands in Tanzania are now in state ownership, all non-freehold lands having previously been declared to be public lands under the Land Ordinance of 1923.[45] However, the practical effect of this ownership is minimal in respect of 95 per cent of the land, which is still held under customary law. Although the rights of the customary holders are only those of occupancy, yet the fact that the conditions of tenure are governed largely by customary law and not by statute has favoured development tending towards private ownership and the landlord—

tenant relationship. However, the extent of land held under customary law is shrinking under the impact of urbanisation; when land is brought within the boundaries of an urban centre, it ceases to be subject to customary law on payment of compensation to the former customary owners, who are then expected to obtain a grant of it from the government, though in fact many of them remain in permissive occupation as 'squatters'. Moreover, the President has statutory power to revoke a customary — or indeed any — right of occupancy if, in his opinion, it is in the public interest to do so.[46] When he does so revoke a right of occupancy, the owner is entitled to compensation not for the land, which does not belong to him anyway, but only for unexhausted improvement. The latter is defined as anything or any quality permanently attached to the land, directly resulting from the expenditure of capital or labour by an occupier or any person acting on his behalf and increasing the productive capacity, the utility or the amenity thereof, including crops or growing produce but not other results of ordinary cultivation. Compensation for improvement is regarded as an inviolable right, though the obligation to pay it is imposed, not on the government, but on the person to whom the right is transferred. In the case of an absent holder, the President may direct that no compensation is to be paid for unexhausted improvement. This is the only instance when compensation may be denied for improvements.

The nationalisation of land is explained as merely re-establishing the position pre-existing in customary law where land is said to belong to the community as a whole, with individuals or groups having only a right to use it. This notion of customary land tenure is not universally true of all African societies, for example those of Southern Nigeria. There, the unit of landholding is not the community, nor ever its primary segment, the village, but rather the family. But even if ownership of all lands by the whole community were prevalent in all African societies, it would still be no justification for the imposition of ownership by the modern state. First the relationship of the constituent groups and individuals to the traditional community is wholly different from their relationship to the modern state. Secondly, ownership of land by the traditional community implies completely different incidents from ownership by the modern state.

The rights of the individual are completely different in each case. Community or family land is owned by all the members as a social collectivity. Each individual has rights in the land which he can enforce against the community or family as represented by the chief — rights to be given an allotment, to share in surplus income, to participate in its management, and in certain circumstances to demand partition or sale of the land. He has none of these rights in state land. What approximates to state ownership in the traditional system is not community ownership, but rather chieftaincy land, which has a limited incidence.

The conversion of private ownership of land into right of occupancy has no doubt contributed to greater social justice, but only to the limited extent of transferring the ownership of all lands to the state. It left the previous owners still in occupation of the full amount of the land they previously owned. It did not attempt any re-distribution by curtailing the existing holdings and transferring part to other persons. Thus the big plantations and farms survived intact as private holdings. Nor did the conversions result in the abolition of private landlordism, although the government strongly disapproves of it as an institution of capitalist exploitation. Most houses in the urban areas still belonged to private owners who let them out on rent to tenants or lodgers. Much agricultural land in the rural areas was in fact cultivated not by the persons to whom the rights of occupancy in it had been granted but by others as tenant-cultivators, with the former becoming absentee holders. The same is true of much building land in the urban areas, where government lessees have sub-let to tenant developers. And in the traditional sector, as has been noted, the landlord—tenant relationship was fast taking root.

Although these features of the land tenure system were viewed as inconsistent with the socialist policy of the government, circumstances seemed to dictate a pragmatic approach rather than a revolutionary one. No general re-distribution was thus embarked upon, except in the island of Zanzibar where, because of the existence at the time of the revolution of 1964 of a powerful ruling oligarchy based on ownership of large landed estates, the government confiscated many such estates and transferred the several lots to the tenant-occupiers.

The pragmatic approach in mainland Tanzania proceeded in four different directions. Some of the former tribal lands granted to expatriate settlers by the colonial administration were repurchased at proper market valuation, either compulsorily or more usually by agreement, and handed to Africans. Secondly, where rural farmland was let by its holder to a tenant who cultivated it, or where a rightholder of urban building land had sub-let it to someone who then developed it, the government might acquire the interest compulsorily and grant it to the tenant-cultivator or developer,[47] the aim being to eliminate 'absenteeism and promote continuity of development in land'.[48] The owner of the right that is extinguished is not entitled to compensation for it. Only the value of improvement carried out on the land by himself will be reimbursed by the new holder, though here the government has a primary responsibility to pay in the first instance from public funds. Tenancies in the traditional sector were subjected to

a compulsory system of enfranchisement under a series of enfranchisement enactments which culminated in the Customary Leaseholds
(Enfranchisement) Act of 1968. The Act is being applied piecemeal to
different parts of the country as and when the need arises. It not only
enfranchises existing customary tenancies, but prohibits the creation of
new landlord-tenant relationships in areas where it has been brought
into force. The landlord of land enfranchised by the Act is entitled to
compensation for unexhausted improvement only, not for the land
itself.

The right of the owner of a rented house was not extinguished in
favour of the occupier(s). However, two forms of restriction were
imposed. One is via the 'Leadership Code' laid down in the Arusha
Declaration of 1967. The purport of the Code is that a leader should
not put himself in a position where his personal interest conflicts with
his responsibility as leader, or which enables him to exploit others. With
certain exceptions the Code therefore forbids a leader *or his spouse* to
draw more than one salary; to employ workers in connection with any
trade, business, profession or vocation, including the running of a hotel,
boarding house or like establishment for gain or profit; to own a house
let out on rent to others; or to be a shareholder or director in a
privately-owned enterprise.[49] To come within the prohibition, a leader
must be the owner of the shares or the rented house not as trustee, but
in a beneficial capacity (a beneficiary by inheritance or by operation of
law or under a trust not created by himself being excepted). However,
'rent' includes 'any fee or other valuable consideration whatsoever
other than lawful deductions from the wages payable to a domestic
servant in respect of occupation by him of any portion of such house or
of any living quarters attached thereto', and 'salary' includes gains or
profits from any trade, business, profession or vocation, and income
accruing to a beneficiary under a trust or *wakf*, though incomes from
any number of trusts or *wakfs* count as one salary. A 'leader' comprises
wide categories of persons: members of TANU National Executive
Committee, ministers, M.P.s, senior officials of organisations affiliated
to TANU and of parastatal bodies, all TANU officials, councillors and
civil servants in high and middle cadres.

Adopted by the resolution of a party conference, the Code becomes
part of the Constitution and rules of the party, binding on party
members who are within the definition of a 'leader'. To rest its binding
force entirely on a party resolution would have made it unenforceable
against leaders who are not party officials or whose offices are not
dependent on party membership. And the sanction for the Code need
not necessarily involve expulsion from the party. The approach adopted
was to incorporate its stipulations into the Constitution by an
amendment as a condition of eligibility for election or appointment to,

and membership of, the national assembly, subject however to certain exceptions and safeguards.[50] The various regulations governing civil servants, councillors and officers of parastatal organisations were similarly amended to incorporate them.[51] Thus, the source of authority of the Code differs for the three categories of leaders: for the M.P.s and ministers it is the Constitution, for public servants the appropriate regulations, and for party officials the party resolution.

It may be noticed here that Zambia is to have a leadership code, but the approach for giving it legal force is different. It is to take the form of regulations to be made by a leadership committee, established by the Constitution, with five members appointed by the President.[52] When the Code is made and put into force, compliance with it will be a condition for election, nomination, or appointment to offices to be specified in it, though the President may, if of the opinion that to do so would be necessary or desirable in the public interest, authorise the nomination or appointment of a person otherwise disqualified, on condition that he complies within three months.[53] Breach of the Code by the holder of a specified office (other than the office of President, judge of the Supreme Court, judge of the High Court, investigator-general, director of public prosecutions and auditor-general) operates to vacate the office, if it is established either on a written admission or by the decision of a tribunal established by the Constitution with a right of appeal to the Supreme Court.[54] The tribunal is to consist of a chairman appointed by the Chief Justice and two other persons appointed by the President; the chairman must be a judge or a person qualified to be a judge of the High Court.[55]

The restrictions on the individual freedom of enterprise and of acquisition in the Tanzanian Code seem rather severe, especially in relation to leaders lower down the hierarchy. President Nyerere's argument is that the restrictions are confined to leaders and that, as no one is obliged to be a leader, everyone is free to choose between retaining his freedom of acquisition and accepting the restrictions which a position of leadership entails. The choice has little reality for those already in positions of leadership, as it means choosing between their career and their investment. No one can be expected lightly to give up a job in which he has made a career, merely because he is a shareholder in a business enterprise and is unwilling to be divested of his interest in it. It is an unwarranted interference with vested rights. Not unnaturally, many of those affected have, with the connivance of the government, evaded the restrictions by creating trusts of their houses or shares in favour of their children while reserving to themselves power of revocation.

The restrictions display an undue pre-occupation with exploitation, forgetting that exploitation is relative, and may not always involve harmful social consequences. The restrictions leave a leader free to acquire any amount of wealth in the form of a bank deposit or government securities, but deny him the opportunity to turn it into a more profitable investment that will add to his own wealth. It may be that, so long as the money is banked and not hoarded in a chest, the restriction on direct investment by the depositor involves no loss to the nation, since the same money may be lent to public bodies for investment by them on behalf of the public. But this assumes that the public bodies have at their disposal sufficient talent and organisational ability completely to replace individual entrepreneurship. Individual initiative is a vital asset in the economic development of an emergent nation, and exclusion from entrepreneurial initiative of a sizeable portion of the population, whose education and income would have enabled them to invest in productive enterprises, must be considered a loss to the nation. It is important that a leader should be prevented from corrupting his position of leadership so as to amass wealth, but it is both morally and economically indefensible to prevent him from investing his legitimate savings in house property or in company shares. Any conflict there may be between a leader's interest in such property or shares and his duty as leader is not so great as to justify a total ban.

The second form of restriction is contained in the Acquisition of Buildings Act of 1971. Under this Act, any building of which the cost of construction or rental value is 100,000 shillings or more may be acquired by the President if he considers it in the public interest — unless it is wholly occupied for residential, commercial or industrial purposes by the owner (individual or corporate) or by any dependent, employee, shareholder or wholly or 90 per cent-owned subsidiary. A house built at a cost of less than 100,000 shillings, and with a rental value less than that amount, is thus outside the Act, though if a person owns two or more such houses and their cost of construction or total rental value totals 100,000 shillings, then the Act applies to them.

The compensation provisions are perhaps the most interesting feature of the Act. Compensation is to be assessed, not on the market value of the building or on the cost of construction less depreciation, but on the cost of construction less an amount arrived at by multiplying 1/120th of the cost of construction by the number of whole months between the date of construction and the date of notice to acquire. In other words, for any house ten or more years old the compensation is nil. In all such cases the acquisition amounts clearly to confiscation. The assumption is that in ten years the owner would have recovered from rents the cost of construction, with perhaps some margin of profit. But even if this assumption were correct in all cases, the value of the house to the owner is surely not what it cost him to build it ten years ago but what it will cost him to build it at the date of the notice to acquire. It is grossly unfair to him to ignore the change that may have taken place in the value of money over the period. Even where, in respect of houses less than ten years old, there is an unexhausted value to be compensated for, payment is not to be made in bulk but by such instalments as the government may direct, after deductions for any outstanding mortgages or charges which the owner may have raised on the house. If, according to the prescribed formula, the house has no unexhausted value for which compensation is to be paid, the President may determine the outstanding mortgage or charge without compensation if he considers it in the public interest. Further, any question arising in the application of the Act, whether concerning the acquisition notice, the terms of the acquisition, the entitlement to compensation or the amount or terms of its payment, is withdrawn from the adjudication of the ordinary courts and vested exclusively in an Appeals Tribunal to be established by the President and consisting of a chairman and not less than two other members appointed by the President.

The practical effect of this Act must be to rule out investment in house property except where it is meant as a residence for the owner. In the short run, the government may have gained through being able to take over rented houses without compensation or with little compensation, but the long-term effect would be to arrest building development for those who already have one house, as well as for anyone aspiring to build and rent out a house worth 100,000 shillings or more. Few people would embark on such investment knowing that after ten years the government can take it over without paying anything for it. What seems to emerge from the socialist reforms in Tanzania is that a bill of rights cannot co-exist with a thoroughgoing socialist programme of development such as is now being pursued there.

2. *Increased National Productivity and Income*

The central point in economic development is increased productivity. All the other objectives either presuppose this or are intended as a means to its attainment. And, because it demands national mobilisation, vigorous action against illiteracy, poverty and disease, and active state intervention in the economy involving various forms of control and nationalisation, it is fraught with a strong likelihood of conflict with individual rights.

One point can be made straight away. The protection of individual rights, whether in the form of a bill of rights or otherwise, cannot be incompatible with state control of the economy. Apart from their property provisions, the Commonwealth African bills of rights contain little to embarrass a government's development efforts. The freedom they guarantee is not that of *unrestrained* free private enterprise based upon a *laissez-faire* conception of society. In this they differ quite markedly from the American bill of rights, which has been held to protect freedom of private enterprise, contract and indeed all the ordinary rights of a citizen under a free government, thus precluding measures of a socialist or welfare character like the regulation of working hours, wages, compulsory workmen's compensation, prices, etc.[56] Indeed the New Deal legislation, aimed at implementing the desirable socialist policies of the Roosevelt administration, initially ran foul of the constitutional guarantee of liberty and was only saved from being completely frustrated by the appointment to the bench of the Supreme Court of progressive-minded judges. In contrast, the liberty guaranteed in the Commonwealth African bills of rights is personal liberty only (i.e. freedom of the person), while the prohibition of forced labour cannot possibly afford protection to freedom of contract generally. Some of the Commonwealth countries in Africa, notably Zambia, came to independence with an inherited system of *laissez-faire* capitalism; yet their having a bill of rights has not prevented them from mounting an effective regulatory system of exchange control, import-export licensing, price control, control over local borrowing by foreign-owned companies, control over the employment of expatriates, etc. The extent of control so far achieved in these countries justifies a description of them as controlled economies.

In particular, there is nothing in the bills of rights to inhibit efforts directed towards the eradication of illiteracy and disease, two of the main impediments in the way of increased national wealth. Compulsory education is undoubtedly desirable as the most effective way of combating illiteracy. Any possible conflict between it and the freedom of thought and conscience guaranteed in the bills of rights is removed by the fact that the guarantee is subject to laws reasonably required in the interests of public morality. It would certainly be against public morality that a person should, on ground of conscience, object to a compulsory scheme of education designed to eradicate illiteracy, for illiteracy is a drag upon the development of a nation's morality. The bills of rights seek to reconcile compulsory education with religious freedom by prohibiting compulsory religious instruction or ceremonies in educational institutions and by permitting the establishment by religious communities of educational facilities in which religious instruction may be provided. Public health, like national security, is a recognised exception to all the guaranteed rights except those that cannot be derogated from either at all or otherwise than during an emergency. So long as what is proposed to be done is both reasonably required in the interests of public health and reasonably justifiable in a democratic society, the bills of rights in no way impede the fight against disease and insanitary conditions or the provision of water and other such facilities.

The guarantee of freedom of association seems to provoke greater objection, on the ground that it might undermine national mobilisation through its protection of the freedom of industrial action and of political association. The right to form trade unions is perhaps admitted as being necessary for the effective organisation of industrial relations. Trade unions serve as a bridge between employers and workers, providing machinery for consultation and settlement of disputes in the common interests of both. But it is argued that the state must not be fettered in its power to regulate the activities of these unions, in order to ensure that freedom of industrial action does not degenerate into industrial anarchy. Demands for wage increases which are not matched by increases in productivity, and strike action to back up such demands, are both things that a new nation can ill afford, because the latter involves the loss of so many man-hours, while often the former can only be met at the expense of the overwhelming majority of the population employed on the land by their own efforts. If, therefore, the guarantee of freedom of association takes away or fetters the power of the government to regulate the wages structure and strike action in the interest of the economy as a whole, then it is an unjustified impediment on progress. Happily, it can be said that this is not the case. What is protected is merely the right to associate with others for the protection of legitimate common interests, but no unfettered freedom is conferred upon individuals to determine what interests they should associate to pursue. The government can determine what interests it is legitimate for workers to associate together to protect, and it is therefore entitled to control the right to strike or to demand wage increases out of keeping with its incomes policy. Further, the bills of rights concede to the government the power to regulate freedom of association in the interests of public safety and public order. As strikes impinge upon these interests, they come also within the government's regulatory authority for this purpose.

The argument against the protection of the right to form political associations has already been considered,[57] and need not be repeated here.

The protection of freedom of correspondence and of the privacy of the home or other property is also said to impede economic development. Such impediment must be of rather limited extent. It is, admittedly, possible for the protection to undermine the effectiveness of, say, a regulatory scheme of exchange control. If, for example, exchange control regulations authorise the searching without warrant of postal packets reasonably suspected of containing currency being illegally exported out of the country, this may well be invalidated by the constitutional protection of private correspondence. This is because the protection is not made subject to economic development, but only to public security, public morality or public health.

Since, as has been said in the last chapter, exchange control bears no proximate relationship to public safety, and *a fortiori* to public morality and public health, it follows that the need for it would not justify interference with freedom of correspondence.[58] This might be considered an undesirable fetter upon social progress. If currency is being illegally exported to the prejudice of the national economy, it does not seem right that the individual's freedom of correspondence should be allowed to stand in the way of effective action to check the drain on the nation's foreign exchange reserves. Yet this is not sufficient for an outright rejection of a bill of rights, on the ground that it undesirably hinders economic development.

This particular hindrance can easily be remedied simply by making the national economy a ground of derogation from the freedom of correspondence. This indeed was done by Uganda in its 1967 Constitution. Freedom not only of expression (including correspondence) but also of assembly, association, conscience and movement was qualified by the demands of the national economy and the running of essential services — so long as the law authorising derogation, and the action taken thereunder, was reasonably required in those interests and was justifiable in a democratic society. The national economy is no less important to a new nation than national security, and there is no reason why it should be any more objectionable as a ground for derogation than the latter. As in Uganda since 1967, the interests of the national economy should be expressly recognised as a ground for derogation in the bills of rights. It should perhaps be stated that the regulation of the technical administration or the technical operation of telephony, telegraphy, posts, wireless, broadcasting and television, which are all part of the necessary infrastructure for development, are not prejudiced by the protection of the freedom of expression.[59] In Uganda (1967) the regulatory power in respect of telephony, telegraphy, posts, etc., was not even limited to their technical administration or technical operation.[60]

The protection of the privacy of the home or other property is qualified by the requirements of town and country planning, the development and utilisation of mineral resources, 'the development or utilisation of property', and by the necessity of the government having to enter private premises for tax or rate purposes or to carry out work on public installations erected on private premises. The qualification relating to the 'development or utilisation of property' has been held to authorise a regulatory scheme of exchange control, on the ground that such a scheme, even when it involves the seizure of contraband, is reasonably required by the development or utilisation of property for a purpose beneficial to the community.[61] It seems clear that, in relation to freedom from arbitrary search, the interests of economic development are adequately safeguarded under this exception.

It may be said that the need to increase national productivity and income provides a stronger motivation for the nationalisations in Africa than the desire for economic independence and social equality. Apart from nationalisation, there are other ways in which the objective of increased national productivity has impinged on the individual right of property. The most telling illustration in Commonwealth Africa is again provided by Tanzania, where agricultural development has been given such a high premium that it has been made to determine security to agricultural holding. A person's title to his holding is dependent on compliance with development requirements, which is thus an integral part of the title, marking out its duration and operating naturally to determine it. Upon such determination no question of compensation for the holding can therefore arise. Unexhausted improvements will of course be compensated for, but only after the holding, together with the improvements thereon, has been sold. When a person accepts a grant with knowledge that his title is dependent on compliance with development requirements, his rights cannot be said to have been violated when the grant is revoked or forfeited for non-compliance. But the retrospective application of development conditions to existing titles which were not previously subject to such conditions means that the title is converted from an unconditional to a conditional one. Herein lies the injustice of the Tanzanian reforms. Freehold titles existed in Tanzania until July 1, 1963, and were never subject to any development requirements. On that date, as will be recalled, all freehold titles were converted to government leaseholds, part of the objective being to enable them to be subjected to development requirements as part of the government's effort to increase agricultural production. The objective was only partly achieved, as many of the converted leaseholds remained free of development requirements. It was to complete this objective that the conversion of all leaseholds into occupancy rights was effected in 1969, thus bringing all such titles compulsorily within the scheme of development requirements. Government has been quite stern in enforcing these conditions by revocation in cases of non-compliance.[62] In the result, a freehold title in Tanzania has changed its character from absolute ownership to a leasehold interest to a conditional right of occupancy revocable by the government for non-development. (Land held under customary law remains still outside the government's development scheme, but there are various local government by-laws which try to implement it by making failure by a farmer to farm his holding effectively, so as to increase production, a criminal offence but without forfeiture of the holding itself.)

In contrast the approach in Kenya, though concerned to increase production, leaves the title independent of development requirements. An owner who does not comply with the development requirements may incur certain penalties and may, in the last resort, have his land compulsorily taken over by the government. But that operates just as in the case of any other compulsory acquisition; the owner is entitled to receive the full market value of his land.[63]

The need to increase national productivity and wealth has led to the co-operativisation and collectivisation of agriculture and of land tenure in Tanzania. Both involve a new kind of social organisation. In place of their scattered households, rural dwellers are brought together in more compact, 'governmentally supervised' village settlements. But they differ in the extent to which they impinge on the life and property rights of the members. Under co-operativisation, the members retained their separate, individual lives in practically all matters; they owned and worked their farms separately, only co-operating in the marketing of their produce. Under collectivisation, the essence of the organisation is communalism or *ujamaa*; the land is owned and worked in common, and the produce belongs to all the members in common, with well-defined principles for sharing.[64] The members either pool their existing holdings together to form a single communally-owned plot of land or, in the case of a completely new settlement, are given a grant of virgin land by the government. Individual enterprise is recognised only in respect of a house garden, which a member can use to supplement his supply of food, so long as this does not grow to an extent where it may interfere with his full participation in communal activity.

Whatever its merits as a method of organising society in order to increase national productivity and eliminate exploitation, this kind of collectivisation is in conflict with individual freedom – the individual's freedom to live and organise his life as he likes and to own property. It is true that membership of an *ujamaa* village is supposed to be on a voluntary basis, it being a declared government policy not to force people to join against their will but only to persuade them. Yet persuasion can sometimes take the form of indirect coercion that leaves the person concerned no real choice. Over-zealousness on the part of some government party functionaries may result in various forms of actual coercion. The attempt to 'persuade' an unwilling farmer to integrate his comparatively prosperous farm into an *ujamaa* farm has already cost the life of a regional commissioner, Dr Klerru. This official may or may not have been over-zealous or too persistent, but, barring personal enmity, it would have taken something more than ordinary persuasion to provoke the farmer into shooting him. Moreover the declared government policy of favouring *ujamaa* villages in the distribution of amenities[65] is apt to nullify the reality of a farmer's choice in the matter.

The government has issued directives to appropriate organisations of government to give priority to *ujamaa* villages in the provision of essential services like credit facilities, water, electricity, roads and schools, and President Nyerere has said that TANU would sponsor no one for nomination as a candidate at the 1970 parliamentary and local government elections who did not show that he lived and actively participated in an *ujamaa* village.[66] All this is a form of pressure, legitimate perhaps, but nevertheless pressure. The voluntary basis of membership of an *ujamaa* village must also be judged in terms of the conditions of withdrawal. If withdrawal entails loss of the benefits of a member's contribution in labour, then his continued membership can hardly be said to be entirely voluntary.

This question, as Professor James has remarked, has proved to be the most controversial in *ujamaa* villages,[67] for it raises in more practical form the whole issue of property rights. It is argued, on the one hand, that a member on resignation or expulsion should not be entitled to compensation for the value of unexhausted improvements on his homestead, on the ground that that would encourage whimsical resignations. The argument in favour of a member's right to compensation asserts that the recognition of such a right is in consonance with the voluntary basis of *ujamaa* and would enhance its attractiveness.[68] Both sides to the argument seem to accept that a withdrawing member is not entitled to any share of the communal assets of the village, though he should be paid for any work performed, and should be given alternative land outside that of the village in substitution for any land he had brought into the village pool. It is little wonder that *ujamaa* is not making a strong enough appeal in rural Tanzania. Most of the so-called *ujamaa* villages are so only in name.

REFERENCES

1. Tanzania, Presidential Commission Report (1964) paras. 102 and 103; Kawawa, Parl. Deb., 28 June, 1962, col. 1088 (Tanganyika); Colin Leys, 'The Constitution of Tanganyika', *Journal of Commonwealth Parliaments* (1963), Vol. 44, p. 135.

2. Julius Nyerere, 'Economic Nationalism' in *Freedom and Socialism* (1968), pp. 262–6.

3. Fenner Brockway, *African Socialism* (1963), p. 14.

4. *Loc. cit.*

5. Ann Seidman, *Comparative Development Strategies in East Africa* (1972), p. 75.

6. *J. U. Patel* v. *Att.-Gen. of Zambia* 1968, S.J.Z. 1.

7. *Ibid.*

8. *Ajakaiye* v. *Lieut-Governor* (1929) 9 N.L.R.I, at p. 5 (P.C.).

9. Fenner Brockway, *African Socialism* (1963), pp. 114 and 115.

10. Bostock and Harvey, ed., *Economic Independence and Zambian Copper* (1972), p. 4.

11. Constitution (Amendment) (No. 5) Act, 1969.

12. *U.S.* v. *Miller* (1942) 317 U.S. 369.

13. *Esi* v. *Warri Divisional Council Planning Authority*, Suit No. M/2/1966 of 20 June, 1969, High Court, Warri (Nigeria).

14. Bostock and Harvey, *op. cit.*, pp. 18 and 19.

15. Bostock and Harvey, *op. cit.*, p. 18.

16. 'African Socialism and its Application to Planning in Kenya', Sessional Paper, No. 10, 1967, para. 142.

17. For a full list, see Julius Nyerere, 'Public Ownership in Tanzania' in *Freedom and Socialism* (1968), pp. 251–6.

18. Bradley, 'Legal Aspects of Nationalisations in Tanzania', *East African Law Journal* 1967, Vol. II, no. 3, pp. 161–2.

19. Ann Seidman, *Comparative Development Strategies in East Africa* (1972), p. 70.

20. Bostock and Harvey, *op. cit.*, p. 42.

21. Quoted from Bostock and Harvey, *op. cit.*, p. 46.

22. Constitution (Amendment) (No. 5) Act, 1969.

23. Bostock and Harvey, *op. cit.*, p. 151; see generally pp. 145–78 for a full discussion of the price of the take-over.

24. S.25(1), (2) and (3).

25. S.25(4) and (6).

26. S.15.

27. Milton Obote, 'The Common Man's Charter', Govt. Printer, Entebbe (1970), para. 1.

28. *Ibid.*, para. 38.

29. Art. 13, Constitution 1967.

30. Companies (Government and Public Bodies Participation) Act, 1970.

31. Established by the Export and Import Corporation Act, 1970.

32. Art. 19 (1).

33. Constitution (Amendment and Supplementary Provisions) Act, 1969.

34. Wraith and Simpkins, *Corruption in Developing Countries* (1963), p. 196.

35. Milton Obote, 'The Common Man's Charter' (1970), para. 27.

36. The Uganda Public Service (Negotiating Machinery) Act, cap. 278, as amended by Act No. 24 of 1968.

37. The Tanzania Civil Service (Negotiating Machinery) Act.

38. Quoted in Fenner Brockway, *African Socialism*, (1963), p. 40.

39. Julius Nyerere, *Ujamaa – Essays on Socialism* (1968), p. 10.

40. Compare President Kaunda's directives to the Constitutional Commission for Zambia (1972).

41. Julius Nyerere, 'Socialism and Rural Development' in *Ujamaa – Essays on Socialism* (1968), p. 115.

42. 'African Socialism and Its Application to Planning in Kenya', Sessional Paper No. 10, 1967, para. 18.

43. Freehold Titles (Conversion) and Government Leases Act, 1963, cap. 523.

44. Government Leaseholds (Conversion to Rights of Occupancy) Act, 1969.

45. For a detailed discussion, see R. W. James, *Land Tenure and Policy in Tanzania* (1971).

46. Land Laws (Miscellaneous Amendments) Act, 1970.

47. Rural Farmlands (Acquisition and Regrant) Act, 1966; Urban Leaseholds (Acquisition and Regrant) Act, 1968.

48. R. W. James, *op. cit.*, p. 215.

49. Arusha Declaration, in J. Nyerere, *Ujamaa – Essays on Socialism* (1968), p. 36.

50. Interim Constitution of Tanzania (Amendment) (No. 2) Act, 1967.

51. See, e.g., Civil Service (Amendment) Regulations, 1969 G.N. 180/69.

52. Arts. 32 and 33 Draft Constitution, 1972.

53. Art. 35 (1).

54. Arts. 35 (2) and 36 (2).

55. Art. 36 (1).

56. Corwin, *The Constitution and what it Means Today* (1958), pp. 218 *et seq.*; pp. 248 *et seq.*; and the cases there cited.

57. Above, ch. VIII.

58. *Patel* v. *Att.-Gen. for Zambia* 1968, S.5.Z.1.

59. S.22(2)(*b*) Zambia; S.79(2)(*b*) Kenya; S.12(2)(*b*) Botswana S.22(2)(*b*) Gambia.

60. Art. 17 (2)(*b*); also Art. 22 (3)(ii), Ghana 1969.

61. *Patel* v. *Attorney-General for Zambia, ibid.*

62. R. W. James, *op. cit.*, p. 175; see generally ch. VII.

63. R. W. James, *op. cit.*, p. 170.

64. Julius Nyerere, 'Socialism and Rural Development' in *Ujamaa – Essays on Socialism* (1968).

65. Julius Nyerere, *op. cit.*, p. 131.

66. R. W. James, *op. cit.*, p. 29.

67. *Ibid.*, p. 242.

68. *Ibid.*

CHAPTER XIII

PRESIDENTIALISM AND CONSTITUENT POWER

1. *Constituent Power and Popular Sovereignty*

Recalling again that the President, under the presidential system in Commonwealth Africa, is the organ that co-ordinates, and therefore dominates, the executive and legislative processes of government — in particular that it is he who, as the executive, has and controls the legislative initiative — we ask the question whether his power in this behalf includes or should include constituent power. The nature and importance of the constituent power need to be emphasised. It is a power to constitute a frame of government for a community, and a *constitution* is the means by which this is done. It is a primordial power, the ultimate mark of a people's sovereignty.

Sovereignty has three elements: the power to constitute a frame of government, the power to choose those to run the government, and the powers involved in governing. It is by means of the first, the constituent power, that the last are conferred. Implementing a community's constituent power, a constitution not only confers powers of government, but also defines the extent of those powers, and therefore their limits, in relation to the individual members of the community. This fact at once establishes the relation between a constitution and the powers of government; it is the relation of an original and a dependent or derivative power, between a superior and a subordinate authority. Herein lies the source and the reason for the constitution's supremacy.

Notwithstanding the earlier pretensions of monarchy, it is not now questioned that in any political community sovereignty in all its three aspects belongs to the people. The fact is indeed formally acknowledged and affirmed in many modern constitutions, notably the French and French-inspired constitutions. In rather significant terms, the Constitution of Ghana, 1960, affirms that 'the powers of the State derive from the people, as the source of power and the guardians of the State, by whom certain of those powers are now conferred on the institutions established by the Constitution and who shall have the right to exercise the remainder of those powers, and to choose their representatives in Parliament now established.'[1] Political theory should not, however, be allowed to cloud the real issue, which concerns the right to the exercise of sovereignty and, in particular, of constituent power. It is not disputed that, for reasons of numbers alone apart from anything else, the people themselves in their great mass cannot all join in governing. Of necessity this must be entrusted to selected individuals, but a power to make the selection must, also indisputably, rest with the people.

This leaves constituent power as the only possible point of controversy. If one imagines a new political community in the process of creating a political order, like the United States of America in 1787, then, there being as yet no state machinery other than the people themselves, the adoption of a constitution must inevitably be by the people, by whatever procedure they may consider most expedient and practicable in their situation. Necessarily, perhaps, they would have to commission a restricted number of individuals to frame proposals, which would then be thrown to the people for their reaction. The procedure of the constitutional commission should ideally involve consultation with the people. It may reasonably be assumed that, in our imaginary political community, the creation of a frame of government for the first time would generate a sense of involvement among the people, and that this in turn would make the proposals a matter of nation-wide concern, exciting active discussion at various levels of the society. But the proposals would also need to be put through an organised and formalised process of discussion in an assembly of the people, a *constituent assembly*, which of necessity again must consist of individuals selected by the people for the purpose. There the proposals would be discussed in detail, and amendments could be made. The final adoption of the proposals as the constitution and supreme law for the government of the community may follow either of two procedures, namely by the constituent assembly (with or without prior reference to the people at large) or directly by the people by means of a plebiscite. A constitution adopted in the way outlined is truly an original act, an emanation of the people from whom it derives its superior authority and its quality as a supreme, overriding law.

No doubt the view of the constitution as law made directly by the people raises some conceptual difficulty. For it was generally thought that law-making was a function *only* of a political community, not of the people in their mass; in other words that only a people organised as a political community can enact law through the machinery of the state. On this hypothesis, while the power of the people in their mass to constitute themselves into a political community is admitted, any such constituent act by which a constitution is established is purely a *political* act, giving the constitution only a political, as distinct from legal, existence. If it is intended that the constitution should also be a law, then it is for the resultant political creation, the state, to enact it as such through its regular procedure for law-making. Thus the American Constitution, as a law 'ordained and established' by the people, is said to have broken with 'the dominant tradition'.[2] Tradition is, however, sought to be reconciled by asserting that 'the agency by which constitutions are nowadays drawn up, namely constitutional conventions, had become such usual phenomena as to have been substantially assimilated to the machinery of organised government, so that one looking back to the State conventions that had in 1787 ratified the Constitution found it natural to regard them as organs of existing political societies, rather than as directly representative of the individuals back of these societies'.[3]

The argument smacks of excessive formalism. If the state is a creation of the people by means of a constitution, and derives its power of law-making from them, it may be wondered why the people who constitute and grant this power cannot act directly, in a referendum or otherwise, to give the constitution the character and force of law. After all, the constitution being the starting-point of a country's legal order, its 'lawness' should not depend on its enactment through the law-making mechanism of the state, but rather on its recognition as such by the people who are to be governed by it. It is today generally accepted that the American Constitution 'obtains its entire force and efficacy, not from the fact that it was ratified by a pre-existent political community or communities — for it was not — but from the fact that it was established by the people to be governed by it.'[4] There can be no doubt that today a referendum or plebiscite is a legally accepted way of adopting a constitution, though adherence to formalism still sometimes requires that, after adoption by the people, the constitution should be *formally* promulgated by a pre-existing state authority, invariably the Head of State. It is pertinent to emphasise, however, that a referendum or plebiscite lacks a genuine constituent and legitimising effect unless it is preceded, at the drafting stage or after, by serious discussion of the constitutional proposals on as wide a platform as possible. This is exemplified by the process followed in America, where the Constitution was drafted by a convention after thorough discussion, followed by even more mature and long deliberation in the ratifying conventions in the various states. An equally genuine process is adoption by a constituent assembly and ratification in a plebiscite, as in the case of the Swiss Constitution of 1848.

The question now is whether the process outlined above ceases to be relevant and applicable after a frame of government has once been constituted and invested with sovereign powers. In other words, are the sovereign powers entrusted to the rulers for the government of the country meant to embrace not only power of ordinary legislation and administration, but constituent power as well? The fact of colonialism in Commonwealth Africa, as elsewhere in the continent and parts of Asia and America, has meant that the people there had not the opportunity of exercising their constituent power at the inception of their political orders. The new states were a creation of the colonising powers, and throughout the colonial period constituent power was the exclusive prerogative of the suzerain power, jealously preserved to emphasise the force of its imperium; this enabled it to dictate the rate of constitutional advance in the dependency. The independence constitution was the product of a final exercise of this power. Deriving the source and the reason for its supremacy from the superior authority of the departing colonisers, this constitution bestowed powers of government upon the organs of government which it created. But what about constituent power? Do the organs of government also succeed to the residual sovereignty (i.e. constituent power) of their imperial creator? This is both a legal and a political question, which requires that the two aspects of constituent power – the strictly amending power and the adoption of a new constitution – be differentiated.

2. *The Strictly Amending Power*

An independence constitution in Commonwealth Africa invariably provides for its amendment. But significantly the conception underlying the provisions is that the power of amendment is a function of government, and so it was invariably conferred on parliament. The procedure for its exercise was of course always entrenched in the sense that a special majority (usually two-thirds, but sometimes three-fourths or even nine-tenths) was required.

The degree of entrenchment varied according to the gravity and importance of the provisions in the light of the political circumstances of the country concerned. Sometimes, as in Ghana (1957), Kenya (1963), Zambia (1964), Gambia (1965) and Botswana (1966), it may, in respect of certain provisions, involve approval by the people in a referendum or, in the federal set-up of Uganda (1962), the approval of the legislative assemblies of the regions. Although the actual power for enacting amendments into law always belonged to an organ of government and never to the people, the fact that a referendum procedure was instituted in as many as five of the countries shows that Britain was not passing its constituent power exclusively to the successor governments. The restrictions on the amending power in favour of the people may not have been inspired by any theory of constituent power as an original power belonging to the people, but simply by a desire to limit the government in order to give practical meaning and reality to the concept of the supremacy of the constitution. For, if parliament is to be able to amend the constitution in the same way as it makes ordinary law, even when such law is not expressed as being an amendment of the constitution but is merely inconsistent with it, then the supremacy of the constitution would have become a sham. Restrictions on the amending power protect and support the supremacy of the constitution, because an amendment or an inconsistent law that is not passed in accordance with them is thereby made *pro tanto* void.

It may be supposed that the more rigorous the restrictions, the better will the supremacy of the constitution be protected. In the context of Africa, with the prevalence of one-party states or of nationalist parties commanding overwhelming support, a restriction based solely on a parliamentary majority, even a two-thirds majority, may have little real effect as a limitation on government, since the special majority can be obtained almost as easily as a simple majority; all the government has to do is to ensure that all its supporters or (in a one-party state) most M.P.s are present at the time of the vote. There is, of course, no suggestion of the requirement for a special majority being entirely without effect in Africa, since if an amendment is so subversive of the spirit of the constitution or of the liberties of the individual, many government M.P.s may feel outraged to the point of rebelling against it and withholding their vote. It would require uncommon courage for a government M.P. to do this, and the occasion is likely to be rare in Africa. A special majority may be supplemented by an amendment being required to be made expressly, as in Ghana (1960) and in West Germany (1949). This ensures that a law inconsistent with the constitution cannot operate as an amendment of it, merely because it was passed by the prescribed majority. The danger about implied amendment is that it can be slipped through unnoticed among a mass of other provisions in a statute dealing with, say, land or some similar subject. There would be none of the publicity and public comment that an express amendment usually attracts. Gradually and surreptitiously, the liberties secured in the constitution can thus be eroded away.

The reality of the African political scene compels the conclusion that constitutionalism would be better safeguarded if the more fundamental provisions of the constitution are made subject to amendment by a procedure involving more than a parliamentary majority, e.g., the participation of some outside body or bodies, like the electorate at a referendum or other legislative assemblies in a federation. It is in the light of this reality that the referendum procedure, instituted in the independence constitutions of some of the countries, is to be considered. A constitution is supposed to be a permanent charter, which is to endure for ages to come, and not be be lightly altered to meet the temporary expediency of party politics. If the procedure for its amendment is not sufficiently rigid, and the temptation to alter it in accordance with the fancy or interest of the party in power is succumbed to over-readily, the constitution loses its sanctity and authority as the bedrock of constitutionalism, and may become instead a mockery of the very idea of a government of laws.

This is not to say that a constitution should be made unduly rigid, since that might invite its overthrow by revolutionary means when a genuine need for change has arisen and cannot be effected constitutionally. Referring to the Cyprus Constitution, 1960, which made some forty-eight articles incorporated from the Zurich Agreement completely unalterable, Justice Vassiliades has remarked upon what he calls 'the sin of ignoring time and human nature in the making of our constitution'. 'Time moves on continuously,' he says; 'man is, by nature, a creature of evolution and change, as time moves on. The constitution was, basically, made fixed and immovable. . . . As time and man moved on, while the constitution remained fixed, the inevitable crack came — perhaps a good deal sooner than some people may have thought — with grave and far-reaching consequence'.[5] Mr Dowuona-Hammond, a parliamentary secretary in Nkrumah's government, has also emphasised the evolutionary character of a constitution. 'The constitution of any country,' he said, 'develops by evolution. No constitution is static.'[6]

It may even be conceded that the need for a constitution that is able to evolve with changing social and political conditions is perhaps greatest in a developing country launched into independent statehood under a constitution made for it by its former imperial masters. Although it has become convenient among African political leaders to make the colonial origin of their constitution the reason for every assault upon it, nevertheless it is true that their constitutions bear unmistakable imprints of colonialism designed to protect foreign (imperialist) business interests, to entrench the rule of a favoured group or to perpetuate a bequeathed political system. Moreover, the society of a developing African country is in a state of flux, modern government itself is at an experimental stage, and the experiment is made all the more difficult by the clash of cultures — between traditional and modern forms and procedures. The conflicts inherent in this situation must be rationalised, and the constitution should be able to lend itself to the process of rationalisation.

The amending power in Africa is thus open to conflicting objectives: the prevention of the constitution from being used as an instrument in the struggle for power, and the need to make it respond to the changing conditions and outlook of the people. It is believed that the independence constitutions struck the right balance in many cases through the procedure of special entrenchment for certain provisions. It may have erred in the range of matters specially entrenched, but that should not invalidate the technique altogether. The really fundamental aspects of a constitution should be immune from alteration without reference to the people. It is interesting to note that Ghana, the greatest opponent of restrictions on the amending power in its Independence Constitution, recognised the truth of this matter by reserving to the people the alteration of seventeen out of fifty-five articles of its Republican Constitution, 1960.

Given the propensity of presidentialism in Africa to aggregate power to the government, we may now enquire into the fate of the restrictions on the amending power since independence. How and for what purposes has the amending power been used, and with what frequency?

(i) *Abolition or Attenuation of Restrictions on the Amending Power*

As always, Ghana was the pace-setter, the first to assault the restrictions on the amending power. It may be recalled that her Independence Constitution of 1957 required a two-thirds majority for constitutional amendment, and, additionally, reference to all regional assemblies and approval by two-thirds of them in case of an amendment of an entrenched provision or one abolishing a regional assembly or diminishing its functions or powers.[7] A regional assembly to be abolished or whose functions or powers were to be diminished had to be among the approving two-thirds, and its approval could only be dispensed with by means of referendum conducted for the purpose in the region, at which the majority of the registered voters voted in favour. A bill amending an entrenched provision had further to be referred to (though not approved by) all houses of chiefs; to enable a house of chiefs to consider the bill and communicate its view thereon to the appropriate regional assembly, consideration of the bill by the latter had to be delayed for one month after reference to it. If a bill affected the traditional functions or privileges of a chief, then, after its first reading in the national assembly, it had forthwith to be referred to the house of chiefs of the region in which the chief concerned exercised his functions, and the national assembly was not to proceed with the second reading of the bill until three months after its first introduction in the house.[8]

There was another type of amendment for which a referendum and the approval of the affected regional assemblies were necessary, namely alteration of regional boundaries involving the transfer of not less than 10,000 persons or the creation of a new region. In every case the Speaker or other person presiding was required to certify compliance with these restrictions. The provisions specially entrenched covered a wide range of matters — executive power, parliament, freedom of conscience and religion, prohibition of racial discrimination, protection of property rights, chiefs, public service, judicature, consolidated fund, auditor-general, the regions and their organs, franchise, general elections and the amending procedure itself.

All these restrictions were abolished in 1958 by the Constitution (Repeal of Restrictions) Act, which was passed strictly in accordance with the prescribed procedure. Thereafter a simple majority sufficed for every constitutional amendment. During the debate on the bill, Nkrumah, then Prime Minister, gave as the reasons for the abolition the need of Ghana as a developing country for certainty and flexibility in its laws, contending that the rigid amending procedure had made it 'difficult to say, with certainty, whether any particular Act of Parliament may or may not indirectly amend the Constitution. It would be easy to challenge much of the legislation required for social development or for industrial development on the ground that it indirectly affected some provision of the Order in Council'.[9] But the leader of the opposition, Dr Busia, pointed to a different but equally important need of a developing country, namely the stability of its constitution. It was, he argued, this particular need that it was sought to secure through rigid entrenchment. 'For if the Constitution can be amended by a simple majority of those present and voting, it would be a fragile document, and no one could place any reliance on any of its provisions, for the provisions could be changed any day, any moment.' Further, the stability of the constitution was necessary to create confidence among foreign investors who would naturally be concerned for the security of their investments.[10]

Writing in 1963, Nkrumah castigated the restrictions as an imperialist imposition, an affront to the sovereignty of the new state, and a perversion of the democratic principle.[11] As we have earlier commented,[12] this new argument amounts to a rejection of the very concept of the supremacy of the constitution and thus of limited government. It seems to regard the constitution as an instrument of a narrow majority, instead of as one that seeks to balance and accommodate competing interests within the nation, with the object of trying to hold the loyalty of all as consenting members of the political community.

When he promulgated his own Constitution in 1960, Nkrumah, interestingly enough, re-instituted restrictions on the amending power of parliament. It has already been noted that only the people, acting directly by referendum, could amend seventeen of the fifty-five articles of the Republican Constitution – i.e. those relating to the powers of the people, the status of Ghana as a unitary, one-party republic, surrender of the country's sovereignty, the executive presidency and the election of its incumbent, appointment of ministers, parliament, taxation, public loans, the courts, armed forces, and special powers of the first President.

The first assault in Kenya was mainly directed, not at the principle of entrenchment as such, but rather at the unnecessarily wide range of matters regulated by the Constitution. The case for constitutional entrenchment is weakened when the Constitution contains matters which by their nature should not be there at all, matters which should more fittingly be dealt with in ordinary legislation. No doubt because of its federal nature, the Independence Constitution of Kenya, 1963, indulged in undue prolixity in an attempt to regulate federal-regional relations down to their minutest details. There were whole sets of detailed and lengthy provisions on land tenure, a central land board and control over transactions in agricultural land (covering twenty pages of print), local government (ten pages) the police (eleven pages), financial relations (twelve pages), etc. Kenya's Independence Constitution was indeed, in the words of Attorney-General Njonjo, 'an unwelcome ... monstrosity of 300 pages',[13] of which 148 pages were schedules. The Kenya government thus felt a justifiable need both to excise the unnecessary matter and reduce the minuteness of the detail of other matter, with the object of simplifying the Constitution to make it readable and intelligible. The basic political motivation for these changes is, of course, another matter, which will be discussed below.

The excision was very wide-ranging. Whole chapters or parts of chapters and schedules were excised, resulting in the shortening of the Constitution by over 200 pages. Speaking on the amendment in October 1964, Tom Mboya, then Minister for Justice and Constitutional Affairs, said that 'the constitutional entrenchment of provisions which in other countries were provided for in the ordinary law is a derogation from the sovereignty of Parliament. A parliamentary democracy is in the hands of Parliament, and Parliament, at election time, is in the hands of the people. Those who fear what Parliament may do, those who fear the powers which we now transfer from the Constitution to this Parliament, do not just fear a tyrant but they are afraid of their own people, they are afraid of democracy itself. They have no confidence in their own people and in their ability through this Parliament to govern and rule over this country'.[14]

The method of entrenchment itself came in for a small measure of attenuation in this first assualt (1964). The original method involved a three-fourths majority in both the house of representatives and the senate, or alternatively popular approval by two-thirds majority of voters in a referendum conducted for the purpose.[15] With such popular approval the amendment could then be re-introduced in parliament and passed by a simple majority. Certain provisions were specially entrenched, i.e. those relating to the senate, citizenship, human rights, the districts of Kenya, the establishment and organs of the regions, the formal division of powers (though not the enumeration of the matters to which the powers extended, the special provisions relating to legislative and executive powers, or the financial relations of the centre and the regions), legislative and financial procedures, the judicature, trust land, control over transactions in agricultural land, and the amending procedure. These required in addition a nine-tenths majority in the senate. For the amendment of the section providing for the appointment of a commission to review the revenue apportionment procedure, only a two-thirds majority in both houses of parliament was required, but the approval of the regional assemblies of at least four regions must be obtained.[16] The procedure for the alteration of the boundaries between regions required agreement in writing between the presidents of the regional assemblies of the two regions concerned, an approving law passed with a two-thirds majority by the assembly of each of the two regions, and the approval by resolution of both houses of parliament.[17]

By the first two amendments in 1964,[18] which came into operation on the same date (December 12, 1964), the provisions on the financial relations between the centre and the regions were repealed in their entirety and with them the procedure for their review. Also repealed were the entrenched provisions for the alteration of regional boundaries; thereafter such alteration was to be simply by Act of parliament enacted in pursuance of the recommendation made after due investigation by a boundaries commissioner (who must be a present or former superior court judge) appointed by the President on the recommendation of the Chief Justice.

In 1965 the remaining restrictions were all but swept away. The majority was reduced from three-fourths to 65 per cent, the referendum requirement, and the special entrenchment with its nine-tenths majority in the senate, were repealed.[19] With the virtual reduction of the regional structure into a system of local government in 1965 (the regions were then re-named provinces), the senate — and hence its participation in the amending process — was abolished in 1967.[20] In 1968 the establishment of provinces, their organs, functions, powers and every other provision relating to the provincial structure, including the new provision (substituted in 1964) for the alteration of provincial boundaries, were excised from the Constitution.[21] The final stage had thus been reached where any amendment could be made by a unicameral national assembly with a 65 per cent majority (less than the usual two-thirds). This is still the position today.[22]

Uganda's Independence Constitution was more federal than Kenya's in that, apart from the legislative lists, a separate constitution for each of the federal states was scheduled to the national constitution. And whereas in Kenya the central parliament could amend the entire constitution, subject to the rigid procedure entrenched, the central legislature in Uganda could not amend the state constitutions; only their own respective legislatures could do this, by a two-thirds majority, and with the consent of the centre (the government, in case of Buganda, and the national assembly, in the case of the other federal states) in respect of certain amendments.[23] Certain other amendments in a federal state (other than Buganda) required a referendum. The national constitution itself was amendable by parliament by a two-thirds majority on the second and third readings, and with the approving resolution (supported by a two-thirds majority) of the legislative assembly of Buganda and/or the other federal states, if the provision to be amended affected either or both of them,[24] e.g., the provision establishing the federal states and their constitutions.[25] But no referendum procedure was instituted, presumably because the requirement of consent by the federal states was special entrenchment enough.

When Prime Minister Obote seized the government in February 1966 and abolished the Independence Constitution, replacing it with a new revolutionary constitution, the amendment procedure underwent a radical change. A quasi-federal structure was retained, with a separate constitution for each of the federal states. However, parliament was given power to amend, by a simple majority vote of its members, both the national and the state constitutions; the only limitation was that the amendment of the provisions establishing the federal states and their constitutions, and those relating to human rights, the status of the rulers of the kingdoms or the ruler of Busoga, *mailo* land tenure, the list of matters within the exclusive competence of the federal states, and the amendment procedure must be consented to by a two-thirds majority of the legislative assembly of the kingdom or territory affected.[26] A further limitation was that the provisions in the constitutions of the federal states relating to the traditional titles, dignities and precedence of the rulers; succession to the throne; regency; and recognition by the President of a new ruler on the death of his predecessor could not be amended at all by parliament. The federal structure was abolished completely in 1967 (the territory of Busoga had been dis-established in 1966 as a federal state[27]); thereafter a simple majority in the national assembly sufficed for ordinary amendment, while a two-thirds majority on the second and third readings was required for the entrenched provisions — namely citizenship, human rights, the judicature, parliamentary votes of no confidence in the government, removal of the President for incapacity, the establishment and definition of parliament, constituencies, the mode of exercising legislative power, and the establishment of the districts of Uganda and their boundaries.[28] A certificate of compliance signed by the Speaker was also necessary before the amendment bill could be assented to by the President.

The device of special entrenchment was also instituted in the Independence Constitution of Zambia, 1964. For ordinary amendments, publication for thirty days in the gazette before first reading, and a two-thirds majority on the second and third readings, were required.[29] An amendment of a specially entrenched provision must in addition be submitted to a referendum and approved by a majority, not of those actually voting, but of all registered voters (i.e. general election registration). And what had to be submitted and approved was a statement of the actual provisions of the amending act, and not just a question framed by the government. The specially entrenched matters were human rights, the judicature, the procedure relating to the presentation of bills for presidential assent and to the making of statutory instruments, and the amendment procedure itself. The referendum procedure proved an unwelcome restraint, and was abolished in 1969.[30] This system – without the referendum procedure – has remained unchanged in the new one-party state Constitution.

The reasons for the abolition given on behalf of the government were most revealing, as they showed its thinking on the question whether constituent power belongs to the people or to the government as part of powers entrusted to it for the government of the community. It was said by Mr Wina, Minister of Information, Broadcasting and Tourism, that a referendum for this purpose was 'an abdication by the government of power that should properly be theirs'[31] – 'theirs' not by the Constitution but solely by right of being the government. It is not clear whether the thinking reflected in Mr Wina's assertion was meant to apply to the two aspects of constituent power – constitutional amendment and adoption of a new constitution. Most likely, in view of later development in the country, it was intended to extend to both. Mr Wina further argued that, in so far as the result was seldom materially different from the votes at the preceding general election, a referendum was a waste of money, energy and time, and therefore useless. Citing both Dicey and Finer,[32] he said it had a 'purely negative effect', in that it only caused 'confusion and personal group collisions, which cost energy to try and overcome; [it would] divert the attention of the people from the programmes of progress and retard the programme of legislative work and inflame antagonisms'.[33] The Vice-President, Mr Simon Kapwepwe, who was in charge of the bill, rested the case for abolition on the grounds that the Constitution was a British creation accepted at the time as a compromise to facilitate independence. But, as the continually changing and developing needs of the country demanded radical changes, a more flexible and less expensive amending procedure was necessary.[34] The opposition viewed the abolition as an attempt by the government to arrogate absolute power and as tantamount to dictatorship.[35]

The amendment procedure in the Independence Constitution of Botswana, 1966, was patterned on that of Zambia, with all the requirements about publication for thirty days in the gazette, a two-thirds majority and a referendum.[36] But there is this difference: a two-thirds majority was necessary only at the final reading and only for the amendment of certain provisions; the provisions for the amendment of which a referendum was required were much fewer (establishment, powers, procedure, life, sessions and dissolution of parliament, parliamentary vote of no confidence in the government, the judicature, constituencies, franchise and elections); final voting on an amendment for which a two-thirds majority and a referendum are required is not to take place before three months after the previous voting. This procedure is still operative at the time of writing.

Gambia is the fifth country where special entrenchment involving a referendum was instituted at independence. An amendment bill must be supported on the final reading by a two-thirds majority and, in so far as it affected any specially entrenched provisions, approved at a referendum by half of the registered voters (general election registration) or by two-thirds of those actually voting.[37] A certificate of compliance with these requirements signed by the Speaker must accompany the bill when it was presented for the assent. The range of matters specially entrenched was wider than in the other countries, covering much the greater part of the Constitution – human rights, constituencies, appointment of a constituency boundaries commission, legislative power, sessions, prerogation and dissolution of parliament, general elections, director of public prosecutions, finance, salaries charged on the consolidated fund, public debt, director of audit, judicature, the public service, and the amending procedure itself.

In view of what has happened elsewhere, it is remarkable that the Republican Constitution of 1970 has re-enacted all the requirements (including referendum), and in two respects even strengthened them, by requiring publication of the bill in at least two issues of the gazette, and by making the two-thirds majority applicable on both the second and third readings.[38] However, it has also reduced the range of specially entrenched provisions, limiting them to the status of the country as a sovereign republic, human rights, the judicature (except appeals to the Judicial Committee), parliament, legislative power and procedure, summoning, sessions, prorogation and dissolution of the national assembly, date of general election after dissolution, and the amending procedure.

The amendment procedure in the Tanganyikan and Malawian Independence Constitution was the least rigid of all, involving only two-thirds majority on the second and third readings.[39] This restriction has survived in the Republican Constitution of Tanganyika, 1962, the Interim Constitution of Tanzania, 1965,[40] and the Republican Constitution of Malawi, 1966; the last (Malawian) also requires an amendment to be express.[41]

The final picture, then, is that the referendum procedure has not survived in two (Kenya and Zambia) of the five countries (Ghana, Kenya, Zambia, Gambia and Botswana) in which it was instituted at independence. The other restrictions on the amending power have either been completely abolished (Ghana) or substantially attenuated (Kenya and Uganda) or preserved (Tanzania, Zambia, Malawi, Botswana and Gambia).

(ii) *Uses of the Amending Power*

Among the presidential regimes of Commonwealth Africa, the frequency of constitutional amendment can rightly be described as excessive in some and moderate in others. Including adoption of a new constitution, there have been no less than seventeen amendments since independence in Zambia, thirteen in Malawi, eleven in Kenya, ten in Tanzania, six in Uganda, five in Ghana and four in Botswana. One would not quarrel with amendment *per se* if a genuine need for it exists, though too frequent amendment may tend to reduce the constitution to the level of an ordinary law, depriving it of any claim to respectability and devotion, which might in time earn for it a status akin to sanctity.

No doubt many of the amendments in the presidential regimes of Commonwealth Africa were motivated by the genuinely-felt needs of the countries concerned. The amendments in Zambia in 1969 and in Uganda in 1970, for example, were intended to facilitate the indigenisation of the economy by making it possible for the government to take over or acquire majority shareholdings in the foreign-owned business concerns without having to pay — as the independence constitution stipulated — 'adequate and prompt' compensation assessed, in default of agreement, by the court, and remittable abroad without restriction.[42]

The establishment of a republic and a presidential system of government can also be said not to have been motivated by party political consideration but by a sincere conviction as to what was best for an independent African country engaged in trying to pull itself up by its bootstrings.[43] The abolition of many of the safeguards instituted in the independence constitution — human rights, public and judicial service commissions, the party system, federalism or regionalism, and bicameralism — may be open to differing evaluation, necessarily subjective, as to whether, in the circumstances of the countries concerned, they were called for by a genuine need. The fact that one entertains a view of the matter different from that of the rulers is not enough to condemn a particular change as politically motivated. The rulers are, after all, entitled to their own judgment as to what political forms and procedures might be best for the country, and to use their position of power to implement that judgment. That is a privilege which they cannot reasonably be denied. However, the circumstances in which some of these changes were introduced raise legitimate doubts as to whether party political considerations were not dominant motives. The arguments have been fully canvassed elsewhere, and it is unnecessary to go over them again here.[44]

While the motivation for certain changes may be a matter for differing interpretation, there are some of which it can confidently be said that the amending power was being used largely, if not solely, to advance the interests of the ruling party as against those of its opponents. For example, the amendments in Kenya and Zambia in 1966 authorising the forfeiture of a M.P.'s seat on his resignation or expulsion from the party on whose platform he was elected were introduced in circumstances that left no doubt that they were politically motivated.[45] It is thus not altogether without justification that an opposition M.P. in Zambia, Mr Liso, charged that most of the amendments were designed to 'suit the ruling party rather than the Zambian public as a whole'.[46] In Kenya after the forfeiture amendment had been passed, the defectors from the ruling party, whom it was sought to unseat through the amendment, argued with apparent conviction that their seats had not in fact been vacated, as the amendment did not in its terms purport to be retroactive. The government immediately rushed through yet another amendment applying the forfeiture amendment to M.P.s who resigned from a party before its commencement.[47] Needless to say, like the one it was amplifying,[48] this amendment contained just this provision. It was also the interest of the ruling party in Kenya in crushing the breakaway Kenya People's Union (KPU) that prompted the Constitution of Kenya (Amendment) (No. 3) Act, 1966. This Act, by repealing the rigorous procedure of the Independence Constitution for the declaration of an emergency, authorised the President to bring into operation, whenever he thought fit, the Preservation of Public Security Act — the provisions of which were by the same amendment Act, radically amended to the same end.[49]

3. *Adoption of a New Constitution*

With the exception of Botswana, all the presidential regimes in Commonwealth Africa have adopted new constitutions since independence. It should be clear from what has already been said that the process described above for the adoption of a new constitution for our imaginary new political community does not cease to be relevant and applicable merely because there already exists a government equipped with sovereign powers. The mandate conferred upon a government by the votes that put it in power is a limited one; it is a mandate to rule in accordance with the existing constitution. And in most democratic countries, the doctrine is accepted that no fundamental change in the political system should be made without a specific mandate from the people.[50]

We may here recall the various steps in that process — the framing of proposals for a constitution, popular consultation, formalised discussion of the proposals in an assembly of the people (i.e. constituent assembly) and, lastly, final adoption by the constituent assembly or by the people at a plebiscite. The methods used in the Commonwealth presidential regimes in adoping their new constitutions will now be considered to see the extent to which they conformed or departed from this procedure.

(i) *The Framing of Constitutional Proposals*

As already stated, this is a job that must necessarily be entrusted to a small group of individuals. And where a government already exists, responsibility for the appointment of the group may be conceded to it, provided the appointment is made objectively with the purpose of obtaining the services of the persons best qualified for the job, and also with due regard to the major interests comprised in the nation. This procedure was not in fact followed in any of the countries except Zambia and Tanzania. In Ghana (1960), Tanganyika (1962), Kenya (1964), Uganda (1966 and 1967), Malawi (1966), Gambia (1970) and Sierra Leone (1971), the proposals for a new republican, presidential constitution were framed by the government. The government's right to initiate proposals was questioned in Uganda in 1967 on the grounds that it had 'outlived its legal life', that 'ten per cent of its members were either in detention or otherwise politically incapacitated.'[51] To the Ghana opposition party's demand for the appointment of a constitutional commission, the government replied that it was 'the duty of the Government and of the elected representatives of the people in the Constituent Assembly to advise what is, in their view, the most suitable form for the Constitution of the Republic of Ghana.'[52] While it may again be conceded that the government has a responsibility in this, yet to treat a constitution like an ordinary law and apply to it the government's right of initiative is to undermine the nature and importance of the exercise. Like other organisations and individuals in the country, the government is perfectly entitled to submit proposals to a constitutional commission. The important point, however, is that the government's proposals should not be the only ones to form the basis of discussions. The advantage of basing the discussions on more than one set of proposals is illustrated by the experience of the United States, where several plans were submitted to the Philadelphia Convention in 1787.

The government proposals in the Commonwealth African presidential regimes took the form of a draft constitution accompanied by an explanatory note. The explanatory note in Ghana and Tanganyika, for example, explained the basic principles underlying the proposals.[53] In Uganda, the explanatory note came after each article, but none enlarged on the general philosophy behind the proposals as a whole. This has been criticised on the ground that the Constitution was thereby made difficult to understand as a whole.[54]

In Tanzania (1965) and Zambia (1972) a commission was appointed by the President to frame proposals. In both cases the independence of the commission appeared to have been somewhat tainted by the fact of being chaired by the Vice-President of the country and of the ruling party. Further, as may be recalled,[55] the central feature of the new constitution, the establishment of a one-party state, had been predetermined by the government and emphatically excluded from the terms of reference of the commission, whose task was merely to recommend the form which the one-party government should take. In the Zambian case the President had directed the commission to 'pay due regard and adhere to the following principles as cardinal, inviolable and built-in safeguards of One-Party Participatory Democracy in Zambia':[56]

1. Zambia shall continue to be a Sovereign Republic.
2. Zambia must continue to build a humanist society.
3. All citizens of Zambia shall continue to enjoy complete equality.
4. The supremacy of the rule of law and independence of the Judiciary shall continue to be maintained.
5. The fundamental rights and freedom of the individual shall be protected as now provided under Chapter III of the Constitution of the Republic of Zambia.
6. The right of the individual to freely choose leaders and representatives to Parliament and many other democratic institutions, national and local, shall be fully preserved.
7. Supreme power must be vested in the people and everything shall be done to ensure that power is exercised by them directly where possible, and indirectly through established democratic representative institutions. There shall, therefore, be complete freedom among the people to participate fully in the running of their affairs at local and national level through institutions under people's own control.

8. Zambia is part and in the front-line of the continent-wide revolutionary movement which seeks to liberate Africa and rid the Continent of all forms of imperialism, colonialism, racism and foreign exploitation which have plagued the African people in the past. Zambia's geo-political position demands a strong and purposeful Government and a united nation if the Zambian revolution is to succeed. There can, therefore, be no room for complacency and for lofty ideas.

9. Zambia is permanently opposed to exploitation of man by man and the people of Zambia will persist relentlessly in their struggle for self-reliance and the establishment of protective measures against possible exploitation by foreign and local economic interests. The people of Zambia will continue to fight against the establishment of economic, social, political and cultural classes in order to guarantee the equality of all human beings in a humanist society.

If an independent commission is used, its proposals should of course be submitted to the government. A difficult point is what should be the powers of the government with respect to the proposals. Should it have unfettered freedom to reject or amend the proposals as it likes? The answer should depend largely on the nature and extent of the popular consultation made by the commission, and on whether the proposals reflect the views merely of the commission or of the majority of the people consulted. A small group of individuals, no matter how eminent and well qualified, has no better right than the government itself to impose its views upon the whole community. For this reason among others, consultation with the public should be on as wide a platform as possible. If the proposals have the support of the public, who have been consulted, then the government cannot justifiably have an unfettered right to modify them as it pleases.

In this respect again the procedure in Zambia seems to have undermined the popular will. For the proposals made by the commission after popular consultation were modified in the most important respects by the government, most of these modifications being designed to remove the limitations which the commission had sought to impose on the powers of the President.[57] These limitations have been discussed above,[58] and need not be repeated here. A *Times of Zambia* editorial rightly questioned the need for the whole exercise — appointment of the commission and popular consultation — if the most vital proposals made by the commission could be modified by the government at its pleasure. This, of course, serves to emphasise the difference between a body of framers commissioned by the people themselves and a presidential commission such as was used in Zambia and Tanzania. It is fair to say that the proposals of the Tanzanian presidential commission were faithfully implemented in the resultant constitution.

(ii) *Popular Consultation*

Popular consultation is necessary if a constitution is to command the confidence, loyalty and obedience of the people. It is on this that the legitimacy of the constitution and of the government largely depends. It cannot be disputed that a major cause of the collapse of constitutional government in many of the new states was the general lack of respect for the constitution among the people and even among the politicians themselves. The state itself is an alien – if also beneficial – creation; its existence is characterised by a certain artificiality in the eyes of the people, and it is remote from their lives and thought.

The constitution embodies ideas that are not part of the native cultural heritage of the people, ideas originating in Roman law and Greek philosophy, but which by a process of reception have become a common heritage of the whole of Europe – but certainly not of Africa. It is not, of course, suggested as a condition for the legitimacy of a system of government that it must be the product of a traditional culture and philosophy. If that were so, no modern system of government could ever have legitimacy in most of the emergent countries whose traditional cultural systems have yielded nothing relevant to the organisation of the central government of a modern complex society. Yet the alien character of the system of government instituted by the constitutions of the new states, and of the ideas underlying it, made it necessary that something should be done to legitimise them in the eyes of the people. What this means is that a constitution should be generally understood by the people, and acceptable to them, because without these two factors it cannot hope to command their loyalty. To achieve this understanding and acceptance, a constitution needs to be put through a process of popularisation, with a view to generating public interest in it and an attitude that everybody has a stake in it, that it is the common property of all. The people must be made to identify themselves with the constitution. Without this sense of identification, of attachment and involvement, a constitution would always remain a remote, artificial object, with no more real existence than the paper on which it is written.

Ideally, consultation should occur at two stages: before and after the framing of the proposals. Over this the countries of Commonwealth African have erred grievously. In Tanganyika (1962), Kenya (1964), Uganda (1966 and 1967), Malawi (1966), Gambia (1970) and Sierra Leone (1971), no popular consultation on the constitutional proposals ever took place. The constitutional proposals as framed by the government were simply tabled before the enacting body. Only in Ghana (1960), Tanzania (1965) and Zambia (1972) did popular consultation take place, but at one stage only – in Tanzania and Zambia before the framing of the proposals, and in Ghana after. But how real and meaningful was the consultation?

The method of consultation used by both the Tanzanian and Zambian commissions provides a useful basis upon which to evaluate the reality and meaningfulness of the consultation. The nature and quality of this method can best be judged if its description in the report of each commission is quoted in full without any attempt at paraphrase. The Tanzanian commission described its method of consultation as follows:[59]

18. The members of the Commission started their work with a heavy sense of responsibility. We had been entrusted with the task of making recommendations for a new Constitution. Our recommendations, if accepted by the President, could affect the happiness and prosperity of the people of Tanzania for generations to come. Our first thought therefore was to turn to the people themselves for help. Accordingly, at our first meeting we decided on a full process of consultation to take place in all parts of the country and at all levels of society. In order to facilitate the process of consultation and give to it a sense of direction we prepared a questionnaire in the light of our terms of reference and the guidance given to us by the President. The questionnaire was in the following terms:

(1) Should TANU be open to all citizens of Tanganyika regardless of their political opinions? If not, should a citizen be entitled to join if he accepts the principles of TANU as set out in the TANU Constitution?

(2) Should the National Assembly and the National Executive of TANU both continue in existence? If so, what should be the relationship and the division of powers between them? If the National Executive and the National Assembly should be amalgamated, how should the members of the amalgamated body be chosen:

(a) be direct elections, like the National Assembly at present? Or

(b) indirectly, like the TANU National Executive at present?

(3) Should local government authorities and district committees of TANU both continue in existence? If so, what should be the relationship and division of powers between them?

(4) Should all candidates for election to the legislature and local government bodies be members of TANU? What other qualifications (if any) should there be for such candidates?

(5) How should candidates for the legislature and local government bodies be elected, given that the people should be able freely to choose the person they wish to represent them from amongst those qualified for election? In particular:

(i) should there be freedom for any qualified person who wishes to stand for election to do so?

(ii) if not, what machinery is necessary to select candidates or limit the number who may submit themselves to the people's choice?

(6) How should the President of the Republic be elected?

(7) Should members of the legislature and local government bodies be subject to Party discipline or should they be allowed to speak and vote as they like?

(8) Should civil servants and other public employees be allowed to join TANU?

(9) Is there any objection to civil servants being members of the legislature or local government bodies? If not, should the terms and conditions on which politicians and civil servants serve the State be identical?

(10) (*a*) Should there be any restrictions on the number of persons in government service who are members of the legislature or a local government?

(10) (*b*) Is it essential that all Ministers and Junior Ministers should be Members of the Legislature?

19. The questionnaire was published as a General Notice in the Tanganyika Gazette on the 21st February, 1964, and the public were invited to submit memoranda before the 25th April, 1964. At the same time the Commission announced that it would be touring the Regions to seek the views of members of the public at a series of meetings. Publicity was given to the work of the Commission in a national broadcast and in the press. Broadcasting to the nation the Chairman emphasised the importance of the Commission's work in framing a constitution which would have as its mainstay the National Ethic. In the same broadcast the Chairman read the whole questionnaire to the people in Swahili and the broadcast was subsequently repeated several times. At a later date, just before the commencement of the tours, the Secretary was instructed to broadcast a message reminding the people of the obligation they owed to the nation to submit their views to the Commission, either orally or by means of written memoranda.

20. The Commission commenced its tours of the Regions on 16th March, 1964. The members divided themselves into Parties A, B and C. The first two had four members each, while Party C consisted of three members. Party A toured Kilimanjaro, Arusha, Dodoma, Singida, Mbeya and Iringa Regions. Tanga, Morogoro, Coast, Ruvuma and Mtwara Regions were visited by Party C, while Party B toured Mara, Shinyanga, Mwanza, West Lake, Kigoma and Tabora Regions. All the tours were undertaken between 16th March and 25th April, 1964. The Chairman of the Commission, the Honourable R. M. Kawawa, M.P., toured the Mara, Shinyanga, Coast, Dodoma and Singida Regions during March and early April, 1964. The Secretary accompanied the Chairman to the Coast, Dodoma and Shinyanga Regions and Party A to the Mbeya Region.

21. The response of the public to the process of consultation was most encouraging. From early in March memoranda began pouring in to the Secretariat of the Commission; other memoranda were

brought from the Regions by the members of the visiting parties. The visiting parties themselves held barazas in the areas toured by them with the object of eliciting from the public their views on the questionnaire. The barazas, without exception, were well attended and characterised by a frank and open discussion of the various issues facing the Commission.

22. The substance of what was said at the barazas was recorded in each case by a member of the visiting party and embodied in a report to the Commission as a whole. Although a very wide variety of views were expressed in the memoranda and at the barazas there was very little divergence in the main trends of opinion appearing from an analysis of the memoranda on the one hand and the reports submitted by the visiting parties on the other. This has suggested to the Commission the encouraging conclusion that the more educated sections of the community who submitted written memoranda were thinking on broadly similar lines to the ordinary men and women who preferred to express their views orally at a baraza.

The method of the Zambia commission, as described in its report, was as follows:[60]

7. We unanimously agreed that as we were dealing with such a crucial national issue it was imperative that supreme power of decision making should be vested in the Zambian people and therefore it was unquestionably desirable to give ample opportunity to as many Zambia citizens as possible to enable them to express their views on this matter either orally or in writing. In order to achieve the above objectives we decided—

    (a) to call for oral and written submissions from all Zambian citizens both at home and abroad. We made it clear at the outset that the nature of our task required that only Zambian nationals participated;

    (b) to visit all provincial headquarters and districts. The itinerary of our visits is shown at Appendix II.

8. We further agreed not to split into groups when touring the country in order to afford ample opportunity to each and every Commissioner to be physically present at every sitting to familiarise himself with the people's feelings and aspirations.

9. A wide and intensive publicity campaign was mounted throughout the country for Zambians to come forward and give evidence. Our programme was widely publicised and the dates and venues of our sittings were advertised in the national and local newspapers and on radio and television.

10. Bearing in mind that the majority of Zambians would not be fully conversant with the official language (English), we decided to translate our terms of reference into the main local languages and posters were distributed throughout the Republic.

11. In order to encourage members of the public to come forward and submit their views, the Chairman of the Commission,

Vice-President Mainza Chona, held a press conference which was covered by both television and radio. In his press conference the Chairman further elaborated on the Commission's task and made an appeal to all Zambians irrespective of their political affiliations, social status, creed or sex, to rise to their national responsibilities by submitting their representations to the Commission.

12. As directed by our terms of reference all our hearings were held in public and accordingly members of the public were free to attend. In order to enable as many people as possible to attend, our hearings were held in the largest available hall at each centre and where the hall was not big enough, the public address system was utilised. At Kaputa, for example, we held our hearings in the open.

13. The procedure which we adopted at our public hearings was that before the submission of representations, the Chairman asked the petitioner for his particulars and explained to him the Commission's terms of reference and its tasks. In most cases we asked petitioners after submitting their views to clarify certain issues arising from their submissions. We allowed petitioners much latitude and freedom in making their submissions. A number of petitioners did not confine themselves strictly to the terms of reference regarding the form of the One-Party Democracy as such and discussed matters relating to the pros and cons of its establishment. We, however, insisted that our task was not to listen to petitioners who gave reasons for or against the establishment of the One-Party System.

14. We are satisfied that we received views from a cross-section of the population including those from political detainees. We then proceeded to consider written and oral evidence presented to us.

Part of the Zambian commission's terms of reference filled the place of the questionnaire used by the Tanzanian commission; it too, therefore, needs to be quoted in full:[61]

(*a*) The nature of the Presidency, methods of election including the important question of whether or not a Presidential candidate shall be eligible for re-election, and if so, after how many terms.

(*b*) The nature and structure of Government in general including the relationship between Cabinet, Parliament and the Central Committee of the Party.

(*c*) The nature and structure of Parliament itself and its relationship to, for example, the National Council of the Party.

(*d*) The relationship between various political and administrative, elected and appointed bodies ranging from Village Productivity and Village Political/Section Committees to the Cabinet and the Central Committee of the Party.

(*e*) The Code of Leadership for Parliamentarians and other leaders in order to qualify for various positions in which supreme power normally vested in the people, is exercised by them indirectly on behalf of the people.

(*f*) The supremacy of the Party *vis-à-vis* Government administration.

(*g*) The amount of freedom of the people to form pressure groups based on tribal loyalties or for particular purposes.

(*h*) The role of the Labour Movement and other specialised organisations in the Nation in the formulation of Government policies.

(*i*) The participation of Public Servants in politics and Government.

(*j*) The system of discipline in the Party, Government and Public Service.

(*k*) Lastly, the freedom of candidates to stand for elections at local or national level.

This is perhaps the most that might be hoped for in the circumstances, and it can rightly be said that the consultation had reality and meaning. The proposals made by the commission were later printed and published and put on sale to the public, exciting some press comments. However, as already stated, they were not submitted to the people in a referendum.

While arrogating to itself the power to frame proposals, the government in Ghana openly admitted that it had no mandate to enact a constitution that would establish both a republic and a presidential system of government, and that it was for 'the people and not primarily for the Constituent Assembly to determine the form of the Constitution'.[62] Admitting the government's lack of a mandate, the Minister of Local Government, Mr Ofori Atta, said in the national assembly:

> The present Members of Parliament were ... not elected by the people for the purpose of enacting a republican constitution and the question of a republic was not an issue at the last general election. At that election, of course, certain constitutional principles were settled. The people voted for a unitary form of government and rejected a federal form of government. Nevertheless, it cannot be said that this House, as at present constituted, has a mandate from the people to adopt or make on their behalf, any particular form of republican constitution.[63]

The consultations in Ghana were on the broad principles underlying the government's draft constitution, though the draft constitution itself, apart from its publication in the government white paper, had been given wide coverage in the daily newspapers, one of which, the *Daily Graphic*, published its text in full.[64] If the broad principles adequately described the main features of the draft constitution, then this would seem sufficient as a basis for meaningful consultation. This method has indeed the advantage that the broad principles would be more easily brought to the notice of the people, and more intelligible to them, than the detailed provisions with their legal phraseology. The newspaper coverage was supplemented by posters, widely distributed throughout the country, which set out the principles of the constitution in English and nine vernacular languages.[65]

Those principles were as follows:[66]

1. That Ghana should be a sovereign unitary republic with power to surrender any part of her sovereignty to a Union of African States.
2. That the Head of State and holder of the executive power should be an elected President responsible to the people.
3. That Parliament should be the sovereign legislature and should consist of the President and the National Assembly, and that the President should have a power to veto legislation and to dissolve Parliament.
4. That a President should be elected whenever there is a general election by a method which insures that he will normally be the leader of the party which is successful in the general election.
5. That there should be a cabinet appointed by the President from among Members of Parliament to assist the President in the exercise of his executive functions.
6. That the system of courts and the security of tenure of judges should continue on present lines.
7. That the control of the armed forces and the civil service should be vested in the President.

These principles can be accepted as adequately embodying the main features of the Constitution and therefore as providing a meaningful basis for consultation.

The form of consultation was by a plebiscite on the draft constitution and on the person who should be first President thereunder. Voting was on the basis of parliamentary constituencies, and was conducted on the lines of a general election. Each voter cast two votes, one for or against the draft constitution, and the other for a presidential candidate, two candidates having been nominated, Dr Nkrumah for the ruling Convention Peoples Party, and Dr Danquah for the opposition United Party. The specific questions voted on were:[67]

1. Do you accept the draft republican Constitution for Ghana as set out in the White Paper issued by the Government on 7th March, 1960?
2. Do you accept Kwame Nkrumah or Joseph Boakye Danquah as the first President under the new Constitution?

The plebiscite was widely publicised, and excited wide interest throughout the country; a 54.6 per cent poll was recorded. The result was overwhelmingly in favour of the proposals and for Nkrumah as first president – 1,009,692 votes to 131,393 for the proposals, and 1,015,740 votes to 124,623 for Nkrumah.[68]

The blanket nature of the question on the draft constitution is open to criticism, on the ground that, by denying the voter the choice of accepting some of the proposals and rejecting others, it deprived the vote of much reality or meaning. It is conceivable too that because of this many people may have been put off from voting at all. It would have been much better to allow the principles to be voted on individually. And many people, while in favour of the proposals as far as they went, might have been unwilling to vote on them without other provisions being added — such as, for instance, a justiciable guarantee of individual rights.

This again underlines the objection, already voiced, of basing discussions on just one set of proposals.

(iii) *Discussion of Proposals in a Constituent Assembly*

It is arguable that, given an existing elected parliament, it is unnecessarily wasteful and disruptive to go through the motion of electing a constituent assembly. The point is conclusively answered by the fact, admitted by the Ghana government in the statements quoted above, that the existing parliament has no mandate to enact a new constitution radically or substantially different from that under which it took office. It is entitled, like anyone else, to originate proposals, but its proposals are no more representative or binding than any others. However, if there had been popular consultation on, and approval of, the proposals, this could have been taken as conferring a mandate on the existing parliament to conduct formal discussions which would carry behind them the representative authority of such a body. In conducting discussions with the mandate of prior popular consultation and approval, parliament is in fact cast in a different role and capacity, that of a constituent assembly, and it seems perhaps more in accord with that role that it should formally assume that name during any proceedings on the proposals.

It was thus perfectly proper for the existing national assembly in Ghana, after the mandate conferred by the vote in the plebiscite, to resolve itself into a constituent assembly for purposes of discussions on the proposals. The opposition in Ghana had demanded a special constituent assembly representing 'all the interests of the country, i.e. the Members of Parliament, Chiefs, the University Colleges of (Legon and Kumasi), the Churches, the Muslim Council, the Professional Associations, the Chambers of Commerce, the Farmers' Unions, the T.U.C., the Co-operative Societies, the Ex-Servicemen's Organisations, the Ghana Women's Federation or Council and the political parties'.[69] In so far as the membership of the proposed constituent assembly would have depended on appointment or indirect election instead of on direct election by the people, it was unsatisfactory, and was rightly rejected by the government.

Without prior popular consultation and approval, it is both pretentious and somewhat disingenuous for a national assembly to resolve itself into a constituent assembly, and in that capacity to assume the constituent power of the people. The position is no different from what it would be if the national assembly in that name just assumed the power without going through the meaningless formality of first resolving itself into a constituent assembly, on the ground that 'the dignity and importance of the proceedings would be enhanced' thereby.[70] The procedure used in Tanganyika (1962) and Uganda (1967) was precisely this. The existing national assembly, without prior popular consultation or approval of the new constitutional proposals, simply resolved itself into a constituent assembly on the authority of its own enactment authorising it in that behalf,[71] and then proceeded to debate and to enact those proposals into law. The attorney-general for Uganda could offer no better justification than that the members of the national assembly had been entrusted with legislative sovereignty by the masses of the country, and that extending the membership of the constituent assembly would do more harm than good, as well as causing unnecessary delay.[72]

In this connection it should be pointed out that the existing national assembly in Ghana had already resolved itself once into a constituent assembly before the plebiscite on the draft constitution, and it was in that capacity that it debated the proposals on the first occasion and by resolution recommended them to the people,[73] and later ordered the holding of the plebiscite.[74] Since, however, the main debates on the draft constitution took place after the plebiscite, the procedure cannot seriously be objected to. And there seemed to have been good reason for proceeding in this way. It had been thought more appropriate to the nature of the exercise and to the desire for constitutional autochthony that the plebiscite should be ordered and conducted by the authority of a constituent assembly rather than by that of the national assembly or the Governor-General under the existing Referendum Act, 1959. Under the enabling enactment in all three countries, the power of the national assembly to resolve itself into a constituent assembly continued until the new constitution came into operation.[75] Until the cessation of the power, the national assembly thus functioned with a dual personality — as the national assembly for ordinary legislative purposes, and as a constituent assembly for proceedings on the new constitution and other matters connected with it. It was expressly provided that the existence of the national assembly as such and its functions under any law should not be affected.[76]

Of greater importance, perhaps, are the procedure adopted in the constituent assembly during the debates and the atmosphere of those debates. More specifically, what impact was the constituent assembly able to exert on the government proposals? It must be said that, though the standing orders of the national assembly provided a ready and convenient procedural framework, the somewhat rigid adherence to them exposed the government's attitude to the proceedings as basically the same as in proceedings on any other government bill. The constitutional bill was in the charge of a minister. The procedure in Uganda best illustrates the government character of the proposals and the proceedings. The Constituent Assembly Act laid down the procedure as follows:[77]

> 59 (1) When the Constituent Assembly meets the Speaker shall call upon the member in charge of the Government proposals for a new Constitution to introduce the proposals and the member shall thereupon move 'that this Constituent Assembly do enact a new Constitution in terms of the proposals laid on the table' and may proceed to outline the policy and principles of the proposals.
> (2) There may then follow a debate on the general merits and principles of the proposals.
> 63. When the motion for the enactment of a new Constitution has been carried, the Constituent Assembly shall proceed to consider the proposals for a new Constitution in the same manner as the National Assembly considers a Bill in committee of the whole Assembly.
> 69. At the end of the deliberations of the Constituent Assembly . . . the member in charge of the Government proposals shall move, 'that the Government proposals be adopted and do constitute and form the Constitution of Uganda'.

The intention appeared to have been to emphasise at every turn that the Constitution was the creation of the government. That intention was manifested equally emphatically in the preamble to the Constitution itself, where it was recited: '. . . We the members of the National Assembly here assembled in the name of all the people of Uganda . . . do hereby resolve on this 8th day of September, 1967, in the name of all the people of Uganda, for ourselves and our generations yet unborn, that the Government Proposals be adopted, and do constitute and form the Constitution of Uganda.' The same kind of emphasis was also noticeable in the proceedings in Ghana and Tanganyika. The procedure was of course not exactly the same in so far as the whole gamut of first and second readings, committee and third reading was gone through in Ghana and Tanganyika.

It needs, however, to be said in favour of the government that there was none of the usual practice of stampeding the house into a hurried acceptance of a bill in one sitting. The proceedings were unhurried, and ample opportunity was given for critical debate by members. The first and second readings in Ghana were taken on the same day (June 13, 1960), the committee stage on June 24, and the third reading on June 29. Altogether the whole exercise from the publication of the government proposals on March 7 to the final passage of the bill occupied four months. The atmosphere of a feud punctuated by numerous and frivolous interruptions, which characterized proceedings in Ghana's national assembly,[78] was absent. The debates were conducted in a calm, tolerant and dignified mood, with a sense of responsibility and gravity on both the government and opposition sides. This was also true of the proceedings in the Tanganyikan national assembly, which at that time was already a *de facto* one-party assembly.

In Uganda the debates in the constituent assembly were begun on June 22, 1967, adjourned on July 27, resumed on September 6, and finally concluded on September 8. The government proposals had been published two weeks before the opening of the debate, on June 9. However, while for the opposition the opportunity for a long debate was ample and appeared to have been fully utilised for informed criticism of the proposals, the government was unwilling to allow its own members freedom to criticise or oppose the proposals as individuals representing constituencies. A letter from the government chief whip warned that 'no member should oppose or vote against the proposals,' and that, since opposition had been dealt with at a private parliamentary group meeting, 'any members who opposed the proposals would be liable to be dealt with severely'.[79] A minister who spoke against the concentration of power in the President was promptly dismissed. President Obote, in the letter dismissing the minister, said he did not accept that members should debate and criticise the proposals as individuals representing constituencies. Frequent interruptions of opposition speakers by government members were said (by the opposition) to be evidence of a plan to bulldoze the proposals through the assembly.[80]

That the debates in the constituent assembly had some impact on the government proposals seems clearly established. For in both Ghana and Uganda, the proposals as enacted incorporated substantial amendments to the original draft, made in response to criticisms raised during the debates.[81] Indeed in Uganda, after the first round of debates which lasted over a month, the proposals had to be withdrawn, and then revised in the light of the criticisms and suggestions made during the debates. In Ghana the leader of the opposition, Mr Dombo, acknowledged that 'most of the criticisms we levelled against this Constitution have been met and for that reason I say well done to the people who have redrafted it'.[82] The extent of this impact must not, however, be exaggerated. First, the amendments were in no case carried against the wishes of the government; they were incorporated because they were acceptable to the government. The controversial Article 55 in Ghana (introduced as an ordinary member's inspired amendment), which gave independent legislative power to the first President, remained in the Constitution in spite of the opposition's violent attack on it. A division on it — the only one in the whole proceedings on the Constitution — was carried by sixty-three votes to seven. Secondly, to acknowledge the government's accommodation of opposition criticisms is not to say that the Constitution was what the opposition would have liked or devised had they been given the opportunity to submit their own proposals. The discussions were conducted on the basis of one set of proposals, and the rules of parliamentary debate precluded departure from those proposals. This was made emphatically clear by the Ugandan attorney-general.[83] The very first stage in the process had been wrong.

In the rest of the countries, Kenya (1964), Tanzania (1965), Uganda (1966), Malawi (1966), Gambia (1970) and Sierra Leone (1971), no pretence was made of a constituent assembly without a mandate; the existing national assembly simply debated and enacted the new constitution in the usual way in which government legislation is enacted.

(iv) *The Enactment of the Constitution*

The power to enact the constitutional proposals into law should rightly belong to the people, and be exercisable by them either directly at a referendum or by a constituent assembly so mandated by them. Such mandate can be implied from earlier popular consultation on, and approval of, the proposals. Enactment directly by the people might have value in enhancing the constitution's legitimacy; it would foster among the people a feeling that the constitution is their own, not an imposition by the government, and that they thus have a stake, a responsibility, in observing its rules. It would serve to give reality to the phrase 'We the people . . . do hereby adopt, enact and give to ourselves this Constitution', which, since the adoption of the American Constitution in 1787, has become a familiar feature of most modern republican constitutions.

In Commonwealth Africa, the enactment of a new constitution has in every case been by parliament or by a constituent assembly. The idea of the people as supreme law-giver does not appear to be accepted. All the new constitutions are acts of government, initiated and finally given force of law through the processes of the government. The significance of the use of a constituent assembly in Ghana, Tanganyika and Uganda is purely political, not legal. The legal power — as distinct from the political mandate — of the constituent assembly to enact the constitution into law was derived from the Constituent Assembly Act which authorised it to 'enact such provisions for or in connection with the establishment of a new constitution as it thinks fit'.[84] Thus, no objection can legally be taken to the fact that in Ghana the Constitution as finally enacted contained provisions (e.g., Article 55) inserted after the plebiscite.[85] The Act also provided that 'any proposals for a new Constitution if adopted by the Constituent Assembly under this Act shall become law and constitute the Constitution of [the country concerned] as by law established, notwithstanding that Her Majesty [or the President in Uganda] has not given Her assent thereto.'[86] Further, the constituent assembly was not required to act by a special majority in adopting a constitution; indeed in Uganda it was specifically authorised to do so by simple majority.[87]

It is necessary to emphasise the character of the Constituent Assembly Act in Ghana and Tanganyika as an amendment of the existing Constitution. Ghana's Independence Constitution was enacted as a British Government order-in-council (the only one in Commonwealth Africa so enacted) while that of Tanganyika was scheduled to an order-in-council.[88] Each Order-in-Council authorised its own repeal or amendment by parliament (i.e. the Queen and the national assembly) by a two-thirds majority in Tanganyika, or – since 1958 by virtue of the Constitution (Repeal of Restrictions) Act – by simple majority in Ghana. It was this power that parliament transferred to a constituent assembly without the Head of State and acting by a simple majority of its members. The transfer amounted clearly to an alteration of the existing Constitution, since the enactment of a new constitution implies the repeal of the old. (This does not necessarily follow; parliament may act by itself to repeal the old constitution with effect from the date the new one comes into operation.) The constituent assembly had thus a dual function; it both enacted a new constitution and repealed the existing order-in-council and the Independence Act.[89] The Constituent Assembly Act in Uganda was not an amendment of the existing constitution (i.e. the 1966 Revolutionary Constitution), because that constitution provided for the establishment of a constituent assembly to enact a new constitution in place of itself.[90]

In the rest of the countries, the enactment of a new constitution was a straightforward exercise by parliament of its power to repeal the Independence Act and the Independence order-in-council in accordance with the procedure (as amended)[91] laid down therein. The government of Kenya minced no words about this: 'This Constitution will depend for its validity on the sovereign will of this Parliament. ... The constitutional system has not compelled us to establish a constituent assembly as has been done in other parts of the world. Our Parliament will make its Constitution and will demonstrate its undoubted sovereignty in so doing'.[92] The Independence Constitution was established by, and scheduled to, the Independence order-in-council;[93] but the procedure for alteration was the same for all three, i.e. the Independence Act, the order-in-council and the Constitution (except in Nigeria and Uganda where the section of the order establishing the Constitution could be amended by a simple majority). To abolish the Constitution and establish a new one, all that was necessary was, using the prescribed procedure, to repeal the section (S.3) of the order-in-council that established it.

An alternative might be, while leaving unrepealed the establishing section and the schedule containing the Constitution, to use the amending power in the Constitution itself. This was the method by which the republic and the executive presidency were introduced in Kenya in 1964.[94] The Independence Constitution, as established by, and scheduled to, the Kenya Independence order-in-council, was simply amended by the deletion of the provisions relating to the Governor-General and replacing them with new provisions that declared the republic and established the office of President; other deletions and additions consequent upon this were made in the appropriate sections of the Constitution whose authority still derived from the Independence order-in-council. Only in 1965, by the Constitution of Kenya (Amendment) Act of that year, was the section in the Independence order-in-council that established the Constitution repealed.[95] This Act re-established the Constitution, while curiously still continuing it as a schedule to the Independence Order.[96] The Constitution, as re-established by an Act of the Kenyan parliament, continued, with numerous amendments, as a schedule to the Independence order until 1969, when all the amendments were consolidated and re-enacted into a completely new Constitution;[97] by that time all the provisions of the Independence Act (in so far as they formed the law of Kenya) and of the order-in-council had been repealed. Section 7 of the establishing Act, the Constitution of Kenya Act, 1969, authorised the printing of the Constitution as a separate document and not as a schedule to an act of parliament.

This alternative method that was used initially in Kenya appears to be legally unimpeachable, since the power to alter the Constitution was rather widely defined to include 'amendment, modification or re-enactment, with or without amendment or modification ... suspension or repeal ... and the making of different provision in lieu'.[98] However, applied to the Independence Constitution (but not the order-in-council itself), it may be doubted whether the spirit of the amending power contemplated the destruction, through the superimposition of a republican, presidential form, of the system of government instituted by the Constitution, namely monarchical, parliamentary government. The so-called amendment in fact established a new constitution, and as such should have been effected by the repeal of the existing Independence Constitution. The change from a two- or multiple-party to a one-party system in Zambia in December 1972 is also regarded in the country as having established a new (i.e. a second) republic. Regarded in that light, its introduction by way of amendment to the Independence Constitution seems inappropriate.[99] However, the change is perhaps not as fundamental and radical as the change from a monarchical, parliamentary government to a republican, presidential one, and in any case the action in Zambia was intended as an interim measure to be formalised by a new constitution as soon as possible.

4. *Government Assumption of Constituent Power by Means of a Coup*

A revolution, whether staged by the military or another group of individuals, by the government itself or by the people is in every case an exercise of constituent power, for its effect is to establish a new legal order in place of the existing one, which is thereby destroyed. A government-staged coup is a somewhat abnormal phenomenon. Usually in Commonwealth Africa, as has been shown, the government has the facilities to bring about constitutionally the changes it desires in the constitution; it would only resort to a coup when it lacks these facilities, i.e. when either the constitution or certain of its vital provisions are not alterable at all or the procedure for alteration is beyond the ability of the government to organise. There have been only three government-staged coups in Commonwealth Africa — in Uganda (1966), Lesotho (1970) and Swaziland (1973).

Obote's government in Uganda clearly disliked the frame of government instituted by the Independence Constitution, particularly its federal structure, but it lacked the ability to change it. It is true that, while amendment to individual provisions in the Constitution needed a two-thirds majority in the national assembly and the consent of the legislative assemblies of the federal states, the entire Constitution itself could have been abrogated by the simple device of a repeal by a simple majority of Section 3 of the Independence order-in-council which established it. Yet in February 1966, when the need for change seemed greatest, even a simple majority was not vouchsafed to Obote, an adverse vote being successfully carried against him. A coup thus seemed the only alternative at that time. So on February 22, 1966, Obote overthrew the Constitution and took over all powers of government. This was a constituent act. Next, in a declaration signed on February 24 by himself and thirteen of his ministers, it was stated that Obote's taking over of all powers on February 22 . . .

... does not ... and shall not affect or be deemed to affect any of the following provisions of the Constitution, that is to say—

(*a*) the powers, dignities, status and privileges of the Rulers of the Federal States and the Constitutional Heads of the Districts;

(*b*) the Constitutions of the Federal States and the Administrations of the Districts and the Councils and Boards of the Municipalities and towns;

(*c*) the powers, duties and functions of the Courts, the Judges, and Magistrates;

(*d*) the National Assembly;

(*e*) the smooth working of the Civil Service;

(*f*) the Armed Forces of Uganda, the Police Force and the Prisons Service.

We hereby further declare that as temporary measure there is hereby established a Security Council of Uganda, of which the Prime Minister shall be Chairman, and a Cabinet of Ministers holding portfolios who shall be appointed by the Prime Minister.[100]

On March 2, yet another declaration, signed this time by Obote alone as Prime Minister, was issued as follows:

Pursuant to the Declaration made by the Government dated the twenty-fourth day of February, 1966, and in exercise of all other powers thereunto enabling it is hereby declared by the Prime Minister acting with the advice and consent of the Cabinet that

(*a*) the executive authority of Uganda shall vest in the Prime Minister acting in accordance with the advice and consent of the Cabinet; and

(*b*) the duties, power and other functions that are performed or are exercisable by the President or the Vice-President immediately before the twenty-second day of February, 1966, shall vest in the Prime Minister and shall be performed or be exercised by the Prime Minister by and with the advice and consent of the Cabinet.[101]

Finally on April 15, a new constitution was promulgated by Prime Minister Obote in the national assembly, i.e. by Obote as Prime Minister in concert with the national assembly. Notwithstanding the saving of the national assembly by the declaration of February 24, and the vesting in the Prime Minister of the functions and powers of the deposed President, the two authorities (i.e. the national assembly and the Prime Minister acting by and with the advice and consent of the cabinet) did not constitute the parliament established by the overthrown Constitution, and even if they did, they would have lacked power to enact a constitution. The Constitution of April 15 was thus clearly a revolutionary constitution enacted, in concert with the national assembly and the cabinet, by Obote as Prime Minister in whom the entire legislative sovereignty of the country was vested by virtue of the revolution of February 22. The consent of the national assembly and the cabinet was necessary in view of the declarations of February 24 and March 2. In making the Constitution, Obote, the cabinet and the national assembly claimed, of course, to have acted in the name of the people, though without pretending to be a parliament or a constituent assembly. No reference to parliament or to a constituent assembly was made at all in the preamble to the Constitution, which recited simply: 'We the people of Uganda here assembled in the name of all the people of Uganda do resolve and it is hereby resolved that the Constitution which came into being on the ninth day of October, 1962, be abolished and it is hereby abolished accordingly and the Constitution now laid before us be adopted and it is hereby adopted this fifteenth day of April, 1966, as the Constitution of Uganda until such time as a Constituent Assembly established by Parliament enacts a Constitution in place of this Constitution.'

In Lesotho, as may be recalled,[102] the occasion for the government-staged coup was the victory of the opposition party in the general election of January 1970. When this became clear, the Prime Minister, Chief Leabua Jonathan, simply declared a state of emergency, annulled the results of the elections, suspended the Constitution, put the King under restriction and assumed the entire executive authority of the country which, under the title of Tona-Kholo, he exercised in his own discretion, with the council of ministers acting only in a consultative capacity.[103] He too, jointly with the council of ministers, acts as the legislature.[104] No new constitution has, at the time of writing, been enacted; recently the assembly met at the summons of the government but it is not clear in what capacity (e.g., as a constituent assembly).

The overthrow of the Constitution in Swaziland was a result of the government's impatience with the restraints which it imposed on its powers. The Constitution had frustrated the government's attempt to have an opposition member of parliament deported as a prohibited immigrant. The last general election in the country had for the first time returned three opposition members, much to the annoyance of the government. The initial deportation order had been declared invalid by the court.[105] A subsequent act of parliament, designed to effect the deportation,[106] met with the same fate[107] on the ground that, being an amendment to the Constitution, it had not been passed in accordance with the procedure for constitutional amendment which, among other things, required a joint sitting of both houses of parliament.[108] Parliament then met and adopted a resolution praying the King to annul the Constitution. On April 12, the King, before an assemblage of the Swazi nation, formally abrogated the Constitution and took over all powers of government, including judicial powers.[109]

REFERENCES

1. Art. 1.
2. Edward S. Corwin, *The Doctrine of Judicial Review*, Gloucester, Mass., (1963), p. 105.
3. Corwin, *loc. cit.*
4. Corwin, *op. cit.*
5. *Att.-Gen. of the Republic* v. *Mustafa Ibrahim and others* (1964) 1, Cyprus L. Rep. 195, 208.
6. Nat. Ass. Deb., 3 Nov., 1958, col. 14.
7. S.32.
8. S.35.
9. Parl. Deb., 3 Nov., 1958, col. 5.
10. *Ibid.*, cols. 9—12.
11. Kwame Nkrumah, *Africa Must Unite* (1963), pp. 60—1.
12. Above, p. 144.
13. Nat. Ass. Deb., Feb. 10, 1969, col. 4770.
14. House of Reps. Deb., Oct. 27, 1964.
15. S.71, Constitution 1963.
16. S.156.
17. S.239.
18. Constitution of Kenya (Amendment) Act, 1964; Constitution of Kenya (Amendment) (No. 2) Act, 1964.
19. Constitution of Kenya (Amendment) Act, 1965.
20. Constitution of Kenya (Amendment) (No. 4) Act, 1966 (operative from 1967).
21. Constitution of Kenya (Amendment) Act, 1968.
22. S.47, Constitution 1969.
23. SS.5(1) and 6, Constitution 1962.
24. S.5.
25. SS.2 and 4.
26. SS.5 and 6, Constitution 1966.
27. Constitution (First Amendment) Act, 1966.
28. S.3, Constitution 1967.
29. S.72, Constitution 1964.
30. Constitution (Amendment) (No. 3) Act, 1969.
31. Nat. Ass. Deb., Hansard No. 17, April 21—23, 1969, col. 2180.
32. Dicey, *The Law of the Constitution*; Finer, *Theory and Practice of Modern Government*.
33. Nat. Ass. Deb., *op. cit.*
34. *Ibid.*, cols. 2169—70.
35. Col. 2172.
36. S.90, Constitution 1966.
37. S.40, Constitution 1965.
38. S.72, Constitution 1970.
39. S.30, Tanganyika 1961; S.46, Malawi 1964.
40. S.35 1962; S.51, 1965.
41. S.97 1966.

42. See above ch. XII, for full discussion.

43. Above, ch. IV.

44. Chs. VI, VII, VIII, IX, X and XIII above.

45. Above, ch. IX.

46. Nat. Ass. Deb. on the Constitution (Amendment) Bill, 1969, Hansard No. 17, 21–23 April, 1969, col. 65.

47. Constitution of Kenya (Amendment) Act, 1967 S.7.

48. Constitution of Kenya (Amendment) (No. 2) Act, 1966.

49. Above, chs. X and XI.

50. Jennings, *The Law of the Constitution* (4th ed.), p. 105.

51. Steve Lino, Letter in *Transition* 34, p. 9.

52. Govt. White Paper No. 1 of 1960, p. 3.

53. Ghana, White No. 1 of 1960; Tanganyika, Govt. Paper No. 1 of 1962.

54. A. W. Bradley, 'Constitution-making in Uganda', *Transition, 32*, p. 25.

55. Above, ch. VIII.

56. Statutory Instrument No. 46 of 1972.

57. Report of the National Commission on the Establishment of a One-Party Participatory Democracy, Lusaka, 1972; Govt. White Paper on the Report, Govt. Printer, Lusaka, 1972.

58. Above, chs. III, IV, VIII, and X.

59. Report 1965.

60. Report 1972.

61. Statutory Instrument No. 46 of 1972.

62. Govt. White Paper No. 1 of 1960, p. 3.

63. Parl. Deb., Feb. 23, 1960, col. 7.

64. Bennion, *Constitutional Law of Ghana* (1962), Ch. 2, for full account.

65. Bennion, *op. cit.*, p. 90.

66. White Paper No. 1, 1960 p. 16. Compare the statement of broad principles in the Tanganyikan Govt. Paper No. 1 of 1962.

67. Constitutional Plebiscite (Questions) Order, 1960.

68. Bennion, *op. cit.*

69. Parl. Deb. 23 Feb., 1960, col. 46.

70. Bennion, *op. cit.*, p. 82.

71. Constituent Assembly Act, 1962 (Tanganyika); Constituent Assembly Act, 1967 (Uganda).

72. Binaisa, Parl. Deb. Hansard, Vol. 69, April 20–28, 1967, pp. 1884, 1888.

73. Proceedings of the Constituent Assembly 1.

74. Constitutional Plebiscite Order, 1960.

75. S.4 Ghana; S.6 Tanganyika; S.9 Uganda.

76. S.2(4) Ghana; S.5 Tanganyika.

77. Schedule — modifying the Standing Order of the National Assembly.

78. See above ch. IX.

79. Nelson Kasfir, 'The 1967 Ugandan Constituent Assembly Debate', *Transition* 33, p. 55.

80. Nelson Kasfir, *op. cit.*, p. 56.

81. For details of the amendments, see Bennion, *op. cit.*, pp. 91–7; Akena Adoko, 'The Constitution of the Republic of Uganda', *Transition* 33, p. 43; Abu Mayanja, 'The Government's Proposals for a new Constitution of Uganda', *Transition* 32, p. 20.

82. Proceedings of the Constituent Assembly, p. 178.

83. Binaisa, Parl. Deb. Hansard, Vol. 69, 20–28 April, 1967, p. 1,888.

84. Ghana S.2(1); Tanganyika S.2(1); Uganda S.1.

85. Bennion, *op. cit.*, p. 97, n. 3; contrast Rubin and Murray, *Constitution and Government of Ghana*, pp. 27–9.

86. S.2(2) Ghana; S.2(2) Tanganyika; S.6(1) Uganda.

87. SS.5(1) and 6(2).

88. Ghana (Constitution) Order-in-Council, 1957; Tanganyika (Constitution) Order-in-Council, 1961.

89. S.4 Republic of Tanganyika (Consequential, Transitional and Temporary Provisions) Act, 1962, cap. 500.

90. S.145 Constitution, 1966.

91. Above, pp. 398–405.

92. Attorney-General Njonjo, Nat. Ass. Deb., 10 Feb, 1969, col. 4775.

93. S.3.

94. Constitution of Kenya (Amendment) Act, 1964.

95. S.5.

96. S.3.

97. Constitution of Kenya Act, 1969.

98. S.72 Constitution of Zambia, 1964, and corresponding provisions in the other independence constitutions.

99. Constitution (Amendment) (No. 5) Act, 1972.

100. Reproduced as Schedule 9 to the 1966 Constitution.

101. Reproduced as Schedule 9 to the 1966 Constitution.

102. Above, ch. IV.

103. The Lesotho Order, Feb. 10, 1970, SS.2 and 4.

104. *Ibid.*, S.10.

105. *Ngwenya* v. *The Deputy Prime Minister and Another*, High Court, August 29, 1972.

106. Immigration (Amendment) Act, 1972.

107. *Ngwenya* v. *The Deputy Prime Minister and Another*, High Court, 9 Jan., 1973; Court of Appeal, CVL.A.1/1973 of 27 March, 1973. 108. S.134.

109. *Rand Daily Mail*, 13 April, 1973.

CHAPTER XIV

EVALUATION OF THE COMMONWEALTH AFRICAN PRESIDENTIAL CONSTITUTIONS

Perhaps the search for an ideal constitution is an elusive enterprise. Yet it can be said that, notwithstanding certain objectionable features, the Commonwealth African presidential constitutions mark quite a significant advance in that quest, for they have blended together what is good in the British and American systems. First, there is the rejection of the split executive — the separation of the nominal Head of State from the Head of Government — with all the conflicts and instability that flow from it. The unification of the two offices in the President conforms to the natural order of things, minimises conflict, and provides a single focal point of leadership and unity in the country.[1] Complementing this is the concentration of executive power in the President, instead of its division among a plurality of persons; in other words, the rejection of cabinet government in favour of presidential rule, with the latter's capacity for unity, energy and despatch, and for the facility with which it enables the public to fix the responsibility for failures in the executive.[2] 'As the functions of government become more complex and urgent', writes Professor Ridley, 'the need for adequate machinery to ensure the continuous formulation of overall policy becomes ever more apparent. Cabinets and cabinet committees are no longer adequate for this purpose. Modern democracy also requires clearly organised political responsibility. This is more easily fixed on one man than on several. The trend to prime-ministerial, presidential or chancellor government appears to be general'.[3]

Thus even the British cabinet system is tending towards prime-ministerial government, and de Gaulle had practically converted the quasi-parliamentary system of the French Fifth Republic into a thoroughgoing presidential government; while in West Germany Konrad Adenauer, by a forceful assertion of his full constitutional power backed by a masterful personality, had made himself the executive in almost the same sense as the American President, but without in any way perverting the Constitution.

However, while instituting a single executive, the Commonwealth African presidential constitutions also establish a cabinet, and by this cast upon the President an obligation to consult it. The influence of the cabinet, to which this consultation exposes the President, might perhaps be expected to create conditions favourable to the minimisation of the danger of personal rule and the development of *de facto* cabinet government, without, however, disabling the President from acting unilaterally when speedy action is needed or when disagreement among cabinet members makes it necessary for him to impose his will. In some of the constitutions, as we have seen,[4] the cabinet is given a role going beyond mere consultation and advice; it shares with the President a concurrent responsibility for policy, the President's being the overriding voice in case of conflict.

The Constitution of the Federal Republic of West Germany, 1948, offers another precedent of a compromise between outright presidential rule on the one hand and outright cabinet government on the other. The system is structured upon the distinction between policy determination, policy formulation and administration. Article 65 provides: 'The Federal Chancellor shall determine, and be responsible for, general policy. Within the limits of this general policy, each Federal minister shall conduct the business of his department autonomously and on his own responsibility. The Federal Government shall decide on differences of opinion between the Federal ministers. The Federal Chancellor shall conduct the business of the Federal Government in accordance with rules of procedure adopted by it and approved by the Federal President.' Under this provision, a minister, unlike in the Commonwealth African countries, administers his department independently of direction or control of the Chancellor. Executive functions within each department belong to the responsible minister; the Chancellor cannot 'substitute his own decision for those of the competent minister in a concrete (i.e. individual) case. Nor can he direct a minister as to the decision he should take in such a case. Even less can he by-pass the minister and issue instructions to a civil servant within the department'.[5] It may be assumed too that the minister's responsibility for his department extends to the determination of departmental policy. In the final analysis, however, policy governs all, and he who determines general policy has the controlling voice, for as Professor Ridley pertinently remarked, policy 'can always be formulated simply to deal with a specific case'.[6] This is not to deny the independence of ministers *vis-à-vis* the Chancellor; policy is not so over-reaching as to absorb the power of the ministers in those of the Chancellor. The relationship can never therefore become that between a minister and his civil service adviser. 'From an administrative point of view, ministers have no superior'.[7]

It is at the cabinet, rather than at the departmental level, that the Chancellor can and does dominate his ministers. The cabinet in

Germany has rather limited function. As far as administration is concerned, it cannot direct or control the ministers except to the extent necessary to resolve differences among them. But it has some responsibility in respect of policy. The extent of its authority over policy depends upon how one draws the line between determination of general policy, for which the Chancellor is solely responsible, and the formulation of policy in the form in which it would be introduced into parliament as a specific legislative measure. This latter falls within the competence of the cabinet, for no legislative measure can be introduced in parliament without the approval of the cabinet. On the other hand, no decision can be taken in the cabinet against the vote of the Chancellor. If therefore he should disagree with the majority, then the matter cannot be proceeded with. Yet a Chancellor, determined to have his way, has the power to secure the approval of the cabinet for his policy, since ministers are appointed and dismissed on his recommendation.[8] Hence the emergence of what has been called 'Chancellor government' under the forceful personality of Adenauer.

The Commonwealth African presidential constitutions mark a further advance upon the American: they avoid the incidence of stalemate between the executive and the legislature and the absence of a well-integrated policy. The causes of the incidence of deadlock are of course the system of checks and balances which enables the Senate to veto presidential action in matters of appointment and foreign affairs, and the somewhat rigid separation between the two primary organs of government, a separation that goes both to the method of their election and to their powers. The President is differently elected from Congress, and is thereby deprived of an assurance of majority support therein. More important than this, perhaps, is the absence in Congress not only of party leaders with sufficient authority to rally the parliamentary party to the support of the government, but also of an effective machinery for enforcing discipline. These features are removed in the Commonwealth African constitutions. The President is given control over appointments and foreign affairs, unfettered by a legislative veto. Foreign affairs have developed into one of the most sensitive and complex areas of government, requiring consistency, speedy action, co-ordinated policy and diplomatic finesse; these are objectives which cannot easily be attained where foreign affairs are made the concurrent concern of the President and the legislature. And, as noted in a previous chapter, one of the greatest frustrations an American President had suffered resulted from the exercise of the Senate's veto in foreign affairs.

By linking the elections of the President and the legislature under a single ballot, the element of popular consent in the choice of the organs of government is maintained, simplicity is achieved and expense reduced; above all, the President is guaranteed an almost certain chance of a legislative majority. But the cardinal merit in this connection is the establishment of a cabinet composed of members of the legislature, thus bringing the government and the legislature into close and regular contact. If, for reasons already noted, it is not practicable or desirable that the President should be in the house, then his ministers ought to be there. The real value of this is not just that their membership enables them to participate in the work of the legislature, to answer questions from members and generally to explain the actions of the government; it lies more importantly in the fact that, since the ministers are the leaders of the majority party, their legislative membership and participation enable them to rally to the government the support of the majority of M.P.s. Their ministerial offices give them the authority which the parliamentary party leaders in America do not have. In the legislature, in the role of leader of the house, is the Vice-President, who is also the President's principal assistant in the government. Together with the other ministers and the party whips, he gives guidance and leadership to the other members, thereby maintaining the party's authority over them and checking an undue assertion of independence, such as characterises American congressmen.

In this connection the President's nominal membership of the house, as in Kenya, may even have some advantage in enabling him to exert influence with the M.P.s in private extra-parliamentary meetings. In Kenya, a Parliamentary Group of the ruling Kenya African National Congress (KANU), which had been inaugurated in pre-Republic days under the chairmanship of the Prime Minister (Mr Kenyatta) in his capacity as party president, emerged under the Republic as an important rapport between M.P.s and the government. The President still remains the chairman of the Parliamentary Group, by right of being an ordinary member of parliament. It had thus been possible for him to meet the Group formally in times of near-stalemate between the cabinet and the M.P.s. He intervened three times in 1965 in this way.[9] On all three occasions the authority of the Vice-President and the ministers as the leaders of the party in the house had proved insufficient to break down the opposition of the M.P.s, but the pre-eminent authority and prestige of the President, exerted at these private meetings with the Parliamentary Group, coupled with the deep respect and loyalty felt for Kenyatta as a person, won the M.P.s over in each case. It is possible that, had the President not been a M.P., he might have achieved the same result through informal meetings with the M.P.s, for such meetings have become a familiar technique by which American Presidents seek to win congressional support for their programmes. Yet the fact that President Kenyatta met with the discontented M.P.s formally as a regularly constituted Parliamentary

Group, of which he himself is part, must have lent a more intimate air to the meetings, which might have conditioned the minds of the M.P.s towards an accommodation with the government.

Modern government should be a co-operative, co-ordinated effort, and not a tug-of-war between antagonistic organs. The cardinal defect in American government is the mutual antipathy and antagonism between the President and Congress, resulting from the rigid separation of powers. This has produced a lack of 'cohesion and rational completeness' in policy. For although, in response to the exigencies and complexities of modern government, the President is now allowed a preponderant role in the initiation of legislation, Congress still considers itself the authority over policy. And an excessive consciousness of its authority often leads it into too minute questioning, through its numerous committees, of policy programmes initiated by the President, so that by the time it has finished with them, the programmes are reduced to a patchwork of disorganised policy. Seldom, if ever, does an American President get his policy programme approved *in toto* by Congress. The result is that the governmental process is rendered incapable of co-ordinated leadership.[10]

This is not of course an argument against any kind of separation of power. On the contrary, some separation of executive and legislative functions is necessary and desirable if limited government and individual liberty are to be secured, but certainly not a rigid separation. John Calhoun has observed that too rigid a separation would result in 'three independent, separate and conflicting departments, without any common point of union, instead of one united authority controlling the whole'. A well-organised system, he argued, ought to have a centre of gravity, serving as 'the stomach and the brain, into which all is taken, digested, and assimilated, and by which the action of the whole is regulated by a common intelligence'.[11] Nowhere is this more necessary than in Africa, where the general poverty, ignorance and disease among the people call for a leadership capable of co-ordinating all the political processes of government. For an African President has to be more than an administrative chief. He has actively to assume the role of chief legislator, and to provide initiative and leadership in the formulation of policy that can usher in the much-needed economic development and national integration. Leadership of this kind is hardly possible within the framework of a rigid separation of powers, since that would make it impossible for the President, through the instrument of legislation, to guide and direct the nation as a whole.

While a co-ordinated governmental process under the control of the executive is a legacy from Westminster, the Commonwealth African presidential constitutions have rejected that aspect of the system which requires the government to resign if it is defeated on an issue of confidence. Since the President and the legislature hold their mandate of office directly from the electorate, any conflict between them should be resolved by the electorate. This desirable position is embodied in the constitutions through the procedure of dissolution, but the real significance of this power, as has been pointed out, lies not in its use, but in the inducement of co-operation which the possibility of its use imposes upon both organs.

Doubtless an executive President who holds and exercises executive power in his discretion and who also controls the process of legislation arouses fear of dictatorship. None the less, the real enemy, it has been said, is not power itself, but insufficient restraint upon power.[12] Presidentialism in Commonwealth Africa has tended towards dictatorship and tyranny not so much because of its great power as because of insufficient constitutional, political and social restraint upon that power, and because conditions in Africa, with the opportunities for total mobilisation of the nation and the greatly enhanced authority which they give to the President, are particularly favourable to the growth of dictatorship.

REFERENCES

1. Above, ch. IV.
2. Above, p. 91.
3. F. F. Ridley, 'Chancellor Government as a Political System and the German Constitution', *Parl. Affairs* (1966), Vol. XIX, No. 4, pp. 453, 461.
4. Above, p. 41.
5. F. F. Ridley, *op. cit.*, p. 457.
6. *loc. cit.*
7. *ibid.*, p. 461.
8. Art. 64(1).
9. For details see C. Gertzel, *The Politics of Independent Kenya* (1970), pp. 139–43.
10. Q. L. Quade, 'Presidential Leadership: Paralysed or Irresponsible', *Parl. Affairs* (1963–4), Vol. XVII, No. 1, p. 65.
11. Speech in Congress, Feb. 1835; quoted in Corwin, *The President: Office and Powers*, 4th revised ed. (1957), p. 322.
12. Q. L. Quade, *op. cit.*, p. 75.

INDEX